The Economic Future in Historical Perspective

The Economic Future in Historical Perspective

Edited by

Paul A. David & Mark Thomas

Published *for* THE BRITISH ACADEMY
by OXFORD UNIVERSITY PRESS

Oxford University Press, Great Clarendon Street, Oxford OX2 6DP

Oxford New York

*Auckland Cape Town Dar es Salaam Hong Kong Karachi
Kuala Lumpur Madrid Melbourne Mexico City Nairobi
New Delhi Shanghai Taipei Toronto*

With offices in

*Argentina Austria Brazil Chile Czech Republic France Greece
Guatemala Hungary Italy Japan Poland Portugal Singapore
South Korea Switzerland Thailand Turkey Ukraine Vietnam*

*Published in the United States
by Oxford University Press Inc., New York*

© *The British Academy 2003*

Database right The British Academy (maker)

*First published 2003
Paperback edition 2006*

*All rights reserved. No part of this publication may be reproduced,
stored in a retrieval system, or transmitted, in any form or by any means,
without the prior permission in writing of the British Academy,
or as expressly permitted by law, or under terms agreed with the appropriate
reprographics rights organization. Enquiries concerning reproduction
outside the scope of the above should be sent to the Publications Department,
The British Academy, 10 Carlton House Terrace, London SW1Y 5AH*

*You must not circulate this book in any other binding or cover
and you must impose this same condition on any acquirer*

*British Library Cataloguing in Publication Data
Data available*

*Library of Congress Cataloging in Publication Data
Data available*

*Typeset by
Hobbs the Printers Limited
Printed in Great Britain
on acid-free paper by
Antony Rowe Limited
Chippenham, Wiltshire*

ISBN 0–19–726347–X   978–0–19–726347–1

Contents

Notes on Contributors — ix

Preface and Acknowledgements — xv

Introduction: Thinking Historically about Challenging Economic Issues — 1
    PAUL A. DAVID & MARK THOMAS

PART ONE: DRIVERS OF LONG-TERM ECONOMIC GROWTH

Overview — 29

1. The Industrious Revolution and Economic Growth, 1650–1830 — 43
    JAN DE VRIES

2. English Apprenticeship: A Neglected Factor in the First Industrial Revolution — 73
    JANE HUMPHRIES

3. Human Capital and Productivity Performance: Britain, the United States and Germany, 1870–1990 — 103
    STEPHEN BROADBERRY

4. General Purpose Technologies and Surges in Productivity: Historical Reflections on the Future of the ICT Revolution — 135
    PAUL A. DAVID & GAVIN WRIGHT

5. Technological Systems and Comparative Systems of Innovation: From Historical Performance to Future Policy Guidelines — 167
    NICK VON TUNZELMANN

Contents

PART TWO: CHANGES IN ECONOMIC REGIMES AND IDEOLOGIES

    Overview   197

6. The East Asian Escape from Economic Backwardness: Retrospect and Prospect   209
   NICHOLAS CRAFTS

7. The Russian Transition through the Historical Looking-glass: Gradual versus Abrupt Decontrol of Economic Systems in Britain and Russia   231
   CHRISTOPHER DAVIS & JAMES FOREMAN-PECK

8. Rational Resistance to Land Privatization: The Behaviour of Russia's Rural Producers in Response to Agrarian Reforms, 1861–2000   267
   CAROL LEONARD

9. Understanding the Past to Reshape the Future: Problems of South Africa's Transition   297
   FRANCIS WILSON

10. Lessons from Italy's Monetary Unification (1862–1880) for the Euro and Europe's Single Market   315
    LEANDRO CONTE, GIANNI TONIOLO & GIOVANNI VECCHI

11. Ideology and the Shadow of History: A Perspective on the Great Depression   339
    BARRY EICHENGREEN & PETER TEMIN

PART THREE: WELFARE, WELL-BEING AND PERSONAL ECONOMIC SECURITY

    Overview   363

12. Economic Welfare Measurements and Human Well-being   371
    AVNER OFFER

13. The Human Body in Britain: Past and Future   401
    RODERICK FLOUD

14. Height and the High Life: What Future for a Tall Story?   419
    TIMOTHY LEUNIG & HANS-JOACHIM VOTH

15. Producing Health in Past and Present: The Changing
    Roles of Scientific and Alternative Medicine   439
    ANNE DIGBY & SHEILA RYAN JOHANSSON

16. An Old Poor Law for the New Europe? Reconciling Local
    Solidarity with Labour Mobility in Early Modern England   463
    PETER M. SOLAR & RICHARD M. SMITH

17. Paying for Old Age: Past, Present, Future   479
    MARK THOMAS & PAUL JOHNSON

Name Index   509

Subject Index   519

Notes on Contributors

Stephen Broadberry is Professor of Economic History in the Department of Economics, University of Warwick. His main research interests are in international comparisons of productivity during the nineteenth and twentieth centuries and structural change and economic growth. Recent publications include *The Productivity Race: British Manufacturing in International Perspective, 1850–1990* (Cambridge University Press, 1997), and 'How did the United States and Germany Overtake Britain? A Sectoral Analysis of Comparative Productivity Levels, 1870–1990', *Journal of Economic History*, 1998.

Leandro Conte is at the University of Pisa. He has written extensively on the history of the Italian financial system, including *La Banca Nazionale 1843–1861* (Naples, 1990).

Nicholas Crafts is Professor of Economic History, London School of Economics. His research interests are comparative study of long-run changes in productive capabilities and living standards. A relevant recent publication is 'Globalization and Growth in the Twentieth Century', International Monetary Fund Working Paper No 00/44, 2000.

Paul A. David is Professor of Economics and Senior Fellow of the Institute for Economic Policy Research at Stanford University; Emeritus Fellow of All Souls College; Senior Fellow of the Oxford Internet Institute and Emeritus Professor of Economics and Economic History in the University of Oxford. His research continues to inquire into the sources and consequences of 'path dependence' in economic processes, particularly those affecting technological and institutional co-evolution. Related recent journal publications include: 'Productivity Growth Prospects and the New Economy in Historical Perspective', *European Investment Bank Papers*, 6(1), 2001; 'The Evolving Accidental Information Super-highway', *Oxford Review of Economic Policy* 17(2), September 2001. Two books are scheduled to appear from Cambridge University Press during 2003: *From the Economics of QWERTY to the*

Notes on Contributors

Millennium Bug and Beyond and *Standards, Markets and Network Evolution*.

Christopher Davis is Lecturer in Russian and East European Political Economy at Oxford University. His main research interests are the theory of the command and transition economies, the economics of the health and defence sectors in the USSR and Russia, and Russian industrialization.

Jan de Vries is Sidney Hellman Ehrman Professor of History and Professor of Economics at the University of California at Berkeley. His current research interests include the role of consumer demand in economic growth, the economics of art production in the seventeenth-century Netherlands, and Asian-European trade in the early modern period. His most recent book, with Ad van der Woude, is *The First Modern Economy. Success, Failure, and Perseverance of the Dutch Economy, 1500–1815* (Cambridge University Press, 1997). He was the recipient of the A.H. Heineken Prize in History, 2000.

Anne Digby is Professor of Social History at Oxford Brookes University. Her current research interests are in medical practice and medical pluralism in Britain and in South Africa. A recent monograph was *The Evolution of British General Practice, 1850–1948* (Oxford University Press, 1999).

Barry Eichengreen is George C. Pardee and Helen N. Pardee Professor of Economics and Political Science, University of California at Berkeley. His current research projects include one on post-World War II European economic growth and one on the evolution of the international financial architecture. Recent publications include 'Labor Markets and European Economic Growth since World War II' (with Torben Iversen), *Oxford Review of Economic Policy* (1999), and *Toward a New International Financial Architecture* (Washington, DC: Institute for International Economics, 1999).

Roderick Floud is Provost of London Guildhall University. An economic historian, his main research interest is anthropometric history. He has recently published *The People and the British Economy, 1830–1914* (Oxford University Press) and is currently editing, with Professor Paul Johnson, *The Cambridge Economic History of Britain since 1700* (Cambridge University Press).

Notes on Contributors

James Foreman-Peck is Professor of Economics at Cardiff Business School and founding Director of the Institute of Economic Research. His current and past research has been concerned with business and management strategy in both the private and the public sector. Recent relevant publications include *European Industrial Policy: The Twentieth Century Experience* (edited with G. Federico, Oxford University Press, 1999).

Jane Humphries is a Fellow of All Souls College, Oxford. She has a long-standing interest in child and juvenile labour in the industrial revolution. She has published articles on this topic both alone and in co-authorship with Sara Horrell and Hans-Joachim Voth.

Sheila Ryan Johansson is a Research Associate at the Cambridge Group for the History of Population and Social Structure at the University of Cambridge. She has a long-standing research interest in the history of health and mortality and is currently completing a book entitled *Death and the Doctors*, examining the role of advances in medical knowledge in the beginnings of the post-1600 mortality transition among the European elites. Her related recent publications include 'Before the Health Transition: Health Policy in Victorian England and After', *Annales de Démographie Historique* 2000; 'Welfare History on the Great Plains: Health and Mortality 1650–1850', in R. Steckel and J. Rose, ed., *The Backbone of History* (Cambridge: Cambridge University Press, 2002).

Paul Johnson is Professor of Economic History at the London School of Economics. His research interests include the history of savings and welfare, the economics of old age and pensions, and the relationship between laws and markets in Victorian England. His publications include *Saving and Spending* (1985) and *Ageing and Economic Welfare* (1992).

Carol S. Leonard, Fellow of St Antony's College, Oxford, is Lecturer in Regional Studies of Post-Communist States at Oxford University. Her research is interdisciplinary, covering economics of transition, the regions of Central and Eastern Europe, and Russian economic history. Her publications include a book on eighteenth-century Russian social history, an edited book on the *Microeconomic Change in Central and Eastern Europe* (Palgrave Macmillan, 2002), and two edited volumes on European and American agrarian and labour history. She has published a number of articles on contemporary agrarian reform and nineteenth-century rural Russian history.

Timothy Leunig is Lecturer in Economic History at the London School of Economics. He works primarily on industrial and business history at the start of the twentieth century, looking at the effects of industrial structure on technological choice, and at the role of skills and worker experience in determining productivity. With Hans-Joachim Voth, he has looked at the role played by the conquest of smallpox in explaining the rise in height in London in the nineteenth century.

Avner Offer is Chichele Professor of Economic History at the University of Oxford and Fellow of All Souls. His main current research interest is in the relation between affluence and subjective well-being in the UK and the USA, especially since World War II. Recent relevant publications include, as editor and contributor, *In Pursuit of the Quality of Life* (1996), 'Between the Gift and the Market: The Economy of Regard', *Economic History Review*, vol. 50 (1997), 'The American Automobile Frenzy of the 1950s', in Bruland and O'Brien (eds.), *From Family Firms to Corporate Capitalism* (1998) and 'Body Weight and Self-Control in the USA and Britain since the 1950s', *Social History of Medicine* (2001).

Richard Smith is Director of the Cambridge Group for the History of Population and Social Structure. His current research interests are concerned with the inter-relationships between demographic change and welfare provisions in England and her continental neighbours before 1850. Recent publications include *The Manor Court and English Medieval Society* (with Zvi Razi), 1996, and *The Locus of Care: Families, Communities, Institutions and the Provision of Welfare since Antiquity* (with Peregrine Horden), 1998.

Peter Solar is Associate Professor of Economics at Versalius College, Vrije Universiteit Brussel. In addition to his work on early modern poor relief, he has published on Irish agriculture and trade in the nineteenth century, Belgian economic growth and industrial policy in the twentieth century, and the European linen and jute industries.

Peter Temin is Elisha Gray II Professor of Economics at MIT. His current research interests include telecommunications and health economics, about current events, and more historical topics such as the economic history of New England, the demographic composition of business elites, the Great Depression, and business history. Recent publications include 'Fateful Choices: AT&T in the 1970s', *Business and Economic History*, Fall 1998; The American Business Elite in Historical Perspective', in Elise S. Brezis and Peter Temin (eds.), *Elites, Minorities, and Economic Growth* (Amsterdam: Elsevier, 1999), 'The Industrialization of New England, 1830–80', in Peter Temin (ed.), *Engines of Enterprise: An Economic History of New England* (Cambridge: Harvard University Press, 2000).

Mark Thomas is Associate Professor of History, University of Virginia. Current research interests include historical perspectives on savings behaviour, income inequality and the evolution of labour markets in the US and UK, as well as methodological questions regarding statistical measurement of historical processes and developments. Recent papers include two co-authored with Charles Feinstein: 'A Plea for Errors', *Historical Methods*, 2002, and 'The Value-Added Approach to the Measurement of Economic Growth', in T. Guinnane, W. Sundstrom and W. Whatley (eds.), *History Matters: Economic Growth, Technology, and Demographic Change* (Stanford, CA: Stanford University Press, 2003 forthcoming). A further collaboration with Charles Feinstein is *Making History Count: A Primer in Quantitative Methods for Historians* (Cambridge University Press, 2002).

Gianni Toniolo is Professor of Economics at both the University of Rome 'Tor Vergata' and Duke University, and Research Fellow, CEPR. His current research interests focus on modern economic growth in Italy and international cooperation by central banks in the twentieth century. Recent books include: *The European Economy Between the Wars*, Oxford, 1997 (with C.H. Feinstein and P. Temin) and *Economic Growth in Europe since 1945*, Cambridge, 1996 (edited with N. Crafts).

Giovanni Vecchi's current research interests at the University of Rome 'Tor Vergata' focus on long-run changes in welfare and income distribution.

Nick von Tunzelmann is Professor of the Economics of Science and Technology, SPRU, University of Sussex. His current research examines the relationship between technological change and organizational change at both macro and micro levels. His most recent book is *Technology and Industrial Progress: The Foundations of Economic Growth* (Aldershot: Edward Elgar, 1995).

Notes on Contributors

Hans-Joachim Voth is Assistant Professor in the Economics Department, Universitat Pompeu Fabra, Barcelona. He is currently working on the economic and social history of working time since the Industrial Revolution as well as the history of poverty traps. Recent publications include *Time and Work in England, 1760–1830* (Oxford: Oxford University Press, 2000); 'Destined for Deprivation? Poverty Traps in Eighteenth Century England', with J. Humphries and S. Horrell, *Explorations in Economic History 2000*; 'Time and Work in Eighteenth Century London', *Journal of Economic History* 1998; 'Human Capital, Equipment Investment, and Industrialization', with J. Temple, *European Economic Review* 1998.

Francis Wilson is Professor in the School of Economics and Director of the Southern African Labour and Development Research Unit (SALDRU) at the University of Cape Town. His current research interests, in addition to globalization and migration, focus on integrated household surveys, both in terms of collection of data and policy analysis. Recent papers (not yet published) include 'Globalization: A View from the South' and 'Unorthodox Migration in Southern Africa'.

Gavin Wright is William Robertson Coe Professor of American Economic History at Stanford University. For some years, his primary research purpose has been to understand the historical origins of the economic performance of the American economy, in comparative and international perspective. Recent publications include: 'Increasing Returns and the Genesis of American Resource Abundance,' with Paul A. David, *Industrial and Corporate Change* (March 1997); 'Les Fondements Historiques de la Domination Economique Américaine', *Annales: Histoire, Sciences Sociales* (Mai-Juin 1998); 'Can a Nation Learn? American Technology as a Network Phenomenon?' in *Learning by Doing in Markets, Firms, and Countries*, edited by Naomi Lamoreaux, Daniel Raff, Peter Temin (Chicago: University of Chicago Press, 1999).

Preface and Acknowledgements

The essays brought together in this volume are based upon papers that were first presented to an International Symposium convened in Oxford, 1–3 July, 1999, on 'The Economic Challenges of the Twenty-First Century in Historical Perspective'. The particular occasion for this gathering was a celebration of the scholarly career of Charles H. Feinstein, FBA, on the eve of his retiring as the Chichele Professor of Economic History in the University of Oxford.

Another, larger academic objective also animated our discussions in Oxford. The Symposium sought to engage economic historians' interest in seeking explicitly to enlighten and inform contemporary economic policy discussions and, by so doing, to encourage a wider acknowledgement on the part of the economics profession of the value of historical approaches to many subjects in their field. To promote in this way a greater appreciation for the value of including some training in economic history as part of the modern economist's academic preparation was an enterprise readily embraced by the participants in the Symposium as being worthy in its own right, as well as a singularly appropriate way to mark Charles Feinstein's contributions in teaching the subject, successively, at the universities of Cambridge, York and Oxford.

This gathering was organized by Paul David, Peter Solar and Mark Thomas, and its celebratory aspects were made possible through the generous support and gracious hospitality of the Warden and Fellows of All Souls College, and the Warden and Fellows of Nuffield College—the two Oxford foundations with which Charles Feinstein has been associated as a Fellow. The staff of each College were wonderfully helpful in accommodating the needs of the large company of Symposium participants during the three-day programme.

Yet without the financial support provided by a grant from the British Academy neither the international assembly of economic historians at the Symposium, nor the subsequent preparation of this volume would have been possible. On behalf of the entire company involved, the organizers and editors wish to express our gratitude to the

Preface and Acknowledgements

Academy. Special thanks are due to Professor Sir Tony Wrigley, the Academy's President at the time, and to Professor F.G.B. Millar, its Publications Secretary, who lent their personal encouragement to this undertaking from its inception. James Rivington, the Academy's Publications Officer, was invariably helpful and, with the Publications Committee, maintained unmatched patience throughout the editorial and publication process.

All those who have contributed directly to the writing of this book also are pleased for us to take this opportunity to acknowledge the important roles played by the following members of the distinguished company of social scientists and historians who acted as discussants of individual papers and commentators on the general themes of the Symposium: Tony Atkinson, Nicholas Dimsdale, Stanley Engerman, Charles Feinstein, John Flemming, Natalia Gurushina, John Habbakuk, Michael Kaser, Jane Lewis, Angus Maddison, Robin Matthews, Peter Mathias, Patrick O'Brien, Peter Oppenheimer, Daniel Raff, Barry Supple, Herman van der Wee, David Vines, Martin Weale, Charles Webster and Tony Wrigley.

The services they performed so conscientiously, both by articulating the issues being addressed and by indicating aspects of the papers that deserved closer consideration, have enhanced the quality of the revised essays and appreciably improved the coherence of the volume as a whole. That contribution was further augmented by the comprehensive set of notes taken during the proceedings by Carol Scott Leonard and made available for editors' use; upon them rested the uncanny (and perhaps not entirely welcome) ability of the editors to remind essay-writers of those suggestions for revisions and elaborations of their work which had surfaced in the course of the Symposium.

We are pleased also to thank most warmly Merilyn Holme for her excellent assistance throughout the entire undertaking. She worked with the organizers and the individual contributors in arranging their travel and accommodations, as well as in preparing their papers for distribution to discussants before the Symposium; she handled all the post-Symposium electronic correspondence between the editors and the contributors concerning revisions, re-formatted and copy-edited the edited papers for the printers and, finally, shared in the task of reading the page proofs. All of this she accomplished with good cheer as well as steady efficiency.

PAD and MT

INTRODUCTION
Thinking Historically about Challenging Economic Issues
PAUL A. DAVID & MARK THOMAS

The Purposes and Organization of this Book

The seventeen chapters contributed to this volume exemplify some of the ways in which studying the economic experiences of societies in the past can contribute to a better understanding of current and future economic questions. What the authors collectively offer is *not* a general epistemological or methodological account of the uses of history, but instead, a variety of particular engagements of 'the historian's craft' — as it was referred to by Marc Bloch — in the service of enlightened discussions of social and economic policy. To do this, they have drawn upon a corpus of more extensive and more detailed historical works (many of them their own) that provide fresh and useful insights into some of the major economic challenges that will continue to concern policy-makers and informed members of the general public in the decades ahead.

The essays have been grouped in three sections within the book, under the respective headings 'Drivers of Long-Term Economic Growth', 'Changes in Institutional Regimes and Ideologies', and 'Welfare, Well-Being and Individual Economic Security'. Each Part thus addresses a major area of policy concern involving complex economic challenges that can be usefully approached from 'an historical perspective'. The focal areas that have been selected are very broad in scope and interrelated: the conditions for sustaining long-term economic growth, the assessment of determinants of the speed of adjustments to particular policy changes and the management of major transitions to alternative institutional regimes, the translation of economies' macro-

Introduction

level performance into improvements in the material welfare and well-being of individuals and families. All of them deal in one way or another with central issues of long-term economic and social change that have preoccupied much of the modern academic literature in the social sciences, as well as figuring prominently in current policy debates.

In Part One, five essays explore the shifting constellation of forces that have sustained economic growth in the West's leading market economies since the era of the Industrial Revolution. Focusing on the historical experiences of Britain, the continental European nations and the US, these studies examine the *linkage* among demand-side and supply-side drivers of growth. Rather than treating increasing factor supplies and productivity-raising innovations as independent 'sources of growth', the particular patterns of their interrelationships and interactions in each of several historical contexts are shown to have been critical determinants of the observed trajectory of long-term growth.

Jan de Vries examines the connections between changing household demand patterns and changes in the supply of work effort, which are shown to have been central in the intensification of production that began with proto-industrialization in north-western Europe during the latter half of the seventeenth century, and continued throughout the century that followed. The essays by Jane Humphries and Stephen Broadberry address the processes of human capital formation and its consequences in early modern England and among industrialized economies (Britain, Germany and the US) during the late nineteenth and early twentieth centuries, respectively. The special institutional arrangements that permitted the financing of apprenticeship and vocational training, and the implications for structural change and productivity growth of the human capital formation that occurred through those channels, provide an illuminating contrast with the emphasis upon formal education in the recent literature on development and growth.

The remaining essays in this section analyse the dynamics of productivity growth. Paul David and Gavin Wright examine the diffusion of new 'general purpose technologies', with special attention to the half-century-long process through which technological systems based upon electric dynamo were elaborated and integrated with other technologies, culminating in the electrification of manufacturing in the interwar era. Nick von Tunzelmann proposes a 'comparative systems' approach to understanding the way in which different institutional regimes affect the 'governance of technological development', arguing that the choice of policy regime has major consequences for productivity performance.

Part Two takes as its common theme the dynamics of transitions to new economic and political regimes, including the ways in which policy responses to unanticipated 'crises' are affected by the realignment of pre-existing ideologies and expectations. The variety of challenges encountered in 'institutional regime transitions' is explored by six studies, each being concerned with a different problem.

The opening essay by Nicholas Crafts reconsiders the state policies and institutional arrangements that figured prominently in the recent East Asian 'economic miracle', employing a historical perspective to examine the implications of the East Asian financial crisis of 1997 for future economic growth among the 'Asian Tigers'. Two essays offer historical perspectives on the post-Soviet Russian economy. They carry some lessons of wider applicability in the design of institutional reform strategies that would avoid mistakes in implementation that result in incomplete transitions and a malfunctioning economic system. Christopher Davis and James Foreman-Peck examine the two episodes during the twentieth century in which Britain made the shift from a wartime command economy to a peacetime market regime. When viewed in the light of the contrasting outcomes of policies that attempted a quick ('big bang') transition versus a gradual government-guided restructuring of the British economy, the failures of the post-1989 policies pursued in Russia become understandable in more generic terms. Carol Leonard provides an analysis of rural opposition to land privatization in the post-Soviet era that draws explicit parallels with the resistance by Russian peasants to early twentieth-century government programmes of land reform, finding a similar economic rationality in both these episodes of agricultural cultivators' recalcitrance.

The other three essays in this section explore various ways in which institutional arrangements, economic structures and modes of thought that persist from a politically discarded economic system can constrain the effectiveness of reform policies or frustrate new policy action entirely. Francis Wilson's essay argues that many of the most difficult policy challenges facing post-apartheid South Africa are the result of deep structures of economic inequality, rather than problems that have arisen due to or subsequent to the fall of the antecedent oppressive regime. A far older system had been developed to exploit

Introduction

the labour of migratory indigenous workers from the rural territories in European-owned enterprises, without permitting the peoples living in those rural areas to invest productively in either physical infrastructures or human capital. That system had set the pattern which was generalized and reinforced under apartheid, and its consequences remain to be addressed by the country's policy-makers.

The essay by Gianni Toniolo, Leandro Conte and Giovanni Vecchi offers a new perspective on the Euro's likely effectiveness in achieving the ('Single Market') goal of European economic integration, by examining the impact of a nineteenth-century national currency reform. Following the unification of Italy's currency in 1861–2, the slow and partial convergence of real wage rates and interest rates in different regions of the country reflected the strong influences exerted by the persistence of local factor market institutions, as well as the counter-reactions of agents who saw their immediate interests as having been harmed by the reform. These findings may serve to temper enthusiastic expectations of the rapid materialization of relative price convergence among the regions of the European Union.

Some equally sobering thoughts about the ability of economic policy-making to respond to new problems in a timely way emerge from Barry Eichengreen and Peter Temin's contribution to Part Two. Their essay closely examines the rhetoric of central bankers' pronouncements during the Great Depression of the 1930s, revealing how tenacious was the hold on those influential policy-makers' thinking of ideas that survived from the pre-1914 era of the Gold Standard. Even when confronted by a radical shock to the world's economy, and surrounded by the facts of the collapse of the old Gold Standard regime, the bankers' interpretations of the current circumstances and their policy prescriptions continued to evince a faith in the operation of automatic monetary readjustment mechanisms. Considering the resulting resistance to the idea of intervening quickly to increase the supply of international liquidity in that era, Eichengreen and Temin see some unsettling parallels in the IMF's actions during the 1997 East Asian financial crisis.

A common theme for Part Three is formed by the nexus of issues arising from modern economic growth's diverse and changing significance for individuals' sense of personal well-being and security, as well as from the uneven distribution of economic welfare among the populations affected. On the basis of his survey of time-series and cross-section data pertaining to per capita real income, various alternative objective indicators of welfare, and indexes of self-avowed levels of satisfaction or 'human happiness', Avner Offer finds that the connection between economic growth and improvements in human welfare altered dramatically over the course of the development process—at least in the case of today's industrially advanced societies. In a closely related pair of essays, Roderick Floud and Timothy Leunig and Hans-Joachim Voth focus on an array of alternative, anthropometric measures (based on age-specific heights and weights) that quantitative economic historians have sought to employ as indicators of material welfare for populations in the past. They debate both the interpretations that should be given to such measures in a variety of historical contexts, and assess the potential for applying them to illuminate welfare trends in the future. Anne Digby and Sheila Ryan Johansson's essay addresses some problematic aspects of interpreting advances in modern medical practice as unambiguous indicators of improvements in people's enjoyment of 'physical wellness'. In particular, they consider some issues raised by historical changes in the positions of 'scientific' and 'alternative' medicine in health care provision, pointing out parallels between the coexistence of 'modern' and 'traditional' healers in some present-day developing countries, and the increasing recourse of Western high-income populations to 'alternative therapies'.

The volume concludes with a pair of essays addressing the challenges of providing economic security, especially for society's vulnerable members. Peter Solar and Richard Smith focus upon welfare and pension benefits in the European Union. Here they see policy-making deadlocked by the conflict between two forces: reforms that would remove restrictions on the cross-border 'portability' of pensions and other welfare entitlements, so as to permit the goal of greater labour mobility; and the rising hostility of tax-payers against proposals that would require them to bear the costs of income transfers to needy 'foreigners'—as would be entailed by harmonizing welfare support throughout the entire region at a reasonable level. Delving into the history of poverty relief in Britain for insights into ways out of this quandary, their essay shows that the set of institutional arrangements governing parish-based relief (the so-called 'Old Poor Law'), which evolved during the early modern era, in effect solved a similar contemporary problem. This problem's features parallel the policy dilemma that is presently confronting Europe's welfare and benefit systems.

Mark Thomas and Paul Johnson's contribution raises the worrisome thought that the political flexibility for innovative reforms affecting welfare support for the elderly may no longer exist. Their comparative

Introduction

study of the history of old age support in the UK and US concludes that despite the quite different beginnings of the public pension and social security systems in the two countries, government policy in both places has become similarly 'locked in' to the continuation of programmes that are headed for financial non-viability. Ironic as it may seem, the successes of the institutional arrangements that had been devised in response to pressing socio-economic problems in the first half of the twentieth century created political constituencies that in each case are making it difficult to save the systems from being wrecked by the mounting financial strains that an ageing population will impose.

The terse, capsule summaries in the preceding paragraphs may convey a sense of the thrust of this volume, and the variety of its contents. But, self-evidently, they will not have captured the scope and depth of the individual essays, or the particular respects in which the authors' historical inquiries illuminate their discussions of present and future policy issues. At this juncture, therefore, readers may be ready and perhaps even eager to turn directly to essays in one or another Part of the book. On having made that choice they will discover that the Editors have not completely abandoned them: each Part is preceded by an overview of the themes that unify and distinguish its constituent essays. Plainly, these overviews are supplemental rather than essential. Their purpose is to explicate and integrate, without venturing to evaluate the contributors' key findings and conclusions. Moreover, the Editors are content to leave it to those who will thoughtfully peruse the individual essays to form their own assessments of the particular benefits and shortcomings of researching the past deliberately for the purpose of better informing future policy analyses.

But there is another option that must be recognized. Some readers at this point may find they have methodological reservations, or even entertain strong doubts as to the value of this volume's declared purpose. It would not surprise us were advanced students of economics and their instructors especially prominent among those who harbour considerable scepticism regarding the value of historical inquiries, especially in a work that aspires to be future-policy-relevant. In thinking about tomorrow's economic challenges, of all things, why should economists need to turn to the study of economic history? What benefit for their discipline to become thus drawn into an uncertain quest for 'historical economics'?

Scepticism is not only a legitimate scientific attitude, it is also essential to the effective functioning of communities devoted to the pursuit of reliable knowledge. So long as the sceptics remain open to rational modes of persuasion, such attitudes are to be commended and encouraged. The remaining pages of this introduction therefore take the foregoing questions seriously and endeavour to respond to them directly. But even those readers who remain less than fully convinced by the arguments for recognizing the study of intrinsically historical processes to be an integral part of the economist's task, will surely find much in the essays that proves interesting, informative and entertaining.

Economic History and the Modern Economist

The historical studies that form the core substance of this book will be seen to aid the modern economic analyst in a number of ways. Firstly, they reveal deep-seated and persisting forces affecting contemporary trends and policy problems. Secondly, they provide a background against which truly new economic phenomena may be identified and examined. Thirdly, they offer a rich array of case-study materials against which one may test the usefulness of current theoretical frameworks, empirical methods and criteria for both private and public decision-making.

In addition, these essays exhibit the considerable pedagogical power of applying 'historical economics' in the writing of economic history itself. By adopting an *analytical narrative* approach, the authors enable students and lay readers alike to absorb the essential economic concepts and data that are required for an appropriately rigorous discussion of the policy issues posed by a variety of complex dynamic processes in the economy—without having first to acquire the formal, highly abstract vocabulary and mathematical concepts that are so prominent a feature of modern-day professional economic writings.

It might well be asked why the contents of this volume have been confined to discussion of the particular major themes and the respective groups of topics treated in each of its three parts. Are there not other important economic challenges, equally worthy of sustained attention, such as the implications of the growing economic importance of knowledge ownership as a source of wealth, or the continuing (and potentially expanding) problems of environmental management? Of course there are. But inasmuch as the task undertaken by the book is

Introduction

to explore the ways in which the fruits of research in economic history can be harvested to inform contemporary policy discussions, this question has a simple answer: we have focused on questions that have been recognized for quite some time as being of continuing importance, long enough for a considerable amount of historical research to have been carried out.

These studies also have been selected to illuminate aspects of the story that typically have to be left out of the mathematical modellers' abstract, caricature-like sketches of the process of growth. A further purpose served by inclusion of explicitly historical treatments of the subject is that of imparting a greater measure of concreteness to the claim that the experience of economic growth can be understood only in terms of the mutual *interactions* and feed-back loops that form among a number of key dynamic processes. Although economists work hard to formulate models in which the distinct sub-processes are more easily disentangled in order to achieve greater clarity, historical accounts can be particularly useful in conveying a more realistic appreciation of the intricacy of those interactions. Equally, comparative historical analysis permits a sharper focus on the complex character and significance of specific institutional details, and the ways in which the sequencing of agents' actions and the timing of exogenous events can make an important difference in the determination of particular economic outcomes.

The topical range of this book, therefore, might be said to have been constrained by the pre-commitment to the animating idea of the volume—the conviction that it is not just useful but truly vital to think historically about the economic future. Without necessarily speaking for the entire company, the editors continue to hold that conviction and believe that the study of economic history has a profound role to play in our understanding of the policy challenges of the new millennium. Since that may be thought to have exacted some cost, in accepting the limitations imposed by the more immediately available supply of historical research, there is a case to answer in regard to the existence of commensurate benefits. What is the good of having economists engage more seriously with history? Why should policy-makers turn to research on the economics of the past history in order to address the problems of the future?

Introduction

Why Ask Economic Historians about the Economic Future?

An answer to that question in the present context needs to be prefaced with a brief but important caveat. The studies presented in this volume, with few exceptions, do not start by setting out a particular contemporary economic problem, much less specific policy questions that are currently being debated and for which suitably detailed answers are sought from an historical inquiry. Instead, what all the contributions have undertaken to offer is in the nature of a commentary on the modern economic concerns to which the subject matter of their respective historical studies appears most immediately germane. Putting this in another way, these essays are motivated by a belief in the value of treating past economic circumstances and problems first on their own terms, within their particular historical contexts. Once that has been done, however, it becomes proper — indeed desirable — for the findings to be reconsidered as a possible vantage point from which to view one or more among the present or prospective issues of economic policy relevance. To be sure, the performance of this second task should not be incumbent upon the economic historian. It so happens that in the present instance, those involved have been intrigued enough to undertake it.

From the viewpoint of traditional historical writing, however, this could still be seen as a consequence of flagrant 'presentism': presenting the past not on its own terms, but with an eye fixed on the concerns of the moment. Accusations of presentism, however, ought to be carefully considered. In some respects, it would hardly be possible for an historian to escape completely the concerns of his or her own milieu; even the choice of an 'escapist' subject must reflect a perception of some salient contemporary questions. Nevertheless, conventional historians regularly caution against the 'error of presentism' — where they do not denounce it as an irredeemable sin. The worry is that indulging in this vice is likely to encourage a misreading of the historical evidence, and the misrepresentation of the concerns — and consequently the larger worldview — of the people who lived in a different age.

Economic historians, no less than historians of other facets of human society, are always subject to the risks of failing to grasp properly the *mentality* of past cultures. But it does not follow that being aware of the concerns of the present exacerbates that risk. Indeed, it may mitigate it; self-consciousness may render the social science

Introduction

historian more alive to the distance that separates her human subjects and their world from the concerns of the moment. Awareness of just such separation itself offers an expanded context in which to consider the particular obsessions of the present, and in just that respect may prove enlightening.

Yet, while presentism *per se* is hardly a defect in historical writing, it is important to be both self-conscious and explicit about what is being attempted, and what is to be expected from an effort to 'apply' economic history to informing the work of modern economic policy analysis. The remainder of this Introduction attempts to do just that, both in the particular context of the studies presented in this book, and at a more abstract and general methodological level.

The Case for 'Historical Economics'

We can make a start by stating our central contention, which is simply that *economics is in some quarters, and more widely should become, an historical social science*. Although some readers may find that a self-evident proposition, many others are likely to regard it as deeply heterodox if not quite baffling. Nevertheless, its immediate import should be clear: were economics generally to be approached as an historical social science, the presumptive distinction between economic history and economics would be harder to maintain. What precisely does that imply, and what would be the gain in it?

Some scholars have cast economic history as an applied form of economics and described the goal of bringing knowledge of the past to bear on present problems as an 'application' of the latter, motivated by the needs of modern policy analysis. But one might ask whether economic history should be conceived of primarily as a branch of applied economics. Our answer is that it should not be. Today, however, many economists view what they are about in more or less the same terms as did the early political economists of the nineteenth century, who took their view of the natural sciences to be the ideal towards which their young discipline should strive. For them the economist's goal was (and is) the discovery of 'iron laws', or as later writers on the philosophy of science put it, 'general covering laws'—except that these were to be about social phenomena rather than 'the laws of nature'. In other words, the aspirations of the discipline were explicitly *ahistorical*.

The argument that might be developed in this vein would assert that the study of economic phenomena observed in times past can serve as theory's handmaiden; the economic historian's role would then be to provide tests of the applicability of the supposed timelessness of the covering laws established by economic analysis. In this view, the past is a museum stuffed with interesting cases, a store of 'wonders and curiosities' that afford new opportunities to demonstrate the range of economists' proven explanatory powers. Moreover, it is a source of data pertaining to an array of economic circumstances more varied than those which can be observed immediately around us, and therefore offers a better empirical basis on which to identify important quantitative regularities about them.

Undeniably, these functions of historical research are valid and important. Where would the systematic study of phenomena that are inherently long-term in nature be without historical research to reconstruct, and so characterize the subject matter? In concrete terms, where would modern economic growth analysis be without Kuznets' programme of historical research on the measurement of national product? Similarly, much of the conceptualization of technological innovation as a form of economic competition, or rivalry in the sense of Schumpeter, derives from detailed historical studies of the origins and impacts of technological change, from the Industrial Revolution onwards.

The study of both historical time-series and cross-section data has provided useful 'tests' of the robustness, or temporal invariance of hypotheses that originally were formulated in more recent contexts of application. Consider the example of recent econometric work on late seventeenth- and eighteenth-century financial markets, or other instances of applications of modern theoretical propositions, such as the classic use by Alfred Conrad and John Meyer of capital theory in explaining the historically observed constellation in the relationships among the price of slaves, the net revenue stream yielded by slave workers, and the interest rate. The analysis of apprenticeship institutions in early modern Britain in this volume, similarly, demonstrates the empirical relevance of contract theory, while simultaneously exploiting it as a source of insights into the workings of pre-industrial labour markets.

Moreover, where would our analysis of the economic past be without the ability to turn to simple, time-invariant propositions about basic features of the workings of markets? Consider the usefulness of these among a host of familiar propositions: that market demand curves for normal goods slope downwards in relative price space, that prices are determined where supply and demand match and so clear the market, that bargained outcomes may be altered by changes in the relative 'threat powers' of the parties (i.e. the level of benefits they would be able to secure for themselves were they to withdraw from the game entirely). These have proved to be dependable aides in making sense of a wide range of historically observed phenomena.

At the same time, our ability to raid the 'curiosity cabinet' of the past to provide support for theories about the fundamental quality of rational behaviour is rather more limited. There is both a simple, empirical element to this later caution, as well as a more sophisticated, theoretical one. At the simplest of levels, the ideal of historical economics if followed to its logical extreme suggests that past actors behaved identically to their current counterparts when faced with a similar problem. On that premise, one might suppose that entrepreneurs faced with the risk and challenge of new technology in 1750, would have acted much as they do today; and consumers in seventeenth-century Holland, if faced with the opportunities to buy new products, would exhibit behaviours not very different from today's household members in the supermarket. The question is whether these are *maintained* hypotheses, or matters for investigation. Historians typically are wiser to the impact exerted by culture and circumstance than 'the economist in the street', and they are thus more disposed to recognize the operation of Hartley's rule — which says that the past is a different place, where things might be done differently. Indeed, one of the main virtues of historical economics may be a greater readiness to work out *how* things were done differently in the past and under what set of prior beliefs and expectations.

But, to repeat, there is a deeper issue in this. The function of historical economics is too often viewed in much the same way as Descartes and his followers regarded history in general. They thought that it was invariant mathematical laws that held the truths about the nature of the world, and so took history's usefulness to consist primarily in supplying illustrations of the workings of those underlying laws. For economic historians to accept that role might be thought suitably modest, but such a view proceeds from serious misconceptions about the relationship of the social systems in which economic events (phenomena) arise, and the physical sciences. This is the more subtle matter that we need briefly to elucidate.

Introduction

The 'open' and consequent 'non-stationarity' of social systems distinguishes them from the systems studied in classical physics and chemistry. This sets definite limitations on the simple, illustrative role assigned to economic history viewed as the handmaiden of economic analysis. By the same token, it also militates in favour of the more general reconceptualization of economics as (properly) an historical discipline.

There are many profound differences between the world of external interactions involving non-sensate physical entities and the world of human social interactions. Among modern philosophers of science, and others concerned with the methodology of economics and other social sciences, it is recognized that a critical difference lies in the absence of effective 'closure' in social systems in general and, therefore, in the mechanisms giving rise to economic phenomena. This refers to our inability to represent the system as being observable in isolation from the consequences of human knowledge about it, and hence from changes in the state of information concerning its workings.

Thus, we should emphasize that the differentiating attribute is not the one often cited in discussions of the specific difficulties that are posed for the classical methodology of science by social systems, viz. that the investigators of such systems cannot perform experiments. On the face of this, at least, a contrary state of affairs holds: today the supposedly paradigmatic 'natural science' mode of investigating the world is being used by behavioural economists working in the tradition of experimental psychology. Social scientists nowadays have become increasingly interested in conducting controlled, laboratory experiments, whereas astronomers cannot do this and so must go on relying upon the observation of 'natural experiments'.

Nevertheless, this reversal is not quite so perfect. Economists' experimental subjects are special, at least when they are humans and not pigeons. Unlike the ordinary rats that run the experimental psychologists' mazes, our undergraduates understand that they are participating in controlled experiments; indeed human subject rules oblige university experimenters to tell them all about it. That inevitably imparts artificiality to the character of laboratory economics. It means that the attempt to isolate the behavioural phenomena of interest has implicitly redefined the nature of the situation, and may thereby have rendered the behaviour other than that found 'in social nature'. By contrast, studying the orbits of the planets and the spectra of starlight does not alter the nature of the phenomena.

Introduction

It could be objected that the foregoing basis for distinguishing between economics and the physical sciences does not extend all the way down to the sub-atomic level, where the Heisenberg uncertainty principle tells us that the action of observation itself enters the system under study. Technically, however, what Heisenberg uncertainty is about is the alteration of the system by the forces that the measurement technique interjects. Therefore, it is wrong to equate this immediately with the 'effect' upon human agents' behaviour of discovering something new about their actions, or observing them in a way that generates inferences about the way they will respond in specified circumstances. There is a temporal order in the latter 'effects'.

Hence, it is proper to insist on the difference between natural systems that are 'stationary' and social systems that are subject to fundamental sources of non-stationarity due to their non-closed character. The latter are disturbed by changes in the knowledge that human agents acquire about their workings. This is the crucial sense in which real social systems cannot be closed. Knowledge about markets affects the behaviour of the knowers, in ways that alter the system itself. Hence, the experimental economics laboratory may be able to prevent the participants within an experimental environment from gaining knowledge about the outcome of the process in which they have participated. But that in itself constitutes an artificiality of the experiment.

One important implication that follows immediately from the foregoing is that the history of social systems' behaviours is the only source of empirical knowledge that allows them to be studied. Abductive and inductive methods of gaining knowledge about economics must thus find their grounding in history. Purely deductive, theoretical methods would have to start somewhere outside the realm of social system interactions. But we have pointed out that importing theoretic constructs from the natural systems remains ungrounded, however frequently mathematically inclined economists have followed that course. Any grounded theory that we can call upon in economics must have sprung from *some* understanding of economic history.

A second point is equally important, as we shall re-emphasize below: economic history is not a chronology of all economic events. It is an interpretation of a stream of events selected from among the myriad possible observations that a mere chronicler could record. As the British economic historian T.S. Ashton rightly remarked: 'The facts do not wear their hearts on their sleeves.' Or, as Joan Robinson, the Cambridge iconoclastic economist, noted, 'Economics is not about finding a 1:1 road map.' Even in making a selection of the facts that are to be interpreted (explained) the historian requires some antecedent analytical framework, a theory that imparts significance to particular observations. Thus we arrive at the view that economic history and economic analysis must be thoroughly intertwined, and in their interrelated, reciprocal interplay there is no warrant for one to claim primacy over the other.

The final point to be made here is that the possibility of non-stationarity in social systems creates a complication in setting purely illustrative tasks for economic historians. The historical system that one seeks to understand might be quite different from that which succeeded it. This means that neither simple projection of present understandings backwards nor simple extrapolations of presently informative models forwards are guaranteed to yield helpful results. The flow of events requires continuous re-examination, and possibly recurring reinterpretation. There is an implied challenge in this to the underpinnings of the rational expectations programme: if the relationships in the economy are not stationary, there may not be sufficient data at any one time to fully identify that structure. Hence, the notion that rational agents will learn their way towards a stable equilibrium presupposes the existence of a condition (the 'fixed point' or globally stable equilibrium), which itself cannot be assumed on *a priori* grounds.

As a practical matter, we carry forward many beliefs about the workings of the economic world around us, based on assumptions about various orders of stationarity in the underlying relations. But there are serious dangers in proceeding solely on faith, for the world does change—and sometimes may do so quite precipitously, as the breakdown of the stable Phillips curve in the 1970s taught macroeconomists. The economic historian's role may therefore include the important task of assisting in the identification of such structural changes.

Path Dependent Dynamics

There is a second and special sense in which 'history matters' in economics, a sense that is somewhat more esoteric than the foregoing propositions. This is the idea of *path dependent dynamics*: of a system whose motion remains under the influence of conditions that are themselves the contingent legacies of events and actions in its history.

Introduction

Sometimes the events in question are recent enough, or obtrusive enough to be integrated into the collective cultural identity of the society. But that is not essential, and in other cases the critical events occurred in a past so remote as to have slipped from the conscious memories of the actors. While their actions may be the deliberate resultants of rational calculation conditioned on presently prevailing circumstances, the particularities of that decision context may well be consequences of the contingent chain of events to which those remote critical events had given rise.

Although the assertion that 'history matters' has come to be coupled frequently with references to the concept of 'path dependence', the precise meaning of the latter term more often than not remains rather cloudy. This is unfortunate as well as unnecessary. The fundamental idea is straightforward enough to be intuitively grasped without any instruction in economics, as the foregoing paragraph may have managed to make evident. (Indeed, a thorough training in modern economics might actually interfere with human intuitions about history, and especially about processes involving historically contingent evolution, but that is another story.)

Even the formalizations of the concept of path dependence that we shall introduce shortly are far from forbidding, and will readily repay the effort spent in absorbing them. They will be seen to lend a useful measure of precision to descriptions of the special class of dynamical systems that are neither completely deterministic nor purely random in their workings, and in which the specific details of history govern the unfolding course of development.

A clearer grasp of what the term 'path dependence' is about ought therefore to be part of the modern economist's tool-kit. One would expect it to figure prominently in the analytical consciousness of economic historians, and be equally familiar to all who are concerned to study the evolution of technologies, institutions, firms' strategies and industry structures. But that hardly measures the extent of the social and behavioural science domains that may be illuminated by a working knowledge of the meaning and implications of this strong formulation of the idea that 'history matters'.

Nevertheless, we must hasten to point out that the case for a more general appreciation of historicity in social and economic processes does not rest on the presumption that path dependence is ubiquitously present and of equal importance everywhere and in every historical epoch. Quite the opposite is true. Many of the problems that properly engage the attention of economists can be tackled perfectly well with the conventional tools of supply and demand analysis, because the situations in question can reasonably be characterized as possessing a globally stable equilibrium that is unique. But neither can that condition be said to hold everywhere, and at all times.

Thus, whether a dynamic process in the economy is or is not path dependent is an empirical question, and one that frequently is not so simple to resolve. It will be seen shortly that the answers supplied to this question will be of interest not only to academics seeking the right narrative mode to use in relating what they have come to understand about the past. In an important respect, identification of the respective properties of the many dynamic processes taking place in the world around us can be viewed as the very first thing one should try to establish before undertaking actions intended to make a change for the better. Yet an elementary prerequisite for deciding such matters is the simple recognition of the question's existence, which is to say, of the possibility that some economic processes are characterized by path dependence whereas others are not.

It should thus be evident that, as the term is being used here, 'path dependence' is *not* a theory, but a label that refers to particular dynamic properties that characterize some but not all resource allocation processes. It may be defined either with regard to the relationship between the process dynamics and the outcome(s) to which it tends; or with reference to the nature of the limiting probability distribution that will eventually govern the movements of the system under consideration.

At the most intuitive level, a distinction can be drawn between dynamic processes that are path dependent and the rest. So the latter can be called path *independent* processes, appropriately enough, because their dynamics guarantee convergence to a unique, globally stable equilibrium configuration regardless of where they start, or how they approach that eventual outcome. In the case of a stochastic system, this eventual limit will be an invariant (stationary) asymptotic probability distribution that is continuous over the entire feasible space of outcomes. That is to say, there will be a positive probability assigned to every imaginable place the system could be within some well-defined space, or to every configuration it could assume.

Systems having this property, evidently, are able eventually to shake free from the influence of their initial conditions or of any other past state(s). If that were not the case, the limiting behaviour of the system would not remain uniquely defined (invariant) throughout the course of their development. There is a technical term for this property: *ergodicity*. In physics, ergodic systems are said to be 'connected', in the sense that it is possible to transit directly or indirectly between any arbitrarily chosen pair of states and hence, eventually, to reach all the states from any one of them. Path-dependent processes may therefore be defined in a negative manner, as belonging to the class of exceptions from the foregoing set processes in which the details of the history of the system's motion 'do not matter'—because eventually the system shakes free of their influence.

For many purposes, however, we would like to say what a path-dependent process is, rather than what it is not. Help from the probability theorists can be invoked in order to do that in a precise way. Focusing upon the limiting (asymptotic) patterns generated by a random process, the positive definition is also simple enough to state: a path-dependent stochastic system is one in which the system's asymptotic distribution evolves as a consequence (function of) the process's own history.

This broader definition applies to certain simple stochastic systems that are represented mathematically by an invariant set of finite (positive) 'transition probabilities' that are *state-dependent*. The latter probabilities express the likelihood of being in any state (or category) i at time t+1, conditional on having been in any state j (including $j = i$) at time t, and they can be concisely arranged in matrix form by listing vertically all the states where the system could be observed at time t, and listing horizontally the (same) set of states to which it could have moved by time t+1. Transition matrices of this general kind define what are referred to as 'first order' or homogeneous *Markov chains*. They are familiarly used in economic models of the evolving distribution of workers among employment states, firms among size categories, family lineages among wealth or socio-economic classes, or economies among relative positions in the international distribution of per capita income levels.

It is quite common in such applications for the *transition matrix* formed by those probabilities to be specified in such a way as to ensure that the dynamic process is ergodic. From the definition of the latter term, already given, it follows that the distribution of the system among the states is governed by the repeated iteration of the transition probability matrix, and therefore will converge eventually to an invariant asymptotic probability distribution in which positive probabilities are assigned to all the possible states.

When there is an 'absorbing state' or subset of connected states from which the probability of escape to the subset of transient states is zero, the system will converge weakly to that particular 'attractor'. Nonetheless, it remains ergodic in the sense that regardless of where it may have started, the motion of the system eventually shakes off its initial conditions and goes to the unique absorbing state. On the other hand, when there are two or more absorbing subsets (distinct states, or regions of equilibria that are locally stable), the homogeneous Markov chain is non-ergodic: it and its outcomes can be said to be path dependent. It is not difficult to see that if there exists at least one transient (non-absorbing) state from which either directly or indirectly any of the multiple absorbing states can be reached, the realization of the random process of the system when it has arrived at such a point in its history ('on its path'), in effect, will select one among the alternative attractors.

The foregoing definition of path dependence also subsumes processes that possess a *multiplicity of limiting distributions*, which generally is the case for 'branching processes' or 'branching systems'. In the latter class of stochastic processes, the prevailing probabilities of transitions among states are functions of the sequence of past transient states that the system has visited. When a branching process is subject to local irreversibilities, it takes on the property of non-ergodicity. That is the case in biological evolution, because speciation is a non-reversible action. But there are other, analogous physical systems that illustrate this property: the simple 'fork in the road' may constitute a critical state, if the diverging trails lead to two or more distinct regions between which there are no other connecting routes.

Thus, even when one is quite precise about it, the defining characteristic of the large class of dynamic phenomena to which the term path dependence refers really is not so esoteric after all. What is more mysterious is that those intuitively plausible characteristics should be deliberately excluded from so many of the dynamic models that economists have developed and sought to apply to the world around them.

Introduction

The Essential Place in Economics of Narratives of 'Motion' and 'Rest'

Consideration of the uses of narrative provides a third and distinct ground on which to base our argument that the discipline of economics will be strengthened and enriched by fusing with economic history. The point here is not the very general one that post-modern proponents of 'discourse analysis' have made about the universality of narrative discourse as a mode of communication. Nor do we want to recycle the contention that scientific discourse is about persuasion, and that the telling of a story is a particularly potent mode of persuasion.

The claim that should be advanced instead is simply that the narrative form, by organizing events in a temporal sequence, provides a natural way of injecting the notion of genetic causation into structures of 'explanation' that would otherwise remain devoid of the requirement that events be preceded by their causes. Philosophers of science have pointed out that the mathematical relationships that describe physical systems—and they might equally have spoken mathematical models in economics—do not venture further at a formal level than to establish correspondences which must be satisfied by the variables that belong to the system.

To illustrate the point, consider the General Gas Law governing the relationship between the volume of a container (V), the temperature of the gas within it (T) and the pressure (P) exerted on the container's inner wall by gas molecules that collide with it. Nothing in the 'Gas Law Equation', i.e. $P = T/V$, says that pressure is 'caused' by T and V, any more than the rearrangement of the terms in the equation would explain how the V was 'caused' by P and T. What we have here is just a relationship that these variables must always satisfy. The same holds for the 'Quantity Theory of Money', which gives us an analogous relationship between the money supply (M), the volume of transactions (T), the velocity of transactions (V) and the commodity price level (P): $MV = PT$; and equally for the equations describing the solution of a demand system derived from the first-order conditions for the maximization of a utility function subject to a budget constraint.

We are able to work with these relationships to obtain answers to the questions that take the form: 'What happens to variable x when we change y...', say, to the quantity of commodity i when we increase its relative price, or reduce the income endowment of the household. But the cause-and-effect part of the story is something that is not in the formal model; it is the narrative we have to supply in order to have the sense that the theory embedded in the model can 'explain' something that could 'happen'. From formal economic theory we may derive the shape of the surfaces that will be traced by the necessary co-movements of its variables, but it is the ad hoc narrative added by the economist that 'puts the model into motion'.

In the familiar mathematical analyses of these relationships, certain derivatives (among all those that may be formed) are selected for interpretation as the isolated 'effects' of particular variables of interest. Obviously such interpretations imply the existence of a particular temporal ordering, which the analyst has imposed as being 'natural'. Thus 'the effects' on production volume of incremental labour inputs and incremental capital service inputs will be derived from a production function representation that typically is perfectly invertable. The latter property implies the possibility of a reversal of the causal relationships among those variables. But that has no correspondence with the real world processes of physical transformation that the model of 'production' purports to describe, so, in order to make sense of it, we must formulate an entirely different narrative in which (through 'derived demand' relationships) an incremental change in (planned) output exerts 'effects' upon the quantities of the inputs.

Economics requires narratives in order to make the concept of 'equilibration' perform some explanatory work. We account for the configurations observed in the world by relating how the system must have reached that position of 'rest' by moving thither from somewhere else. That the notion of 'equilibrium' underlies the foregoing presentation of the concept of path dependent dynamic processes in the economy should not be at all surprising, because equilibrium is so pervasive a methodological construct in economics.

Equilibrium conceived as a balance of forces can have a correspondence with both 'stasis' and dynamics. Stasis is pertinent in descriptions of homeostatic systems that are self-equilibrating and tend to restore their initial state (or configuration) when they are perturbed by exogenous shocks. Consequently, one popular conceptualization of historical change is that there exists a unique stable state for the system that is periodically or aperiodically shocked by exogenous forces. One may think of the simple case of an island that has a fixed carrying capacity for a human population, save that it may be seriously degraded by exogenous environmental changes such as the melting of the polar glaciers, shifts in ocean currents (e.g. El Niño), or by

Introduction

devastating cyclones. The economic and demographic history of such a place may then be written as the narrative of the disturbance and subsequent restoration of the equilibrium—with or without entertaining the possibility that a catastrophe might totally depopulate the territory. Members of the *Annales* school in France, to cite one well-known example, have undertaken to present episodes in the history of population and the economy in the Mediterranean region in just such terms, using a simple version of the Malthusian dynamic model which suggests that the system would possess a unique equilibrium. Evidently, this approach is strictly not one in which 'history matters' in the strong sense associated with notion of a contingent dynamic evolution.

Of course, whether or not the economic relationships that obtain in a particular place and historical epoch give rise to a unique equilibrium, or to multiple equilibria, is really the empirical question worth asking first. But the question's importance does not make it any the easier to answer, especially when the course of history has not actually displayed very different persisting configurations of the economy within any comparatively brief time span. Were the latter observations to have been available, they would tend to support at least the presumption that more than one situation of economic equilibrium was attainable without fundamental alterations having occurred in the nature of the society, or in its technologically and environmentally determined constraints.

A seemingly different conceptualization from the one just reviewed allows for 'equilibrium change'. Physiologists have developed the concept of 'homeorrhesis'—or channelled change—to describe the tendency for certain sequences of (organic) development to be self-stabilizing: thus there may be continual, recurring change rather than stasis, but it proceeds in the same manner. There are analogies to this in political science where, say, reform scenarios are found to exhibit constancy, even though the subjects of the reform efforts vary widely in nature.

One illustrative view of such a process envisages a multiplicity of constituencies that could be mobilized to back a change in the status quo pertaining to a particular social institution, or a legal regime, such as that affecting the safety inspection and licensing of consumption goods. We might suppose that the advocates of different reform measures are so separated in their respective interests that they cannot form a politically potent coalition to back any one proposal for change.

Introduction

Then there comes a 'shock', a disaster such as widespread alcohol poisoning from the unregulated sale of methylated spirits, or chemically induced deformities in newborns due to inadequate testing of a new medicinal substance (e.g. thalidomide). Overnight, public awareness of a danger is raised to the point that some proposal for a change in the regulatory regime will now be perceived as likely to succeed. Consequently, those who have favoured any of the changes under consideration in the past (and yet despaired of finding effective backing for one of them) might think it worthwhile to seize the opportunity to score some form of 'victory', and possibly in doing so to create a precedent for future reforms that they particularly advocate. This scenario might have to be repeated over and over until an adequate array of protective legislation had been put in place.

In macroeconomic dynamics the notion analogous to homeorrhesis is that of 'steady-state growth' — possibly punctuated by episodes in which exogenous technological or political events shock an economy off a path in which the structural relations within the economy are being preserved while its output continues to grow in relationship to its population. Steady-state growth alone, whether fast or slow, is not useful as a description of the long-run trajectory of any growing economy that has been carefully documented; structural change turns out to be a concomitant of sustained improvements in productivity and rising average income levels. Rather, this formulation of the equilibrium concept serves to allow one to consider the possibility of different steady-state (equilibrium) *paths*, the dynamical counterpart of stable levels of per capita real product. Exogenous events (world wars, major technological advances) could disturb the growth equilibrium sufficiently that the previous configuration would not be restored, even if it was 'locally' stable.

Were the new situation also to introduce stronger positive feedback forces, however, the immediate effect of the shock would be self-reinforced by the reactions it induced. That instability of the dynamics would thus initiate an extended transition towards some new equilibrium configuration, which would become established only as a result of the gradual weakening of the positive feedback, or the appearance of new, counter-balancing sources of negative feedback.

In all stories of the latter sort one will find both continuity (equilibrium) and change (the movements towards different equilibria). The existence of a multiplicity of locally stable equilibria (dynamic attractors of the system) poses two generic explanatory challenges for the

Introduction

historian. First, what reason is there to suppose that there is more than a single equilibrium, especially when the stability and continuity observed around us suggests that there is only one? This is the part of the challenge that requires analysis of the existing structure to demonstrate the plausibility of a counterfactual state. Second, if another state might have obtained, how did we arrive in this one? This is the problem of identifying the mechanism(s) of 'selection' — which in the conceptualization of path dependence as a branching process corresponds to looking for critical bifurcations in the sequence of development, and for the factors that conditioned the actions taken at those historical junctures.

The drama of an historical narrative becomes more acute when the presence of just such a critical juncture, 'a forking of the road', has been identified in the flow of events. In the tragic form of narrative, the action of the player or players when they reach that point are foreordained, and so it really does not matter whether they can or cannot be said to have seen what would befall them on each of the paths that lie ahead. This is not so in the stories that economic historians typically wish to tell. Economic analysis is essentially about human choices among what the philosopher William James termed 'real options', and the question of what the actors knew, and when they knew it or sought to know it, are understandably of interest. Therefore the quintessential, most satisfying form for an 'historical' economic history narrative to take should rightly involve circumstances in which alternative local states of the world are conceivable. Further, for a tale to emphasize the highly contingent nature of eventual outcome, the actors who are being followed until their arrival at that critical branch-point, or others who might have been in their place, ought to have been capable of choosing either of the paths forward. Then, as a poem by Robert Frost relates, their actual choice at the fork in the road can be seen to have 'made all the difference'.

Where History has Mattered Most for Mainstream Economists — Path Dependence and Market Failures

As has been said, the core content of the concept of path dependence as a dynamic property refers to the idea of history as an irreversible branching process. One must logically distinguish from this the idea that it is possible that some branchings in the course of a market-

Introduction

guided process were 'regrettable' because they created inextricable economic inefficiencies or other difficulties that could have been averted (in some counterfactual but equally feasible world). The two notions are logically quite separable. Plainly, it is a confusion between them that has led some commentators to impute to the notion of path dependence in economics *as such* the set of analytical propositions upon which rests the possibility that a competitive market process could yield a sub-optimal outcome.

For one thing, although the formal concept of path dependence has arrived only lately on the scene, the concept of a 'market failure' has been around in the literature for a long time. 'Effect' before 'cause'? No, not really. Indeed, it was within the context of static general equilibrium analysis that economists developed the concept of 'market failure' — namely, that the Pareto optimality of allocations arrived at via atomistically competitive markets is not guaranteed *except* under a stringent set of convexity conditions on production and preference sets; and further that it requires the existence of markets for all extant and contingent commodities. One may or may not accept the usefulness for pragmatic policy purposes of defining market failure in a way that takes those conditions as a reference ideal. Analytically, however, it remains a total *non sequitur* to assert that the essence of path dependence — a property defined for analyses of dynamical and stochastic processes — consists in asserting propositions regarding the possibility of market failure that were first established in the context of purely static and deterministic models.

Path dependence does not imply that competitive markets fail. Quite the contrary proposition holds: it can be shown that under full conditions of convexity in preference and production sets a *non-tâtonnement* general equilibrium process (in which costless re-contracting is not available to the agents) will converge in a strictly path-dependent manner on one among the continuum of valid 'core' solutions — thereby satisfying the criterion that the outcome is socially efficient in the Paretian sense. This well-known theoretical result should be sufficient to expose the logical error of taking market failure to be among the defining properties of path-dependent economic processes.

To be sure, it should be recognized that among the conditions that give rise to the existence of multiple equilibria and path-dependent dynamics, there are some that would also prevent the workings of competitive markets from arriving unerringly at allocations that are socially efficient in the sense of Pareto. Prominent in that company are

Introduction

micro-level irreversibilities in the behaviour of agents, due to learning by doing and the habituation of tastes; and externalities affecting non-market interactions in the spheres of consumption and production that give rise to co-ordination games which end in 'co-ordination failures'. Consequently, while the logical relationship between path dependence and market failure is neither one of necessity nor sufficiency, there are some important underlying connections between the two.

The latter observation undoubtedly adds to the potential policy relevance of historical research that undertakes to identify where and when economic processes exhibit the property of path dependence. One certainly has to agree that among economists at large most of the interest in path dependence has tended to focus upon possibilities that sub-optimal equilibria will be 'selected'—almost to the exclusion of every other consideration. Nevertheless, there is more to economic life than welfare losses due to static inefficiencies. Market structures in some areas of the economy—especially those where network externalities and bandwagon dynamics are especially important—are particularly susceptible to the shaping influence of specific historical events in the evolution of the industries concerned. Insofar as market structure itself strongly conditions entrepreneurial behaviour and managerial strategies of innovation, path dependence then must be reckoned among the conditions that govern *dynamic* efficiency.

But questions of distribution also matter and, indeed, in private and public policy deliberations these often exert an influence more powerful than that of pure efficiency considerations. The identities of winners and losers in market rivalries are obviously matters of intense interest to the owners and employees of the enterprises involved, and to the governments of countries and regions where those agents are situated. More generally, all manner of political and social sequelae, as well as issues of equity and social justice, are attached to the dynamics governing the evolution of income and wealth distributions and related processes of socio-economic stratification. The analysis of positive feedback mechanisms that impart path-dependent properties to those processes can significantly enhance economists' abilities to understand and predict distributional phenomena of the kind that have recurrently occupied the centre of economic policy debate, and most likely will continue to do so in the future.

Envoi

Having set out the more abstract points of the rationale for seeking to advance research and writing in economic history as a contribution to a policy-relevant form of historical economics, we now present the strongest part of the case: leaving our readers the enjoyment of sampling the work of outstanding social scientists who have mastered the historians' craft.

PART ONE
Drivers of Long-term Economic Growth

Historical experience has often been invoked as a guide to the future course of economic development and growth, even in countries and regions of the world where neither of those processes are firmly established. The question of how the West grew rich is posed not simply out of curiosity, but in the belief that a proper understanding of that story would provide pertinent lessons for economic policy-makers in either the presently advanced economies or in those now undergoing development. There is a presupposition in this practice, namely, that the study of the past will expose some important and generic characteristics of the structural transformations involved in economic development, and of the sources of the sustained rise in real output per capita that we associate with modern economic growth. The emergence of cumulative and sustained economic growth as a salient feature of the modernization of societies entailed dramatic changes in the organization of economic activity. Many economic historians have looked to alterations in the institutions of the market place (in commercial organizations, financial practices, and legal codes) as the source of the fundamental break with 'pre-modernity' that initiated this process. Others have emphasized the role played by technological innovations, seeing in these the inducement for the restructuring of the relationships among the factors of production, and the removal of previous constraints upon productivity. Jan de Vries takes a less traditional tack in his essay on the 'industrious revolution', by focusing attention on changes in the economics of the household after 1650.

De Vries' thesis is that modern growth was launched in Northern Europe by a revolution in attitudes and behaviours that took place within the household rather than in business organizations and market institutions. The household was the most important unit of social and economic organization, for within it, typically, production, consumption and capital formation activities were centred. Reconsideration of the complex of developments observed within the sphere of the household, particularly in the higher income regions of northern Europe, leads de Vries to identify changes in consumption demands as having played a primary initiating role in the process of industrialization. Rather than attributing the expansion of productive potential to the effects of technological improvements at this time, he points to the intensification of labour efforts on the part of the population.

To state the argument starkly, households reorganized themselves in order to take advantage of the opportunities to enjoy new and attractive commodities, market goods that were becoming available from sources outside as well as within Europe. Initially, it was as much the enhanced attraction of novel consumption items as it was the effects of a reduction in their relative supply prices that was critical in stimulating consumption demand. To acquire these goods required greater real income and that led in turn to the intensification of work on the part of male household heads, and to the fuller exploitation of the labour supply potential of their wives and children. The growth of 'cottage industry' and the increasingly elaborate organization of the proto-industrial 'putting out system' in this era are seen by de Vries as reflections of the expanded readiness of households to sacrifice leisure in order to satisfy their new consumption wants.

The altered terms of that exchange were thus tantamount to the launching of a self-reinforcing 'industrious revolution'. As this new regime of intensified household production took root, it imparted critical impetus to just such a virtuous spiral as that described by Adam Smith in the *Wealth of Nations* (1776). The increased scale upon which the business of providing the new consumption goods was being conducted permitted progressively finer specialization and division of labour. This yielded cost savings which helped avoid the relative prices of these items being driven upwards by the growing quantities that were being demanded; indeed, in some cases it led eventually to relative price reductions that further stimulated growth in the quantities demanded.

In turn, the first 'industrious revolution' within the household sector both impelled and was reinforced by significant changes in business organization, affecting both the international wholesale trade and the retail provision of consumables. A commercial economy was adapting to and reshaping consumption opportunities at the same time that families were rearranging their work-routines in order to realize those opportunities. It was the interaction of these two spheres that created the simultaneous shifts in labour supply and final product demand that led towards the Industrial Revolution.

What is perhaps most striking about this interpretation is that it recognizes a central role for the households that were ranged towards the bottom as well as towards the top of the income distribution. As de Vries points out, there was a bond between the 'luxury of the middling sort' and the developing 'plebeian consumer culture'. The former is now well known from studies of the revolution in consumption that was associated with the rise of 'breakables' such as pottery and glassware, and complex domestic consumer durables such as clocks. The latter, however, was based on the diffusion of tropical goods such as sugar and tobacco, the shift in grain consumption from rye, oats and unbolted wheat to finer cereals, and an increased demand for lighter clothing fabrics which were, of course, produced by the very same domestic industry that was generating the plebeian household cash-income to support the new consumption standards. In each case, the penetration of a new commodity culture effected a transformation in household structure and behaviour that contributed to the emergence of positive feedback and self-reinforcing development dynamics.

In reflecting on the significance of the historical emergence and growth of new forms of consumption demands, and their ability to launch a cumulative dynamic expansion of the economy, there is a connection that might well be drawn between past experience and prospects for the economic future. Some modern analysts have foreseen precisely that potentiality in the swarms of new information-goods and information-services that are being created by the convergence of digital computing technologies and computer-mediated telecommunications. The growing use and enjoyment of digital videos, music, Internet chat-rooms and cyber-shopping, not to mention the appetite of teenagers for vastly expanded volumes of text messages, is eliciting not only the development of new business practices, but the increasing allocation of household members' time to these 'consumption cum production' activities. Seen in that light, the transformations taking place in the 'New Economy' perhaps should not be regarded as being so historically unprecedented, or distinct from the dynamics of the old 'Industrious Revolution'.

Increased labour supply was the key means by which productivity constraints in the economies of Northern Europe were overcome during the first half of the eighteenth century, and at still later dates. In this respect, Europe's 'industrious revolution' presents features that are very different from the growth prospect of today's developed economies, where the sustained growth of labour productivity has been and is likely to remain the mainstay of rising material standards of living. But the story related by de Vries is one that should not come as a surprise to students of the US economy's growth during the nineteenth century or to observers of the East Asian miracle in the late twentieth century. In both of those instances, the rising average intensity of work—gauged in terms of average annual hours of market work per member of the population—played a significant part in raising the growth rate of per capita real income. Of course, the extent to which that aspect of economic growth should be held to have been welfare-enhancing, rather than simply a sacrifice of leisure for goods, forms just the kind of question that is addressed by the essays in Part Three.

Human capital accumulation figures prominently in discussions of the sources of economic growth among the developed countries since the end of World War II. The positive correlation between the level of human capital per worker and the average pace of growth in productivity emerges quite strongly from international cross-section comparisons at the economy-wide level. On the other hand, econometric studies based upon international data are much more ambiguous regarding the impact that variations in the pace of human capital formation have upon rates of economic growth.

Growth theory tends to focus upon the possible complementarities between human capital and other productive assets, thereby emphasizing the supply-side relationship between investment in education and rising average real income levels. But, educational attainments also appear to have an independent complementary relationship with some modes of consumption, particularly those that are comparatively income-elastic. The simultaneous existence of this demand-side connection might well be an important source of the robust positive correlations found between average educational and income levels, whereas it would not contribute similarly to creating a positive relationship between the rate of human capital formation and the rate of economic growth.

This is an area in which the longer-run perspective of the economic historian ought to be particularly valuable. Inasmuch as the demand-side and supply-side connections between human capital and economic development may have evolved differently in different epochs, projecting contemporary conditions backwards can seriously distort our understanding of the dynamics of historical growth. By the same token, widening the temporal window of observation and analysis provides greater opportunities to identify the distinct processes through which demand-side and supply-side connections were forged between human capital formation and rising levels of output per person.

Indeed, stimulated by these possibilities, economic historians are beginning to take a fresh look at the variety of ways in which human capital was created in the past, for what purposes, under what institutional arrangements, and with what effects upon the lives and livelihoods of the individuals concerned. Two of the essays in this Part take the examination of human capital formation and its influence in earlier historical epochs as their core concern, and two others have much to say about the evolving role of education and training in the technologically advanced economies of the twentieth century.

All of these studies find it important to distinguish explicitly between general 'schooling' and kindred modes of formal education on the one hand, and vocational training (in the manual arts) on the other hand. There is a consensus that if the goal is to understand the way that human capital formation shaped the process of early industrialization and modern economic growth, it would be a misleading anachronism to associate investment in human capital exclusively or even primarily with participation in formal schooling. Furthermore, the distinction between vocational training and formal education in previous epochs appears important in clarifying the nature of the supply-side connections between human capital formation and economic development in different economies, as well as in separating demand-side from supply-side relationships.

The essay by Jane Humphries undertakes to reassess the role of apprenticeship in the British Industrial Revolution with a dual purpose in mind. Inasmuch as the system of apprenticeship provided the major source of vocational training in Britain before the expansion of schooling in the late nineteenth century, her aim, first, is to establish a proper appreciation of the significance of this preparatory factor among the historical conditions that contributed to that country's emergence as the first industrial nation. Second, to understand the microeconomics of apprenticeship institutions is important in revealing the influence of public policy in structuring private contracts governing investment in specific forms of human capital, contracts that for a long time remained outside the orbit of the institutions of education.

The problem of market failure in the provision of formal education to free agents is well known. Quite apart from the existence of 'externalities' or 'spillovers' that would benefit members of society other than the individuals and families who bear the direct and indirect costs of education, in early modern Britain the imperfect condition of capital markets and the skewed distribution of income and wealth meant that for the mass of the population the impediments to private financing of such investments were particularly severe. Humphries shows very clearly how in that setting the apprenticeship system created a structure of contract enforcement which ensured that both masters and trainees would derive the benefits from human capital accumulation — the apprentice by having legal recourse if the master failed to teach and train; the master by keeping the apprentice in bondage for a full seven years when the time spent to learn a craft was significantly shorter than that. The incentive for the apprentice to stay in place, even after the net benefit from the contract had ceased to be positive, was partly due to the power of the guilds to control access to mastery; it was partly due to the benefits provided in the form of completed apprenticeship access to 'social security' under the settlement clauses of the Old Poor Law.

Humphries concludes that although the system of apprenticeship had been reinforced by the Tudor State and its successors with quite different intentions in mind, it played a central role in Britain's economic development for three reasons. Firstly, it assisted in the transfer of resources from low-productivity agriculture to higher-productivity industry and services. Secondly, it promoted the formation of necessary skills in the newer sectors, whose importance grew continuously as the economy expanded. Thirdly, it helped overcome some of the inherent inadequacies of the competitive market in allocating investment to the formation of intangible assets of the sort that are necessarily embodied in people. But the gains from the system of apprenticeship were neither immediate, nor automatic, nor fully anticipated. The historical irony brought out by Humphries' account is that a form of labour control initially designed to advantage agriculture, and hence the nation's rural land-owning class, in the end turned out to be a major factor in the displacement of workers from village to town, and from farm to shop and workshop.

The net effect of the apprenticeship system in Britain in contributing to the early movement of labour out of agriculture appears also as a central aspect in Broadberry's analysis of the role that human capital accumulation played in shaping the economy's growth in the post-1870 era. In this analysis, the rise of compulsory public schooling in Britain after 1870 did not replace apprenticeship immediately. Vocational training remained an important source of human capital accumulation, shaping as well as reflecting the particular features of Britain's industrial economy. Broadberry's approach in this essay is explicitly comparative, examining the process by which the first industrial nation was overtaken at the beginning of the twentieth century by the upstart economies of the US and Germany. Whereas scholars and pundits have been quick to indict under-investment in human capital as a crucial factor in Britain's loss of economic leadership, Broadberry cautions that the story is rather more complicated than that.

To arrive at a proper assessment of the possible bearing that differences in labour-force training investment may have had upon the comparative labour productivity levels in these countries, Broadberry proceeds by distinguishing vocational training from formal schooling among the sources of human capital formation, and disaggregates the national economies into their three principal sectors: agriculture, industry and services. (It may be noted that the comments in Nick von Tunzelmann's essay on the comparative quality of vocational training in Britain's chemicals and electrical engineering industries suggests that further disaggregation could be enlightening.)

This approach reveals that a crucial mechanism by which Germany and the US caught up with and overtook Britain was through their sloughing off of agriculture and the relative shift of resources into sectors where the average level of labour productivity was higher. Indeed, the persisting shortfall in aggregate skills in Germany vis-à-vis Britain prior to 1945 can be proximately attributed to the former country's super-abundance of low-skilled rural labour. As those workers were shifted towards 'modern' sectors, average skill levels in the economy rose, accompanied by rising labour productivity.

In the US, by contrast, the greater commitment to industrial technologies of mass-production led to less and less emphasis being placed on the creation of a labour force equipped with traditional craft skills. At the same time, the larger organizational scale and management-driven transformations of the nature of work within US industrial and commercial enterprise were generating a demand for adaptable workers who could quickly adjust to new work-routines; and for managers with general problem-solving capabilities to staff the hierarchical control structures of the emerging multi-establishment firms.

Broadberry sees the precocious commitment of US society to public education first at the secondary and then at the tertiary level both as a response to those needs and as a crucial creator of 'social capabilities', whose effect was to encourage further the elaboration of a distinctively American technological trajectory.

This interpretation is supported by Paul David and Gavin Wright whose essay notes that, even when secondary schooling expanded in the early twentieth century, the contribution that the High School movement made to raising the human capital endowments of America's workers was not primarily in the information and skills they received in the classroom. More important was the effect of secondary education in equipping graduates with the necessary cognitive capacities to readily absorb job-relevant instruction in the workplace, and thereby reduce the costs of the kinds of firm-specific human capital investments that employers were more likely to finance.

In the two concluding essays of this Part, attention focuses squarely on the uses of history in illuminating the dynamics of economic growth along new technological trajectories, and the implications of changes in the systems of innovation within which new technological opportunities are created. David and Wright analyse the connections been the diffusion of 'general purpose technologies' (GPTs) and surges in the growth of productivity. Taking the experience of electrification during the first third of the twentieth century as a significant illustrative episode, they ask what lessons it may hold for current thinking about the future trajectory of economic growth driven by the continuing elaboration and deployment of computers. The significance of GPTs and the formation of technological systems more generally also figure in Nick von Tunzelmann's broad exploration of secular changes that have transformed the creation and implementation of new knowledge in the technologically advanced branches of the developed economies.

David and Wright identify the years between 1919 and 1929—the decade of the 'Roaring Twenties'—as the era in which the trend rate of growth in total factor productivity (TFP) in the US economy underwent a significant acceleration, initiating a half-century-long epoch of rapidly rising labour productivity and high real wages that continued until the crises of the mid-1970s. A surge of productivity growth in the manufacturing sector during the 1920s underlay the discontinuity in the trends evident at the level of the domestic economy. That development, in turn, is shown by David and Wright to have been directly connected with the diffusion throughout the manufacturing sector of a new 'general purpose technology' — the electric motor.

The 'dynamo revolution' did not get under way in American industry until four decades after the introduction of the first extensive commercial applications of electricity for commercial and domestic lighting at the beginning of the 1880s. Although most of the ways in which the new power source would come to be implemented in factories had already been foreseen at the turn of the century, the realization of those industrial engineering visions was delayed by conditions that often impeded the immediate implementation of fundamental innovations. The existence of extensive mechanical power capacity in the established centres of manufacturing that utilized water and steam power was prominent among these. A lengthy period of gestation was required before the building of large-scale power plants and the formation of extensive regional electricity supply networks could bring down the relative cost of electric power. Yet that was required to warrant the refitting of plant embodying the older power technologies, or their scrapping and replacement with thoroughly modernized facilities. Further investment, and further learning, were required before the advantages of the new technology could be fully exploited through the introduction of new modes of organizing production within the redesigned, electricity-powered factory.

David and Wright present the experience of factory electrification as a paradigm of the way that GPTs stimulate complementary technological and organizational innovations to form new and more efficient systems of production that pervade many branches of industry; as well as the respects in which their transformative impact in any particular industrial context may be dependent and thus contingent upon the realization of supporting changes in other quite distinct sectors of the economy. Installation of electric motors in manufacturing establishments alone would not have yielded the simultaneous boost in the average productivity of capital and labour that occurred in almost every branch of US manufacturing after 1919. It needed complementary innovations in organization and management across a wide array of industrial enterprises, as well as co-ordinated investments in public utilities and transportation infrastructures and equipment such as those that permitted the relocation of the new, sprawling industrial facilities to green-field sites outside the high-rent core of the cities where manufacturing was previously concentrated.

The evidence that David and Wright introduce to supplement the US story, regarding the roughly contemporaneous experiences of factory electrification in Britain and France, underscores their arguments in regard to the generic features of the dynamics of GPT diffusion. But it also illuminates a number of the contrasts between the 'background conditions' in these economies that may have been responsible for the observed differences in the strength of the accompanying 'surges' of industrial TFP growth.

David and Wright suggest that the story of 'the dynamo revolution' offers a number of useful insights into the future potentialities for productive capabilities throughout the economy to be transformed and augmented by a modern-day GPT—namely, the digital computer and the cluster of complementary information and telecommunications technologies that are forming around it. They do not hold that information and electricity are similar, but, rather, point to the parallels in the dynamics of introducing 'general purpose engines' that explain why such a process should not be expected to be completed overnight, and why it is more likely that they will tax the patience of optimists, and afford great (albeit transient) room for sceptics to doubt that there is any 'productivity payoff' in sight.

There is a further, more profound lesson to be drawn from the story of electrification during the opening third of the twentieth century. It concerns the importance of both market and non-market mechanisms to co-ordinate the formation of complementary technical and organizational innovations. Because their effects will not be fully 'internalized' in many instances, to accelerate the diffusion process and bring forward the resulting productivity gains may well require policies of public intervention to achieve the appropriate levels and timing of private investment commitments.

Thus, while David and Wright take a cautiously optimistic view of the future course of the ICT revolution, they argue that full realization of its potential will require major physical, organizational and institutional reconfigurations affecting the conduct of economic activities well beyond the domain of the industries that produce computer hardware and software, telecommunications equipment and digital information goods and services. In this view, the payoffs in terms of conventionally measured gains in productivity will come not so much from the growth of a 'new economy' sector, but as was seen in the US during the 1920s from a 'renewal' of production and distribution operations taking place throughout the economy's many branches.

Nick von Tunzelmann's discussion of the ways in which emerging technological opportunities have driven the growth process in the developed economies also places major emphasis upon *systems*: not only technical systems of the kind treated in David and Wright's essay, but 'systems of innovation'. This analysis turns upon a set of key distinctions—between knowledge and information, between creating technologies and putting them into actual use, between markets and networks of actors—that affect the realization and the distribution of economic benefits from technological and organizational change. On the basis of the time-series movements in aggregate-level indicators of inventive activity (patenting and R&D expenditure rates) and productivity indexes, von Tunzelmann generalizes on the point made by David and Wright that substantial delays may indeed separate investments in new knowledge from the payoffs that are discernible in terms of macroeconomic performance.

It is the conditions affecting the intervening processes through which complementary productive assets are mobilized that concerns von Tunzelmann, and his essay introduces the term 'governance of technological development' to refer to these. In other words, if we are to understand why some sectors and some societies have responded with greater success than others to new technological opportunities, attention needs to be focused on the institutional structures within which inventors and producers were acting. Von Tunzelmann focuses on four institutional constraints, which he characterizes as market failure, government failure, corporate failure and network failure. Each of them has the potentiality to impede, or interpose a total 'disconnect' of the linkage between the creation or discovery of new technological possibilities and their successful exploitation. Although, ideally, each form of failure ought to be readily recognizable and averted, or at least mitigated in its adverse consequences, both theory and history suggest that generally this is not what happens.

Thus, while market systems may not create sufficient protection for inventors to benefit fully from their creative achievements, at the same time the knowledge concerned with inventions has the characteristic of a public-good, whose free and open dissemination and availability for application would be optimal for the economy. Thus patents can afford protection for the rewards of inventors, and they do so at the expense of innovators and the consumers of new goods and services. The more general purpose the technology, the greater the disadvantages of a regime of liberal patent issuance and strong enforcement of the monopoly rights of the patent-owners. Similarly, governments can overcome the constraints associated with 'big-ticket', public-goods projects, and may often thereby unleash beneficial spillovers from 'essential' technology. Yet bureaucracies (and not only those in centrally planned economies) are notoriously unwieldy and often respond to political pressures to create 'technological rents' that special interest groups can appropriate. Mixed systems of public and private investment for the co-development of new technologies have emerged historically, as in the US, but their ability to meld successfully the advantages of both approaches has been repeatedly found to be limited, as von Tunzelmann's survey points out.

Indeed, a central contention of this essay is that inefficiencies in resource allocation may be inevitable even in the best designed of 'innovation systems'. This is not a matter of there being some or even numerous projects that simply fail; uncertainty is inescapable in the creations of novelty, whether in invention and discovery or in business innovation. Von Tunzelmann's concern stems from the recurring history of 'co-ordination-failures' or 'network-failures'. These have not been confined to societies where it can be said that market institutions have still to be developed that would effectively provide signals to guide decentralized decision-making, as remains the case in post-transition Eastern Europe, or in modern African and Latin American states. Network failures may also occur when the institutional components of an innovation are fully elaborated and mature, but have different targets and conflicting purposes. Von Tunzelmann points to this having been exemplified by the structural situation in twentieth-century Britain, where long-standing tensions exist between the needs and aspirations of producers in the industrial districts and the competitive objectives of banking and financial interests concentrated in the City of London.

The implication is that practical policy solutions must be of a second-best, rather than the first-best sort. Von Tunzelmann suggests that most current government policy measures in the area of technology are geared excessively towards promoting invention and initial commercialization, and should be 're-balanced' by giving greater consideration to means to improve the ability of firms to assess, access and adapt existing technological information to their production and management needs. In this regard the thrust of this contribution resonates with a central theme of the essay by David and Wright: it is the structural adaptation of the system to technological opportunity that is crucial for the unleashing of increasing returns, and only as such complementarities come to be established will the full benefits of technical progress be realized for society as a whole.

1.
The Industrious Revolution and Economic Growth, 1650–1830
JAN DE VRIES

Consumer Theory

How do economies achieve growth? How was sustained growth initiated in the first modern economies? These classic questions of economic history have long been answered with arguments that emphasize the forces of production. Scholars have not agreed on which of the 'supply-side' factors have been most important. Technological change,[1] augmented supplies of capital, energy and raw materials,[2] and institutions[3] that increase the efficient deployment of all the above factors, all have persuasive advocates. In most of these accounts, the locus of decision-making is the entrepreneur and the basic unit of analysis is the firm.

The supply of labour also figures prominently in studies of economic growth, but here causal mechanisms relating labour supply to growth are far from clear. So long as Malthusian forces are thought to be strong, the growth of population is assumed to halt and undermine the growth of per capita income; only with the advent of 'modern' growth is the causal arrow reversed. Indeed, population growth is then held to be 'closely associated with', if not essential for, the achievement of economic

---

[1] Landes, *Unbound Promethius*; Mokyr, *Lever of Riches*.
[2] Wrigley, *Continuity, Chance, and Change,* advances the cause of energy supply; Maddison, *Dynamic Forces*, adheres to a model in which capital accumulation plays a central role.
[3] North has led the movement to establish a 'new institutional economic' that emphasizes the importance of property rights, including intellectual property, in making economic growth possible.

growth.[4] The measurement of labour inputs appears, at first sight, to offer fewer challenges than the measurement of other inputs, but the opposite is more commonly the case, for there are many dimensions to the effective scope of labour's productive contribution. Measuring the duration and intensity of past labour is a challenge to the historian, but the larger issue is not only historical. This paper is a contemplation of a dimension of economic performance that is resistant to measurement: the scope and intensity of productive labour and its relationship to consumer aspirations. I hope to demonstrate that — in the past as well as in the future — the impulse to market-oriented work is closely connected to the organization of households and the character of consumer aspirations. This is a theme that directs the economist's attention from the familiar terrain of production to the less well-charted thickets of consumption and the patterns of demand.

This is not to say that economic historians have ignored demand-side issues in long-term economic growth. While maintaining the supply side as the *primum mobile*, they have explored such issues as the conquest of foreign markets (since it appeared to offer an external demand-led force to break into the circular flow of the domestic economy) and the distribution of income and the preferences of different classes of consumers.[5] Foreign demand seemed particularly promising as a means of breaking out of the circular flow of economic life in an age of large European colonial empires, while the distribution of income seemed promising as a means distinguishing 'good' from 'bad' consumer demand. Underlying this latter approach is the belief that a strong demand focused on 'strategic goods' can stimulate future economic growth like the lever of Archimedes. Demand for goods possessing strong linkages with other sectors of the economy, goods whose increased production induces learning effects that speed the pace of productivity improvement, and goods whose increased output exposes bottlenecks in existing production processes,[6] has been thought to

---

[4] The concept of 'modern economic growth' as described here is closely associated with the pioneering work of Simon Kuznets, *Modern Economic Growth*. For a critique, see De Vries, 'Economic Growth'.

[5] On foreign demand see, Hobsbawm, 'General Crisis'; Deane and Cole, *British Economic Growth*; On income distribution see, Hirschman, *Strategy of Economic Development*. For an application, see Fishlow, 'Brazilian Size Distribution'.

[6] Landes emphasizes the importance of bottlenecks in production processes as focusing devices that stimulated technological improvement, especially in the British cotton textile industry. *Unbound Prometheus*: 'To sum up: it was in large part the pressure of demand

possess 'strategic' qualities. Conversely, consumers who devote their augmented incomes to the perpetuation of traditional consumption patterns — more food, drink, banquets, servants, ritual gift exchange — are incapable of reinforcing the growth process.[7]

In all these accounts, demand for strategic goods remains a distinctly 'second order' effect when compared to the forces of production, and there is reason to doubt that it was very strong in the early stages of European industrialization.[8] Yet, one hesitates to dismiss the role of demand in economic growth, for however little its role impresses modern economists, its hold over the imagination of seventeenth- and eighteenth-century contemporaries was enormous. Indeed, it is often remarked that the dramatic events of the British Industrial Revolution escaped the attention of even the most acute economic thinkers of the time (Smith, Malthus and Ricardo).[9] But many of the most influential writers of the time, both in Britain and on the Continent, were convinced that consumer behaviour was undergoing fundamental changes, and that these changes were full of meaning for society as a whole.

This historical 'reality check' is, for an historian, justification enough to re-examine markets and consumer behaviour in the seventeenth and eighteenth centuries. But there is also reason for the economist to do so. Conventional consumer theory is based on a set of assumptions that seems designed to confine the study of consumption to limited, short-term questions: the individual is utterly autonomous, with unchanging tastes, perfect knowledge of all goods and prices, and capable of effortless and costless maximization. It is, then, no accident that economists applying such a theory have been unable to detect any but a passive, adaptive role for consumer choice in dynamic economic processes. There are, however, newer approaches to the study of consumer behaviour that have, without abandoning the foundations of conventional theory, extended the range of human activities over which economic reasoning can be fruitfully applied.

---

on the mode of production that called forth the new techniques in Britain, and the abundant, responsive supply of the factors that made possible their rapid exploitation and diffusion', pp. 77, 84–6.

[7] For an exploration of the potential 'modernity' of pre-industrial consumer demand see De Vries, 'Peasant Demand Patterns'.
[8] Horrell, 'Home Demand'; Horrell and Humphries, 'Old Questions, New Data'.
[9] For a skeptical survey of these claims see Mokyr, 'Editor's Introduction', pp. 3–5.

One of these innovations was the distinction introduced by Kelvin Lancaster between 'goods', which are purchased, and their 'characteristics', which give rise to utility and are consumed. This allows one to distinguish goods, their prices and the budget constraints that govern consumer behaviour in conventional theory from the characteristics of goods (goods typically possess multiple characteristics) which give utility and are the qualities for which individuals have preferences. Just as goods have multiple characteristics, so characteristics can be shared by more than one good. Indeed, 'goods in combination may possess characteristics different from those pertaining to the goods separately.'[10] This invites the economist to inquire into the complex processes by which goods are converted into the consumed characteristics, a process Lancaster called the 'consumption technology'.

These insights were developed further by Gary Becker and led to a body of theory called the 'new household economics'. Instead of focusing on the individual as an autonomous decision-maker, Becker took as his unit of study the household. The household purchases goods on the market, subject to a money income constraint, and combines these goods with the labour and other resources of the household to produce what Becker called 'Z, the more basic commodities [or 'characteristics'] that directly enter utility functions'.[11] This formulation invites us to consider the household (typically, but not exclusively, a family) as an entity that must allocate its resources, chiefly time, in such a way as to maximize the utility of its members. This allocation is a complex one, involving labour to acquire the money income to purchase goods, labour within the household to transform goods into Z-commodities, and leisure, which includes the time actually to consume the commodities.[12] Households must select 'consumption technologies' to transform goods into consumed commodities, which they do with varying degrees of efficiency.[13] Apart from the knowledge needed to be an 'efficient consumer' there is the question of whether the decision-makers adequately comprehend the preferences of other household members

---

[10] Lancaster, *Modern Consumer Theory*, p. 13.
[11] Becker, 'Theory of the Allocation', p. 495.
[12] This last claim on time, consumption time, is not considered by Becker, but is explored in Linder, *Harried Leisure Class*.
[13] In this approach, the household is treated as a firm. However, a firm's inefficiency in converting inputs into finished products is subject to the discipline of a competitive market while the household's conversion of goods into consumed goods is not. See Schultz, 'Economic Demography'.

in their actions. The household context of this theory makes unavoidable a consideration of how decisions are made concerning the ultimately consumed commodities, who makes the decisions, and how the commodities are allocated among the household members.

The innovations in consumer theory have been developed with contemporary problems in mind, and have not, to my knowledge, been applied to historical questions. Yet, they provide a framework that seems well suited to the study of basic questions of historical change. The unit of analysis is the household, the basic economic unit of pre-industrial societies. The household is viewed *simultaneously* as both a producing and a consuming unit, which offers a way to address the 'chicken or egg' question that has plagued studies of consumer-led economic growth. A framework is established to investigate the productive activities *internal* to the household, which are often overlooked by economists, but certainly loomed large in the past. The investigator is also alerted to the importance of the decisions made concerning the deployment of the time of household members across the several categories of its use, and to the distribution of commodities to those members. Finally, by focusing on the *oikos* as an autonomous economic unit, the interaction of individuals (as husbands, wives, children, servants) with the larger market economy is placed in a new, potentially fruitful, light.

My effort to turn these theoretical contributions towards problems of historical explanation has led to a model of household behaviour over time that identifies a coherent period, beginning in the second half of the seventeenth century and ending in the first half of the nineteenth century, that I have called the 'industrious revolution'.[14] This name was chosen because a driving force of economic development in this long era was an increased supply of market-oriented labour effort. This supply, in turn, was closely linked to a new desire to consume more market-supplied goods (or, more correctly, to use more market-supplied goods in the production of Z-commodities).[15]

---

[14] See De Vries, 'Industrial Revolution'.

[15] The ultimately consumed 'Z' can be achieved via a variety of consumption technologies, combinations of x (purchased goods) and T (household labour time). Consequently, the household's money income (I) might be exhausted in the purchase of goods ($\Sigma\ x_i\ p_i$), yet it will ordinarily be significantly less than the 'full income' of the household, which equals $\Sigma\ \pi_i\ Z_i$, where π is the shadow price of Z.

The Industrious Revolution, the Division of Labour, and Economic Growth

My historical argument, in a nutshell, is this: in the 'long eighteenth century' consumer demand grew because of reallocations of the productive resources of households. This reallocation of resources stands at the heart of the division of labour that Adam Smith held to be the driving force in economic improvement. In this era the division of labour cannot be understood only, or even primarily, as a matter of the organization of work at the firm level (that is, Smith's pin factory), or as a macroeconomic phenomenon that increased the range of intermediate inputs. Rather, it was a reorganization achieved primarily at the level of the household, where it can be identified as a *simultaneous* rise in the percentage of household production sold to others and the percentage of household consumption purchased from others.

The methods available to households to become more market-dependent in this period included (i) agricultural specialization, (ii) proto-industrial production, (iii) wage labour and (iv) commercial service. As some or all family members engaged in such market-oriented activities, the household economy became more specialized, drawing its total household support from a narrowed range of activities, but with the expectation of achieving higher levels of productivity. At the same time, it became more dependent on the market for goods and services necessary to achieve its consumption goals. That is, its consumption technologies moved towards a mix with more purchased goods and less household labour. The household could hope to benefit from the greater productivity with which these goods could be supplied by other specialists, but against these expected future benefits the household-as-consumer faced *immediately* the high transaction costs that attached to securing a diverse consumption packet via the market.[16]

Described in this way, the economy's ability to secure 'increasing returns from a progressive division of labour'[17] depends on the solution of a major coordination problem. A multitude of households must choose a level of specialization in production, the outcome of which will help determine the speed with which the transaction costs of market consumption will decline. Thus, as Allyn Young famously

---

[16] Yang and Borland, 'Microeconomic Mechanism'.
[17] Young, 'Increasing Returns', pp. 527–42.

remarked, not only does 'the division of labour depend on the extent of the market, but the extent of the market also depends on the division of labour.'

The advantages of specialization surely were not revealed for the very first time to Adam Smith. Yet, the coordination problem standing between the 'universal poverty' where 'every man provides everything for himself' and the 'universal opulence' where 'the joint labour of a great multitude of workmen' is required for 'the woollen coat ... which covers the day-labourer', was rarely solved satisfactorily.[18] Most households remained only marginally involved in market production and as consumers they faced markets that were both limited and costly. Yet, significant parts of Western Europe (and Colonial North America) overcame this coordination problem in the course of the long eighteenth century. A series of household-level decisions increased the supply of marketed goods and labour as it intensified and redirected the demand for market-bought products. This complex of changes in household behaviour constituted an 'industrious revolution', a commercially-driven phenomenon that preceded and prepared the way for the Industrial Revolution, which was advanced by new technologies and changes in organization.

The Industrious Revolution: The Supply of Labour

Is it possible to marshal sufficient historical evidence to render plausible the proposition that households earned more (in the absence of significantly increased labour productivity) and spent more, igniting what some have called a 'consumer revolution' in the long eighteenth century? And further, can it be shown empirically that these household members were motivated in their industrious behaviour by new consumption aspirations?

The first problem that must be faced is the question of earnings. I will not rehearse here the large literature that began in the nineteenth century as the 'condition of England' debate and extended into the twentieth as the 'standard of living' debate. The debate continues, and it does so in large part because it is very difficult to demonstrate con-

---

[18] Smith, *Wealth of Nations*, pp. 672, 259, 11. Smith describes with these words the difference between the first and fourth (and final) stages of economic life: hunting, herding, farming and commerce.

clusively that the wages of labour rose sufficiently over the course of the eighteenth and early nineteenth centuries to provide increased purchasing power to the bulk of the labouring population.[19] And what is difficult in England is doubly difficult in Continental Europe. The recent literature revising sharply downwards the rate of economic growth in the early decades of the British Industrial Revolution raises doubts that labour productivity rose significantly, even as a 'wave of gadgets' swept over England.[20]

The industrious revolution model argues for a shift of attention from the daily wages of individuals to the annual earnings of households. In so doing, the key variables shift from the wage rate to (i) the number of days of paid employment per year, (ii) the participation of wives and children in market-oriented labour, and (iii) the intensity of work effort. Various combinations of more regular work, more intense work and greater paid labour force participation—a more elastic supply of labour—could have overcome the limitations of the wage rate to secure households the means to act on new consumer aspirations.

There is considerable evidence, direct and indirect, in support of changes in all three dimensions of industrious behaviour. Indeed, many of the most ferocious 'pessimists' in the standard of living debate offered evidence of prolonged work hours, expanded child labour, and so on, in order to argue that the real incomes of workers must have been deteriorating and their freedom restricted. An obvious alternative to the industrious revolution model is the model of the 'traditional' pre-capitalistic worker, who must be forced to greater industry—trained to obey the cash nexus—by poverty, the employer and the law.[21]

The evidence for a longer work year, and more regular work in general, is both prescriptive (abolition of religious holidays) and empirical. It is well known that the Protestant Reformation brought with it a rationalization of the religious calendar that, in extreme cases, lengthened the potential work year from 260 to 307 days.[22] In most countries, including those remaining loyal to the Roman Catholic Church, saints' days were removed in stages extending through the

---

[19] Feinstein, 'Pessimism Perpetuated'.
[20] Crafts and Harley, 'Output Growth', pp. 703–30.
[21] The 'external constraints' school is described and discussed in De Vries, 'Between Purchasing Power', pp. 116–17.
[22] This increase of up to 18 per cent in the length of a full work year was mandated in the Netherlands, all at once, upon the introduction of the Reformed religion in 1574. See Noordegraaf, *Hollands welvaren?*, pp. 57–61. See also, Freudenberger, 'Das Arbeitjahr'.

eighteenth century. Obviously, this process must be regarded as a background factor *enabling* rather than mandating more industrious behaviour. But there is direct evidence showing that the work year was extended in fact. In the Netherlands the payroll records of public employers (polder administrations, admiralty wharves and rope works) show that the 'labour potential' offered by the stroke of a clergyman's pen in 1574 was being made use of regularly by the second half of the seventeenth century.[23] For London, Hans-Joachim Voth has demonstrated with an ingenious methodology that Londoners increased their hours of annual labour by over 20 per cent in the course of the second half of the eighteenth century. Voth concluded that, 'Abstention [from leisure] was more important than ingenuity' in advancing the Industrial Revolution.[24]

The evidence for greater market-oriented labour force participation in this period is primarily indirect, but it is abundant. The spread of proto-industrial activities to fill the winter months and employ wives and children has long been the object of historical research. Indeed, the seventeenth-century spread of such market-oriented by-employments noted by Joan Thirsk assumed such an importance by the following century that it has allowed a vast feminist literature to emerge that deplores the withering of women's engagement with the market economy in the course of the nineteenth century.[25]

Daniel Defoe, who may fairly be called the chronicler of the industrious revolution, put the matter directly:[26]

> A poor labouring Man that goes abroad to his Day Work, and Husbandry, Hedging, Ditching, Threshing, Carting, etc. and brings home his Week's Wages, suppose at eight pence to twelve pence a Day . . .; if he has a Wife and three or four children to feed, and who get little or nothing for themselves, must fare hard, and live poorly . . .
> But if this Man's Wife and Children can at the same time get Employment, if at next door, or at the next Village there lives a clothier, or a Bay Maker, or a Stuff or Drugget Weaver; the Manufacturer sends the poor Woman combed Wool, or carded Wool every week to spin, and she gets eight pence or nine pence a day at home; the Weaver sends for her two little children, and they work by the loom, winding, filling

---

[23] De Vries, 'Labour Market', p. 62.
[24] Voth, 'Time and Work', pp. 29–58. Voth is here turning on its head the elegant dictum of Donald McCloskey that 'Ingenuity rather than abstention governed the industrial revolution'. See also, Bienefeld, *Working Hours*, pp. 15–19.
[25] Thirsk, *Economic Policies*; Hill, *Women, Work and Sexual Politics*.
[26] Defoe, *Plan of the English Commerce*, pp. 89–91.

Quills, etc. and the two bigger Girls spin at home with their Mother, and these earn three pence or four pence a day each: So that put it together, the family at home gets as much as the Father gets Abroad, and generally more ... The Father gets them food, and the Mother gets them Clothes ...

The earliest budget studies of English agricultural labourer's families confirm that women and children commonly contributed to household money income, but they do not show that these contributions were as large as Defoe suggested: instead of contributing half of total household earnings, they tended to hover around 25 per cent.[27] Sara Horrell and Jane Humphries' analyses of these and later household budgets also suggest that Defoe was rather exuberant in his estimates, but they confirm that such supplemental earnings were common in the 1790 to 1840 period, and would become much less so thereafter.[28]

The intensity of work effort is the most difficult dimension of the industrious revolution to measure. Indeed, it is a topic that even economists working with contemporary data prefer to sidestep. Most historical work on this topic concerns agriculture, where piece rate payment for agricultural tasks offers opportunities to observe work intensification and output changes under conditions of constant technology. This permits the inferring of changes in work intensity. Here, recent studies of French agriculture suggest that work intensification tended to be paired with greater market orientation in the eighteenth and early nineteenth centuries. Indeed, George Grantham summarized his findings with the observation that 'it is the history of markets rather than the history of technology which explains the growth of agricultural labour productivity in the "late organic economy".'[29]

One might expect that a market-incentive-driven intensification of work observed in parts of France in the eighteenth and nineteenth centuries would have arisen in England and Holland rather earlier. Indeed, Gregory Clark sometimes argues that the largest shift had occurred already in fourteenth-century England.[30] There is much that remains obscure on this topic, even though critics of the 'industrious revolution' approach generally assume that such labour intensification took place.

---

[27] Sokoll, 'Early Attempts', pp. 34–60.
[28] Horrell and Humphries, 'Women's Labour Force Participation', pp. 89–117.
[29] Grantham, 'Division of Labour', pp. 478–502; See also, Hoffman, *Growth in a Traditional Society*.
[30] Clark, 'Labour Productivity', pp. 211–35. See also, Clark 'Too Much Revolution', pp. 226–9.

Whether one turns to the 'pessimist' interpretations of Sidney Pollard or E. P. Thompson (where the new rhythm of capitalist enterprise imposes harder, more regular work),[31] or to the biomedical approach of Robert Fogel (where improved nutrition lifts the ceiling on work effort), work intensification is assumed to exist.[32] Thus, the debate turns not so much on the existence of intensification as on the question of whether this was a symptom or a cause of economic growth.

There were many margins at which the time of the household could be re-deployed towards market-oriented labour. The trade-offs were not simply between labour and leisure. They were also, and crucially, between household labour and marketed labour and between work and education. The scope for increasing marketed labour came from reducing the daily, weekly and seasonal irregularities in the rhythm of work; filling the time of the young, old and housebound; intensifying the pace of work itself. Not all of these margins were worked by all types of households, but over the course of the long eighteenth century the 'per capita work effort' rose considerably, and in so doing, the course of annual household money earnings diverged from the daily adult male wage. In Becker's vocabulary, money earnings came closer to approximating the 'full income' position.

The Industrious Revolution: Consumer Demand

The new character of consumer demand during the industrious revolution was not a 'consumer revolution' if this is understood as an explosive rise in the volume of purchased goods, and of goods that triggered, or at least sustained, the production in the 'leading sectors' of the Industrial Revolution. Nor was it primarily a phenomenon driven by emulation, where rising incomes allowed progressively lower socio-economic layers to adopt the fashions and comforts of their superiors.[33]

Rather, the consumer demand of this era was associated with a broadened choice in the selection of 'consumer technologies' whereby the ultimately consumed 'Z-commodities' could be produced. This made possible substantial redistributions of the productive resources

---

[31] Pollard, *Genesis of Modern Management*; Thompson, *Making*.
[32] Fogel, 'Conquest of High Mortality'.
[33] McKendrick, Brewer and Plumb, *Birth of a Consumer Society*.

(primarily time) of the household as it encouraged renegotiation of the distribution of consumption resources within the household. The emergence of 'incentive goods' — goods that answered persuasively to the wants of specific communities — acted as a focusing device, supporting distribution networks despite their high transaction costs. The interaction of household members with an expanded range of goods, and more numerous venues for purchase and consumption, led to the more frequent exercise of individuated choice, consolidating over time the practices of consumption recognizable to us today.

This, in a nutshell, constitutes the transformation of consumer demand associated with the industrious revolution as experienced in north-western Europe and the North American seaboard in the long eighteenth century. What evidence exists to sustain such a vision? The probate inventory is the place to begin, not only because it is a rich source of information about material culture, but because the contemplation of its evidence of steadily richer, more diverse and more refined material surroundings initially spurred my interest in explaining how such a phenomenon could be reconciled to the much more sombre image of eighteenth-century economic life presented by the record of wage and price trends.[34]

A considerable number of detailed regional studies now exists, and others are ongoing, for Colonial America (New England and the Chesapeake region), England, Scotland, the Netherlands, Belgium, Germany and France. The motivating questions of investigators vary across these countries, as do the specific forms of the inventories. Moreover, the very richness of the inventories, each with scores, often hundreds, of entries, possess methodological challenges that no two investigators have resolved in just the same way. Yet, wherever it proves possible to achieve a chronological coverage that spans the late-seventeenth century to mid- or late-eighteenth century, these studies have revealed a steady rise, generation-by-generation, of the number, range and quality of material possessions. This was true of expansive, newly settled areas of North America as well as of declining provincial towns in Holland (Delft) and France (Chartres).

Johan Kamermans' recent study of a Dutch rural area (the Krimpenerwaard) quantified this growing material profusion: the average inventory of 1630 to 1670 numbered 47 separate types of goods and 241 separate items; the averages for 1700 to 1795 (holding social

---

[34] De Vries, 'Between Purchasing Power', pp. 89–107.

categories constant) were 71 types of goods and 538 items. 'As the number of different items rises', Kamermans concludes, 'it is especially domains of exotic consumption goods, comfort, interior decoration, and dining table culture that assume a larger place in the household.'[35] His description concerns a wholly rural district of farmers and villagers, and most of these improvements were achieved in a protracted period of falling agricultural prices.

An important limitation of probate inventories, of course, is that they were ordinarily drawn up only for decedents leaving sufficient movable assets to make the exercise worthwhile. While the social 'depth' to which they reach is not the same everywhere, an argument for an industrious revolution among a labouring population can hardly be illustrated with probate inventory data, since their coverage does not extend far below the middling sort.

What they *can* show, however, is two broad trends in durable and semi-durable goods among the middle ranks: an increase in standards of domestic comfort, privacy, and refinement, and a shift towards 'breakability', that is towards goods that depreciate quickly because of their materials and their embodied fashions. The first of these developments involved expenditures that made them largely inaccessible to the poorer half of the population until well into the nineteenth century. Indeed, I will argue below that consumer expenditures among the lower ranks constructed lifestyles that had little in common with the new domesticity and respectability of the middling sorts.

The second development was far more widespread. Here, the probate inventories reveal a portion of a much broader sphere of consumer behaviour, one that characterized both the middle ranks and lower orders: the gradual replacement of expensive, durable products possessing a high secondary market value by cheaper, less durable, more fashion-sensitive goods.[36] Examples are numerous and varied: dinner plates evolve from pewter and wood to china and earthenware; drinking vessels similarly shift from metal to glass and chinaware; furniture, to take a Low Countries example, moves from the 'Spanish chair' (long-lasting, suited to repair and resale) to the more short-lived rush-seated chair; wall decoration shifts from paintings and tapestries to wall paper hangings. I leave for last the well-known shift in the

---

[35] Kamermans, *Materiële cultuur*, pp. 137–8, 284.
[36] A clear presentation of this position is offered in, Blondé, 'Birth of a Consumer Society?'

composition of wardrobes towards lighter woollens, cotton and mixed fibres, and to articles of apparel that embodied a shortened fashion life cycle.

In the early seventeenth century the members of every social class lived their lives in material worlds they inherited, surrounded by consumer goods they would not survive.[37] Recycled consumer durables supported an important trade in second-hand goods, including clothing. The decline of this trade was a gradual thing, but it left an unmistakable mark on the probate inventories: the decline of inventory valuations. Old goods depreciated faster in the course of the long eighteenth century because they wore out faster and they went out of fashion sooner.

Of course, another feature affecting inventory valuations in many cases was a decline in the original purchase cost of goods. Mark Overton and Carole Shammas have both reported a long-term decline of the prices of consumer durables that preceded the technological innovations of the Industrial Revolution.[38] Many factors will have played a role in this, but 'lower quality' is likely to have been one. This certainly must be acknowledged in the case of what Cissie Fairchild calls 'populuxe' goods: cheap copies of aristocratic luxury items. Her study of lower-middle- and lower-class Parisian decedents in the period 1725 to 1785 found only a small rise in average value over this interval of considerable price inflation, from 1286 to 1565 livres. 'Yet', she continued, 'because prices for many items favoured by consumers fell, the later inventories show more goods in greater variety than ever before.'[39]

The probate inventory is not ideally suited to study consumer demand. It does not illuminate sufficiently the lower reaches of the social order and it describes only the more durable items of the 'world of goods'. More generally, it describes the *stock* of possessions at a point in time rather than what most interests us, the *flow* of purchases that constitute consumer demand. The probate inventories of the long eighteenth century reveal stocks of consumer durables whose valuations rise but little, but the combination of speeded devaluations (reduced resale value) and speeded depreciation (more frequent replacement) requires that we apply progressively larger multipliers to these stock values in

---

[37] Dibbits, 'Between Society and Family Values', pp. 125–45.
[38] Shammas, 'Decline of Textile Prices', pp. 483–507.
[39] Fairchild, 'Production and Marketing', p. 229.

order to translate them into measures of consumer demand. What these documents show — in a distorted and hazy way — is a proliferation of durable and semi-durable goods in the homes of a broad middle range of the North-west European societies. The new consumer cultures were urban in origin, but in most of this region they were not confined to urban populations. Indeed, they spread quickly.

Since the probate inventories can take us only so far, one would like to examine consumer behaviour directly, by measuring the volume and value of purchases. There is little hope that the sales of the highly varied assortments of home furnishings and decoration, cooking and eating utensils, and items of apparel can usefully be measured. Here the probate inventories remain our best hope. But at least a few of the non-durable consumer goods, which leave no direct trace in the inventories, can be measured because they were imported (paying import duties, if not smuggled) and/or subject to excise tax. Happily, the most important objects of non-durable consumer expenditure in the long eighteenth century fall into these categories: sugar, tea, coffee, cocoa, cotton/imported cotton piece goods, and distilled spirits.

The elastic European demand for tropical products from Asia and the New World is a familiar theme of early modern economic history. It bears repeating, however, that Europe as a whole, which barely knew tobacco in 1620, consumed some 40 million kilograms of the substance a century later, or nearly 1 kilogram per capita; that its consumption of sugar, a commodity long familiar to Europeans, rose from perhaps 15 million kilograms in the 1650s to 200 million kilograms by the 1770s, or nearly 2 kilograms per capita; that coffee consumption, which stood at less than 1 million kilograms in 1720, had risen to 50 million kilograms by the eve of the French Revolution (just under 0.5 kilogram per capita); and that tea consumption, negligible in 1700, rose to 14.5 million kilograms in 1795 (0.12 kilogram per capita).

These and other products of the East and West Indies — porcelain, silk, cotton cloth, drugs, spices, dyestuffs — all found their ultimate consumers in Europe via complex networks of shippers, processors, distributors and retailers. And with few exceptions these tropical products were consumers' goods rather than producers' goods. Consequently, the total value of the goods landed in Europe by the Asian trading companies and by traders with the Western Hemisphere will indicate in broad outline the course of consumer expenditure for these novel goods. As import volumes of the initially exotic commodities rose, prices fell — often spectacularly. Thus, while the imported *vol-*

umes of the chief commodities each sustained growth rates of between 2.5 and 4.0 per cent over at least a century of expansion, the *value* of total imports rose more slowly, at 1.6 per cent per annum across the 110 years ending in the 1750s.

Table 1. Import value of intercontinental trade in Europe (thousands of guilders).

Period	Asia	New World	Total	Per Capita
1640s	12,000	[12,000]	24,000	f. 0.32
1750s	52,000	88,000	140,000	1.50
1780s	63,000	171,000	234,000	2.03

Sources: Asia: Sales revenue of all Asian trading companies, De Vries 'Connecting Europe and Asia', New World: 1640s, estimate based on volumes of tobacco and sugar imports; 1750s and 1780s, import values (excluding specie) of Spain, Portugal, Britain, France and the Netherlands, Morineau, *Incroyables gazettes*, p. 487; De Vries and Van der Woude, *First Modern Economy*, p. 478.

But a trend sustained for over a century, even if 'only' 1.6 per cent, is no small matter. In the 1640s European consumption of non-European goods still consisted primarily of pepper, spices and exotica, and touched but lightly all but elite consumers. By the mid-eighteenth century every European household (west of a line stretching from Konigsberg to Vienna to Trieste) was consuming non-European goods valued (wholesale, at the ports) at some 11 shillings (or six Dutch guilders) per annum. The actual retail cost of these goods to the ultimate consumers will have been much greater, certainly well over one pound sterling.

These goods were not distributed equally over the surface of Europe. They arrived at the Atlantic ports of the chief colonial powers, and were distributed from there in complex ways shaped by tariff policies and consumer demand. Our knowledge of this distribution is still far from sufficient, but it is possible to indicate its broad contours towards the end of the eighteenth century.

Table 2 will suffice to demonstrate that Great Britain consumed all the commodities except coffee at levels far above average, and that the Netherlands was also a major market for these commodities. The low French averages probably hide large regional differences, since it is known that all French tobacco processing factories were in the north, and Parisian sugar consumption on the eve of the French Revolution may have been over 5 kilograms per capita. It is likely that rather irregular concentric circles emanated from a North Sea epicentre, causing British consumption of non-European products to stand at three to four times the average, north-western Europe to stand at perhaps two times the average, while eastern and southern zones consumed at levels far below average. While the new non-European products will have touched daily life in these last zones but lightly, in Britain they may have absorbed some 15 per cent of the annual income of lower-class households by the second half of the eighteenth century.

Table 2. Per capita consumption of selected commodities, end of eighteenth century.

Country	Sugar kg	Tobacco kg	Coffee kg	Tea kg	Spirits litres
Great Britain	9.0	2.0	0.03	0.9	5.5**
France	0.8	0.5	0.24		0.9
Paris	4.9	1.9			
Netherlands	3.75*	4.0	2.8	0.7	7.0
Belgium	1.65*	6.0			
Europe	2.0	1.0	0.5	0.12	n.a.

* The Netherlands and Belgium also consumed significant quantities of sugar-based syrup.
** English domestic distilled spirits consumption in the 1740s. Thereafter taxed domestic production declines while imports rise. In 1833 consumption stands at 3.3 litres per capita.

Sources: France: Toutain, 'La consommation alimentaire', pp. 1913–75. Paris: A.-L. Lavoisier, *Richesse Territoriale*, p. 141ff.
Belgium: C. Vandenbroeke, *Agriculture et alimentation*.
Netherlands: De Vries and Van der Woude, *First Modern Economy*, 480; Jansen, 'Wilt U koffie of thee?' pp. 36–68; Voskuil, 'Verspreiding van koffie en thee', pp. 77–83.
Great Britain: Mitchell and Deane, *Abstract of British Historical Statistics*, pp. 355–56; Shammas, *Pre-industrial Consumer*.
Tobacco: Goodman, *Tobacco in History*.
Coffee: Schneider, 'Effects of European'.

This was no marginal phenomenon. It reorganized the structure of meals and the timing of meal-taking;[40] it attracted poor and remote householders to retail shops, the only source of these goods; it increased the utility of cash income, the only way to acquire these goods; and it reoriented the fiscal regimes of England, and to a lesser extent the Netherlands and France, as governments learned to levy customs tariffs and excise taxes on commodities exhibiting such high income elasticities of demand.[41] Patrick O'Brien reckoned that the various taxes and tariffs on wine, spirits, beer, sugar, tobacco and tea accounted for about 60 per cent of total British public revenue by 1788–92.[42]

Before considering what could have motivated ordinary householders to undertake such a far-reaching renovation of their quotidian lives, a few words must be said about the changing consumption of 'old commodities'. English beer consumption declined as the combination of spirits and tea rose, but not nearly so far as to compensate for the expenditures on the new commodities. Moreover, the types of beer drunk and the increasing resort to public venues probably tended to increase the per-unit expenditures on beer.[43] In Paris, the consumption of wine declined slightly over the course of the eighteenth century, but it was increasingly drunk in cafés and *guinguettes*: 3000 in Paris by 1750, or 1 per 200 inhabitants.[44]

Finally, we can consider the staff of life: bread. Both England and northern France experienced a large shift from the 'lesser grains' and unbolted wheat breads towards fine wheat bread in the course of the eighteenth century. Gregory King supposed wheat to make up only 20 per cent of total English bread consumption in 1688. By 1800 wheat

---

[40] In the Netherlands, the shift from the 'two-meal system' common to much of Europe in the early modern period, to a three- or four-meal system, began earlier than in most other parts of Europe—before the introduction of tea and coffee. But those commodities redefined the concept of breakfast in the Netherlands, and sped the replacement of meals based on porridges and pancakes, which were very labour-intensive, with meals based on tea or coffee and bread. Jobse-van Putten, *Eenvoudig maar voedzaam*, pp. 260–8. For Germany, 'the crucial changes in our meal system were not initiated merely by urbanization and industrialization after the middle of the nineteenth century. The "proto-industrialization" in the countryside was in general more important for this alteration. [This is] correlated with the appearance of food and meal innovations: potatoes, beet sugar, chicory coffee, and spirits . . .' Teuteberg, 'Food Consumption in Germany', p. 235.
[41] Shammas, 'Eighteenth-Century English Diet', p. 258.
[42] O'Brien, 'The Political Economy of British Taxation', p. 11, Table 5.
[43] Clark, *English Alehouse*, pp. 292–3.
[44] Brennan, *Public Drinking*, p. 76.

accounted for 66 per cent of English grain consumption, and even more in southern England.[45] Fernand Braudel supposed that the French had led the way in 'a wheat bread revolution', but in truth it was a broader movement, which Hollanders passed through in the seventeenth century and the (northern) French and (southern) English experienced in the eighteenth century.[46] Bolted wheat bread was, and was perceived to be, a very different product from other types of bread. The yield per bushel of grain was far lower, making fine wheat bread much more expensive per pound than the coarser loaves, and it was much more likely to be bought from a baker rather than prepared at home. Yet, even as grain prices tended upward in the second half of the eighteenth century, the drift toward the most expensive breads continued. This consumer behaviour endured the scolding of reformers and faced regulation by officials who sought to force the consumption of coarser wheat breads in order to increase the available bread supply.[47] In 1801, after noting that half the bread consumed in London was bought the same day and eaten hot, Parliament enacted the Stale Bread Act, forbidding the sale of fresh (warm) bread. This 'was said to have reduced metropolitan consumption by a sixth'.[48]

A feature all these new forms of consumption had in common was, expressed in Beckerian terms, the heavy weight of purchased goods (x) in the consumer technologies used to achieve the ultimate 'Z-consumption'. Relatively little household labour entered into the new forms of consumption. Indeed, much of it did not occur primarily within the household at all. Consumers came to depend much more on retail shops and venues of sociable consumption than had been the case under the consumption patterns of earlier times; the century after 1650 can fairly be said to have witnessed a retailing revolution. Retailing, like so many services, has not received sufficient attention from economic historians, but the scraps of available evidence support the view that the 1650–1750 century witnessed a major shift from markets, fairs and direct artisanal sales towards pedlars and, especially, retail shops. Excise records allow Mui and Mui to estimate that England possessed one such shop per 52 inhabitants in 1759. They believe the density must have been much

---

[45] Collins, 'Dietary Change', p. 105.
[46] Braudel, *Civilization and Capitalism* Vol. 1, p. 137. 'Wittebroodskinderen' (white bread children) was a seventeenth-century Dutch term roughly equivalent to 'yuppie'. Voskuil, 'De weg naar Luilekkerland', p. 476.
[47] Petersen, *Bread and the British Economy*, pp. 105–06; Kaplan, *Bakers of Paris*, pp. 536–9.
[48] Wells, *Wretched Faces*, pp. 29, 218.

lower in 1688, at the time of Gregory King's social arithmetic exercises.[49] For the Netherlands, no national estimates are available, but regional data reveal a comparable density of shopkeepers: 1 per 50 in Holland's cities in 1742; 1 per 66 in the rural Krimpenerwaard in 1795.[50] While the French took some pleasure in calling the English a nation of shopkeepers, they too were moving in this same direction. 'Although the retailing network lacked the sophistication of that of England, a great many localities witnessed "the rise of the shopkeeper"'.[51]

This multitude of shops—far more per capita than in the twentieth century—alerts us to the specific form that the division of labour took in the long eighteenth century. E. A. Wrigley noted that 'the majority of those living in the countryside but no longer able to find work on the land went, not into industry, but to the traditional trades and services . . . [As late as 1831] adult employment in manufacturing was only 10 per cent of adult male employment, whereas retail trade and handicrafts comprised 32 per cent.'[52]

The turnover of these shops will, on average, have been very modest. Many must have been the part-time undertakings of our 'industrious' households, serving literally as the pantries of a consuming public unable to purchase goods in large quantities and/or dependent on credit that only those with local knowledge could provide. Here we confront the high transaction costs that ordinarily impeded the shift towards specialized production and consumption. The high mark-ups of retailers were a major theme of Sir Frederic Morton Eden's critique in his *State of the Poor* of 1797. He organized his investigation as a comparison of northern and southern rural labouring families: the former retaining old patterns of self-provisioning, while the latter depended on retailers for their food, clothing and almost everything else. His pioneer budget studies showed these poor households spending over 11 per cent of their earnings on sugar, treacle and tea. The high prices they willingly paid, often for foods of inferior nutritional quality, caused him to conclude that the poverty problem of southern England was founded on improvident spending rather than inadequate pay.[53]

---

[49] Mui and Mui, *Shops and Shopkeeping*, pp. 135–47.
[50] De Vries and Van der Woude, *First Modern Economy*, p. 581; Kamermans, *Materiële cultuur*, pp. 33–4.
[51] Jones, 'Bourgeois Revolution Revivified', p. 88. Jones cites Dewald, *Point-Saint-Pierre*, pp. 20–1.
[52] Wrigley, 'Men on the Land', pp. 296, 97.
[53] Eden, *State of the Poor*.

What Motivated Consumers in the Industrious Revolution?

The changes in consumer behaviour in north-western Europe and Colonial North America that began in the late seventeenth century cannot be understood as marginal adjustments to changes in relative prices. Nothing in the movement of wages and prices experienced by these societies made inevitable the new consumption regime observable in the second half of the eighteenth century. Rather, it should be seen as a jump from an old to a new state, requiring simultaneous changes in the productive organization of the household and its desired 'consumption bundles'. The new regime formed the context in which the Industrial Revolution unfolded rather than being itself the cause of that sequence of events.

This new consumption regime was not uniform across social classes. The two sources I have relied on to chart the changes tend to illuminate consumption of two distinct, though overlapping, ranges of society. For those with some sort of property, the new forms of consumption were integrated into a domestic setting that featured greater comfort, domestic sociability, symbols of respectability, and steps towards the achievement of privacy. Developing side by side with this luxury of the middling sort was a plebeian consumer culture in which the domestic setting played as yet but a minor role. It pursued the cultivation of sociability outside the home, used the widened choice in food and drink to simplify meal preparation, and shifted from jointly-consumed to more individuated forms of consumption. In all these developments, the long-term needs of the household as a unit had a relatively low priority.

The consumer culture of the industrious revolution shaped what Nicholas Crafts has called the 'peculiar type of prosperity' that 'accompanied industrialization'.[54] It was a peculiar prosperity because of its abysmal nutritional standards, which were inversely related to real incomes;[55] the declines in stature that were in part the price of the

---

[54] Crafts, 'Some Dimensions', pp. 617–39.
[55] Clark, Huberman and Lindert, 'British Food Puzzle', p. 234. The puzzle addressed here is the gap between food output (and net imports) and final food consumption. The authors account for the difference by a growing consumption of foods that have endured extensive transportation, processing, and marketing costs. See also Shammas, *Pre-industrial Consumer*: 'The abysmal dietary situation of the early nineteenth century industrialization period . . . may well have had its origins a century earlier', p. 145.

increased energy expenditures of an industrious population;[56] and the internal distribution of income that skimped on the human capital and nutrition of children.[57]

Against all these negative features of the plebeian version of consumer culture in an industrious household economy stood the positive achievement: the exercise of choice across a widened array of available goods to construct clusters of consumption with the appeal sufficient to activate intensified market production. By increasing the offer of labour this phenomenon supported an extensive growth of the economy, and through the focused demand on certain 'incentive goods' it speeded the construction of distribution and retailing systems that supported an extensive division of labour. Recall that the dense network of retail shops that undergirded an economy of industrious households emerged in a century in which population growth was close to zero. It emerged not because of greater consumer density but because of a greater demand per consumer, and it was triggered by the colonial groceries that could be distributed no other way. As Shammas observes,[58]

> Once shopkeepers stocked tobacco, sugar and caffeine drinks that were bought frequently in small amounts, it made sense to stock other provisions purchased in the same way, such as salt, soap, starch, candles, butter, cheese, flour, and bacon.

The prominence of colonial groceries in new consumer cultures of the long eighteenth century raises the question of their role in motivating this whole complex phenomenon. Were these 'irresistible' commodities that 'seduced' the consumer, drawing him into the market and forcing her to industrious behaviour? The rapid growth of European markets for sugar, coffee, tea and tobacco has given rise to two distinct lines of explanation. Some point to the substantial decline in prices to suggest that nothing more than conventional consumer demand theory is required to explain the growth in demand for these commodities. Others believe more is required and emphasize their

---

[56] The relative importance of the multiple determinants of net nutritional status remains a matter of debate. See Voth, 'Height, Nutrition, and Labour', pp. 627–36 and Komlos, 'Shrinking in a Growing Economy?', pp. 779–802; Steckel, 'Stature and Living Standards', pp. 1903–40.

[57] Weir, 'Parental Consumption Decisions', pp. 259–74. On human capital formation, see Mitch, 'Role of Education', pp. 241–79.

[58] Shammas, *Pre-industrial Consumer*, p. 258.

novelty, addictive qualities and, in the case of sugar the 'energy rush' and the political symbolism that adhered to, and recommended, its consumption.[59]

In my view, the reception of these commodities needs to be seen in a larger context. The recent study of Sucheta Muzeumdar reminds us that irresistible consumer desire does not adhere intrinsically to sugar and tea, or, for that matter, cotton textiles. All of these commodities were produced and traded in Asia without altering the behaviour of regional consumers. Sugar and tea were both produced in China, but 'by the nineteenth century... the British worker not only ate more sugar but also drank more tea than the Chinese peasant, whose usual drink was the so-called *baicha*, "white tea", that is, hot water... The market for Chinese sugar was to emerge overseas.'[60] Furthermore, the timing of the rapid advance of all these colonial groceries except tobacco (which had reached a level of use by the early eighteenth century that it would not exceed until the invention of the cigarette) cannot be taken as an exogenous fact, determined entirely by autonomous changes in supply. Beginning in the late seventeenth century these and other commodities could begin to play new roles as part of 'consumption bundles' that appeared to increasing numbers of people to fit better than old alternatives in household strategies to secure the ultimately consumed 'Z-commodities'.

By the late seventeenth century, a commercial economy was altering consumption opportunities at the same time that households were acting to integrate new consumer goods into their lives. It is the interaction of these two spheres that created the simultaneous labour supply and consumer demand conditions that led towards the Industrial Revolution.

As noted earlier, the eighteenth-century contemporaries who had such great difficulty in discerning the productive achievements of modern industry were fully cognizant of the changing character of consumer behaviour. Beginning around 1690, the venerable concept of 'luxury' as inevitably corrupting morally and debilitating socially came under attack. Gradually, luxury, or a new luxury, could be defended as

---

[59] Shammas, *Pre-industrial Consumer*, emphasizes addiction and energy; Sidney Mintz advanced the view that the method and source of production (colonial plantations worked by slaves) caused the consumer to value sugar not only as a food but also for its political symbolism, an interesting transferral of the doctrine of transubstantiation to the study of consumer behaviour. Mintz, *Sweetness and Power*.

[60] Muzumdar, *Sugar and Society*, pp. 57, 59.

constructive of prosperity and even human fulfilment. It now seemed possible to move from a luxury of excess and arbitrariness, filled with food, drink and servants to a form admired by Sir William Temple, English ambassador to the Dutch Republic in 1673, where money 'is laid out in the fabrick, adornment, or furniture of their houses; things not so transitory, or so prejudicial to Health and to Business as the constant excesses and luxury of tables; nor perhaps altogether so vain as the extravagant expenses of clothes and attendance'.[61] From a perception that the new luxury could be less prejudicial than the old, the hope gradually arose that a 'good consumption' could support economic development. Indeed, these speculations went further, to imagine that the new consumer practice was part of a 'civilizing process', altering the capacities of a broad public to imagine new ways of life and to act effectively to pursue those desires. As Sir James Steuart put it in 1767, men who had once been forced to work out of poverty 'are forced to labour now because they are slaves to their own wants'.[62]

This 'long eighteenth century' experience raises the question whether there exists a history of consumer preferences. By this I do not mean simply the chronicle of substitution and income effects driven by changes in relative prices and incomes, nor the capricious history of fashion, advertising and the like. Rather, the question is whether economic growth gives rise to a coherent, endogenous pattern of changing preferences resulting from changes in personal and social capital.[63] The pre-Smithian political economists certainly sensed a transformation in the behaviour of people as consumers that was shaped by the changing economic settings in which they lived. That behavioural change, in turn, helped advance the specialized, interdependent commercial economy in which an industrial revolution could take place.

This episode in western economic development alerts us to the ongoing importance of the household as an economic organization and the market economy with which it interacts. These interactions do not appear to result in linear processes of growth, or in the erosion of the household. Their continued interactions in the twenty-first century may yet surprise us.

---

[61] Temple, *Observations upon the United Provinces*, p. 87.
[62] Steuart, *Inquiry into the Principles*, p. 67.
[63] Becker, *Accounting for Tastes*, pp. 18–19.

References

Akkerman, Tjitske. *Women's Vices, Public Benefits. Women and Commerce in the French Enlightenment*. Amsterdam: Amsterdam University Press, 1992.

Becker, Gary. *Accounting for Tastes*. Cambridge, Mass: Harvard University Press, 1996.

Becker, Gary. 'A Theory of the Allocation of Time.' *Economic Journal* 75 (1965): 493–517.

Bienefeld, M.A. *Working Hours in British Industry: An Economic History*. London: Weidenfeld and Nicolson, 1972.

Blondé, Bruno. 'The Birth of a Consumer Society? Consumption and Material Culture in Antwerp, Seventeenth and Eighteenth Centuries.' Unpublished paper, University of Antwerp, 1997.

Braudel, Fernand. *Civilization and Capitalism. Fifteenth to Eighteenth Centuries, Vol. 1, The Structures of Everyday Life*. New York, Harper and Row, 1981.

Brennan, Thomas. *Public Drinking and Popular Culture in Eighteenth-Century Paris*. Princeton: Princeton University Press, 1988.

Clark, Gregory. 'Labour Productivity in English Agriculture, 1399–1860.' In *Land, Labour, and Livestock: Historical Studies in European Agricultural Productivity*, edited by Bruce Campbell and Mark Overton, 211–35. Manchester: Manchester University Press, 1991.

──────. 'Too Much Revolution: Agriculture in the Industrial Revolution, 1700–1860.' In *The British Industrial Revolution. An Economic Perspective*, edited by Joel Mokyr, 206–40. Boulder: Westview Press, second ed., 1999.

Clark, Gregory, M. Huberman and P.T. Lindert. 'A British Food Puzzle, 1770–1850.' *Economic History Review* 48 (1995): 215–37.

Clark, Peter. *The English Alehouse: A Social History 1200–1830*. London: Longmans, 1983.

Collins, E.J.T. 'Dietary Change and Cereal Consumption in Britain in the Nineteenth Century.' *Agricultural History Review* 23 (1975): 97–115.

Crafts, N.F.R. 'Some Dimensions of the Quality of Life during the British Industrial Revolution.' *Economic History Review* 50 (1997): 617–39.

Crafts, N.F.R., and C.K. Harley. 'Output Growth and the Industrial Revolution: A Restatement of the Crafts-Harley View.' *Economic History Review* 45 (1992): 703–30.

Deane, Phyllis, and W.A. Cole. *British Economic Growth, 1688–1959*. Cambridge: Cambridge University Press, second ed., 1967.

Defoe, Daniel. *A Plan of the English Commerce*. London: 1728.

De Vries, Jan. 'Between Purchasing Power and the World of Goods: Understanding the Household Economy in Early Modern Europe.' In *Consumption and the World of Goods*, edited by John Brewer and Roy Porter, 85–132. London: Routledge, 1993.

———. 'Connecting Europe and Asia: A Quantitative History of the Cape Route Trades, 1497–1795', In *Monetary History in Global Perspective*, edited by Richard van Glahn, Dennis Flynn and Arturo Giraldo. London: Macmillan, forthcoming.

———. 'Economic Growth before and after the Industrial Revoluton: A Modest Proposal.' In *Early Modern Capitalism*, edited by Maarten Prak, 177–94. London: Routledge, 2001.

———. 'The Industrial Revolution and the Industrious Revolution.' *Journal of Economic History* 54 (1994): 249–70.

———. 'The Labour Market.' *Economic and Social History in the Netherlands* 4 (1992): 55–78.

———. 'Peasant Demand Patterns and Economic Development: Friesland, 1550–1750.' In *European Peasants and their Markets*, edited by William N. Parker and Eric L. Jones, 205–65. Princeton: Princeton University Press, 1975.

De Vries, Jan and Ad van der Woude. *The First Modern Economy: Success, Failure and Perseverance of the Dutch Economy, 1500–1815*. Cambridge: Cambridge University Press, 1997.

Dewald, Jonathan. *Point-Saint-Pierre*. Berkeley and Los Angeles: University of California Press, 1987.

Dibbits, Hester. 'Between Society and Family Values: The Linen Cupboard in Early-modern Households.' In *Private Domain, Public Inquiry. Families and Life-styles in the Netherlands and Europe, 1550 to the Present*, edited by Anton Schuurman and Pieter Spierenburg, 125–45. Hilversum: Verloren, 1996.

Eden, Sir Frederic Morton. *The State of the Poor* (3 Vols., London, 1797) abridged ed., edited by A.G.L. Rogers. New York: Dutton, 1929.

Fairchild, Cissie. 'The Production and Marketing of Populuxe Goods in Eighteenth-Century Paris,' In *Consumption and the World of Goods*, edited by John Brewer and Roy Porter, 228–48. London: Routledge, 1993.

Feinstein, Charles H. 'Pessimism Perpetuated: Real Wages and the Standard of Living in Britain during and after the Industrial Revolution.' *Journal of Economic History* 58 (1998): 625–58.

Fishlow, Albert. 'Brazilian Size Distribution of Income.' *American Economic Review* 62 (1972): 391–402.

Fogel, Robert W. 'The Conquest of High Mortality and Hunger in Europe and America: Timing and Mechanisms.' In *Favorites of Fortune: Technology, Growth, and Economic Development Since the Industrial Revolution*, edited by Patrice Higonnet, David S. Landes, and Henry Rosovsky, 33–71. Cambridge, Mass.: Harvard University Press, 1991.

Freudenberger, Herman. 'Das Arbeitjahr.' In *Wirtschaftliche und Soziale Strukturen im säkularen Wandel*, edited by Ingorma Bog et al., 307–20. Hanover: Verlag Mund H. Schaqper, 1974.

Goodman, Jordan. *Tobacco in History. The Cultures of Dependence*. London: Routledge, 1993.

Grantham, George. 'Division of Labour: Agricultural Productivity and Occupational Specialization in Pre-industrial France.' *Economic History Review* 46 (1993): 478–502.
Hill, Bridget. *Women, Work and Sexual Politics in Eighteenth Century England.* Oxford: Oxford University Press, 1989.
Hirschman, Albert. *The Strategy of Economic Development.* New Haven: Yale University Press, 1958.
Hobsbawm, E.J. 'The General Crisis of the Seventeenth Century.' *Past and Present* 5 & 6 (1954–55): 33–53; 44–65.
Hoffman, Philip. *Growth in a Traditional Society: The French Countryside 1450–1815.* Princeton: Princeton University Press, 1996.
Horrell, Sara. 'Home Demand and British Industrialization.' *Journal of Economic History* 56 (1996): 561–604.
Horrell, Sara, and Jane Humphries. 'Old Questions, New Data and Alternative Perspectives: Families' Living Standards in the Industrial Revolution.' *Journal of Economic History* 52 (1992): 849–80.
———. 'Women's Labour Force Participation and the Transition to the Male-Breadwinner Family, 1790-1865.' *Economic History Review* 48 (1995): 89–117.
Jansen, J.C.G.M. 'Wilt U koffie of thee? Consumentengedrag in Maastricht in de achttiende eeuw.' *NEHA Jaarboek* 60 (1997): 36–68.
Jobse-van Putten, Jozien. *Eenvoudig maar voedzaam. Cultuurgeschiedenis van de dagelijkse maaltijd in Nederland.* Nijmegen, SUN Uitgeverij, 1995.
Jones, Colin. 'Bourgeois Revolution Revivified: 1789 and Social Change.' In *Rewriting the French Revolution*, edited by Colin Lucas. Oxford: Oxford University Press, 1991.
Kamermans, John A. *Materiële cultuur in de Krimpenerwaard in de zeventiende en achttiende eeuw.* Wageningen: AAG Bijdragen 39, 1999.
Kaplan, Steven. *The Bakers of Paris and the Bread Question, 1700–1775.* Chapel Hill: University of North Carolina Press, 1996.
Komlos, John. 'Shrinking in a Growing Economy? The Mystery of Physical Stature during the Industrial Revolution.' *Journal of Economic History* 58 (1998): 779–802.
Kuznets, Simon. *Modern Economic Growth: Rate, Structure and Spread.* New Haven: Yale University Press, 1966.
Lancaster, Kelvin. *Modern Consumer Theory.* Aldershot, Hants: Ashgate, 1991.
Landes, David. *The Unbound Prometheus.* Cambridge: Cambridge University Press, 1969.
Lavoisier, A-L. *De la richesse territoriale du royaume de France.* Reprint edition, edited by J. C. Perrot. Paris: Editions du C.T.H.S. 1988.
Linder, Staffan B. *The Harried Leisure Class.* New York: Columbia University Press, 1970.
McKendrick, Neil, John Brewer and J.H. Plumb. *The Birth of a Consumer Society: The Commercialization of Eighteenth-Century England.* Bloomington, Indiana: Indiana University Press, 1982.

Maddison, Angus. *Dynamic Forces in Capitalist Development. A Long-run Perspective.* Oxford: Oxford University Press, 1991.
Mintz, Sidney. *Sweetness and Power.* New York: Viking, 1985.
Mitch, David. 'The Role of Education and Skill in the British Industrial Revolution.' In *The British Industrial Revolution,* edited by Joel Mokyr, 241–79. Boulder: Westview Press, 1999.
Mitchell, B.R., and P. Deane. *Abstract of British Historical Statistics.* Cambridge: Cambridge University Press, 1962.
Mokyr, Joel. 'Editor's Introduction: The New Economic History and the Industrial Revolution.' In *The British Industrial Revolution. An Economic Perspective,* edited by Joel Mokyr, 1–127. Boulder: Westview Press, second ed., 1999.
_____. *The Lever of Riches.* Oxford: Oxford University Press, 1990.
Morineau, Michel. *Incroyables gazettes et fabuleux métaux.* Cambridge: Cambridge University Press, 1985.
Mui, Hoh-Cheung, and Lorna H. Mui. *Shops and Shopkeeping in Eighteenth-Century England.* Kingston and Montreal: Queens University Press, 1989.
Muzumdar, Sucheta. *Sugar and Society in China. Peasants, Technology, and the World Market.* Cambridge, Mass.: Harvard University Press, 1998.
Noordegraaf, Leo. *Hollands welvaren?* Bergen: Octavo Uitgeverij, 1984.
O'Brien, Patrick K. 'The Political Economy of British Taxation, 1600–1815.' *Economic History Review* 41 (1988), 1–32.
Petersen, Christian. *Bread and the British Economy, c. 1770–1870.* London: Scolar Press, 1995.
Pollard, Sidney. *The Genesis of Modern Management.* London: Penguin, 1965.
Schneider, Juergen. 'The Effects on European Markets of Imports of Overseas Agriculture: The Production, Trade and Consumption of Coffee (15th to late 18th Century).' In *Economic Effects of the European Expansion, 1492–1824,* edited by J. Casas Pardo, 283–306. Frankfurt: Franz Steiner Verlag, 1992.
Schultz, T.P. 'Economic Demography and Development: New Directions in an Old Field.' In *The State of Development Economics,* edited by Gustav Ranis and T.P. Schultz, 416–51. Oxford: Oxford University Press, 1988.
Shammas, Carole. 'The Decline of Textile Prices in England and British America prior to the Industrial Revolution.' *Economic History Review* 47 (1994): 483–507.
_____. 'The Eighteenth-Century English Diet and Economic Change.' *Explorations in Economic History* 21 (1984): 254–69.
_____. *The Pre-industrial Consumer in England and America.* Oxford: Oxford University Press, 1990.
Smith, Adam. *An Inquiry into the Nature and Causes of the Wealth of Nations* (1776), edited by Edwin Cannan. New York: Modern Library, 1937.
Sokoll, Thomas. 'Early Attempts at Accounting the Unaccountable: Davies' and Eden's Budgets of Agricultural Labouring Families in Late Eighteenth Century England.' In *Zur Ökonomik des Privaten Haushalts,* edited by Toni Pierenkemper, 34–60. Frankfurt: Campus 1991.

Steckel, Richard. 'Stature and Living Standards,' *Journal of Economic Literature* 33 (1995): 1903–40.
Steuart, Sir James. *An Inquiry into the Principles of Political Œconomy.* London: 1767.
Temple, Sir William. *Observations upon the United Provinces of the Netherlands* (1673), edited by Sir George Clark. Oxford: Oxford University Press, 1972.
Teuteberg, Hans J. 'Food Consumption in Germany since the beginning of Industrialization: A Quantitative Longitudinal Approach.' In *Consumer Behavior and Economic Growth in the Modern Economy*, edited by H. Baudet and H. van der Meulen, 231–78. London: Croom Helm, 1982.
Thirsk, Joan. *Economic Policies and Projects: The Development of a Consumer Society in Early Modern England.* Oxford: Oxford University Press, 1978.
Thompson, E.P. *The Making of the English Working Class.* New York: Vintage Books, 1963.
———. 'Time, Work, Discipline and Industrial Capitalism.' *Past and Present* 38 (1967): 56–97.
Toutain, Jean-Claude. 'La consommation alimentaire en France de 1789 à 1962.' *Economie et Société* (1972): 1913–75.
Vandenbroeke, C. *Agriculture et alimentation dans les Pays-Bas Autrichiens.* Ghent: Centre Belge d'Histoire Rurale, 1975.
Voskuil, J.J. 'De verspreiding van koffie en thee in Nederland,' *Volkskundig Bulletin* 14 (1988), 68–93.
———. 'De weg naar Luilekkerland.' *Bijdragen en mededelingen van de geschiedenis der Nederlanden* 98 (1983): 460–90.
Voth, Hans-Joachim. 'Height, Nutrition, and Labor: Recasting the "Austrian Model".' *Journal of Interdisciplinary History* 25 (1995): 627–36.
———. 'Time and Work in Eighteenth-Century London.' *Journal of Economic History* 58 (1998): 29–58.
Weir, David. 'Parental Consumption Decisions and Child Health during the Early French Fertility Decline,' *Journal of Economic History* 53 (1993): 259–74.
Wells, Roger. *Wretched Faces. Famine in Wartime England, 1763–1803.* Gloucester: Sutton, 1988.
Wrigley, E.A. *Continuity, Chance, and Change. The Character of the Industrial Revolution in England.* Cambridge: Cambridge University Press, 1988.
———. 'Men on the Land and Men in the Countryside.' In *The World We Have Gained*, edited by L. Bonfield et al. Oxford: Blackwells, 1986.
Yang, X., and J. Borland. 'A Microeconomic Mechanism for Economic Growth.' *Journal of Political Economy* 99 (1991): 460–82.
Young, Allyn. 'Increasing Returns and Economic Progress.' *Economic Journal* 38 (1928): 527–42.

2.
English Apprenticeship:
A Neglected Factor in the First Industrial Revolution
JANE HUMPHRIES

Introduction

The English Industrial Revolution is increasingly understood as precocious structural change. 'The main features of the period . . . are slow income growth and rapid structural change starting from an early eighteenth century position which was already relatively industrialized'.[1] English exceptionalism involved an early reduction in the relative proportions of agricultural output and employment and an early increase in the weight of industrial, or at least non-agricultural, output and employment. Output growth in both aggregate and per capita terms was reliant on the preemptive exploitation of the productivity gap between agriculture and industry at low levels of income. ' . . . the triumph of the industrial revolution lay in getting a lot of workers into industry rather than in obtaining high productivity from them once there'.[2]

Much energy has been devoted to the demonstration of this precocious structural change and its implications for our broader understanding of British economic development. In contrast, little attention has been given to how it was achieved and, in particular, to the institutions that facilitated the transfer of resources. Peter Solar's reinterpretation of the Old Poor Law (OPL) is an exception.[3] Solar argued that the OPL ' . . . underpinned the growth of an economically mobile wage labour force; encouraged the consolidation of farms and facilita-

---
[1] Crafts, *British Economic Growth*, p. 61; see also Mathias, *First Industrial Nation*, p. 2; and Deane, *First Industrial Revolution*, p. 1.
[2] Crafts, *British Economic Growth*, p. 156.
[3] Solar, 'Poor Relief'.

ted the separation of smallholders from the land; provided local initiatives for agricultural capital formation and industrial development; and kept population under control. All these elements contributed to the distinctiveness of the English economy... '[4]

The English system of apprenticeship is another institution 'ripe for inclusion in this new political economy of English development in the seventeenth and eighteenth centuries'.[5] Apprenticeship contributed in four ways. First, apprenticeship provided training in skills directly relevant to the expanding areas of employment and to the increasing need to transport commodities and people. However, the market under-produces general training. So second, this paper argues that several characteristics of the English system of apprenticeship, characteristics that may have been historical accidents, nudged masters and men towards efficient training. Third, apprenticeship reduced the transactions costs involved in transferring resources from agriculture to non-agriculture and facilitated the expansion of networks across sectors which promoted trade and commerce. Finally, apprenticeship saved the children of the poor from social exclusion and, by providing them with basic maintenance and some general training, enabled them to become productive adults. The second and fourth points involve the inter-connections between apprenticeship and the Poor Law which go back to the Tudor origins of both institutions and their shared purpose in poverty reduction and social control. The paper suggests that training and human capital formation may have played a more important role in early industrialization than is generally allowed.[6]

A Brief History of English Apprenticeship[7]

Although apprenticeship existed as early as the fourteenth century, its structure and functioning in the period under review can be traced

---

[4] Ibid., p. 16.
[5] Ibid., p. 1.
[6] This paper concentrates on what were mainly beneficent links between apprenticeship, poor law and economic growth in the eighteenth century. Later developments combined to produce a different, more exploitative version of these same links—see Rose, 'Social Policy'.
[7] Dunlop (with Denman), *English Apprenticeship*, is the classic treatment of English apprenticeship. Margaret Gay Davies, *Enforcement*, provides a rare study of the enforcement of apprenticeship legislation. Several recent books and papers approach the topic in

back to the Statute of Artificers of 1563. The Tudor legislation, while originating in the rules of medieval craft guilds, created a national system of technical training. The apprentice was bound by indentures to a tradesman or artificer who was covenanted to teach him his trade. The apprentice contributed to the costs of his training and maintenance by working for the master during the contract and, from the seventeenth century, by paying a premium up-front. During the apprenticeship, the apprentice lived with the master as part of the family. Training extended to learning the way of life associated with the future occupation.

For a match to be made between master and apprentice there had to be a mutual gain. The apprenticeship contract designed a mutually acceptable division of the gain. There are two obvious problems. First, the exchanges are not synchronized in time; either the master trains first and the apprentice works subsequently as skilled labour, or the unskilled apprentice works first to be trained subsequently. If a premium is involved the worker pays initially and the training is delivered afterwards. Second, the commodities to be exchanged, training and maintenance on the one hand and service on the other, are difficult to define and specify. In these circumstances the party who is paid first has an incentive to renege on the contract and seize more of the mutual gain than was specified by the original terms and is assisted in this by the difficulties of demonstrating that either training or service has been delivered.

The Elizabethan legislation can be read as codifying the numerous laws on the employment of apprentices to provide a legal framework within which these problems could be addressed. Thus early legislation (5 Elizabeth 1) limited the number of apprentices that masters could take on, fixed the term of apprenticeship at seven years, and required written indentures in all private contracts.[8]

---

new ways. Earle, *Making of the English Middle Class*, uses data for London to interpret apprenticeship as a building block of 'the middling sort'. Snell, *Annals*, uses settlement examinations to explore apprenticeship's importance to the labouring poor, and Deakin, 'Legal Origins', links apprenticeship to the evolution of modern labour markets. Lane's *Apprenticeship* provides rich empirical detail. Grubb's extensive work on contracts and indentured servitude has informed my approach (see Grubb, 'Bonded Labour').

[8] 5 Elizabeth 1 refers to specific Elizabethan legislation. The first number denotes the year in Elizabeth's reign in which the law was passed.

Elizabethan attempts to codify apprenticeship were overlaid with anxieties about the social consequences of under-employment, especially among the young, and hence accompanied by measures to force apparently idle youngsters into work. The Elizabethan legislation built on the political tradition that apprenticeship was a remedy for vagrancy and that the possession of a trade would keep a man from poverty.[9] While apprenticeship was intended to promote English industries by requiring technical training before the practice of a trade, it also facilitated social control. As Jocelyn Dunlop notes: ' . . . there is no doubt that apprenticeship was an integral part of the new system for the relief of the poor, and that in addition it was used by the Government as a means both to maintain the rural population and to resuscitate the waning prosperity of corporate towns'.[10] Thus 5 Elizabeth 1 also enabled Justices of the Peace to bind the offspring of pauper vagrants or 'those overburdened with children'. Indeed anyone under 21 'refusing to be an apprentice and to serve in husbandry or any other kind of art, mystery or science' could be imprisoned. Householders fulfilling a property requirement were obliged to take apprentices.

Other laws followed, some specific to pauper apprentices. In 1597 (39 Elizabeth 1 c. 3), overseers were permitted to raise a rate to cover the costs of apprenticeship premiums for poor children, and 14 years old was stipulated as the maximum age at which a parish child might be bound. In 1601 (43 Elizabeth c. 2), the Elizabethan Poor Law Act returned to the issue of indenturing poor children, and empowered the 'Churchwardens and overseers . . . by the assent of any Two Justices of the Peace . . . to bind any such children . . . to be apprentices, where they shall see convenient'. Girls were to serve until aged 21 or until they married and boys until 24. Perhaps initially Justices of the Peace did not make great efforts to 'seek out' poor children to indenture. But once such children actually became chargeable, apprenticeship was an economic option. It also provided some advantages for the children, though sometimes at the cost of foisting parish apprentices on reluctant parishioners.

---

[9] Dunlop, *English Apprenticeship*, charts the developing political belief that apprenticeship was a remedy for vagrancy and that the possession of a skilled trade would keep a man from poverty (see pp. 68–70). See also Davies, *Enforcement*.

[10] Dunlop, *English Apprenticeship*, pp. 61–2. The state also appears to have had population control in mind. Service until 24 years of age for example was designed to prevent 'the over hastie marriages and over sone setting up of householdes of and by young folk . . .' (quoted in Dunlop, *English Apprenticeship*, p. 70).

Moreover in Charles I's reign, the activities of the Privy Council led to the better administration of the laws, and JPs were now required to make reports on their work, stimulating activity.[11] These returns show the regular use of apprenticeship in almost every parish.[12] Finally the Settlement Act of 1692, by providing that a settlement could be gained by a completed apprenticeship, created an incentive to apprentice pauper children or those at risk of indigence out of the parish. 'Poor law officers could now no longer rid themselves of their poor with a bribe to remain hidden in a neighbouring parish. But they could induce petty craftsmen and other poorer inhabitants by the payment of a premium to receive their pauper children as apprentices, and so free themselves for ever not only from the maintenance of the child, but also from the possibility of supporting his wife and children'.[13]

In 1709 with the Stamp Act, apprenticeship premiums were taxed. Tax inspectors had to be appointed, indentures listed and financial records kept. Originally these arrangements were for five years but they yielded such a regular source of income that in 1710 they were made perpetual. Legislative refinements continued into the eighteenth century. A law of 1747 enabled any allegedly abused apprentice whose premium had been less than £5 to complain to two Justices of the Peace. If the accusation was upheld the child was released from his indentures, but the master was not punished and retained the premium! The upper limit on the premium, while covering most pauper apprentices, excluded the majority of private placements. The same act enabled masters too to complain, providing a loophole for unscrupulous masters wanting to be rid of apprentices to manufacture false charges.

In 1757 indentures were replaced by a stamped deed, increasingly a printed one. The duties and tasks of both master and apprentice were reaffirmed, implying that behaviour was a contested terrain. Apprentices absconding seems to have been a perennial problem. A law of 1766 added absences to the term of service. In 1768 the usual term for male apprentices was cut to end at 21 years old and premiums could be paid in instalments, though the latter practice was probably already widespread. Further statutes in 1780–1800 reaffirmed the duties of masters, ameliorated the conditions of boy chimney sweeps, and extended the power of justices over apprentices. Justices

---

[11] Ibid., see also Davies, *Enforcement*.
[12] Dunlop, *English Apprenticeship*, p. 250.
[13] Ibid., p. 256.

were permitted to reassign apprentices whose masters had died and to discharge children for whom masters could not find employment or maintenance if they had less than £4 premium. Legislation in the reign of George III increased the range of children covered by right to resort to the JPs. All children whose premiums were under £10 could complain of harsh treatment and for the first time there was a deterrent to masters in the form of a £2 fine if the complaint was upheld.

The 1802 Health and Morals of Apprentices Act provided comprehensive and detailed regulation of the small proportion of child apprentices who worked in textile mills, although none of the Act's provisions were enforceable. More important was the requirement in 1802 for Overseers and Guardians to keep a register of the children bound or assigned by them as apprentices.

The repeal of the Statute of Artificers in 1814 meant that it was no longer possible to prosecute anyone practising a trade without completing a legal apprenticeship, and removed the barriers to entry that had seemingly upheld the central legislation at local level. However, repeal did not abolish apprenticeship itself and large numbers of children continued to be trained in the traditional way.[14]

The Quantitative Importance of Apprenticeship

While the legal history of apprenticeship is well known, few historians have been willing to estimate its quantitative significance. How many children passed through the system and what proportion of the high

---

[14] The timing of the decline of apprenticeship is unclear—see Snell, *Annals*. Dunlop, *English Apprenticeship*, and Marshall, *English Poor*; see decline from about 1720, with the diminishing control of the guilds. Kellett, 'Breakdown', and Kahl, 'Apprenticeship', perhaps associating the health of apprenticeship too closely with the strength of the guilds, push decline forward into the seventeenth century. Peter Clark, 'Migration', accepts this chronology. Snell is one of the few historians to attempt to document the decline of apprenticeship, in terms of the declining length of the term actually served, and the growth of illegal apprenticeships as revealed in settlement examinations. His evidence suggests regional differences in the timing of the decline and a different chronology between guilded towns and more rural contexts. In terms of the declining length of the term served, Snell dates the decline from the mid-eighteenth century, especially after 1780 and with 1811–1820 seeing most change (see *Annals*). See also Rushton, 'Matter'. Lane takes a particularly strong position, though without citing quantitative evidence. She charges that the repeal of the Statute of Artificers ' . . . in no way abolished apprenticeship but only modified its legal enforcement and the numbers of children apprenticed do not appear to have been affected', *Apprenticeship*, p. 7.

growth rates of industrial labour derived from this source? Dunlop asserts: 'No determinate figures can be given for the number of children employed in the various trades and in agriculture. The employment books of some towns are preserved and from them can be gathered the number of apprentices in those places but there is no record for the country as a whole'.[15]

Less documentation of non-poor apprenticeship than of pauper or charity apprenticeship has survived. Liability for Stamp Duty means that apprenticeship registers inevitably undercount. Some 250,000 apprentices were registered in the years 1710–1762.[16] If the majority of these non-poor apprentices were non-agricultural, this figure provides for one non-poor apprentice per twelve manufacturers, merchants and tradesmen identified in Massie's social table for England and Wales in 1759.[17]

Scattered data available for individual towns probably give a more accurate picture. According to Malcolm Graham, 282 boys on average were apprenticed in Oxford each decade, 1711–1780.[18] Assuming each worked out a full seven-year term, and with an 85 per cent survivorship rate, 213 of Oxford's 5–7,000 population were apprentices (approximately 4.3–2.1 per cent).[19] London was a special case, with thousands of boys coming every year.[20] Estimates of their numbers in the second half of the seventeenth century range from 11,000 to 40,000.[21] In some parishes, they represented as much as 10 per cent of the population.[22] Apprentices always comprised a higher proportion of the labour force than of the local population—perhaps twice as high. Table 1 brings together the scattered evidence of this kind. The numbers are consistent with Lawrence Stone's conjecture that domestic, agricultural or industrial apprentices and live-in servants made up 15–20 per cent of the adult male population in early modern England.[23] If the sectoral breakdown of apprentices and live-in servants roughly

---

[15] Dunlop, *English Apprenticeship*, p. 100.
[16] Lane, *Apprenticeship*.
[17] This calculation assumes each apprentice served a seven-year term and takes no account of mortality. Massie's estimate of the number of manufacturers, merchants and tradesmen is from Mathias, 'Social Structure'.
[18] Graham, *Oxford City Apprentices*.
[19] This survivorship rate is based on London's mortality (see Finlay, *Population*) and so probably underestimates the numbers in Oxford.
[20] S.R. Smith, 'London Apprentices'.
[21] Finlay, *Population*, on the basis of data provided in V.B. Eliott, 'Mobility'.
[22] Earle, *Making of the English Middle Class*.
[23] Stone, 'Social Mobility'.

Table 1. Estimates of the proportion of apprentices in the population of various towns and cities.

	London 1600	London 1700	Oxford 1701–10	Oxford 1751–60	Oxford 1791–1800	Northampton 1654–1715	Northampton 1716–76	Coventry 1781–1806
Total population	200,000	575,000	5,000–7,000	5,000–7,000	5,000–7,000	4,000–5,000	4,000–5,000	16,000
Annual number of apprentices bound	4,000–5,000	3,400–4,080	57	24	34	19	28	174
Apprentices serving a minimum seven-year term	28,000–35,000	23,800–28,560	399	168	238	133	194	1,218
Total Apprentices	32,000–40,000	27,200–32,640	456	192	272	152	222	1,392
After depletion, 85% survivorship during term	27,200–34,000	23,120–27,744	388	163	231	129	189	1,183
Percentage of total population	13.6–17.0	4.0–4.8	5.5–7.8	2.3–3.3	3.3–4.6	2.6–3.2	3.8–4.7	7.4

Sources: Elliott, 'Mobility'; Everitt, *Ways and Means*; Finlay, *Population*; Graham, *Oxford City Apprentices*; Lane, *Coventry Apprentices*; Wrigley, *Continuity*.

followed the aggregate distribution of the labour force, non-agricultural apprentices made up between 7.5 and 10 per cent of the adult male population.

Another way to appreciate the quantitative importance of apprenticeship is to consider the proportion of the male population that had served. Again piecemeal evidence is all that is available. Rushton calculates that 50 per cent of the male population of Newcastle had been through apprenticeship to become freemen of the town.[24] More must have served out apprenticeships but remained journeymen. As far as the growth of the industrial labour force itself is concerned, Dunlop rightly highlights the apprenticeship gateway. 'The industrial labour market depended for its fresh supplies of labour almost entirely upon one source, the boys who at about fourteen years old joined the ranks of industry as apprentices'.[25]

Apprenticeship and Efficient Levels of Training

General training is crucial in raising labour productivity and its role was probably particularly important in craft production.[26] In a competitive economy with no market imperfections workers invest in and firms provide efficient levels of general training.[27] But in the real world markets are less than perfect. The case for policy intervention has focussed on the consequences of imperfect capital markets, and in particular workers' inability to borrow. Unless workers pay up-front for training, firms are reluctant to supply it because trained workers can earn wages equal to marginal products elsewhere and will quit unless the training firm matches the external wage offer. This classic hold-up inhibits firms from training, as they are unable to recoup the costs through paying wages below marginal products. But as is implicit in the description of the complex nature of training and the difficulties identified in contracting for its provision, workers' lack of capital is not the only reason for inefficient general training. Even if workers had access to capital markets and could pay for training,

---

[24] Rushton, 'Matter'.
[25] Dunlop, *English Apprenticeship*, p. 134.
[26] Soskice, 'Reconciling Markets and Institutions'.
[27] Becker, *Human Capital*.

81

hold-up could operate in reverse. Trainees may be reluctant to pay in advance if they know that there is a chance that some masters will not provide the training promised and the money will be wasted.

Training involves a long-term relationship where a considerable amount of time elapses between the *quid* and the *quo* and where competition *ex ante* is replaced by monopoly *ex post*.[28] In these circumstances a contract becomes an essential part of the trading relationship, specifying rules that define how the partners have decided to share the returns in various possible future circumstances. But it is very difficult to write contracts that induce efficient relationship-specific investments.[29] A contract is the outcome of an optimization process in which the relative benefits and costs of additional length are traded off. Costs include the costs of writing the contract in a sufficiently clear and unambiguous way so that the terms can be enforced, and the legal costs of enforcement. There are, of course, circumstances that are not explicitly covered, either because they are not *observable* at reasonable cost, or because they are thought unlikely to occur, or because states of the world, quality and actions even if *observable* (to the contracting parties) are not *verifiable* (to outsiders).[30] Exchange, here training, requires credible low-cost contracts. Recently theorists have emphasized the practical importance of self-enforcing contracts, that is contracts that are enforced by custom, good faith and reputation.[31] The theory of repeated games has demonstrated the value of 'reputation' in completing a contract. 'A party may behave "reasonably" even if he is not obliged to do so in order to develop a reputation as a decent and reliable trader'.[32] Reputation works best to enforce implicit contracts if the time horizon is fairly long or the future important relative to the present.

Third-party enforcement is also possible in the form of a monitor, arbitrator or court of law. Adjudication by third parties can be very costly though its availability is essential for contracts to be credible, and the more informed the third parties are, the lower cost policing

---

[28] Hart, 'Incomplete Contracts'.
[29] Williamson, *Economic Institutions*.
[30] Asymmetry of information between the parties on the one hand and the parties and outsiders on the other is the root of the problem (see Hart, 'Incomplete Contracts').
[31] Azariadis, 'Implicit Contracts'.
[32] Hart, 'Incomplete Contracts', p. 751. But note that if there is asymmetric information within the contract, the parties do not have access to the same information and cannot observe whether reasonable behaviour is being maintained, reputation cannot help.

may be. Legal coercion tends to be a last resort. Extra-legal physical or social coercion in which society evolves customs and norms so that contract breakers can be punished by the wronged parties sufficiently to deter contract breaking often proves more efficient. Interested groups organize to monitor and apprehend contract breakers. The collective institutions (guilds, corporations, trade associations, professional associations) may wield powers related to membership to deter contract breakers. Punishment often involves the same enforcement mechanisms as market sanctions, only with defamation demonstrated and publicized through the collective institutions.

Apprenticeship indentures provide a low cost way of specifying the timing and levels of training and the standard of maintenance to be provided and the reciprocal nature of service including its duration. The actual form of the apprenticeship indentures covering the reciprocal rights and duties of the two parties was fairly standard.[33] Where the negotiation lay was in the details such as the length of service, which was usually seven years but more for certain trades, for younger apprentices or *in lieu* of a lower premium. Other issues included the specification of the wardrobe to be provided by the master, security monies to indemnify the master against dishonesty by the apprentice, and the premium, an innovation of the seventeenth century said to indicate the increasing value of apprenticeship.[34] While apprenticeship was a legal contract, it was incomplete in the economist's sense outlined above. The position argued here is that English apprenticeship contracts were self-enforcing and therefore low cost and so induced efficient general training. Moreover when disputes arose, both insider (informal, group) and outsider (formal, legal) adjudication were available. How did apprenticeship work in practice and what mechanisms held apprentice and master together even in adverse circumstances?

Apprenticeship was an attractive institution to masters. Premiums, which could be substantial, were a source of liquidity and capital.[35] Apprentices, whose marginal products exceeded their maintenance costs, made a net contribution to their masters' incomes. The English

---

[33] Earle, *Making of the English Middle Class*, p. 93.
[34] Ibid., pp. 93–4.
[35] Ibid.; Lane, *Apprenticeship*; Collyer, *Parents' and Guardians' Directory*; Campbell, *London Tradesman*.

evidence suggests that when boys started their apprenticeships aged 14 and where the trade did not require seven years to learn, apprentices were valuable to masters as soon as two years into their service.[36]

Masters' priorities were to ensure that their apprentices served long enough to repay the training costs and contribute to profits. The need to deter runaways provided a constraint on masters' behaviour, in a context where traditional patriarchal values gave them substantial authority, authority that they could interpret quite brutally. But should masters have problems, they had a variety of enforcement agencies on which to call, starting with the family and friends of the apprentice who had been party to the deal and who could mediate and adjudicate. The location of apprenticeship within the framework of the guilds and corporations provided an important semi-legal adjudication mechanism staffed by fellow practitioners who were more able to assess idiosyncratic detail. In the last instance the master could appeal to the law. The balance of power within the everyday life of the contract was undoubtedly on the master's side. Contesting the details of the contract must have been beyond the powers and confidence of most apprentices. Running away may have seemed the only option and here masters had recourse to exogenous agency. The integration of apprenticeship within the broader institutions governing the practice of trades and occupations again had self-enforcing features. Apprentices who broke their contracts were prevented by the Statute of Artificers from practising their trade and collective solidarity mediated through the trade organization would inhibit alternative employers from taking on such workers as journeymen even if they could thereby benefit from training provided by others. Early modern industrial organization, and particularly the persistence of owner-proprietor firms, probably militated against apprentices breaking their contracts to take work as illegal journeymen by limiting the number of such berths available. This is consistent with Davies finding that prosecutions under the apprenticeship clauses of the Statute, at least in the period 1563–1642, were almost always of independent craftsmen and rarely of journeymen. Prosecution of the employer made more sense as the chance of collecting composition was better and because the wording of the Act identified the employer as liable. But prosecutions of masters either for employing men who had not completed an apprenticeship or for

---

[36] Earle, *Making of the English Middle Class*.

practising the trade illegally were also infrequent.[37]

Although changes in industrial structure increased the demand for journeymen, making it easier for apprentices to threaten masters, the general framework of apprenticeship mitigated against hold-up by frowning on the receipt of wages during training. For example, taking wages disbarred apprentices from acquiring the freedom of the City of London. However many economic historians hold that the payment of wages, especially towards the end of the term, became common.[38] Earle's description of the pressures sounds like a classic hold-up. 'However, by the early eighteenth century, the payment of wages towards the end of an apprentice's term was quite common, the threat of desertion on the grounds of the master's cruelty or some other pretext being a common bargaining point. And indeed by this stage, most apprentices would be worth wages since their skills were likely to be equal to those of journeymen long before the end of their terms'.[39] Self-enforcement suggests a search for other ways to lock apprentices in.

Apprentices' main objective was to secure general training. Indentures provided them with some security against default. Apprentices too could use the array of enforcement mechanisms from market sanctions through collective semi-legal third party policing to the long (but costly) arm of the law to ensure the training was delivered. In addition apprentices had a strong interest in other features of the contract often left implicit (wardrobe, quality of food, and kindliness of treatment). They had more to quibble about than masters did and much less in the way of support from the immediate patriarchal environment. Although they might appeal to guild or corporate authorities to mediate and rule, helped here by their family and friends, this machinery too was likely biased towards the master's interpretation of mutual obligations. Formally too apprentices had appeal to law. The threat to go public (or semi-public) with grievances may have been persuasive. Defamation of masters could reduce access to apprentices in the future. On the other hand apprentices who complained

---

[37] Davies suggests that this pattern of prosecutions was 'possibly explicable' in terms of an 'economic organization in which the "one man business" was typical . . . [and] . . . with the hired servant playing a small part outside agriculture and the life of the gentry', *Enforcement*, p. 264.

[38] Minchinton, (ed.), *Wage Regulation*; Rushton, 'Matter'; Earle, *Making of the English Middle Class*.

[39] Ibid., p. 100.

could be thought truculent or undisciplined. Not surprisingly, when charges were made in semi-public or public arenas they were both pursued and resisted with vigour.

The frequency of legislation concerning apprenticeship in the seventeenth and eighteenth centuries and the evidence from court records suggest that the long-term relationships between masters and their apprentices did not always progress smoothly. What is most interesting is the apparent impulse within the adjudication machinery towards reconciliation: the efficient outcome. If the contract was mutually beneficial when completed, the individuals and society were worse off if it disintegrated. Moreover, breakdowns might deter future potentially beneficial exchanges. Peter Rushton's analysis of disputes between masters and apprentices in the local courts in north-east England, 1600–1800, maps the path of 'variance' and identifies the bones of contention.[40] Both are predictable.

Apprentices were more prone to complain to the courts than masters were. Masters brought only 12.5 per cent of cases involving apprentices.[41] Clearly the companies offered the masters sufficient scope for correcting their apprentices, while the apprentices had to appeal to the more public forum of the quarter sessions for redress.[42] Apprentices needed help to bring a case and it was usually kin or the bondsmen who had stood surety for good behaviour at the time of indentures who became involved. Legal counsel was rare and apprentices usually acted on their own initiative.[43] Rushton concludes that although formally subordinated young people were capable of acting in their own interests.[44]

The causes of the disputes are instructive. Masters' complaints related overwhelmingly to desertion, confirming other evidence, for example from church courts. From the apprentices' perspective the contract had left more issues implicit. Thus, apprentices complained of a range of deviations from appropriate masterly behaviour including physical abuse. But again the single most important issue concerned the delivery of training. Recurring problems were that bankruptcy or death of the master could disrupt apprenticeships, leaving boys stran-

---

[40] Rushton, 'Matter'.
[41] But Ben-Amos finds a higher proportion of cases instigated by masters in Bristol albeit for a much earlier period (1600–1645), see 'Service'.
[42] Rushton, 'Matter', p. 92.
[43] But see Ben-Amos, 'Service'.
[44] Rushton, 'Matter', p. 94.

ded socially and economically. Both circumstances prompted judicial interventions to standardize responses as noted earlier. Apprentices were more likely to win their cases if failure to train was charged, reflecting the authorities' prioritizing of the training provisions of the contract and their tolerance of conduct by masters that apprentices held to be inappropriate.

Rushton's evidence suggests that there was no mass judicial rebuff for the young; apprentices won their cases surprisingly frequently.[45] Given the contemporary acceptance of patriarchal authority and the masters' local dominance, it was helpful to reassure apprentices and their families of judicial review. But winning his case did not solve the apprentice's problems. Discharge left the boy and his family back where he had started only probably poorer. Forced transfers were expensive and could bring new problems. Significantly 20 per cent of apprentices who had won their cases were ordered to stay. Even at this stage arbitration and reconciliation were the socially preferred solutions, salvaging the training process and attempting to restore discipline to both master and apprentice.

Thus the apprenticeship contract, buttressed by guild control of entry into trades, upheld by reputation, and subject in times of difficulty to peer review, and in the last instance to legal judgement, reduced the threat of hold-up by both apprentices and masters. But if, as is suggested in the literature, apprenticeship contracts ceased to be effective in imposing additional penalties for premature quits as guild controls weakened, this role for apprenticeship disappears.[46] Why then did apprenticeship contracts survive through the eighteenth century and on into the nineteenth? Closer inspection reveals other efficiency-inducing characteristics.

A second reason why general training may be under-produced arises from asymmetric information about workers' productivities.[47] If apprentices absconded and took employment as journeymen, the usual adverse selection argument predicts that, on average, their wages would be less than their marginal products.[48] Their new employers would capture part of the return to general training as an external benefit. According to Malcomson et al., apprenticeships mitigate this

---

[45] Ibid.
[46] Snell, *Annals*. Elbaum, 'Why Apprenticeship Persisted'.
[47] Chang and Wang, 'Human Capital'; Malcomson et al., 'General Training'.
[48] Greenwald, 'Adverse Selection'.

externality.[49] Malcomson et al. argue that an apprenticeship contract commits the parties to do something ahead of time that they might not otherwise do when the time arrived, with long-term beneficial effects. Their example is the practice, well-documented in modern Germany, for training firms to retain some trainees as skilled workers at the end of their apprenticeships.[50] By committing in advance to a high wage for these retained trainees, a training firm ensures that it retains only the better workers whose productivity is at least as great as the promised wage. Retention at the end of the apprenticeship then reveals information about the productivity of those retained and thus increases their wages if and when they subsequently quit. Because workers do not know their own type until it is revealed by the firm, their expected wage after the end of the contract is greater than the productivity of the less productive type, which is also the wage available to those who quit. Consequently their wage during the contract can be reduced below this level without inducing them to quit. By using a contract that makes it credible to reveal workers' types at the end of the contract, a training firm induces trainees to accept lower wages during the contract period. As a result, training firms make higher profits from training than they would if they made no commitment to future wages but merely determined them day to day.[51] This role for apprenticeship contracts, unlike that of reducing hold-up, exists even if an apprenticeship is no more effective at preventing trainees from quitting than training without one.

English apprenticeship contracts bear a functional resemblance to the contracts described by Malcomson et al. as effective against this kind of externality. It was a lucky apprentice who could expect to graduate straight into freeman status and set up as a master.[52] Set-up

---

[49] Malcomson et al., 'General Training'.

[50] See Soskice, 'Reconciling Markets and Institutions'.

[51] The shorter the contract length, the sooner the firm reveals its information about workers' marginal products and ensures that hiring firms cannot benefit from their training. But the shorter the contract length, the sooner retained workers receive a wage equal to their trained marginal products and so the less time the training firm has to recoup the costs of training. The profit-maximizing contract length trades off these two effects (see Malcomson et al., 'General Training').

[52] A high proportion of apprentices never became citizens or set up as masters, probably prevented by lack of capital. Yarbrough finds that only one-third of sixteenth-century Bristol apprentices became citizens, see Yarbrough, 'Apprentices'. Smith quotes seventeenth-century evidence to show that the majority of apprentices did not become freemen, see Smith, 'London Apprentices'.

costs for many trades were considerable and a period working as a journeyman was often necessary to accumulate capital.[53] Although masters did not promise ahead of time to retain some workers at high pay, retention was not an unreasonable expectation for a dutiful apprentice. It was not only in fairy stories that lucky apprentices married the daughters of their masters and graduated to partnerships. R.D. Lang estimated that in the early seventeenth century some 8 per cent of London Aldermen had been apprentices who had married their masters' daughters.[54] Marrying into the master's family, a strategy analogous to vertical integration, may have been mutually beneficial, restraining a talented apprentice from setting up in competition and creaming off the clients. If daughters were not available nieces and sisters could serve the same purpose. Marrying the master's widow was a less socially approved but perhaps more immediate route to the top, though as a strategy it required outside help! Partnership was possible even without marriage into the family. Lane reports that sometimes masters took apprentices into partnership without money changing hands.[55] Even something less than partnership could be of real value. In trades where a large capital was required apprentices from modest origins could never hope to become masters, but could aspire to rise in the firm where they were trained. Several of Matthew Boulton's department heads at Soho had once been his apprentices, young plain country lads 'who had become gifted craftsmen and designers'.[56]

Even when an apprentice was able to set up on his own, it was important to retain the goodwill of the master. Lane cites numerous examples of men who advertised the name of their former master as an indication of their own skills.[57] In exceptional cases masters might even help their ex-apprentices to set up in business, putting custom their way and lending them money. Even at the bottom end of the economic scale there were rewards for completion. Pauper apprentices could expect 'double apparel' and sometimes the provision of basic tools.[58]

---

[53] Earle, *Making of the English Middle Class*; Lane, *Apprenticeship*.
[54] Lang, 'Greater Merchants'. See also Peter Clark, *Transformation*, for similar evidence for Gloucester.
[55] Lane, *Apprenticeship*.
[56] Quoted in Lane, *Apprenticeship*, p. 232.
[57] Lane, *Apprenticeship*.
[58] Grubb rejects this explanation for double apparel in the contracts of indentured servants, see 'Statutory Regulation'.

In addition to the occupational advantages, discussed above, in some communities, apprenticeship brought with it franchise rights, access to specific charities and local privileges such as common grazing. Freedom of the city denoted social prestige in itself. Perhaps most important of all the completion of an apprenticeship marked a man out as trustworthy and dutiful. It provided a market signal equivalent to the retention at higher wages in the Malcomson et al. model, and it was therefore worth paying for with years of service at wages less than marginal products.

Apprenticeship contracts cannot, however, in general, prevent some of the return to non-specific training being captured by trainees and, if they quit, by their new employers. As a result even with apprenticeship contracts, trainees receive less training than is efficient. Moreover when firms vary in the cost of providing training places, too few workers are trained. These two inefficiencies provide a natural role for regulation. Malcomson et al. show that by increasing the length of the training contract, regulation can increase the amount of training towards the efficient level. But regulating the duration of apprenticeships reduces the profits from training and so the number of firms that train. Malcomson et al. show that it is still socially worthwhile, because at the profit-maximizing level of training, a small change in that level has only a second order effect on profit, and, hence only a second order effect on the number of workers trained. But it has a first order effect on the amount of training received by each trainee and, because of the externalities, this has a first order effect on social welfare.[59] Moreover the adverse effect of regulation on the number of workers trained can be mitigated by a subsidy to firms for each completed contract. Can the historical case be interpreted as regulated in these ways?

Malcomson et al. note themselves that the regulation of contract length is characteristic of historical regulation of apprenticeship.[60] What has not hitherto been appreciated is that the weaving together of apprenticeship with settlement functioned to provide a subsidy for completed apprenticeship. Historians have been puzzled about why apprentices, especially those who had no hope of setting up in business for themselves, submitted to indentures that lasted longer than appeared necessary to impart skills. Earle even contends that 'in most trades seven years' apprenticeship was merely a racket which provided

---

[59] Malcomson et al., 'General Training'.
[60] Ibid.

masters with cheap labour'.[61] One additional incentive to complete the contract has been forgotten. From the late seventeenth century the completion of an apprenticeship was one of the routes to obtain a legal settlement with all that settlement entailed in terms of a claim on poor relief in times of need due to unemployment, sickness and old age. The vital importance of legal settlement to working people and the social and economic exclusion that haunted those whose settlement was in doubt, is now well established.[62] Large numbers of working people made use of apprenticeship as a condition for obtaining settlement. Snell has shown that between one-eighth and one-tenth of settlement examinations were of artisans claiming settlement through apprenticeship.[63] The proportion was higher in market towns and urban parishes though probably declining everywhere after the Napoleonic wars. My own analysis of a sample of settlement examinations of adult males from Rochford in Essex, 1728–1830, identifies 12.1 per cent as settled via apprenticeship for the years after 1790 (n = 138) compared with 24.7 per cent in the years before 1790 (n = 78). These ex-apprentices cited many trades not all of which were at the bottom end of the economic scale. Among examinees for settlement, Snell finds chimney sweeps, gunflint makers and fellmongers, but he also finds merchant jewellers and coach makers![64] Only *legal* apprenticeships conferred settlement and so examinations reviewed length, conditions and other details to establish legality. An incomplete apprenticeship was not legal and settlement examinations were strewn with the sorry details of broken contracts which left men later in life not legally settled and in danger of removal. It mattered not that the individual regretted the high spirits which had caused him to abscond, nor that he had been driven to run away by a master's brutality, nor even that the term was incomplete because the master had gone bankrupt and fled the country. In all these cases settlement was in doubt and with it the working man's insurance and pension. There was incentive enough here to lock an apprentice in. The costs of broken contracts were widely understood. One poor lad in Rushton's sample

---

[61] Earle, *Making of the English Middle Class*, p. 100.
[62] Taylor, *Poverty*.
[63] Snell, *Annals*.
[64] Ibid.

notes that his master's imprisonment during bankruptcy charges meant that he was 'like to lose him his trade but also the Freedom of the Town'.[65]

Since settlement insured the apprentice and was paid for out of the local poor rate raised through property taxation, it amounted to a subsidy paid out of lump sum taxation benefiting the apprentice. But the master could well have demanded a share in this subsidy through the terms of the apprenticeship contract. Hence the association of settlement with the completion of an apprenticeship made training more profitable and so increased its supply. It is interesting to note that premiums became standard practice at about the same time as the settlement law, which introduced apprenticeship as a condition for obtaining settlement. Perhaps apprentices shared the lifetime subsidy obtained through settlement with their masters via this payment.

Of course it was the inclusion of apprenticeship as a condition for obtaining settlement that provided the incentive to overseers and guardians to apprentice the poor children of the parish in some other jurisdiction. This unpleasant aspect of the Old Poor Law has received much attention in the literature although there is some evidence that at least until the late eighteenth century, when poor relief costs spiralled, the export of pauper apprentices was not widespread.[66] The practice of paying premiums with pauper and charity apprentices appears to have anticipated their payment with non-poor apprentices. The former children were on average younger and so masters needed to be compensated for the upkeep of youngsters who were not immediately productive. But if pauper apprentices were also thought more likely to become a burden on the rates, masters who accepted them from outside the parish might have been locally unpopular and needed premiums to compensate. Indeed sometimes masters were required to give surety that their apprentices would not fall on the local rates at least during training, a responsibility that was often passed back to the parish of origin.

---

[65] Rushton, 'Matter', p. 93.
[66] Emmison, 'Relief'; see also, Snell, *Annals*.

Apprenticeship and the Reallocation of Labour to Industry

The Statute of Artificers had originally via rules about the social standing of apprentices and a property qualification sought to restrict access to apprenticeships in certain occupations to the sons of freemen, and particularly to exclude the sons of labourers or men engaged in husbandry. But the Elizabethan property qualifications were soon rendered nugatory by inflation and other restrictions appear readily breached.[67] It is possible to find many instances of the apprenticeship of sons of labourers or husbandmen, contrary to the Act, in the seventeenth century.[68] 'A fair number of the boys apprenticed to Oxford tradesmen were the sons of labourers and husbandmen. In Bristol a certain number of labourers' sons were apprenticed throughout the seventeenth century and the bakers of York accepted the sons of husbandmen. These are but a few instances of what was going on throughout the country; any town where the enrolments are detailed will afford similar examples'.[69] Thus apprenticeship provided a route out of agriculture not only for the sons of yeomen and farmers (perhaps younger sons) but for the sons of men lower down the rural hierarchy. Urban apprentices, even if they only became journeymen rather than masters, faced better prospects than did farm servants destined for lives as rural labourers.

Apprenticeship registers illustrate the exodus of labour from agriculture into the growing urban and industrial centres. The Coventry records cover 545 boys (12.5 per cent of the total number) whose fathers were employed in agriculture at different social levels (yeomen, farmers, husbandmen and labourers) in the parishes near Coventry and all these were apprenticed out of agriculture.[70] The drift from the land is evident in the Oxford City registers. Agriculture was the largest single occupation of fathers, accounting for 21.5 per cent (417 fathers) before 1750 and 17.4 per cent (175) thereafter. But only 1 per cent of apprentices (20 boys) entered land-work before 1750 and 1 per cent (12

---

[67] Davies, *Enforcement*.
[68] Dunlop, *English Apprenticeship*; Davies, *Enforcement*, notes that the clause which might have been a real obstruction if enforced was section 25, the £3 estate qualification for the parents of an apprentice to a country weaver but she concludes that the evidence suggests that it was 'largely disregarded' (p. 10).
[69] Dunlop, *English Apprenticeship*, p. 139; see also, Ben-Amos, 'Service', p. 50.
[70] Lane, *Coventry Apprentices*.

boys) after 1750.[71] The much more rapid increase in Northampton's apprentices than its general population illustrates the town's development as an urban centre where it was known that boys could be apprenticed to a wide variety of trades.[72] In consequence many boys from outside the town came to be trained as well as the sons of townsmen themselves. Norwich, York and Bristol played similar roles in the seventeenth century and Coventry, Nottingham and Manchester in the eighteenth. London's pull was exceptional throughout.

The number and distribution of apprenticeships can be read as simply reflecting market forces with apprenticeship playing only a passive role. But the argument here is that the institution itself really did matter. By credibly reducing the possibility of hold-up and by militating against the externality associated with asymmetric information, it increased the level of general training undertaken. To the extent that settlement was a functional equivalent to a subsidy financed from lump-sum taxation, the number of apprenticeships provided was increased. But the institution particularly fostered non-agricultural apprenticeships and the geographical movement that such training required of boys originating in the country. It trimmed the transaction costs, pecuniary and non-pecuniary, that boys and their families faced when contemplating such a career choice. How?

First, apprenticeship was a parallel institution to farm service. The institutional similarities must have made apprenticeship less of a daunting prospect to a farm boy and his family.[73] Second, the financial investment involved in apprenticeship was reduced by the tradition of paying through subsequent service. Even when premiums became customary it was possible for the sons of labourers to enter poorer trades. Parents could also pay premiums in instalments, easing financial demand on them and reducing the dangers of hold-up by masters. Wider kin, friends and local charities might also contribute to premiums. There is intriguing evidence to suggest that charities often favoured the sons of yeomen in allocating their subsidies and that the sons of husbandmen worked out a longer term to increase their desirability. Maybe also boys from the countryside had advantages in terms of health and strength. Urban masters may have found these attractive enough to waive their financial demands. Third, although finding a

[71] Graham, *Oxford City Apprentices*.
[72] Everitt, *Ways and Means*.
[73] Ben-Amos, 'Service'.

master (apprentice) was generally an informal process in which family and friends participated, more formal machinery was available. Both masters and boys advertised for suitable matches in papers and journals, for example.[74]

Finally, apprenticeship as an institution provided a package deal of training, housing and supervision that cut the transaction costs of negotiating all of these separately. Boys migrating to urban centres in search of training outside the economic (and protective) structures of apprenticeship were liable to encounter problems. Benjamin Bangs was originally apprenticed to a local shoemaker in the early seventeenth century. He faced a bitter decision when his master decided to move to a larger town. Bangs preferred to stay close to his widowed mother but could not afford to write off the investment that he had with his master and so decided to move under the latter's aegis. But even with this semi-protection Bangs found London economically and socially treacherous. The unprotected could be lured into selling themselves into indentured service or press-ganged or simply exploited.[75]

Apprenticeship contributed to the establishment of geographical and industrial networks that then served to reduce transaction costs of trade and commerce. Many authors describe the geographical patterns of migration associated with apprenticeship and note their coincidence with trading routes. In provincial centres such as Norwich, York and Bristol, apprentices arrived in large numbers from regions in which rural industries proliferated. Even in smaller towns trading routes were decisive. In Great Yarmouth, for example, many apprentices came from the towns and villages along the coastal coal route all the way to Dorset.[76] Many apprentices never became freemen in the towns where they had trained. These men probably migrated again back to the countryside or to some other expanding region. But it does not follow that they did not practice their trade or that they practiced illegally. The Statute of Artificers was enforced outside corporate towns as well as therein, and professional informers prosecuted country as well as town offenders, at least before the civil war.[77] But under the Statute, a legally completed apprenticeship gave a young man the right to practice his trade without distinction of place, that is he was not required

---

[74] Lane, *Apprenticeship*.
[75] Bangs' career is described by Ben-Amos, 'Service', p. 53.
[76] Ben-Amos, 'Service'; Rushton, 'Matter'; Lane, *Coventry Apprentices*; Patten, 'Patterns'.
[77] Davies, *Enforcement*.

to trade in the same place where the term of apprenticeship had been served. This aspect of the Statute, which distinguished it from continental legislation, perhaps recognized that industrial skills had ceased to be a prerogative of the town craftsman and become a characteristic of the intermingled agricultural-industrial life of the countryside.[78] The mobility it encouraged promoted networks of interconnected tradesmen throughout the commercial and trading regions linking urban centres with rural hinterland.

The development of commercial networks is detectable too in occupational choices. Although kin ties have been clearly documented as playing a role in identifying a match in the apprenticeship market, and boys were apprenticed to both paternal and maternal kin, training by fathers was less common than expected.[79] Families probably utilized apprenticeship to diversify occupations, to move into trades that were seen as profitable, and to establish sons in vertically or horizontally linked trades. Thus the sons of yeomen, farmers, husbandmen and labourers were particularly likely to become millers, bakers, butchers and grocers. Their parents probably had first-hand experience of the profits that such middlemen made out of agricultural producers. By placing their own sons in such trades they not only sought to share this advantage but also to establish commercial connections, which they had reasons to trust.

Pauper Apprenticeship and the Alleviation of Poverty

Classic accounts of English apprenticeship have sought to distinguish industrial training from the apprenticeship of the children of the poor, especially insofar as the latter shaded into the practice of boarding underprivileged children in the houses of better-off parishioners, and associated the perceived abuses of pauper apprenticeship in the late eighteenth century with the deteriorating reputation of apprenticeship more generally. While it is important to distinguish pauper, charity and non-poor apprenticeship and to draw a line between apprenticeship proper and boarding out, the treatment accorded poor children by way

[78] Ibid.
[79] Rushton, 'Matter'.

of these overlapping systems, although harsh by modern standards, had some redeeming features. There were benefits for the children and for society more generally.

Under the Old Poor Law, officials intervened in a variety of direct and indirect ways to shore up the health and human capital formation of children in poor households. In Tysoe in 1827, the overseers paid for the parish children to be inoculated, and in both Tysoe and Ardleigh, clothes and shoes were frequently purchased for the children of the poor.[80] The activism of the overseers went further. They ' ... frequently made decisions in the interests of parentally deprived children and acted on them—whether in support or defiance of parents and guardians'.[81] Not only orphans but also other vulnerable children were sometimes removed from their homes and placed as boarders with wealthier families. While to contemporary sensibilities this seems a terrible infringement of parental rights it was probably a sensible way of safeguarding the diet and health of the vulnerable. Boarding out poor children may have exposed some to exploitation and abuse. But, as Ashby points out, it maintained the children within a family circle, 'and it may be doubted whether they were called upon to work at an earlier age than the children of the families into which they were thrown by the bargains made on their behalf by the overseers'.[82] Even Dunlop concedes that boarding out provided 'support and training' and helped launch children into the world.[83]

But the overseers were also encouraged to seek formal apprenticeships for the children of the poor. Indeed the origins of apprenticeship, as already noted, were clearly intertwined with the Elizabethan Poor Law: ' ... although apprenticeship was adopted primarily in the interests of trade and manufactures, it was regarded by the Government with additional favour as a partial solution of the problem of pauperism'.[84] Although it appears that it was customary to give a small premium with parish apprentices even in the seventeenth century, before premiums were paid in private arrangements, apprenticeship was the cheapest way of dealing with pauper children. Initially there was little incentive for Justices to seek out and apprentice the children of poor parents unable to train them until such children became paupers. But

---

[80] Erith, *Ardleigh*; Ashby, *One Hundred Years*.
[81] Snell, *Annals*, p. 284.
[82] Ashby, *One Hundred Years*, p. 137.
[83] Dunlop, *English Apprenticeship*, p. 248.
[84] Ibid., p. 68.

in the reign of Charles I, when these laws became better administered, the Justices were required to make reports on their efforts to apprentice the children of the poor. From these returns it appears that a certain number of such children were apprenticed each year in every parish. Collections of poor law documents from a large number of parishes with a range of economic bases confirm that pauper apprenticeship was very frequent. Apprenticeship registers suggest that between 10 per cent and 20 per cent of all apprentices had premiums paid by the overseers. 'The total number [of children] who acquired their training and start in life by this means must have been very large'.[85]

Nor were these apprenticeships mere time-fillers. Snell's investigation of the biographical information contained in settlement examinations suggests that those apprenticed by the parish or charity were generally taught the trade and later practised it.[86] Undoubtedly there was mistreatment of parish apprentices especially among children unlucky enough to be 'apprenticed' to manufacturing establishments at the end of the eighteenth century. But in the family-based trades and when apprenticeship was conducted through the localized administration of the Old Poor Law, the system provided training in a humane context for otherwise deprived children. Parish authorities often investigated the reputations of prospective masters and mistresses and extensive legislation covering parish apprentices at times provided greater legal protection than that available to other apprentices.[87]

The retreat of the Old Poor Law in the face of spiralling costs in the late eighteenth century had implications for assistance to children. Economies involved harsher treatment of lone mothers, especially unmarried mothers, and more frequent attempts to pass responsibilities on to others.[88] Paul Carter's study of the changing strategies of the poor law administrators of Hanwell, Middlesex, from 1780 to 1816, shows how pauper apprenticeship degenerated.[89] In the 1780s placements were to local or land-based crafts where treatment could be harsh but children remained in a known environment and close to their family of origin. But in the face of rising costs the parish sought to banish pauper children to the new industrial mills. Mothers who

---

[85] Ibid., p. 250.
[86] Snell, *Annals*, p. 285.
[87] Ibid.
[88] Song, 'Landed Interest'; Lane, 'Apprenticeship in Warwickshire'; Rose, 'Social Policy'.
[89] Carter, 'Poor Relief Strategies'.

resisted were denied relief.[90] Changing demand for child labour in conjunction with pressure on poor rates created a systematic traffic in pauper apprentices between many urban centres and the early cotton factories.[91] Long before 1834, the Old Poor Law had ceased to act in a symbiotic way with the apprenticeship system to provide a supply of skilled labour, and to breach if not overcome the barriers to social mobility embedded in deprived origins.

Conclusion

English apprenticeship was codified and formalized simultaneously with the Elizabethan Poor Law and it shared many of the latter's objectives: social control, mercantilism and the reduction of mendacity. But the most important consequences of the apprenticeship system were unintended, indeed ironic in view of its pro-agrarian origins. Apprenticeship in tandem with poor relief worked to promote rather than retard general industrial training and to transfer labour into non-agricultural occupations. A key feature of the founding legislation, the lack of restriction on the location of the craftsman, helped to check the more extreme restrictive measures of some corporations. As Davies says, 'Without it there might not have been free entry into occupations in a period in which the claims of private privilege were so strong'.[92] The institution did more than passively reflect market signals, it actively contributed to the premature exodus of labour out of agriculture that is the hallmark of English exceptionalism.

References

Ashby, A.W. *One Hundred Years of Poor Law Administration in a Warwickshire Village*. Oxford: Clarendon, 1912.

Azariadis, C. 'Implicit contracts.' In *The New Palgrave: A Dictionary of Economics*, vol. 2, edited by John Eatwell, Murray Milgate and Peter Newman, 733–7. London: Macmillan, 1987.

Becker, Gary S. *Human Capital*. New York: Columbia University Press, 1964.

---

[90] Ibid; see also, Lane, 'Apprenticeship in Warwickshire'.
[91] Rose, 'Social Policy'.
[92] Davies, *Enforcement*, p. 267.

Ben-Amos, J.K. 'Service and the Coming of Age of Young Men in Seventeenth Century England.' *Continuity and Change* 3, no. 1 (1988): 41–64.

Campbell, Robert. *The London Tradesman*. London: T. Gardner, 1969 (first published 1747).

Carter, Paul. 'Poor Relief Strategies—Women, Children and Enclosure in Hanwell, Middlesex, 1780–1816.' *Local Historian* 25, no. 3 (1995): 164–77.

Clark, Peter. 'Migration in England during the Late Seventeenth and Early Eighteenth Century', *Past and Present* 83 (May 1979): 57–90.

Clark, Peter (ed.). *The Transformation of English Provincial Towns, 1600–1800*. London: Hutchinson, 1984.

Chang, Chun and Wang, Yijiana. 'Human Capital Investment under Asymmetric Information: The Pigovian Conjecture Revisited.' *Journal of Labour Economics* 14, no. 3 (1996): 505–19.

Collyer, J. *The Parents' and Guardians' Directory*. London, 1761.

Crafts, N.F.R. *British Economic Growth during the Industrial Revolution*. Oxford: Clarendon, 1985.

Davies, Margaret Gay. *The Enforcement of English Apprenticeship: A Study in Applied Mercantilism, 1563–1642*. Cambridge, MA: Harvard University Press, 1956.

Deakin, Simon. 'Legal Origins of Wage Labour.' Unpublished, 1988.

Deane, Phyllis. *The First Industrial Revolution*. Cambridge: Cambridge University Press, 1979.

Dunlop, O.J., with a supplementary section on the modern problem of juvenile labour by O.J. Dunlop and Richard D. Denman. *English Apprenticeship and Child Labour: A History*. London: T. Fisher Unwin, 1912.

Earle, Peter. *The Making of the English Middle Class: Business, Society and Family Life in London, 1660–1730*. London: Methuen, 1986.

Elbaum, Bernard. 'Why Apprenticeship Persisted in Britain but not in the United States.' *Journal of Economic History* XLIV, no. 2 (1989): 337–49.

Eliott, V.B. 'Mobility and Marriage in Pre-industrial England.' Ph.D. diss., Cambridge University, 1978.

Emmison, F.G. 'Relief of the Poor at Eaton Socon, Bedfordshire, 1706–1834,' *Bedfordshire Historical Record Society* 15 (1933): 14–19.

Erith, F.H. *Ardleigh in 1796*. East Berholt, 1978.

Everitt, Alan. *Ways and Means in Local History*. London: National Council of Social Service, 1971.

Finlay, Roger. *Population and Metropolis: The Demography of London*. Cambridge: Cambridge University Press, 1981.

Greenwald, Bruce C. 'Adverse Selection in the Labour Market.' *Review of Economic Studies* 53, no. 3 (1986): 325–47.

Graham, Malcolm. *Oxford City Apprentices 1697–1800*. Oxford: Clarendon, 1987.

Grubb, Farley. 'Does Bonded Labour have to be Coerced Labour?' *Itinerario: European Journal of Overseas History* XXI, no.1 (1999): 28–51.

———. 'The Statutory Regulation of Colonial Servitude: An Incomplete Contract Approach.' *Explorations in Economic History* 37, no 1 (2000): 42–75.

Hart, Oliver. 'Incomplete Contracts.' In *The New Palgrave: A Dictionary of Economics*, vol. 2, edited by John Eatwell, Murray Milgate, and Peter Newman, 752–9. London: Macmillan, 1987.

Kahl, W.F. 'Apprenticeship and the Freedom of the London Livery Companies, 1690–1750,' *Guildhall Miscellany* VII (1960): 17–20.

Kellett, J.R. 'The Breakdown of Guild and Corporation Control over the Handicraft and Retail Trade in London', *Economic History Review* X (1957–8): 381–94.

Lane, Joan. *Apprenticeship in England, 1600–1914*. London: UCL Press, 1996.

———. 'Apprenticeship in Warwickshire Cotton Mills, 1790–1830.' *Textile History* 10 (1979): 161–74.

Lane, Joan (ed.). *Coventry Apprentices and their Masters, 1781–1806*. Coventry: Dugdale Society, vol. XXXIII, 1983.

Lang, R.D. 'The Greater Merchants of London in the Early Seventeenth Century.' D. Phil. diss., Oxford University, 1963.

Malcomson, James, James W. Maw and Barry McCormick. 'General Training by Firms, Contracts, and Public Policy.' *European Economic Review*, forthcoming.

Mathias, Peter. *The First Industrial Nation*. London: Methuen, 1983.

———. 'The Social Structure in the Eighteenth Century: A Calculation by Joseph Massie.' *Economic History Review* X (1957–8): 30–45.

Marshall, Dorothy. *The English Poor in the Eighteenth Century*. London: Routledge, 1926.

Minchinton, Walter (ed.). *Wage Regulation in Pre-industrial England*. Newton Abbot: David and Charles, 1972.

Patten, J. 'Patterns of Migration and Movement of Labour to Three Pre-industrial East Anglian Towns.' *Journal of Historical Geography* 2 (1976): 128–34.

Rose, M.B. 'Social Policy and Business: Parish Apprentices and the Early Factory System, 1750–1834.' *Business History* XXI (1989): 5–32.

Rushton, Peter. 'Matter in Variance': Adolescents and Domestic Conflict in the Pre-Industrial Economy of North-east England 1600–1800.' *Journal of Social History* 25 (Fall 1991): 89–107.

Smith, S.R. 'The London Apprentices as Seventeenth-century Adolescents.' *Past and Present* 61 (Nov. 1973): 149–61.

Snell, K.D.M. *Annals of the Labouring Poor: Social Change in Agrarian England. 1600–1800*. Cambridge: Cambridge University Press, 1985.

Solar, Peter M. 'Poor Relief and English Economic Development Before the Industrial Revolution.' *Economic History Review* XLVIII, no. 1 (1995): 1–22.

Song, Byung Khun. 'Landed Interest, Local Government, and the Labour Market in England, 1750–1850.' *Economic History Review* LI, no. 3 (1998): 465–88.

Soskice, David. 'Reconciling Markets and Institutions: The German Apprenticeship System.' In *Training and the Private Sector: International Comparisons*, edited by Lisa M. Lynch, 25–60. Chicago: University of Chicago Press, 1994.

Stone, Lawrence. 'Social Mobility in England, 1500–1700.' *Past and Present* 33 (1966): 16–55.

Taylor, James Stephen. *Poverty, Migration and Settlement in the Industrial Revolution: Sojourners' Narratives*. Palo Alto: Palo Alto Society for the Promotion of Science and Scholarship, 1989.

Yarbrough, Anne. 'Apprentices as Adolescents in Sixteenth Century Bristol.' *Journal of Social History* 13 (1979): 67–81.

Wrigley, E.A. *Continuity, Chance and Change*. Cambridge: Cambridge University Press, 1988.

3.
Human Capital and Productivity Performance:
Britain, the United States and Germany, 1870–1990

STEPHEN BROADBERRY

Introduction

Human capital has widely been seen as playing a crucial role in Britain's relative economic decline since the late nineteenth century. For the period 1870 to 1914, many writers point to low levels of education amongst the labour force, argue that industrial workers had insufficient technical training, and portray managers as amateurish and even anti-scientific.[1] These views have been extended into the post-1914 period by other writers.[2] An important problem with much of this literature is a presumption that things were always much better abroad in all important respects, particularly in the United States and Germany, which are confusingly held up as a single idealized example of modernity. In fact, this is misleading, because Germany and the United States have been very different from one another in terms of both productivity history and human capital accumulation strategy.[3]

To understand the relationship between human capital and productivity performance among these three economies, it is necessary to disaggregate the productivity performance and to take account of vocational training as well as formal schooling. For comparative productivity performance has varied across sectors as well as through

---
[1] Landes, *Unbound Prometheus*, pp. 326–58; Levine, 'Industrial Retardation', pp. 57–78; and Aldcroft, 'Introduction', pp. 34–5.
[2] Wiener, *English Culture*; Barnett, *Audit*; and Aldcroft, *Education*.
[3] Broadberry, *Productivity Race* and 'How did the United States?'; Pollard, *Britain's Prime*, pp. 115–213.

time, as noted by Broadberry (1998), while the standard data on levels of education have shown little difference between rich countries, despite the large gap identified between rich and poor countries.[4]

The picture becomes more comprehensible if data on school enrolments are augmented with data on vocational training, and if account is taken of the sectoral composition of the labour force. In the late nineteenth century, Britain had one of the most skilled labour forces in the world, but this was largely a result of the early contraction of agriculture, so that Britain had a high proportion of workers in industry and services performing specialized tasks and using vocational skills. This is reflected in the data on apprenticeships and membership of professional bodies. For much of the twentieth century, however, human capital accumulation in Britain has fallen between higher levels of formal education in the United States and higher levels of vocational training in Germany, and Britain has fallen behind both countries in terms of aggregate productivity. Using a framework that treats capital and vocational skills as substitutes, skills are shown to account for a large part of the German overtaking of Britain since World War II, but little of the US forging ahead during the first half of the twentieth century. However, if general education and capital are seen as complements, with education providing 'social capabilities', human capital can also account for a part of the US labour productivity lead.

Sectoral Productivity Performance, 1870–1990

Table 1 presents sectoral estimates of comparative labour productivity levels for the US/UK and Germany/UK cases over the period 1870 to 1990.[5] The concept of labour productivity used here is output per person engaged. At the whole economy level, we see that in about 1870, aggregate labour productivity in the United States was about 90 per cent of the British level, and that the United States overtook Britain as the aggregate labour productivity leader during the 1890s and continued to forge ahead to the 1950s. Since then, there has been a slow process of British catching-up, but by 1990 there was still a substantial aggregate Anglo-American labour productivity gap of more than 30 per cent. Turning to the Germany/UK comparison, we see that at the

---

[4] Maddison, 'Growth and Slowdown'; Barro and Sala-i-Martin, *Economic Growth*.
[5] Figures derived from Broadberry, 'Forging Ahead' and 'Anglo-German Productivity'.

whole economy level, German labour productivity in 1871 was about 60 per cent of the British level, and had still reached only about 75 per cent of the British level by World War I. After a setback across the war, Germany again reached about 75 per cent of the British level by the mid-1930s, rising to about 80 per cent by the late 1930s. After another setback across World War II, Germany continued to catch up, overtook Britain only during the mid-1960s and by 1990 had a labour productivity advantage of about 25 per cent.

The sectoral patterns of comparative productivity performance are quite varied. Here the nine-sector analysis provided in an earlier study has been simplified onto a three-sector basis, distinguishing between agriculture, industry and services.[6] Industry includes mineral extraction, manufacturing, construction and the utilities, while services includes transport and communications, distribution, finance, professional and personal services and government. Both Germany and the United States caught up with and overtook Britain in terms of aggregate labour productivity largely by shifting resources out of agriculture and improving their comparative productivity performance in services rather than by improving their comparative productivity performance in industry.

In an earlier study, I established that comparative labour productivity in manufacturing has remained stationary in both the US/UK and the Germany/UK cases since the late nineteenth century, and Table 1 shows that this result generalizes to industry as a whole.[7] By contrast, in both cases the aggregate labour productivity ratio moves broadly in line with the labour productivity ratio for services. Although both Germany and the United States have improved their labour productivity performance relative to Britain in agriculture, there has also been a dramatic decline in the importance of agriculture, which can be seen in Table 2. Whereas in 1870 agriculture accounted for about half of all employment in Germany and the United States, by 1990 this had fallen to under 3.5 per cent. The shift out of agriculture has nevertheless had an important impact on comparative productivity performance at the aggregate level. This is because in the late nineteenth century Britain already had a much smaller share of the labour force in agriculture, which has had a substantially lower value added per employee than in industry or services. Hence the large share of

---

[6] Broadberry, 'How did the United States?'
[7] Broadberry, 'Manufacturing and the Convergence Hypothesis'.

resources tied up in agriculture in the United States exercised a significant negative influence on the aggregate US productivity performance relative to Britain in the late nineteenth and early twentieth centuries, and as the importance of agriculture declined this negative influence was removed. Similarly, the relatively large share of resources in German agriculture had a negative effect on Germany's aggregate productivity performance relative to Britain until after World War II. Note that Germany in 1950 had a bigger share of the labour force in agriculture than Britain in 1871.[8]

Table 1. Comparative US/UK and Germany/UK labour productivity levels by sector, 1869/71 to 1990 (UK=100).

	Agriculture	Industry	Services	Aggregate economy
A. US/UK				
1869–71	86.9	153.6	85.8	89.8
1889–91	102.1	164.5	84.2	94.1
1909–11	103.2	193.5	107.3	117.7
1919/20	128.0	198.2	119.0	133.3
1929	109.7	222.9	121.2	139.4
1937	103.3	190.6	120.0	132.6
1950	126.0	243.9	140.8	166.9
1973	131.2	215.1	137.3	152.3
1990	151.1	163.0	129.6	133.0
B. Germany/UK				
1871	55.7	86.2	66.1	59.5
1891	53.7	92.5	71.9	60.5
1911	67.3	122.0	81.3	75.5
1925	53.8	97.4	78.2	69.0
1929	56.9	101.7	84.3	74.1
1935	57.2	99.1	85.7	75.7
1950	41.2	95.8	83.1	74.4
1973	50.8	128.9	111.0	114.0
1990	75.4	116.7	130.3	125.4

Sources: Derived from Broadberry, 'Forging Ahead' and 'Anglo-German'.

Part of the labour productivity differences in Table 1 may be explained by differences in capital intensity, so before we turn to the estimates of human capital it will be useful to provide estimates of

---

[8] Conventional shift-share analysis fails to capture the importance of structural change because it is based on the assumption that the high rates of productivity growth in the shrinking agricultural sector would still have been achieved even if labour had not left the sector. For an alternative calculation, see Broadberry, 'How did the United States?', p. 390.

Table 2. Sectoral shares of employment in the United States, the United Kingdom and Germany, 1870–1990 (%).

	Agriculture	Industry	Services
A. US			
1870	50.0	24.8	25.2
1910	32.0	31.8	36.2
1920	26.2	33.2	40.6
1930	20.9	30.2	48.9
1940	17.9	31.6	50.5
1950	11.0	32.9	56.1
1973	3.7	28.9	67.4
1990	2.5	21.8	75.7
B. UK			
1871	22.2	42.4	35.4
1911	11.8	44.1	44.1
1924	8.6	46.5	44.9
1930	7.6	43.7	48.7
1937	6.2	44.5	49.3
1950	5.1	46.5	48.4
1973	2.9	41.8	55.3
1990	2.0	28.5	69.5
C. Germany			
1871	49.5	29.1	21.4
1913	34.5	37.9	27.6
1925	31.5	40.1	28.4
1930	30.5	37.4	32.1
1935	29.9	38.2	31.9
1950	24.3	42.1	33.6
1973	7.2	47.3	45.5
1990	3.4	39.7	56.9

Sources: Derived from Broadberry, 'Forging Ahead', 'Anglo-German' and 'How did the United States?'

comparative levels of total factor productivity (TFP), where TFP measures the productivity of labour and physical capital, weighted by their respective shares in income.[9] Comparing Table 3 with Table 1, we see that although capital explains a part of the labour productivity differences between the three countries, it is not sufficient to eliminate differences in TFP, some of which may be explained by human capital.

For the US/UK case, trends in comparative TFP and labour productivity at the aggregate level are similar, but with TFP differences generally smaller than labour productivity differences. One point

---

[9] The share of capital declines from 0.4 before World War I to 0.25 after World War II. These shares are derived from Matthews et al., *British Economic Growth*; Kendrick, *Productivity Trends*; and Hoffmann, *Das Wachstum*.

Table 3. Comparative US/UK and Germany/UK total factor productivity levels by sector, 1869/71 to 1990 (UK=100).

	Agriculture	Industry	Services	Aggregate economy
A. US/UK				
1869/71	98.4	153.8	86.3	95.1
1889/91	122.9	139.7	64.3	83.3
1909/11	117.8	151.1	71.7	90.5
1919/20	132.4	158.4	92.2	108.2
1929	117.6	187.8	92.0	112.7
1937	118.8	161.1	89.1	105.9
1950	132.5	218.0	110.2	138.1
1973	127.2	202.4	120.6	137.5
1990	142.0	157.5	119.9	125.5
B. Germany/UK				
1871	58.3	86.0	69.7	61.6
1891	59.8	86.1	71.9	63.2
1911	71.4	102.6	83.2	75.3
1925	57.1	98.0	85.5	74.3
1929	59.4	100.5	92.2	78.5
1935	59.7	97.1	89.6	78.3
1950	44.6	93.3	89.2	76.2
1973	48.1	112.4	118.0	108.2
1990	65.4	103.5	134.3	116.1

Sources: Derived from Broadbery, 'Forging Ahead' and 'Anglo-German'.

worth noting here is that whereas the United States overtook Britain before World War I in terms of labour productivity, it was only between the wars that the United States gained a TFP advantage. This would be consistent with the emphasis of Moses Abramovitz and Paul David on the importance of capital rather than TFP in American economic growth during the nineteenth century.[10] It is also consistent with D.N. McCloskey's claim that Victorian Britain did not fail, in the sense that the United States was still catching-up in terms of aggregate TFP levels.[11] In services, too, note that the US overtaking of Britain also occurred later in terms of TFP than in terms of labour productivity. For the Germany/UK case, again comparing Tables 1 and 3 we see that trends are very similar for comparative TFP and labour productivity at the aggregate level, with differences in TFP generally smaller than differences in labour productivity. Note that in industry, Germany had caught up with Britain in terms of TFP as well as labour productivity before World War I.

[10] Abramovitz and David, 'Reinterpreting' and 'Convergence'.
[11] McCloskey, 'Did Victorian Britain?'

Formal Education

The most widely used indicator of human capital in comparative growth studies is the average number of years of formal educational experience of the population aged 15–64. Table 4 presents the standard data for Britain, the United States and Germany over the twentieth century, distinguishing between primary, secondary and higher education. A weighted total is provided in addition to the unweighted total, with the weights given by the relative earnings of workers with different educational levels.[12] Table 5 presents the same data on a comparative basis. Whether we use the weighted or the unweighted total, it is clear that there is no simple relationship between comparative levels of educational experience and comparative labour productivity at the aggregate level.

Whereas the United States already had a small aggregate labour productivity lead over Britain by 1913 and pulled further ahead to 1950, since when Britain has narrowed the productivity gap, there has been a monotonic improvement in the US/UK comparative educational level, with the US slightly behind in 1913 and slightly ahead in 1989. The comparative US/UK level of higher education follows a similar time profile to comparative labour productivity at the aggregate level, but the scale of the US superiority in higher education has been substantially greater than in labour productivity.[13] The information for the above estimates is obtained from population censuses, where people are asked to state their educational experience. However, as this question was not typically asked in censuses until after World War II, the historical estimates are obtained by working backwards in time with the educational experiences of different age cohorts.[14] This has recently been criticized in a US context by Claudia Goldin, who notes the propensity of older individuals to overstate their educational attainments when the average attainment is rising.[15] Her conclusion would be that the US data obtained in this way overstate pre-war educational experience and understate the increase in formal schooling during the first half of the twentieth century. However, Angus Maddison's figures for the United States, used here, are

---

[12] Maddison, *Monitoring*, p. 37.
[13] Greasley and Oxley, 'Comparing'. Also note the time series relationship between university education and the comparative US/UK labour productivity level.
[14] Hence, for example, the educational experience of people aged 50–60 in 1950 is used as an estimate of the educational experience of people aged 40–50 in 1940, and aged 30–40 in 1930 etc.
[15] Goldin, 'America's Graduation', p. 367.

consistent with those of Edward Denison, who made some allowance for this bias.[16] Furthermore, it is not clear that we should expect the bias significantly to affect international comparisons where the data have been obtained on a similar basis for all countries.

Table 4. Average years of formal eductional experience of the population aged 15–64, 1913–1989.

	Primary	Secondary	Higher	Unweighted total	Weighted total
A. United Kingdom					
1913	5.30	1.90	0.08	7.28	8.12
1950	6.00	3.27	0.13	9.40	10.84
1973	6.00	3.99	0.25	10.24	12.09
1989	6.00	4.75	0.53	11.28	13.71
B. United States					
1913	4.90	1.83	0.20	6.93	7.86
1950	5.61	3.40	0.45	9.46	11.27
1973	5.80	4.62	0.89	11.31	14.05
1989	6.00	5.72	1.67	13.39	17.35
C. Germany					
1913	3.50	3.35	0.09	6.94	8.37
1950	4.00	4.37	0.14	8.51	10.40
1973	4.00	5.11	0.20	9.31	11.55
1989	4.00	5.20	0.38	9.58	12.04

Notes: These figures refer to full-time formal schooling only and exclude post-formal apprentice training combined with part-time education; Weights based on relative earnings of groups with different educational levels: primary = 1, secondary = 1.4, higher = 2.
Sources: Maddison, 'Growth and Slowdown', Table A-12, updated to 1989 from Maddison, *Dynamic Forces*, Table 3.8. Weights from Maddison, *Monitoring*, p. 37.

Turning to the Germany/UK case, we see that whereas Germany has come from a labour productivity level that was only about three-quarters of the British level in 1913 to a small productivity lead by 1989, the comparative Germany/UK educational level has declined somewhat. Indeed, weighting the different educational levels by earnings differentials, Germany has gone from a small educational advantage to a sizeable educational deficit. However, the apparent German disadvantage is largely because these figures omit post-formal apprentice training combined with part-time education.[17] The next section will examine comparative data on apprentice training, which will pre-

---

[16] Denison, *Sources*, pp. 70–2.
[17] Maddison, *Dynamic Forces*, p. 64.

sent a more favourable view of German intermediate level skills. We will then examine data on professional training, which will give a more favourable view of British higher level skills.

Table 5. Comparative US/UK and Germany/UK levels of schooling per person, 1913–1989 (UK=100).

	Unweighted total schooling	Weighted total schooling	Higher education
A. US/UK			
1913	95.2	96.8	250.0
1950	100.6	104.0	346.2
1973	110.4	116.2	356.0
1989	118.7	126.5	315.1
B. Germany/UK			
1913	95.3	103.1	112.5
1950	90.5	95.9	107.7
1973	90.9	95.5	80.0
1989	84.9	87.8	71.7

Source: Derived from Table 4 above.

Vocational Training: Intermediate Level Skills

The paper will proceed on the basis of a distinction between higher level and intermediate level vocational training. Higher level training is taken to cover vocational qualifications at the standard of a university degree, including membership of professional institutions, while intermediate level training is taken to cover craft and technician qualifications above secondary level but below degree level, including non-examined time-served apprenticeships.[18] We begin with intermediate level skills, paying particular attention to the industrial sector before 1945 and developments in the service sector since World War II.

Table 6 provides apprentice-to-employment ratios in Britain, Germany and the United States. As well as economy-wide ratios, estimates are also provided on a sectoral basis where available. Data are taken from official sources including occupational censuses for all three countries and various enquiries into apprenticeship training. Traditionally, apprenticeships have been concentrated in the industrial sector, and this is reflected in Table 6. The most striking finding is the much lower proportion of apprentices in US industry compared with

[18] Prais, *Productivity*, p. 17.

both Britain and Germany throughout the period.[19] The most important factor here is the different approaches to training in manufacturing on the two sides of the Atlantic.

Table 6. Apprentices as a percentage of persons engaged in Great Britain, Germany and the United States, 1895–1991.

	Agriculture	Industry	Services	Whole economy
A. Great Britain				
1906		4.19	0.65	2.48
1925		5.02	0.50	2.54
1951	0.17	3.22	0.59	1.87
1961	1.41	4.61	2.69	3.56
1966	1.34	5.08	3.18	4.01
1971	1.11	4.05	2.74	3.28
1981	0.56	3.67	1.98	2.58
B. Germany				
1895		7.67	1.60	2.99
1907		6.38	1.60	2.87
1925		7.64	0.40	3.18
1933		6.48	0.48	2.28
1950	0.50	7.87	3.89	4.75
1957	0.73	6.95	6.33	5.70
1962	0.77	4.78	5.65	4.62
1969	1.60	4.99	5.50	4.89
1980	3.47	7.94	5.29	6.34
1988	3.89	7.39	5.31	6.08
C. United States				
1880		0.95	0.07	0.25
1900		0.87	0.06	0.28
1920		0.91	0.06	0.34
1930		0.56	0.03	0.19
1940		0.47	0.02	0.16
1952		0.74	0.03	0.26
1960		0.72		0.24
1970		0.98		0.31
1975		1.00		0.29
1991		0.84		0.20

Sources: Britain: 1906: More, *Skill*, pp. 98–103, based on data from the *Report of an Enquiry by the Board of Trade into the Earnings and Hours of Labour of Workpeople of the United Kingdom*, supplemented with information from the Report of an Enquiry by the Board of Trade into the Conditions of Apprenticeship and Industrial Training in Various

[19] A transatlantic difference also exists in the apprentice-to-employment ratio in construction, but on a much smaller scale. Indeed, the figures in Bolino, *Century*, suggest that throughout the twentieth century, about half of all US apprenticeships have been in construction.

Trades and Occupations of the United Kingdom, (printed but not published by the Board of Trade, 1915).
1925: Derived from *Report of an Enquiry into Apprenticeship and Training for the Skilled Occupations in Great Britain and Northern Ireland, 1925–26*.
1951: *Census of England and Wales, Industry Tables*, Table 4.
1961: *Census of England and Wales, Industry Tables, Part I (10% Sample)*, Table 2.
1966: *Census of Great Britain, Economic Activity Tables, Part I (10% Sample)*, Table 14.
1971: *Census of Great Britain, Economic Activity, Part II (10% Sample)*, Table 16.
1981: *Census of Great Britain, Economic Activity, (10% Sample)*, Table 9.
Germany: Apprentices: 1895: Berufs- und Gewerbezählung vom 14. Juni 1895. Gewerbestatistik für das Reich im Ganzen, *Statistik des Deutschen Reichs*, Neue Folge, Band 113 (Berlin, 1898); 1907: Berufs- und Gewerbezählung vom 12. Juni 1907. Berufsstatistik, *Statistik des Deutschen Reichs*, Band 202 (Berlin, 1909); 1925: Volks-, Berufs- und Betriebszählung vom 16. Juni 1925, Gewerbliche Betriebszählung. Die gewerblichen Betriebe und Unternehmungen im Deutschen Reich, *Statistik des Deutschen Reichs*, Band 413 (Berlin, 1929); 1933: Volks-, Berufs- und Betriebszählung vom 1933. Das Personal der gewerblichen Niederlassungen nach der Stellung im Betrieb und die Verwendung von Kraftmaschinen, *Statistik des Deutschen Reichs*, Band 462 (Berlin, 1936); 1950, 1957: 'Die Lehrlinge und Anlernlinge 1950 bis 1957/58', Beilage zum Heft 11/57 der *Arbeits- und sozialstatistischen Mitteilungen* (Bonn, 1957); 1962, 1969: 'Auszubildende in Lehr- und Anlernberufen in der Bundesrepublik Deutschland', Beilage zum Heft 12/70 der *Arbeits- und sozialstatistischen Mitteilungen* (Bonn, 1970); 1980, 1988: *Statistisches Jahrbuch für die Bundesrepublik Deutschland* (Wiesbaden, 1990), Tab. 16.7.
Employment: Hoffmann, *Das Wachstum*, Tab. 14, 15, 20; Kohler & Reyher, *Arbeitszeit*, Tab. 5.2; *Statistisches Jahrbuch für die Bundesrepublik Deutschland* (Wiesbaden, 1982, 1990).
United States: Bolino, *Century*; *Historical Statistics of the United States: Colonial Times to 1970* (Department of Commerce, 1975); *Statistical Abstract of the United States* (Department of Commerce); Department of Labor.

To understand the relationship between human capital and labour productivity in manufacturing, it is essential to take account of the distinction between 'mass production' and 'flexible production' technology.[20] In mass production, special purpose machinery was substituted for skilled shopfloor labour to produce standardized products, while flexible production relied on skilled shopfloor labour to produce customized output. It would be an over-simplification to identify American manufacturing with mass production and European manufacturing with flexible production. Since in practice both systems coexisted on both sides of the Atlantic, mass production has been more prevalent in America and flexible production more prevalent in Britain and Germany, for reasons associated with both demand and supply conditions.[21] On

---

[20] Piore and Sabel, *Second*; Sabel and Zeitlin, 'Stories'; Broadberry, 'Technological Leadership'.
[21] See Scranton, 'Diversity', for a discussion of flexible production in an American context, and Herrigel, *Industrial Constructions*, for an analysis of German industrial performance stressing the co-existence of mass production and flexible production.

the demand side, standardization was facilitated in the United States by the existence of a large homogeneous home market, compared with the fragmentation of national markets and greater reliance on exports in Europe. On the supply side, mass production machinery economized on skilled shopfloor labour (relatively abundant in Europe) but was wasteful of natural resources (relatively scarce in Europe).[22]

These transatlantic differences in technology have important implications for the accumulation of human capital in the three countries under study here.[23] In Britain and Germany, with an orientation towards flexible production, we see an emphasis upon the accumulation of intermediate level skills for shopfloor workers through apprenticeship. In the United States, however, with an orientation towards mass production, we see much more emphasis on higher level skills, with management hierarchies to supervise the relatively unskilled shopfloor workers, and research capabilities to produce the standardized designs and oversee the development process to volume production.[24]

It should be emphasized that flexible production has been more labour intensive than mass production, and has therefore been associated with lower labour productivity. Hence we can understand the persistent US labour productivity lead in manufacturing in terms of the greater reliance on mass production methods than in Britain and Germany.[25] Note, however, that the continued use of flexible production methods in Britain and Germany should not be seen as inefficient or irrational, since conditions have been different.

Although it is sometimes suggested that the quality of training received by British apprentices left something to be desired, it should be noted that contemporary enquiries from the 1920s to the early 1960s generally concluded that Britain was not out of step with other European countries in this regard.[26] Similarly, Roderick Floud adopts a

---

[22] For a thorough discussion of these issues, including a detailed analysis of individual industries, the reader is referred to Broadberry, *Productivity Race*.

[23] Broadberry and Wagner, 'Human Capital'.

[24] Although Goldin and Katz ('Technology') argue that US manufacturing increasingly employed workers with some high school education during the first half of the twentieth century, they did not have intermediate level skills in the sense used here.

[25] Broadberry, *Productivity Race*.

[26] Ministry of Labour, *Report of an Enquiry into Apprenticeship*; Williams, *Recruitment*; Liepmann, *Apprenticeship*; Organization for European Economic Co-operation, *Vocational Training*.

comparative framework to reject accusations of inadequate technical training of British apprentices before World War I.[27] This is consistent with the findings of later research for the 1980s and 1990s, which suggests that Britain's skills gap has more to do with the quantity than the quality of trained workers.[28]

Table 6 allows us to compare apprentice-to-employment ratios in Britain and Germany on the basis of the three broad sectors, agriculture, industry and services. In industry, there was a higher apprentice-to-employment ratio in Germany before World War II. This is consistent with the fact that Germany had already overtaken Britain before World War I in terms of labour productivity in all the industrial sectors.[29] Although apprentices also formed a larger proportion of the service sector workforce in Germany before World War I, the absolute numbers involved were small, and we shall see in the next section that this was offset by a British lead in higher level training. After World War II, however, the German lead in the provision of intermediate level vocational training in services became substantial. Given the importance of developments within services for the German overtaking of Britain in terms of aggregate labour productivity during the post-World War II period, this German lead in the provision of intermediate level vocational skills in services is of major significance.

Vocational Training: Higher Level Skills

The Higher Professions

An important aspect of human capital accumulation was the early development in Britain of professional bodies, an important function of which was to oversee professional training.[30] The majority of these qualified professionals worked in the service sector, where Britain had a labour productivity lead over Germany and the United States in the late nineteenth century. Table 7 presents data on the employment of professionals in the three countries since 1881. The British data allow a distinction between higher and lower professions, and data on the higher professions are shown in panel A. The definition is taken from

---

[27] Floud, 'Technical Education'.
[28] Prais, *Productivity*.
[29] Broadberry, 'Anglo-German'.
[30] Carr-Saunders and Wilson, *Professions*; Reader, *Professional Men*.

Guy Routh, and corresponds broadly with the concept of higher level skills employed elsewhere in this paper, requiring a qualification at the standard of a university degree.[31] Although the key higher professions in the nineteenth century were in the church, medicine and law, the twentieth century has seen the growing importance of engineering, science and accounting. Increasingly, these professions have come to be restricted to graduate entry, so that in recent times information on professional associations does not substantially alter the picture of human capital levels gleaned from data on higher education.

Table 7. Professionals in Britain, the United States and Germany, 1880–1991.

A. Higher professionals in Great Britain, 1881–1991 (thousands)

	1881	1911	1931	1951	1971	1991
Church	38	44	48	49	41	34
Medicine	21	35	46	62	80	115
Law	20	26	23	27	39	82
Engineering	24	24	51	138	343	542
Writing	7	15	21	26	51	79
Armed Forces	8	14	16	46	40	34
Accounting	13	11	16	37	127	171
Science	1	7	20	49	95	114
Total	132	176	240	434	816	1173

B. Higher and lower professions as a % of total employment in Great Britain, the United States and Germany, circa 1880 to 1950 (%)

	1880	1890	1900	1910	1920	1930	1950
Great Britain	3.6	3.7	4.0	4.1	4.3	4.4	6.1
United States	3.1	3.7	4.0	4.4	5.0	6.1	7.5
Germany			2.6	2.8	2.6	3.0	3.5

Notes: Church includes Anglican, Roman Catholic and Free Church clergy; Medicine includes doctors and dentists; Law includes barristers and solicitors; Engineering includes engineers, surveyors and architects; Writing includes editors and journalists; Armed Forces includes commissioned officers; Accounting includes accountants and company secretaries; Science includes pure scientists.
Lower professions include: Nurses; Others in Medicine, including veterinary surgeons, pharmacists and opticians; Teachers; Draughtsmen, including industrial designers; Librarians; Social welfare workers; Navigating and engineering officers, aircrew; Arts, including painters, producers, actors and musicians.
Dates for Great Britain are 1881, 1891, 1901...; Dates for Germany are 1895, 1907, 1925, 1933, 1950.

---

[31] Routh, *Occupation and Pay*.

Sources: Great Britain: 1881–1911: *Census of England and Wales; Census of Scotland;* 1911–1951: Routh (1965: 13–15); 1951–1991: *Census of Great Britain;* United States: 1880–1910: Edwards, *Comparative Occupation;* 1910–1950: Routh, *Occupation and Pay,* p. 13; Germany: 1895: Berufs- und Gewerbezählung vom 14. Juni 1895. Gewerbestatistik für das Reich im Ganzen, *Statistik des Deutschen Reichs,* Neue Folge, Band 113 (Berlin, 1898); 1907: Berufs- und Gewerbezählung vom 12. Juni 1907. Berufsstatistik, *Statistik des Deutschen Reichs,* Band 202 (Berlin, 1909); 1925, 1933: *Statistisches Jahrbuch für das Deutsche Reich;* 1950: *Statistisches Jahrbuch für die Bundesrepublik Deutschland.*

To measure the growth of the professions on a comparative basis, it is necessary to include the lower professions as well as the higher professions, in panel B of Table 7. Although Britain started the period with a higher share of the occupied population in the professions, the United States had pulled ahead by the end of the nineteenth century. Although much of the existing literature on the professions concentrates on social aspects and eschews quantification, the idea of a leading role for Britain in the professionalization of society during the nineteenth century and a leading role for the United States during the first half of the twentieth century does seem to be widely accepted.[32] In Germany, we see the effects of the large agricultural sector and low per capita incomes restricting the growth of the professions. Figures for the inter-war period suggest a substantially smaller professional sector in Germany through to 1950.[33]

Professional Qualifications

For some professional groups, it is possible to chart the growth of qualifications on a comparative basis. Data on the development of the accountancy profession in Britain, Germany and the United States are provided in Table 8. Here, we see that Britain currently has a substantially larger number of accountants than Germany, despite the similarity of the size of the labour force in the two countries.[34] Note, however, that if all accountants rather than just chartered accountants are considered, the British lead is not as great as is sometimes suggested.[35] Although the historical information is rather more sketchy for Germany, it seems that the British reliance on professional accountants is of long standing, and can be explained at least in part by the nature of the British capital market, which generated an early and growing need for independent

---

[32] Perkin, *Third Revolution;* Gilb, *Hidden Hierarchies.*
[33] McClelland, *German Experience.*
[34] The German figures refer to the former Federal Republic, even after 1990.
[35] Although Matthews et al. ('Rise', p. 409) note that in some countries taxation work is the province of lawyers rather than accountants, they provide figures only on the narrowest definition of chartered accountants in their Table 2.

Drivers of Long-term Economic Growth

auditors.[36] Note that the growth of professionally qualified accountants in Britain mirrors the growth of the number of accountants enumerated in the higher professional occupational group in the Census.

Table 8. Qualified accountants in Britain, Germany and the United States, 1882–1991.

A. United Kindgom

	ICAEW	Other UK bodies	Total UK membership	Professional accountants in Census (000)
1882	1193	290	1486	
1891	1737	1092	2829	9
1901	2776	2951	5727	11
1911	4391	6950	11,341	11
1921	5337	9932	15,269	9
1931	9213	16,340	25,553	16
1941	13,694	21,994	35,688	
1951	16,079	28,667	44,746	37
1961	35,228	30,174	65,402	110
1971	51,660	41,633	93,293	127
1981	72,695	67,726	140,421	142
1991	96,208	100,367	196,575	171

B. Germany

	Chartered accountants	Tax advisers	Total
1932	540		
1943		22,588	
1945	3043		
1955		22,000	
1961	2741	23,761	26,505
1971		26,294	
1981		39,171	
1986	4925	43,905	48,830
1991	10,787	49,176	59,963

C. United States

	Certified public accountants
1896	56
1901	303
1911	1780
1921	5143
1931	13,774
1941	25,242
1951	47,224
1958	64,887

[36] Matthews et al., 'Rise'.

Human Capital and Productivity Performance

Notes: UK: ICAEW = Institute of Chartered Accountants in England and Wales.
Germany: Chartered accountants includes 'Wirtschaftsprüfer' and related occupations; Tax advisers includes 'Steuerberater' and related occupations.
United States: Stocks of certified public accountants calculated from data on CPA certificates issued.
Sources: UK: Matthews et al., 'Rise', p. 408; Table 7 above.
Germany: Wirtschaftsprüferkammer, Düsseldorf; Bundessteuerberaterkammer, Bonn.
United States: Edwards, *History*, pp. 362–3.

The US data are derived from flows of Certified Public Accountant (CPA) certificates, which were established in 1896 following the British lead in professionalization.[37] The flow data have been converted to a stock basis using the perpetual inventory method, assuming an average working life of 35 years after qualifying. Allowing for the much greater population in the United States, it is clear that the density of qualified accountants was much greater in Britain, and this remains true today.[38]

Industrial Managers and Researchers

Although data exist on the educational qualifications of American industrial managers in the late 1920s, comparable British and German data are available only from the early 1950s. These figures, which are presented in Table 9, suggest that the proportion of graduates among British and German management in the early 1950s was at about the level of American managers in the late 1920s, with Britain and Germany lagging equally behind America.[39]

Table 9. Proportion of industrial managers who were graduates in industrial companies, Great Britain, the United States and Germany, 1928–1954 (%).

	Great Britain	United States	Germany
1928		32	
1950–4	36	62	37

Sources: Copeman, *Leaders*; Warner and Abegglen, *Occupational Mobility*; Hartmann, *Authority*.

Historical data on research and development are available for Britain, the United States and Germany, reaching back as far as the

---

[37] Edwards, *History*, p. 69.
[38] Handy et al., *Making Managers*.
[39] Figures for a longer time span, extending the figures in Table 9 from the 1950s to the 1980s are provided in Broadberry and Wagner, 'Human Capital'. However, they are not presented here because detailed data on stocks of workers with higher level qualifications are available for later years from labour force surveys.

1930s for Britain and the United States.[40] For manufacturing, where the vast bulk of R&D has been concentrated, there has been for much of the twentieth century a substantial gap between Britain and the United States in the ratio of researchers to all employees and in the ratio of R&D expenditure to net output. However, as David Edgerton and Sally Horrocks have recently pointed out on the basis of firm level data for the inter-war period, there has been little difference between Britain and Germany, with Britain even ahead until the 1980s.[41] This is a far cry from the allegations of an anti-technological bias in British society in much of the declinist literature.[42]

The large transatlantic R&D gap confirms the concentration of American industry on higher level skills compared with the greater emphasis on intermediate level skills in European industry. It also illustrates the American commitment to science and technology that has been seen as an important factor in US industrial supremacy in the early post-World War II period.[43] However, we should be careful in moving from explanations of industrial performance to the situation in the economy as a whole.

Accounting for Labour Productivity Differences

Stocks of Qualified Persons

From the 1970s, it is possible to obtain from official sources reliable estimates of the proportions of the labour force with higher and intermediate level qualifications on a sectoral basis for the British, US and German economies. For earlier years, it is possible to piece together estimates from the fragmentary data on stocks and flows of qualified persons surveyed in the previous sections. These estimates should be regarded as tentative, but sufficient to indicate broad orders of magnitude.

Parts A to C of Table 10 provide estimates of the proportions of the labour force with higher and intermediate level qualifications circa 1910, 1930 and 1950. The intermediate level qualifications are obtained by taking the apprenticeship flow data in Table 6 and converting them

---

[40] The data are available in Broadberry and Wagner, 'Human Capital'.
[41] Edgerton and Horrocks, 'British'.
[42] Wiener, *English Culture*; Barnett, *Audit*.
[43] Nelson and Wright, 'Rise and Fall'.

onto a stock basis using estimates of the ratio of journeymen to apprentices, obtained largely from the British sources.[44] For the higher level qualifications in industry, estimates of the proportion of industrial managers who were graduates have been taken from Table 9 and applied to data on the numbers of industrial managers from the occupational censuses. In services, higher level qualifications have been obtained for Britain by using the number of higher professionals from Table 7.[45] For Germany and the United States, the same proportion of higher to lower professionals has been assumed as in Britain.[46] Before 1950, there is no clear indication of a British shortfall of vocational skills. Although Germany was ahead in intermediate skills, particularly in industry, this was offset by a British advantage in higher level skills, especially in services. And although Britain lagged behind the United States in higher level skills, this was offset by a British advantage in intermediate level skills.

Parts D and E of Table 10 provide the official estimates based on labour force survey data available from the 1970s onwards. By the late 1970s, Britain had a substantially smaller fraction of the labour force with higher level qualifications than the United States, but there was little difference between Britain and Germany at the higher level. At the intermediate level, however, although Britain clearly had no shortfall relative to the United States, there was a massive skills gap between Britain and Germany. The key developments here have been the expansion of higher education in the United States since World War II and the expansion of apprenticeship training in Germany, particularly in services. During the 1980s and into the 1990s, there has been a significant expansion of higher education in Britain, so that the higher level skills gap with the US has been narrowed and Britain has pulled ahead of Germany in this aspect of training.[47] There has also been a significant expansion of vocational training in Britain, so that the intermediate level skills gap with Germany has been narrowed,

---

[44] Although this may not be a particularly accurate method of estimation for the United States, where apprenticeship was much less widespread, it is equally clear that the US stock of skilled workers was so much smaller than in Britain or Germany that even a serious error would not significantly affect the comparative results.
[45] Note that the number of accountants in the census grows in line with the membership of professional accountancy bodies.
[46] This is probably an overestimate of the higher level qualifications in the United States and Germany in 1910, given the much slower development of professional associations in these countries.
[47] O'Mahony, *Britain's Productivity*.

and Britain remains significantly ahead of the United States in this dimension of human capital accumulation. However, such policy changes cannot bring instantaneous results, and it is a long time before changes in the flow of investment feed through to significant changes in the stocks of qualified workers.[48]

Table 10. Stocks of qualified persons as a percentage of employees, by sector and skill level in the United Kingdom, the United States and Germany, 1910–1990 (%).

	Higher level			Intermediate level		
	UK	US	Germany	UK	US	Germany
A. 1910						
Agriculture	-	-	-	-	-	-
Industry	-	-	-	15.1	2.8	19.8
Services	2.0	3.0	2.4	2.0	0.2	1.6
Total	0.9	1.1	0.6	7.5	0.9	9.7
B. 1930						
Agriculture	-	-	-	-	-	-
Industry	-	4.1	-	15.6	1.9	23.7
Services	2.6	3.5	2.1	1.5	0.1	1.2
Total	1.3	2.8	0.7	7.9	0.6	9.8
C. 1950						
Agriculture	-	-	-	0.5	-	0.5
Industry	5.7	10.5	5.7	12.9	1.6	24.4
Services	3.8	4.0	3.1	1.8	0.1	3.9
Total	4.5	5.7	3.4	7.2	0.6	11.7
D. 1978/79						
Agriculture	2.0	6.0	0.7	11.3	5.8	31.5
Industry	4.4	8.4	3.2	26.0	8.9	58.8
Services	8.8	19.8	11.2	18.8	12.3	61.5
Total	6.8	15.8	6.9	21.8	11.0	58.5
E. 1989/90						
Agriculture	3.7	10.4	2.0	20.0	7.7	50.8
Industry	6.2	14.2	6.1	37.1	10.1	68.3
Services	12.3	25.8	15.1	23.1	12.9	65.0
Total	10.1	22.4	11.0	27.7	12.1	65.8

Sources: See text.

Accounting for labour productivity differences

Tables 11 and 12 provide estimates of the contributions of skills and capital to labour productivity differences for the US/UK and

---

[48] *Competitiveness: Creating the Enterprise Centre of Europe*, pp. 34–53.

Germany/UK cases, respectively. The first step is to provide a measure of relative skills, using the method of Mary O'Mahony.[49] For each country, the proportions of the labour force in each category of higher, intermediate and lower or no skills are aggregated into a single unskilled labour equivalent. This is done by weighting each category according to its wage relative to the unskilled category:

$$H = \Sigma \, (w_s/w_1) \, (L_s/L) \tag{1}$$

where w_s is the wage of skill category s, w_1 is the unskilled wage, L_s/L is the employment share of skill category s and H stands for human capital. The ratio of H for the two countries provides the estimate of relative skill levels, which is presented in the first column of Tables 11 and 12 for the US/UK and Germany/UK cases, respectively. Relative wage rates for workers with intermediate skills declined from 1.6 times the unskilled wage in 1910 to 1.4 times in 1990, while relative wage rates for workers with higher skills fell from 4.2 times the unskilled wage in 1910 to 1.8 times in 1990.[50]

The first point to note in Tables 11 and 12 is that in 1910, Britain had higher aggregate labour force skills than either Germany or the United States. This is despite the fact that Germany had higher skill levels than Britain in both industry and services. The British advantage overall arose in this case from the small size of the agricultural sector in Britain, since agriculture was more dependent on unskilled labour than industry or services. The second point to note is that relative skills defined in this way did not change much over time in the US/UK case, despite the large changes in comparative labour productivity levels. Furthermore, in industry, where we see the largest US labour productivity lead, Britain has apparently had a skills advantage in recent decades. Third, however, note in Table 12 that relative skill levels did change fairly substantially in the Germany/UK case, with a decisive German skills advantage emerging as Germany overtook Britain in terms of aggregate labour productivity after World War II.

One question which naturally arises in this context is why Britain did not choose to follow the German path of extending intermediate level vocational training to services after World War II, and even allowed the apprenticeship system within industry to decline. Two points can be made here. First, Britain retained a labour productivity

---
[49] O'Mahony, *Britain's Productivity*.
[50] Based on estimates in Routh, *Occupation and Pay*; and O'Mahony, *Britain's Productivity*.

lead over Germany in services until the 1970s, so it was not obvious at this stage that the German model was successful in services. Second, it seems clear that for much of the post-World War II period there was greater enthusiasm in British industry for American mass production methods, which did not require so much shopfloor labour with intermediate level skills.[51] This greater attempt at Americanization in post-war Britain may be understood in the context of the integration of the two economies in the Allied war effort, with many British industrialists witnessing at first hand the much higher levels of labour productivity achieved in American industry. Furthermore, wartime visits by British industrialists to the United States were followed up after the war by the Anglo-American Council on Productivity, which sponsored visits by productivity teams made up of managers and trade unionists in a wide range of industries.[52]

Let us turn now to the contribution of skills and capital to the US/UK labour productivity differences in Table 11. The accounting procedure of O'Mahony can be thought of as applying the standard growth accounting formula to compare two economies at the same point in time rather than a single economy at two points in time.[53] The total contribution in the final column is calculated as the comparative US/UK labour productivity ratio minus 100, and this is taken directly from Table 1. The contribution of skills is given by:

$$\{\exp((1-\alpha)\ln H) - 1\}.100 \qquad (2)$$

where α is capital's share in income.[54] The contribution of capital is:

$$\{\exp(\alpha \ln K/L) - 1\}.100 \qquad (3)$$

where K/L is capital per person engaged. The residual is the total difference in labour productivity levels minus the sum of the contributions of skills and capital. At the aggregate level, the biggest contribution to the US/UK labour productivity difference before 1929 was made by capital. After 1929 the biggest contribution was made by the residual. At the sectoral level, however, note that the residual was also important in industry and agriculture before 1929. In particular, it is worth emphasizing the transatlantic technological differences in

---

[51] Broadberry and Wagner, 'Human Capital'.
[52] Hutton, 'We Too'.
[53] O'Mahony, *Britain's Productivity*.
[54] As in Table 3, this is assumed to decline from 0.4 before World War I to 0.25 after World War II.

industry that have conventionally been noted for the nineteenth as well as the twentieth century.[55] Using the same accounting procedure for the Germany/UK comparison in Table 12, we see that at the aggregate level, the residual made the most important contribution to the total labour productivity difference between 1910 and 1950, but that skills were the most important factor in 1973 and 1990, although the situation was more complex at the sectoral level.

Table 11. Contribution of skills and physical capital to US/UK labour productivity differences, 1910–1990.

	Relative skills (UK=100)	Percentage point contribution of:			Total
		Skills	Capital	Residual	
A. 1910					
Agriculture	100.0	0.0	-12.4	15.6	3.2
Industry	93.2	-4.1	28.0	69.6	93.5
Services	102.0	1.2	49.7	-43.6	7.3
Total	96.9	-1.9	30.1	-10.5	17.7
B. 1929					
Agriculture	100.0	0.0	-6.7	16.4	9.7
Industry	105.5	3.8	18.7	100.4	122.9
Services	101.9	1.3	31.8	-11.9	21.2
Total	100.9	0.6	23.6	15.2	39.4
C. 1950					
Agriculture	99.8	-0.2	-5.0	31.2	26.0
Industry	106.3	4.7	11.9	127.3	143.9
Services	99.8	-0.2	27.8	13.2	40.8
Total	100.4	0.3	20.9	45.7	66.9
D. 1973					
Agriculture	100.9	0.7	3.2	27.3	31.2
Industry	96.8	-2.4	6.3	111.2	115.1
Services	105.4	4.0	13.9	19.4	37.3
Total	102.5	1.9	10.8	39.6	52.3
E. 1990					
Agriculture	100.4	0.3	8.6	42.2	51.1
Industry	88.1	-9.1	3.5	68.6	63.0
Services	105.6	4.2	8.1	17.3	29.6
Total	103.0	2.2	6.0	24.8	33.0

[55] Habakkuk, *American*; Broadberry, *Productivity Race*.

Table 12. Contribution of skills and physical capital to Germany/UK labour productivity differences, 1910–1990.

	Relative skills (UK=100)	Skills	Capital	Residual	Total
A. 1910					
Agriculture	100.0	0.0	-5.8	-26.9	-32.7
Industry	102.6	1.6	18.9	1.5	22.0
Services	100.9	0.5	-2.3	-16.9	-18.7
Total	99.8	-0.1	0.2	-24.6	-24.5
B. 1929					
Agriculture	100.0	0.0	-4.2	-38.9	-43.1
Industry	103.8	2.6	1.2	-2.1	1.7
Services	98.4	-1.1	-8.6	-6.0	-15.7
Total	99.2	-0.6	-5.6	-19.7	-25.9
C. 1950					
Agriculture	100.0	0.0	-7.7	-51.1	-58.8
Industry	103.9	-2.9	2.7	-9.8	-4.2
Services	99.2	-0.6	-6.8	-9.5	-16.9
Total	99.2	-0.6	-2.6	-22.6	-25.6
D. 1973					
Agriculture	106.7	5.0	5.5	-59.7	-49.2
Industry	110.7	7.9	14.6	6.4	28.9
Services	116.6	12.2	-5.9	4.7	11.0
Total	112.9	9.5	5.4	-0.9	14.0
E. 1990					
Agriculture	109.8	7.3	15.2	-47.1	-24.6
Industry	100.9	0.7	12.7	3.3	16.7
Services	116.0	11.8	-3.0	21.5	30.3
Total	113.3	9.8	8.0	7.6	25.4

There is some evidence, then, to suggest that skills played a role in the German overtaking of Britain after World War II. For the US/UK case, however, there appears to be no obvious relationship between relative skills and comparative productivity performance. Should we, then, conclude that the US productivity lead throughout the twentieth century has had little to do with human capital? This would surely not be appropriate, since, as we have seen, the United States has increasingly provided more formal schooling for its population, and the US/UK comparative productivity ratio does appear to move in line with relative years of higher education. However, it is more in keeping with the spirit of the literature to posit a complementarity between education and capital, rather than to see them as substitutes, as required by the growth accounting formulation. Hence the importance of mass education in the United States has been in the provision of what Kazushi Ohkawa and

Henry Rosovsky called 'social capability' rather than specific skills.[56] American technology has largely been deskilling seen from the perspective of the European skilled worker, as Harry Braverman and others have noted, but effective participation in this technological system has nevertheless required the transmission of more general capabilities.[57]

Table 13. Contribution of skills and physical capital to US/UK labour productivity differences, 1910–1990.

	Percentage point contribution of:		
	Education	Residual	Total
1910	-3.2	20.9	17.7
1950	4.0	62.9	66.9
1973	16.2	36.3	52.3
1990	26.5	6.5	33.0

Notes: The total contribution is calculated as the comparative US/UK labour productivity level minus 100. The contribution of education is relative US/UK education levels minus 100 and the residual is the total difference in labour productivity levels minus the contribution of education.
Sources: Total labour productivity difference derived from Table 1. Comparative education levels from Table 5.

Table 13 provides estimates of the contribution of general education to the US labour productivity lead over Britain during the twentieth century on the assumption of complementarity between education and capital. Hence the weight on education is set equal to one rather than labour's share in income, and the contribution of education is simply relative education levels from Table 5 minus 100. The weighted total schooling variable has been used, although results would be qualitatively similar using unweighted total schooling. The education variable accounts for an increasing proportion of the labour productivity difference over time. This would be broadly consistent with the views of Paul David and Gavin Wright, who stress lags in the process by which employers learned to use the more educated labour force effectively and the provision by the educational system of social capabilities rather than specific skills.[58] It is rather harder to square with the claims of Claudia Goldin and Lawrence Katz to have identified a decisive shift to capital-skill complementarity in the early years of the twentieth century with the diffusion of batch and continuous-process methods.[59]

---

[56] Ohkawa and Rosovsky, *Japanese*; Abramovitz, 'Catching Up'.
[57] Braverman, *Labor*.
[58] David and Wright, 'Early Twentieth Century'.
[59] Goldin and Katz, 'Technology'.

Concluding Comments

At the beginning of the twentieth century, the key institutions of human capital accumulation in Britain were the system of apprenticeships and the body of professional associations. Given the small scale of the agricultural sector in Britain, Britain still had one of the most skilled labour forces in the world on the eve of World War I. Although some writers have tried to see the forging ahead of the United States between the wars as based on human capital accumulation, this is hard to square with an alternative literature based on the deskilling nature of Fordist technology. However, the development of mass secondary and higher education in the United States can still be seen as playing a role in the development of social capabilities, and stimulating future endogenous technical change that made effective use of the better educated labour force. A more straightforward role for human capital accumulation can be seen in the German overtaking of Britain after World War II, as the German agricultural labour force declined sharply and the vocational training system was extended to services and strengthened in industry.

Note. I am grateful to Mary O'Mahony for making available unpublished data on recent stocks of human capital. I would also like to thank Brian A'Hearn, Nick Crafts, Roderick Floud, Gianni Toniolo, Gavin Wright and participants in seminar and conference presentations at Chapel Hill, Copenhagen, Lund, Oxford and Wassenaar for helpful comments on earlier versions. The usual disclaimer applies.

References

Official Publications and Reports

United Kingdom
Census of England and Wales. Office of Population Censuses and Surveys.
Census of Great Britain. Office of Population Censuses and Surveys.
Census of Scotland. Office of Population Censuses and Surveys.
Competitiveness: Creating the Enterprise Centre of Europe. Department of Trade and Industry, 1996, Cm 3300.
Report of an Enquiry by the Board of Trade into the Earnings and Hours of Labour of Workpeople of the United Kingdom. Board of Trade, 1909.
Report of an Enquiry by the Board of Trade into the Conditions of Apprenticeship and Industrial Training in Various Trades and Occupations of the United Kingdom. (Printed but not published by the Board of Trade, 1915).

Report of an Enquiry into Apprenticeship and Training for the Skilled Occupations in Great Britain and Northern Ireland, 1925–26. Ministry of Labour, 1928.

United States
Historical Statistics of the United States: Colonial Times to 1970. Department of Commerce, 1975.
Statistical Abstract of the United States. Department of Commerce.

Germany
'Auszubildende in Lehr- und Anlernberufen in der Bundesrepublik Deutschland.' Beilage zum Heft 12/70 der *Arbeits- und sozialstatistischen Mitteilungen.* Bonn, 1970.
'Berufs- und Gewerbezählung vom 14. Juni 1895. Gewerbestatistik für das Reich im Ganzen.' *Statistik des Deutschen Reichs.* Neue Folge, Band 113. Berlin, 1898.
'Berufs- und Gewerbezählung vom 12. Juni 1907. Berufsstatistik. *Statistik des Deutschen Reichs.*' Band 202. Berlin, 1909.
'Die Lehrlinge und Anlernlinge 1950 bis 1957/58.' Beilage zum Heft 11/57 der *Arbeits- und sozialstatistischen Mitteilungen.* Bonn, 1957.
Statistisches Jahrbuch für die Bundesrepublik Deutschland. Statistisches Bundesamt.
Statistisches Jahrbuch für das Deutsche Reich. Statistisches Reichsamt.
'Volks-, Berufs- und Betriebszählung vom 16. Juni 1925, Gewerbliche Betriebszählung. Die gewerblichen Betriebe und Unternehmungen im Deutschen Reich.' *Statistik des Deutschen Reichs.* Band 413. Berlin, 1929.
'Volks-, Berufs- und Betriebszählung vom 1933. Das Personal der gewerblichen Niederlassungen nach der Stellung im Betrieb und die Verwendung von Kraftmaschinen.' *Statistik des Deutschen Reichs.* Band 462. Berlin, 1936.

International Organizations
Organization for European Economic Co-operation. *Vocational Training in the Footwear Industry.* Paris: OEEC, 1960.

Books and Articles

Abramovitz, Moses. 'Catching Up, Forging Ahead and Falling Behind.' *Journal of Economic History* 46 (1986): 385–406.
Abramovitz, Moses and Paul A. David. 'Reinterpreting Economic Growth: Parables and Realities.' *American Economic Review* 63 (1973): 428–39.
Abramovitz, Moses and Paul A. David. 'Convergence and Deferred Catch-up.' In *The Mosaic of Economic Growth*, edited by Ralph Landau, Timothy Taylor and Gavin Wright, 21–62. Stanford, CA: Stanford University Press, 1996.

Aldcroft, Derek H. 'Introduction.' In *The Development of British Industry and Foreign Competition, 1875–1914*, edited by Derek H. Aldcroft, 11–36. London: Allen & Unwin, 1968.

———. *Education, Training and Economic Performance, 1944–1990*. Manchester: Manchester University Press, 1992.

Barnett, Corelli. *The Audit of War: The Illusion and Reality of Britain as a Great Nation*. London: Macmillan, 1986.

Barro, Robert J. and Xavier Sala-i-Martin. *Economic Growth*. New York: McGraw-Hill, 1995.

Bolino, August C. *A Century of Human Capital by Education and Training*. Washington, DC: Kensington, 1989.

Braverman, Harry. *Labor and Monopoly Capital: The Degradation of Work in the Twentieth Century*. New York: Monthly Review Press, 1974.

Broadberry, Stephen N. 'Manufacturing and the Convergence Hypothesis: What the Long Run Data Show.' *Journal of Economic History* 58 (1993): 375–407.

———. 'Technological Leadership and Productivity Leadership in Manufacturing Since the Industrial Revolution: Implications for the Convergence Debate.' *Economic Journal* 104 (1994): 291–302.

———. *The Productivity Race: British Manufacturing in International Perspective, 1850–1990*. Cambridge: Cambridge University Press, 1997.

———. 'Forging Ahead, Falling Behind and Catching-Up: A Sectoral Analysis of Anglo-American Productivity Differences, 1870–1990.' *Research in Economic History* 17 (1997): 1–37.

———. 'Anglo-German Productivity Differences 1870–1990: A Sectoral Analysis.' *European Review of Economic History* 1 (1997): 247–67.

———. 'How did the United States and Germany Overtake Britain? A Sectoral Analysis of Comparative Productivity Levels, 1870–1990.' *Journal of Economic History* 58 (1998): 375–407.

Broadberry, Stephen N. and Karin Wagner. 'Human Capital and Productivity in Manufacturing During the Twentieth Century: Britain, Germany and the United States.' In *Quantitative Aspects of Post-war European Economic Growth*, edited by Bart van Ark and Nicholas F.R. Crafts, 244–70. Cambridge: Cambridge University Press, 1996.

Carr-Saunders, A.M. and P.A. Wilson. *The Professions*. Oxford: Oxford University Press, 1933.

Copeman, G.H. *Leaders of British Industry*. London: Gee & Co, 1955.

David, Paul A. and Gavin Wright. 'Early Twentieth Century Productivity Growth Dynamics: An Inquiry into the Economic History of 'Our Ignorance.'' Unpublished, All Souls College, Oxford, 1999.

Denison, Edward F. *The Sources of Economic Growth in the United States and the Alternatives Before Us*. New York: Committee for Economic Development, 1962.

Edgerton, David E.H. and Sally M. Horrocks. 'British Industrial Research and Development Before 1945.' *Economic History Review* 47 (1994): 213–38.

Edwards, Alba M. *Comparative Occupation Statistics for the United States, 1870–1940.* Washington, DC: US Bureau of the Census, 1943.

Edwards, James Don. *History of Public Accounting in the United States,* University, AL: University of Alabama Press, 1978.

Floud, Roderick. 'Technical Education and Economic Performance: Britain 1850–1914.' *Albion* 14, (1982): 153–71.

Gilb, Corinne Lathrop. *Hidden Hierarchies: The Professions and Government.* New York: Harper & Row, 1966.

Goldin, Claudia. 'America's Graduation from High School: The Evolution and Spread of Secondary Schooling in the Twentieth Century.' *Journal of Economic History* 58 (1998): 345–74.

Goldin, Claudia and Lawrence Katz. 'Technology, Skill, and the Wage Structure: Insights from the Past.' *American Economic Review, Papers and Proceedings* 86 (1996): 252–7.

Greasley, David and Les Oxley. 'Comparing British and United States' Economic and Industrial Performance 1860–1993: A Time Series Perspective.' *Explorations in Economic History* 35 (1998): 171–95.

Habakkuk, H. John. *American and British Technology in the Nineteenth Century.* Cambridge: Cambridge University Press, 1962.

Handy, Charles, Colin Gordon, Ian Gow and Colin Randlesome. *Making Managers.* London: Pitman, 1988.

Hartmann, Heinz. *Authority and Organization in German Management.* Westport, CT: Greenwood, 1959.

Herrigel, Gary. *Industrial Constructions: The Sources of German Industrial Power.* Cambridge: Cambridge University Press, 1996.

Hoffmann, Walther G. *Das Wachstum der deutschen Wirtschaft seit der Mitte des 19. Jahrhunderts.* Berlin: Springer-Verlag, 1965.

Hutton, Graham. *We Too Can Prosper: The Promise of Productivity.* London: Allen & Unwin, 1953.

Kendrick, John W. *Productivity Trends in the United States.* Princeton, NJ: National Bureau of Economic Research, 1961.

Kohler, Hans und Lutz Reyher. *Arbeitszeit und Arbeitsvolumen in der Bundesrepublik Deutschland, 1960–1986: Datenlage-Struktur-Entwicklung.* Nürnberg: Institut für Arbeitsmarkt und Berufsforschung der Bundesanstalt für Arbeit, 1988.

Landes, David S. *The Unbound Prometheus: Technological Change and Industrial Development in Western Europe from 1750 to the Present.* Cambridge: Cambridge University Press, 1972.

Levine, A.L. *Industrial Retardation in Britain, 1880–1914.* New York: Basic, 1967.

Liepmann, Kate. *Apprenticeship: An Enquiry into its Adequacy in Modern Conditions.* London: Routledge and Kegan Paul, 1960.

McClelland, Charles E. *The German Experience of Professionalization: Modern Learned Professions and their Organizations from the Early Nineteenth Century to the Hitler Era.* Cambridge: Cambridge University Press, 1991.

McCloskey, D.N. 'Did Victorian Britain Fail?' *Economic History Review* 23 (1970): 446–59.

Maddison, Angus. 'Growth and Slowdown in Advanced Capitalist Economies: Techniques of Quantitative Assessment.' *Journal of Economic Literature* 25 (1987): 649–98.

———. *Dynamic Forces in Capitalist Development*. Oxford: Oxford University Press, 1991.

———. *Monitoring the World Economy, 1820–1992*. Paris: Organization for Economic Co-operation and Development, 1995.

Matthews, Derek, M. Anderson and J.R. Edwards. 'The Rise of the Professional Accountant in British Management.' *Economic History Review* 50 (1997): 407–29.

Matthews, Robin C.O., Charles H. Feinstein and John C. Odling-Smee. *British Economic Growth, 1856–1973*. Oxford: Oxford University Press, 1982.

More, Charles. (1980), *Skill and the English Working Class, 1870–1914*. London: Croom Helm.

Nelson, Richard R. and Gavin Wright. 'The Rise and Fall of American Technological Leadership: The Post-war Era in Historical Perspective.' *Journal of Economic Literature* 30 (1992): 1931–64.

O'Mahony, Mary. *Britain's Productivity Performance, 1950–1996: An International Perspective*. London: National Institute of Economic and Social Research, 1999.

Ohkawa, Kazushi and Henry Rosovsky. *Japanese Economic Growth: Trend Acceleration in the Twentieth Century*. Stanford, CA: Stanford University Press, 1972.

Perkin, Harold *The Third Revolution: Professional Elites in the Modern World*. London: Routledge, 1996.

Piore, Michael J. and Charles F. Sabel. *The Second Industrial Divide: Possibilities for Prosperity*, New York: Basic, 1984.

Pollard, Sidney. *Britain's Prime and Britain's Decline: The British Economy, 1870–1914*. London: Arnold, 1989.

Prais, S.J. *Productivity, Education and Training: An International Perspective*. Cambridge: Cambridge University Press, 1995.

Reader, William J. *Professional Men: The Rise of the Professional Classes in Nineteenth-Century England*. London: Weidenfeld & Nicolson, 1966.

Routh, Guy. *Occupation and Pay in Great Britain, 1906–1960*. Cambridge: Cambridge University Press, 1965.

Sabel, Charles F. and Jonathan Zeitlin. 'Stories, Strategies, Structures: Rethinking Historical Alternatives to Mass Production.' In *World of Possibilities: Flexibility and Mass Production in Western Industrialization*, edited by Charles F. Sabel and Jonathan Zeitlin, 1–33. Cambridge: Cambridge University Press, 1997.

Scranton, Philip. 'Diversity in Diversity: Flexible Production and American Industrialization.' *Business History Review* 65 (1991): 27–90.

Warner, W. Lloyd and James C. Abegglen. *Occupational Mobility in American Business and Industry, 1928–1952*. Minneapolis, MN: University of Minnesota Press, 1955.

Wiener, Martin J. *English Culture and the Decline of the Industrial Spirit, 1850–1980*. Cambridge: Cambridge University Press, 1981.

Williams, Gertrude. *Recruitment to Skilled Trades*. London: Routledge and Kegan Paul, 1957.

————. *Apprenticeship in Europe: The Lesson for Britain*, London: Chapman and Hall, 1963.

4.
General Purpose Technologies and Surges in Productivity:
Historical Reflections on the Future of the ICT Revolution

PAUL A. DAVID & GAVIN WRIGHT

Introduction

In this essay we reflect on the relevance of early twentieth-century American experience for understanding the more general phenomenon of recurring prolonged swings in the TFP growth rate in advanced industrial economies. After a 'productivity pause' of some three decades, during which gross manufacturing output in the US grew at less than one per cent per annum relative to inputs of capital and labour, TFP in this sector expanded at more than five per cent per annum between 1919 and 1929. This remarkable discontinuity has been largely overlooked by modern productivity analysts and economic historians alike; yet it contributed substantially to the absolute and relative rise of the US domestic economy's TFP residual, and in many respects may be seen as the opening of the high-growth era that persisted into the 1970s.[1]

The shift in the underlying technological regime that is implied by this statistically documented discontinuity can be traced to critical engineering and organizational advances connected with the electrification of industry. These developments marked the culminating phase in the diffusion of 'the dynamo' as a general purpose technology (GPT)

---

[1] This paper builds upon the detailed re-examination of manufacturing productivity in David and Wright, 'Early Twentieth Century Growth'. We are grateful to Sir John Habakkuk, Angus Maddison and R.C.O. Matthews for their comments and suggestions on a previous draft.

that made possible significant fixed-capital savings, while simultaneously increasing labour productivity. Yet, a narrow technological explanation of the post-World War I industrial productivity surge proves to be inadequate. It neglects the concurrence of those developments with important structural changes in US labour markets. It fails to do justice to the significance of complementarities that emerged between managerial and organizational innovations and the new dynamo-based factory technology, on the one hand, and on the other, between both forms of innovation and the macroeconomic conditions of the 1920s.

We explore the latter, more complex formulation of the dynamics of GPT diffusion by considering the generic and differentiating aspects of the US experience with industrial electrification in comparison with that of the UK and Japan. The cross-national perspective brings to light some differences between leader and follower economies in the dynamics of GPT diffusion, and its relationship to the strength of surges in productivity growth. Our Anglo-American comparison serves also to underscore the important role of the institutional and policy context with respect to the potential for upgrading the quality of the workforce in the immediately affected branches of industry.

The concluding sections of the essay offer some reflections on the analogies and contrasts between the historical case of a socio-economic regime transition involving the electric dynamo and the modern experience of the information and communications technology (ICT) revolution. Contextualizing the GPT concept in explicitly historical terms sheds light on the paradoxical phenomenon of the late twentieth-century productivity slowdown, and also points to some contemporary portents of a future phase of more rapid ICT-based growth in total factor productivity.

A Brief Recapitulation

In his introduction to John Kendrick's study of productivity trends in the United States, Solomon Fabricant noted:

> A distinct change in trend appeared some time after World War I. By each of our measures, productivity rose, on the average, more rapidly after World War I than before ... The change in trend ... is one of the most interesting facts before us. There is little question about it. It is visible not only in the indexes that Kendrick has compiled for the private

domestic economy... It can be found also in his figures for the whole economy, including government, as well as in his estimates for the groups of industries for which individual productivity indexes are available.[2]

The historical break was heavily though not exclusively concentrated in the manufacturing sector. Kendrick's estimates put the decadal growth of TFP at approximately 22 per cent for the whole of the private domestic economy, while the corresponding figure for manufacturing was 76 per cent, and for mining 41 per cent. TFP growth in transportation, communications and public utilities exceeded the private domestic average by lesser amounts, while the farm sector was in last position with a relatively low gain of 14 per cent. At the heart of the story was manufacturing, where the discontinuity was particularly marked (Figure 1).[3]

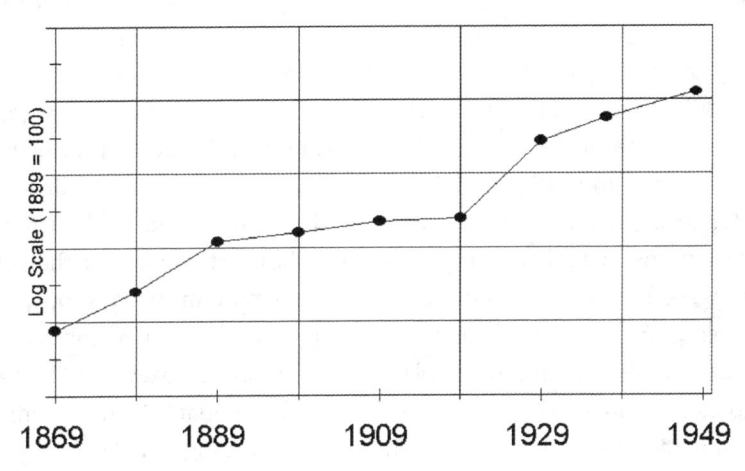

Figure 1. Total factor productivity in U.S. manufacturing, 1869–1948.
Source: Computed from data presented in David, 'Computer and Dynamo', p. 323.

---

[2] Kendrick, *Productivity Trends*, p. xliii.
[3] The discontinuity in decadal measures was not an artefact of cyclical fluctuations accentuated by wartime and post-war demand conditions. Although we do not have annual TFP data, logarithmic regressions using data on labour productivity show that trend growth jumped from 1.5 percentage points per annum during 1899 to 1914, to 5.1 during 1919 to 1929. See David and Wright, 'Early Twentieth Century Growth', Figure P3.

Having pinpointed manufacturing, we may ask whether the productivity surge of the 1920s was broadly based within that sector, reflecting common forces at work in the economy; or whether instead it was concentrated in a small number of rapidly changing industries. The distinction may be illustrated with the terms deployed by Arnold Harberger in his 1998 Presidential address to the American Economic Association: 'yeast-like' processes expand uniformly under a common fermenting agency; whereas 'mushroom-like' innovations reflecting 'real cost reductions stemming from 1001 different causes', and being highly localized and idiosyncratic to particular industries and even to individual firms, tend to pop up at random places in the field of industry. Although Professor Harberger finds that the 'mushroom' metaphor better describes the distribution of TFP growth among industries in the late twentieth-century (slow productivity-growth) US economy, we find, in contrast, that the 1920s was a decade of yeast-like manufacturing productivity advances.

When the branches of US manufacturing are aggregated into standard industrial groups, it appears that 13 of the 14 major categories experienced an *acceleration* in the growth of multi-factor productivity between 1909 and 1919, and 1919 and 1929.[4] When the categories are further disaggregated, to identify the fastest-growing individual industries in terms of real net output per man-hour, we find that the high-fliers were broadly dispersed among nine larger industry groups; six of these aggregates boasted two or more high-growth members. The flat Lorenz-like diagram displayed in Figure 2 (developed using Harberger's method) makes immediately apparent the contrast between the 1920s and the 'pro-mushroom' findings of the 1970s and 1980s. Evidently the post-1919 industrial productivity surge reflected broad, generic developments that were impinging widely upon US manufacturing activities.

---

[4] The lone exception, Transportation Equipment, was deviant only because of its exceptional productivity growth during the previous decade, not because it was below average for the 1920s. These findings, previously reported by David in 'Computer and Dynamo', (and presented also in David and Wright, 'Early Twentieth Century Growth'), account for purchased energy inputs in the multi-factor productivity measurement. This is appropriate, especially in view of the substitution of purchased electricity for the services of on-site capital equipment in the form of prime movers, which was taking place during the era in question.

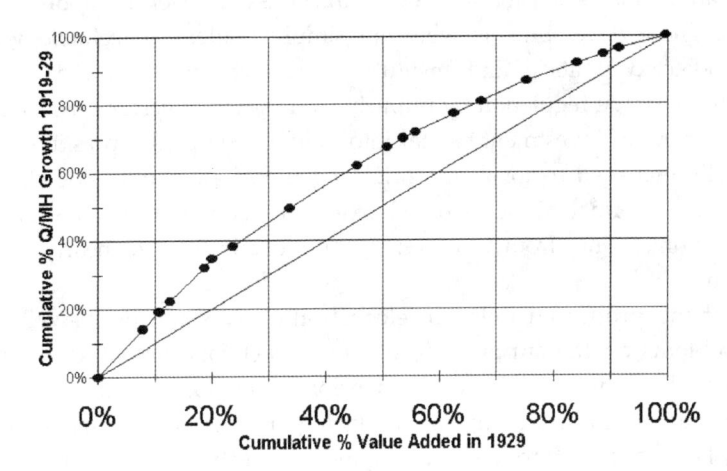

Figure 2. Cumulative percentage of productivity growth 1919–1929, versus cumulative percentage of value added by industry, 1929.
Source: Productivity Growth by Industry from Kendrick, *Productivity Trends*, Tables D-I and D-IV; cumulative proportions of value added from U.S. Commerce Department, *Historical Statistics of the United States to 1970*, Series P-65 with interpolations. For fuller discussion, see David and Wright, 'Early Twentieth Century Growth Dynamics', Note and Sources for Table 2.

What sorts of forces were sufficiently pervasive and potent as to have these far-reaching effects? We highlight two: first, the culmination of the dynamo revolution that had been underway as a technological trajectory since the nineteenth century, but which did not realize its engineering potential for major productivity gains until the 1920s; and second, the restructuring of US manufacturing labour markets, in the wake of the closing of mass European immigration after 1914. Each of these developments had its own prior history; but the productivity surge reflected the confluence of these two largely independent streams of development.

As recounted by David in 'Computer and Dynamo', the transformation of industrial processes by electric power technology was a long-delayed and far from automatic business. It did not acquire real momentum until after 1914 to 1917, when the rates charged consumers by state-regulated regional utilities fell substantially in real terms, and central station generating capacity came to predominate over generating capacity in isolated industrial plants. Rapid efficiency gains in electricity generation during 1910 to 1920 derived from major direct investments in large central power plants, but also from the scale economies realized through integration and extension of power transmission over expanded territories. These developments were not simply matters of technology, but also reflected political and institutional changes that allowed utilities largely to escape regulation by municipal and town governments, facilitating the flow of investment capital into holding companies presiding over centrally managed regional networks. Together these supply-side changes propelled the final phase of the shift to electricity as a power source in US manufacturing, from just over 50 per cent in 1919 to nearly 80 per cent in 1929.[5]

But the protracted delay in electrification was not exclusively due to problems on the supply side of the market for purchased electrical power. The slow pace of adoption prior to the 1920s was attributable largely to the unprofitability of replacing still serviceable manufacturing plants adapted to the old regime of mechanical power derived from water and steam. Coexistence of older and newer forms of capital often restricted the scope for exploiting electricity's potential. Prior to the 1920s, the 'group drive' system of within-plant power transmission remained in vogue. With this system — in which electric motors turned separate shafting sections, so that each motor drove related groups of machines — primary electric motors often were merely added to the existing stock of equipment.[6] When the favourable investment climate of the 1920s opened up the potential for new, fully electrified plants, firms had the opportunity to switch from group drive to 'unit drive' transmission, where individual electric motors were used to run machines and tools of all sizes. The advantages of the unit drive extended well beyond savings in fuel and in energy efficiency. They also made possible single-storey, linear factory layouts, within which reconfiguration of machine placement permitted a flow of materials through the plant that was both more rapid and more reliable. According to the surveys of American manufacturing directed by Harry Jerome, rearrangement of the factory contributed to widespread cost savings in materials handling operations, serializing machines and thereby reducing or eliminating 'back-tracking'.[7]

The package of electricity-based industrial process innovations just described could well serve as a textbook illustration of *capital-saving*

---

[5] David and Wright, 'Early Twentieth Century Growth', Figure E1, derived from DuBoff, *Electric Power*.
[6] See Devine, 'From Shafts to Wires'; Devine, 'Electrified Mechanical Drive'.
[7] Jerome, *Mechanization*, pp. 190–1.

General Purpose Technologies and Surges in Productivity

technological change. Electrification saved fixed capital by eliminating heavy shafts and belting, a change that also allowed factory buildings themselves to be more lightly constructed, because they were more likely to be single-storey structures whose walls no longer had to be braced to support the overhead transmission apparatus. The faster pace of material throughput amounted to an increase in the effective utilization of the capital stock. Further, the frequency of downtime was reduced by the modularity of the unit drive system and the flexibility of wiring; the entire plant no longer had to be shut down in order to make changes in one department or section of the factory.[8] Notice too that Henry Ford's transfer-line technique and the speed-up of work that it permitted was a contributory element of the high throughput manufacturing regime, as were the new continuous process technologies that grew in importance during this era.

These effects are confirmed by the sharp fall in the capital-output ratio during the 1920s, reversing the long-term trend. As with TFP growth, the pattern was pervasive: All but two of the seventeen major industry groups show a fall during this decade, whereas the ratio had been rising in every one of these groups during 1899 to 1909, and in twelve of seventeen during 1909 to 1919. A scatter plot demonstrates

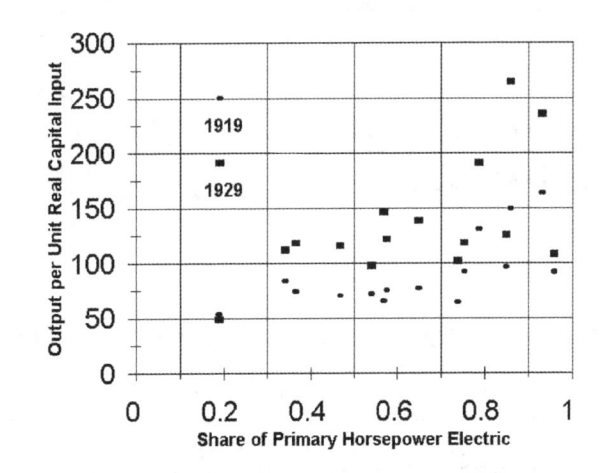

Figure 3. Output/capital versus percentage of horsepower electric, 1919 and 1929.
Source: DuBoff, *Electric Power in American Manufacturing*, Tables 26, E-22.

---

[8] Schurr et al, *Electricity in the American Economy*, esp. pp. 29–30 and 292–3.

141

that this increase in capital productivity was directly associated with the electrification of primary horsepower, a correlation that strengthened across the 1920s (Figure 3).

A proper historical account of the 1920s productivity revolution, however, cannot be confined to the cluster of manufacturing techniques that were diffusing into use in that decade. Equal notice must be taken of a second broad force operating on the US economy at that time, namely the sharp increase in the relative price of labour. Relative to the general price level, the hourly wage of industrial labour was 50 to 70 per cent higher after 1920 than it had been a decade before (Figure 4). This change was most immediately associated with the end of mass European immigration, which had averaged more than one million per year during the decade prior to 1914, but was blocked during the war and then decisively closed by legislation in 1920 and 1924. The rise in real wages ushered in a sweeping change in the functioning of labour markets, reflected in a fall in turnover and an upgrading of hiring standards. As we interpret these events, reinforcing changes on both sides of the labour market generated a 'regime transition', towards a new set of relationships that we may call the High Wage Economy.

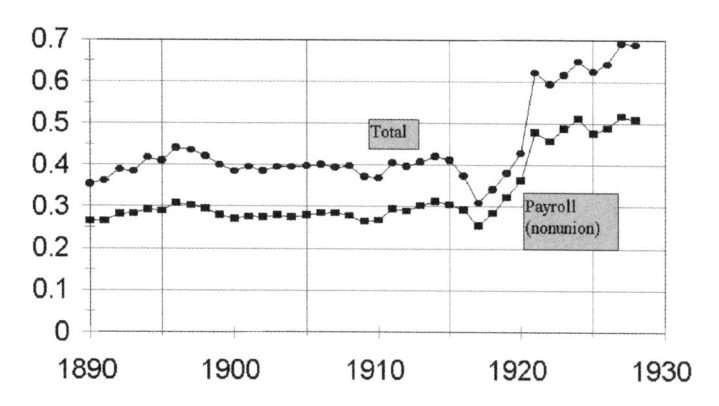

Figure 4. Real hourly wages in US manufacturing, 1890–1928.
Source: US Department of Commerce, *Historical Statistics of the United States to 1970*, Series D766, D768 (originally from Douglas *Real Wages in the United States*), deflated by wholesale price index (Series E40); 1927–1928 from Douglas and Jennison, *The Movement of Money and Real Earnings*.

Although this history was largely independent of electric power technology, it was the confluence of these two streams that gave the decade of the 1920s its truly extraordinary character. Both were facilita-

General Purpose Technologies and Surges in Productivity

ted by favourable macroeconomic conditions, including the high rate of investment in new plant and equipment; the new flexibility in plant location and design facilitated the reorganization of job assignments and labour systems as well as physical arrangements. Indeed, we would go further, suggesting that there were positive micro-level interactions between electrification and rising labour productivity. Another scatter diagram, relating the growth of capital and labour productivity across the array of industries during the decade, shows that there was a *positive* correlation between the two—not the negative association that one would expect using a simple factor substitution model (Figure 5). We argue that the technological and organizational changes just reviewed also exerted a positive influence on the efficiency of labour inputs, through at least three channels:

(a) An increase in the effective utilization of labour capacity, by improving the speed and reliability of materials transmission;
(b) A higher premium on mature, reliable, longer-term employees, because of the vulnerability of electrified plant systems to disruption;
(c) Increased scope for individual specialization and the exercise of discretion, made possible by the localization of power supply under the unit drive system.

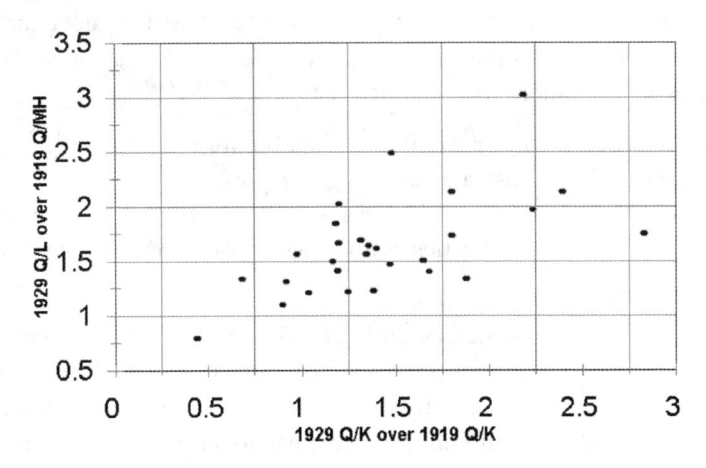

Figure 5. Change in output per manhour versus change in output per unit of capital, 1919–1929.
Source: Kendrick, *Productivity Trends in the United States*, Table D-VI.

Generalizing the Dynamo: Generic Features of General Purpose Technologies

The diffusion of the dynamo has served as something of a paradigmatic example for economists working in the spirit of the new growth theory who have sought to generalize the idea of 'general purpose technologies' with applications in diverse sectors of the economy. As formulated by Bresnahan and Trajtenberg:

> Most GPTs play the role of 'enabling technologies,' opening up new opportunities rather than offering complete, final solutions. For example, the productivity gains associated with the introduction of electric motors in manufacturing were not limited to a reduction in energy costs. The new energy sources fostered the more efficient design of factories, taking advantage of the newfound flexibility of electric power. Similarly, the users of micro-electronics benefit from the surging power of silicon by wrapping around the integrated circuits their own technical advances. This phenomenon involves what we call 'Innovational complementarities' (IC), that is, the productivity of R&D in a downstream sector increases as a consequence of innovation in the GPT technology. These complementarities magnify the effects of innovation in the GPT, and help propagate them throughout the economy.[9]

The interest in generalization has in turn stimulated efforts to consolidate our understanding of the defining features of GPTs, and to extend the list of historical examples. According to the most carefully developed criteria proposed by Lipsey, Bekar and Carlaw, GPTs are technologies that share four characteristics:

(a) Wide scope for improvement and elaboration;
(b) Applicability across a broad range of uses;
(c) Potential for use in a wide variety of products and processes;
(d) Strong complementarities with existing or potential new technologies.[10]

Using these criteria, Lipsey and his co-authors identify an extensive list of historical and contemporary GPTs, from power delivery systems (waterwheel, steam, electricity, internal combustion) and transport innovations (railways and motor vehicles) to lasers and the internet. They also extend the concept to such 'organizational technologies' as

---

[9] Bresnahan and Trajtenberg, 'General Purpose Technologies', p. 84.
[10] In Helpman (ed.), *General Purpose Technologies*, pp. 38–43.

the factory system, mass production and flexible manufacturing. In the same volume, Nathan Rosenberg extends the application still further into the institutional structure of knowledge itself, arguing that the rise of Chemical Engineering in the US may be usefully viewed as a GPT.[11]

One has only to consider the length of such proposed lists of GPTs to begin to worry that the concept may be getting out of hand. History may not have been long enough to contain this many separate and distinct revolutionary changes. On closer inspection, it may be that some of these sweeping innovations should be better viewed as sub-categories of deeper conceptual breakthroughs in a hierarchical structure. Alternatively, particular historical episodes may be fruitfully understood in terms of interactions between one or more GPTs on previously separate historical paths. Quite clearly, an important aspect of the 'dynamo revolution' was the technological confluence, or convergence, of electrification with other trajectories of industrial innovation, each of which might be considered a species of GPT. Three among these are especially notable in the present connection:

(a) The fixed transfer-line layout of assembly operations that came into full fruition in the Ford Highland Park plant on the eve of World War I diffused rapidly and widely during the 1920s, because, as Hounshell points out, Ford was deliberately open in promoting the logic and engineering specifics of this system of mass production by means of interchangeable parts. Electric power transmission by wire, rather than by drive-shafts, was better suited to this new manufacturing regime (as one can see from the use made of group and unit drives at Highland Park itself.)[12]

(b) Automated materials handling was a generic labour-saving development that featured prominently among the new innovations of manufacturing mechanization reported in Jerome's survey; these too did not require electrification, although in some cases, such as the use of battery-powered fork-lifts, the availability of cheap purchased power for recharging was important.

(c) Continuous process chemical technologies, which as Rosenberg emphasizes implemented the unit system principles of A.D. Little, made extensive use of electro-mechanical and electro-chemical

---

[11] Ibid., pp. 167–92.
[12] Hounshell, *American System to Mass Production*, pp. 260–1.

relays for control. Many of these processes were heat-using and so were dependent upon purchased electricity for large-scale operations.

For the sake of brevity and the thematic unity provided by considering the dynamics of the diffusion of a broad GPT, however, we prefer to regard the foregoing streams of technical development as subsidiary, or perhaps 'tributary'. Hence, we focus our discussion on the productivity impact of electric power technology and its applications, regarding the dynamo technology as a GPT of a higher order and a more pervasive and transformative agent than the others.

But we do see the explosive productivity growth of the 1920s as the result of a confluence between the dynamo GPT and the clustering of electricity-based or -enhanced manufacturing process technologies on the one side. On the other side we see the emergence of a new organizational regime that created what might be called the High Wage Path for the mid-twentieth-century US economy. This development was triggered by a particular conjunction of macroeconomic and labour market conditions, and insofar as it became institutionalized in the practices and expectations upon which the strategies of major US industrial corporations were premised, it might itself have a certain claim to be regarded as a GPT. But we prefer not to burden formulations of the GPT concept with this degree of historical specificity. We hold to the view that appropriate *applications* of the concept should be explicitly historical in the sense that the impact of a new technology is typically conditioned by just such conjunctions in timing.

Inevitably, some of the sense of historical context is lost in the more abstract theoretical treatments. In the recent collection of essays edited by Helpman, GPTs are variously characterized in terms of inter-industry linkages, R&D investments, scale economies, coordination problems, spillover and other structural features, often applied to perfect-foresight, general-equilibrium models that seem to deny the premise of historical technological trajectories. But this may be a necessary phase in the early diffusion of a concept within the discipline of economics. And it is noteworthy that even in models that are stripped down and simplified, GPT phenomena readily generate alternating phases of slow and rapid productivity growth, and corresponding phases of slowed or accelerated real wage growth. Depending on the formulation, the 'output slowdown' phase may be attributed to the diversion of resources into knowledge investment during the gestation phase; to increased rates of obsolescence in the older capital stock and in labour force skills; to measurement problems with respect to both the capital stock and new goods and services; to the need for industry-specific adaptations, which have to wait upon progress in the GPT itself; or to risks and uncertainties facing adopters, which decline only with improvements and cost reductions by suppliers.[13]

Virtually all of these aspects of discontinuity may be observed in our historical case of American electrification. We would add to this list, however, the need for organizational and above all for *conceptual* changes in the ways tasks and products are defined and structured. And because major technological revolutions can be expected to have social and distributional consequences, political adjustments may also be required, if the full potential of the new technology is to be realized. Changes of this sort are intrinsically subject to delay and discontinuity. As noted above, the historical US episode saw such transformations in immigration policy, education and the recruitment and retention policies of industrial employers.

Was this Phenomenon Uniquely American? Evidence from Comparative Electrification

Was the experience of delayed and then accelerated TFP growth, associated with electrification, a uniquely American phenomenon, or do we find similar patterns elsewhere?[14] A truly global analysis would be a vast project, but an appropriate place to begin is with the United Kingdom. Of course, there were so many contrasts in economic conditions between these two countries during the period of interest, that there is no assurance that any simple comparisons would be at all meaningful. As a self-sufficient continental power, the US escaped damage during World War I and was largely insulated from the travails of the international economy during the 1920s. Britain, on the other hand, was afflicted during that decade by the loss of traditional markets for manufactured goods and the overvaluation of the pound.

---

[13] See, particularly, the essays by Helpman and Trajtenberg, and by Aghion and Howitt, in Helpman, *General Purpose Technologies*.

[14] Special thanks are due at this point to Angus Maddison and R.C.O. Matthews for their privately communicated comments on David and Wright, 'Early Twentieth Century Growth', in which both suggested that we take notice of the experiences of industrial nations other than the US.

In view of these differences, it comes as something of a surprise to find a remarkable number of qualitatively similar patterns in the British productivity data. These emerge when the record for the period 1924 to 1937 is contrasted with that for the pre-war era. Matthews, Feinstein and Odling-Smee report that TFP for the economy as a whole rose at 0.70 per cent per year during 1924 to 1937, compared to 0.45 per cent per year for 1873 to 1913, the acceleration being led by manufacturing, where TFP growth jumped from 0.6 per cent to 1.9 per cent per year.[15] A particularly striking feature of this surge was that the capital-output ratio in manufacturing declined at the rate of 2.4 per cent per annum during 1924 to 1937, reversing the trend of the entire period stretching from 1856 to 1913.[16] Not only did the productivity of manufacturing capital increase for the sector as a whole, but the authors go on to note:

> It is remarkable that a fall in the capital-output ratio between 1924 and 1937 is found in every manufacturing group without exception, including rapidly growing industries such as vehicles and electrical engineering, where a legacy of old excess capacity can hardly have been important.[17]

Inspection of cross-section relationships within manufacturing suggests that, as in the US, there was a positive correlation between the growth of capital productivity and of labour productivity during this period.[18]

When we turn to the text of Matthews, Feinstein and Odling-Smee for an explanation of these patterns, we find that at the top of the list is electrification, 'a change that extended over the whole range of manufacturing ... a development that was accompanied by an increase in the proportion of electricity purchased as opposed to generated within the firm'. The authors note that

> ... apart from this straightforward capital-saving effect (as far as manufacturing was concerned), it is likely that a capital-saving effect also resulted because electrification permitted the more flexible and efficient use of any given horsepower. One of these consequences was the extension of the use of (relatively cheap) machine tools.[19]

---

[15] Matthews, Feinstein and Odling-Smee, *British Economic Growth*, p. 229.
[16] Ibid., p. 378.
[17] Ibid., p. 384.
[18] Ibid., p. 240.
[19] Ibid., p. 385.

More recently, Feinstein, Temin and Toniolo identify electrification as one of the key forces behind the movement known in Europe as 'rationalization' of industry, entailing 'closer control over the pace and continuity of effort by the labour force'.[20] This latter formulation resonates with the observations of David and Wright concerning the confluence during the 1920s of technological developments and the diffusion of new managerial practices.

What does this remarkable parallelism imply for our thinking about general purpose technologies? First, it is encouraging confirmation that factory electrification was indeed a GPT, with pervasive effects across virtually all manufacturing industries. Because central-source power generation required large fixed-capital investments, which in turn opened opportunities for capital-saving conversions across a wide range of industries, we should expect to see many common features in the experience, even in countries that differed in many other respects. Secondly, however, once underway, the diffusion of electricity as a primary power source in manufacturing establishments seems to have proceeded more rapidly in the UK than in the US during the post-World War I era. The electricity supply industry in Britain had started down a very different and more decentralized course during the period 1880 to 1914, and the development of large central generating plants serving regional networks was a comparatively late phenomenon, initially confined to the Northeast.[21] The Central Electricity Board was established by Parliament only in 1926, but progress thereafter was rapid, with the bulk of the national power grid being constructed between 1929 and 1933.[22]

Consistent with this lag behind the US in the widespread availability of cheap purchased electric power for its industrial districts, in Britain the growth of TFP in manufacturing was slower during the 1924 to 1929 interval than it was over the course of the following cyclically comparable period, 1929 to 1937.[23] Furthermore, it appears that

---

[20] Feinstein, Temin and Toniolo, *European Economy*, p. 80.
[21] See Hughes, *Networks of Power*, for comparisons between Britain, Germany and the US, which highlights the early lead of the latter in developing extensive regional universal electrical supply networks based upon 3–phase AC current, particularly in the Midwest. On the continuing entry during 1900 to 1913 of many small DC-based electrical supply companies in Britain—to which the North East regional network built by Mertz was the exception—see Hannah, *Electricity*, esp. p. 38.
[22] Feinstein, Temin and Toniolo, *European Economy*, p. 181.
[23] Matthews, Feinstein and Odling-Smee, *British Economic Growth*, p. 610.

by the end of the 1930s the extent of diffusion of electric power in British manufacturing as a whole essentially matched that in the US.[24] We interpret this rapid catch-up as an aspect of the experience of a 'follower' country, which can adopt a well-developed technology from abroad relatively quickly, without having to retrace all the steps and mis-steps of the social learning trajectory that had occurred in the country that pioneered the application of the technology in question.

Thus a second point brought out by this comparative approach to the subject is that the pace of GPT diffusion may be very different in leader and follower nations, a consideration that GPT theorists have thus far largely overlooked. This observation, of course, can be read as lying squarely within the tradition of historical analysis springing from Thorstein Veblen's remarks on 'the penalties of taking the lead', and made familiar in the literature of development economics by Alexander Gerschenkron's more elaborate formulation of 'the advantages of economic backwardness'.

Ryoshin Minami's account of factory electrification, *The Power Revolution in the Industrialization of Japan*, offers us another case in point. Electricity was employed as motive power in the Japanese cotton spinning industry at least as early as 1903, and the first industrial use of purchased electricity followed within a few years as the development of electric utilities reduced the cost of purchased power. The timing and sequencing of subsequent developments closely matched those in the US. From the end of World War I up to the mid-1920s the group drive system continued to be used in electrified spinning factories, with unit drive being introduced in those departments where the machinery required variations in speed. Beginning in the 1920s, however, increased domestic production of small 6–8 hp induction motors (so-called 'ring motors') facilitated the more general diffusion of unit drive throughout the industry.

While both contemporaries and later analysts in Japan agree in identifying the same range of advantages associated with the transition to the unit drive system as those observed in US factories, the available direct quantitative evidence on the magnitude of the impacts upon productivity in Japan is quite limited. Minami cites a study based upon 1938 data, which found that the switch to unit from group drive in the production of 20–count yarn raised output per spindle while reducing

---

[24] *Ibid.*, p. 385, note 5.

power consumption by 7–8 per cent.[25] But, the greater profitability of weaving factories in Japan that were employing electric motors to drive their power-looms, in comparison with those using steam engines or petroleum-powered engines, is firmly documented by Minami's net profit rate estimates for 1910 and 1926 (see *Power Revolution*, pp. 252–3). Electrification in this era yielded essentially the same higher rate of return in small as in large factories, whereas the high fixed costs of steam power made it far less suited for use by the country's many small-scale weaving establishments. Consequently, Minami's discussion of the weaving industry concludes:

> In small plants, the introduction of electric motors made mechanization possible; it promoted the transition from hand looms to power looms, which raised production efficiency and improved cost performance. In large plants, the transition from non-electric engines to electric motors decreased production costs and improved output quality.

A similar observation can be made regarding the role played by small electric motors in the mechanization of Japan's match industry during the 1920s. This was a 'modern' (which is to say a Western, non-traditional) branch manufacturing that had been established as an export activity during the closing quarter of the nineteenth century—based on the availability of low-wage labour. The formation of the Swedish Match Trust in 1921 soon led to a crisis, as Japanese matches were driven out of foreign markets and two large match-making companies were founded with the intention of dominating the home market. That outcome, however, failed to eventuate, because the mass of small-scale factories was able to survive by introducing match-making machines (of German design) which could be profitably powered by small electric motors.

In comparison with the US, and *a fortiori* with Britain, Japan's 'age of steam power' was 'historically compressed' by the rapid process of factory electrification. Thus, although the timing was coincident with, and the order of diffusion by industry closely resembled, that of the United States, Minami points out that by 1930 the transition to the new

---

[25] Moriya, *Boskei Seisanhi Bunseki*, p. 80. is the source discussed by Minami (*Power Revolution*, p. 213–14). In the same place, Minami takes note also of a 1923 study of Japanese spinning mills that were using steam-generated electric power, in which it was found that the costs of installing the equipment needed for the unit drive system were 10 to 27 per cent above those required for the group drive. This, of course, does not consider the capital-savings in building a new plant designed for the unit-drive system.

power regime was actually more complete in Japan. This was despite having been—or perhaps because it had been—'entirely dependent on borrowed technology'.[26] Thus, the impact of factory electrification on productivity was augmented in the case of Japan by the special circumstance that this transition was already underway before the mechanization of manufacturing plants had been completed. It was through the introduction of small electric motors and the unit-drive that the modernization and mechanization of small-scale industry was accomplished.

In view of this history, a close parallelism between the time path of productivity growth experienced by the Japanese manufacturing sector as a whole and that observed for the US during the opening third of the twentieth century is what one might well have anticipated would be observed. That expectation is reassuringly fulfilled: over the period 1908 to 1938, according to Minami's estimates, the average total factor productivity growth rate was about 2.9 per cent per annum, whereas in the US the corresponding growth rate for the 1909 to 1937 interval was slightly slower, averaging 2.5 per cent per annum.[27] The acceleration in TFP growth up to the peak in the 1920s is present in both cases, although the productivity growth surge in Japanese manufacturing was far less discontinuous. The rates there averaged 2.2 per cent per annum in the period 1908 to 1920, 4.3 per cent per annum during 1920 to 1930, followed by a decline back to the 2.2 per cent level during 1930 to 1938. By contrast, the variations of the average TFP growth rates in US manufacturing (corresponding to the series in Figure 1) were more pronounced: they show a rise from the negligible level of 0.2 per cent per annum during 1909 to 1919 to 5.3 per cent per annum during 1919 to 1929, and then drop back to slightly under the 2 per cent per annum mark in the period 1929 to 1937. Viewed against the

---

[26] Minami, *Power Revolution*, pp. 9, 138–41.

[27] The trend TFP growth rates presented by Okhawa and Rosovsky, *Japanese Economic Growth*, Table 4–2, are similar to those in Minami, *Power Revolution*, Table 1–3, over the period as a whole, averaging 3.3 per cent per annum during the 1912 to 1938 interval. But they display a quite different temporal pattern, suggesting that manufacturing productivity growth in the 1920s was *slower* than that during the surrounding years. Clearly, the Okhawa-Rosovsky estimates do not correlate well with the course of Japanese factory electrification that has been described here. But neither do they square with the more recent estimates provided by Minami's work, which depend upon different underlying data. The latter departs from the procedures of Okhawa and Rosovsky in making adjustments for changes in hours of work and capital utilization, as well as in making use of more appropriate factor income share estimates as weights for the input growth rates.

benchmark provided by the Japanese experience, the US pattern suggests that effects of World War I on industrial investment may well have delayed the diffusion of the unit-drive system and attendant factory reorganizations. They thereby created a potential for more rapid 'catch-up' that was exploited during the next decade.

On the other hand, it does not follow that the process of 'catch-up' in the aftermath of developments that delay the diffusion of a new GPT will automatically translate into higher average rates of growth in labour productivity and TFP. In Britain, even during the 'surge' period 1924 to 1937, the average pace of growth in manufacturing TFP remained (at 1.9 per cent per annum) far under both the Japanese and the US rates recorded during the 1920s.[28] A proximate explanation for the larger, American-British 'gap' may be found in the faster pace of increases in average man-hour productivity that had become established in US manufacturing following World War I. This suggestion directs our notice to another underlying aspect of difference between the experiences of these two industrial economies.

Where the US and British records in this era diverged most sharply was in regard to the labour market. An upward jump in the real hourly wage between 1913 and 1924 was in fact common to both countries, and indeed to many other countries at that time. It was occasioned in a proximate sense by global economic developments in the form of the inflation during the years 1915 to 1920 and the subsequent sharp deflation of 1920 to 1921.[29] About the same (4.5 per cent per

---

[28] The TFP calculations for US manufacturing without allowance for purchased energy inputs perhaps are those most directly comparable with the estimates for Britain from Matthews, Feinstein and Odling-Smee (*British Economic Growth*), which were cited in the text above. That US rate for the long period from 1889 to 1909 averages 0.7 percentage points, and corresponds closely to the 0.6 per cent per annum pre-1914 trend rate in Britain. The same productivity growth measures for the US show a rise to 5.3 per cent per annum during 1919 to 1929. See David, 'Computer and Dynamo', Table 2, Cols. 4, 7, for these TFP estimates, which have already been cited in connection with the US-Japanese comparison. Note that whereas the acceleration to the 1920s peak in these rates involved a jump of 4.7 percentage points, the weighted average of the multi-factor productivity growth rates (adjusted for purchase energy inputs) in US manufacturing industries indicate a still greater acceleration, involving a jump of 5.1 percentage points.

[29] According to Matthews, Feinstein and Odling-Smee, *British Economic Growth*, Table 6.5, the domestic (UK) economy-wide rise in real unit labour costs between 1913 and 1924 averaged 3.2 percentage points per annum when calculated on a manhour basis, but only 1.3 percentage points per annum on a manyear basis. This difference reflects the shortening of the work year in Britain, which, however, was not a factor in the US experience during the same period.

annum) average rate of increase in real unit labour costs was experienced by the manufacturing sectors of both countries over this 1913 to 1924 interval, even though the rise of the real wage rate in Britain was accentuated by the one-time national reduction in hours of work, enacted in 1919—a development that had no counterpart in the US prior to the 1930s.[30] But, as has been noted, the rise in real unit labour costs in the US was followed closely by a spectacular (5 percentage point) jump in the annual growth rate of TFP, whereas Britain's TFP acceleration was far less pronounced in both absolute and relative terms.[31]

Undoubtedly there were many factors contributing to the observed contrast in the proportionate relationship between the movement of real wage rates and the productivity of labour in the two countries. Thus there are no compelling reasons to expect the quantitative impact of the diffusion of the same capital-embodied GPT to be identical across economies, just because its qualitative effects were similar. Because US manufacturing firms had long experience with adapting to high-wage conditions, it is quite plausible to suppose that they were more readily able to accelerate the restructuring of labour relations that was already underway in many industries. An additional country-specific feature of the American economy that may also account for the differentially stronger US response to the altered state of the labour market might be found in the better match between the technologies advanced by electrification and the country's institutions of education and worker training.

On this latter point, recent research by Claudia Goldin and Lawrence Katz suggests that the new manufacturing technologies of this era were, indeed, well adapted to the attributes of the high school graduates emerging from educational reforms in the US in the decades just prior to the 1920s. Our examination of the data they have developed, and other related evidence, indicates that this was not because the American secondary school systems of the day were supplying

---

[30] The average annual rates of increase in manufacturing money wages inflated by the wholesale price index are found to be 4.5 per cent and 4.4 per cent, for Britain and the US, respectively. The underlying industrial money wage rate and price series for Britain are drawn from Mitchell, *International Historical Statistics*, Tables B4 and H1; the corresponding US data are those described in David and Wright, 'Early Twentieth Century Growth', Figure L1 and the accompanying text discussion (p. 20).

[31] During the decade of the 1920s, the US increased its already large labour productivity lead vis-à-vis Britain, and also Germany. See Stephen Broadberry, 'Manufacturing and the Convergence Hypothesis'.

industry with a workforce whose members had received specific cognitive information and particular skills required by the new, electrified manufacturing technologies. Rather, the new factory regime increasingly called for workers who were literate and numerate enough to be readily 'instructable' on the shop and factory floor; employers in the technologically more sophisticated industries sought workers who could accustom themselves to a succession of work routines, and who would be reliable in the execution of mechanically assisted tasks where consistency of performance had become more important in the context of integrated, high-throughput systems of production. High school attendance and high school completion appear to have constituted signals of these attributes and of the motivation to respond to experience-based wages and job promotion incentives that were designed to stabilize and upgrade the quality of the workforce employed by the leading manufacturing firms in this era.[32]

In contrast, the same decade has been identified as one of missed opportunity for the British educational system, as the older apprenticeship institutions were in decline, yet were not replaced by new forms of technical and continuation schooling.[33] Thus, a third broad implication of these cross-country comparisons is that the impact of any particular GPT diffusion may be strongly conditioned by circumstances affecting the supply of complementary productive inputs. To the extent that GPTs have a capability for widespread applications across many branches of the economy concurrently, if they successfully percolate and are able to take hold in that fashion, they will most likely give rise to synergetic interactions and positive feedbacks. The availability of correspondingly generic complementary inputs therefore is likely to constitute a critical constraint, not only upon the extent of the GPTs' diffusion, but upon the impact this has upon productivity growth. The historical case at hand suggests that critical factors in differential productivity performance may have been the management competencies rooted in the prior industrial experience, and policies affecting access to 'educational attainment' signals of general worker quality (as

---

[32] See Goldin and Katz, 'Technology-Skill Complementarity'; David and Wright, 'Early Twentieth Century Growth', section 4.
[33] M. Sanderson, 'Education and Economic Decline'; Stephen Broadberry and Karin Wagner, 'Human Capital and Productivity'.

distinguished from traditional craft apprenticeship) sought by employers in establishments that were becoming committed to factory electrification.[34]

Dynamos and Computers: Uses of History and Historical Analogy

By drawing an explicit analogy between 'the dynamo and the computer', David's essay of that title sought to use the US historical experience to give a measure of concreteness to the general observation that an extended phase of transition may be required to accommodate fully and hence elaborate a technological and organizational regime built around a general purpose digital computing engine. This 'regime transition hypothesis' has suggested itself as a possible resolution of the so-called 'productivity paradox', wherein new computer and information technologies (now commonly designated as ICT) have been rapidly and visibly diffusing through the economy at the same time that the growth rate of TFP has fallen to historic lows, in the US particularly. An understanding of the way in which the transmission of power in the form of electricity came to revolutionize industrial production processes tells us that far more was involved than the simple substitution of a new form of productive input for an older alternative. In both the past and current regime transitions, the pace of the transformation may be seen to be governed by the ease or difficulty of altering many other technologically and organizationally related features of the production systems involved.

Recent estimates of the growth of computer stocks and the flow of services therefrom are consistent with the view that when the 'productivity paradox' began to attract attention, the US economy could be

---

[34] In 'The Rise of Intangible Investment', Abramovitz and David discuss some aspects of the reciprocal historical relationships between the emergence of educational-attainment based hiring standards in US labour markets and the formation of perceptions of material advantage associated with extended schooling, and the growth of popular support for the movement towards public provision of mass secondary education—even at the appreciable costs to many families of foregoing earnings from their children's labour. This dynamic process is one in which there are positive feedback externalities of the kind found more generally at work in market-driven, *de facto* 'standards-setting for network industries'. See David, 'Some New Standards', for further discussion of the latter subject.

said to have still been in the early phase of the deployment of ICT. Figures developed by Dale Jorgenson and Kevin Stiroh reveal that in 1979, when computers had not yet evolved so far beyond their limited role in information processing machinery, computer equipment and the larger category of office, accounting and computing machinery (OCAM) were providing only 0.56 per cent and 1.5 per cent respectively of the total flow of real services from the (non-residential) producer durable equipment stock. But these measures rose at 4.9 per cent in 1985, and had ballooned to 13.8 per cent by 1990 and 18.4 per cent two years after that.[35] Thus, the extent of 'computerization' that had been achieved in the whole economy by the late 1980s was roughly comparable with the degree to which the American manufacturing sector had become electrified at the beginning of the twentieth century. When the historical comparison is narrowed more appropriately to the diffusion of secondary motors, a proxy for the spread of the unit drive, the growth rate for 1899 to 1914 is almost precisely the same as that for the ratio of computer equipment services to all producers' durable equipment services in the US.[36]

Although there seems to be considerable heuristic value in this historical analogy, a cautious, even sceptical attitude is warranted regarding the predictions for the future that some commentators have sought to extract from the quantitative resemblance between the two transition experiences. For one thing, statistical coincidences in economic performance are more likely than not to be mere matters of coincidence, rather than indications that the underlying causal mechanisms are really one and the same. One may use the historical evidence quite legitimately when suggesting that it is still too early to be disappointed that the computer revolution has not unleashed a sustained surge of readily discernible productivity growth throughout the economy. But that is not the same thing as predicting that the continuing relative growth of computerized equipment must eventually cause a surge of productivity growth to materialize, nor does it say anything whatsoever about the future pace of the digital computer's diffusion. Least of all does it tell us that the detailed shape of the diffusion path that lies

---

[35] Jorgenson and Stiroh, 'Computer Investment', pp. 3–4.
[36] David, 'Understanding Digital Technology's Evolution', provides this and other quantitative indicators, including comparisons of the decline in the real price of computer services with that of purchased electricity, that dispose of criticisms brought against the dynamo analogy's relevance, based on the argument that the much greater rapidity of innovation in the computer revolution renders the two cases incomparable.

ahead will mirror the curve traced out by the electric dynamo during the early decades of the twentieth century. One cannot simply infer the detailed future shape of the diffusion path in the case of the ICT revolution from the experience of previous analogous episodes. The very nature of the underlying process renders that path contingent upon events flowing from private actions and public policy decisions, as well as upon the expectations that are thereby engendered—all of which still lie before us in time.

Eschewing blind faith in historical repetition, we nonetheless can draw insights from the record of analogous past experiences that help us to understand the so-called 'productivity paradox' by indicating relevant margins and constraints governing the linkage between new information technologies and the rise of measured productivity. Here there is a case to be made for viewing the path taken up the present as one among a number of available alternatives—a path whose selection, viewed in retrospect, was responsive to considerations that led away from a tight coupling between new technological artefacts and the task productivity of the individuals and work groups to whom those tools were offered.[37]

The widespread diffusion of the stored program digital computer is intimately related to the popularization of the personal computer as a 'general purpose' technology for information processing and the incremental transformation of this 'information appliance' into the dominant technology of information processing. For the personal computer, as for its parent the mainframe and its cousin the minicomputer, adaptation and specialization have been required to apply a general purpose information processing machine to *particular* purposes or tasks. It is something of an historical irony that the core elements of the adaptation problems attending this GPT's diffusion into widespread business application may be seen to derive from a trajectory of innovation that emphasized the 'general purpose' character of the paradigmatic hardware and software components.

During the 1970s it was recognized that a general purpose integrated circuit, the microprocessor, afforded the flexible means of solving the problems of electronic system designers who found themselves

---

[37] The following draws upon David ('Understanding Digital Technology's Evolution', Section 4), and the more detailed treatment by David and Steinmueller ('Understanding the Puzzles and Payoffs', Section 7) of the productivity implications of the general purpose formulation computer technology that has characterized the personal computer revolution.

confronted by an ever-growing array of application demands. At the same time, efforts to down-scale mainframe computers to allow their use for specialized control and computation applications supported the birth of the minicomputer industry. These two developments provided the key trajectories for the birth of the personal computer. As microprocessors became cheaper and more sophisticated, and applications for dedicated information processing continued to expand, a variety of task-specific computers came into existence.

One of the largest markets for such task specific computers created during the 1970s was that for dedicated word-processing systems. These appeared as an incremental step in office automation, aimed at the task of producing documents repetitive in content or format such as contracts, purchase orders, legal briefs and insurance forms, that could be quickly modified and customized based upon stored formats and texts. They became attractive and were often adopted where the production of forms and texts generated full-time work for more than a single employee. But the inability of the vendors of the pioneer dedicated word-processing hardware to furnish their customers with new software—for they had adopted a strategy of providing only proprietary software—led to both a perceived and actual absence of flexibility; the technology was not responsive to the proliferating user needs arising from the growing number of product installations.

The displacement of dedicated word processors by personal computers thus came relatively rapidly in the mid-1980s, driven by the apparent superiority of the latter in a number of the relevant dimensions of comparison. The personal computer was quickly perceived to be more 'flexible' and more likely to be 'upgrade-able' as new generations of software were offered. Moreover, personal computers could use many of the same peripherals, such as printers: because the widespread adoption of the new technology raised the demand for compatible printers, the dedicated word processors found themselves unprotected by any persisting special advantages in printing technology.

The dedicated word processor's demise was re-enacted in numerous markets where dedicated 'task-specific' data processing systems had begun to develop.[38] The elimination of task-based computing in favour of general purpose computers and or multi-purpose software packages was in a sense the main thrust of the 'PC revolution' that

---

[38] See the discussion in Steinmueller, 'US Software Industry'.

was completed in the course of the 1980s.[39] The 'general purpose' software produced for the emerging standard platforms (IBM PC and Apple Macintosh) not only discouraged task-specific software, it also created a new collection of tasks and outputs specifically driven by the new capabilities such as 'desk top publishing', 'presentation graphics' and 'advanced word processing'. All of these changes improved the 'look and feel' of information communication, its quality and style, the capability for an individual to express ideas, and the quantity of such communications. But, singly and severally, they made very little progress in changing the structure of work organization or the collective productivity of the work groups employing these techniques.

The early trajectory of the personal computer's evolution thus may be seen as having cut across the development of an entire family of technically-feasible information processing systems focused on the improvement of 'task-productivity' in applications ranging from word processing to manufacturing operations control. In many cases, it also precluded effective development of collective 'work group' processes whose synergies would support multi-factor productivity improvement. Instead of 'breaking free' from the mainframe, these general purpose engines often wound up 'slaved' to the mainframe, using a small fraction of their capabilities to emulate the operations of their less expensive (and less intelligent) cousins, the 'intelligent' display terminals. The information systems departments of large organizations soon faced a growing array of demands for access to databases and reporting systems, so that managers might construct reports more to their liking, using their new spreadsheet tools.

Although the 'personal computing' revolutionaries had kept their promise that the new hardware would soon match the computing performance of the mainframes of yesteryear, what they had not achieved, and could not achieve by this technological leap was a radical, rapid reconstruction of the information processing activities of the organizations to which the equipment and software was being sold. Rather

---

[39] In the medium and large enterprises of 1990, what remained was a deep chasm between the 'mission critical' application embedded in mainframe computers and the growing proliferation of personal computers. The primary bridge between these application environments was the widespread use of the IBM 3270, the DEC VT-100 and other standards for 'intelligent' data display terminals, the basis for interactive data display and entry to mainframe and minicomputer systems. From their introduction, personal computers had software enabling the emulation of these terminals, providing further justification for their adoption.

than contributing to the rethinking of organizational routines, the spread of partially networked personal computers supported the development of new database and data entry tasks, new analytical and reporting tasks, and new demands for 'user support' to make the general purpose technology deliver its potential.

This is not to claim that the process should be regarded as socially sub-optimal, or mistaken from a private business perspective. No clear basis for such judgements, one way or the other, presently exists. It appears that what was easiest in an organizational sense tended to be the most attractive thing to undertake first. The local activities within the organization that were identified as candidates for personal computer applications often could and did improve the flexibility and variety of services offered by the company internally and externally to customers who, through the intermediation of personnel with appropriate information system access, would receive an array of service quality improvements. Arguably, many of these quality improvements contribute to the problems of productivity measurement. The reason is that they fail to be captured in the real output statistics of the services sector, even though they might enhance the revenue-generating capacity of the firms in which they are deployed. The availability of 24–hour telephone reservation desks for airlines, or the construction of world-wide networks for securing hotel, rental automobile or entertainment reservations, represent welfare improvements for the customer. But these do not appear in the measured real GDP originating in those sectors, nor in the real value of expenditures on final goods and services. Of course, the same point may be, and has been, made about the tendency of service quality improvements to slip through the national income and product statisticians' net.[40] These improvements include safety improvements connected with the switch from gas lamps to electric lighting, and the replacement of horse-drawn trams by electric railways.

---

[40] See, e.g., David, 'Computer and Dynamo', Nordhaus, 'History of Lighting'.

Historical Reflections on 'General Purposeness' and the Future of the ICT Revolution

The historical trajectory of computer technology development now appears poised to take a portentous change of direction. At least three new dimensions are emerging strongly enough in commercial applications to deserve brief notice. None of these developments are likely to displace the use of personal computers in the production and distribution of information that must be highly customized, or that arises from the *ad hoc* inquiries similar to the research processes for which the general purpose computer was originally invented. What they do promise is greater and more systematic efforts to integrate information collection, distribution and processing efforts. In attempting to take advantage of these opportunities, enterprises and other institutions are forced to re-examine workflow and develop new methods for information system design.

Firstly, a growing range of information technologies has become available that is purpose-built and task-specific. Devices such as supermarket scanners were applied to a wide range of inventory and item tracking tasks and related 'data logging' devices were to be found in the hands of maintenance, restaurant and factory workers. The environmental niches in which these devices were able to achieve a foothold are ones where the mass produced personal computer was neither appropriate nor robust. These more 'task specialized' devices have become sufficiently ubiquitous to provide the infrastructure for task-oriented data acquisition and display systems, in which up-to-date and precise overviews of the material flows through manufacturing and service delivery processes.

Secondly, the capabilities of advanced personal computers as 'network servers' have become sufficiently well developed that it is possible for companies to eliminate the chasm between the personal computer and mainframe environment by developing the intermediate solution of client-server data processing systems. This development is still very much in progress and reflects the more complete utilization of the local area networks devised for information and resource sharing during the personal computer era. In this new networked environment, the reconfiguration of work organization becomes a central issue, strategic and practical issues surrounding the ownership and maintenance of critical company data resources must be resolved, and these are often compelling enough to force redesign of the organizational structure.

Thirdly, the development of Internet technology has opened the door to an entirely new class of organization-wide data processing applications as well as enormously enhanced the potential for collective and cooperative forms of work organization. Applications and their maintenance can be controlled by the technical support team who would previously have been responsible for the company's centralized data resources. The common standards defining Internet technology have the fortuitous feature that virtually all personal computers can be similarly configured, facilitating not only intra-company network but also *inter*-company networking.

The 'general purpose' trajectory followed by the spectacular development of personal computer technology has greatly reduced the price-performance ratio of the hardware, without effecting commensurate savings in the resource costs of carrying out many specific, computerized tasks. Some part of the limited resource savings clearly has been transitional, as personal computers were added to existing mainframe capacity, rather than substituted for it, and indeed were underutilized by being allocated the role of intelligent terminals. This aspect of the story bears some striking similarities with the early progress of factory electrification, wherein the use of the group drive system supplemented without replacing the distribution of power within factors by means of shafts and belting; this added capital to an already highly-capital-using industrial power technology, without instigating any reorganization of factory layout and routines for materials handling. It was not, however, until the dynamo could be effectively integrated into individual tools under the unit drive system that the major capital-saving contributions to multi-factor productivity growth from thoroughgoing factory redesign could be realized.

A similar structural change seems likely to emerge, based on the development and diffusion of digital information appliances — robust and specialized tools that are embedded in hand-held devices, carried on belts, sown into garments or worn as head-gear — and linked through sophisticated networks to produce complex and interactive systems.[41] This may indeed be a promising trajectory of ICT development that will impinge directly upon specific (and hence more readily measurable) task performance.

---

[41] See, for example, the vision presented recently by Norman in *The Invisible Computer*, esp. Ch. 11.

Other portents for the future may be seen in the expansion of inter-organizational computing for the mass of transactions involving purchase ordering, invoicing, shipment tracking and payments, all of which continue at present to absorb much specialist white-collar labour time. Such service occupations might be viewed as the modern-day counterparts of the ubiquitous materials-handling tasks in the manufacturing sector that became the target of mechanization innovations during the 1920s. A continuation of the presently still-limited growth of 'tele-working' in the US—where only about one-fifth of the workforce time in large service sector firms is now provided via data communications networks with employees' homes—would eventually yield significant capital-savings in the reduced requirement for commercial office space and transport infrastructure facilities.

Major physical and organizational reconfigurations of this kind lend themselves to application across a wide array of specific branches of the economy, as was the case in the dynamo revolution of the early twentieth century. They would seem to hold out the most promising prospects for the early twenty-first century to see the potentialities of the information technology revolution realized in a sustained, 'yeast-like' surge of productivity growth.

References

Abramovitz, M., and P.A. David. 'The Rise of Intangible Investment: the US Economy's Growth Path in the Twentieth Century.' In *Employment and Growth in the Knowledge-Based Economy*, edited by D. Foray and B.-A. Lundvall, 35–60. Paris: OECD, 1996.

Aghion, P. and P. Howitt. 'On the Macroeconomic Effects of Major Technological Change.' In *General Purpose Technologies and Economic Growth*, edited by E. Helpman, 121–44. Cambridge, MA: MIT Press, 1998.

Bresnahan, T., and M. Trajtenberg. 'General Purpose Technologies: Engines of Growth.' *Journal of Econometrics* 65 (1995): 83–108.

Broadberry, S. 'Manufacturing and the Convergence Hypothesis.' *Journal of Economic History* 53 (1993): 772–95.

Broadberry, S., and K. Wagner. 'Human Capital and Productivity in Manufacturing during the Twentieth Century.' In *Quantitative Aspects of Post-War European Economic Growth*, edited by B. van Ark and N.F.R. Crafts, 244–70. Cambridge: Cambridge University Press, 1996.

David, P.A. 'Some New Standards for the Economics of Standardization in the Information Age.' In *Economic Policy and Technological Performance*, edited by P. Dasgupta and P. Stoneman, 206–39. Cambridge: Cambridge University Press, 1987.

———. 'Computer and Dynamo: The Modern Productivity Paradox in a Not-too-distant Mirror.' In *Technology and Productivity: The Challenge for Economic Policy*, 315–47. Paris: OECD, 1991.

———. 'Understanding Digital Technology's Evolution and the Path of Measured Productivity Growth: Present and Future in the Mirror of the Past.' In *Understanding the Digital Economy: Data, Tools and Research*, edited by E. Brynolfsson and B. Kahin, 49–95. Cambridge, MA: MIT Press, 2000.

David, P.A., and W.E. Steinmueller. 'Understanding the Puzzles and Payoffs of the IT Revolution: The "Productivity Paradox" after Ten Years.' Ch. 1 of *Productivity and the Information Technology Revolution*, edited by P. A. David and W. E. Steinmueller. Harwood Academic Publishers, forthcoming.

David, P.A., and G. Wright. 'Early Twentieth Century Growth Dynamics: An Inquiry into the Economic History of "Our Ignorance".' Stanford: SIEPR Discussion Paper No. 98–3, 1999.

Devine, W. Jr. 'From Shafts to Wires.' *Journal of Economic History* 43 (1983): 347–72.

———. 'Electrified Mechanical Drive: The Historical Power Distribution Revolution.' In *Electricity in the American Economy*, edited by S. Schurr et al. New York: Greenwood Press, 1990.

Douglas, Paul H. and Jennison, Florence Tye. *The Movement of Money and Real Earnings in the United States, 1926–1928*. Chicago: University of Chicago Press, 1930.

DuBoff, R. *Electric Power in American Manufacturing 1889–1958*. New York: Arno, 1979.

Feinstein, C.H. *Domestic Capital Formation in the United Kingdom 1920–1938*. Cambridge, England: Cambridge University Press, 1965.

Feinstein, C.H., Peter Temin and Gianni Toniolo. *The European Economy Between the Wars*. Oxford: Oxford University Press, 1997.

Gerschenkron, A. *Economic Backwardness in Historical Perspective*. Cambridge, Mass: Harvard University Press, 1969.

Goldin, C., and L. Katz. 'The Origins of Technology-Skill Complementarity.' *Quarterly Journal of Economics* 113 (1998): 693–732.

Gordon, Robert J. 'US Economic Growth Since 1870: One Big Wave?' *American Economic Review* 89 (May 1999): 123–8.

Harberger, A. 'A Vision of the Growth Process.' *American Economic Review* 88 (1998): 1–32.

Helpman, E., ed. *General Purpose Technologies and Economic Growth*. Cambridge, MA: The MIT Press, 1998.

Hannah, L. (1979). *Electricity Before Nationalisation*. London: Macmillan, 1979.

Hounshell, D. *From the American System to Mass Production*. Baltimore: JHU Press, 1984.

Hughes, T.P. *Networks of Power: Electrification in Western Society, 1880–1930*. Baltimore: JHU Press, 1983.

Jerome, H. *Mechanization in Industry*. New York: National Bureau of Economic Research, 1934.

Jorgenson, D., and K. Stiroh. 'Computers and Growth.' *Economics of Innovation and New Technology 3*, no. 3–4 (1995): 295–316.

Kendrick, J. *Productivity Trends in the United States*. Princeton: Princeton University Press, 1961.

Lipsey, R. G., C. Bekar, and K. Carlaw. 'What Requires Explanation?' In *General Purpose Technologies and Economic Growth*, edited by E. Helpman, 15–54. Cambridge, MA: MIT Press, 1998.

Matthews, R.C.O., C.H. Feinstein and J.C. Odling-Smee. *British Economic Growth 1856–1873*. Stanford, CA: Stanford University Press, 1982.

Minami, R. *Power Revolution in the Industrialization of Japan, 1885–1940*. Tokyo: Kinokuniya Co, 1987.

Mitchell, B.R. *International Historical Statistics of Europe, 1750–1988*, Third Edition, Basingstoke, England: MacMillan, 1992.

Moriya, Fumio, *Boskei Seisanhi Bunseki*. Kokyo: Nippon Hyoronsha, 1948.

Nordhaus, William D. 'Do Real Output and Real Wage Measures Capture Reality? The History of Lighting Suggests Not.' In *The Economics of New Goods*, edited by T.F. Bresnahan and R.J. Gordon, 25–66. Chicago: The University of Chicago Press, 1997.

Norman, Donald A. *The Invisible Computer: Why Good Products Can Fail, the Personal Computer is So Complex, and Information Appliances are the Solution*. Cambridge, MA: MIT Press, 1998.

Okhawa, Kazushi, and Henry Rosovsky. *Japanese Economic Growth: Trend Acceleration in the Twentieth Century*. Stanford, C.A.: Stanford University Press, 1973, Table 4–2.

Sanderson, M. 'Education and Economic Decline, 1890s–1980s.' *Oxford Review of Economic Policy* 4 (1988): 38–50. Reprinted with postscript in *The Economic Development of the United Kingdom since 1870*, edited by C.H. Feinstein. Cheltenham, UK: Edward Elgar.

Schurr, S.H., et al. *Electricity in the American Economy*. New York: Greenwood Press, 1990.

Steinmueller, W.E. 'The US Software Industry: An Analysis and Interpretative History.' In *The International Computer Software Industry*, edited by D.C. Mowery, 15–52. Oxford: Oxford University Press, 1996.

Veblen, T. *Imperial Germany and the Industrial Revolution*. New York: MacMillan, 1915.

5.
Technological Systems and Comparative Systems of Innovation:
From Historical Performance to Future Policy Guidelines

NICK VON TUNZELMANN

Introduction

To approach the question of how different societies both produce and use technology involves cross-relating two rather different parts of the economics literature. One concerns the nature of technological development and its relationship with economic growth at large. The second concerns comparisons among economic systems. Much of Charles Feinstein's work has been associated with precisely these two fields, and my intention in this paper is to link them quite directly. Although there are many elements of continuity as well as contrast across economic systems, there is also an underlying historical evolution of technological systems that is disruptive of economic systems, and often of growth.

The view presented in this paper is that a linear kind of economic model of technology production and use has some validity as a first approximation to such historical evolution, but in the end has to be rejected as an inadequate context for assessing the interaction between technology and growth over the long term. Instead the paper draws on two rather disparate modes of analysis. The study of technological systems departs from work on innovation studies, with which my own work and institution is primarily associated. The study of economic systems is drawn from the literatures on political and economic governance. This paper can be no more than a start on trying to effect a union between such strange bedfellows.

A key issue emanating from the innovation studies literature is that technology is primarily a matter of knowledge rather than information. There is of course a relationship between information and knowledge, but they are conceptually quite different. Knowledge is accumulated in individuals and in organizations and other structures through processes of learning. Much of this accumulated knowledge is 'tacit', that is uncodified, and part of it perhaps uncodifiable. The codified part, on the other hand, becomes potentially available as information, which can be communicated through market or other mechanisms. Thus knowledge can generate and supply information in somewhat similar fashion to the way a capital stock generates output. Equally, on the receiving end, new information can be an input into the recipient's knowledge base. Absorbing the new items of information therefore expands the latter's stock of knowledge. A peculiarity of knowledge, however, is that the impact of most items of information is likely to be greater, the *greater* is the already existing relevant knowledge base of the recipient. A new theorem in Galois theory in mathematics is likely to have much less impact on the present author, being not at all sure what Galois theory is, than on a mathematician already working at the forefront of that area of study. This contrasts with usual diminishing returns assumptions relating to, say, physical capital in economics. The capacity for *absorption* is thus crucial to technological development and technology transfer. This absorptive capacity is not independent but in practice intimately linked to experience and learning in the firm.[1]

Analysing both the production of technology, which in the knowledge dimension can be seen as its codification—either 'embodied' in an artefact or 'disembodied' in a description such as a patent registration—and the use of technology, seen as its absorption, is the main focus of this paper. Different economic systems have very different capacities to generate and especially to absorb technological information, which reflects the relative adequacy of their learning systems for knowledge accumulation. As already implied, the developments in the technological system themselves impose new requirements on economic systems, and these will become critical in any projection into the future.

---

[1] Cohen and Levinthal, 'Innovation and Learning' and 'Absorptive Capacity'.

The Production of Technology Versus the Use of Technology

In two recent papers, the author has attempted to show that the production of technology and the use or adoption of technology, though often conflated, need separate consideration.[2] This is not just a matter of innovation versus diffusion, though of course that comes into the story. The main point here is that the use of technology requires adaptations and extensions to the technology, so that the use phase itself is one of broad-ranging production of innovations. A technological advance becomes significant when it is assimilated into a variety of user contexts.

Innovations such as the aircraft represent the coming together of a variety of preceding technological components in a radically new *design architecture*, rather than springing fully conceived into the world. The main point here is to emphasize the complex causal patterns that go into the evolution of a 'macro-innovation'.[3] It is not just followed by a swarming of micro-innovations but often preceded by them as well. Such a process is captured by the Kline-Rosenberg model of 'chain-linked' technological development, characterized by multiple interactions and feedbacks at all levels.[4]

Even so, the technological evolutions of both particular products and of technological systems at large are heavily 'front-loaded', as the author's papers have tried to demonstrate. Among these interacting relationships, there remain observable historical sequences. In a recent paper, Hariolf Grupp has shown how the laser, an 'invention in search of a purpose', began with a wave of associated patenting in the 1960s, but then fell into a period of 'slump' when it appeared that it would become a scientific curiosity, until rescued in the mid-80s by the emergence of major economic applications, as with the semiconductor laser.[5]

While these results for the laser might have been predicted from common sense, it is less expected to find that much the same occurs in the opposite context, when technology leads science. The case of petroleum refining, using data developed by Jacob Schmookler in his

---

[2] Von Tunzelmann, 'Technology Generation'; von Tunzelmann and Anderson, 'Technologies and Skills'.
[3] See Mokyr, *Lever of Riches*.
[4] Senker, 'Tacit Knowledge'; Kline, *Conceptual Foundations*.
[5] Grupp, 'Appropriation of Innovation Rents'.

well-known analyses of the economics of invention,[6] was re-examined.[7] Schmookler linked disaggregated data on patents with economic data on investment and so on, to show that *fluctuations* in investment preceded fluctuations in patents by several years, which in turn supports a demand-driven view of the innovation process. If instead we examine the *trends* in the data, we find a somewhat different picture emerging. On the basis of Schmookler's data when rendered as trends, there is an unsurprising tendency for inventions to lead patents. There is, however, an after-wave of inventions in the inter-war period, which clustered around the development of catalytic cracking, so we can speak here of a feedback from *use* into the *production* of major new process technologies. Moreover, the major burst of patenting *precedes* the major growth in output. That is, once one shifts attention from fluctuations to trends in the comparative patterns, the sequence of causation reverses.[8]

Other product-related studies in the same vein, using similar or more original data, show basically similar results, for example for patenting in railroad systems.[9] Work on telephone and telegram patents equally shows two-way linkages in the long-term patterns.[10]

Perhaps more striking is the result that these findings about sequential relationships between supply, demand and innovation also show up at a macroeconomic level. Again, some of the patterns have been more carefully analysed in the companion papers, but Figure 1 indicates the kind of result that has been obtained on the basis of patent data. It shows the ratio between numbers of patents and industrial production in three of the leading industrial countries in the First and Second Industrial Revolutions, namely the UK, USA and Germany.

Relative to industrial production and based on a comparison with 1913 as the base year, patenting in the UK in the top panel is at low levels before the Industrial Revolution, then rises very sharply around the period conventionally allocated to the onset of industrialization. It remains at high levels throughout the Industrial Revolution years, down to the mid-nineteenth century, before falling away somewhat. The pattern is even sharper when compared to the production of

---

[6] Schmookler, *Invention*; Schmookler, *Patents*.
[7] In von Tunzelmann and Anderson, 'Technologies and Skills', Fig. 11.
[8] Freeman and Soete, *Economics of Industrial Innovation*.
[9] In von Tunzelmann and Anderson, 'Technologies and Skills', Fig. 12.
[10] Ibid., Fig. 13.

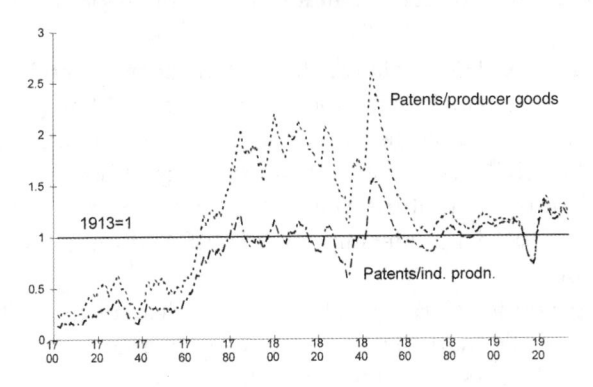

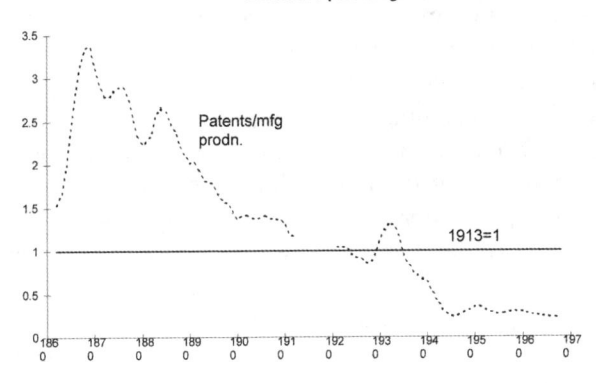

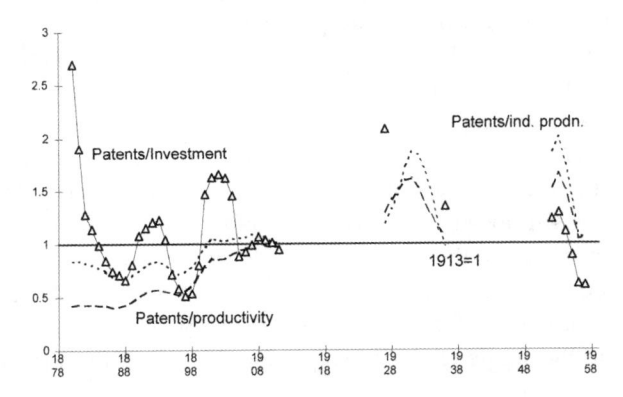

Technological Systems and Comparative Systems of Innovation

Figure 1. Patenting compared to industrial production and investment, USA, UK and Germany.
Sources: Panel 1 (UK): Hoffmann, *British Library*, fold-out appendices; Panel 2 (USA): *Historical Statistics*, pp. 667, 958–9; Panel 3 (Germany): Hoffmann, *Das Wachstum*, Tables 15, 35, 45, 76.

171

capital goods, using Hoffmann's index for all three of these indicators.[11]

Patenting in the USA relative to manufacturing production is shown in the middle panel. Using the same base of 1913 as for the UK, the picture is dominated by the rapid rise in relative patenting around the time of the Civil War, which then stays high though dropping down to the turn of the century. The pattern clearly relates well to the rise to world industrial leadership by the USA during the Second Industrial Revolution.

The third panel, for Germany, shows a less clear picture. The data are made problematic by the fact that Germany had no uniform patent law until 1878 (of course the country itself was not unified politically until 1871). Before that date, the figures consist of patenting by individual German states[12] and are not compatible with the later data, so they are excluded here. The high early levels c. 1880 shown here probably represent a short-term 'catching-up' in extending patenting rather than an explosion of new inventions. Missing data especially for wartime and fluctuations even in the smoothed data make the assessments somewhat ambiguous, but the impression is one of a build-up in relative patenting to a peak after World War I. On top of short-term catching-up in patenting (after the 1878 law, after 1945, and so on), there appears to be a longer-term catching-up process linked to Germany's more delayed emergence as a leading industrial power.

These long-term spurts are suggestive of a burst of *production* of new technologies at an early stage in the principal industrial revolutions experienced by each of these major countries, with the patenting spurt preceding the major growth of output, just as occurred at the micro level of individual product areas. However they also exhibit some aspects of 'reverse causation', in which the growth of output itself drives inventive activity through the spreading usage of the new technologies. Some indication of causation patterns can be obtained by estimating time series in 'error-correction model' (ECM) format, in which the change in the supposed 'dependent variable' is regressed not only against the change in the supposed 'independent variable' but also against lagged levels of both 'dependent' and 'independent' variables. This neatly allows collapsing short-term responses and long-term responses into the single regression equation. The short-term response is

---

[11] Hoffmann's patents index (from Hoffmann, *British Industry*) takes into account major legislative overhauls of the UK patents system in 1852 and again in 1883.
[12] Taken from Federico, 'Historical Patent Statistics'.

given by the coefficient on the lagged change in the 'independent variable' in the usual way; the long-term response by the inverse of the coefficient on the lagged level of the 'independent variable' divided by that on the lagged level of the 'dependent variable'. The latter can be shown to be equivalent to the 'cointegration' between the two series.

Table 1. ECM regulations of GDP of patents by country, 1860/1961 (t-values).

Country	Dep. Var.*	Start Year	Constant	Level of Dep. Var.	Change of Indep. Var.	Level of Indep. Var.	R-bar Sqd.	Short term**	Long term**
UK	DGDP	1860	-.800	.987	-1.224	1.441	.083		
	DPat	1860	.280	-2.133	-1.224	2.290	.046		+
USA	DGDP	1860	-.869	1.365	.558	1.233	.100		
	DPat	1860	2.151	-2.286	.558	1.928	.026		+
Germany	DGDP	1880	-.942	5.801	-.578	-1.437	.372		
	DPat	1880	1.275	-2.160	-.578	1.708	.027		+
France	DGDP	1860	-.674	-1.122	2.797	2.537	.117	+	
	DPat	1860	-.657	-5.249	2.797	4.413	.225	+	+
Belgium	DGDP	1860	-.207	-.327	10.198	1.137	.518	+	
	DPat	1860	.453	-1.909	10.198	1.256	.526	+	
Neths.	DGDP	1915	.274	1.420	2.975	-1.020	.240	+	
	DPat	1915	1.069	-2.508	2.975	1.803	.307	+	+
Denmark	DGDP	1866	-.911	-.642	4.693	2.392	.226	+	
	DPat	1866	1.693	-2.985	4.693	1.914	.210	+	+
Sweden	DGDP	1860	1.542	2.634	.934	-1.385	.111		
	DPat	1860	1.645	-1.790	.934	1.317	.020		
Norway	DGDP	1866	-.929	4.155	-.156	-.350	.261		
	DPat	1866	1.489	-1.612	-.156	.535	.008		
Finland	DGDP	1860	-1.944	4.069	.889	.727	.373		
	DPat	1860	1.205	-2.563	.889	1.386	.040		
Italy	DGDP	1860	-1.291	2.822	.398	-.864	.132		
	DPat	1860	-1.164	-5.843	.398	4.512	.253		+
Australia	DGDP	1860	-.398	1.849	1.722	-.849	.081	+	
	DPat	1860	.850	-3.688	1.722	3.336	.148	+	+
Canada	DGDP	1871	1.029	3.692	1.289	-1.200	.248		
	DPat	1871	1.051	-2.091	1.289	2.378	.093		+
Japan	DGDP	1886	-.507	1.202	5.354	.890	.443	+	
	DPat	1886	-3.175	-3.479	5.354	3.745	.517	+	+

* DGDP = Change in GDP; DPat = Change in Patents.
** Short term = sign of significant coefficient on change in 'independent' variable
Long term = negative of sign of significant coefficient on level of 'independent' variable divided by significant level of 'dependent' variable (cointegration factor)

These equations can be run with either variable as the supposed 'dependent variable'. In Table 1, the data are patents as the measure of technology and GDP as the measure of the economy.[13] The equations are estimated separately for each country over the period 1860 to 1961. The values quoted in the Table are all t-values, to allow a ready assessment of levels of significance. For most countries, the traditional 'linear' relationship of patents leading GDP, shown in ordinary type, gives better R-squareds. However the reverse causation, shown in italics, appears to work better for some countries, and also for generating significant coefficients on the levels variables. The short-term and long-term relationships, where statistically significant at the 5 per cent level, are set out in the final two columns; it will be observed that all of these are positive.[14] While bursts of patenting may precede bursts of growth as already implied, it may be concluded that in the long term levels of patenting are driven by levels of output and growth rates.

Patents are obviously an imperfect measure of the amount of effort devoted to innovative activity, though they may more accurately reflect this than other purposes, such as measuring competitiveness to which patents data are often applied. Only since the 1960s do we have macro-level data on R&D across a sizeable range of countries, thanks to the labours of OECD statisticians as well as national statistics units. While R&D expenditures are nowadays considered a more useful measure of innovative effort, it should be noted that formal R&D is in reality a very narrow concept.

Nevertheless, time-series estimates of the average level of 'R&D intensity' in the group of countries comprising the OECD in 1990, as shown in the lower panel of Figure 2, reveal the persisting upward trends in the proportions of GDP devoted to total R&D expenditures (GERD%). The relative increases in business R&D expenditures (BERD%) in the first half of the 1980s are particularly evident as a source of the rise in the overall intensity measure (GERD%), because it was not paralleled by an expansion of R&D expenditures in the Higher Education sector (HERD%). Some part of this acceleration in R&D intensities, however, is the result of slowed growth of the denominator

---

[13] Annual patents data are taken from Federico, 'Historical Patent Statistics'; GDP data from Maddison, *Dynamics*. The data for UK were re-estimated for post-1885 and for Germany post-1860, to assess the sensitivity to the changes in patenting practice noted above; the results differed very little.

[14] The short-term impacts of course show the same level of significance in either direction.

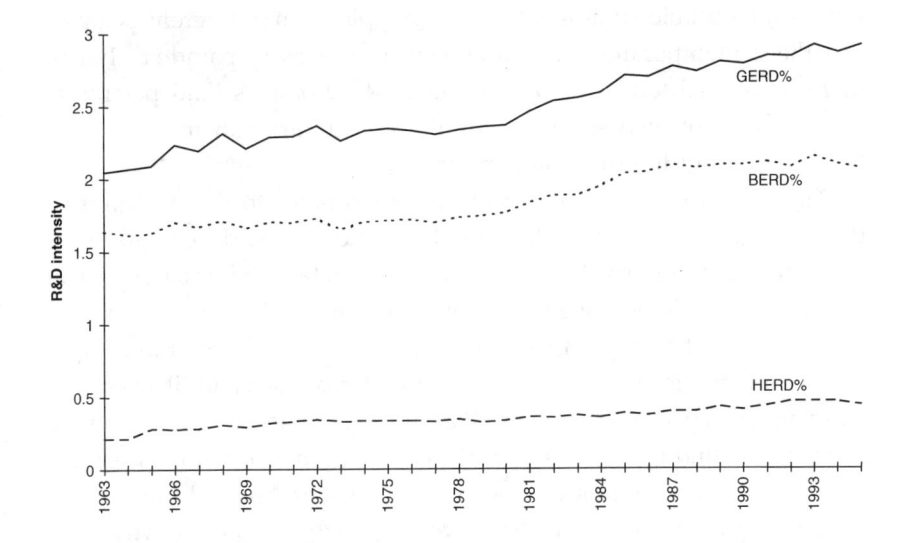

Figure 2. Predicted 'average' values for real R&D expenditures, 1963–1995, 22 OECD countries, USA base.
Source: Author's database, from OECD and related data.

across the leading industrial countries at the beginning of the 1980s. Nonetheless, it remains noteworthy that R&D intensities are counter-cyclical in the recession of the early '80s, but more procyclical in that of the early '90s. Recession or no recession, countries in general diverted quite a lot more of their GDP to formal R&D during the 1980s.[15]

The available evidence for 15 OECD countries suggests that this greater commitment to R&D was reflected in the advance of high-technology industries associated with the 'Third Industrial Revolution', and particularly those associated with information and communication technologies (ICTs). The increase in the proportions of GDP going into computing and communications R&D between the late 1970s and the mid-1990s accounted for somewhat more than one-half of the 0.6 percentage point rise in the overall proportion of GDP devoted to R&D expenditures during the same period.

The picture suggested by the conjuncture of rising R&D investment rates from the mid-1970s onwards, the slowing down in the rates of growth of aggregate real output, and a declining rate of investment in

---

[15] Figures for patenting (similarly calculated, but without such problems of missing data) show a rise through most of the observable period, though with an upturn in the 1980s that comes about three years later than for R&D.

175

producers' durable equipment, is one that places in a different perspective the contemporaneous, well-known 'productivity paradox'. Put in more traditional terms, the expansion of R&D outlays (and patenting) in this era betokened short-run 'diminishing returns' in respect of the failure of output to grow commensurately.

This observation seems to run directly counter to the nostrums of the 'new growth theory', which hold that R&D should generate some gains that are non-rivalrous and non-excludable and thus represent positive externalities, albeit allowing for some gains to be privately captured by patenters and so on. There are also some important implications for public policy which, however, I shall defer until after considering the governance issues. For the meantime, it is sufficient to remark that findings for the recent period are in line with earlier historical experience: efforts to develop technologies rise early in the historical sequence, whereas the payoff in output, productivity, and ultimately in living standards, may be considerably postponed.

The latter pattern, however, does seem at face value to fit with the conclusions of a rather different body of theory about the sequencing of economic gains, especially productivity gains, from R&D. One recent line of analysis follows the neo-Austrian approach explored in the work of Hicks on *Capital and Time* (1973). Amendola and Gaffard have recently reinterpreted and applied this in a model that envisages a period of 'technological knowledge-construction' followed by a period of 'operation', or 'knowledge-utilization'.[16] From the foregoing discussion, it appears that the commitment to the generation of technology is relatively more important even than the commitment to construction of capital (in the manner that Rostow and others stressed) during the industrialization spurt. The 'innovative choice', referred to in the title of Amendola and Gaffard's book, is the decision to embark on a major programme of technological development prior to its application, and these authors consider that to be essentially an irreversible investment in developing suitable human resources (technological skills).

---

[16] Amendola and Gaffard, *The Innovative Choice*. The Hicksian schema for 'The Industrial Revolution' (set out first in *The Theory of Economic History*) featured heavy fixed tangible capital formation in the initial phase, accompanied by a slowing of output growth and a lowering of per capita consumption. Evenutally, however, the new capacity raises labour productivity and a surge of faster consumption per capita ensues.

A second approach, which is nearer the economics mainstream, is the recent work on 'general purpose technologies' (GPTs) by Bresnahan, Helpman, Trajtenberg and others. This has antecedents in the new growth and new trade theories on the one hand, and in work in economic history on the other.[17] Central to the theoretical development of the associated model is the notion of an R&D sector, in which the technologies (particularly GPTs) are generated. This, too, is seen as a diversion of labour away from production activities, with short- and medium-term sacrifice in total output. Helpman and Trajtenberg accordingly develop the notion of 'a time to sow and a time to reap'.[18] Lasers—which have now been admitted to the ranks of a GPT—evidently fit this chronology well, but so do broader areas of technological development in which learning was more practical than scientific.[19]

Both the above sets of authors are aware that there is a demand side attached to their models, which emerges more powerfully during the 'time to reap'. In this stage there emerge major 'applications sectors' across which the technologies spread.[20] However, the models are basically supply-driven. To date, the empirical support has been predominantly very descriptive historical accounts of GPTs, alongside reference to older work in economic history such as on the steam engine. The work I have covered so far in this paper can be thought of as stronger empirical support for the highly formalized model-building.

Cross-country Comparisons and Sources of Failure

When we bring in cross-country comparisons, however, a rather different picture begins to emerge. Different economic systems perform very variously in their ability to engage with the two phases of technology generation and technology application, and particularly with the latter. To locate this, we need to take into account some of the literature on the governance of technological development.

The seminal papers of Richard Nelson and Kenneth Arrow posed the problem as one of 'market failure'.[21] The public-good character and

---

[17] See also the discussion of the GPT concept by David and Wright, Chapter 4 of This Volume.
[18] Helpman and Trajtenberg, 'A Time to Sow'.
[19] Lipsey et al., 'What Requires Explanation?'
[20] Bresnahan and Trajtenberg, 'General Purpose Technologies'.
[21] Nelson, 'The Simple Economics'; Arrow, 'Economic Welfare'.

lack of appropriability of much invention established a case for government intervention to support innovation. Arrow, in particular, argued in favour of the 'socially managed economy', in which invention was rewarded by 'prizes', allowing the fruits of invention to be disseminated freely to all users, thus benefiting the economy at large to the maximum. Arrow drew attention to the Lenin Prizes in the USSR as an example of what he had in mind. Subsequently the contrast between prizes and profits became central to comparisons between the economics of science and the economics of innovation.[22] Much innovation could in fact be appropriated, through patenting or other means. Work in the new growth theory clarified the distinction between the non-rivalrous character of innovation, as knowledge, and its varied degree of excludability.

The bigger issue was the implied role for governments if technological knowledge was indeed non-excludable or only partially excludable. This ran into the opposition of those from the 'public choice' school and others, who argued for the contrary notion of 'government failure'. While the 'free market' had its undoubted shortcomings in practice, these paled into insignificance alongside the depredations arising out of uninformed and frequently corrupt governments, hence 'government failure'. Without necessarily becoming fundamentalist about this, the notion of government failure also drew empirical support from those working on innovation, including some who were strongly linked to the 'market failure' perspective.[23] As Nelson described in his book, *The Moon and the Ghetto*, there was a complex balancing act to be performed by the state. In the political economy and political governance arena, however, views polarized between adherents of market failure and adherents of government failure.

Market Failure

In the UK and USA, market failure arguments underpinned the role of the governments in technological development, especially in the years from about 1940 to about 1980. In both countries the exigencies of war first acted to promote and focus the role of government. In the UK, World War I had already had an important effect of experiencing elements of a command economy, which in the sphere of concern to us

---

[22] Dasgupta and David, 'Information Disclosure'.
[23] For example Eads and Nelson, 'Government Support'.

here had led to the organizing of public science and technology (S&T), through the creation of the Department of Scientific and Industrial Research (DSIR) in 1916, and the coordination of technological effort in some of the more fragmented industries in the private sector, through the rise of Engineering Research Associations.[24] World War II renewed the attention paid by the state to technology, embodied in such well-known examples as the jet engine, radar and computing (encryption and code-breaking). There was a corresponding drastic reorganization of technological development in the private sector, whose main effect was relocating R&D functions geographically distant from production activities in many companies.[25] While a number of good reasons were given for this, especially in wartime, it did serve to sharpen demarcations between technology as being suitable for 'gentlemen' while production was for the 'players', to take up the vivid analogy of Donald Coleman and Christine MacLeod.[26]

World War II developments in the USA were more dramatic, linked to the Manhattan Project and the emergence of 'Big Science'.[27] In the aftermath of war, and through the proselytizing efforts of public figures such as Vannevar Bush at the Office of Scientific Research and Development,[28] science came to find a role for itself as a new — and 'endless' — frontier, now that the territorial frontier had long since disappeared. To an extent that is often seriously underestimated, the post-war US government came to lead the development of large-scale technology as well as science in the bulk of science-intensive activities.[29]

These two countries thus developed 'mission-oriented' approaches to new technologies,[30] built around notions of market failure via the so-called 'linear model' of technological development noted above, in which science led invention, which led innovation and commercialization, in turn giving rise to diffusion of the technology and the eventual embodiment of it in production. There were at the same time important differences in the role of government in technology between the US

---

[24] Mowery, 'Industrial Research'.
[25] Heim, 'Industrial Organization'.
[26] Coleman and MacLeod, 'Attitudes to New Techniques'.
[27] Mowery and Rosenberg, *Technology and the Pursuit*, and 'The US National Innovation System'.
[28] Bush, *Science*.
[29] Computing was a case in point. See Flamm, *Targeting the Computer*, and *Creating the Computer*. On US government support for basic research in computer science and non-military applications, see also NRC/CSTB, *Funding a Revolution*.
[30] Ergas, 'The Importance'.

and the UK. In part this was just a matter of resources, where post-war American governments were obviously much better endowed than their British counterparts. But there were deeper differences interfused with this difference in sums of money commanded. One was a question of scale, in which the US system of innovation conceived of S&T as primarily the province of big programmes with big teams ('Big Science'). A second lay on the demand side, with the importance of the government as purchaser, including procurement areas not immediately related to military activities, for example technology for public health.

While it is difficult to measure, there are indications that S&T policy was more strongly motivated in the USA than in the UK. As my colleague, Keith Pavitt, puts it, American governments were driven by fear of the two 'big Cs' — Communism and Cancer. The scale of federal-funded basic research programmes in physics and biomedicine reflected these obsessions, founded not just on the relative political ease of securing resources from the US Congress to satisfy them, but also the model of corporate governance in the USA, so extensively described by Chandler, which was by then becoming dominant.[31] S&T became buried within an organizational system built on 'big business'. To a much greater extent than in most other leading industrial countries, the US federal government has been willing to fund R&D that is actually carried out in laboratories located in the private sector, again first emerging as a wartime exigency. As a typical example, in 1985, 73 per cent of all federally-funded R&D was performed in private industry and only 12 per cent in federal intra-mural laboratories, with the rest being made up of universities and so on; even for basic research only 15 per cent was performed within the federal research establishment.[32] This has the evident effect of giving a more commercial slant to public research programmes and decreasing the risk of 'government failure'.[33]

In addition, the corporate-funded research carried out in the private sector can be organized around larger and better-organized teams, capable of obtaining Marshallian-Schumpeterian economies of scale in R&D. This argument can perhaps be pushed too far. The packaging of

---

[31] Chandler, *The Visible Hand*, and Chandler, *Scale and Scope*.
[32] Mowery and Rosenberg, 'The US National Innovation System', pp. 40–2.
[33] Whether this counts politically as a 'level playing field' is more open to doubt. Arnold and Guy, *Parallel Convergence*; Mowery and Rosenberg, *Technology and the Pursuit*.

R&D functions inside separate corporate divisions oriented to specific product development in many cases led to loss of generic capabilities, even in Chandler's exemplar of Du Pont.[34] Moreover, studies of major corporate laboratories have shown the continuing importance of individuals, who often fitted unsuitably into corporate structures, like Nobel prize-winner Irving Langmuir at General Electric.[35] Louis Galambos's superb study of a century of vaccine development at Merck and its predecessors shows the importance of 'entrepreneurial' technology leaders equipped with both vision and persistence.[36]

The picture can, of course, be easily overstated on the British side as well. Recent research on business history has somewhat reinstated the emergence of big business in the UK, if not to the levels then achieved in the USA, at least well ahead of Continental European rivals such as Germany.[37] But until the advance of new pharmaceuticals firms around the 1960s and 1970s, the indications are that R&D in UK firms remained scattered and individualistic, even if the total outlays involved were respectable.[38] The model for most was typified by the work of Alistair Pilkington on float glass at his eponymous glass company — eleven years of being left alone to do his own thing. While this case was dramatically successful, it does not appear to be overstating things to regard much of this individualistic work as making little progress towards commercial application.

Why Britain eventually scored so successfully in pharmaceuticals, having long lagged in the field, is an unresolved question. Part of it had to do with the arrival of new competitors tapping into the British science system, such as Glaxo when it relocated its HQ from Wellington, New Zealand, to the UK in 1948. But this does not explain the 'pull' effect of British chemistry. A major factor was almost certainly the creation of the UK's National Health System (NHS), which greatly expanded the demand for prescription drugs within the country. In addition, I would add to this oft-stated view that it came about because R&D in chemistry in the private sector is so similar to research in chemistry in the public sector. New chemistry graduates

---

[34] Mowery, 'The Boundaries'.
[35] Wise, *Willis R. Whitney*.
[36] Galambos with Sewell, *Networks of Innovation*. The same author also, it may be noted, takes pains to emphasize the interaction between private and public sectors in the supposedly free-market economy of the USA.
[37] Cassis, *Big Business*.
[38] Edgerton, *Science, Technology*.

from British universities could take their skills from the university lab bench into industry with very little need to adapt to corporate conditions. In effect, the system of research and development in the private sector was modelled on that in the public sector, rather than the other way around. Moreover, production processes were relatively unimportant in an industry where intellectual property rights were the foundation of market success. The creation of 'gentlemen' in the universities thus lost little in transition into industry.

This was not the case in medium-tech industries such as electrical equipment or motor vehicles, where a corporate orientation of R&D was crucial and where Britain performed much more poorly. In such sectors the weakness of British vocational training was severely felt.[39] Whereas in engineering, the US system from early days focused on producing graduates to work at middle levels in large corporations,[40] the UK engineers from similar times (in the late nineteenth century) sought professional status, not least as a way to social status—escaping the popular identification of engineers with dirty-handed mechanics. The rise to centrality of professional institutes and the importance of university degrees testified to this British form of obsession.[41] Despite continuing and even accentuated efforts, it failed to achieve its objective. The most important recent government report on British engineering, the Finniston Report of 1980 (*Engineering Our Future*), pointed this out repeatedly.

It is a stereotype to argue that Britain was good at inventing but weak at commercializing and profiting from invention. Like all stereotypes this is defective, as can be shown not just from the case of chemicals but also more recently from rapid and successful commercialization of new technologies in many service sectors. It does, however, seem to apply to industries in which production processes are critical. In these areas, learning by doing and learning by using and interacting appear to be the cornerstones of technological advance, as opposed to *a priori* formal learning. Britain fell short, seemingly because of inadequate systems for inculcating learning and interaction.

The American mass-production system in principle instituted the corporate hierarchy, and pushed production processes and outputs down to workers who were seen as basically passive. By the 1980s this

---

[39] Walker, 'National Innovation Systems'.
[40] Calvert, *The Mechanical Engineer*.
[41] Von Tunzelmann, 'Engineering and Innovation'.

system was under heavy criticism for its inability to learn and act competitively, when compared with the then rapid advance of East Asian countries. The take-up of advanced processing systems such as robotics or computer-integrated manufacturing was and is notably lower than in some of its major competitors.[42] A decade later, however, the picture looks to most very different. Many reasons have been advanced to explain this. It did not help that countries such as Japan tried to imitate the American system of finance and money markets, and produced a bubble economy. The points here, however, relate more closely to technology.

On the American side, the shortcomings in learning in production processes were partially 'solved' by removing such processes offshore, to cheaper-labour countries in the Far East or the Caribbean, and since NAFTA to or near Mexico. In other words, cost competitiveness was maintained by downgrading wages rather than upgrading methods. But more important, in all probability, has been the rise of *product* applications of new technologies, which are intensive in the use of 'cognitive skills' (to use the terminology of Edward Wolff[43]).

Four elements have combined to bring this about. One is the high levels of human capital formation especially at the college (university) level in the USA, overwhelmingly publicly-funded and for so long a lynchpin of the US system of innovation, which produced people in abundance with the requisite cognitive skills.[44] This has gone with a rebirth of interlinkages between universities and industry.[45] A second is the advantages of an early *scientific* start engendered by the commitment of large-scale government funds to technologies which finally seem to be paying off, as noted above. A third is the natural focus of the American system of corporate governance on product development, as represented for example in the Chandlerian M-form company, with its divisions being based on product ranges rather than functional differences.[46] A fourth, however, is the emergence of upstart firms capable of either rapid growth to large size (Compaq, Amgen, Cisco Systems, and so on) or of being acquired for their ideas by older and slower-moving firms (for example dedicated biotechnology and genomic firms). Some of the new entrants, it is true, were initially protected

---

[42] Mowery and Rosenberg, 'The US National Innovation System'.
[43] Wolff, 'Technology'.
[44] Nelson, 'US Industrial Competitiveness'.
[45] Mowery and Rosenberg, 'The US National Innovation System', pp. 53–4.
[46] See von Tunzelmann, *Technology and Industrial Progress*, and sources therein.

by monopolistic supply arrangements with older firms from whom they later cut loose (for example Intel and Microsoft supplying IBM), but in general this emergence of new giants contradicts the Chandler position of the stability of established corporations in the face of new technologies. Many of the more dynamic firms such as Hewlett-Packard in effect dismantled their M-form structures and replaced them with more 'organic' systems that were being constantly reconfigured. The high mobility of American business society was a significant determinant of this fluidity.

On the Asian side, a major problem was being 'locked into' dependence for commercial success on leadership in manufacturing processes. By the mid-1990s these were becoming less and less important in overall added value of the goods and services finally sold. Competition from cheaper-labour countries and globalized supply systems undercut margins in production, while the very success of new technologies in leader countries such as Japan had a similar effect. Profit margins were shifting towards marketing and distribution, especially in attached services, while they were being whittled away in production. Prospects for radical change in countries such as Japan or Korea were limited by the long separation between universities and industry in those countries, and the relative absence of a base in frontier science, to which scholars such as Nathan Rosenberg had for some time been drawing attention.[47]

The results suggest that complementarity between technology generation and technology application is ultimately required, though either can be commercially effective in the medium term. Germany has been castigated by its own scholars for the inadequacy of its university system for innovation, though this has to be set against the achievements of the Max Planck institutes and their predecessors.[48] On the other hand, what especially promote the German system are first, the well-recognized depth of training offered further down the technical scale, and second, the existence of bridging institutions for technology transfer. The various bodies—Fraunhofer institutes, Steinbeis foundations, AN institutes, and so on, partly complement but also partly compete with one another to engage in technology transfer. The more they succeed in this, the more funds they obtain to carry on.

---

[47] Rosenberg, *Exploring*.
[48] Keck, 'The National System', p. 147.

The South Korean case is another example of how government technology policies appear to work better when the resources are distributed according to objective outcomes—the chaebol were rewarded in terms of concessionary finance according to their relative success in expanding exports, and equally such subsidies were withdrawn if their exports failed. By the early 1990s, however, clientism was seen as becoming rife in Korea, and the more pernicious sides of 'government failure' were becoming evident.

Government Failure

The supreme example of government failure of recent times, at least among industrialized or partially industrialized countries, may be taken to be the USSR and the collapse of Communism in Eastern Europe. This is popularly seen as an economy (or set of economies) that tried to dispense with the powers of the market, and thus laid itself open to excessive reliance on the government and the Communist party regime. In the perspective of Hayek,[49] Communism through the one-party state ignored the benefits of decentralized decision-making through markets and overburdened itself with the sheer extent of information required to set targets centrally using non-market criteria.[50] There arose the 'shortage economy', in which demand was equated to supply through queuing.[51]

No doubt there is much validity in these views, but in turning to the technology system, the author would argue that there were more similarities than contrasts with problems in western economies, and especially in those of the 'mission-oriented' countries such as the USA and UK. If anything, the USSR practised more decentralization, or at least division of labour, than in the West. Yet equally there is no doubt that the technology system in the Former Soviet Union failed dismally. The situation clearly needs some care in analysis.[52]

The regime maintained a high commitment to technology—as well as to capital formation—throughout. Most estimates reckon R&D intensities in the post-war period to be higher than the top western countries, though to be sure somewhere between one-half and three-

---

[49] Hayek, 'The Use of Knowledge'.
[50] Nove, *The Soviet Economic System*, ch. 4.
[51] Kornai, *Economics of Shortage*.
[52] This section draws heavily on the chapter on the USSR in von Tunzelmann, *Technology and Industrial Progress*.

quarters of this was military R&D, and the intensities tailed off as economic problems grew during the 1980s.[53]

In relation to the precepts advanced by Arrow, the USSR system envisaged technological development as a matter of acquiring information. In the case of the military R&D it would have to accumulate this itself or obtain it from the West through espionage. Much the same applied to civilian technology, with the domestic R&D system intended to supply incremental product innovations, and borrowing from the West to supply more radical product innovations. In terms of the latter, the USSR fell further and further behind, especially in the high-tech sectors such as computers, semiconductors and chemicals. Transferring technology was, as the successful countries of East Asia were showing, much more than a matter of acquiring information, and involved accumulating *knowledge*.

The fundamental inadequacy of the Soviet system lay in the segregation of science and technology from industry, a practice which dated back to Tsarist times. A strictly 'linear' process of S&T feeding through into industrial expansion was envisaged. The division of R&D labour was rigidly hierarchical. At the top was the Academy of Sciences, responsible for basic research (and separated from teaching). Below this came the proliferation of research institutes, intended for applied research. Below these again there came to be added a tier of design bureaux, with the task of specific product development. At the bottom came the manufacturing enterprises, which were construed as passive users of technologies rather than their producers. This was about as far removed from the 'chain-linked' model of feedback in R&D as it was possible to get.

Except in military R&D, where state support was far more generous and special considerations applied, the system was unable to deliver what was wanted. Design bureaux spewed out designs that no manufacturers implemented—during the 1960s and 1970s only 17 per cent of designs in the important control and instruments sector were actually utilized.[54] Manufacturers were forced back on their own limited in-house capabilities ('dwarf workshops') to keep machinery working, quite apart from improving it.

---

[53] The USSR figures are also probably overstated by comparison with Frascati Manual definitions in the West, see Glaziev and Schneider, *Research and Development Management*.
[54] Amann and Cooper, *Industrial Innovation*.

Spillovers were even more difficult to attain horizontally. The 'branch' system of inter-war commissariats and post-war ministries imposed equally rigid horizontal demarcations between industries. Each maintained its own vertical system of research institutes, design bureaux and enterprises, with no cross-communication and hence more waste. The kinds of horizontal applications envisaged by the 'applications sectors' phase of the GPT framework were seriously restricted.

Despite throwing relatively large amounts of money at problems of industrial technology, the Soviet system achieved remarkably little, and in general went backwards from the 1950s in its position vis-à-vis the advanced industrial countries. This stemmed from its disconnection between the generation of technology and its use, both downstream in the directly associated sector and laterally in other sectors. The boundaries between manufacturing and services, in which for example the service content of goods was becoming increasingly important—boundaries which were weakening in the West—were maintained in the centrally planned economy. Learning by interacting was almost totally absent, as manufacturers struggled to meet urgent plan targets. The Arrow prognosis for the technologically progressive 'socially managed economy' failed in practice, in part because the enterprises were only weakly coupled to market signals on the demand side, and because technological accumulation was treated as a matter of producing and acquiring *information*, when what was needed was the accumulation of effective *knowledge* in the context of production. This held above all in using, adapting and extending technology to new areas of application.

'Networking Failure' and the System of Innovation

Thus, during the 1980s, on the one side lay a communist technology system that was constructed upon a rigid division of labour—not a market system to be sure, because of centrally imposed prices, but one which in other respects had a market-like structure. On the other side, in the USA, was a capitalist technology system which, to the extent it was successful, greatly depended on injections of funding and other support from governments. While facing competition in the military sector from the former, this was encountering serious competitive threats from the Asian system which placed primary emphasis on process innovation in the industrial sector.

While it seems reasonable to describe the USSR as a classic case of government failure, and the USA as exemplifying certain cases of market failure, there is also a sense in which neither label really captures the basic issue. Let me give another example, drawn from work with which I have been more personally involved. This is the case of New Zealand, which, under a Labour government from the mid-1980s, set out to reform its technology system, and indeed its entire industrial and governmental system, on the combined presumptions of market failure and government failure. Reasoning from contemporaneous developments in economic theory, especially 'public choice' theories of political governance, principal-agent and transaction cost theories of corporate governance, and contestability theories of competitive structure, New Zealand's government decided on a radical, top-down reorganization of an economic system that was widely regarded as having failed to deliver adequate economic performance.

In the sphere of technology, the combined effects of market failure and government failure were to be addressed by perfecting markets for technology. In a small country, there were limits as to how much overt competition could be introduced, but ideally the 'markets' could be made more contestable by threatening a (monopolistic) incumbent with being supplanted by a new entrant. Although this policy produced dramatic changes in the organization and responsibilities of research institutes and associated bodies, it focused almost exclusively on the *production* of S&T. Its weaknesses in providing inducements for the application and adoption of the technologies thus generated or adapted have become evident in the past few years. In many respects, the drive for a market-based system paradoxically reproduced some of the deficiencies of the state-based Soviet system, especially its over-reliance on a vertical division of S&T labour.

It is only now coming to be realized that such a system must place equal if not greater emphasis on the take-up of technologies and on feedback. Recent policy recommendations made to the New Zealand government stress paying greater attention to 'absorptive capacity', especially in the private sector. While some of this is out of the hands of the government, the latter does not simply have to be passive in this arena; it might follow the example of the German innovation system, described briefly above. A broader and in some ways more relevant example is that of Taiwan.[55] The Taiwanese spurt into high-tech

---

[55] This discussion is drawn from Kim and von Tunzelmann, 'The Dynamics and Alignment'.

industry was initiated by the arrival of foreign multinational companies, as in many other parts of the globe. The national government then moved in to try to commandeer some of these developments, which it did through an intensive technology policy. The policy created the research institute, ITRI, which brought back overseas Chinese, especially from North America, but also encouraged its skilled employees to go forth and set up their own small companies. High inward and outward mobility of human capital was thus at the top of the agenda. Finally, local governments underpinned these efforts through establishing science parks which served as a base for the spin-off companies. Essentially what happened in Taiwan was that three types of networks—the foreign companies, the national government, and the local governments—'aligned' with one another to overcome 'coordination failures' in the system of innovation.

'Network failures' as defined in the author's recent work are of two kinds. The simpler form is the failure to form networks in situations where linkages might prove to be an effective form of governance. For these purposes, networks are very broadly defined as any form of interconnection between organizations that does not take the form of either a market or a (simple) hierarchy (in some of the governance literature, networks are allocated a much more precise role, but for simplicity this is overlooked here). The failure of economic development in Latin America over the past half-century, for instance, is often ascribed to the near-absence of the 'right sort' of networks. The more complex form of network failure is the one discussed—several networks pertaining to the issue do exist, but they do not 'align' with one another in the sense of pulling in the same directions. For example, British banking and British industry both developed important networks over the past century or more, but are often accused of clashing with each other and thus contributing to economic retardation. Situations where the 'wrong sort' of networks emerge—for instance, the British 'old boy network' or the Mafia—often give rise to alignment problems and therefore networking failure in this sense. In the case of Taiwan, the networks generated by foreign multinationals, by the state, and by local governments, each had different objectives, but these objectives were all compatible rather than conflictual.

'Market failure' deals with failure in markets, 'government failure' with failure in state hierarchies, and 'corporate failure' with failure in corporate hierarchies. 'Networking failure' deals with failure in the remaining form of governance, i.e. networks in this broad sense of the term, and the present argument is that for technology use this may be more significant than any of the other types of failure, still more so when technology use requires chain-linked feedbacks into technology generation. The UK based its post-war technology policy on a 'market failure' view similar to that in the US, but only in certain areas like pharmaceuticals could it overcome 'network failures' defined by social and institutional as well as technological determinants.

Implications and Conclusion

The prognostications follow from the foregoing analysis of historical experience. The diffusion of new information and communication technologies in modern times has been very different across sectors. Their diffusion within some service sectors has been rapid — not only in relatively advanced service sectors such as finance, but in others previously regarded as more backward, such as retailing or tourism. Yet, it seems likely that in manufacturing we are at present only scratching the surface, especially in the so-called 'low-tech' and 'medium-tech' branches of manufacturing.

It thus appears that we are entering a period in which the focus may shift from generating IT to applying it across a widened spectrum of economic activities. In doing so, the 'diminishing returns' period of increasing R&D costs per unit of output, which according to the figures above characterized the 1980s and earlier decades, might be expected to give way to the kind of 'increasing returns' from (horizontal) spillovers predicted by the new growth theory and so on. Further down the line, other new technological paradigms (or GPTs) such as biotechnology and 'smart materials', which also hold out prospects of cross-sectoral applications, may be expected in the future to move from developments in depth to developments in breadth, and ultimate productivity benefits.

The message of the second part of this paper is that such spillovers are by no means automatic. They require firstly high mobility, as seen in their different ways in the cases of Taiwanese networks or the American high-tech sectors. This is because some technologies prove difficult to transfer purely in the form of codified knowledge. Systems like that of the USSR (or more recently New Zealand) that have tried to rely on codification alone have done poorly. Knowledge is best embodied in people rather than in artefacts or information, so if people move, knowledge is more likely to move too. Bruland's study of the attempts to create a cotton industry in nineteenth-century Norway, however, suggests that even movement of people may not suffice.[56] The second factor has to be 'absorptive capacity' on the part of the technology user. Encouraging the employment of people equipped with knowledge may help this, but the context may differ so much as to render the existing knowledge scarcely relevant. Carrying out one's own R&D may be integral to absorbing technology, even if it does not appear to be doing anything remarkably new.[57]

The third requirement, which serves to combine these two, is for the pervasiveness of learning. Hayek was quite right that a centrally planned economy such as the USSR could not handle the amount of information (or knowledge) required to produce an economically efficient system. The 'centrally planned' M-form corporation which Chandler describes has, however, similar weaknesses of its own. Separation into quasi-autonomous product divisions subject to an overriding financial constraint can create problems similar to the branch system in the Soviet economy; the incentive for division managers to gain more of the corporation's financial pie, and so expand their own spheres of influence, may actually reduce the tendency to allow spillovers of knowledge across divisional boundaries, rather than promoting it. This has allegedly been particularly serious in the UK.[58] Corporate as well as political systems which encourage both transfer out and transfer in of knowledge can be expected to perform much better.

Governments have to share in learning, just as much as the corporate sector.[59] During the stage of technology generation ('the time to sow'), it may have to be accepted that the costs of R&D are going to rise relative to resulting output. Diminishing returns from R&D, as appear to have arisen during the 1980s, are not an argument for ducking these obligations, although this is how the UK sometimes seems to have viewed things. During the ensuing applications phase—'the time to reap'—it is evident that policies should be geared as much, or more, towards adoption of technologies as to their generation.[60] It is striking that, although there is a small but serious literature that con-

---

[56] Bruland, *British Technology*.
[57] Cohen and Levinthal, 'Innovation and Learning'.
[58] Tylecote, 'Time Horizons'.
[59] Von Tunzelmann, 'Government Policy'.
[60] See, for example, David and Foray, 'Accessing', and Smith, 'Interactions'.

trasts technology policies for production with those for their use, almost all the discussion at governmental level is about the former (tax credits for R&D, venture capital, and so on). For the future, it seems to me that countries that focus their policies upon extending the adoption of technologies will be those that fare best. These will be those that gain most from any 'increasing returns'.

At the same time, simply concentrating on technology applications without paying comparable attention to generating technology is unlikely to be entirely successful, either. Such strategies run the risk of creating a repeat of the Japanese situation, of being boxed into old corners when the world is moving into new pastures. To complete the structure and avoid 'networking failures', it would seem essential to maintain close links between technology production and technology use.

Note. This paper draws in part on two previous papers which are mentioned below, though taking them in a different direction. I am grateful to the many people who gave useful suggestions relating to those papers.

References

Amann, R., and J. Cooper (eds). *Industrial Innovation in the Soviet Union.* New Haven: Yale University Press, 1982.
Amendola, M., and J.-L. Gaffard. *The Innovative Choice,* Oxford: Blackwell, 1988.
Arnold, E., and K. Guy. *Parallel Convergence: National Strategies in Information Technology.* London: Pinter, 1986.
Arrow, K.J. 'Economic Welfare and the Allocation of Resources of Invention.' In *The Rate and Direction of Inventive Activity: Economic and Social Factors,* edited by R.R. Nelson, 164–81. Princeton: Princeton University Press, 1962.
Bresnahan, T., and M. Trajtenberg. 'General Purpose Technologies: "Engines of Growth"' *Journal of Econometrics,* 65 (1995): 83–108.
Bruland, K. *British Technology and European Industrialization: Norwegian Textile Industry in the Mid-Nineteenth Century.* Cambridge: Cambridge University Press, 1989.
Bush, V. *Science: The Endless Frontier.* Washington: National Science Foundation, 1945.
Calvert, M.A. *The Mechanical Engineer in America, 1830–1910: Professional Cultures in Conflict.* Baltimore: Johns Hopkins Press, 1967.

Cassis, Y. *Big Business: The European Experience in the Twentieth Century*. Oxford: Oxford University Press, 1997.
Chandler, A.D., Jr. *The Visible Hand: The Managerial Revolution in American Business*. Cambridge MA: Belknap Press, 1977.
———. *Scale and Scope: The Dynamics of Industrial Capitalism*. Cambridge MA: Belknap Press, 1990.
Cohen, W.M., and D. Levinthal. 'Innovation and Learning: The Two Faces of R&D.' *Economic Journal* 99 (1989): 569–96.
Cohen, W.M., and D. Levinthal. 'Absorptive Capacity: A New Perspective on Learning and Innovation.' *Administrative Science Quarterly* 35 (1990): 128–52.
Coleman, D.C., and C. MacLeod. 'Attitudes to New Techniques: British Businessmen, 1800–1950.' *Economic History Review* 39 (1986): 588–611.
Dasgupta, P., and P.A. David. 'Information Disclosure and the Economics of Science and Technology.' In *Arrow and the Ascent of Modern Economic Theory*, edited by G. Feiwel, 519–42. London: Macmillan, 1987.
David, P.A., and D. Foray. 'Accessing and Expanding the Science and Technology Knowledge Base.' *STI Review* 16 (1995): 13–68.
Eads, G., and R.R. Nelson. 'Government Support of Advanced Civilian Technology.' *Public Policy* 19 (1971): 405–27.
Edgerton, D. *Science, Technology and the British Industrial 'Decline', 1870–1970*. Cambridge: Cambridge University Press, 1996.
Ergas, H. 'The Importance of Technology Policy.' In *Economic Policy and Technological Performance*, edited by P. Dasgupta and P. Stoneman, 51–96. Cambridge: Cambridge University Press, 1987.
Federico, P.J. 'Historical Patent Statistics 1791–1961.' *Journal of the Patent Office Society* 46 (1964): 89–171.
Finniston, M. *Engineering Our Future: Report of the Committee of Inquiry into the Engineering Profession*, Cmnd 7794. London: HMSO, 1980.
Flamm, K. *Targeting the Computer: Government Support and International Competition*. Washington: Brookings Institution, 1987.
———. *Creating the Computer*. Washington DC: Brookings Institution, 1988.
Freeman, C. and L. Soete. *The Economics of Industrial Innovation*, 3rd edn., London: Pinter, 1997.
Galambos, L. with J.E. Sewell. *Networks of Innovation: Vaccine Development at Merck, Sharp & Dohme, and Mulford, 1895–1995*. Cambridge: Cambridge University Press, 1995.
Glaziev, S. and C.M. Schneider (eds). *Research and Development Management in the Transition to a Market Economy*. Laxenburg: IIASA, 1993.
Grupp, H. 'Appropriation of Innovation Rents in a Science-driven Market.' *Industrial and Corporate Change* 9 (2000): 143–72.
Heim, C.E. 'Industrial Organization and Regional Development in Inter-war Britain.' *Journal of Economic History* 43 (1983): 931–52.
Helpman, E. (ed.). *General Purpose Technologies and Economic Growth*. Cambridge MA: MIT Press, 1998.

Helpman, E. and Trajtenberg, M. 'A Time to Sow and a Time to Reap: Growth Based on General Purpose Technologies.' In *General Purpose Technologies and Economic Growth*, edited by E. Helpman, 85–120. Cambridge MA: MIT Press, 1998.

Hicks, J.R. *Capital and Time*, Oxford: Clarendon Press, 1973.

Historical Statistics of the United States: Colonial Times to 1970. Washington: U.S. Bureau of the Census, 1975.

Hoffmann, W.G. *British Industry, 1700–1950*, transl. W.O. Henderson and W.H. Chaloner. Oxford: Blackwell, 1955.

_____. *Das Wachstum der Deutschen Wirtschaft seit der Mitte des 19 Jahrhunderts*. Berlin: Springer, 1965.

Keck, O. 'The National System for Technical Innovation in Germany.' In *National Innovation Systems: A Comparative Analysis*, edited by R.R. Nelson, 115–57. Oxford University Press: New York, 1993.

Kim, S.R., and N. von Tunzelmann. 'The Dynamics and Alignment of 'Networks of Networks': Explaining Taiwan's Successful IT Specialization.' Mimeo, SPRU/SEI, Sussex, 1998.

Kline, S.J. *Conceptual Foundations for Multidisciplinary Thinking*. Stanford: Stanford University Press, 1995.

Kornai, J. *The Economics of Shortage*. Amsterdam: North-Holland, 1980.

Lipsey, R.G., C. Bekar and K. Carlaw. 'What Requires Explanation?' In *General Purpose Technologies and Economic Growth*, edited by E. Helpman, 55–84. Cambridge MA: MIT Press, 1998.

Maddison, A. *Dynamic Forces in Capitalist Development*, Oxford: Oxford University Press, 1991.

Mokyr, J. *The Lever of Riches: Technology Creativity and Economic Progress*. Oxford: Oxford University Press, 1990.

Mowery, D.C. 'Industrial Research, Firm Size, Growth, and Survival, 1921–1946.' *Journal of Economic History* 43 (1983): 953–80.

_____. 'The Boundaries of the US Firm in R&D.' In *Coordination and Information: Historical Perspectives on the Organization of Enterprise*, edited by N.R. Lamoreaux and D.M.G. Raff, 147–82. Chicago: University of Chicago Press, 1995.

Mowery, D.C., and N. Rosenberg. *Technology and the Pursuit of Economic Growth*. Cambridge University Press: New York, 1989.

_____. 'The US National Innovation System.' In *National Innovation Systems: A Comparative Analysis*, edited by R.R. Nelson, 29–75. Oxford University Press: New York, 1993.

Nelson, R.R. 'The Simple Economics of Basic Scientific Research.' *Journal of Political Economy* 67 (1959): 297–306.

_____. *The Moon and the Ghetto*. New York: W.W. Norton, 1977.

_____. 'US Industrial Competitiveness: Where Did It Come From and Where Did It Go?' *Research Policy* 19 (1990): 117–32.

Nelson, R.R. (ed.) *National Innovation Systems: A Comparative Analysis*. Oxford University Press: New York, 1993.

Nove, A. *The Soviet Economic System*. London: Allen & Unwin, 1977.

Rosenberg, N. *Exploring the Black Box: Technology, Economics, and History*. Cambridge: Cambridge University Press, 1994.

Schmookler, J. *Invention and Economic Growth*. Cambridge MA: Harvard University Press, 1966.

———. *Patents, Invention, and Economic Change: Data and Selected Essays*, edited by Zvi Griliches and Leonid Hurwicz. Cambridge MA: Harvard University Press, 1972.

Senker, J. 'Tacit Knowledge and Models of Innovation.' *Industrial and Corporate Change* 4 (1995): 425–48.

Smith, K. 'Interactions in Knowledge Systems: Foundations, Policy Implications and Empirical Methods.' *STI Review* 16 (1995): 69–102.

Tylecote, A. 'Time Horizons of Management Decisions: Causes and Effects.' *Journal of Economic Studies* 14 (1987): 51–64.

von Hayek, F.A. 'The Use of Knowledge in Society.' *American Economic Review* 35 (1945): 519–30.

von Tunzelmann, G.N. *Technology and Industrial Progress: The Foundations of Economic Growth*, Aldershot, UK: Edward Elgar, 1995a.

———. 'Government Policy and the Long-run Dynamics of Competitiveness.' *Structural Change and Economic Dynamics* 6 (1995): 1–20.

———. 'Engineering and Innovation in the Industrial Revolutions.' *Interdisciplinary Science Reviews* 1 (1997): 67–77.

———. 'Technology Generation, Technology Use and Economic Growth.' *European Review of Economic History* 4, no. 3 (2000): 121–46.

von Tunzelmann, G.N., and E. Anderson. 'Technologies and Skills in Long-run Perspective.' Mimeo, SPRU/IDS, Sussex, 1999.

Walker, W. 'National Innovation Systems: Britain.' In *National Innovation Systems: A Comparative Analysis*, edited by R.R. Nelson, 158–91. Oxford University Press: New York, 1993.

Wise, G. *Willis R. Whitney, General Electric, and the Origins of US Industrial Research*. New York: Columbia University Press, 1985.

Wolff, E. 'Technology and the Demand for Skills.' *OECD STI Review* 18 (1996): 95–123.

PART TWO
Changes in Economic Regimes and Ideologies

The challenge of understanding *transitions* is the unifying theme that runs through the six essays that comprise this Part. One of the most obvious ways in which historical studies can improve our grasp of the workings of economic systems is by focusing upon the dynamics of adjustments and transitions in response to 'shocks' that disrupt established regimes. Mainstream economic theory focuses, largely for analytical reasons, upon equilibrium states of markets and economies. It has less to say about the general nature of the behaviour of economic systems that are 'pushed out of equilibrium' by exogenous disturbances, and in particular about the 'out of equilibrium' behaviour of systems in which there is a multiplicity of equilibrium regimes towards which the system could move.

Simplistic notions of path dependence might suggest that 'historical events' — such as the breakdown of political structures or of informal social norms, or radical advances in scientific and technological knowledge — could propel the economy onto an entirely new course, which would be sustained until the next 'shock'. The reality, however, is different in many respects. One quite basic point concerning the dynamics of transitions to new regimes that warrants closer study than it usually receives is this: in the aftermath of the most major economic disruptions the influence of the past is almost never swept away entirely.

Thus, just as new policies are usually predicated on the failures or inadequacies of the old, so governments and other actors in transitional economies evaluate the procedures and organizational arrangements that were previously in place, discarding only those that appear to be grossly dysfunctional from an economic standpoint, or symbolically associated in inextricable ways with political or social features of a rejected regime; for the rest, modification and amelioration is the path of least resistance. Moreover, new institutional directives are likely to respond to historical success stories elsewhere—in other countries or in other times.

A further way in which continuity shapes responses to change and crisis is via the actions of the actors towards whom the policies are directed—the consumers, entrepreneurs and workers in a new economic system, for example. For the mass of these participants, who may well be motivated more by pragmatism than principles, the transition to new *modi operandi* and *vivendi* is likely to be gradual, incomplete and governed by cultural background and memories of previous disappointments, rather than unreservedly impelled by ideological promise. Sometimes the reaction to past experience takes the form of conscious rational calculation, whereas elsewhere it is simply latent in the habituated behaviours of individuals, including their associations and patterns of social communication.

Nicholas Crafts' study is concerned with dynamic reconfigurations of state policies and institutions that occur as developing economies pass successfully through initial industrialization and begin competing effectively in international markets for more complex manufactured products and services. This is the vantage-point from which he proposes to re-examine the institutional foundations of the East Asian 'economic miracle', and assess the significance of the crisis that overtook these newly industrializing countries (NICs) at the end of the 1990s.

Crafts' essay is explicit in arguing for the usefulness of adopting a broader historical perspective within which to view the rapid transition of the NICs in the final quarter of the twentieth century. As a point of departure for understanding the institutional requirements of 'catch-up' modernization, he takes Alexander Gerschenkron's well-known model of 'economic backwardness', modifying and updating it in the light of recent work on the microeconomics of economic development. Gerschenkron's classic schema was first proposed as an interpretation of the ways in which the industrializing economies of western Europe during the second half of the nineteenth century managed to respond to the challenges of their 'later-comer' status vis-à-vis Britain. The core idea is that the 'follower-nations' of that era, eschewing attempts at institutional imitation, took paths whose main features diverged markedly from the liberal, laissez-faire policies and export-market orientation that had been central in Britain's ascent as 'the workshop of the world'. In other words, they were able to begin to catch up with the leader by embracing proactive State policies and developing new institutional forms that linked banking and finance with industrial enterprise.

Gerschenkron's framework has been elaborated in an important dimension by Crafts' recognition that, just as there can be institutional innovation and adaptation, institutions and policies that serve well in launching a 'catch-up process' may also be subject to obsolescence. Moreover, at a later stage they may begin to exert effects that actually inhibit continuation of rapid economic growth. Thus the bureaucratic machinery of State-led planning and control, through which savings were formerly mobilized and channelled into the formation of infrastructure capital and directly productive industrial facilities, can grow too cumbersome to respond effectively to changing international market opportunities. Networks that arrange financing for mutually supporting projects may cease to co-ordinate investments that yield large positive spillovers and instead become defensive instruments to avert or postpone the exposure of bad investment decisions, which have the potential to cause embarrassingly heavy financial losses. Similarly, the very same means by which government agencies promoted the transfer of technologies from the more advanced economies, and their adaptation for local application, eventually may be perceived to be inhibiting the development of indigenous firms' capabilities to produce significant technological innovations.

This line of argument leads Crafts towards a cautiously optimistic interpretation of the shock that overtook the East Asian economies in the 1990s. Although the 'Asian Tigers'' developmental regimes were likely eventually to have been substantially transformed by the waning importance of state-directed initiatives and the concomitant restructuring of their banking and capital market institutions, that outcome was not foreordained. The resumption of vigorous growth might well have been seriously impaired during a long-drawn-out, partial and uncertain process in which entrenched institutional interests resisted radical reforms — were it not for the precipitating cathartic events of the 1997 financial crisis.

The study of comparative economic systems makes use of an alternative conceptualization of transitions, one that is not less concerned with institutional change, but is temporally more sharply demarcated and less bound up with institutional innovations and adaptations of the kind that Gerschenkron (and Crafts) regard as essential for the process of economic development and long-term growth.

This notion of 'transition' is grounded upon the classification of economic systems according to multiple criteria, such as (a) the architecture of decision-making for resource allocation (centralized or decentralized); (b) the nature of the mechanisms for information and co-ordination (plan or market); (c) property rights arrangements (state or private); and (d) characteristic organizational incentives (conducive or detrimental to effective corporate governance). Therefore, a transition in this sense refers to the process whereby an economy moves between two distinctive system configurations defined in those dimensions.

Comprehensive regime changes of that kind, almost necessarily, are propelled by events originating in the politico-military sphere, which makes the foregoing schema well suited for the purposes of Christopher Davis and James Foreman-Peck's approach to understanding the transition process in the post-Soviet Russian economy. Characterizing the situation prevailing in the late Soviet era as one that exhibited hallmarks of a typical wartime 'shortage economy' created by a centralized, non-market 'command' system, the authors undertake a comparative historical analysis of the two post-World War episodes in which Britain's economy underwent conversion from its wartime 'command' configuration back to a decentralized market regime.

Davis and Foreman-Peck show that the rapid demobilization and liberalization of the extensive wartime system of controls in 1918 led to a speculative surge in prices in Britain, followed by a slump as the Treasury reacted to quench the inflation. All this added significantly to the unavoidable disorganization and 'noise' that would have been likely to accompany the return to peace-time production; the haste to re-establish sterling convertibility at the pre-war exchange rate made it even more difficult to re-employ ex-servicemen in the sectors of the economy linked to the export industries. By comparison with that painful 'big bang' style of transition, the government in 1945 pursued a gradualist policy, in which wartime rationing and exchange controls were removed sequentially. This yielded a comparatively benign transition for Britain, and a post-war decade of macroeconomic performance that — perhaps because of the currency devaluation, forced by the premature removal of exchange controls — was very respectable, especially when judged by the historical standard of the preceding half-century.

Commenting on the post-Soviet transition from the historical perspective of Britain's two quite different experiences of readjustment from a wartime economy, Davis and Foreman-Peck remark upon the two-fold respect in which the failures associated with the commitment to a 'big bang' policy rather than a gradualist strategy can be ascribed in good measure to the absence of a credible state that could have effectively intervened and guided the process of transition. Initially, the Russian state's loss of legitimacy and the desire of the 'democratic' forces to avoid policies that would provide any role sustaining the power of the old political apparatus encouraged the belief that spontaneous generation of markets would suffice in lieu of positive state action. This meant that there was little guidance for the productive allocation of resources during the initial phase of price liberalization and deregulation, which exacerbated the losses of output due to co-ordination failures, and opened the door to the misappropriation of raw materials and intermediate goods for quick conversion into sequestered bank deposits.

A still more serious source of failures lay in the poor sequencing of reforms, and the slowness with which the state moved to re-establish a secure fiscal base, put in place legal and other market facilitating institutions, and introduce effective governance structures for the nominally privatized enterprises that had passed into the control of their former 'inside' managers. The lesson from this experience, which might well be the lesson of other failed regime transformations, is that these rarely succeed as spontaneous processes in the absence of sustained impetus and guidance from some quite 'visible (political) hands'. Moreover, the rapid emergence of a functioning decentralized economy without a supporting scaffolding of pre-existing market institutions, however rudimentary, is an historical rarity indeed.

Carol Leonard's essay focuses on a particular aspect of the post-Soviet transition from collectivized modes of production, one that is not discussed in Davis and Foreman-Peck's comparative historical analysis of industrial restructuring. This is the failure of the effort to extend the policy of privatization to farmland, and the collapse of marketed output from the agricultural sector's large *koholz* units. Leonard shows the two phenomena to have been interrelated in a number of ways. Rather than seeking private holdings on which they could become independent farmers, agricultural cultivators who maintained their attachment to the former state farms were thereby afforded access to land for market gardens, as well as supplies of fertilizers and other inputs for use in expanding vegetable production. That is exactly what they did, at the expense of grain production. Another connecting factor was the exogenous fall in world grain prices, which pushed the terms of trade more strongly in favour of vegetable production, and so enhanced the value of the benefit provided by free access to commune resources for market gardening. Retention of such benefits was therefore one among the motivations to resist privatization.

But, as Leonard argues, such resistance would be an economically rational act only where embarking upon independent farming did not promise corresponding larger net benefits for the individual cultivator. Here is where the risks surrounding the irreversible decision to exit from the collective farming community became a critical consideration, especially for people who had no prior experience as independent cultivators and limited access to information about the costs that that might entail. The increased volatility of market prices, and the uncertainties surrounding the access that an independent producer might have to rural transportation and marketing facilities, were considerations that became more and more worrisome with the increasing disorganization of the economy at large, and so further weakened the attractions of land privatization.

Leonard finds that similar, rational grounds existed on previous occasions in Russian agrarian history, when the peasantry resisted government directed agrarian reform programmes whose effect would have been the attenuation or complete extinguishing of cultivator's rights to communal land and their replacement by private property holdings. Early in the twentieth century, the peasantry's reaction against the Stolypin reforms was reinforced by a climate of uncertainty surrounding the security of private property, and adverse external market conditions that diminished expectations of net gains from the expanded productive capacity that the proposed restructuring of commune arrangements was intended to achieve.

Historically, such resistance typically manifested itself in outbursts of violence on the part of commune members who, lacking other means to register their opposition to the policy dictates of distant government ministers, were stirred to collective action by local leaders. In the post-Soviet era, however, resistance was channelled politically — to the representatives of the agricultural block in the Duma, which effectively stymied the programmes of land privatization in the farm sector that had been initiated by reformers in the executive branch with the encouragement of Western economic advisers and international agencies such as the World Bank. Thus the story related by Leonard cannot be read as one of a doggedly irrational agrarian population's ability repeatedly to block efforts to introduce more efficient institutional arrangements in Russian agriculture. Quite the contrary, for the existence of rational grounds for the observed behaviour of the cultivators suggests the hopeful conclusion that the basis for opposition could be removed by better-designed programmes of reform.

In the historical episodes discussed in Leonard's essay, the details of timing also mattered. The chances for successful restructuring appear to have been adversely affected by the length of the preceding period during which cultivators remained without opportunities to acquire independent farming skills and market experience; the policies of implementation exposed an initially slow and halting privatization campaign to the emergence of negative feedback conditions that further increased individual agents' reasons to cling to the *status quo ante*. Leonard's observations regarding the microeconomics of the process, and the resulting highly contingent and path dependent character of its transition dynamics, show that sometimes 'history matters' in the small, rather than in the macro-level aspects of institutional regime transitions. These observations also lead Leonard to suggest strategies whereby government agencies might create a more supportive economic environment, and provide more complete information about both costs and benefits of independent farming, thereby creating an initial movement into privatization that would itself have the effect of dissipating rather than strengthening the attachment of the remaining members of the community to the old institutional regime.

To be sure, the legacies of the past may also exert an influence over the larger dynamics of transitions between economic regimes. The effects of structural features of the economy that had been formed under a previous institutional regime often endure long after the political collapse of that regime. In the ensuing confusion and disorganization of the period when new institutional arrangements are taking shape, those persisting conditions form the constraints with which economic policy-makers must contend. This is strikingly illustrated not only by the recent experiences of post-Soviet Russia but by the situation of post-apartheid South Africa, which is the subject of the fourth essay in this Part.

As Francis Wilson points out, the roots of many of the most difficult economic policy choices presently confronting South Africa's government lie in the long-standing distortion of the region's development path. There is a sense in which that also could be said of the Russian story, where the prior concentration of investment resources upon heavy industry and the military-industrial complex had left the civilian consumer goods market badly served by obsolete plants and the inefficient and increasingly corrupt management of the large state enterprises. On the other hand, while memory of the ruthlessly oppressive character of the Soviet political regime cannot lightly be put to one side, it is important here to acknowledge the existence of a marked contrast between the extreme inegalitarian thrust of the old economic regime in South Africa, and the conditions that had been achieved by the Russian people during the post-World War II era. Before the withering of a functional public sector in the chaotic period of liberalization and privatization presided over by the Yeltsin government, the population by and large was protected from the extremes of poverty. Indeed, a significant degree of real income security was provided for families in the form of state subsidized housing, medical care, preschool facilities, and the old age pension and welfare benefits that were provided through affiliation with the industrial enterprises and state farms. Moreover, access was provided to an effective system of free public education that extended through generally high-quality university and post-graduate training.

The pre-transition situations in the Russian and South African cases were thus fundamentally different: the mass of the indigenous population in South Africa, both before and under the regime of apartheid, had suffered the consequences of systematic, politically structured strategies of economic exploitation. The result was high levels of income and wealth among the country's White minority population, while the Black majority was reduced to conditions of widespread poverty and material insecurity, as well as the deprivation of personal liberty and dignity under a racially discriminatory political and legal regime.

Apartheid was only the last stage of a historical process of exploitation. A far older system had been used to mobilize the labour of migratory indigenous workers from the rural territories for the benefit of European-owned enterprises that, initially, were engaged in mining activities. That system of labour exploitation was progressively expanded, and applied in ways that prevented the peoples living in the rural areas whence the workers were recruited to invest in productivity — either in the form of physical infrastructures or human capital. This system had set the pattern that eventually was generalized and institutionally reinforced under apartheid.

Thus, the dysfunctional features of the present-day economy did not derive solely from the economics of apartheid and could not be swept away simply by the removal of that oppressive regime. The extended prior history of under-investment in physical facilities and the denial of educational opportunities to the mass of the indigenous peoples of southern Africa's rural regions was responsible for creating the country's deep-seated economic problems: continuing immigration into urban areas despite the persistence of woefully inadequate housing conditions, widespread lack of clean drinking water and consequent health problems for millions of people, lack of industrial and cognitive skills in the workforce that exacerbates structural unemployment in the cities. These fundamental problems have been aggravated by a new array of social ills, such as the spread of AIDS and the ubiquity of crime that now beset South African society, and which make the challenges of reform all the more difficult.

This historical diagnosis leads Wilson to suggest that public and private investment programmes should be redirected towards the rural homeland regions. It motivates his call for a more general acknowledgement of the truth that the accumulated wealth enjoyed by the country's white population and the concentration of productive assets under the control of foreign-owned corporations are the other side of the materially impoverished conditions in which the mass of the South African people celebrated the dawning of freedom and democracy.

A rather different and less sweeping instance of persisting effects of old institutional arrangements upon the dynamics of the transition to a new regime emerges from the study of the effects of monetary unification on market integration, by Leandro Conte, Gianni Toniolo and Giovanni Vecchi. Their essay begins by noting that the textbook presumption of price equalization in a 'single market' appears not to be borne out in recent European experience. Almost a decade after the signing of the Maastricht Treaty committing the member states of the EU to the creation of the 'Single Market', substantial variations in relative and absolute prices are observed across European commodity and financial markets, even for items as homogeneous and instantly tradable as stocks and shares. Will the final step of institutional integration, the replacement of national monetary systems by a uniform currency, the Euro—which took place at the beginning of 2002—provide the missing element required to bring about price convergence throughout the regions of Europe? The authors approach this question by looking back to the experience of Italian monetary unification after 1861 and asking how rapidly and how completely in the aftermath of the introduction of a national currency the prices of the basic factors of production, wages and interest rates began to converge towards the common levels that theory would predict.

Their study of the movements of the prices quoted in the leading financial markets for the Consol-like (i.e. irredeemable fixed-yield) debt instrument of the Italian state shows no secular reduction of the dispersion in the two decades that followed monetary and political unification. Although quite clearly the integration of money markets promoted more efficient arbitrage, and despite a tendency towards core-periphery convergence, other forces in the economy tended to widen the dispersion between asset prices in different regional centres. A conflict between stockbrokers and government regulatory authorities in the mid-1870s was the source of a distinct disturbance that emptied the stock exchanges for several years, during which time price-setting became impossible, resulting in a huge increase in dispersion that persisted for a number of years.

The labour market story is even more complex. Focusing upon skilled (master masons) and unskilled (hod-carriers) workers in the building trades as two reasonably homogenous categories of labour, Conte et al. report that the trend in the dispersion of wage quotations for each class of workers across the country suggests that gradual post-unification convergence was indeed taking place. But closer examination reveals that rather than this being a ubiquitous national tendency, the phenomenon of decreasing wage dispersion was concentrated within the southern region that included Sicily and Sardinia. The authors' explanation of the latter puzzle centres upon the greater elasticity of the labour supply available to the urban building trades in that region, which in turn can be ascribed to special features of the organization of agriculture and the land tenure institutions there. These permitted unskilled male labourers to leave their rural holdings for more extended sojourns of employment in the building trades of distant centres. Elsewhere, particularly in the north, local labour markets remained segmented and the dispersion of wage rates among them persisted.

This historical experience serves to illustrate the proposition that *de facto* monetary unification is a more complex and longer process than *de jure* currency unification. The integration of factor markets is likely to remain quite incomplete even when a common currency has been accepted in widespread use. Perhaps more striking still is the demonstration of the ways in which the dynamics and eventual pattern of market integration are shaped by pre-existing economic conditions, institutions and long-standing social conventions. These findings may serve to temper enthusiastic expectations that the advent of the Euro will soon bring about price equalization throughout the provinces of the European Union.

The hold of the past on the minds of economic policy-makers is perhaps nowhere more starkly illustrated than in Barry Eichengreen and Peter Temin's examination of international monetary policy formation during the Great Depression of the 1930s. Here was a major economic disturbance that eventually generated an entirely new conception of the workings of the macro-economy, local and global. Yet, the immediate response on the part of the international community of central bankers was not a re-assessment of the norms of policy-making in the light of the unfolding crisis conditions, so much as an intensified commitment to their faith in the value of adhering to the 'rules of the game' that had prevailed under the old Gold Standard. The rhetoric of central bankers' policy pronouncements during the critical period of the early 1930s reveals the hold of the prevailing ideology about the self-correcting capabilities of the international monetary regime. These pre-committed views were a legacy of the experience acquired by their respective institutions before World War I and were apparently unaffected by the actual alterations in international monetary arrangements that had occurred following 1914.

Eichengreen and Temin present a historical parable about the pernicious consequences that may ensue from the resilience of 'received wisdom' in economic policy-making. In most cases, macro-economic policy shocks can be readily handled within established policy structures. Such structures, and the decision criteria associated with them, have evolved over time with the benefit of experience, much of it derived from dealing with previous minor shocks. But a disturbance of extraordinary magnitude, or of an unusual character, challenges the capabilities of a 'routine-bound' regulatory system to comprehend its true nature and respond in appropriately new ways. One might think that faced with a challenge that presents significant novel elements, the sensible response of policy-makers would not be to follow the conventional course of action for dealing with broadly similar situations, but, instead to withhold action, or to act circumspectly until they fully understand the dimensions of the new problem.

But this is too simplistic. The true nature of a problem may be slow to emerge, making it difficult for policy-makers to recognize that they are actually confronting something new. Moreover, waiting for more data to arrive so that the situation can be more thoroughly studied is likely to be perceived as a departure from the normal course of institutional response, which may have its own unsettling effects upon economic agents in the affected markets. Inaction, therefore, may appear a luxury in which responsible authorities cannot indulge, especially during 'crisis' conditions. Moreover, policy-makers with the longer term in view are understandably inclined to proceed conservatively, rather than risking bold innovative moves in an atmosphere of uncertainty and potential panic. It is much easier and may appear safer to operate within conventional norms of behaviour. In certain cases, such norms are so deep-rooted as to take on the character of an ideological commitment. Indeed, the more these norms are viewed as central to the smooth operation of the economy, the more deep-seated the ideological commitment is likely to be. Thus, paradoxically, the more severe the shock, the less likely the desire for policy innovation.

The parable represents a cognitive form of 'sunk cost' hysteresis, in which commitment to a pre-formed mode of thought entrenches patterns of behaviour that fail to address worsening problems; the intensification of the crisis further reinforces commitment to the traditional form of (increasingly inadequate) response. Eichengeen and Temin suggest that a modern example of 'cognitive lock-in' can be observed in the tenacity with which the international bankers and financial advisers associated with the IMF clung to that institution's formulaic requirements for budgetary and other structural reforms as a condition for its provision of international reserves—seemingly ignoring the pressing needs for liquidity during the Asian exchange rate and financial crisis of the mid-1990s. The parable suggests that authorities entrusted with regulatory responsibilities, whether in the macroeconomic sphere or elsewhere, should be wary of the 'blinkering' effects of the received wisdom that becomes codified in well-rehearsed decision procedures and pre-determined criteria for action. Critics of policy-making, at the same time, should acknowledge that codified routines make for efficient responses in the 'normal' run of problem-situations with which, by definition, such authorities will typically be dealing, and that structural discontinuities or fundamental aberrations are often revealed clearly only in hindsight.

6.
The East Asian Escape from Economic Backwardness:
Retrospect and Prospect

NICHOLAS CRAFTS

Introduction

Through the early 1990s discussions of economic growth in East Asia were characterized by competing claims about the reasons for success in achieving spectacular economic development from a low initial income level. In particular, the debate surrounding the publication of *The East Asian Miracle* was notable for contrasting interpretations stressing either that the 'developmental state' had triumphed or that 'the market works, God Bless It'.[1] In fact, East Asia seems to encompass both types of economic development, including Korea as an example of the former and Hong Kong representing the latter.

Recently, the so-called 'miracle' has been viewed more sceptically, notably since the widely read paper by Paul Krugman.[2] The original scepticism stemmed from growth accounting exercises that suggested that fast East Asian growth was based primarily on factor accumulation while total factor productivity (TFP) growth was quite modest. Subsequently, the crisis of 1997/8 has prompted a great deal more pessimism about the sustainability of growth in East Asia.

Relatively little has been written about recent East Asian economic growth from the vantage point of mainstream economic history. This seems unfortunate since a central theme in the historical literature since the seminal work of Alexander Gerschenkron has been the analy-

---

[1] World Bank, *East Asian Miracle*.
[2] Krugman, 'Myth'.

sis of development from conditions of initial economic backwardness.[3] Gerschenkron argued that rapid growth could be achieved in these circumstances but would depend much less on the market institutions familiar from British or American industrialization and much more on a proactive state. In particular, this perspective would draw attention both to the role of institutional innovation in embarking on the early stages of development and also to the challenge of subsequent transition to a more orthodox market economy en route to full catching up of the leading economies.

Economic historians have always been aware that catch-up was by no means automatic and often remains incomplete even among OECD countries. Historical experience is that TFP levels vary considerably and that catch-up involves much more than the elimination of a (broad) capital to labour gap in the style of a traditional neoclassical growth model. Moses Abramovitz underlined the importance of 'social capability' to productivity performance in catch-up growth.[4] This involves not only accumulation of the human capital necessary to assimilate advanced technology but also the establishment of incentive structures that promote innovation and investment but discourage rent-seeking and the survival of inefficient producers.

The insights from these economic history classics can be reinforced by making explicit connections with economic theory. Abramovitz's framework for thinking about catch-up growth connects readily with the endogenous innovation school of endogenous growth economics which stresses the importance of appropriation of returns and control of agency problems in productivity performance. Gerschenkron's backwardness paradigm maps into recent work in development economics on overcoming coordination failures and also links to microeconomic analysis based on asymmetric information and transactions costs that explains why both the role for hierarchy rather than the market in economic activity and also the design of the financial system may well be different in the early stages of development.

Informed by this perspective and a review of the growth accounting results mentioned above, the present paper then goes on to examine two questions:

[3] Gerschenkron, *Economic Backwardness*.
[4] Abramovitz, 'Catching Up'.

(a) How has the 'escape from backwardness' shaped East Asian economic growth ?
(b) Can East Asia continue to catch up ?

The discussion suggests that mechanical extrapolation of recent performance by the Tigers is likely to be seriously misleading, just as it was in the case of Japan at a similar stage in its development.

Economic Backwardness in a Modern Microeconomic Perspective

Many students associate Gerschenkron's backwardness perspective with his summary statement that higher degrees of backwardness at the start of industrialization were associated with more dramatic initial spurts of growth, with larger plants and enterprises and less competitive market structures, and with a more organized direction of credit based on investment banks and/or bureaucratic control.[5] This is somewhat unfortunate since in many specific aspects these generalizations have appeared somewhat vulnerable when tested in the context of European economic history, especially in terms of his key cases, Germany and Russia.[6]

The more robust component of Gerschenkron's account is his concept of 'substitutes for prerequisites' in which he stressed that backwardness entailed the absence of factors that served as preconditions for development in more advanced countries and highlighted the importance of examining the ways in which, in conditions of backwardness, substitutions for the absent factors were achieved.[7] Knick Harley suggested that this might largely be construed as the endogenous substitution of hierarchies for markets in backward areas as the transactions costs analysis of Oliver Williamson suggests would be appropriate.[8] This would account for the greater role of large firms and bureaucracies in circumstances where markets were less well-

---

[5] Gershenkron, *Economic Backwardness*, p. 44.
[6] Useful assessments of the evidence can be found in Crafts et al., 'Measurement', Fohlin, 'Financial System', and the various contributions in Sylla and Toniolo, eds., *Patterns*.
[7] Gerschenkron, *Economic Backwardness*, p. 46.
[8] Harley, 'Substitution'; Williamson, *Economic Institutions*.

211

developed, and the transaction specificity of assets thus intensified, with greater attendant risks of opportunistic hold-up deterring investment and innovation.

A similar argument might be made using an incomplete contracts approach.[9] Here the point might be that internalizing control over complementary economic activities is especially beneficial when it is not possible to write a complete contract that covers all contingencies, is verifiable, and enforceable. This argues for more hierarchy in conditions of backwardness when the legal system is unreliable. Both theories indicate, however, that these market-substituting arrangements have a downside in terms of reduced incentives for cost reduction and innovation within the hierarchical organization.

Central to Gerschenkron's account of development is the role of the financial system. Here a deeper understanding can be obtained by a reconsideration in terms of analysis based on the importance of asymmetric information. This suggests that two problems — adequate information and adequate recourse — are at the heart of the finance process.[10] To combat effectively the endemic diseases of adverse selection and moral hazard which threaten to undermine the supply of credit in financial markets, it is necessary to overcome the free-rider problem in collection of information especially where disclosure rules are lax and firms are small and young. This potentially gives a leading role to banks that can profit from the production of information in their own loan activities and, especially, to relationship banking. Even better information is needed if poor functioning of the legal system makes it hard to use collateral or restrictive covenants to mitigate the difficulties.[11]

Problems of excessive risk-taking due to moral hazard also infect banks themselves. In practice, monitoring by depositors is unlikely to be an adequate solution and prudential regulation and supervision by government is desirable if private sector banking is to flourish and provide a stable financial environment. Not surprisingly, cross-country differences in the legal rights of creditors and the efficiency with which those rights are enforced explain much of the variation that is observed in banking sector development.[12] It is easy then to understand

[9] An introduction to these ideas is in Hart, *Firms*.
[10] White, 'Financial Infrastructure', p. 123.
[11] Mishkin and Eakins, *Financial Structure*, pp. 310–11.
[12] Levine, 'Legal Environment'.

Gerschenkron's claim that in conditions of moderate backwardness investment banking might play a major part in promoting industrialization but that in extreme backwardness the state may have to substitute for the banks.

Gerschenkron also stressed the importance of complementarity and indivisibilities in developing economies and seems to have had in mind a big-push view of industrialization.[13] Mainstream economists are now inclined to take these issues rather more seriously and there has been considerable interest in modelling the economics of co-ordination failures in the early stages of development.[14] Dani Rodrik argues that there are three conditions (which applied in much of East Asia in the 1960s) that together make co-ordination failure a serious problem, namely, imperfect tradability of some key inputs and/or technologies used in the modern sector, economies of scale in these activities and an abundance of skilled labour relative to physical capital.[15] In such circumstances, by ensuring the production of a sufficiently large number of intermediate inputs, appropriate government intervention may facilitate the transition to a high income equilibrium.

While modern economics can provide strong support for many of Gerschenkron's ideas, at the same time it also underlines some of the downside risks in relying on the state to spearhead the escape from backwardness. State-owned enterprises are notoriously subject to agency problems that undermine productivity performance. The state itself may be predatory and unable credibly to commit itself not to expropriate the returns from private sector investment. Rent-seeking behaviour tends to flourish in circumstances of industrial policy and protected markets.

It also seems clear that, as development progresses, ideally, the institutions devised to cope with economic backwardness should be replaced by more orthodox market-orientated arrangements. Directed credit and relationship banking may have advantages in encouraging a high initial volume of investment. However, later on, the relative attraction of financial liberalization is likely to increase as a way to improve allocative efficiency, to discipline policymakers and to create the equity finance that research and development intensive activity

---

[13] Gerschenkron, *Economic Backwardness*, p. 10.
[14] Recent theoretical contributions include Ciccone and Matsuyama, 'Start-Up Costs', and Murphy et al., 'Industrialization'.
[15] Rodrik, 'Co-ordination Failures'.

requires. Similarly, while the high profits associated with market power may underpin the finance of early industrialization, in the longer run competition is likely to be a valuable pressure on managers to improve productivity performance in hierarchical firms with agency problems.[16]

Overall, Gerschenkron's backwardness perspective can be interpreted to suggest that institutional innovation, probably involving a relatively big role for the state, can promote high levels of investment in the early stages of modern economic growth. However, there is likely to be a downside in terms of weaknesses in productivity performance. For continued strong catch-up growth, it will be desirable to move eventually to market-based institutions that strengthen the incentives for cost reduction and allocative efficiency. Yet, as North has pointed out, there is no natural selection process that ensures the replacement of inefficient with efficient institutions.[17]

Developmental States in East Asia

Although East Asia comprises a wide variety of developmental strategies, it seems clear that in many cases the state played a considerably greater role than is envisaged in neoclassical models of development. In a much-cited paper, Rodrik points to the key role of the Korean and Taiwanese governments in raising the returns to private investment by using strategic interventions, including investment subsidies, administrative guidance and public enterprise, to address co-ordination failures.[18] Chung Lee explicitly develops the theme of hierarchical organization as an alternative to the market in Korean development by seeing the relationship between government and large enterprises as reducing uncertainty in a 'quasi-internal organization' akin to an M-form structure with an internal capital market.[19]

Well-known accounts of East Asian development that stress an active role for the state can also be found in Alice Amsden, who stresses the importance of 'getting prices wrong', and in Robert Wade, whose theme is that of 'governed markets'.[20] Wade emphasizes capital

---

[16] Nickell, 'Competition'.
[17] North, *Institutions*.
[18] Rodrik, 'Getting Interventions'.
[19] Lee, 'Visible Hand'.
[20] Amsden, *Asia's Next Giant*; Wade, *Governing*.

accumulation as the key to superior East Asian performance and argues that, in countries like Korea and Taiwan, state intervention changed both the level and composition of investment, supported infant industries and dealt with co-ordination failures in small markets with imperfect access to international trade. The underlying story is of an authoritarian state able to confer enough autonomy on a centralized bureaucracy to influence resource allocation in the long-term national interest.[21] Amsden in her account of Korean development highlights the role of the *chaebol* as a solution to transactions costs problems and state direction of investment.[22] She stresses the unusual discipline that the state exercised over large firms through credible commitment to export targets.

All these discussions of East Asian growth can be interpreted as invoking a Gerschenkronian escape from backwardness. They recognize the potential downside risks to the developmental role of the state but argue that these were mitigated by policies of outward orientation that stressed the importance of industrial exports as a disciplinary device. The successful developmental states are seen as distinguished not so much by the policies that they embraced but by their unusual success in implementing them efficiently rather than succumbing to rent-seeking and agency problems.

This view is at least somewhat contentious. Detailed econometric investigation of the Korean case, which has typically been seen as a prime exhibit of the virtues of a developmental state in promoting rapid growth, has started to uncover evidence of policy failures. Thus, in the context of corruption and the clout of the *chaebols*, the use of directed loans appears to have distorted credit flows to the detriment of both profitability and productivity growth.[23] Similarly, an analysis of industrial productivity growth across sectors in Korea for the period 1963–83 found that tax and financial incentives did not enhance productivity growth while non-tariff barriers to trade reduced both capital accumulation and TFP growth.[24]

---

[21] Wade, *Governing*, p. 29.
[22] Amsden, *Asia's Next Giant*.
[23] Borensztein and Lee, 'Credit Allocation'.
[24] Lee, 'Government Interventions'.

Changes in Economic Regimes and Ideologies

Table 1. Growth accounting: comparisons of sources of growth (% per year).

		Capital (%)	Labour (%)	TFP (%)	Output
1913–1950	France	0.6 (55)	-0.2 (-19)	0.7 (64)	1.1
	Japan	1.2 (55)	0.3 (13)	0.7 (32)	2.2
	UK	0.8 (62)	0.1 (7)	0.4 (31)	1.3
	USA	0.9 (32)	0.6 (21)	1.3 (47)	2.8
	West Germany	0.6 (46)	0.4 (31)	0.3 (23)	1.3
1950–1973	France	1.6 (32)	0.3 (6)	3.1 (62)	5.0
	Japan	3.1 (34)	2.5 (27)	3.6 (39)	9.2
	UK	1.6 (53)	0.2 (7)	1.2 (40)	3.0
	USA	1.0 (26)	1.3 (33)	1.6 (41)	3.9
	West Germany	2.2 (37)	0.5 (8)	3.3 (55)	6.0
1973–1992	France	1.3 (57)	0.4 (17)	0.6 (26)	2.3
	Japan	2.0 (53)	0.8 (21)	1.0 (26)	3.8
	UK	0.9 (56)	0.0 (0)	0.7 (44)	1.6
	USA	0.9 (38)	1.3 (54)	0.2 (8)	2.4
	West Germany	0.9 (39)	-0.1 (-4)	1.5 (65)	2.3
1978–1995	China	3.1 (41)	2.7 (36)	1.7 (23)	7.5
1960–1994	Hong Kong	2.8 (38)	2.1 (29)	2.4 (33)	7.3
	Indonesia	2.9 (52)	1.9 (34)	0.8 (14)	5.6
	Korea	4.3 (52)	2.5 (30)	1.5 (18)	8.3
	Malaysia	3.4 (50)	2.5 (37)	0.9 (13)	6.8
	Philippines	2.1 (55)	2.1 (55)	-0.4 (-10)	3.8
	Singapore	4.4 (54)	2.2 (27)	1.5 (19)	8.1
	Taiwan	4.1 (48)	2.4 (28)	2.0 (24)	8.5
	Thailand	3.7 (49)	2.0 (27)	1.8 (24)	7.5
	South Asia	1.8 (43)	1.6 (38)	0.8 (19)	4.2
	Latin America	1.8 (43)	2.2 (52)	0.2 (5)	4.2
	Africa	1.7 (59)	1.8 (62)	-0.6 (-21)	2.9
	Middle East	2.5 (56)	2.3 (51)	-0.3 (-7)	4.5

Sources: These growth accounting estimates have been devised to facilitate international comparisons as each of the main sources imposes common assumptions about factor shares across countries. G7 countries from Maddison, 'Macroeconomic Accounts'. East Asia derived from Collins and Bosworth, 'Economic Growth' except for Hong Kong which is based on Young, 'Tyranny' and China based on Maddison, *Chinese Economic Performance*, both with factor shares adjusted to match Collins and Bosworth's assumptions. South Asia, Latin America, Africa, Middle East from Collins and Bosworth, 'Economic Growth'.

The assessment in *The East Asian Miracle* provides a good starting point as an early 1990s mainstream development economics view of East Asia which largely accepted the optimistic account of the role of the developmental state. High-performing East Asian economies were seen as benefiting from excellent TFP growth linked to their outwardly orientated policies and the unusual success of these economies was attributed to governmental success in solving co-ordination problems while adopting policy frameworks that contained rent-seeking and were generally market-friendly. Rapid deepening of financial markets was taken to be a big stimulus to investment and growth while industrial and directed credit policies were not seen as damaging. The World Bank evaluation of the growth record was backed up by first generation growth regressions in which dummy variables suggested that high-performing East Asian economies had outperformed the world sample by about 1.7 per cent per year, compared with underperformance of 1.3 and 1.0 per cent signalled by the Latin American and African dummies, respectively.[25]

The miracle years were already the subject of some reassessment prior to the recent crises as economists turned to the standard economic history methodology of growth accounting.[26] The messages were somewhat different from those coming from growth regressions, since the impact on labour inputs of the demographic transition in East Asia and on capital stock growth of initially low capital to output ratios had not been reflected in regressions that used investment shares and population growth as right-hand side variables.[27] When put in an historical context, the clear message of the growth accounting studies, which appears robust to arguments about the data, is that East Asian TFP growth is far from outstanding, although obviously it compares well with Africa or Latin America.[28]

Taking columns 1 and 2 of Table 1 together, it is clear that East Asian growth has relied much more on the contribution of rapid factor accumulation, of both capital and labour, than did Europe's fast growth of its Golden Age. Conversely, East Asian TFP growth has been less strong than in the European countries which experienced rapid catch-up growth in the early post-war decades. Indeed, the Tigers have also fallen well short of what Japan achieved in this aspect of growth. Certainly, countries such as Hong Kong and Singapore lacked the opportunity to transfer labour from low productivity agriculture and the estimates of Angus Maddison suggest that this may have reduced their TFP growth compared with Golden Age France and Germany by about 0.5 per cent per year.[29] Even so, normalizing for the oppor-

---

[25] World Bank, *East Asian Miracle*, p. 54.
[26] Growth accounting is reviewed in Collins and Bosworth, 'Economic Growth', who supply estimates for East Asia; see also, Young, 'Tyranny'.
[27] On age structure and labour inputs, see Bloom and Williamson, 'Demographic Transitions'; on capital to output ratios, see Fukuda, 'Sources'.
[28] Possible biases are fully discussed in Crafts, 'East Asian Growth'.
[29] Maddison, 'Macroeconomic Accounts'.

Changes in Economic Regimes and Ideologies

tunities for catching up presented by the initial productivity gaps and levels of education, the Tigers' TFP growth appears in a much less favourable light and seems rather disappointing.[30]

Table 2. Annual hours worked and real GDP/hour worked ($1990int).

	Per Worker 1973	Per Worker 1996	Per Person 1973	Per Person 1996	GDP/HW 1996
Austria	1778	1710	741	725	24.76
Belgium	1872	1637	720	595	29.84
Denmark	1742	1644	842	797	24.85
Finland	1915	1790	900	732	21.67
France	1904	1666	783	600	28.47
Greece	2000	1733	724	641	17.08
Ireland	2199	1694	763	622	25.43
Italy	1885	1830	781	641	26.23
Netherlands	1751	1487	692	592	31.26
Norway	1721	1407	728	686	32.46
Portugal	1900	2009	768	853	14.09
Spain	2238	1810	818	559	23.50
Sweden	1571	1554	749	693	25.35
Switzerland	1930	1643	982	874	23.17
UK	1929	1732	861	764	22.68
West Germany	1865	1558	817	661	29.68
Hong Kong	2400	2259	1008	1127	18.81
Indonesia	2010	2200	754	903	3.75
Japan	2201	1898	1065	976	20.06
Korea	2428	2453	798	1099	11.70
Philippines	2235	2110	776	679	2.87
Singapore	2410	2318	872	1193	15.87
Taiwan	2690	2339	930	988	14.28
Thailand	2606	2546	1232	1394	4.51

Source: Crafts, 'East Asian Growth'.

The most powerful reason for supposing that these estimates understate East Asian TFP growth would be that, as in nineteenth-century America, the capital to labour ratio has been rising, technological change has been labour-saving and the elasticity of substitution between factors is less than 1. However, simulations of the likely bias in TFP growth if the elasticity of substitution is set at 0.6 suggest that the order of magnitude in Korea, Singapore and Taiwan in Table 1 is around 0.7 to 0.9 per cent per year. This would still leave their TFP growth short of the rates achieved in Golden Age Europe. In any case,

[30] Crafts, 'East Asian Growth'.

similar corrections for bias in estimated TFP growth probably apply during the European Golden Age when capital deepening was also considerable.

One obvious retort to the suggestion that East Asian productivity performance has been below par is to note that real GDP per person on a purchasing power parity adjusted basis in the leading Tigers such as Hong Kong and Singapore has overtaken that of most of Western Europe during the 1990s. This is not true, however, for levels of labour productivity as is reported in Table 2, which compares purchasing power parity adjusted real GDP per hour worked. The key to the difference lies both in age structure differences and also in the much higher number of hours worked per worker per year in the Asian countries. Table 2 not only offers some further support for the view that productivity performance has not been outstanding in East Asia but also shows considerable scope for further catch-up growth.

This analysis tends to the conclusion that the Asian developmental state has been much more successful in promoting high levels of investment than in achieving exceptional productivity performance. At least for the more successful Asian economies, this should not detract from their unusually successful efforts to accumulate human capital and improve and develop imported technology.[31] Imports of capital goods and foreign direct investment have clearly been central components of technology transfer and far outstrip those of less successful regions such as Latin America.

This suggests that the Tigers' disappointing TFP growth may have its roots in the escape from backwardness. The economic analysis of the preceding section predicted that the substitution of hierarchy for market, of state for private enterprise and of policy directed lending for capital market discipline would give a strong impetus to investment at the expense of some dulling of the incentives for innovation and cost reduction. This suggests that for full catch-up of the leading OECD economies it may be more urgent to reform some of the distinctive aspects of the East Asian model than the World Bank recognized.[32]

Problems of asymmetric information and market failure imply that effective regulation of banks is essential to the well-being of the financial system both to prevent excessive risk-taking and to reduce the likelihood both of bank insolvencies and bank runs. Recent appraisals of

---

[31] Dahlman, 'Technology Strategy'.
[32] World Bank, *East Asian Miracle*.

East Asian banking systems have commented on a number of serious weaknesses that were common, with differing severity, through much of the region, although not in Hong Kong or Singapore. These include low capital-adequacy ratios of banks, excessive exposure of banks to single borrowers, unduly lenient provisioning rules for non-performing loans, weak supervision, absence of proper auditing and accounting, and so on, which combined with high leverage of the corporate sector have implied vulnerability to financial shocks.[33] It should be noted also that this is not the wisdom of hindsight—just the same view can be found in assessments made before the crisis.[34]

East Asian growth has, of course been rudely interrupted by the financial crises which started in 1997. This should not be so surprising since economic history offers many examples of financial crises leading to severe downturns occurring in basically sound and strong economies with high growth potential but exposed to macroeconomic shocks where the banking system was inadequately regulated. The classic case is surely the United States in the nineteenth and early twentieth centuries, most notoriously in the Great Depression of the 1930s.[35] In each case, however, resolution of the crisis permitted the resumption of strong growth.

In many cases, East Asian financial systems were initially set up in conditions of economic backwardness. Problems of asymmetric information were dealt with outside the framework of regulation and legal recourse in an environment not yet exposed to financial liberalization. The financial sector policies of a developmental state had tended to place little weight on proper auditing, accounting, credit rating, disclosure requirements or experienced and independent regulators.[36] As development progressed, financial liberalization seemed attractive but the importance of reforming financial regulation was either not perceived or impeded by interest groups. Moreover, the developmental state was perceived by markets to offer bailout guarantees in the event of bank failures. When the prospective fiscal deficits from this implicit insurance rose sufficiently high currency crises were triggered.[37] Thus,

---

[33] World Bank, *East Asia*.
[34] See, for example, White, 'Financial Infrastructure'.
[35] Helpful accounts can be found in Grossman, 'Macroeconomic Consequences', and Mishkin, 'Asymmetric Information'.
[36] Park, 'Concepts'.
[37] Burnside et al., 'Prospective Deficits'.

the recent trauma in countries such as South Korea can be seen as illustrative of the difficulties of making the transition from the first phase of a Gerschenkronian-style development.

Recent Japanese economic history also illustrates rather clearly the potential difficulties of this transition. The Golden Age was characterized by spectacular economic growth, as Table 1 reported. That period can be thought of as an escape from backwardness built around institutional innovations that emerged as a result of the wartime experience that led to enhanced social capability for catch-up, namely, the main bank system, the *keiretsu* and lifetime employment. All of these can be seen as responses to transactions costs problems.[38] Now these institutional arrangements are increasingly seen as obstacles to overcoming the present economic difficulties and resuming catch-up of the United States.[39]

Most obviously, this is true of the banking system, which since the flawed liberalization of the 1980s has developed serious and persistent problems that have their roots in moral hazard and inadequate regulation. The collapse of asset prices in the early 1990s crippled bank lending but was met by regulatory forbearance and thus has severely curtailed the effectiveness of conventional macroeconomic policy in effecting recovery from recession.[40] In failing to address the banking crisis, Japanese policy compares unfavourably with Roosevelt's America.[41]

The fundamental weaknesses of the Japanese financial system have a longer history. In particular, the post-war bank finance arrangements were established to deliver a low cost of finance to industry rather than to promote the efficient use of capital or shareholder value. The outcome was effective mobilization of resources but tolerance for low efficiency and profitability and a bias towards over expansion.[42] These arrangements needed a well-designed reform but the incentives delivered by the changes of the 1980s appear mainly to have encouraged real estate speculation and excessive lending.

---

[38] Noguchi, 'The 1940 System'.
[39] See, for example, Ito, 'Japan'.
[40] On policy response, see Cargill et al., *Political Economy*; on the impact of asset price falls on the supply of loans and investment, see Bayoumi, 'Morning After'.
[41] Crafts, 'Implications'.
[42] Ide, 'Financial System'.

Tables 1 and 2 show faltering Japanese TFP growth in the most recent period and output per hour worked in 1996 below that of Britain or Finland. Japan has notably weak productivity performance outside of tradable manufactures but, even in manufacturing, Japan did not close the TFP gap with the USA between the mid-1980s and the mid-1990s. In part, poor Japanese productivity performance reflects excessive and wasteful investment and thus weaknesses in the financial system and in corporate governance. Beyond this, however, policy errors have also played a part, notably industrial policies that appear to have diverted resources away from high-growth sectors towards declining industries and excessive regulation that has impeded productivity performance.[43] This experience underlines the point that catch-up is not automatic, as the neoclassical model would have us believe, but depends on social capability and can be eroded by poor policy choices.

Three main points emerge from the discussion of this section. First, the East Asian escape from backwardness has tended to be accomplished through institutional arrangements that generally delivered more by way of factor accumulation than outstanding TFP growth. Second, attempts to move from the financial systems set up to facilitate industrial take-off to those more appropriate to a mature economy have been much more difficult than was foreseen. Third, further supply-side reform will be required to deliver full catch-up of leading economies like the United States, as the Japanese example underlines.

Future Prospects

Extrapolating recent growth performance is a popular way of projecting future growth prospects. As earlier sections imply, it is, of course, potentially seriously misleading. Yet it is fairly close to what international agencies tend to do, at least in their scenario planning. Table 3 reports some results from a recent OECD exercise, completed not long before the Asian crisis broke. This probably corresponds reasonably closely to what the person in the street might have guessed at that time; now public opinion would perhaps be more pessimistic about 'dynamic Asia', although not perhaps about China.

---

[43] On counterproductive industrial policy, see Beason and Weinstein, 'Growth'; on excessive regulation, see Blondal and Pilat, 'Economic Benefits'.

Table 3. OECD Growth projections (% per year).

	Output	Capital	Labour	TFP	Share World GDP (%) 1995	2020
High Growth						
China & Hong Kong	8.0	4.1	0.5	3.4	9.3	19.5
Indonesia	7.0	3.4	0.8	2.8	1.9	3.2
Other Dynamic Asia	6.9	3.0	1.1	2.8	3.6	5.8
Low Growth						
China & Hong Kong	5.6	3.3	0.3	2.0	9.3	16.9
Indonesia	4.4	2.6	0.6	1.2	1.9	2.6
Other Dynamic Asia	4.8	2.0	0.8	2.0	3.6	5.4

Source: 'Other Dynamic Asia' comprises Malaysia, Philippines, Singapore, Taiwan and Thailand; projections from Richardson, 'Globalization'.

Table 3 is derived essentially on a growth accounting basis and incorporates assumptions about the future growth of factor inputs and TFP. Compared with the recent past, as reported in Table 1, it envisages a marked slowdown in the contribution of labour inputs throughout the region as the demographics become less favourable. On the other hand, the projections anticipate the possibility in the high growth scenario of a significant improvement in TFP growth and in the low-growth scenario that TFP growth will be sustained at a slightly higher rate than for the average of 1960–94. The contribution of capital stock growth varies with TFP growth; diminishing returns set in relatively quickly in the low growth scenario, as Krugman foresaw.[44]

There is nothing intrinsically infeasible about these scenarios in that they are within the range of historical experience and the rapid growth that they contemplate is underpinned by the substantial scope for catch-up that is implied by current levels of labour productivity, as shown in Table 2. Growth accounting is enormously valuable for benchmarking past performance. It is not, however, a very reliable tool for the purpose of growth projections. At the end of Japan's Golden Age, Edward Denison and William Chung undertook a similar exercise in which they projected an average growth rate of 6.2 per cent for real GDP from 1971–2000 with growth in the early 1990s still up at over 5 per cent per year.[45] They were wrong basically because they vastly

---

[44] Krugman, 'Myth'.
[45] Denison and Chung, *How Japan's Economy*, p. 126.

overestimated TFP growth from continued catch-up, which has been inhibited in practice by problems in the financial sector and by unfortunate supply-side policies.

In other words, history tells us that catch-up depends on social capability, which means that we cannot use simple growth models to anchor the growth accounting exercise with TFP and capital growth projections, especially where economic and social reform is required to sustain catch-up growth. For the East Asian economies, including Japan, full catch-up of the USA requires that attention is paid to non-tradables and other sectors as well as manufacturing. It seems likely that the traditional Asian developmental state model with its emphasis on export targets and performance to limit rent seeking and to inform the allocation of credit is not particularly well-suited to this requirement. The industrial policy prescriptions of the developmental state, which are liable to result in the support of declining industries at the expense of the rapid exploitation of new service sector opportunities, are likely to be still less helpful to the next phase of catch-up.

In the longer term, it seems likely that in the later stages of development it will be desirable for East Asian countries to move away from bank-dominated finance and to develop better methods of corporate governance. In most cases, this will entail the establishment of better legal rights for outside shareholders and will be facilitated by the emergence of ownership characterized by large and powerful investors.[46] Investor protection and availability of equity finance appear to be especially important in fostering growth in R&D-intensive activities that are starting to be important in the leading Tiger economies.[47]

In the absence of effective control by shareholders, the best restraint on inefficient management of firms is competition.[48] This implies that it is important that policies of greater openness to international trade and foreign companies are pursued. In particular, the Japanese example suggests that this should extend to the relatively backward services sector, important parts of which such as telecommunications, utilities and transportation have generally been government dominated. Yet competition policy in East Asia has been seriously neglected; for example, ASEAN countries with the exception of Thailand do not

---

[46] La Porta et al., 'Legal Determinants'.
[47] Carlin and Mayer, 'Finance'.
[48] Nickell, 'Competition'.

have anti-trust laws. In the Thai case the law has been used as an instrument of price control rather than to promote economic efficiency.[49] This is also an area where reform to the developmental state model seems to be urgently required.

The American example of the 1930s argues that even a massive financial crisis need not damage long-term growth potential, provided that the banking system is rehabilitated and re-regulated. However, this does not detract from the case for wider-ranging reforms to the conduct of both firms and governments in East Asia if future growth potential is to be fully realized. In any event, there is clearly a wide range of growth outcomes depending on the success that East Asian countries have in modifying the developmental state model. It is likely, however, that this range has been widened somewhat by the current financial crisis, even though the ingredients necessary to deal with the banking crisis and the longer term reforms to banking systems in East Asia are well understood and there are encouraging signs that some progress is being made.[50] As Japanese experience shows, carrying this through may not be easy politically and there exists the temptation to react, as Malaysia unfortunately has, by reversing financial liberalization.

As Rodrik points out, it has become commonplace to assert that crisis is the instigator of reform but it is less clear what are the analytic or empirical underpinnings of such a claim despite its intuitive appeal.[51] Rodrik himself suggests that one justification may be that the opportunity provided by deep crisis is to deliver widespread income gains by policies to revive economic activity. This allows reformist policymakers to add on microeconomic and structural reforms that would be difficult to implement in normal circumstances because of their distributional implications.[52] Given that microeconomic reform to the Asian development state model is clearly required, it is even possible then that the crisis will actually be helpful to long-run growth despite its devastating short-term impact.

China has largely escaped the Asian financial crisis and that might lead the unwary to conclude that here at least the OECD growth projections are on safe ground. Sadly, this is not the case because China

---

[49] Lall, 'ASEAN Approaches'.
[50] Goldstein, *Asian Financial Crisis*.
[51] Rodrik, 'Understanding'.
[52] Ibid., pp. 28–9.

also needs to make a transition from a first phase escape from backwardness to an economy capable of improved productivity performance, as the very disappointing TFP growth reported in Table 1 underlines. This transition is fraught with political difficulty and might easily fail to be achieved satisfactorily.

Since 1978, China has relaxed the command economy and benefited from rapid agricultural and industrial growth. It has not, however, established an effective financial or legal system, nor has it developed a tax base that will facilitate adequate public expenditure on infrastructure and human capital accumulation. State interference has led to serious misallocation of funds, the four major banks are insolvent and standards of bank regulation are abysmal.[53] Transforming state enterprises and commercial banks into market-oriented institutions has yet to be achieved.[54] As a recent detailed study of Chinese economic policy put it, 'many of the painful aspects of restructuring have been postponed'.[55]

Concluding Comments

The main message of this paper is that economies that achieve a rapid escape from backwardness typically carry a legacy of institutional arrangements that have served them well initially but need substantial reform before full catch-up of the leading economies can become a realistic prospect. This is clearly the case for the developmental states of East Asia. This makes projection of growth prospects for these economies much more difficult than is generally realized, even without the current financial crisis, because economic historians tend to argue that the replacement of outmoded institutions is a very uncertain and often painfully slow process while political economy provides no solid generalizations about the likelihood of successful reform.

There is still very substantial scope for rapid catch-up growth throughout the region provided that supply-side reform is achieved. The Japanese example illustrates that this may actually be quite difficult. Financial crisis has added to the difficulties in the short term but, if met by an appropriate policy response, need not reduce trend

---

[53] Lardy, *China's Unfinished Economic Revolution*.
[54] World Bank, *China 2020*.
[55] Naughton, *Growing*, p. 324.

growth in the medium term. Factor accumulation in East Asia has been hugely impressive during the last 30 years; what is needed now is to improve productivity performance through improvements to institutional and policy design. China is clearly in urgent need of substantial further reform if its recent growth is to be sustained and its growth prospects are far less secure than the bald facts of its recent track record might seem to suggest.

Note. I am grateful to the editors and especially to Angus Maddison for helpful comments on an earlier version. I am, of course, responsible for all errors.

References

Abramovitz, Moses. 'Catching Up, Forging Ahead, and Falling Behind.' *Journal of Economic History* 36, no. 2 (1986): 385–406.

Amsden, Alice H. *Asia's Next Giant*. New York: Oxford University Press, 1989.

Bayoumi, Tamim. 'The Morning After: Explaining the Slowdown in Japanese Growth in the 1990s.' *Journal of International Economics* 53, no. 2 (2001): 241–59.

Beason, Richard and David E. Weinstein. 'Growth, Economies of Scale, and Targeting in Japan, 1955–1990.' *Review of Economics and Statistics* 78 no. 2 (1996): 286–95.

Blondal, Sveinbjorn and Pilat, Dirk. 'The Economic Benefits of Regulatory Reform.' *OECD Economic Studies* 28, no. 1 (1997): 7–45.

Bloom, David E. and Jeffrey G. Williamson. 'Demographic Transitions and Economic Miracles in Emerging Asia.' *World Bank Economic Review* 12, no. 3 (1998): 419–55.

Borensztein, Eduardo and Lee, Jong-Wha. 'Credit Allocation and Financial Crisis in Korea.' International Monetary Fund Working Paper No. 99/20, 1999.

Burnside, Craig, Martin Eichenbaum and Sergio Rebelo, 'Prospective Deficits and the Asian Currency Crisis.' *Journal of Political Economy* 109, no. 6 (2001): 1155–97.

Cargill, Thomas F., Michael M. Hutchison and Takatoshi Ito. *The Political Economy of Japanese Monetary Policy*. Cambridge, Mass.: MIT Press, 1997.

Carlin, Wendy and Colin Mayer. 'Finance, Investment and Growth.' Department of Economics, University College, London Discussion Paper No. 98–09, 1998.

Ciccone, Antonio and Kiminori Matsuyama. 'Start-Up Costs and Pecuniary Externalities as Barriers to Economic Development.' *Journal of Development Economics* 49, no. 1 (1996): 33–59.

Collins, Susan M. and Barry P. Bosworth. 'Economic Growth in East Asia: Accumulation versus Assimilation.' *Brookings Papers on Economic Activity* 2 (1996): 135–91.

Crafts, Nicholas. 'East Asian Growth Before and After the Crisis.' *IMF Staff Papers* 46, no. 2 (1999): 139–66.

———. 'Implications of Financial Crisis for East Asian Trend Growth.' *Oxford Review of Economic Policy* 15, no. 3 (1999): 110–31.

Crafts, N.F.R., Steven J. Leybourne and Terence C. Mills. 'Measurement of Trend Growth in European Industrial Output before 1914: Methodological Issues and New Estimates.' *Explorations in Economic History* 27, no. 4 (1990): 442–67.

Dahlman, Carl. J. (1994), 'Technology Strategy in East Asian Developing Countries.' *Journal of Asian Economics* 5, no. 4 (1994): 541–72.

Denison, Edward. F. and William Chung. *How Japan's Economy Grew So Fast*. Washington, DC: Brookings Institution, 1976.

Fohlin, Caroline. 'Financial System Structure and Industrialization: Reassessing the German Experience before World War I.' California Institute of Technology Social Science Working Paper No. 1028, 1998.

Fukuda, Shin-ichi. 'Sources of Economic Growth in East Asian Countries: Why Did Capital Stock Grow So Rapidly?' In OECD, *Structural Aspects of the East Asian Crisis*. Paris: OECD, 29–56, 1999.

Gerschenkron, Alexander. *Economic Backwardness in Historical Perspective*. Cambridge, Mass.: Belknap Press, 1962.

Goldstein, Morris. *The Asian Financial Crisis: Causes, Cures and Systemic Implications*. Washington, DC: Institute for International Economics, 1998.

Grossman, Richard S. 'The Macroeconomic Consequences of Bank Failures under the National Banking System.' *Explorations in Economic History* 30, no. 3 (1993): 294–320.

Harley, C. Knick. 'Substitution for Prerequisites: Endogenous Institutions and Comparative Economic History.' In *Patterns of European Industrialization*, edited by Richard Sylla and Gianni Toniolo, 29–44. London: Routledge, 1991.

Hart, Oliver. *Firms, Contracts, and Financial Structure*. Oxford: Clarendon Press, 1995.

Ide, Masasuke. 'The Financial System and Corporate Competitiveness.' In *Japanese Firms, Finance and Markets*, edited by Paul Sheard, 191–221. New York: Addison-Wesley, 1996.

Ito, Takatoshi. 'Japan and the Asian Economies: A "Miracle" in Transition.' *Brookings Papers on Economic Activity* 2 (1996): 205–72.

Krugman, Paul. 'The Myth of Asia's Miracle.' *Foreign Affairs* 73, no. 6 (1994): 62–78.

Lall, Ashish. 'ASEAN Approaches to Competition Policy.' In *Competition and Regulation: Implications of Globalization for Malaysia and Thailand*, edited by Frank Flatters and David Gillen, 7–32. Kingston: Queen's University Press, 1997.

La Porta, Rafael, Florencio Lopez-de-Silanes, Andrei Shleifer and Robert W. Vishny. 'Legal Determinants of External Finance.' *Journal of Finance* 52, no. 3 (1997): 1131–50.

Lardy, Nicholas. *China's Unfinished Economic Revolution*. Washington, DC: Brookings Institution, 1998.

Lee, Chung. H. 'The Visible Hand and Economic Development: The Case of South Korea.' In *The Economics of Cooperation: East Asian Development and the Case for Pro-Market Intervention*, edited by James A. Roumasset and Susan Barr, 157–73. Oxford: Westview Press, 1992.

Lee, Jong-Wha. 'Government Interventions and Productivity Growth in Korean Manufacturing Industries.' NBER Working Paper No. 5060, Cambridge, MA, 1995.

Levine, Ross. 'The Legal Environment, Banks, and Long-Run Economic Growth.' *Journal of Money, Credit and Banking* 30, no. 3 (1998): 596–611.

Maddison, Angus. 'Macroeconomic Accounts for European Countries.' In *Quantitative Aspects of Postwar European Economic Growth*, edited by Bart van Ark and Nicholas Crafts, 27–83. Cambridge: Cambridge University Press, 1996.

―――. *Chinese Economic Performance in the Long Run*. Paris: OECD, 1998.

Mishkin, Frederic S. 'Asymmetric Information and Financial Crises: A Historical Perspective.' In *Financial Markets and Financial Crises*, edited by R. Glenn Hubbard, 69–108. Chicago: University of Chicago Press, 1991.

Mishkin, Frederic S. and Eakins, Stanley G. *Financial Markets and Institutions*. New York: Addison-Wesley, 1998.

Murphy, Kevin M., Andrei Shleifer and Robert W. Vishny. 'Industrialization and the Big Push.' *Journal of Political Economy* 97, no. 5 (1989): 1003–26.

Naughton, Barry. *Growing Out of the Plan*. Cambridge: Cambridge University Press, 1995.

Nickell, Stephen J. 'Competition and Corporate Performance.' *Journal of Political Economy* 104, no. 4 (1996): 724–46.

Noguchi, Yukio. 'The 1940 System: Japan under the Wartime Economy.' *American Economic Review Papers and Proceedings* 88, no. 2 (1998): 404–07.

North, Douglass C. *Institutions, Institutional Change and Economic Performance*. Cambridge: Cambridge University Press, 1990.

Park, Yung-Chul. 'Concepts and Issues.' In *The Financial Development of Japan, Korea and Taiwan: Growth, Repression and Liberalization*, edited by Hugh. T. Patrick and Yung-Chul Park, 3–26. New York: Oxford University Press, 1994.

Richardson, Pete. 'Globalization and Linkages: Macroeconomic Challenges and Opportunities.' *OECD Economics Studies* 28 (1997): 49–152.

Rodrik, Dani. 'Getting Interventions Right: How South Korea and Taiwan Grew Rich.' *Economic Policy* 20 (1995): 55–107.

―――. 'Coordination Failures and Government Policy: A Model with Applications to East Asia and Eastern Europe.' *Journal of International Economics* 40, no. 1 (1996): 1–22.

———. 'Understanding Economic Policy Reform.' *Journal of Economic Literature* 34, no. 1 (1996): 9–41.

Sylla, Richard and Gianni Toniolo, eds. *Patterns of European Industrialization*. London: Routledge, 1991.

Wade, Robert. *Governing the Market*. Princeton: Princeton University Press, 1990.

White, Lawrence J. 'Financial Infrastructure and Policy Reform in Developing Asia.' In *Financial Sector Development in Asia*, edited by Shahid. N. Zahid, 123–59. Hong Kong: Oxford University Press, 1995.

Williamson, Oliver. E. *The Economic Institutions of Capitalism: Firms, Markets, and Relational Contracting*. New York: Free Press, 1985.

World Bank. *The East Asian Miracle*. New York: Oxford University Press, 1993.

World Bank. *China 2020*. Washington, DC: World Bank, 1997.

World Bank. *East Asia: the Road to Recovery*. Washington, DC: World Bank, 1998.

Young, Alwyn. 'The Tyranny of Numbers: Confronting the Statistical Realities of the East Asian Growth Experience.' *Quarterly Journal of Economics* 110, no. 4 (1995): 641–80.

7.
The Russian Transition through the Historical Looking-glass:
Gradual versus Abrupt Decontrol of Economic Systems in Britain and Russia

CHRISTOPHER DAVIS & JAMES FOREMAN-PECK

Introduction

Throughout the 1990s governments under President Yeltsin attempted to transform the Russian economic system on the basis of a strategy that entailed liberalization of prices and markets, macroeconomic stabilization, and rapid mass privatization. Although some aspects of economic performance had improved by 1997, severe economic problems developed thereafter, culminating in the crash of August 1998. This was triggered by the Asian economic collapse and falling oil prices, but policy errors and neglect of flaws in the economic system underlay the crisis. By the end of the decade it was generally accepted that the attempt to make an abrupt transition to a market economy in Russia had produced a hybrid, malfunctioning economic system.

The reasons for the initial failures of the Russian economic transition have been clarified by new theoretical, empirical and comparative studies. This paper attempts an additional contribution to the analysis of the Russian economic experience by comparing the transition in the 1990s with economic decontrol in Britain following two world wars. The three cases involved a similar challenge of shifting the economic system from a centrally controlled one, with negligible or attenuated private property rights, that was focussed on military production to a market-oriented peacetime economy.[1] But the transition policies adopted and the results obtained varied considerably.

Economic Systems, Decontrol and Transition

Economic transition involves a revolutionary transformation of the characteristics of an economic system, changes in economic policies and environments, and alteration in performance standards of an economy. Economic systems conventionally are classified according to four features: decision-making structure (centralized or decentralized); mechanisms for information and co-ordination (plan or market); property rights (state or private); and incentives (conducive or detrimental to effective corporate governance).[2]

Any viable economic system has to solve fundamental informational problems.[3] Even in a capitalist market economy not all information is conveyed by prices. The price system must be supplemented by implicit or explicit social contracts. Economies require an effective legal infrastructure and transactions inevitably are based on social trust and civil norms, as well as market or plan signals. Any economic system has an intricate institutional fabric and relies on social and organizational capital that takes time to produce. Effective governments are of crucial importance in ensuring the proper functioning of an economic system, although the scale of state intervention can vary substantially.

All economic systems possess the markets and related prices shown in Table 1. The influence of the market mechanism can range from negligible to dominant, depending on the economic system and the prevalence of administrative controls.[4] For example, in most war economies labour allocation is centrally managed and the distribution of commodities is rationed.

Economic performance is determined by the features of an economic system, economic policies (such as fiscal, monetary, exchange rate), and the economic environment (for example, wars, oil prices). Performance measures include economic growth, price and output stability, static and dynamic efficiency, living standards, income distri-

---

[1] This paper is similar in spirit to the study by Feinstein, *Historical Precedents*, which analysed several historical cases of transitions from centralized economic systems. Among his main conclusions were: transition was likely to take an extended period of time; the state would play an important role in transition; an effective financial sector would be needed; and foreign direct investment would be influential in restructuring the economy.
[2] Gregory and Stuart, *Comparative Economic Systems*.
[3] See Stiglitz, 'Whither Reform?'
[4] Kornai, *The Socialist System*.

bution, and attainment of development objectives. Ideally, an economy would achieve economic growth with price and output stability, while raising living standards and maintaining inequality within acceptable limits. Chronic failure to achieve performance objectives can undermine the viability of an economic system and can contribute to revolutions (as in Russia in 1917 and in the USSR in 1991).

Table 1. Markets, prices and administrative controls in economic systems.

Markets	Prices	Administrative Controls
Labour	Wages	Wage Setting, Labour Allocation
Retail Trade	Consumer Prices	Price Controls, Rationing
Wholesale Trade	Producer Prices	Price Controls, Rationing
Capital Market	Interest Rates	Capital Rationing
Foreign Currency	Exchange Rates	Targets, Restriction of Convertibility
Foreign Trade	World Market Prices	Import Controls, Tariffs
Property	Property Prices	State Ownership, Rent Control

The present study considers four economic systems in the UK, the USSR and Russia in peace and war. Their main features are shown in Table 2. The Soviet peacetime command economy relied on central direction, quantity control mechanisms (for example, planning and rationing), state ownership of productive assets, and a mixture of incentives (state-determined material, ideological, coercive) intended to make managers as agents act in the interest of their principal, the state.[5] Its priority system accorded the highest ranking, and best conditions, to heavy industry and defence.[6] The essential processes of this system are described by the shortage economy model.[7]

The British peacetime capitalist economy before and after World War I was a prototype of the open, liberal market economy (column 2). Decision-making was decentralized, transactions were governed by prices determined in free markets, most property was privately owned, and incentives were material and provided primarily by markets. Corporate governance was beginning to be based on equity markets. Although the British economic system deviated from the liberal model following World War II because of the substantial state intervention, for the purposes of this paper it can be roughly described by column 2.

---

[5] See Table 13.6 in Davis, 'Russian Industrial Policy' for a more detailed description of the Soviet command economic system.
[6] See Davis, 'The High Priority'; 'The Defence Sector'.
[7] See Davis and Charemza, *Models*; Kornai, *The Socialist System*.

Table 2. Features of UK, Russian and USSR economic systems.

Feature	Type of Economic System			
	U.K. Peacetime Capitalist	U.K. Wartime Capitalist	Russia Transitional Capitalist	U.S.S.R. Peacetime Command
Decision Making Structure	Decentralized	Centralized	Chaotically Decentralized	Centralized
Mechanisms for Information and Coordination	Primarily Market, but with State Regulation	Plans, Rationing, Import Controls, Restricted Markets	Weak State and Imperfect Markets	Compulsory Plans, Restricted Labour and Retail Markets
Property Rights	Primarily Private Ownership	Nationalization and Requisitioning, but Primarily Private Ownership	State, Legal Private and Organised Crime	State Ownership of All Productive Assets
Incentives and Corporate Governance	Material (cash) and Moral (social trust, civil norms). CG based on Equity Markets.	Moral (patriotism), Material (cash and in-kind benefits). CG based on State.	Predominantly Material (cash). Ineffective CG due to Weaknesses of State, Banks and Equity Markets.	Material (cash, privileges), Moral (communist ideology), Coercion

Source: Adapted from Gregory and Stuart, *Comparative*, p. 27 and Davis, 'Russian Industrial'.

The characteristics of the contemporary Russian transition economic system are outlined in column 4.[8] Decision-making is more decentralized than in the Soviet system, however powerful central organs intervene in economic processes frequently but unpredictably. In principle, transactions are determined by markets and prices, but in reality state intervention and quantity controls play dominant roles. Most assets have been privatized, but in industry they have been sold to 'insiders' and legal protection of property rights is weak. Incentives are based on material rewards, but often these are not related to productive economic activities. Corporate governance is largely ineffective because of weakness of the state, banks and equity markets.

In wartime any basic economic system can be mobilized to support the military effort. If this mobilization proceeds beyond a critical point, a transition is made to a war economy. This type of economic system inevitably has many of the features of the command economy, although the degree of administrative intervention has varied between

---

[8] The Russian economic system is described in greater detail in Table 13.7 in Davis, 'Russian Industrial Policy'.

countries. The British war economies during both World War I and World War II (column 3) were closer in many respects to the Soviet command economy than to the US market-oriented war economy in that they relied on pervasive rationing, *de facto* nationalization, and non-price control mechanisms.

Reduction in the degree of state intervention in an economic system is economic decontrol.[9] Its measures include privatization, elimination of administrative oversight, liberalization of prices and foreign trade, and relaxation of exchange controls. Pursued far enough, decontrol can alter the nature of an economic system, initiating an economic transition.

The transition process involves the movement of an economic system from an initial state along a path to an end state associated with a different economic system. For most of the twentieth century economic transition referred to the shifts of 'modes of production' from Feudalism to Capitalism to Socialism to Communism. Systemic transformations were caused by clashes between classes (for example, capitalists, proletariat) with the ascendant class usually being led by a revolutionary group (Bolsheviks, for instance). Since 1990, economic transition usually describes the change from a centralized, state-owned, planned economy to a market economy that is predominantly privately owned, decentralized and governed by market mechanisms.

A transition strategy determines the path from the initial state to the desired end state and the speed of movement. It involves the choice of reforms to develop or create institutions, as well as of economic programmes (for example, privatization) and policies (for example, macroeconomic stabilization) to facilitate movement towards established objectives. In the early post-Communist transition the main strategic options were 'big bang' and 'gradualism'.[10] Within a given strategy there is scope for variations in policies, such as orthodox versus heterodox stabilization. Strategic and policy errors (such as maintaining an over-valued exchange rate) can adversely affect the outcomes of the transition.

Both command and war economies allocate resources administratively in accordance with the preferences of the political elite. They distribute significantly more capital and labour to heavy and defence

---

[9] See Tawney, 'The Abolition'.
[10] See Roland, 'On the Speed'; Sachs, *Understanding*; Gros and Steinherr, *Winds*; Blanchard, *The Economics*.

Changes in Economic Regimes and Ideologies

industries than would an open market economy in peacetime. In the centrally planned economies the over-developed branches of industry typically had low productivity and their products were uncompetitive in world markets. In consequence, one of the main tasks of transition from a command/war economy to a market one is the reallocation of resources within manufacturing to competitive sectors and from industry to services.

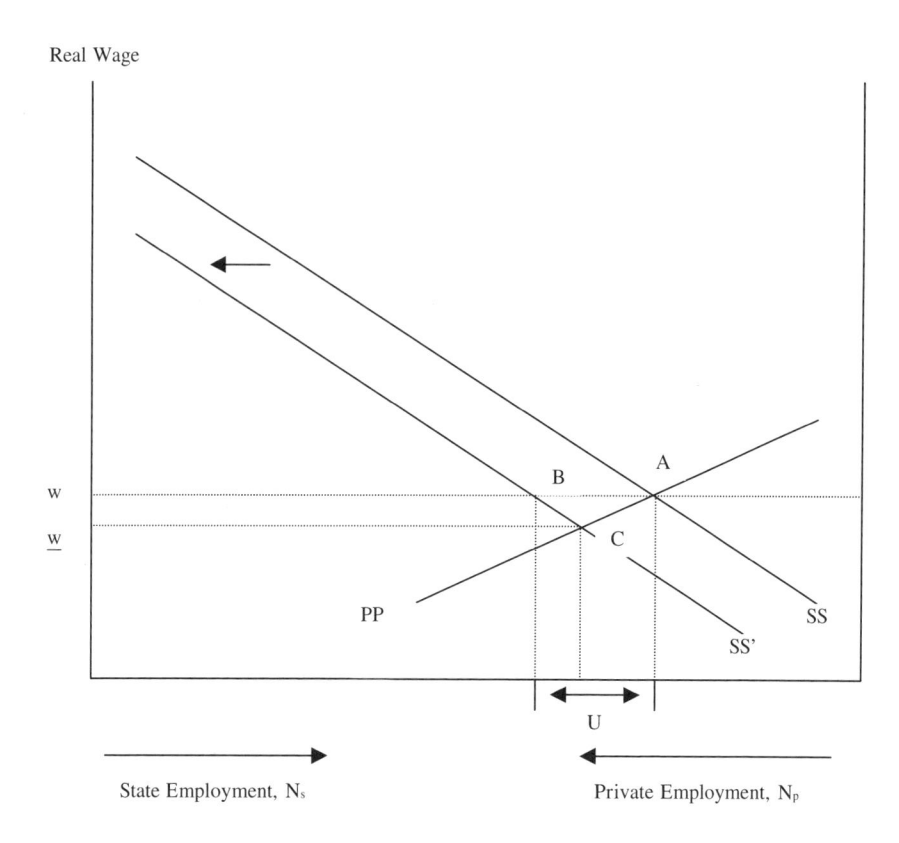

Figure 1. Reallocation of Labour During Economic Transition.
Source: Blanchard, *The Economics*, p. 30.

The reallocation is described in simple form in Figure 1 from O. Blanchard's *The Economics of Post Communist Transition*. The equilibrium position pre-transition is denoted by point A. The demand for labour by state firms, SS, is measured from left to right on the horizontal axis, whereas private sector demand, PP, is measured right to left. The equilibrium real wage is w and full employment is achieved at A. Assume that transition policies initially involve a removal of subsidies to the state sector but no significant change for the private sector. For example, the private sector goes on paying taxes because the debt incurred to pay for the war must be serviced and redeemed, whereas the purchase of armaments and war-related stores by the government ceases. The state sector demand curve for labour will shift to the left (SS') and the demand for labour at the existing wage, w, will drop to B. Private sector employment, N_p, will continue to be that associated with point A. In this case, unemployment will increase to U. Over the longer term, in an optimistic case, surviving state firms will restructure and the real wage will decline to w̲. State and private demands for labour approach point C and unemployment falls from the early phase of transition peak. This would be a positive benefit from the process of 'creative destruction' in the economy.

This reallocation problem suggests that former war/command economies undergoing decontrol could exhibit similar 'double cycles' without state intervention.[11] After the forced participation of labour in the war/command economy, decontrol allows some workers to leave the workforce and others to work less hard or put in shorter hours (again, a decline in state employment in Figure 1). Physical output therefore should fall, although that may not be true of the market value of output, other things being equal. This slump will be reinforced by the cancellation of government orders (the process already discussed). A contrary tendency should soon come into play as a result of reconstruction, however. In both market and planned economies after a war there is worn-out or destroyed physical equipment to be replaced or repaired, and there are many areas of neglect to be remedied. The demand for investment should generate increases in output and employment. Once immediate reconstruction has been completed in a market system, it is likely that there will be a second 'pause' while assessments are made of where resources should be directed in changed post-war/transition conditions. Market signals, especially volatile floating exchange rates in a world of inconsistent national policies and substantial shocks, may be misleading or inadequate to ensure rapid adjustment. The economy may become trapped in the underemployment equilibrium of Figure 1. In these circumstances the state

---

[11] See Pigou, *Aspects*.

could play a useful role in identifying sectors with promising future employment prospects and in encouraging resource shifts.

A second important process in transition, according to Blanchard, is restructuring.[12] This involves finding dynamic managers, identifying profitable product lines, closing unviable plants, reducing labour hoarding and renewing capital. Blanchard assumes that state firms are capable of engaging in defensive restructuring at the start of transition, but that privatization, in particular on an outsider basis, is necessary to promote the strategic restructuring that is essential for the survival of firms in the new market economy. Institutional and cultural shifts matter greatly at this stage, and depend on the historical legacy.[13] The four million men demobilized in Britain at the end of World War I to join a male workforce of eight million often experienced this acutely, albeit in less extreme form than former Soviet workers. One returning former army officer wrote that, after nearly five years on active service:

> I still had the army habit of commandeering anything of uncertain ownership that I found lying about; also a difficulty in telling the truth—it was always easier for me now, when charged with any fault, to lie my way out in army style.[14]

During transitions in the aftermath of wars or in Eastern Europe/FSU in the 1990s, reallocation and restructuring are impeded by 'noise' that distorts price signals and 'disorganization'. The latter is caused by the breakdown in traditional links between industrial firms and their suppliers, both within the country and abroad.[15] It takes time for markets to develop and for price signals to direct resources. This confusion, and the resulting adverse impacts on output and efficiency, is connected with 'transformational recession', which accompanies the shift in economic systems from a resource-constrained (shortage) economy to a demand-constrained (market) economy.[16]

Disorganization in a transition process creates bottlenecks due to deficiencies in infrastructure and/or insufficient production of key goods and services. During the debate over the industrialization strategy in the USSR in the 1920s, those who believed in gradualism and genetic planning argued that bottlenecks should be avoided by ensur-

---

[12] Blanchard, *The Economics*.
[13] See Rapcyzynski, 'The Roles'.
[14] Graves, *Goodbye*, p. 254.
[15] Blanchard and Kremer, 'Disorganization'.
[16] See Kornai, *The Socialist System* and 'Transformational Recession'.

ing the economy developed towards socialism in a balanced and flexible manner. Advocates of teleological planning, however, claimed that attainment of Party-determined goals was of over-riding importance and that bottlenecks should be 'broken through' when they are engendered by rapid unbalanced development. Similar debates arose in the 1990s. Economists in favour of gradualist (genetic) transition urged caution in the face of bottlenecks. In contrast, the advocates of the 'big bang' strategy favoured attacking them simultaneously on all fronts.

Throughout the twentieth century there have been debates over whether transition from one economic system to another is best advanced by the 'ideological, fundamental and root-and-branch approach to reform as opposed to an incremental, remedial, piecemeal and adaptive approach'.[17] Both Karl Popper and Friedrich von Hayek criticized the utopian, brutal social engineering that the Bolsheviks employed in their attempt to construct socialism. In contrast, Soviet theorists and their Western supporters, such as E.H. Carr and M. Dobb, defended Bolshevik methods with the argument that they were inevitable in light of the domestic and foreign challenges confronting the USSR. Somewhat similar disputes arose in the West following both world wars. Liberals in Britain and the USA consistently prescribed policies intended to decontrol war economies as rapidly as possible and to transfer resources back to the private sector if they had been nationalized. In contrast, the dominant European opinion was that the best strategy would involve a gradual transition from the war economy with maintenance of price, import, and capital controls and nationalized industries for a lengthy period of peacetime.[18]

When the anti-communist revolutions in Eastern Europe and the USSR occurred in the period 1989 to 1991 the economic orthodoxy in the West was of an unusually liberal character for a combination of intellectual and political reasons. The early thinking about transition by reformers in the East, such as L. Balcerowicz in Poland, was dominated by liberal ideas.[19] According to the neo-liberal doctrine, transition could be most effectively advanced on the basis of a programme of rapidly introduced, comprehensive reforms that included: price liberalization; mass privatization; macroeconomic stabilization using hetero-

---

[17] See Stiglitz, 'Whither Reform?'.
[18] See Foreman-Peck and Federico, *A Century*.
[19] See Balcerowicz, *Socialism*; Murrell, 'How Far?'; Wedel, *Collision*; Stiglitz, 'Whither Reform?'.

dox packages (for example, using the exchange rate as a nominal anchor); foreign trade liberalization (for example, elimination of the state monopoly of foreign trade and adoption of low explicit tariffs); and currency convertibility.[20] The liberal reformers considered that governments in the transition countries were inefficient, obstructive and corrupt. Economic processes therefore should be governed by markets and free prices in the private sector. They argued that countries that rigorously implemented the liberal strategy would achieve the best economic results. The economic recoveries in countries that adopted variants of 'shock therapy', notably Poland, appeared to validate their position.[21]

Many area specialist economists criticized neo-liberal doctrines concerning the transition strategy and policies.[22] Subsequent theoretical and empirical work undermined many of the arguments of the liberal reformers and demonstrated that failures in programmes of macroeconomic stabilization and voucher mass privatization were due primarily to design flaws rather than to improper implementation. In 'Whither Reform?' the former Chief Economist of the World Bank, Joseph Stiglitz, claims that many liberal reformers misunderstood the essential nature of the existing market economies and based their policy prescriptions on outmoded, simplistic neoclassical economic models.[23] They placed great faith in private property, markets and prices but ignored many key features of capitalist economies that ensure their effective functioning. Among the deficiencies of relevance to this paper are:

[20] See World Bank, *From Plan to Market*.
[21] See EBRD, *Transition Report 1999* for a comprehensive review of the contrasting experiences of 26 countries in Eastern Europe and the Former Soviet Union that have been engaged in transition. On p. 22 the report states that 'Over the past decade, two broad patterns in transition have emerged. In more advanced countries, rapid liberalization, sustained macroeconomic stabilization and comprehensive small-scale privatization have laid the basis for the gradual development of the institutions that are necessary to support markets and private enterprise...In the less advanced countries, progress in liberalization has been slow and uneven. Moreover, macroeconomic stabilization in these countries has been jeopardized by the persistence of soft budget constraints for 'old' enterprises and banks and their continuing structural weaknesses, while the business environment for new private enterprises remains difficult.' This paper is not making a general argument that abrupt transition ('shock therapy') cannot work, since the Polish case provides evidence to the contrary. Rather, it was not likely to succeed in Russia given the unfavourable initial political and economic conditions.
[22] Murrell, 'The Transition'; Ellman, 'The State'; Sapir, *Le Chaos*; Brada, 'Privatization'.
[23] See Mau, *Russian Economic* for a critique of Stiglitz, 'Whither Reform?'

(a) neglect of institutions, social and organizational capital and the legal infrastructure;
(b) failure to recognize that the price system is not the only conveyor of information;
(c) naive belief in the efficacy of privatization on its own;
(d) misunderstanding of the investment process and the roles of financial institutions; and
(e) neglect of the contribution of the state to managing an economy.

By the mid-1990s it was evident that weaknesses of the states in many of the transition countries were undermining economic programmes. Macroeconomic stabilization was jeopardized by failures to collect taxes, industrial restructuring was hamstrung by inadequate legal safeguards of private property, competition policy was blocked by regulatory capture and development of adequate social safety nets was stillborn. A new, more centrist, orthodoxy was outlined in World Bank, *The State in a Changing World*, which acknowledged the constructive role of state institutions in market economies. Overall, the consensus concerning transition shifted from the liberal end of the economic policy spectrum towards the middle.

Abrupt Decontrol of the British War Economy after 1918

The transition from a war economy in Britain after 1918 was primarily governed by liberal economic policies and a 'big bang' stabilization programme. Free markets and private enterprise were expected to direct economic activities almost immediately, despite the massive changes in the structure of the economy caused by the war effort and the fragile state of many market-related institutions. This abrupt decontrol of an administered economic system created problems in reallocation of resources and restructuring.

As World War I intensified, it had become clear that a comprehensive mobilization of resources was needed. Britain developed a war economy with the features summarized in Table 2.[24] The government assumed control of much activity. The Ministry of Munitions supervised 20,000 establishments and managed the iron mining industry. The coal mining industry operated under the Coal Controller.

[24] See Dearle, *An Economic Chronicle*; Tawney, 'The Abolition'; Ministry of Munitions, *History*.

Administrative methods typical of command economies replaced the markets and prices shown in Table 1 as a means of coordination. The state nationalized private property crucial for the war effort or assumed use rights to it. The state dominated the labour market. By 1918 4.7 million people were serving in the armed forces, about one-quarter of those in civilian work in 1913. About two-thirds of civilian employees were working in industries that were subjected to wartime regulation. For example, the Ministry of Munitions employed directly and indirectly 3.4 million people. The government transferred workers from 'non-essential' to 'essential' jobs and held them there by a system of leaving certificates. Wage rates were set within centrally determined bands.

In retail markets more than four-fifths of all food consumed by civilians was bought and sold by the Ministry of Food and over nine-tenths was subject to maximum prices fixed by the Ministry.[25] The wholesale market was carefully controlled and industrial supplies were allocated according to state priorities and administrative prices. Capital markets were highly restricted and the state directed the flow of investment into sectors of the economy that were vital for the war effort. Freedom of international trade was suspended. Ninety per cent of imports were purchased on the Government's account and shipping was controlled.[26] The British economy's dependence on imported food and raw materials gave the state a powerful instrument of economic influence. Tight controls were placed on the convertibility of sterling and the exchange rate was managed in accordance with war aims. Private property rights in industry continued to exist, but they were radically attenuated. The Ministries of Food and Agriculture determined the utilization of land. The Railway Executive, the Ministry of Shipping, and the Canal Control Committee directed transport. Many private residences and commercial buildings were requisitioned for war uses.

National output and employment rose during the war while price stability was maintained by administrative means. Annual production of artillery pieces rose from 91 in 1914 to 8,039 in 1918, while aircraft production increased from 200 to 32,000 over the same period. Although government followed prudent macroeconomic policies, it was not possible to finance its cumulative (imperial) war expenditure,

---

[25] See Beveridge, *British Food*; Lloyd, *Experiments*.
[26] See Fayle, *The War*.

amounting to 40 per cent of the Allied total, with tax revenue and sale of assets.[27] It had to borrow heavily in world capital markets and to guarantee loans for financially weaker allies, such as Italy and Russia.

When the war ended, the British government was confronted by a multitude of tasks. One was to transform the economic system, with its accompanying reallocation and restructuring (Figure 1). Others included maintaining domestic political control in a revolutionary period, rebuilding international economic relations in a severely disrupted global economy, and servicing a massive war debt. Inevitably, alternative strategies were debated. Many members of the government and public had become accustomed to the wartime economy, with its extensive state intervention, and were in favour of gradual change to an economic system with greater government involvement than had been the case before the war. The War Cabinet received reports listing advantages of the wartime controls. *De jure* state ownership of industry controlled by government, and already nationalized *de facto*, was a popular solution, especially for transportation, electricity and coal. Indeed, Winston Churchill advocated the nationalization of railways in his 1918 election campaign.[28]

In contrast, influential representatives of business and banking were in favour of rapid decontrol and a reversion to the pre-war system. The 1919 Cunliffe Committee advocated a speedy return to normality in the economy and to the Gold Standard. Although advice from the USA concerning post-war economic policies was not especially important in influencing the British debate on transition, it was based on liberal prescriptions (market-determined prices, free trade, promotion of competition) and therefore supported those in favour of rapid decontrol.

However, initial economic and social policies were primarily influenced by the government's determination to maintain political stability in a chaotic world. The revolutions in Russia had attracted considerable interest. For example, the leader of the Labour Party, Ramsay MacDonald, supported discussions about the formation of workers' and soldiers' councils in Great Britain. By the end of the war most armed forces were experiencing difficulty in maintaining discipline as unrest increased among the troops and occasional mutinies occurred. In January 1919 a 'soldiers' council' was formed at the Army Service

---

[27] See Kennedy, *The Rise*, p. 274.
[28] See Mowat, *Britain*, p. 16.

Corps depot at Kempton Park, and soldiers demonstrated near Whitehall demanding to be demobilized. Taking these factors into account, Churchill accelerated demobilization. Within a year over 4 million men had been released.[29] Lloyd George wrested control of the public finances from the Treasury, and ordered an expansion of demand in order to absorb the newly released labour.[30] As a result, industrial output rose in the period 1919/20 and unemployment was kept low (Table 3). The social safety net was improved to ensure that the unemployed received relatively generous benefits. A reaction to the effort of war work was a spontaneous labour-led reduction of the length of the working week in industry, as well as withdrawal from the labour force of many workers, especially women.[31]

Table 3. The UK economy during abrupt decontrol, 1918–1925.

Indicator	Units	1918	1919	1920	1921	1922	1923	1924	1925
Industrial production	1918=100	100	110	122	100	115	122	136	141
Investment/GDP	%	NA	NA	NA	8.9	8.7	8.0	8.8	9.2
Unemployment	%	0.8	5.4	3.5	17.2	13.0	11.5	10.8	11.0
Cost of living	1918=100	100	106	123	111	90	86	86	87

Sources: Unemployment (among insured) from Pigou *Aspects*; Industrial Production and Cost of Living from Mitchell, *Abstract*, and converted, respectively, from 1924=100 and 1914=100. Investment/GDP from Feinstein, *Domestic Capital*.

While this boom was occurring, the debate over the transition strategy was resolved in favour of a 'big bang' by inertial forces. The legislation that had allowed the government to intervene comprehensively in the wartime economy had also provided for the termination of special powers within a short period of the cessation of hostilities. Although arguments were put forward to maintain key aspects of the war economy, parliament did not pass supportive legislation. As a result, by 1920 most administrative controls affecting the markets and prices shown in Table 1 had disappeared. Food rationing and tight regulation of capital markets were quickly eliminated.

The peacetime economic system that emerged in Britain had many of the characteristics of the pre-war one, but the war had generated

---

[29] See Pigou, *Aspects*.
[30] See Howson, *British*.
[31] See Broadberry, 'The Emergence'; Dowie, '1919–20'.

significant changes in both the domestic and world economy.[32] Much social and organizational capital had been degraded during the war, along with physical capital. The re-establishment of the conventions and customs on which markets depend required considerable time, especially without government involvement. There was substantial 'noise' and 'disorganization' in the economy that impeded microeconomic adjustments in markets. This caused confusion even among those who had been the strongest advocates of rapid decontrol:

> It was difficult for [businessmen] to realize, especially in a continent accustomed for nearly half a century to take an ordered routine of existence for granted, that the very possibility of economic activity depends on the maintenance of an elaborate framework of economic habits, social conventions, rules of law and political organization which is a highly artificial product, and with the crumbling of which, the operations of business are arrested or stultified.[33]

Although most property was transferred back to the private sector rapidly, this was not sufficient in itself to ensure effective corporate governance and necessary restructuring.

Another key economic objective was to return to the gold standard. The exchange rate was allowed to float up at the end of the war (rather than adopting rigorous controls around a fixed rate as after World War II). This facilitated British inflation during the post-war boom and subsequently required extensive price deflation to return to the gold standard at the pre-war rate. Meanwhile, confused signals about optimal movements of labour and capital were transmitted, exacerbating the unemployment problem described in the preceding section. A speculative stock-market boom over-capitalized a large number of companies and required subsequent painful restructuring.

While the economic system was adjusting to the rapid decontrol, macroeconomic policies abruptly changed. Once demobilization was completed in 1920, the Treasury regained its influence and attempted to combat the growing inflation by tightening fiscal and monetary policies. The demand-suppressing macroeconomic policies generated deflation and a fall in output (Table 3). Industrial production collapsed to its 1918 level in 1921, but increased in subsequent years. However, unemployment rose abruptly to 17.2 per cent in 1921 and remained above 10 per cent until the next war boom in the late 1930s (Figure 2).

[32] Foreman-Peck, *A History*.
[33] Tawney, 'The Abolition'.

Changes in Economic Regimes and Ideologies

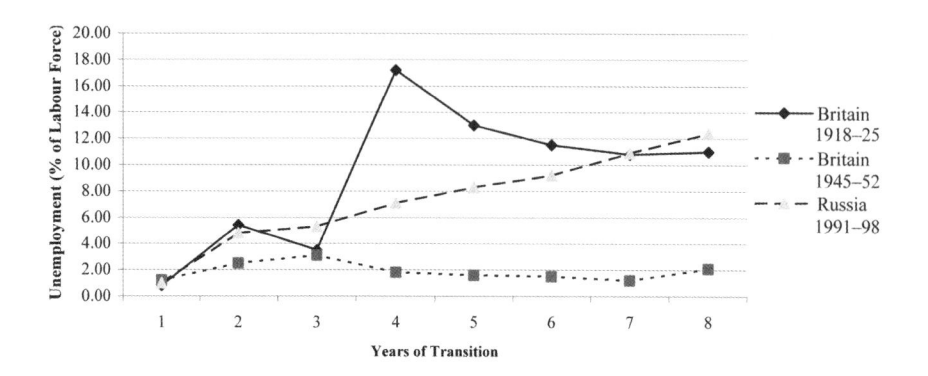

Figure 2. Unemployment During Abrupt and Gradual Economic Transitions.
Sources: Britain 1918–25 Pigou (1948); Britain 1945–52 LCES and *Annual Abstract of Statistics*; Russia 1991–98 GKRFS (1998) and EBRD (1999).

In terms of Figure 1, this represented a sudden drop in state sector (war economy) demand for labour with only a slow compensating growth in private sector (civilian) demand.

The combination of disorganization in the economic system together with unstable and incorrect economic policies (such as an over-valued exchange rate) undermined the reallocation of resources and restructuring of industry. Sectors that had over-expanded during the war in response to administrative signals (for example, shipbuilding, engineering, coal and cotton) did not adjust to weak and confusing signals from markets. Keynes' former intellectual adversary Pigou observed that 'many persons for many years were clinging to occupations in which their services were not, and were not likely to be wanted...there was a role for a well managed state to signal the change in the world pattern of industry'.[34] The consequences of these adjustment problems plagued the British economy throughout the inter-war period.

Gradual Decontrol of the British War Economy After 1945

In contrast to the transition after 1918, and in part because of the lessons learned from it, the transition after 1945 was much more gradual. The state maintained administrative controls for much of the initial

---

[34] Pigou, *Aspects*, p. 4.

post-war decade and its macroeconomic policies were more expansive. The outcomes of this shift from a war economy were more benign.

During 1939 to 1945 Britain again developed an effective war economy in which all the features identified in Table 2 and the administrative controls listed in Table 1 were more pronounced than was the case in World War I.[35] The armed forces and defence-related industries were given highest priority. Civilian investment and consumption were severely reduced. At the peak of the war, over two-thirds of national resources were directly employed on government work.[36] Wartime planning was based on physical output targets and rationing. As in the USSR, central planning was not infallible and plans were never fulfilled exactly because of second thoughts, errors or changes in circumstances. However, the administrative system did ensure the economy effectively attained vital targets.[37]

By 1944, 22 per cent of the British labour force was in the armed forces and another 33 per cent was in war-related employment. The manpower survey and manpower allocation provided the foundation for central planning in the later phases of the war. The Control of Engagement Order required employers to hire labour and workers to take jobs in accordance with instructions of the national employment service.[38]

The retail market was heavily regulated. Food and clothing were rationed. At the end of the war, one-half of total consumer spending was on goods and services affected by price controls. Virtually all producer goods that were normally traded in wholesale markets were either rationed by the state or traded in prescribed quantities at controlled prices.

Banks were tightly regulated and their main function was to mobilize resources for state directed investment. Domestic capital and equity markets became dormant. Sterling was made inconvertible for the private sector during the war. The government manipulated the exchange rate and used available foreign currency to achieve war objectives. Foreign trade by individuals was prohibited. The state

---

[35] In *Audit of War*, Barnett condemns the war economy and transition in the light of the economic failures of the later 1960s and 1970s. This ignores the substantial achievement of the years immediately after 1945 in contrast to those after 1918.
[36] Robinson, 'The Overall Allocation', p. 35.
[37] Detailed histories of the British war economy are to be found in Hancock and Gowing, *British*; Hurstfield, *The Control*; Scott and Hughes, *The Administration*; Hall and Wrigley, *Studies*; and Hornby, *Factories*.
[38] See Cairncross, *Years*.

governed the flows of resources into and out of the country on the basis of quantity-based import and export controls.[39]

The war economy of Britain differed radically from that of the United States. The US was under less pressure to mobilize resources and it did not rely significantly on nationalization and physical planning. The American economy, at least five times the size of the British, was more able to maintain markets in relatively free forms and relied on monetary controls.[40]

The British war economic system achieved its main goals. The production of all major weapons systems increased dramatically. Annual aircraft output rose from 7,940 in 1939 to a peak of 26,461 in 1944 (compared with 96,318 in the USA and 38,807 in Germany). The value of British armaments production in 1944 was close to that of Germany and the USSR, and one-third that of the USA. However, British armaments output per head of population was as high as the US measure, despite a much lower peacetime industrial productivity.

By early 1945 it became clear that both Germany and Japan were heading for defeat and that planning for peacetime should be accelerated. The problems that would confront Britain during the transition in the reallocation of resources and industrial restructuring would be more acute than those following World War I because the economy had become more distorted by the higher intensity and longer duration of World War II. Furthermore, there was considerable international disorganization. Continental Europe had been devastated by the conflict, as had large areas of Asia. There was a realignment of the global political system. The Soviet Union was expanding control into Europe and revolutionary communist movements were strong in major European countries, notably France and Italy, and in the Third World.

In the policy debate the right-left conflict was more acute than after 1918. The Conservative Party and liberal economists were critical of central planning and public ownership, which were associated with the Stalinist system, and argued for a rapid return to a market economy with predominantly private ownership and uncontrolled prices. The 'big bang' approach to transition was supported by the influential US government, which advised Britain to decontrol quickly, emphasize macroeconomic stabilization and move rapidly to currency convertibility and a flexible exchange rate. This strategy was opposed by the

---

[39] See Allen, 'Mutual Aid'.
[40] Robinson, 'The Overall Allocation', p. 54.

Labour Party and by a wide section of British policy-making opinion. During the war, the civil service commissioned the study of decontrol after World War I by Cambridge economics professor A.C. Pigou (the 1948 published version is cited above). R. H. Tawney at the London School of Economics at the same time undertook and published in 1943 a similar assessment.[41] The Labour Party's policy in favour of state ownership of key industries, controls on capital and foreign currency markets, state-directed investment and a tax-financed, comprehensive social safety net was therefore not merely partisan.

The debate was resolved by the victory of the Labour Party in the election of 1945. The new government was committed to cutting defence spending as soon as possible, improving the social safety net while controlling private consumption, and channelling investment into restructuring.[42] Unlike the government after World War I, it intended to keep in place many of the administrative controls over markets shown in Table 1. The Chancellor of the Exchequer of this time, Sir Stafford Cripps, believed in long-term plans for basic industries and the *Economic Survey for 1947* included output targets for the main branches of the economy.[43]

However, the Labour government's freedom of manoeuvre was constrained by its financial dependence on the United States. Although the Americans could not determine domestic economic policies, they were able to influence Britain to adopt liberal trade and convertibility policies as the price of a post-war loan. The adverse consequences are discussed below. But the emergence of the Cold War led to a reversal of the free market orientation of US foreign policy and thereby supported Britain's gradualist transition. For the Americans, preventing Europe going Communist assumed higher priority than propagating liberal policies. Consequently, instead of imposing reforms on Europe that would have squeezed demand and opened the economies to US competition, the Marshall Aid programme facilitated a rapid post-war expansion.[44]

---

[41] Tawney, 'The Abolition'.
[42] The 'social safety net' that Sachs identifies in *Understanding* as a key element of contemporary transition was prominent in the British transition after 1945.
[43] The *Economic Survey of 1947* contained the first and only attempt in an official British publication to explain what economic planning entailed. It discussed the need to match resources and requirements, either manpower or national income, but no explanation was offered of how a balance would be reached. Detailed investment targets had disappeared from the *Economic Surveys* by 1951. See Cairncross, *Years*, p. 302.
[44] See Foreman-Peck, *A History*, pp. 245–9.

In the labour market the government acquired powers to direct labour shortly after the *Economic Survey for 1947* was published, and these were not formally abandoned until 1950. However, it was loath to use labour controls in practice and never succeeded in linking them with the manpower budget. The much-maligned post-war social contract seems to have yielded labour harmony dividends in the short run.[45] Industrial disputes in the nationalized coal industry were absent in the transition period (unlike in the transition after 1918), despite the decline in the labour force, in contrast to the free enterprise inter-war years and to the strike-prone 1950s. That the devaluation of 1949 was not followed by a rise in wages may be interpreted as further evidence of the effectiveness of Labour's labour and social safety net policies (notably the introduction of the National Health Service in 1948) in maintaining social cohesion during a disruptive reallocation of resources. Conversion of war industries into civilian ones capable of producing goods to satisfy peace-time demands, and absorption of demobilized servicemen, were not the only challenges confronting the economy. In addition, the structure of industry and employment needed to be changed from the 1938 pattern in order to manufacture the extra exports that would pay for the foreign exchange costs of the war.

The government kept controls in retail markets, for most of the first decade after the war, that were designed to align consumption with administratively determined supplies (as in Soviet consumption planning).[46] One-third of consumer spending was on rationed products in 1948, but from 1949 the proportion was never more than one-eighth. Despite the excess demand for consumer goods at the fixed prices, the black market appears to have been relatively unimportant in Britain after the war, presumably due to the population's ideological commitment.[47] Wholesale markets were similarly constrained. Coal was rationed until 1958. Investment, timber, steel and building were all affected by raw material allocation controls. Car producers in 1948 were required to export 70 per cent of their output as a condition of receiving a steel allocation.[48]

---

[45] See Barnett, *The Audit*, and Eichengreen, 'Institutions'.
[46] See Cairncross, *Years*, pp. 305, 334.
[47] Ibid., p. 351.
[48] Foreman-Peck, Bowden and McKinlay, *The British Motor*, pp. 101–2.

Britain, like most European countries, maintained tight restrictions on financial markets during the transition period (1945 to 1949). Credit was rationed and the state attempted to influence the flow to projects deemed useful for economic recovery. Foreign direct investment did not play a significant role in the British economy immediately after the war.

As mentioned, Britain moved rapidly to sterling convertibility, which was inconsistent with a gradual transition. This liberal policy was maintained for five weeks in 1947, which was the period necessary to exhaust British dollar reserves.[49] Controls were re-imposed after the failure of this premature experiment. However, the run on sterling traumatized British policy-makers and made them acutely sensitive about exchange rate policies for many years afterwards.

Quantitative import controls remained in place after the war. In 1946 the government imported 80 per cent of food and raw materials. Although Britain obtained some short-term benefits from the trade restrictions, in the longer term they probably discouraged competitiveness and reorganization in British industry, and possibly repressed unemployment. Trade controls were removed in the 1950s, just as competition from war-damaged European economies intensified.[50]

Table 4. The UK economy during gradual decontrol, 1945–1952

Indicator	Units	1945	1946	1947	1948	1949	1950	1951	1952
Industrial production	1945=100	100	106	112	122	129	136	141	138
Investment/GDP	%	NA	10.4	12.7	13.5	14.2	14.5	14.6	15.0
Unemployment Rate	%	1.2	2.5	3.1	1.8	1.6	1.5	1.2	2.1
Cost of Living	1945=100	100	104	110	116	120	124	137	149

Source: Industrial Production from *Economic Trends* (1969) with index changed from 1963=100. Unemployment from LCES and *Annual Abstract of Statistics*; Cost of Living from Department of Employment *Gazette* with index changed from 1963=100; Investment/GDP from HMSO, *National Income*.

Immediately after the war many properties under the control of the government were returned to their private owners. However, the Labour government nationalized several important industries (coal, electricity, telecommunications, steel). This state control enabled the government to carry out some reactive restructuring without labour

---

[49] Cairncross, *Years*, Chap. 6; Pressnell, *External*, pp. 366–7.
[50] See Milward and Brennan, *Britain's Place*.

unrest, as discussed above. But more radical, strategic restructuring was deferred because of political constraints.

As a result of the gradual systemic changes and expansionary macroeconomic policies linked to the Cold War rearmament, the British economy performed quite well in the initial years after World War II (Table 4 and Figure 2). The government was able to demobilize a large army and reallocate resources quickly to meet immediate needs while increasing output, maintaining full employment, and keeping inflation under control. Over the seven years after World War II the UK did not experience a major slump and high unemployment rates as it did in the aftermath of World War I, although prices were kept under tighter control in the earlier period (Table 3 and Figure 2). Since recessions damage confidence and generate 'noise' that distorts entrepreneurial decisions, the stability that accompanied the gradual transition undoubtedly was beneficial. Nonetheless, government policy was not necessarily optimal. The manufacturing sector was expanded to a historically unprecedented size to gain foreign exchange earnings to pay Britain's foreign debts. As a consequence of the neglect of radical restructuring, the sector later had to be run down as German and Japanese competition recovered, and high productivity service trades were encouraged to grow in its place.

Economic Transition in Russia in the 1990s

The liberal policies that were adopted by successive Russian governments in the 1990s to promote transition to a market economy were analogous in many respects to those in Britain after 1918. However, initial conditions were more unfavourable in Russia (for example, severe repressed inflation) and the command economic system was more entrenched. Most economic agents lacked any experience with a free market system. Due to these factors, the consequences of abrupt decontrol were more adverse.

The Soviet command economy evolved out of the Stalinist system. Its main characteristics are summarized in Table 2.[51] One salient feature was highly centralized control of economic processes. All the markets and prices identified in Table 1 were either tightly regulated or

[51] The Soviet economic system is described in detail in Gregory and Stuart, *Soviet Economic* and in Davis, 'Russia'.

inactive. There was some freedom in the labour market, but wage rates were determined centrally and mobility was constrained by inflexibility in the housing market. Retail markets existed, but prices tended to be set below market clearing level, so they were afflicted by chronic excess demand and shortages. Industrial supplies were distributed by centralized rationing; wholesale markets were of negligible significance. Banks operated in accordance with state instructions, interest rates were unimportant and no equity market existed. The currency was inconvertible, citizens could not hold foreign currency, and administratively determined currency conversion coefficients were used to link world market prices to ruble prices. The government held a monopoly of foreign trade and used planning to govern exchanges. All productive assets were owned by the state. The government, as principal, made use of material and moral incentives to control the behaviour of its managers (agents). Resources were allocated in accordance with the preferences of the Communist Party elite. Their main objectives were to develop science and industry in order to promote growth and to support a powerful military. The Soviet economy was dominated by a large military-industrial complex that had highest priority and, at a minimum, absorbed about 16 per cent of GDP in the mid-eighties.[52]

Although the Soviet command economy was successful in achieving a number of objectives (expansion of industry, attainment of superpower status, creation of a comprehensive social safety net), it was plagued by the problems characteristic of a shortage economy.[53] Of particular concern to the leadership were the deceleration of growth, the failure to shift to intensive growth, and the widening technological gaps between the USSR and the West, especially in the military sphere. Among the key tasks of General Secretary Mikhail Gorbachev in the *perestroika* period were to reallocate resources between sectors (as discussed above), improve efficiency and restructure industrial firms. A major defence industry conversion programme was adopted and the defence budget was cut. Numerous enterprise reforms were introduced with the objectives of decentralizing decision-making and raising productivity. However, the failure to introduce complementary reforms meant that firms operated in an economic environment with weakening planning, malfunctioning markets and absence of scarcity prices. By 1989 severe external and internal disequilibria had developed.

[52] See Davis, 'The High Priority', and 'The Defence Sector'.
[53] See Davis and Charemza, *Models*; Kornai, *The Socialist*.

Economic performance deteriorated at an accelerating pace and the politico-economic system entered a terminal crisis.[54]

In the final years of the Soviet system it was recognized that it would be necessary to make a transition to an economy based on markets with a large, if not dominant, private sector. Gorbachev and his advisers remained committed to a gradualist reform strategy due to concerns about imbalances, the likely slow responses of institutions to remedial policies, and political opposition. Alternative proposals in favour of abrupt decontrol of the deteriorating command economy were advanced by neo-liberals, led by Yegor Gaidar, who had been impressed by the 1990 Polish 'shock therapy' programme that was achieving good results.[55]

When the USSR disintegrated and Boris Yeltsin became undisputed leader of Russia, he asked Gaidar to design and manage a 'big bang' transition to a market economy.[56] The reformers believed that the state was weak, intrusive and corrupt. They were determined to minimize its interventions in the economy and to rely primarily on markets, prices and decentralized decision-making. Labour markets were allowed to establish wage rates. Domestic trade in most goods and services was legalized and the majority of retail prices were freed. The creation of wholesale markets was encouraged and about 80 per cent of prices were decontrolled (but not energy prices). Banking reforms were accelerated and the foundation for an equity market was established. The ruble was made convertible for current account purposes and controls on capital flows were loosened. The reformers floated the exchange rate, abolished the state monopoly of foreign trade, liberalized trade and set tariffs at low levels. Small-scale privatization of retail trade establishments was immediately authorized. In late 1992 the government initiated the programme of mass privatization of medium and large enterprises on the basis of vouchers.

These systemic reforms were complemented by macroeconomic stabilization measures. The Russian programme, unlike that in Poland, was not heterodox in that no incomes policy was adopted nor was the exchange rate fixed and used as a nominal anchor. Reliance was placed on tight fiscal and monetary policies. The government drastically cut state budget expenditure on subsidies and on defence. Little attention

---

[54] See Mau, *The Political History*.
[55] See Aslund, *How Russia Became*.
[56] See Aslund, *How Russia Became* and Mau, *The Political History*.

was paid to restructuring of the military-industrial complex. It was assumed that the nascent market forces would govern the necessary reallocation of resources.

The Russian 'big bang' transition programme was strongly supported by leading Western governments, the major multinational institutions (IMF, World Bank, EBRD), and many prominent economists. Western aid programmes poured money into projects that supported neo-liberal economic policies, especially privatization and stabilization.[57]

The initial macroeconomic stabilization programme proved unsustainable, in part due to flaws in its design and mistakes in implementation. In early transition there were weak connections between macroeconomic control instruments and microeconomic behaviour because of 'state desertion' and the sluggishness in the development of vital institutions, such as the central bank and the tax service. Lower level actors in Russia ignored taxation and interest rates, while the government routinely violated its adopted budget expenditure laws.

In this period 'noise' and 'disorganization' increased markedly as consequences of the collapse of the old command system, the instability and distorted nature of prices, and the breakdown of trading links with traditional partners in former CMEA and other FSU countries. Much of the social and organizational capital that was necessary for a market economy was either destroyed or not developed.[58] Economic institutions operated primarily in accordance with inertia and quantity signals. Old patterns of production and supply were maintained. In place of sales revenue, bank loans and budget allocations, firms made use of uncontrolled inter-enterprise credit and barter. In order to cope with the growing indebtedness of firms, the central bank loosened controls on credit in the summer of 1992, which resulted in high rates of inflation over the following year (Table 5).

The Gaidar government was more successful in implementing its radical policy of mass privatization.[59] During 1993/94 the Russian government and its economic advisers reported on the inexorable increase in the private share of industry in a manner similar to Gosplan officials boasting about increases in the production of cement. However, it turned out that the overwhelming majority of firms were

---

[57] See Wedel, *Collision*.
[58] See Stiglitz, 'Whither Reform?'.
[59] See Blasi, Kroumova and Kruse, *Kremlin Capitalism* and Freeland, *Sale of the Century*.

privatized on an 'insider' basis and no effective corporate governance mechanisms were established. Banks had emerged as powerful institutions that regularly intervened in political and economic processes. However, neither banks nor the fragile equity market channelled much investment into industry for restructuring. Prices remained distorted, necessary market infrastructure was missing, and the legal system proved unable to protect private property rights. Given these circumstances, the economic recession and political instability, a substantial share of privatized assets was stolen by 'entrepreneurs' with links to the government and the proceeds were spirited abroad. The privatization scheme resulted in minimal reallocation of resources between sectors and restructuring of industry. Unemployment rose from a negligible rate in the Soviet period to 7.8 per cent in 1994.

Table 5. The Russian economy during transition, 1992–1999.

Indicator	Units	1992	1993	1994	1995	1996	1997	1998	1999
GDP Growth	%	-14.5	-8.7	-12.7	-4.1	-3.4	0.9	-4.9	5.4
Industrial Production	1991=100	82	70	56	54	52	53	50	54
Investment Growth	%	-41.5	-25.8	-26.0	-7.5	-19.3	-5.7	-9.8	4.7
Unemployment	% LF	5.3	6.0	7.8	8.5	9.6	10.8	11.9	12.6
Change in Consumer Prices	Annual %	1,526	875	311	198	48	15	28	86
Budget Deficit	% GDP	-18.9	-7.3	-10.4	-6.1	-8.9	-8.0	-8.0	-3.3

Sources: EBRD, *Transition Report 2000; Transition Report 2002.*

A second major effort at macroeconomic stabilization was made in the period 1994 to 1997. Considerable progress was achieved in meeting economic targets that the reformers considered to be of prime importance. Inflation decelerated, real interest rates were positive, the exchange rate was stable, surpluses were being achieved in foreign trade, and the budget deficit was financed in a non-inflationary manner using GKOs (treasury bills). The stock market grew robustly; the Moscow Times index increased from 150 in December 1996 to 450 in September 1997. These developments engendered positive appraisals of the Russian economy and optimistic forecasts of the future.[60]

---

[60] Optimistic assessments of economic transition in Russia include Aslund, *How Russia Became*; Granville, *The Success*; and Layard and Parker, *The Coming*. International organizations such as the IMF and EBRD also presented optimistic appraisals of the Russian economy. The EBRD *Transition Report 1997*, published in August, forecast GDP growth of 3.0 percent for Russia in 1998.

However, numerous analysts in Russia and the West were consistently critical of the neo-liberal transition strategy and specific policies, such as the illegal sequestering of budget funds to meet IMF deficit targets, the 'loans-for-shares' deal with the oligarchs in 1996, and the defence of an over-valued rigid exchange rate after late 1997.[61] These critics tended to focus on developments in the real sectors of the economy (for example, industry and agriculture), and their problems, such as continuing negative growth of production, the inadequacy of investment, rising unemployment, and the deterioration in the population's health (Table 5 and Figure 2). In their view, there was substantial evidence of systemic failure in the Russian economy, even in the 'golden years' of 1996–7.

A key problem in Russia identified by both the liberal reformers and their critics was 'state desertion'. The weakness of the government impeded efforts to reform institutions and to implement economic policies. For example, the state proved incapable of collecting approved taxes, which led to arbitrary budget sequestrations, failure to pay the wages of its employees and bills for supplies, and chronic budget deficits. The weakness of the state contributed to the arbitrariness and ineffectiveness of the legal system and to rampant corruption, which undermined property rights and the reliability of contracts.

In any event, a major economic crisis developed in Russia from autumn 1997, triggered by both internal weaknesses and exogenous shocks. The equity market bubble burst first, the index dropping from the peak of 450 to 50 in August 1998. Over the same period the unwise investments and speculative activities of most major Russian banks increased their vulnerability to shocks. One duly struck in August as a result of the decision of the liberal Kiriyenko government to devalue the ruble ('widen the exchange rate corridor') and to renege on payment of the government's debt (the GKOs). The banking system became paralysed, the exchange rate crashed, and Russian banks refused to honour forward exchange contracts with Western banks.[62]

The Russian economic crisis has stimulated re-evaluations of general theoretical positions and policy recommendations concerning transition economies, as well as reinterpretations of the nature of the

---

[61] Critical studies of Russian economic developments included Goldman, *Lost Opportunity*; Nolan, *China's Rise*; and Sapir, *Le Chaos*.
[62] See EBRD, *Transition Report 1998*; Ellman and Scharrenborg, 'The Russian'; Sapir, 'Russia's Crash'; and Freeland, *Sale of the Century*.

malfunctioning hybrid economic system in that country. According to Davis, it has evolved from the politico-economic system of shortage described in Kornai, *The Socialist System*, which was characterized by five blocks of inter-related phenomena:

(a) Communist political power;
(b) state domination (public ownership);
(c) bureaucratic coordination (planning);
(d) microeconomic behaviour (soft budget constraints);
(e) shortage-related problems.

The liberal reform policies destroyed certain elements of the old system, such as the power of the Communist Party, and created new ones, such as private property. However, the Russian economy entered a transformational recession and, unlike some countries in Eastern Europe, did not achieve sufficient systemic reform to emerge from it. Instead, Russia has been left with a politico-economic system headed by a weak and corrupt state, decentralization of power, mass privatization of lucrative assets with an ineffective legal system, and survival of 'shortage economy' phenomena, such as bureaucratic control, non-price signals, soft budget constraints, shortages in the state sector (for example, in the medical system and the military-industrial complex), and barter.[63]

A second interpretation is that Russia has had a politico-economic system committed to sustaining economically unviable manufacturing branches of industry.[64] This is a 'virtual economy' because it is based on illusions about important economic variables: prices, sales, wages, taxes and budgets. At its heart is a mechanism that enables the government to redistribute value from value-adding, resource-producing industry (for example, Gasprom) to value-subtracting manufacturing. This redistribution process is inextricably tied in with others, including demonetization of transactions and corruption.

A third alternative interpretation with a historical resonance is that the Russian economy has developed into a form of industrial feudalism. R. Ericson argues that its features are: a weak centre with strong

---

[63] See Davis, 'The Health Sector' and 'The Defence Sector'.
[64] The issue of negative value added in industries of the transition economies has been discussed throughout the nineties. It was assumed that this phenomenon would disappear as transition progressed due to the hardening of budget constraints and restructuring of industry (Gaddy and Ickes, 'Russia's Virtual Economy'). As with barter, though, this has not happened in Russia (Commander and Mumssen, 'Understanding Barter').

local authorities; parcelization of sovereignty; personalized authority and discretion; no separation of public and private roles; absence of factor markets; highly regulated commodity markets; diffuse property and contract rights; and control over the primary capital asset (land) as the source of power and wealth.[65]

In the years since the August 1998 crisis there have been significant developments in the political sphere, economic policy and performance, and transition strategy. Vladimir Putin has replaced Yeltsin as President, the Duma elected in December 1999 is more supportive of the government than was its predecessor, and steps have been taken to re-assert federal control over the regions. Successive governments under Prime Ministers Primakov, Stepashin, Putin and Kasyanov have maintained prudent fiscal and monetary policies and gradually have improved the effectiveness of policy instruments. As a result of the government's actions, the recovery in the price of oil to $25 per barrel, and the stimulating effect on domestic industry of the devaluation, industrial production rose by 8.1 per cent in 1999 and GDP increased by 5.4 per cent. Inflation rose to 86 per cent in 1999, but decelerated to 20.1 per cent in 2000. Russia's balance of payments improved substantially. These positive developments continued through 2002.

The evaluation of Russia's economic experiences in the 1990s by the Putin administration has led to a consensus concerning the transition process and the appropriate strategy. The new ideas are reflected in the economic reform package that the government adopted in June 1999, which was designed by the reformer Germain Gref, and in President Putin's speech to the Federal Assembly in July.[66] In brief, these documents argue that while many of the liberal policies promoted in the past, such as price liberalization and privatization, were correct in principle, they could not achieve the intended beneficial effects because of the weakness of the state and absence of the rule of law.[67] The new strategy is simultaneously to improve the effectiveness of the state (for example, by both reforming taxes and strengthening tax collection powers), promote reforms of institutions that are necessary for a

---

[65] Ericson, 'The Post-Soviet'.
[66] See Gref, 'Prioritetnye zadachi' and Putin, 'Vystuplenie'.
[67] Putin, in 'Vystuplenie', states that: 'An ineffectual state is the main cause of the lengthy and profound economic crisis...We need to draw lessons from our experience and admit that the key role of the state in the economy is, without any doubts, to defend economic freedom...The task of the authorities is to regulate the work of state institutions that ensure the work of the market.'

market economy (such as banks, the equity market and the legal system), promote competition, harden budget constraints by restricting subsidies and shift to a welfare system with targeted benefits. The new strategy that will govern economic transition over the initial decade of the twenty-first century is therefore a synthesis of the neo-liberal and gradualist programmes of the 1990s.

Conclusions

The British war economies and the peacetime Soviet economy were more similar in important aspects than is usually recognized. Their transitions therefore can be usefully compared. Both economic systems evolved in times of acute crisis to mobilize scarce resources for the achievement of military objectives. Combinations of ideology, coercion, planning and rationing were substituted for material incentives, prices and market mechanisms. Of course, the British war economies and the Soviet economic system remained different in fundamental respects. Even in wartime conditions Britain remained a democracy with a long tradition of private property and free market activity. In contrast the USSR had a dictatorship, a supply-constrained (shortage) economy and a tradition of pervasive state intervention. Nonetheless, the experiences of these economies demonstrate that central direction possesses substantial advantages over market systems when there is a single overriding purpose of the system: the development of a powerful military machine for total war.[68]

The British and Russian governments faced similar challenges in their transitions from war/command economies based on administrative controls and dominated by military-industrial complexes. They had to return to, or construct, economic systems relying on prices and markets while carrying out substantial re-distributions of capital and labour between sectors and restructuring of state-owner or controlled enterprises.

In the initial stages of transition in all three cases there was considerable 'noise' and 'disorganization' in the economy. This may be attributed in part to the dependence of any economic system on social

---

[68] However, the Soviet case suggests that the maintenance of a closed command economy in a rapidly developing, open global economic system is not viable over the long term.

and organizational capital to function properly. A rapid transition destroys the capital essential to the war/command system without providing the replacement social assets necessary for the new market arrangements. There were also major disruptions in both domestic and foreign supply links. Prices were unable immediately to convey necessary market data, and time was required for institutions to develop the contracts that provided vital supplemental information.

'Big bang' strategies and policies achieved limited successes in transforming war/command economic systems into properly functioning, peacetime market economies and reallocating resources. Abrupt shifts in systems and policies in the UK in the 1920s and Russia in the 1990s disrupted co-ordination and contributed to economic difficulties. The imperfect market mechanisms of early transition were not able to reallocate resources efficiently or ensure that firms were restructured into competitive unit. As a result, unemployment rose to high levels (Figure 2). The shortcomings of this strategy also contributed to malfunctions in the emerging economic systems, most notably in Russia in the 1990s. One difference between these two cases is that the Russian economy in the 1990s did not exhibit the 'double cycle' discussed previously, primarily because it failed to recover enough to complete the initial cycle.

A related finding is that governments should focus on developments in the real sphere of the economy, and not become overly sensitive to financial variables. In the post-World War II case the British government maintained controls over real domestic and foreign flows to good advantage. In contrast, the governments of both post-World War I Britain and Russia in the 1990s relinquished such controls abruptly and oriented their policies to financial variables that were conveying imperfect information about economic processes in a chaotic transitional period. The rapid transitions in Britain after World War I and Russia in the 1990s were associated with numerous problems in reallocation of resources and restructuring. In contrast, the successful transition of the British economy in the post-World War II period was based on continued government intervention and control. This case indicates that the state can provide useful interim guidance in the reallocation process in the initial phase of transition, which is dominated by 'noise' and disorganization. State-directed conversion programmes were, on the whole, effective in directing resources into exports essential to pay Britain's foreign debts, maintaining full employment, and providing a social support system that improved the well-being of the population. The findings of this study and others cited suggest that a gradualist transition with better sequencing of policies by an effective state would have produced more sustainable institutional change and superior economic performance in Russia than did the attempt to decontrol the economy abruptly in an environment with imperfect markets and a weakened state.

Note. The authors would like to thank Antoni Chawluk, Cyril Lin and Terry O'Shaughnessy of Oxford University and the Editors for their comments.

References

Allen, R.G.D. 'Mutual Aid between the United States and the British Empire 1941–45.' *Journal of the Royal Statistical Society* 110 (1946): 243–71.
Aslund, A. *How Russia Became a Market Economy.* Washington DC: The Brookings Institution, 1995.
Balcerowicz, L. *Socialism, Capitalism, Transformation.* Budapest: Central European University Press, 1995.
Barber, W.M. 'British and American Economists and Attempts to Comprehend the Nature of War, 1910–20.' *History of Political Economy* 23, supplement (1991): 61–86
Barnett, C. *The Audit of War: The Illusion and Reality of Britain as a Great Nation.* London: Macmillan, 1986.
Barnett, M.L. *British Food Policy in the First World War.* London: Allen & Unwin, 1985.
Beveridge, W.H. *British Food Control.* London: Oxford University Press, 1928.
Blanchard, O. *The Economics of Post Communist Transition.* Oxford: Clarendon Press, 1997.
Blanchard, O., and M. Kremer. 'Disorganization.' *Quarterly Journal of Economics* CXII, no. 4 (1998): 1091–1127.
Blasi, J.R., M. Kroumova and D. Kruse. *Kremlin Capitalism: Privatizing the Russian Economy.* London: Cornell University Press, 1997.
Brada, J. 'Privatization is Transition—Or is it?' *Journal of Economic Perspectives* 10, no. 2 (1996): 67–86.
Broadberry, S.N. 'The Emergence of Mass Unemployment: Explaining Macroeconomic Trends in Britain during the Trans-World War I Period.' *Economic History Review* 43 (1990): 271–82.
Cairncross, A. *Years of Recovery; British Economic Policy 1945–51.* London: Methuen, 1985.
Commander, S., and C. Mumssen. 'Understanding Barter in Russia.' EBRD Working Paper 37, London, 1998.
Davis, C. 'The High Priority Military Sector in a Shortage Economy.' In *The Impoverished Superpower: Perestroika and the Burden of Soviet Military*

Spending, edited by H. Rowen and C. Wolf Jr., 155–84. San Francisco: Institute for Contemporary Studies, 1990.

―――――. 'Russia: A Comparative Economic Systems Interpretation.' In *European Industrial Policy: The Twentieth-Century Experience*, edited by J. Foreman Peck and G. Federico, 319–97. Oxford: Oxford University Press, 1999.

―――――. 'The Health Sector: Illness, Medical Care, and Mortality.' In *Russia's Post-Communist Economy*, edited by B. Granville and P. Oppenheimer, 45–538. Oxford University Press, 2001.

―――――. 'The Defence Sector in the Economy of a Declining Superpower: Soviet Union and Russia, 1965–2001.' *Defence and Peace Economics* 13 (2002): 145–77.

Davis, C., and W. Charemza (eds.). *Models of Disequilibrium and Shortage in Centrally Planned Economies*. London: Chapman and Hall, 1989.

Dearle, N.B. *An Economic Chronicle of the Great War for Great Britain and Ireland 1914–1919*. London: H. Milford, 1929.

Dowie, J.R. '1919–20 is in Need of Attention.' *Economic History Review* 28 (1975): 429–50.

EBRD, *see* European Bank for Reconstruction and Development

Eichengreen, B.J. 'Institutions and Economic Growth: Europe after World War II.' In *Economic Growth in Europe since 1945*, edited by N. Crafts and G. Toniolo, 38–72. Cambridge: Cambridge University Press, 1996.

Ellman, M. 'The State under State Socialism and Post-socialism.' In *The Role of the State in Economic Change*, edited by H.J. Chang and R. Rowthorn, 215–36. Oxford: Clarendon Press, 1995.

Ellman, M., and R. Scharrenborg. 'The Russian Economic Crisis.' *Economic and Political Weekly* (India), 26 December 1998.

Ericson, R. 'The Post-Soviet Russian Economic System: An Industrial Feudalism?' Paper presented to the Conference on 'Economies in Transition at the Turn of the Century.' Institute of European Studies, University of Macau, 1999.

European Bank for Reconstruction and Development. *Transition Report 1996, Transition Report 1997, Transition Report 1998, Transition Report 1999, Transition Report 2000, Transition Report 2002*. London: EBRD, 1996, 1997, 1998, 1999, 2000, 2002.

Fayle, C. E. *The War and the Shipping Industry*. London: Oxford University Press, 1927.

Feinstein, C.H. *Domestic Capital Formation in the United Kingdom, 1920–1938*. Cambridge: Cambridge University Press, 1965.

―――――. Historical Precedents for Economic Change in Central Europe and the USSR. Oxford: Oxford Analytica, 1990.

Foreman-Peck, J. *A History of the World Economy: International Economic Relations since 1850*. London: Harvester-Wheatsheaf, 1995.

Foreman-Peck, J., S. Bowden and A. McKinlay. *The British Motor Industry*. Manchester: Manchester University Press, 1995.

Foreman-Peck, J., and R. Millward. *Public and Private Ownership of British Industry 1820–1990.* Oxford: Clarendon Press, 1994.
Freeland, C. *Sale of the Century. The Inside Story of the Second Russian Revolution.* London: Little, Brown and Co., 2000.
Gaddy, C., and B. Ickes. 'Russia's Virtual Economy.' *Foreign Affairs* 77, no. 5 (1998): 53–67.
GKRFS = Gosudarstvennyy Komitet Rossiiskoi Federatsii po Statistiki
Goldman, M. *Lost Opportunity: Why Economic Reforms in Russia Have Not Worked.* London: W.W. Norton & Co., 1994.
Gosudarstvennyy Komitet Rossiiskoi Federatsii po Statistiki. *Rossiskii Statisticheskii Ezhegodnik: 1998, ...1999, ...2001.* Moscow: Statistika, 1998, 1999, 2001.
Granville, B. *The Success of Russian Economic Reforms.* London: Royal Institute of International Affairs, 1995.
Graves, R. *Goodbye to All That* London: Guild Publishing, 1979.
Gref, G. (ed.) 'Prioritetnye zadachi pravitel'stva Rossiiskoi Federatsii na 2000–2001 gody po realizatsii Osnovnykh Napravlenii Sotsial'no-ekonomicheskoi Politiki Pravitelstva Rossiiskoi Federatsii na Dolgosrochnuyu Perspektivu'. http://www.kommersant.ru/Docs/, June 2000.
Gregory, P.R., and R.C. Stuart. *Soviet Economic Structure and Performance* (Fourth Edn.). London: Harper & Row, 1990.
Gregory, P.R., and R.C. Stuart. *Comparative Economic Systems* (Fifth Edn.). Boston: Houghton Mifflin, 1995.
Gros, D., and A. Steinherr. *Winds of Change: Economic Transition in Central and Eastern Europe.* London: Longman, 1995.
Hall, H.D., and C.C. Wrigley. *Studies of Overseas Supply.* London: HMSO, 1956.
Hancock, W.K., and M.M. Gowing. *British War Economy.* London: HMSO, 1953.
HMSO. *National Income and Expenditure 1970.* London: HMSO, 1971.
Hornby, W. *Factories and Plant.* London: HMSO, 1958.
Howson, S. *British Monetary Policy 1919–1939.* Cambridge: Cambridge University Press, 1975.
Hurstfield, J. *The Control of Raw Material.* London: HMSO, 1953.
Kennedy, P. *The Rise and Fall of Great Powers.* London: Unwin Hyman, 1988.
Kornai, J. *The Socialist System: The Political Economy of Communism.* Oxford: Clarendon Press, 1992.
―――. 'Transformational Recession: The Main Causes.' *Journal of Comparative Economics* 19, no. 1 (1994): 39–63.
Layard, R., and J. Parker. *The Coming Russian Boom.* London: The Free Press, 1996.
Lloyd, E.H.M. *Experiments in State Control at the War Office and the Ministry of Food.* Oxford: Clarendon Press, 1924.
Mau, V. *The Political History of Economic Reform in Russia, 1985–1994.* London: Centre for Research into Communist Economies, 1996.
Mau, V. *Russian Economic Reforms as Seen by an Insider: Success or Failure?* London: Royal Institute of International Affairs, 2000.

Milward, A .S., and G. Brennan. *Britain's Place in the World*. London: Routledge, 1998.
Ministry of Munitions. *History of the Ministry of Munitions* (8 vols). London: HMSO, 1918–1922.
Mitchell, B.R. *Abstract of British Historical Statistics*. Cambridge: Cambridge University Press, 1962.
Mowat, C.J. *Britain Between the Wars*. London: Methuen, 1955.
Murrell, P. 'The Transition According to Cambridge, Mass.' *Journal of Economic Literature* 33, no. 1 (1995): 167–78.
_____. 'How Far Has the Transition Progressed?' *Journal of Economic Perspectives* 10, no. 2 (1996): 25–44.
Nolan, P. *China's Rise, Russia's Fall: Politics, Economics and Planning in Transition from Stalinism*. London: Macmillan, 1995.
Pigou, A.C. *Aspects of British Economic History 1918–1925*. London: Macmillan, 1948.
Pressnell, L.S. *External Economic Policy Since the War: Vol. 1 The Post War Financial Settlement*. London: HMSO, 1986.
Putin, V. 'Rossiya na rubezhe tysyacheletii'. *Nezavisimaya Gazeta* (30 December 1999): 4.
Putin, V. 'Vystuplenie pri predstavlenii ezhegodnogo Poslaniya Prezidenta Rossiiskoi Federatsii Federal'nomu Sobraniyu Rossiiskoi Federatsii.' http://president.kremlin.ru/events/42.html, 8 July 2000 (see also 'Putin's address to Federal Assembly — Text.' *Summary of World Broadcasts* SU/3888 B/1–9. 10 July 2000).
Rapacyzynski, A. 'The Roles of the State and the Market in Establishing Property Rights.' *Journal of Economic Perspectives* 10, no. 2 (1996): 87–103 .
Robinson, E.A.G. 'The Overall Allocation of Resources.' In *Lessons of the British War Economy*, edited by D.N. Chester, 34–57. Cambridge: Cambridge University Press, 1951.
Roland, G. 'On the Speed and Sequencing of Privatization and Restructuring.' *Economic Journal* 104 (1994): 1158–68.
Sachs, J. *Understanding 'Shock Therapy'*. London: Social Market Foundation, 1994.
Sapir, J. 'Macroeconomic Stabilization in Russia: Why Traditional Macroeconomics Have Failed.' IRSES-MSH Working Paper, Paris, 1994.
_____. *Le Chaos Russe: Désordres Economiques, Conflits Politiques, Décomposition Militaire*. Paris: Editions La Découverte, 1996.
_____. 'Russia's Crash of August 1998: Diagnosis and Prescription.' *Post-Soviet Affairs* 15, no. 1 (1999): 1–36.
Scott, J.D., and R.A.W. Hughes. *The Administration of War Production*. London: HMSO, 1955.
Stiglitz, J. 'Whither Reform?: Ten Years of Transition.' In *Proceedings of the World Bank Annual Conference on Development Economics 1999*, 27–56. Washington DC: The World Bank, 2000.

Tawney, R.H. 'The Abolition of Economic Controls 1918–1921.' *Economic History Review* 13 (1943): 1–30.

Taylor, L. 'The Market Met its Match: Lessons for the Future from the Transition's Initial Years.' *Journal of Comparative Economics* 19, no. 1 (1994): 64–87.

Wedel, J. *Collision and Collusion: The Strange Case of Western Aid to Eastern Europe, 1989–1998*. New York: St. Martin's Press, 1998.

World Bank. *From Plan to Market: World Development Report 1996*. Oxford: Oxford University Press, 1996.

World Bank. *The State in a Changing World: World Development Report 1997*. Oxford: Oxford University Press, 1997.

8.
Rational Resistance to Land Privatization:
The Behaviour of Rural Producers in Response to Agrarian Reforms, 1861–2000

CAROL SCOTT LEONARD

Introduction

This paper argues that rural opposition to land reform in transition Russia is a consequence of individually rational decisions by members of former state and collective farms about whether to support further land reform, or preserve the status quo—collective farming. Evidence from survey data shows that despite the government's efforts to promote a land market and independent farming in the 1990s, preferences in 1996 still favoured the largely unreformed agricultural system.[1] The worsening effects of adverse terms of trade facing agriculture (itself a consequence of stalemated reforms in the Russian economy) led to a prolonged decline of agricultural output and widespread 'bankruptcy' of large farm entities. The latter's debts were in turn written off by the government. In this environment, there was little stimulus for agrarian producers to undertake the transition to independent farming.[2]

Rural opposition to land reform is of general interest in the social sciences as an example of persistent collectivism. In Russia, collectivism was thought to emerge in part from religious national tradition (*sobornost'*) and in part from peasant tradition. The most salient historical parallel in Russia, although not the only one, is widespread rural

---

[1] See Leonard, 'Rejecting Land Reform'. Compare similar circumstances in Carlson, *Indians*, and Kantor, *Politics*.
[2] Leonard and Serova, 'The Reform'.

opposition to the Stolypin reforms at the turn of the last century, when peasant communes resisted enclosures and restructuring of rights to land.[3] Secure property rights and market infrastructure, which the current transition reforms seem to promise, just as the Stolypin reforms did in the past, would seem obviously necessary for the improvement of the sector. Yet opposition, seemingly irrational, has recurred and lasted throughout the reform era.

Opinion polls demonstrate the strength and nature of opposition to land reform, suddenly emerging mid-way through transition.[4] This paper argues that opposition to land reform and its failure to be fully implemented can be rationalized within a decision-theoretic framework, given the existence of uncertainty about the costs that individual cultivators will incur. Under uncertainty, a crucial determinant of the decision outcome will be particular structural features of the economy that impinge on rural risk perceptions. In other words, there are particular domestic and external conditions—such as fiscal and financial crises that may accompany governments' attempts at land reform—which elevate producers' perceptions of both the economic and political risk entailed by entrepreneurial behaviour. In such circumstances, rural social organization can develop informal rules to inhibit out-migration, which can, in turn, lead to the institutionalization of sharecropping and diverse forms of labour bondage. Furthermore, the resulting abundance of labour and low-yield cultivation practices has the effect of discouraging technological innovation in the village. Under these conditions, reform will be the impetus for the less risk-averse and those with skills and knowledge to choose to leave the village in search of better opportunities elsewhere. It turns out that the consequences of initial decisions can have decisive impact on rejection of reform later on. When the initial 'enthusiasts' have left the farm, those remaining will, more and more, perceive fewer opportunities and a greater likelihood of high costs of accepting the reform regime. This self-reinforcing dynamic process serves further to entrench the (surviving) rural community's commitment to maintenance of the status quo. It is argued from other empirical and theoretical study that if a larger group were initially to leave, the likelihood of a more positive opinion of reform in the group remaining behind would be raised.

[3] Pallot, *Land Reform*.
[4] Leonard, 'Rejecting Land Reform'.

In Russia, the current rejection of reform by rural producers bears a similarity to historical resistance to agrarian reform, especially in the post-Emancipation period and Stolypin era. In both the contemporary and the historical periods, the Russian government failed to adjust the legal and financial infrastructure sufficiently, after redistributive reforms, to make allotments of arable securely the property of individual rural households and therefore encourage the land market. In addition, in both the contemporary and historical eras, among the further effects of unclear property rights, overuse of the collectively controlled resources and free-riding by community members made it necessary to monitor labour. By tradition, the collective controlled labour discipline by social pressure and other reputation mechanisms, and by centralized allocation of goods as an incentive for hard work. The resulting homogeneity of the populace and historical pattern of collective action meant that there was little cost when leaders sought to mobilize resistance to reform. Individual agents thus perceived risks not only from arbitrary and excessive state intervention, but also from the lack of legally guaranteed portions of land and the absence of protections against actions of the organized opponents of the land reform. Thus peasant and farm communities in nineteenth- and twentieth-century Russia were readily mobilized to defend the pooling of production at primary levels, under the circumstances of unclear property rights, even when offered small compensatory benefit packages, including subsidized loans, by the government for accepting farm restructuring.

Failed Land Reform in Russia, 1861–2000

Rural Preference for Collective Farming in Transition

Opposition to land reform did not surface immediately in the wake of price and trade liberalization on 2 January 1992. Spontaneous decentralization of farm assets, with households claiming a share of the collective livestock holdings, led to the reallocation of labour to vegetable subsidiary plots, which were a source of commercial income. Some households developed this secondary form of employment; others, among the most skilled and well-connected younger farmers, left the collective to start independent farms, which had been permitted since the 1980s.[5] To assist these processes, early in transition, reformers sought guarantees of private landownership and obtained them in the

Constitution.[6] Then, as monetary and fiscal tightening drastically lowered agricultural budget subsidies, and as the terms of trade shifted against agriculture, increasingly harsh conditions slowed the movement to set up independent farms. Independent farms had grown by 1994 to roughly 280,000 and they did not exceed that number over the next six years; these farms occupy only 5 per cent of the arable land in the Russian Federation.

The slow-down also reflected skills and experience. Collective farmers lacked work experience needed for the range of tasks required of independent farmers, but they had both organizational skills and the expectation that lobbying generated funds. As shown in the new literature on transition economics, socialist expectations (for example, of subsidies and benefits) can hinder the popular understanding and implementation of a range of reforms in post-socialist societies.[7] Responding to the opportunity to enhance their local authority, the regional governments took some of the responsibility for subsidies from the centre, and rural opinion began to shift fully against independent farming.

Meanwhile, the government's reform in 1992/1993 had fully preserved many aspects of the socialist structure of farming. The former state and collective farms could retain their assets by nothing more elaborate than re-registration as private joint stock companies. The continued strength of their representatives in parliamentary parties, especially the Communist and Agrarian blocs in the Duma, enabled the farm managers to halt reform. The extent of this reversal was described by a Russian economist, considering the second round of discussions of a proposed Land Code in the summer of 1996 (a draft vetoed by President Yeltsin),

> The situation is astonishing. Originally conceived as a document that officially introduces unrestricted commercial transfers of land, the Land Code, in the version that has been approved as of now, explicitly prohibits commercial transfers of agricultural land and basically negates the right of private landownership established in the Constitution.[8]

---

[5] Leonard, 'Resistance'.
[6] Van Atta and Macey, *The 'Farmer Threat'*.
[7] Csontos, Kornai, et al., 'Tax Awareness'.
[8] Boiko, 'Russian Land Ownership', p. 2.

The Russian Constitution of 1993 guarantees individual landownership, yet the Duma has repeatedly rejected the right of the individual to sell arable land.[9] Little could be done to implement the presidential decrees that confirmed the right to buy and sell agricultural land. Farm reorganization could not be imposed from above, since reformers were unwilling to act as 'Bolsheviks in Reverse' (impose land auctions by force where they are not wanted).[10] As the deputy head of the State Land Committee, Valery Alexeev, described the stalemate,

> The striving to prod the collective and state farms to engage in active privatization of land has run into tough resistance on the part of farm management and, surprisingly, farmers themselves. Whatever the explanation, the reform in that direction proceeds painfully. Only some regions (e.g. Nizhnii Novgorod) have something to boast, and even there the reform has been progressing under strong pressure on the part of local authorities, something which is reminiscent of the tragic collectivization campaign of the 1930s.[11]

The opposition to land reform is best modelled as a decision-making process, in which the initial stage was marked by government support (in the form of budgetary resources for credit institutions and infrastructure development) for those who started independent farms. The second stage was marked by three elements working in tandem: a general reduction of subsidies to the farm sector; political difficulties over the passage of the Land Code guaranteeing the right to buy and sell arable land; and the price repercussions of 2 January 1992. Input prices rose and producer prices, in tandem with global commodity prices, fell. Meanwhile, in many urban areas across the Russian Federation, consumer prices for food were fixed and grain export was prohibited. In general, with the influx of cheap imported food goods from the EU, conditions were highly adverse to the less competitive domestic production. Tight monetary policy, introduced in the third quarter of 1994, reduced inflation but raised nominal interest rates to as high as 210 per cent. Meanwhile, directed credits from the Central Bank were eliminated. The effect was crippling. The loss of investment resources was visible in continuing depletion of the soil of nutrients—

---

[9] Leonard and Serova, 'The Reform'.
[10] See *Doklad*, *'O Sostianii'*. This was the view of V.F. Vershinin, Duma Deputy of the Agrarian Lobby, in 1995, and Maksim Boyko, Deputy Head of the Russian Privatization Center.
[11] Valery, 'Land Reform'.

the cost/price squeeze forced producers to cut fertilizer usage. Output steadily dropped. Agriculture's share of GDP declined from 15.3 per cent in 1990 to 6.3 per cent in 1996, even as overall output was falling. Land under crops fell by 17 per cent between 1985 and 1995. Livestock production halved in value between 1990 and 1996. The removal of subsidies, the retreat from mechanization, the decline in fertilizer usage and the drop in demand for forage caused cereal production to fall by 25 per cent between 1992 and 1995.[12] The share of the population engaged in agricultural production meanwhile remained roughly the same, putting pressure on wages and resulting in a sharp decline in per capita income. The wage of agricultural workers relative to the average wage in the economy fell from 95 per cent in 1990 to 50 per cent in 1995.[13]

The opportunity costs of leaving the collective were perceived to be very large. Collective farm members expected to retain state support for community services, including education, health care and pensions, programmes that had been delivered through Soviet state and collective farms. In transition, these services continued to be provided on farms, albeit at much reduced levels as fiscal tightening took hold. Over time, benefits tended more and more to be provided privately, which placed even greater strain on household income.

The status quo in rural Russia promised continued access to communally held land and a minimum subsistence, in a legal environment where land improvement was not encouraged. According to Russian property rights law in the 1990s, enterprise shareholders of the former state and collective farms had titles to the land. However, they did not have the actual shares, which most often were not distributed. The lack of clear, accessible and simple formal procedures for households to buy and sell land was due, as in the period after Emancipation in the nineteenth century, in part to the inadequacy and inexperience of state agencies in handling transactions in land. In both periods, there were no existing facilities for land cadastres and no market-based mechanisms for establishing land prices. In the 1860s and 1870s, land could be exchanged via the Russian commune; in the 1990s, land could initially be exchanged only through local soviets, and when these were

---

[12] Leonard and Serova, 'The Reform'; Liefert, 'Grain Sector Reform'.
[13] Leonard and Serova, 'The Reform'.

abolished, only through the state agency, the National Land Committee, and its local branches, which managed state reserves. Landowners cannot receive rents or obtain a profit by selling the land.

Low productivity to some extent rationalizes the 'survivalist' orientation of the management of large farm enterprises, which lobbies for direct budgetary subsidies and relies on the inherent subsidies that are masked as barter arrangements and soft loans with quasi-state agencies, such as Gasprom.[14] The latter allow a fiction of state ownership to persist in a world where competitiveness depends upon full engagement with private sector activities, such as the production of seeds, the purchase of appropriate machinery, and marketing. The perpetuation of survivalist management is a form of resistance to restructuring. Although 98 per cent of the 26,878 former state and collective farms were privatized as joint stock companies by the mid-1990s, restructuring has been slow: no more than 1000 farms have undergone significant restructuring.[15] Agrarian reform has been one of the most significant failures of the transition era in Russia, not because of its design, but because the Duma failed to complete it. Management reform, smaller-scale production techniques, and more efficient use of labour and capital inputs have been very limited due to the long- as well as short-term immobility of the main factors of production, land and labour.[16] To a great extent, then, even the continuing grain output decline can be attributed directly to stalemated reform of the legal framework.[17]

Under severe transition conditions both the negative and positive effects of unclear property rights were enhanced. Without the investment funds or skills for restructuring and improved management, large farms lacked crop portfolios; they suffered from seasonal volatility in prices due to the lack of information about international and domestic prices, and they accumulated arrears on wage payments as a consequence of their losses. The household, in turn, was also vulnerable to price volatility due to dependence on farm wages. Apart from

---

[14] Commander and Mumssen, 'Understanding Barter'; Leonard, 'The Political Economy'.
[15] Leonard and Serova, 'The Reform'.
[16] For the laws on reorganization, see *Land Privatization, Annexes*; see also Kuznetsov, *Organizatsionno-ekonomichekie*.
[17] Too often, the output decline is discussed in terms of single sectors within agriculture and demand and supply effects (Liefert, 'Grain Sector Reform'). However powerful those effects may be, such as the decline in demand for livestock production, on the supply side, there are structural problems causing market failure.

wages, which tended to be in arrears for months or years, and the earnings from subsidiary plots, households had few outside cash earnings.[18] Isolated by poor transportation networks from urban centres, farm members had no non-agricultural employment opportunities and no interest in entrepreneurship.[19] The household had recourse only to the private subsidiary plot, from which vegetables can be grown for subsistence and marketing.

That the possession of a subsidiary plot was guaranteed by remaining in the collective farm entity made it a free good, and that it was a clear reason for remaining in the collective, despite the bankruptcy of the farm, was a sign of how profitable it was. Unclear property rights caused rent from such assets to be captured by farm members and this led to their excessive use. Turning to the plot for primary as well as supplementary income, households reallocated labour from crops to vegetable cultivation even during seasons when the labour was required for field crops. The institutional feature of this is in the laws: they failed to define as separable and freely disposable the farm subsidiary plot, as distinct from subsidiary plots located near urban centres, and they failed clearly to specify readily available mechanisms for its purchase and sale.

The conduct of households in allocating labour to the subsidiary plot may seem secondary in importance by comparison with the deteriorating situation of field crops. In transition Russia, however, the private subsidiary plot produced over half of Gross Agricultural Output (GAO) with significant shares of meat as well as vegetables. Excess use of the free good thus created inefficiencies not only on the collective farm but also across the economy. Other adverse outcomes included the slow-down of out-migration of the relatively large farm population (roughly 22 per cent of the populace, by contrast with most western countries, where it amounts to 1 or 2 per cent). Rural emigration was explicitly held in check by residuals of the 'propiska' registration regime (by which work permits were required for residence in an area). Workers according to the Constitution of 1993 were not bound to the land; however, it was not easy to acquire residence permits in towns. Another outcome was that under conditions of low

---

[18] Perotta, 'The Higher Up'.
[19] Ibid.

world grain prices and high vegetable prices, there was misallocation of labour: the population was trapped in labour-intensive vegetable gardening, rather than being released for commercial farming.[20]

Preferences for Communal Landholding in the Nineteenth Century

In the course of Russian industrialization, after Emancipation of the serfs in 1861 and before the Russian Revolution in 1917, preference for the pooling of production resources was as common as it was during and after collectivization in Soviet Russia.

After having been nearly total under serfdom, the share of villages governed by communes in Russia before the turn of the twentieth century dropped gradually, beginning when peasants obtained access to credit after the creation of a Peasants' Land Bank in 1883. Even afterwards, the government's support for the commune through 1903 hindered the process of enclosure. The government used the commune for its quasi-governmental role in the collection of taxes and maintenance of stability.[21] What is important for the process discussed in this paper is the stalling of land reform after 1903, when the government abolished the system of mutual guarantees of the commune, and especially after the Stolypin Reforms of 1906 to 1911, when the commune itself was abolished. The government sought market reform to encourage larger agricultural exports than was the outcome of pooled production under conditions of technological backwardness. By 1913, there was considerable evidence that the medium and large private farms and even the small peasant farms were more productive than the collectives. The communes, nevertheless, resisted reform and communal forms of production and governance were preserved in over half of Russian villages, despite vigorous intervention by the government.

As in the 1990s, there were political and legal hindrances to peasant landownership in the post-Emancipation period. Protracted and complex arrangements for peasants' redemption payments prevented the emergence of a land market immediately after Emancipation. For a nine-year period, peasants continued to pay dues to the landlord, and instructions for settling the contractual issues between the commune and the landlord were only advisory. It was only in 1883 that redemption itself was made obligatory. Also, the liberation of peasants from

---

[20] Leonard, 'The Political Economy'.
[21] Danilov, 'Ob istoricheskikh'; Dubrovskii, Sel'skoe khoziastvo.

the landlords' personal and juridical control was incomplete. Landlords retained management rights over the commune, with rights to expel peasants.

Only technically, then, were peasants liberated. In fact, land remained a collectively owned good, and the disposal of it was tied to complex procedures involving the entire commune. The land market, as a consequence, developed very slowly. Before Emancipation, nobles, the state and the crown owned most of the arable land in Russia, but land was generally not sold; rather, it was exchanged by inheritance or mortgaged to the state. After Emancipation, allotment land (*nadel*), along with tax obligations, were held collectively by the commune. Virtually every peasant producer had to lease land in order to have access to any meadows, forests or water that were separated from peasant allotment land by the terms of liberation. But land sales accumulated slowly. The exchange of contracts averaged annually only 0.2 per cent of all the arable in the Russian empire; by 1900, only 5 per cent of all land changed hands by land sale, or roughly the annual rate of market exchange of land in Germany.

Tenancy arrangements not only slowed down the land market, but made departure difficult. Exit from the collective was possible after Emancipation, but it was accompanied by liabilities and procedural difficulties. It took four decades for migration to become a sustained high flow to urban and frontier areas, and even then much of it (one-third) was not permanent migration.[22] The residual claims to land through the commune worked simultaneously to slow down out-migration and to pull migrants back to the land, where at least a subsistence income was secured by means of that primary pooling of resources.

Adverse economic conditions reinforced preferences for collective production. The minimum size of allotment land that the households received, determined by the state according to territorial zones, led to non-market allocations that inhibited the sale of land. In the densely settled central black-earth *gubernii* (provinces), peasants on average were left with as little as a quarter of their former *nadel* (allotment) and, since the landlords retained the right to determine what land peasants obtained, the quality of the allotment was misaligned with the payment owned. In the north, land allotments were larger. Regional income differences were further affected by the amount of redemption

---

[22] Rashin, *Formirovanie*.

fees owed per household. These fees, to be paid over 49 years (calculated at a capitalization of the land's 'value' at 6 per cent), were valued at the level of monetary dues paid by serfs before emancipation in the region — a non-market price. After 20 years, over 20 per cent of all serfs had still not been allotted land.[23]

Peasant preferences for collective production also reflected state policies to inhibit migration of taxpayers and consequent loss of control over villages. Peasants were taxed both for regular and ad hoc needs. There were chronic shortages in the budget in the nineteenth century, linked to wars and the costs of borrowing. Before Emancipation, the rural populace paid roughly 63 per cent of direct tax revenues in the poll tax and in monetary dues on state lands and excise taxes.[24] After Emancipation, as the state gradually recovered from financial destabilization during the Crimean War, the need for ad hoc taxes grew, especially since Russia lacked a stable currency. There were new levies of indirect taxes to expand the resource base (regressive taxes such as on salt, kerosene, tobacco, spirits, sugar). Peasants paid the bulk of the land tax (on average, 20 per cent more than nobles paid). Excluding local taxes, the per capita tax burden (nominal) doubled between 1885 and 1913, while the total per capita excise tax burden tripled.[25] To be sure, the state reviewed the poll tax and abolished it between 1883 and (in Siberia) 1899, but the share of excise revenues continually increased. In the 1890s, a lucrative state monopoly replaced the spirits excise, and repayment of foreign loans continued to be onerous (amounting by the 1890s to 40 per cent of expenditures).[26]

Rural communities also lacked formal financial institutions until the mid-1880s. In 1883 the Peasant Land Bank was created in order to assist peasants to buy land. By the Stolypin era, it was a powerful enabling instrument by which the government encouraged both the sale and the reform of the land. Peasant purchases of land expanded, and peasants had new access to short-term credit, like merchants, in mutual credit societies for the deposit of savings and short-term loans. By 1914 almost half of all peasants were members of cooperative savings institutions. Yet, despite some evidence of the beginning of a

[23] Anfimov, Danilova, et al., *Sistema*.
[24] Pogrebinsky, *Ocherki istorii*, p. 18.
[25] Kahan, *Russian Economic History*, p. 93.
[26] Shvanebakh, *Nashe podatno delo*; Fridman, *Nasha finansova*.

transformation, lack of resources was severe in the most agricultural regions, and peasants continued to pool production resources as well as input supplies.[27]

Moreover, the extraction of investible surplus from the agricultural sector intensified in the Soviet era, reinforcing pre-revolutionary peasant expectations about their vulnerability as individuals and collective liability for taxation for the next six decades. Both historically and in the present, one of the key constraints on agricultural development has been the structure of transportation networks across the vast expanse of Russian territory.[28] In medieval and early modern times, landlords' grain was transported on barges by boat haulers along riverways, particularly the Volga. On the Volga's upper reaches, the grain was transferred to carts for travel along overland winter roads and canals to Moscow and St Petersburg. The rivers flowed south to north, enriching both the agricultural regions along the lower and middle Volga, which supplied Moscow and St Petersburg and the non-agricultural provinces further en route along the Volga.[29] Trade routes were altered in mid-century, as new railways linked the more fertile grain-producing regions in western Siberia and the South-east more directly with Moscow and from there to St Petersburg. Within a decade, this had impoverished some regions lying along the Volga. It also assisted the state to enforce agricultural procurement through the monitoring and pricing of storage at rail centres, and of rail transport. It was not until the early twentieth century that regionalization of machinery production allowed mechanization to spread across the central farm areas. Here advancement had been delayed both by the legal framework of unclear property rights and the transportation 'improvements' that liberated the grain trade from the riverways and canals, as beneficial on aggregate as that was to the economy as a whole.[30]

The dominance of servile production required in some areas guarantees of landlord and state aid during emergencies to ensure subsistence. The lack of adequate transportation and scarcity of officials required the centralization of such procedures. Access to networks and knowledge of channels by which emergency aid could be provided were an essential element in village/state relations, and this reinforced

---

[27] Gatrell, *The Tsarist Economy*; Kahan, *Russian Economic History*; Dubrovskii, *Sel'skoe khosiastvo*; Fridman, *Nasha finansova*.
[28] Symons and White (eds.), *Russian Transport*.
[29] White, 'The Impact'.
[30] Spechler, 'The Regional Concentration'.

the need on both sides for collective management of resources. The particular skills and contacts required also led to rents that could be captured on the part of those who handled emergency resources, and this reinforced the political structures that benefited from collective agriculture.

In the Soviet era, collective and state farms depended for many decades on centralized distribution of off-farm supplies of feed, fuel, fertilizer and machinery (and machine maintenance), deliveries paid for by non-market centralized exchange. Input supply bottlenecks caused by delays in production and transportation were decisive in their negative impact on production plans on-farm. This was combined with the failure of the system to mobilize services and parts at the levels needed on-farm, which led to waste and had a large impact on farm efficiency.

Coordination failure in the collective and state farm system was acknowledged by Khrushchev and Brezhnev era reformers. At that time, the Soviet state cut the costs of inputs and arranged for extensive new investments, which concentrated almost exclusively on input supply.

However, this produced further coordination failure in downstream activities, including processing and retailing, which were undeveloped and insufficient to meet the needs of an advanced society.[31]

In the post-Soviet transition era, former collective farm directors and members, unused to private marketing channels that have developed slowly and been inhibited by both the prevalence of barter and quasi-governmental activities of monopoly suppliers in the grain market, find their access to markets and transportation, as well as the monopoly of storage infrastructure, a major constraint on production decisions. Where the situation is eased by better access, that is, where the potential rewards may outweigh the risks, independent farming has spread more widely than in areas where transportation and marketing are inhibited by the state or other monopoly suppliers.[32] Failure to overcome these inherent geographical problems has been a striking continuity over long periods of Russian history, and it has recently been the subject of special study.[33]

---

[31] Brooks, 'Agricultural Reform'.
[32] Leonard, 'The Political Economy'.
[33] Ioffe and Nefedova, *Continuity and Change*.

Resistance: 1860–2000

The balking of farm communities at the idea of selling land in the 1990s seems, at first glance, to have little in common with the violent confrontations between peasants and landlords in the nineteenth and early twentieth centuries. Yet both reflect a culture of resistance to change perceived as undesirable. Historically, any kind of state intervention where the promised benefits were not well understood could evoke resistance. Indeed, when rural welfare seemed threatened, virtually the entire rural populace could be mobilized, and so it was in the interests of the state and the landlords to use the collective to prevent that from happening. In the nineteenth century, resistance also took the form of labour slow-downs, absenteeism, and accumulation of household arrears to landlords and the state. To be sure, in the 1990s, the protest of farm communities is expressed mainly by voting behaviour and through local political leaders who negotiate for regional and local budgets and farm policies with ministers. Farm communities, through their directors, also apply pressure through private lobbies at the federal and regional levels to raise subsidies and avert restructuring and other forms of state support to individual entrepreneurship, including the free disposal of land.

These protests are well organized rather than spontaneous, and non-violent. The major point of comparison is that like classic solidarity in agrarian opposition to local and central authority, in a dynamic familiar to historians, sociologists and anthropologists, rural producers can easily be mobilized by communal leadership. The collective as a relatively isolated unit, represented by its political leaders, preserves its isolation from market information in a self-reinforcing process. In the Stolypin era, numerous communes resisted reform in a collective response against government intervention.[34] And transition circumstances have been sufficiently harsh to renew strong preferences for the status quo under the leadership of collective organization.

The resurfacing of resistance to land reform shows how a pattern of social political behaviour might take root, disappear and then reorganize itself, even though its economic performance is sub-optimal and even financially destabilizing to the economy. The state and collective farms of the Soviet era were by no means the same kind of organization as the Russian commune, and the two had different kinds of pro-

---

[34] Danilov, 'Ob istoricheskikh'; Pallot, *Land Reform.*

duction procedures. Their similarity rested in the constraint on market coordination of downstream and upstream activities through producers who did not entirely make their own decisions. Beginning in the 1950s, the Soviet government began to rethink this aspect of collectivization and launched a variety of partial, incentive-based reforms without going so far as to dismantle the system. But the basic system remained in place. Private agriculture was expanded within bounds, sufficient to satisfy rural and urban demand for additional income through entrepreneurship and to improve the food supply. Similarly, in the nineteenth century, the peasant *mir* was left relatively unaltered in regard to its constraints on population mobility after the abolition of serfdom in 1861, despite the government's awareness of its impact on the rural economy. The government exploited the commune rather than dismantled it.

In the tsarist and Soviet eras, the commune and both state and collective farms became agencies for monitoring production and providing the state with what was owed to it. Although the notion of collective responsibility lost force in law briefly under Stolypin, when the commune spontaneously re-emerged in the 1920s under the NEP, it was again appropriated by the state as a mechanism for control. The codex of 1 December 1922 (1925 in Ukraine, Georgia, Belarus) made land the collective property of the worker/peasant state. Limitations were placed on private (*kulak*) rights, and as the agencies through which the state and land committees regulated disputes and levied taxes, collective and *artel'* (cooperative) forms of production were given tax relief. After collectivization in the 1930s, rural communities were more directly subordinated to central authority, without rights of planning production or even out-migration (passports permitting departure from the collective were issued to collective farmers only in 1974).

The subordination of the collective peasant or rural producer entity to the government, then, in each successive era, was promoted by the commune's dual function. In a classic example of how the principal-agent problem can be resolved at low cost by reputational means, it simultaneously served to control and to represent the rural community. Belonging to the commune/collective was, in a sense, as close as rural dwellers came to having the protection of statutes and rights in successive land codes. Although it was an entity that could be taxed, it was a convenient vehicle for the distribution of subsidies. The collective farm (like the industrial firm) was easily used for the delivery of a variety of federal benefits to the rural population. There were, of course, a myriad of other persisting norms of behaviour, also called 'peasant institutions', ranging from periodic repartition of holdings, strip farming, household division, patriarchal family structure, universal marriage and high fertility, casual non-agricultural labour and target earnings, subsistence farming and self-exploitation. Whereas many of the rural commune's institutional features were transformed or discarded under the influence of rural per capita income growth — for example, universal marriage and high fertility — the commune remains the natural mediating institution for economic control and resistance in relations between the individual cultivator and the Russian state.

Modelling Resistance to Reform with Adaptive Learning

The Fernandez-Rodrik Model

Recent theoretical papers by R. Fernandez and D. Rodrik deal with an issue of wide policy relevance in the developing world and are also germane for understanding the Russian transition experience: why might reform that is in principle efficiency-enhancing, such as trade liberalization, be opposed by a majority, even though the majority would stand to benefit from its general implementation?[35] The Fernandez-Rodrik analysis focuses on individual specific uncertainties, mainly about the costs of retooling to adapt to the post-reform environment, and shows how individual decisions under uncertainty can frustrate rational collective response to reform measures.

The link between individual rationality and collective action is critical in economic theory. Efficient collective 'choice' is distinct from individually rational behaviour. As defined by K. Arrow, rationality in individual decision-making and behaviour can lead to irrational outcomes in collective behaviour.[36] But how? Although acting rationally as individuals, peasants in collectives can produce outcomes that dampen the impact of market forces; by voting or other means of influence, peasants can succeed in retaining collective/corporative institutions, based on extended kinship and common property as well as

---

[35] Fernandez and Rodrik, 'Resistance'.
[36] Arrow, *Social Choice*.

redistributive institutions.[37] J.C. Scott was among the first to examine the rational aspect of peasant resistance by introducing the concept of risk aversion into the analysis of such behaviour.[38] He argued that peasants generally would prefer organizational arrangements that provide low but certain incomes over ones that yield a higher average income but also increased risk. Since Scott's view fails to link this individual behaviour to the possibility of individual participation in collective action, another line of explanation is drawn from the theory of collective action.[39] Collective organizations can exhibit strategic behaviour within the guise of ethnic or peasant demands. The theory of collective action thus would account for rebellions in response to reform measures by the state as the actions of organized interest groups through historically based ethnic or cultural institutions: the transactions costs of organizing are steep, and the appropriation of existing social organization helps to overcome the free-riding behaviour that would otherwise block collective action.[40]

In this paper, rural producers' behaviour at both the individual and group level is presented as rational from the perspective of the evolutionary accumulation of 'knowledge' about complex and imperfectly observed economic and political processes.[41] Ultimately, redistributive collectives persist precisely because they are exploited organizationally by group leaders and lobbies at the level of the government to achieve political interests, and this is strategic behaviour on the part of the leaders who can offer benefits in return for concessions by the state.[42] What is contended here, however, is that an explicitly dynamic framework of analysis is called for, in contrast to the static theories that have dominated the economic literature on this subject. Only the first stage of an extended interactive process occurring between the state, the individual producers and the collectives, set in motion by a reform initiative, will have taken place when further decisions by individuals that could either accept or halt successful implementation are made.

---

[37] Bates, 'Macropolitical Economy'; Scott, *The Moral Economy*; Popkin, *The Rational Peasant*.
[38] Scott, *The Moral Economy*.
[39] Olson, *Logic*; Hardin, *Collective Action*.
[40] Bates, 'Macropolitical Economy'.
[41] David, 'Path Dependence and Varieties'.
[42] Olson, *Logic*.

The minimal framework of analysis must allow for a second stage, in which resistance to reform either dissipates or becomes stronger, possibly through opposing collective action.

The basic choice facing individual economic agents is whether to remain within the collective farm entity or switch to another kind of farming or sectoral employment. This choice resembles in some respects the one in Fernandez and Rodrik to illustrate the possible defeat of trade liberalization and other similar reforms in the developing world, regardless of whether these policies are introduced by a legislative process or by an authoritarian ruler.[43] The argument here begins with their model, according to which individuals are initially uninformed but subsequently gain more information about alternative choices and decide accordingly on the basis of a calculation of expected net benefits. The cost that individuals face in accepting reform in the Fernandez-Rodrik model is that of retooling for a new job in another sector, which, it is supposed, would be collectively efficient for them to enter under the reformed regime. This cost can be determined exactly only after a preliminary screening activity, which requires an initial non-recoverable investment by each agent. If agents do not expect that the initial investment will be justified because, then, the uncertain additional costs of retooling will be revealed (a second stage) to be too high, they will not accept the reform in stage one, because the screening 'investment' will appear to be a pure tax. The individual agents can represent a firm that is unsure about the future structure of its costs, or an individual who is unsure about the nature and costs of retraining for an unknown position in a firm, to which re-location would be required after the liberalizing reform. Thus, the Fernandez-Rodrik model directs our attention to the role of agents' beliefs about the distribution of unknown costs, the eventual realization of which will either justify or fail to justify incurring an initially known investment cost. It thereby opens a way in which the role of experience-based learning in belief-formation may be brought into the analysis, as an historical factor conditioning responses to economic reform proposals.

---

[43] Fernandez and Rodrik, 'Resistance'.

The Russian Case

The relevance of the Fernandez–Rodrik model to the case of Russian land reform should be quite transparent from our preceding analysis. The individual state and collective farm members face a two-part investment decision: the first part involves applying for a private holding of land, and that entails withdrawal from the state or collective farm, and thereby sacrificing access to the resources that are being distributed to the members, essentially as common rights. These include not only the particular 'subsidiary plot' that the family has been cultivating on the collective's land, the fertility of which, typically, would have been raised by their past cultivation practices in applying fertilizer, growing legumes and other nitrogen-fixing crops, and so forth. Also sacrificed would be the annual allotments of supplies of fertilizers and other marketed farming inputs (for example, insecticides, tools) that the individual households have been accustomed to receiving from the collective or state farm's management—or, more realistically, that by common consent of the community and the manager are being taken for private use from the input provisions that the state delivers to the collective.[44]

We may suppose that the value of those inputs transferred from the collective for private use, along with the sacrificed 'common rights' in the form of the differentially greater fertility of garden plot land (vis-à-vis the arable fields that they might expect to receive as their holding of private land) are known *ex ante*. Those costs would be sunk, or largely irreversible, whether the ex-farm member were to leave agriculture altogether and move away to pursue some urban occupation, or were to carry on as an independent farmer.

In the situation of the Russian village in transition, the agrarian community can be supposed to start with little direct experience of the costs of adjusting to, and continuing on as independent farmers. The initial array of opinions about the costs that this will entail would, therefore, be likely to reflect a mixture of other considerations. Some opinion would be coloured by memories of the experience of *kulak* farming in the era before collectivization under the Soviet regime, whereas others would represent extrapolations from the experience of commercial marketing of surplus produce from private plots in more

---

[44] For discussion of the effects on official state farm production of the reallocation of inputs from collective farming to private plot use, see Leonard, 'The Political Economy'.

recent times. In addition, the initial distributions of opinions would most likely have been shaped by the expressed 'expert' views of the local manager of the collective or state farm. The latter, however, are not neutral experts, and so their views about the costs of adjustment that operating as individual entrepreneurs would impose upon those individuals whose efforts as workers they have been responsible for directing, are likely to be biased upwards. Even if such exaggeration were not motivated by a personal economic interest in perpetuating their own managerial roles, which it would tend to do by reinforcing individual commune members' resistance to privatization, it is not implausible to suppose that managers harbour an inflated impression of the gap between their own competence and the managerial capabilities of the workers, and they therefore would quite 'naturally' offer an upward-biased estimate of the adjustment costs that the latter would incur in switching to the independent owner-cultivator sector. These aspects of the context in which the initial distribution of opinions about the second stage costs of privatization help to account in rational terms for the limited initial subscription to land privatization and related 'reforms' among the collective's members.

So much for the initial response. What may we suppose the agents in our model would learn subsequently? Adaptive belief formation is what is at issue here, and while such a process must be viewed as taking place at the level of the individual, we should recognize that the households are embedded in a social (community) network that acts to filter, pool and retain such 'knowledge' in collective memory, whence it will be presented for the guidance of the individual decision-takers.[45]

Once the privatization reforms are initiated, there would be some change in the state of the remaining members of the collective with regard to their information. It is possible that further data would become available from the experiences of those members who have left the corporative farm. That supposes, to be sure, that they still maintain communications with former members who are engaged in indepen-

---

[45] In David and Sanderson, 'Making Use', and David, 'Path Dependence and Varieties', the significance of adaptive belief formation for evolutionary interpretations of 'learning' is examined. further discussed in David, op. cit. Added to such path dependent models of learning for the individual agents, in this project is also important the effects of information pooling among them. Information pooling might tend to smooth out the sharp peaks in individual's prior probability distributions on the alternative states of nature that are under consideration.

dent farming. It is questionable, however, how good those communication links with former members will be and how heavily the information they transmit would be weighted by those receiving it on the corporative farm. Notice, then, that if such data are lost, or tend to be filtered out, there will be a biasing effect upon the mean of the distribution of beliefs among the remaining villagers, because those who left the collective would tend to have been drawn disproportionately from the part of the opinion distribution that initially believed that (for them at least) the costs would be low. Their departure, therefore, would make it increasingly likely that the lowest estimate of the costs appearing among the opinions in the population of survivors would have been shifted upwards from its initial level.

This constitutes a form of negative feedback that would tend to operate to discourage further 'defection' from the collective (acceptance of privatization reform), especially if the initial response had been numerically limited so that only a few households left the collective when the option first became available. By the same token, were a large group to have left at the outset, it would be less likely that their experiences would be filtered out from the information affecting the beliefs among the surviving collective (corporative) farm members. So, if their expectations of low costs of adjustment had proved justified, the flow of that information would have had an effect opposite to that of the selective exit process considered above. This would moderate, and conceivably more than offset, the tendency for the expected cost estimates to move upwards over time.

What this analysis suggests is that the dynamic evolution of the response to land reform, to the extent that it is dependent upon or driven by a process of revised expectations about the costs (and benefits) of opting for privatization, may be highly 'path dependent'. The eventual outcome is contingent but strongly governed by events along its path. Furthermore, as is characteristic of a large class of dynamic stochastic processes that cannot shake off the influence of past events, the dynamics of reform implementation—as we have modelled the adoption process here—appear to be strongly conditioned by events at or close to the outset of the implementation process.

The crux of this explanation for stalled implementation of land privatization rests upon the idea that with differentially greater exposure to 'stayers' than to 'movers', the views about the economic attractiveness of independent farming among those remaining part of the collective/corporative farm would tend to diverge further and further from the perceptions and opinions of those who have already exited the collective/state farm sector. That such a difference exists has been found from opinion survey results.[46] The views of nationally sampled independent farmers surveyed in 1996 differed markedly from those of members of the former collective and state farms and of farm directors in regard to the benefits of land reform and land sales. It is of course possible that this divergence would be induced by the well-known psychological phenomenon of minimization of cognitive dissonance. This, in view of the irreversible nature of the investment entailed in exiting from the collective, would lead those who had left to find good *ex post* reasons for their having chosen independent farming.[47]

Yet, this is not the only likely mechanism that yields a divergence of opinion between the 'stayers' and the 'movers'. It is found, not surprisingly, that the surviving corporative farm members (the 'stayers') tended to be older than those who had left. So their pessimistic outlook in this regard would be more likely to have been coloured by sharper historical memories preserved in the commune concerning the political and economic risks to which individual entrepreneurs were exposed in the early Soviet era, and before that in the time of Stolypin's reforms. That the village commune actively preserves folk memories reaching back to the historically remote events of the immediate post-Emancipation epoch of Russian agrarian experience seems rather more far-fetched. But it may be pointed out that insofar as those memories were recent enough to have affected collective resistance among the peasantry to land reforms in the early twentieth century, their influence would persist indirectly, being embedded in later recollections of such resistance.

The latter argument serves to make it clear that the information effects of selective exit is hardly the only set of considerations germane to the 'learning process' that affects the dynamics of adoption of the independent farming option. Yet we have not exhausted the range of influences that should be included in the analysis. The political outlook for the success of privatization must also matter, if only because it would influence expectations about the security of tenure of private land holdings. To the extent that the reform is resisted at the outset,

---

[46] See Leonard, 'Rejecting Land Reform'.
[47] On path dependence, see, for example, Arthur, *Increasing Returns*, and 'Competing Technologies'; David, *Path-Dependence*, 'Why Are Institutions', and 'Path Dependence and the Quest'.

the prospects that the state will adopt credible safeguards for the property rights of former collective and state farm members who have become independent farmers are diminished. That, in turn, would have the effect of raising the expected costs of 'private ordering', organizing some defence—whether individual, or in collective action among an emergent *kulak* element in the countryside—against subsequent efforts at re-collectivization. Strong initial resistance to land privatization based on perceptions of high second-stage costs, therefore, would operate via this channel as a self-reinforcing effect, thereby contributing to the path dependent character of the dynamics of the land reform/privatization process.

The immediate conclusion to which the foregoing arguments lead is that the recent rejection of land privatization reforms by the overwhelming majority of the Russian rural populace ought not be interpreted as a manifestation of irrational preferences for collectivized production and all that it entailed. Instead, it is more plausibly the consequence of rational micro-level calculations that have been conditioned by historically formed expectations and a self-reinforcing process of opinion revision. This interpretation may also apply equally in the case of previous episodes in Russian agrarian history, as well as to other instances of resistance to land reform in the developing world. One important background condition may be seen to have been common to the recent experience and to the late nineteenth-century episodes of peasant resistance to pressures for dissolution of the agrarian commune regime in Russia. Both during the transition period, and in the era 1870 to 1900, producers were confronted with trade liberalization and plummeting international prices of grain products. These background conditions surely contributed expectations of weak benefits, which, when added to the adverse expectations of adjustment costs upon which the discussion here has been focused, served to reinforce the rural population's rejection of reform measures and adherence to the status quo.

Conclusion: The Russian Rural Community and Market-Based Land Reform

The policy implications of this conclusion are that the households' response to reforms is likely to be a further retreat into the safety of income smoothing from the output of their subsidiary plots. Russian peasants had struggled in the past against confiscatory policies by the tsarist governments and activities of landlords under the condition of unclear property rights. In the 1990s, similarly, rural producers sought to retain control over their limited assets, a free good, given that the prospective property rights in land were insecure.

That Russian rural dwellers should now resist de-collectivization, after having resisted collectivization in the 1930s and held on to their allotment land against the party line for 60 years, would seem to be evidence of inconsistent preferences, which is the definition of the kind of irrational behaviour that challenges the viability of microeconomic models and predictions.[48] In this paper it has been argued that the rejection of land reform is a complex phenomenon. For both the historical and the modern period of Russian history, communal institutions survived in part because they served strategic purposes of community leaders and of the state itself under conditions of financial crisis and inadequate property rights legislation. Equally important, however, they survived because as the reform proceeded, opinions were formed and formed again on the basis of informal conversations within a sample increasingly biased towards a single, negative extreme. Some policy implications seem clear enough. For further land reform and restructuring to appeal to the larger rural community, the government should focus on reinforcing the security and clarity of procedures for selling the land and on reducing barriers to information flows between those who are successfully established in the independent farming sector and those who remain on collectives. This may not be enough to persuade the older, more risk-averse 'stayers'. So further measures might well be directed towards providing subsidies for retraining, loss offsets and other targeted, non-distortionary rural income support for those who undertake the move to private farming.[49]

The larger policy message, which may be pertinent in designing land reform programmes elsewhere, concerns the importance of providing timely incentives and loss limitation provisions designed to secure a large positive initial response from the rural population. That

---

[48] Instrumental rationality is defined as making consistent choices, or those that satisfy a preference ordering.

[49] This suggestion was made out of concern for the high capital start-up costs in a discussion paper by Brooks and Lerman, 'Land Reform'.

strategy is one that would seek to use the path dependent nature of the dynamics of adoption to overcome the feedback effects that might otherwise result in a 'stalled' land reform.

Note. I am grateful for comments by Paul David, Daniel Field and Judith Pallot and for the understanding and technical assistance provided by Evgenia Serova, Elena Efimenko, Renata Ianbykh and Aleksandr Tarasov. None of those who have helped bear responsibility for any deficiencies that remain, or the conclusion I have drawn here.

References

Agrarian Institute. 'Agrarnaia Reforma v Rossii.' *Zemlia Rossii* [Agrarian Reform in Russia. The Land of Russia], No. 1. Moscow: Agrarian Institute, 1993.
Agricultural Policies, Markets and Trade in the Central and Eastern European Countries, Selected New Independent States, Mongolia and China, Monitoring and Outlook. Paris: OECD, 1995.
Alexeev, Valery. 'Land Reform.' *Executive and Legislative Newsletters RF*, no. 46. Moscow, 1998.
Anfimov, A., and M., L.V. Danilova, et al. *Sistema gosudarstvennogo feodalizma v Rossii: sbornik* [System of State Feudalism in Russia: Collection]. Moskva: Rossiiskaia Akademiia Nauk RF, 1993.
Arrow, K. *Social Choice and Individual Values.* New Haven, Conn: Yale University Press, 1951.
Arrow, K., E. Colombatto, M. Perlman, et al. *The Rational Foundations of Economic Behavior: Proceedings of the IEA Conference held in Turin, Italy.* London: Macmillan Press Ltd, 1996.
Arthur, W.B. *Increasing Returns and Path Dependence in the Economy.* Ann Arbor: University of Michigan Press, 1994.
_____. 'Competing Technologies, Increasing Returns, and Lock-In by Historical Events.' *Economic Journal*, 99 (1989): 116–31.
Bates, R. 'Macropolitical Economy in the Field of Development.' In *Perspectives on Positive Political Economy*, edited by J.E. Alt and K.A. Shepsle, 31–56. New York: Cambridge University Press, 1990.
Boiko, B. 'Land Legislation: Russian Land Ownership, an Endless Story.' *Current Digest of the Post-Soviet Press* 47 (1995): 12–14.
Borodkin, L., and C.S. Leonard. 'The Russian Land Commune and the Mobility of Labour during Industrialization, 1885–1913.' In *Economics in a Changing World: Proceedings of the Tenth World Congress of the International Economic Association*, 167–78. Moscow: St. Martin's Press, 1994.

Brooks, K. 'Agricultural Reform in the Soviet Union.' In C.K. Eicher and J.M. Staatz, eds., *Agricultural Development in the Third World*, 459–79. Baltimore and London: The Johns Hopkins University Press, 1990.

Brooks, K., and Z. Lerman. 'Land Reform and Farm Restructuring in Russia.' World Bank Discussion Papers, No. 233. Washington, DC, 1994.

Carlson, L. *Indians, Bureaucrats, and Land: the Dawes Act and the Decline of Indian Farming*. Westport, Conn.: Greenwood Press, 1981.

Commander, S., and C. Mumssen. 'Understanding Barter in Russia.' EBRD Working Paper No. 37. London, 1999.

Current Statistical Survey, No. 10, Moscow: Goskomstat, 1995.

Csontos, L., J. Kornai, et al. 'Tax Awareness and Reform of the Welfare State: Hungarian Survey Results.' *Economics of Transition* 6, No. 2 (1998): 287–312.

Danilov, V.P. 'Ob istoricheskikh sud'bakh krest'ianskoi obshchiny v Rossii.' In *Ezhegodnik po agrarnoi istorii, vyp. VI, Problemy istorii russkoi obshchiny* [About the Historical Fate of the Peasant Obshchina in Russia, Agrarian History Annual, issue VI, Issues in the History of the Russian Obshchina], 6 (1976): 103–6.

_____. *Sovetskaia dokolkhoznaia derevnia*. Moscow: 'Nauka', 1977.

David, P.A. 'Fortune, Risk and the Microeconomics of Migration.' In *Nations and Households in Economic Growth*, edited by P.A. David and M.W. Reder, 21–88. New York: Academic Press, 1974.

_____. *Path-Dependence: Putting the Past into the Future of Economics*. IMSSS, Stanford University, 1988.

_____. 'So, How would it Matter if 'History Mattered'? Path-Dependence in Economics and Its Long Run Implications.' In *Historical Analysis in Economics*, edited by G.D. Snooks, 29–40. London: Routledge, 1992.

_____. 'Why Are Institutions the 'Carriers of History'?: Path Dependence and the Evolution of Conventions, Organizations and Institutions.' *Structural Change and Economic Dynamics* 5, No 2 (1994): 205–20.

_____. 'Path Dependence and the Quest for Historical Economics: One More Chorus of the Ballad of QWERTY.' Oxford University Discussion Papers in Economic and Social History, No. 20. Oxford, 1997.

_____. 'Path Dependence and Varieties of Learning in the Evolution of Technological Progress.' In *Technological Innovation as an Evolutionary Process*, edited by J. Ziman, 118–345. Cambridge: Cambridge University Press, 2000.

David, P.A., and G. Rothwell. 'Standardization, Diversity and Learning: Strategies for the Coevolution of Technology and Industrial Capacity.' *International Journal of Industrial Organization* 14 (1996): 181–201.

David, P.A., and W.S. Sanderson. 'Making Use of Treacherous Advice: Cognitive Process, Bayesian Adaptation, and the Tenacity of Unreliable Knowledge.' In *The Frontiers of the New Institutional Economics*, edited by J.N. Drobak and J.V.C. Nye, ch 14. New York: Academic Press, 1997.

Doklad (See Gosudarstvennyi...)

Dubrovskii, S.M. *Sel'skoe khoziastvo i krest'ianstvo Rossii v period imperializma* [Agriculture and the Peasantry in Russia in the Period of Imperialism]. Moscow: Nauka, 1975.

Euroconsult Centre for World Food Studies. 'Farm Restructuring and Land Tenure in Reforming Socialist Economies: A Comparative Analysis of Eastern and Central Europe.' World Bank Discussion Paper No. 238. Washington, DC, 1995.

Fernandez, R., and D. Rodrik. 'Resistance to Reform: Status Quo Bias in the Presence of Individual-Specific Uncertainty.' In *Monetary and Fiscal Policy*, edited by T. Person and G. Tabellini, vol. 2: 371–86. Cambridge, MA: MIT Press, 1994.

Fridman, M. *Nasha finansova i à sistema* [Our Financial System]. St Petersburg: Obshchestsvennaia Pol'za, 1905.

Galbi, D. 'The Significance of Credits and Subsidies in Russian Agricultural Reform.' World Bank Policy Research Working Paper No. 1441. Washington, DC, 1995.

Gatrell, P. *The Tsarist Economy, 1850–1917*. New York: St Martin's Press, 1986.

Gosudarstvennyi (Natsionalnyi) Doklad 'O Sostianii i ispol'zovanii zemel' Rossiiskoi Federatsii za 1994' (1995). *Komitet Rossiiskoi Federatsii po zemel'nym resursam i zemleustroistvu* [Government (National) Report 'About the State of Land Use in the Russian Federation for 1994, Committee of the Russian Federation for Land Use and Land Construction]. Moscow, 1994.

Gumbell, E.J. *Statistics of Extremes*. New York: Columbia University Press, 1958.

Hardin, R. *Collective Action*. Baltimore: Johns Hopkins University Press, 1982.

Hounshell, D.A. 'The Medium is the Message, or How Context Matters: The Rand Corporation Builds an Economics of Innovation, 1946–1952.' In *Systems, Experts, and Computers* edited by A.C. Hughes and T.P. Hughes, 255–310. Cambridge, MA: MIT Press, 2000.

Ioffe, G., and T. Nefedova. *Continuity and Change*. Boulder, Colorado: Westview Press, 1997.

Kahan, A. *Russian Economic History: The Nineteenth Century*. Chicago: The University of Chicago Press, 1989.

Kantor, Shawn. *Politics and Property Rights : The Closing of the Open Range in the Postbellum South*. Chicago: University of Chicago Press, 1998.

Kuznetsov, V.V. (ed.). *Organizatsionno-ekonomichekie faktory razvitiia regional'nogo APK* [Organizational and Economic Factors in the Development of the Regional APK]. Rostov-on-Don: Vserossiiskii NII ekonomiki i normativi, 1996.

Land Privatization and Farm Reorganization in Russia, Annexes. Washington, DC: International Finance Corporation, 1995.

Leonard, C.S. 'Resistance to Land Reform.' Paper presented at BASEES, Cambridge, MA, 1998.

———. 'The Political Economy of the Subsidiary Plot in Transition Russia.' Paper presented at the Institute of Economics and Statistics, Oxford University, February, 1999.

Leonard, C.S., 'Rejecting Land Reform in Russia: A Strategic View of Status Quo Reference, 1861–2000.' Paper presented at Oxford University, 2000.

———— and E. Serova. 'Braking and Entering: Transition to a Market Economy in Agriculture, 1992–1995.' Paper presented at the American Economics Association Meeting, San Francisco, 8 January, 1996.

————. 'The Reform of Russian Agriculture, 1990–1998.' In *Russia's Post Communist Economy*, edited by B. Granville and P. Oppenheimer, 367–96. London: The Royal Institute for International Affairs, 2001.

Lewin, M. *Russian Peasants and Soviet Power: A Study of Collectivization*. NY: Norton, 1968.

Liefert, W.M. 'Grain Sector Reform and Food Security in the Countries of the FSU.' In *Cereals Sector Reform in the Former Soviet Union and Central and Eastern Europe*, edited by L.D. Smith and N. Spooner, 93–107. Wallingford, Oxon: CAB International, 1997.

Narodnoe khoziastvo SSSR v 1989 g. Statisticheskii ezhgodnik [The Economy of the USSR in 1989, Statistical Annual]. Moscow: 'Financy i Statistika,' 1990.

Nifontov, A.S. *Zernovoi priozvodstvo Rossii vo vtoroi polovine XIX veka* [Grain Production in Russia in the Second Half of the Nineteenth Century]. Moscow: Nauka, 1974.

Nove, A. *An Economic History of the USSR*. Harmondsworth: Penguin Books, 1969.

Olson, M. *Logic of Collective Action*. Cambridge, MA: Harvard University Press, 1965.

Pack, H., and L.E. Westphal. 'Industrial Strategy and Technological Change: Theory Versus Reality.' *Journal of Development Economics*, 22 (1986): 87–128.

Pallot, J. *Land Reform in Russia, 1906–1917: Peasant Responses to Stolypin's Project of Rural Transformation*. New York: Oxford University Press, 1998.

Penny, D.H. 'Farm Credit Policy in the Early Stages of Agricultural Development.' In *Rural Financial Markets in Developing Countries*, edited by J.D. Von Pischke, et al, pp. 58–66. Baltimore, Md.: The Johns Hopkins University Press, 1983.

Perotta, L. 'The Higher Up Don't Want to and the Lower Down Cannot: Analysis of Focus Groups Village Community.' *CPER Staff Paper*, Issue 49. Ukraine, 1998.

Persson, T., and G. Tabellini. *Monetary and Fiscal Policy*. Volume 2. Cambridge, MA: MIT Press, 1994.

Popkin, S. *The Rational Peasant*. Los Angeles: University of California Press, 1979.

Pogrebinsky, A.P. *Ocherki istorii finansov dorevoliutsionnoi Rossii* (19–20,vv). Moscow: Gosfinizdat, 1954.

Rashin, A.G. *Formirovanie promyshlennogo proletariata v Rossii* [Formation of the Industrial Proletariat in Russia]. Moscow: Gosudarstvennoe sotsial'no-ekonomicheskoe izdatel'stvo, 1940.

Scott, J.C. *The Moral Economy of the Peasant*. New Haven, Conn: Yale University Press, 1976.

Sel'skoe khoziastvo Rossii [Agriculture of Russia]. Moscow: Goskomstat, 1995.
Shepsle, K. 'Institutional Arrangements and Equilibrium in Multi-dimensional Voting Models.' *American Journal of Political Science* 23 (1979): 27–59.
Spechler, M.C. 'The Regional Concentration of Industry in Imperial Russia 1854–1917.' *Journal of European Economic History* (Fall 1980): 401–19.
Statistical Report. Moscow: Interfax News Agency, 1995.
Statisticheskii Biulleten' No. 1 (APK), *Osnovnye pokazateli funktsionirovaniia agropromyshlennogo kompleksa Rossiiskoi Federatsii v 1994 goda* [Statistical Bulletin, Fundamental Indicators of the Functioning of the APK in the Russian Federation for 1994]. Moscow: Goskomstat Rossii, 1995.
Statisticheskii Biulleten' No. 10 (APK), *Osnovnye pokazateli funktsionirovaniia agropromyshlennogo kompleksa Rossiiskoi Federatsii v ianvare-sentiabre 1995 goda*. Moscow: Goskomstat Rossii, 1995.
Shvanebakh, P.K. *Nashe podatnoe delo* [Our Taxes]. St Petersburg: Tiografiia M.M. Stasiulevicha, 1903.
Symons, L., and C. White (eds.). *Russian Transport: An Historical and Geographical Survey*. London: G. Bell & Sons Ltd, 1975.
Townsend, R. Y. 'Consumption Insurance: An Evaluation of Risk-Bearing Systems in Low-Income Economies.' *Journal of Economic Perspectives* 9, No. 3 (1995): 83–102.
Van Atta, D., and D.A.J. Macey. *The 'Farmer Threat': The Political Economy of Agrarian Reform in Post-Soviet Russia*. Boulder: Westview Press, 1993.
White, C. 'The Impact of Russian Railway Construction on the Market for Grain in the 1860s and 1870s.' In *Russian Transport: An Historical and Geographical Survey*, edited by L. Symons and C. White, 1–45. London: G. Bell & Sons Ltd, 1975.

9.
Understanding the Past to Reshape the Future:
Problems of South Africa's Transition

FRANCIS WILSON

Introduction

The fundamental theme of this paper is simple. History matters. Although there are flat-earth economists who profess to believe that economic problems can be tackled without reference to the historical and institutional circumstances within which they occur, they are happily less influential than they have been. Certainly for South African economists, understanding the peculiar pattern of industrialization in a racially divided society leads to a firm belief in the importance of including the historical dimension in their analysis.

In this paper we shall consider the fundamental economic problem[1] with which South African policy-makers are currently grappling, in order to show the necessity of historical analysis in the process of formulating possible solutions. The structure of the paper is straightforward. The first part explores the problem briefly but with sufficient detail to enable those who do not know South Africa to grasp the main issues. Part two attempts to uncover the historical roots of the current difficulties. And in the third part we assess the ways in which a historical perspective illuminates the search for effective policies to resolve the problems.

---

[1] There is, of course, a number of other no less critical (and urgent) issues, including the tidal wave of AIDS that is threatening to engulf the whole region and the degree of violence, especially against women, in the society as a whole, but this paper focuses on the one that is of particular concern to economic historians and economists.

The Problem

It is generally agreed that the political transition that took place in South Africa during the five short years between 1989 and 1994 was one of the most remarkable in an eventful century. For those of us who lived in South Africa through the deeply depressing apartheid decades of the 1950s, 60s, 70s and 80s the achievements of the past ten years, however clouded by the spectre of escalating crime, have been such that nobody in 1989 (apart, it would seem, from Nelson Mandela himself) would have believed them possible. The secretly negotiated release of all political prisoners and unbanning of their political parties; the dismantling of the legal apparatus of *apartheid*; the relatively peaceful transition to fully democratic rule in the elections of 1994; the formulation and adoption of one of the most enlightened constitutions in the world; and the ongoing commitment to democratic practices in the ensuing years including the elections of 1999 are extraordinary achievements recognized by all but the most cynical or those blinded in some way by the proximity of events.

With hindsight, it is easy enough to explain the multiple causes of this transition, although it is important to record that for virtually all concerned (including this writer)[2] such wisdom was acquired only after the event. Such explanation lies beyond the scope of this paper. But it is important to note that the combination of reasons, which includes a wide spectrum ranging from the fall of the Berlin Wall to the reaching of the historic limits on any further growth of the apartheid economy, itself requires historical understanding. What is of more immediate concern for us in this paper, however, is recognition of the fact that whilst such changes were and are fundamentally necessary conditions for the shaping of a more just society in South Africa, they are not by themselves sufficient. To put it another way, the dismantling of South Africa's racist laws has to be seen more as the removal of the scaffolding that enabled apartheid to be built and maintained rather than the undermining of the foundations of the building itself.

Let me not overstate the point. The deeply wounding assault on human dignity visited daily on black South Africans by all manner of classification and control laws has been stopped in its tracks by the victory of the liberation movement. This is a magnificent achievement

---

[2] See Wilson and Ramphele, *Uprooting Poverty*, p. 6, for a prediction that proved embarrassingly wrong only 12 months after it was published.

to be celebrated for ever. At the same time it is important not to allow the brilliance of this very process to blind oneself to a fundamental problem that remains.

Essentially, the difficulty lies in the potential political instability and fundamental injustice inherent in the fact of deep economic inequality where the fault line runs largely (although not entirely) along colour or 'racial' lines. Inextricably, part of this core is the problem of overwhelming poverty endured by so large a proportion of the population as revealed in stark statistical terms.[3] South Africa's Gini index, officially measured at 59.3, is fourth only to that of Sierra Leone (62.9), Brazil (60.1) and Guatemala (59.6), indicating a level of inequality far deeper than that of such countries as India (29.7) or the Russian Federation (48.0).[4] Another estimate, based on a 1993 national survey, placed South Africa as the most unequal country of those then measured in the world.[5] In that year, whilst the top 10 per cent of households earned almost exactly half (50.1 per cent) of the total income, the poorest 10 per cent accounted for less than half of one per cent (0.4 per cent) of the total. Indeed the poorest half of the households, most of which are black, earn less than one-tenth (8.9 per cent) of total income.[6] Either way the basic data indicate a profound problem. So too the statistics on poverty, whilst also best interpreted as approximations, point to a deep malaise. In 1993, 45 per cent of the population was below the widely agreed Minimum Living Level whilst 53 per cent of the population lived in the poorest 40 per cent of households.[7] In comparative terms 21 per cent of South Africans fell below the international rule-of-thumb measure of absolute poverty of $1 per person per day.[8] This in a country whose average income, measured as GNP per capita, placed it in the upper-middle-income range, 80 countries or more from the bottom, on the world scale.[9] After deconstructing these numbers in order to understand the complexity a little more deeply, the following realities emerge from the data.

---

[3] The main sources from which this information is drawn are: (a) May (ed.), *Poverty*; (b) Central Statistical Service (now StatsSA), *Living*; (c) Project for Statistics on Living Standards and Development, *South Africans*; (d) Wilson and Ramphele, *Uprooting Poverty*.
[4] World Bank, *Entering*, table 5.
[5] Whiteford, Posel and Kelatwang, *A Profile*, table 15.
[6] Ibid., p. 13.
[7] Ministry in the Office of the President, *Reconstruction*, table 3.
[8] May (ed.), *Poverty*, p. 30.
[9] World Development Reports, 1990–1997.

First is the extent to which poverty is a racial phenomenon. The median household annual income for different groups in 1995 was Black (African) R12,400 ($4,500); Coloured R19,400 ($7,040); Indian R40,500 ($14,700); White R60,000 ($21,780).[10] Against this background it is perhaps not surprising to find that the proportion of people living in poverty varies widely, with African 61 per cent; Coloured 38 per cent; Indian 5 per cent; White 1 per cent.[11]

Second is the extent to which it is concentrated in the rural areas. In terms of income, nearly three-quarters (71 per cent) of people living in rural areas are classified as poor compared with only 29 per cent of those in urban areas.[12] But poverty is not only a matter of inadequate income: in the rural areas there is a chronic lack of basic services. For example, in 1995, whilst three-quarters (74 per cent) of urban people had running water inside their homes, only one-sixth (17 per cent) of rural homes had inside taps.[13] And many people still have to walk long distances for water. Similarly, in terms of access to energy for cooking, heating and lighting, there is an enormous difference between life in urban and rural areas with many country women having to scour the countryside for fuel, often walking hours bearing heavy loads of wood. This in a country which produces approximately 60 per cent of the electricity in the African continent and which is criss-crossed from top to bottom by a national grid.

The third aspect of the poverty and inequality that characterize South Africa is the extent to which they affect women more than men. The gender bias to which many analysts have referred can be seen, for example, in the fact that whilst 31 per cent of all households headed by men are classified as poor, no less than 60 per cent of households headed by women are in the same condition.

Finally there is an age perspective. Children are vulnerable in all societies but in South Africa there seems to be mounting evidence that they suffer unduly from poverty and the consequences of poverty. Approximately 60 per cent of all children live in poor households where stress levels are high and alcoholism is widespread. In such conditions children may be abused in numerous ways including beatings and sexual assaults. Nor is it only children. Young adults too seem to

---

[10] May (ed.), *Poverty*, p. 27. For consistency the Rand figures are converted to US dollars at the then existing exchange rate of R3.63 to the dollar.
[11] Ibid., p. 32.
[12] Ibid., p. 30.
[13] Ibid., p. 31.

be peculiarly vulnerable in South Africa today. For they are growing to maturity in an educational system that is woefully inadequate in an economy unable to use them in a meaningful way.

Table 1. Unemployment in South Africa, 1993, by Major Dividing Lines.

Race	Black 39%	White 5%
Geography	Rural 40%	Urban* 22–26%
Gender	Women 35%	Men 26%
Age	16–24 53%	55-64 15%

*Metropolitan areas, 22 per cent; other urban areas, 26 per cent.

Indeed the figures of unemployment in South Africa throw into sharp relief the contours of poverty sketched above.[14] When categories overlap, inequality is reinforced. Thus, for example, the combination of race and age, without taking account of geography or gender, shows unemployment rates of 65 per cent for young blacks compared with 2 per cent for older whites in the decade before retirement.

Historical Roots

The facts are not new and for those who know their history such realities are not surprising. Yet it is worth considering, again briefly, some of the major factors which helped to shape the South Africa which President Nelson Mandela inherited when he took office in 1994 and which the country's first democratic government has been attempting to reshape since then.

First: The Land

We do not yet know enough of the history to be sure of earlier struggles that may have taken place between Khoi, San, Sotho and Nguni speakers moving around the land that is now South Africa. But after 1652 there was a long process of conquest whereby people coming

---

[14] Project for Statistics on Living Standards and Development, *South Africans*, pp. 141–3.

from Europe moved into the Cape and then north to take control of the land, the water and, when they were found, the minerals. The Land Act of 1913, as subsequently amended and consolidated, the mineral rights legislated after the diamond and gold discoveries of the latter half of the nineteenth century, and the riparian rights developed to ensure that whoever controlled the land controlled the water effectively meant that the accumulation of wealth was confined almost exclusively to whites. The reality is blindingly obvious. Yet it was not until 1994 and the democratic appointment of a minister of Water Affairs that the fundamental consequences of the control of water for both home consumption and agricultural production became a matter of public consciousness and debate.[15]

Second: Labour

Within a decade of arriving to stay in the Cape, the Dutch imported slaves. For nearly 200 years slavery was part and parcel of economic life and set the tone for labour relations, particularly along colour lines. Although abolished in 1836 slavery continued to exert its influence in a way that is almost without parallel. Pass laws, vagrancy laws and master and servant laws enacted in the years that followed provided a framework of control. This enabled the political rulers to bend the process of industrialization in such a way that it gave employers (white) in the diamond and gold mines of South Africa a power over the lives of their workers (black), which was effectively a modernized form of slavery. Turrell has described in meticulous detail the process whereby the early diamond diggings with their motley crew of adventurers became a highly organized, white-run, mining industry in which black workers (but not white) were compelled to stay in closed, single-sex, compounds for the duration of their contract in the mines.[16] The outcome of the seminal battles fought within the first two decades of the diamond discoveries in 1867 set a pattern of labour organization that was not to change for a full hundred years. For what happened in Kimberley was repeated on the Witwatersrand. The system of oscillating migration, with workers housed, several thousand at a time, in huge compounds or labour batteries and treated effectively as labour units without families, social aspirations, or political preferences was

---

[15] See, for example, Department of Water Affairs and Forestry, *Water Supply*.
[16] Turrell, *Capital*. See also Worger, *South Africa's City*.

entrenched at the heart of South Africa's industrial revolution. Men were drawn from different rural parts of the region, from both inside and outside South Africa, on contracts that varied from a few months to a maximum of two years. Many of those who might have settled in town did not do so given the pressure of the pass laws, which increased over the years to prevent either workers or their families from moving out of the rural areas. Whilst the system was never so water-tight as to prevent completely the process of urbanization, there is no doubt that the process was both retarded and distorted by a labour system that has no parallel in the history of industrialization. Centred in the mining industry, the system was expanded, particularly during the apartheid years after 1948, into many other parts of the urban economy.

Thus, in mines affiliated to the Chamber of Mines, employment of black African workers between 1906 and 1986 rose from 81,000 to 536,000. All of them, save a tiny percentage, were housed as temporary contract workers in the single-sex compounds. It is interesting to note the changing patterns in terms of areas from which the men came. In 1906 two-thirds (65 per cent) of the miners came from Mozambique and only one-quarter (23 per cent) from inside South Africa, mainly from the eastern Cape. By 1936, when employment had risen to over 300,000, just over half (52 per cent) came from rural South Africa with Mozambique (28 per cent) and Lesotho (15 per cent) supplying most of the rest. By 1966, with employment risen to 383,000, South Africa's contribution had fallen to one-third (34.1 per cent). In addition to Mozambique (28 per cent) and Lesotho (17 per cent), countries north of South Africa, notably Malawi, had become major suppliers (15 per cent). The proportion of South Africans continued to fall until 1973 at which time Malawi, Mozambique and Lesotho all sent more men to the South African mines than did the rural areas of South Africa. But the risk was high and in the period of one month, April 1974, two events occurred that made action necessary. The first was that the President of Malawi — in response to an aircrash in which more than 70 miners died — started to withdraw all Malawian labour from the mines. The second was a coup in Lisbon, which served notice that the Portuguese had lost the will to rule their empire meaning that Frelimo (which then opposed the recruiting of Mozambicans for the mines) would shortly be in power. Facilitated by a rapidly rising price of gold and stimulated by the burgeoning of trade unions within secondary industry around them, mine management embarked on a series of dramatic pay increases. These saw real wages of black miners treble within five years. Expansion of the industry that followed the rising price of gold meant that by 1986 employment on the mines had risen to 536,000. Of these no less than 315,000 (60 per cent) were recruited within the country as a result of wages having risen to a level that was competitive with the manufacturing sector. Apart from Lesotho (20 per cent) and Mozambique (down to 10 per cent), no other countries were supplying more than 3 or 4 per cent, although even such relatively small proportions implied considerable foreign exchange earnings for the countries concerned. Although the diamond mines began to phase out the compound system in the early 1970s, the gold mines continue to this day to house the vast majority of their workers as oscillating migrants. The one change that has taken place in recent years is that men tend to go home more often, whilst regarding the job as more permanent than was generally the case in the past. But the urbanization of wives and families that normally accompanies the long-term development of a major mining industry has not happened on the South African gold mines.

The consequences of the systemic control over black labour by means of the structure of oscillating migration were profound and have been detailed elsewhere.[17] For our purposes it is sufficient to note three important points.

First, the system was part of a process that generated poverty whilst simultaneously producing wealth for others. The conditions under which rural-urban migration can stimulate rural development have long been a matter of debate in the literature. A recent paper by Dorrit Posel constructs a model to show how migration 'can lead either to higher level equilibrium in sending communities with investment out of remittances, or to a lower level equilibrium where remittances are primarily consumed'.[18] Clearly there are conditions (even in South Africa) where migration provides funds for investment in rural development, but the historical evidence points to the fact that a process of oscillating migration involving a large proportion of the able-bodied males in the sending area over a long period of time is more likely to impoverish that area in the sense of reducing its capacity to generate income for those who live there. The argument is not new but bears

---

[17] Wilson, *Labour*; Wilson and Ramphele, *Uprooting Poverty*, chapter 10; Crush, Jeeves and Yudelman, *South Africa's Labor*; Moodie, *Going for Gold*.
[18] Posel, 'Migration'.

repeating as part of the process of understanding the historical perspective that illuminates the economic challenges of the coming century. Essentially what happened was that a system developed whereby an increasing proportion of able-bodied black males was drawn out of those rural areas (both inside South Africa, for example, Transkei, and outside, for example, Lesotho), which had not been occupied through white conquest. Inside South Africa these areas, first defined in terms of the Land Act of 1913, were the core of what became the 'Bantustans' or 'Black' National States of post-1948 apartheid. When the migrant system first began, it is clear that the earnings from the mines provided rural societies with much-needed cash not only for consumption but also for investment, including the purchase of guns. But as time went on and more and more men were drawn into mining, there was a steady shift in the pattern of production as men (but not women) shifted the focus of their work from cattle and maize to diamonds and gold.

Colin Murray has documented[19] with great clarity what this process meant in terms of production in Lesotho (then the Protectorate of Basutoland) where, until the end of World War I, the country produced more than enough grain to feed itself and was able, in most years, to export a surplus. From about 1920 to the great drought of 1930 to 1932 the country was more or less able to feed itself. Since that time Lesotho has had to import increasing quantities of food. Whilst there is less data available to prove it, it would seem that the trends in rural reserve areas of South Africa were much the same.[20]

Such evidence does not, of course, by itself imply an increase of poverty. Just as Britain moved, after the abolition of the Corn Laws, out of food into textile production whilst increasing its imports of American wheat paid for by industrial exports, it arguably made economic sense for the people of Basutoland to shift productive resources (that is, labour) from agriculture into mining and to pay for grain imports with the earnings from diamonds and gold. But analogies, like truths, can be misleading if they come in halves. And this particular half-analogy obscures the fundamental question as to the geographic location and control of the accumulation, over a long period of time, of productive capital and infrastructure. For the diamond and gold mines in which the workers of Basutoland/Lesotho (as well as others) pro-

---

[19] Murray, *Families*.
[20] Bundy, *The Rise*.

duced so much wealth were situated in another country to which neither they nor their families had any rights of citizenship or access. And the common wealth of that other country derived, *inter alia*, from the taxes on those same diamond and gold mines was used to build the vital economic infrastructure, such as roads and telecommunications, on only one side of the border. What was true of the independent country of Lesotho was no less true of those rural areas such as the regions in the Eastern Cape where, by means of pass laws and the politics of a racist state, populations were confined to places in which there was little investment whether private or public and from which people could only get permission to leave as oscillating migrants without their families.

And so, over the years, the process of 'development' in South (and southern) Africa had an in-built bias which distorted the pattern of accumulation in such a way as to exacerbate the imbalance between rural people in the reserves and the capital and infrastructure to which they had access. This led in time to rural situations all over the country where the capacity of sending areas to generate wealth for those who lived there seems over time to have declined on a per capita basis as the areas became increasingly dependent on the urban areas for jobs and remittances to meet basic consumption needs.

The second consequence of the oscillating migrant labour system as it was developed in the gold mines at the end of the nineteenth century was the fact of its becoming the model for the architects of apartheid.[21] We shall not dwell on that theme here except to note how misleading it is to assume, as so many do (not least in the English-speaking world), that the system of apartheid was simply a matter of racism enforced by prejudiced whites, mainly Afrikaans-speaking, against blacks by means of legislation to segregate residential areas and beaches and to prevent inter-marriage. It was, of course, partly that. But the way in which the underlying dynamics of the long-entrenched system of oscillating migration was re-inforced, expanded and used to provide a fig-leaf of 'eiesoortige ontwikkeling' (one's own type of development), whilst maintaining a cheap labour supply for the country's unique path to industrialization, should not be ignored.[22] It

[21] Wilson, *Labour*, p. 13.
[22] Wilson, *Migrant Labour*.

was a fundamental component of apartheid and it came originally not from slightly backward rural racists but from what were then the sophisticated cosmopolitan exponents of modern industrial capitalism.

The third consequence of the country's migrant labour system has already been implicitly discussed above. It relates to the fact that throughout the century of industrialization workers were drawn from well beyond the political boundaries of the nation state that South Africa became in 1910. The relations thus forged between South Africa and her neighbours, from almost all of whom she has drawn significant numbers of workers on an oscillating basis, are complex in a way which in Europe perhaps only the Irish would understand. In the case of Lesotho, the ending of the migrant system in the diamond mines in the early 1970s, as De Beers moved to stabilize its labour force in family housing, meant the effective exclusion of Basotho men from jobs in Kimberley. So too on a wider scale, as South Africa plagued by unemployment has moved to reduce the flow of oscillating migrants from across its political boundaries, countries that for decades have helped to build the wealth of the Republic have found themselves increasingly excluded from the economy of which they were an integral part. Yet, in the not-so-long run, it is clearly in the interests of South Africa to collaborate effectively with her neighbours in the development of a regional economy in which political boundaries do not become another fault line marking the deep and destabilizing inequalities which characterize the area.

So much then for the consequences of South Africa's racially biased institutional arrangements for allocating resources (land, water and minerals) and controlling black labour during most of the first century of industrialization.

Third: Government Expenditure

A third source of bias may be traced to the way in which the tax revenue of the state was used by those who controlled it to make investments, not least in human capital, in order to benefit primarily whites. As early as the 1890s, the area that is today the Free State Province introduced compulsory education for all white children. It was to be another 100 years before the state did the same for black children. It is thus not surprising to find that in 1993 of those aged 18 and above nearly two-thirds (61 per cent) of whites had completed standard 10 (12 years of schooling) or more, whilst only one-tenth (11 per cent) of blacks had done the same.[23]

Table 2. Human Capital, by Race, in South Africa 1993.

Age	Completed	All	White	Black
14 or more	Standard 6 or more	55	90	46
16 or more	Standard 8 or more	38	83	27
18 or more	Standard 10 or more	20	61	11

It is this basic difference in human capital investment by race that explains why, in 1985, when blacks formed 75 per cent of the population, they constituted only 0.1 per cent of engineers, 2.9 per cent of architects/surveyors, 5.5 per cent of scientists, and 7.4 per cent of accountants/auditors. Only in nursing (60 per cent) and teaching (63 per cent) were blacks anywhere near the 75 per cent that would have implied equal opportunity.[24]

Insights for the Twenty-first Century

How then does the historical perspective that we have considered, albeit so briefly, illuminate the search for effective policies to resolve the problems identified above as South Africa, in the aftermath of its second democratic election, stands poised to move into the new millennium?

I would suggest five insights. None are original but as at least three of them are widely contested for one reason or another it is worth arguing their case. Some are as much to do with consciousness as they are with specific policies.

1. This is primarily a political point and relates to the perception seemingly held by a large proportion of those white South Africans who did not support apartheid in the sense of voting for the National Party during the half century of its rule after 1948. In a trenchant attack on the Truth and Reconciliation Commission, not least for the attention it was devoting to the business sector, one of the country's leading white English-speaking political leaders in 1997 utterly rejected 'the notion of collective, community or group guilt'. There could be no

---

[23] Project for Statistics on Living Standards and Development, *South Africans*, tables 3.5–3.7.
[24] Commonwealth Expert Group, *Beyond Apartheid*, p. 15.

such thing he argued, '[a]s group liability, or, even worse racial liability'. But what he and so many of the representatives of the business sector who gave evidence to the Commission failed to recognize was that the functioning of the apartheid state as it evolved from conquest and slavery was such as to be of primary benefit to one group only in the society. And whether or not individual whites opposed the National Party at the polls, all of them were beneficiaries of the system. If then the benefits which flowed their way were determined in part by the colour of their skin, could they, could we, deny a common liability?[25] Understanding the racial bias in the whole process of accumulation in South Africa over the past century is, it could be argued, a necessary condition for creating the political conditions for tackling the problems of distribution that challenge South Africa as we enter the twenty-first century.

2. The second observation is also related to consciousness. It too has to do with blindness, a failure to perceive. It has to do with the presence, or rather the absence, of water in so much of South Africa's past political and economic thinking. For decades those battling for democracy and justice in South Africa focused on 'the land question'. Yet only a moment's thought is necessary to make one realize that the key problem with regard to agricultural production in the country is not so much land as water. Nor is it only a matter of water for irrigation. When the new government came to power, there were some 17 million black South Africans, nearly half the total population, who did not have access to clean drinking water through a tap either in the house or in the yard. Yet these needs of water for basic household use are fundamental and it was not really until the 1980s that they began to be discussed with any sense of urgency. Given the lack of consciousness that economists and others have shown about such an issue in the past, all those concerned with development issues have to ask themselves as to what other critical issues they/we have failed to see clearly.

3. Linked to the issue of lack of water for irrigation by black farmers is the matter of rural investment. One insight that analysis of the past suggests is the realization that South Africa's peculiar pattern of urbanization during its first industrial century has been one that has kept people on the land, whilst simultaneously restricting investment in productive activities by those living there. Rural areas have become

---

[25] For further discussion on this point see Wilson, Graduation Address.

dormitory suburbs and the economic base to sustain them is elsewhere. Much thinking in South Africa now tends to the view that investment in job creation needs to take place in the urban areas. The argument that emerges from this paper is that the emphasis has to shift to a much greater focus on investment, both public and private, to establish the conditions for the creation of jobs, many of them possibly part-time, in the rural areas.

To put it another way, South Africa's crippling unemployment rate of 30 per cent and more is unlikely to be significantly reduced through any combination of growth policies that focus only on the urban areas. To be successful, strategies of development will have to find ways of enhancing the existing assets of the poor. Apart from human capital, the most important assets of the poor still include (for a significant proportion of them) some stock, access to some grazing land and the possibility of a little arable land as well as a relatively cheap garden plot, near the homestead, plus a network of kinship and neighbourhood connections. From an urban perspective in a modern industrial economy these assets seem to be hardly worth counting. But looked at again, in terms of potential resources in a situation where the only possible way out of poverty for those enduring it is to harness their own energies and assets, there is perhaps more here than meets the eye.

Two recent ventures provide signs — no more than that at this stage — of what might be possible. One is the production, in a former homeland or 'reserve' area in the Northern Province, of strawberries aimed at the export market for Japan; the other is a scheme put into effect by government agricultural officers in the Eastern Cape Province to facilitate a process whereby owners of small flocks of sheep, sometimes only two or three animals, are able to improve the quality and marketing of their wool so as to increase by 50 per cent, 100 per cent or more the income they derive from this product. Of course, starting at a very low base, the absolute increase in income is not yet all that noteworthy. But the growth potential of such a revolution in the organization of production by small-scale farmers is vast, as the half-century of experience of buffalo-owning milk producers in the Amul dairy of Gujarat in India can testify. Nor is it only in agricultural production that the potential of the rural areas lies. South Africa's strong telecommunications infrastructure, combined with the technological revolution of the 1990s, means that the potential exists, albeit unexploited as yet, to develop information-processing centres away from the major metropolitan areas, not least in the currently under-utilized old agricultural towns such as Adelaide or Bedford in the Eastern Cape. The consequences of the telescoping of space made possible by the World Wide Web have not yet been adequately explored, let alone exploited, in the new South Africa.

4. The fourth insight is not contentious, but a sense of history helps to emphasize its relevance and urgency. Appropriate investment in human capital is a necessary condition to overcome the twin legacies of inequality and poverty in South Africa today. Analysis of current economic trends, not least with regard to globalization, points to the fact that a fundamental cause of widening inequality within and between nations is the relative shift in the demands for skilled and unskilled labour. The requirements of the new competitive economies, with their computer technology and the software to run it, are increasingly for people with numeracy and literacy skills rather than for those (as was the case until relatively recently) with the physical strength and stamina to work long hours at the bottom of a mine or in the harsh environment of a metal foundry. In this environment it is clear that South Africa has to pay particular attention to creating an educational system which is able, as rapidly as possible, to ensure that the young women and men emerging from secondary school are properly numerate and literate. The country's tragedy is that the educational system it inherited from its apartheid past was designed with almost exactly the opposite intentions. Overcoming the legacy of 'Bantu education' and of the disruptions of the struggle-years in the schools is perhaps the single greatest challenge facing the South African government as it enters the new century. The importance of finding effective ways of improving the country's stock of human capital is underlined by our understanding as to how education policy in the past impacted on the shape of today's political economy. Nor is it only education that is important. Given the history of poverty in South Africa, the need for investment in human capital has to include the body as much as the mind. The extent of malnutrition, for example, and its impact on the capacity to learn in school or elsewhere highlights, for even the most tough-minded of economists, the need for investment in health.[26]

5. Finally there is an issue already discussed above. Awareness of the functioning of the oscillating migrant labour system across the political boundaries of Southern Africa for a full century helps drive

---

[26] See Digby and Johansson; Floud; Leunig and Voth in this Volume.

home the point that the countries surrounding the Republic of South Africa are more than just neighbours. They have contributed materially to the development of the economy centred on the gold mines of the Witwatersrand. In this context, policies for immigration cannot be simply xenophobic; strategies for infrastructural investment cannot be confined within a political boundary. South Africa's development has to take into account the region as a whole. Here too a sense of history has an important bearing on shaping appropriate policies for dealing with the problems of South Africa's transition.

Conclusion

The theme of this volume is that wise policy-makers in the new century must understand the historical roots of the problems they seek to address. This is true even when current events seem to indicate a break with the past. South Africa, which for so long seemed to be stuck in the nineteenth century, now finds itself in the midst of great change. The political transition has gone extraordinarily well. But the economic challenges that remain are formidable. Understanding of the country's history is surely important in searching for ways to meet those challenges.

References

Beyond Apartheid: Human Resources in a New South Africa. Report of a Commonwealth Expert Group. London: The Commonwealth Secretariat, 1991.

Bundy, Colin. *The Rise and Fall of the South African Peasantry*. London: Heinemann, 1979.

Central Statistical Service (now StatsSA). *Living in South Africa: Selected Findings of the 1995 October Household Survey*. Pretoria, 1996.

Crush, Jonathan, Alan Jeeves and David Yudelman. *South Africa's Labor Empire: A History of Black Migrancy to the Gold Mines*. Boulder, Colorado: Westview Press, 1991.

Department of Water Affairs and Forestry. *Water Supply and Sanitation Policy*. White Paper, Cape Town, November, 1994.

May, Julian (ed.). *Poverty and Inequality in South Africa: Meeting the Challenge*. Cape Town: David Philip Publishers, 2000.

Ministry in the Office of the President: Reconstruction and Development Programme. 'Key Indicators of Poverty in South Africa.' Pretoria, 1995.

Moodie, T. Dunbar, with Vivienne Ndatshe. *Going for Gold: Men, Mines and Migration*. Johannesburg: Witwatersrand University Press, 1994.

Murray, Colin. *Families Divided: The Impact of Migrant Labour in Lesotho*. Cambridge: Cambridge University Press, 1981.

Posel, Dorrit. 'Migration, Poverty Traps and Development: A Tale of Two Villages.' Paper presented at workshop on Immigration and Migration in Southern Africa, University of Cape Town, May 1999.

Project for Statistics on Living Standards and Development. *South Africans Rich and Poor: Baseline Household Statistics*. Cape Town: Southern Africa Labour and Development Research Unit (SALDRU), 1994.

Turrell, Rob. *Capital and Labour on the Kimberley Diamond Fields, 1871–1890*. Cambridge: Cambridge University Press, 1987.

Whiteford, Andrew, Dori Posel and Teresa Kelatwang. *A Profile of Poverty, Inequality and Human Development*. Pretoria: Human Sciences Research Council, 1995.

Wilson, F. Graduation Address. University of Cape Town, December, 1997.

_____. *Labour in the South African Gold Mines, 1911–1966*. Cambridge: Cambridge University Press, 1972.

_____. *Migrant Labour in South Africa*. Johannesburg: South African Council of Churches and Spro-cas, 1972.

Wilson, F., and M. Ramphele. *Uprooting Poverty: The South African Challenge*. Cape Town: David Philip, 1989.

Worger, William H. *South Africa's City of Diamonds: Mine Workers and Monopoly Capitalism in Kimberley, 1867–1895*. Craighall: Ad. Donker, 1987.

World Bank. *Entering the Twenty-first Century. World Development Report 1999/2000*. New York: Oxford University Press, 1999.

10.
Lessons from Italy's Monetary Unification (1862–1880) for the Euro and Europe's Single Market

LEANDRO CONTE, GIANNI TONIOLO & GIOVANNI VECCHI

Monetary Unions and Market Unification

More than thirty years have passed since the completion of the customs union among the original six signatory countries of the Rome Treaty of 1957, and ten years since the signing of the Single Market Agreement.[1] It is, nevertheless, a common observation by Europeans that individual commodities, labour skills, and capital assets do not fetch a single price throughout the union. Volkswagen Passats are priced 25 per cent higher at authorized VW dealerships in Munich than at such dealerships in Copenhagen.[2] University professors' salaries, while almost uniform within individual countries, for given seniority levels, differ to no small extent across the EU. Perhaps more surprisingly still, the closing price of Bayer shares was fixed on 3 June 1999 at euro 37.20 in Frankfurt, and at 37.87 in Milan.[3]

The Monetary Union, on the other hand, is still in its infancy. Actual euro-denominated banknotes only substituted for individual countries' currencies in March 2001. The question then remains open as to the effect the single currency will have on the pace of the EU's

---
[1] The Treaty contained transitory provisions that allowed member countries slowly to lower their respective tariff barriers and adopt a common external tariff. The Common Market was fully operative by the late Sixties.
[2] *Business Week* (30 August 1999).
[3] *Il Sole-24 Ore* (4 June 1999).

movement towards the actual realization of a single market in factors of production (labour and capital). In a slightly more technical fashion, the question can be rephrased as follows: under what conditions is the Monetary Union likely to accelerate factor price convergence in the EU?

History, as we all know, is no *Magistra Vitae*. It does not provide blueprints readily applicable to current situations. It is, however, of great help in framing the relevant questions about the present and the future. As far as monetary unions are concerned, economic history provides at least three types of cases from which 'lessons' may be drawn or, rather, sophisticated questions may be asked:

1. A weak form of monetary union can be found in the so-called classical gold standard (from 1873 to 1914).[4] Such scholars as Jeffrey Williamson and his numerous co-authors have contributed to our understanding of price convergence, and of the creation of a large Atlantic, or even 'global', market during the classical gold standard.[5]

2. A second type of monetary union emerged in the nineteenth century as the result of formal international agreements among sovereign states. Foremost among these are the Austro-German, the Scandinavian and the Latin Monetary Union. Neither the supranational unions nor the gold standard, however, provide satisfactory historical proxies for the EMU. In both cases, individual participant states retained their customs' sovereignty, and did not create a common central bank. Moreover, membership in the gold standard was not irrevocable—individual countries could, and did, 'opt out'. And the rules of the game were not always adhered to by members of the monetary unions, a behaviour that led to the *de jure* or *de facto* dissolution of all three unions by the early 1900s.

3. The most relevant 'lessons' for the EMU come from monetary unions created soon before, during or in the wake of the creation of new sovereign states. In these cases, a common external tariff existed for all the territories involved in the monetary union, no 'opt out' clause could be invoked, and embryo central banks were either planned or created. Particularly interesting in these respects promise to be the German and the Italian cases where monetary union was

---

[4] Weak because 'membership' was not formally sanctioned and an implicit opt-out clause existed which was very often exercised.

[5] See, for example, Williamson, 'Globalization'; and O'Rourke and Williamson, 'Late Nineteenth-Century'.

achieved at the same time as steps were taken to fulfill the legal and economic prerequisites for market unification. In this chapter we discuss the relevance to the on-going creation of Europe's single market of the similar Italian experience in the twenty-odd years following the 1862 legislation for currency unification.

The Monetary Unification of Italy

At the beginning of 1859, Italy was divided into six separate states. Each levied its own customs duties, circulated its own currency, and often chartered its own bank(s) of issue. Additionally, institutions differed considerably between the states in such areas as weights and measures, property rights protection, taxation, and government expenditures. Nevertheless, a slow process of economic unification, due to improved communications and a revival in trade, had been under way during the previous decades. In particular, the 1850s saw Vienna abolish the customs barrier between Lombardy and the Venetia, the completion of the Venice-Milan railway in 1857 (the Ferdinandea), the 1855 tariff opening the Kingdom of Sardinia to the benefits of free trade, and the Grand Duke of Tuscany championing the policy of *laissez faire*.

The Kingdom of Italy was created between 1859 and 1861. The military defeat of Austria by the allied armies of France and Piedmont (officially called the Kingdom of Sardinia) resulted in the annexation of Lombardy by the latter. This was followed by uprisings and plebiscites in most of Central Italy, sanctioning the decisions of the region's constituent provinces to apply for membership in the enlarged Piedmontese State. Garibaldi's expedition to Sicily and his march towards Naples prompted the abdication of the Bourbon King, and Piedmont's annexation of the Kingdom of the Two Sicilies. The new Kingdom of Italy was proclaimed in March 1861. Italy then gained Venice and its territory, ceded to her by Austria in the wake of the Prussian war of 1866. Finally, Italian troops entered Rome in 1870, thereby completing the political unification of the Peninsula in a single sovereign state.[6]

---

[6] The regions of Trento and Trieste were added to the Kingdom as a result of World War I.

The first step to foster market integration was taken by extending the Piedmontese tariff to the new provinces, upon their joining the Kingdom of Sardinia. At the time of the proclamation of the new kingdom, therefore, Italy was, *de jure*, a large customs union with free trade within its borders and a mild uniform external tariff. A huge array of non-tariff barriers to the movement of goods and production factors, however, remained in place for a long period of time. Some of them will be discussed in the following section.

In many ways, a parallel may be found between the Italian situation of the 1860s and 1870s and that of the EEC in the late 1960s. In both cases, the legal creation of a 'common market' was only the first necessary step, and not a sufficient one, in the creation of a single market for goods and factors of production. Indeed, the single market is still far from being an accomplished fact in the European Union. Two questions arise from this comparison. Firstly, did monetary union speed up market unification in mid-nineteenth century Italy? Secondly, can we learn anything from that experience? Before discussing these issues, a brief account of Italy's monetary unification in the 1860s and 1870s is appropriate as its history may shed light on the on-going process of European monetary unification.

The monetary regimes existing in Italy immediately preceding political unification are summarized in Table 1.

The reorganization of the payments system was one of the first tasks of the new state. In July 1861 the Piedmontese Lira, re-named *Lira Italiana*, was made legal tender in all the territories of the kingdom. The government, however, had to compromise with a Parliament that reflected the resistance of local populations to currency unification: it was therefore agreed that the divisional coins of the pre-unity states would retain the status of legal tender within their respective territories.[7] This transitory provision was legally overcome in 1862 when an Act of Parliament made the gold Italian Lira the kingdom's sole legal tender. At the same time, the new kingdom's monetary standards were better specified, and clearly defined exchange rates for the lira with the currencies of the old Italian states, France and Belgium were established.[8] The southern provinces were allowed to continue using pre-unity bank notes for local payments.[9]

---

[7] See De Mattia, *Unificazione monetaria*.
[8] The parity being 1 to 1.
[9] See Spinelli and Fratianni, *Storia monetaria*; Pittaluga, 'Monetizzazione'.

Table 1. Italian Monetary Systems Before Unification.

Provinces	Year of annexation	Monetary regime Multiple	Monetary regime Regime	Monetary regime Gold/silver	Unit of account Denomination	Unit of account Gold content (grams)	Unit of account Silver content (grams)	Metal content	Exchange rates Actual[a]	Exchange rates Legal[b]
Piedmont, Liguria, Sardinia	1859	decimal	bimetallic	1 : 15.5	lira piemontese	0.322	5.000	900	1.00	1.00
Lombardy	1859	other	monometallic	silver	fiorino	–	12.346	900	2.47	2.47
Modena	1859	–	–	–	–	–	–	–	–	–
Parma	1859	decimal	bimetallic	1 : 15.5	lira di Parma	0.322	5.000	900	1.00	1.00
Tuscany	1859	other	monometallic	silver	lira toscana	–	4.103	916	0.82	0.84
Romagna, Marche, Umbria	1859–1861	decimal	bimetallic	1 : 15.5	scudo romano	0.322	5.000	900	5.37	5.32
South	1860	other	monometallic	silver	ducato	–	22.943	833	4.25	4.25
Venetia	1866	other	monometallic	silver	fiorino	–	12.346	900	2.47	2.47
Papal states	1870	decimal	bimetallic	1 : 15.5	lira pontificia	0.322	5.000	900	5.37	5.32

[a] Exchange rate based on metal content of the Italian lira (gr. 0.290 of fine gold, and gr. 4.50 silver).
[b] Legal parity established by the Italian government.
Source: De Mattia, *Unificazione*.

If we identify monetary unification with legislation introducing a new payment instrument as sole legal tender, and establishing an official conversion rate between the old and new legal tenders, then Italy's monetary unification was in most respects achieved in 1862. If, on the other hand, we define a monetary union as an area where agents are endowed with the quantity of legal tender they demand, and prefer it for payments over and above other existing currencies, then monetary unification took much longer than two years to be completed.[10]

At the beginning of 1862 there were as many as 270 types of legal-tender metal coins in circulation, all of different weight and metal content.[11] The decimal system was not predominant. It is therefore little wonder that — according to Mint records — the conversion of old coins into Italian lire was not completed until around 1874. The suspension of the convertibility of paper money into gold or silver in 1866 boosted monetary unification as the new banknotes had all been issued in lire. By 1874, paper money accounted for about 70 per cent of total circulation (up from about 10 per cent in 1862). In April 1874 an Act of Parliament reorganized the issue of banknotes by forming the six banks of issue into a consortium, with each bank contributing to total circulation in proportion to its own capital and reserves.[12] This Act, together with the balancing of the state budget (achieved in 1876), stabilized expectations about the value of the lira which finally became universally accepted, even before the resumption of convertibility in 1883. It is safe to assume, therefore, that the monetary unification of the country was not realized *de facto* until the mid-1870s.

Labour Market Unification

In what follows the authors deal with the space and time patterns of market unification for the factors of production (labour and capital). A discussion of factor, rather than commodity, markets will allow us to draw better analogies to the current creation of a single market in the European Union, after the introduction of the euro. While the completion of the single market deals both with products and factors of pro-

---

[10] See De Cecco, *Italia*; Roccas, 'Italia'; and Ripa di Meana and Sarcinelli, 'Unione monetaria'.
[11] See Martello and Montanari, *Stato*; and Supino, *Storia*.
[12] Sannucci, 'Molteplicità'.

duction, it is undoubtedly on the latter that most of the policy-makers' attention is now focusing. Goods have circulated quite freely in the European Community since the late 1960s while, until relatively recently, most member states maintained a good grip on capital movements, and social security legislation still provides a powerful barrier to labour mobility.

To economists, a market is typically a place where a single price applies to homogeneous commodities. Whenever the rule of one price is not verified, we are in the presence of different (or segmented) markets. The process of market unification entails the creation of conditions whereby, at any given time, homogeneous commodities fetch close to single prices at different points in space. Unfettered traders typically bring about a single market by taking advantage of price differentials between localities (a process called 'arbitrage'). By definition, arbitrage takes place only when price differentials make it profitable to buy a commodity in market A and sell it at a higher price in market B. The larger the price gap, the less integrated the markets are said to be. By measuring price differentials we can tell how close we are to the realization of a single market. It must be remembered, however, that price differentials across regional markets will never disappear given the existence of positive transaction costs to arbitrage. The latter can in fact be quite large and determine the limits to price convergence.

A synthetic measure of market integration is given by the coefficient of variation (CV) of prices across points in geographical space.[13] By studying the direction and pace of changes in the CVs over time, we can assess the speed of the market-unification process.

Measuring price convergence, however, is not as simple as it may seem. To start with, we must make sure that we are measuring like with like. In the second place, goods or factors of production taken into account must be frequently and sizably traded in as great a number of local markets as possible. More technically, price convergence must be measured for items — commodities, capital goods, labour services — that are both homogeneous and ubiquitous. These two conditions are seldom, if ever, simultaneously met. Empirical and historical investigations must, by necessity, find practical and acceptable compromises between these two features. Since 1986, *The Economist* has measured world-wide price convergence with the cost of

---

[13] On alternative approaches for examining labour market integration, see Boyer and Hatton, 'Regional Labour'.

a McDonald's 'Big Mac' hamburger in the main cities across the globe, suggesting that it satisfies both requirements of homogeneity and wide representation.[14] In assessing the pace of factor-market unification in nineteenth-century Italy, the first question to be asked is the following: what was the Big Mac for the Italian labour market? In other words: among the occupations for which wage data are available over the period 1860 to 1880, what are the ones most suited to testing the 'law of one price'?

The search for a nineteenth-century labour-market Big Mac leads us to focus on the construction industry. There are at least three good reasons for this choice:

1. Contrary to most industries, particularly in the manufacturing sectors, construction was one of the most ubiquitous trades, not being constrained by specific location advantages. It was, furthermore, one of the most important industries, employing roughly 14 per cent of the total industrial workforce.[15]
2. Technological innovations were slow relative to other sectors and likely to affect job descriptions uniformly within the whole industry. (Whatever the region, job descriptions are likely to better preserve a relative consistency over time.)
3. Data on hourly wages of construction workers (i) turn out to be relatively abundant, and (ii) clearly distinguish between skilled and unskilled workers.

Skilled and unskilled wage convergence was measured on the basis of two samples of adult male workers: 'hodmen' and 'master masons'.[16] Hodmen were workmen assigned to very basic activities, such as carrying bricks, digging, moving masses of soil and the like.[17] Master masons 'were required to possess a licence certifying their qualification, and guaranteeing some knowledge of arithmetic, geometry, drawing and architecture'.[18] On the building site they occupied a position somewhere in between the architect and the most highly skilled masons.

[14] Pakko and Pollard, 'For Here or To Go?'
[15] Ercolani, 'Documentazione'.
[16] Ministero di Agricoltura, Industria e Commercio, *Salari*.
[17] Levi, 'Salari'.
[18] Di Rollo, 'Retribuzioni', p. 6.

In order to assess the speed of the creation of a single Italian labour market after monetary unification, we estimated the CVs of nominal hourly wages for skilled (master masons) and unskilled (hodmen) labour, for each individual year, between 1862 and 1874. The observed trend of the CVs over time provides evidence on price convergence across the country and on its speed (a downward-sloping trend suggesting the occurrence of convergence).[19] We also estimated numerical approximations of the standard errors associated with the CVs.[20] The results are summarized in Figure 1.

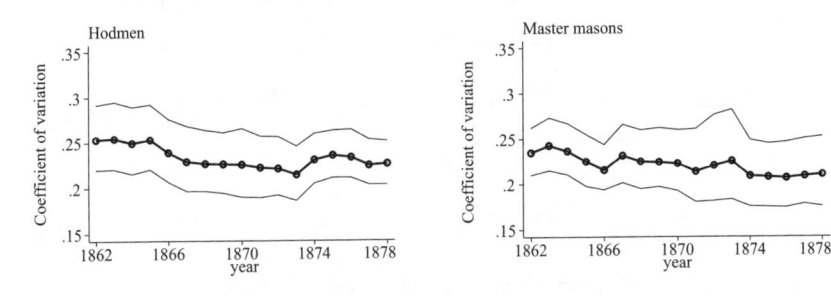

Figure 1. Dispersion of nominal wages, Italy 1862–1878.

Figure 1 shows the estimated CVs of hourly wages for the whole Kingdom of Italy, together with their 90 per cent confidence intervals. It depicts a downward-sloped trend in the dispersion of both the hodmen's and the master masons' wages, indicating a slow but steady convergence. Confidence intervals illustrate that the CV point estimates are accurate up to a 15–20 per cent factor (approximately).

Taken in isolation, the results summarized in Figure 1 go in the expected direction. They seem to tell a story of slow but steady integration of the national market for the services of masons, both skilled and unskilled. If, however, as in Figures 2 and 3, the national market is broken down into four macro-areas, we get surprising results. They reveal an underlying mechanism in national labour market unification that is in need of explanation.

---

[19] More precisely, what is being measured is the rate of σ-convergence, as defined by Barro and Sala-i-Martin, *Economic Growth*.

[20] Standard error estimates allow assessment of the extent to which the observed intertemporal differences are due to statistical noise, for instance to sampling variation, and errors of measurement. The authors used a non-parametric bootstrap procedure, which allows them to obtain numerical approximations of the standard errors associated with the CVs. For details, see Conte et al., 'Factor Price'.

Changes in Economic Regimes and Ideologies

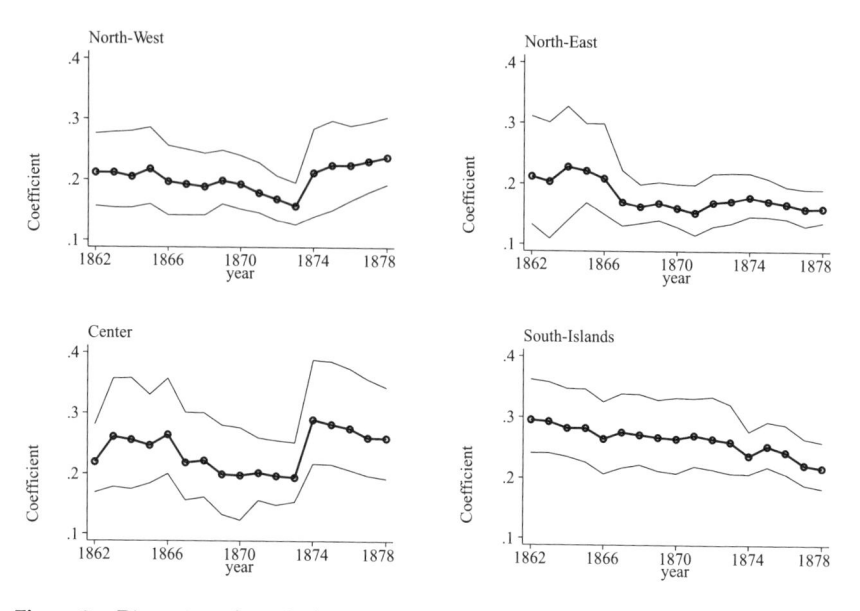

Figure 2. Dispersion of nominal wages, by macro-area—Hodmen, 1862–1878

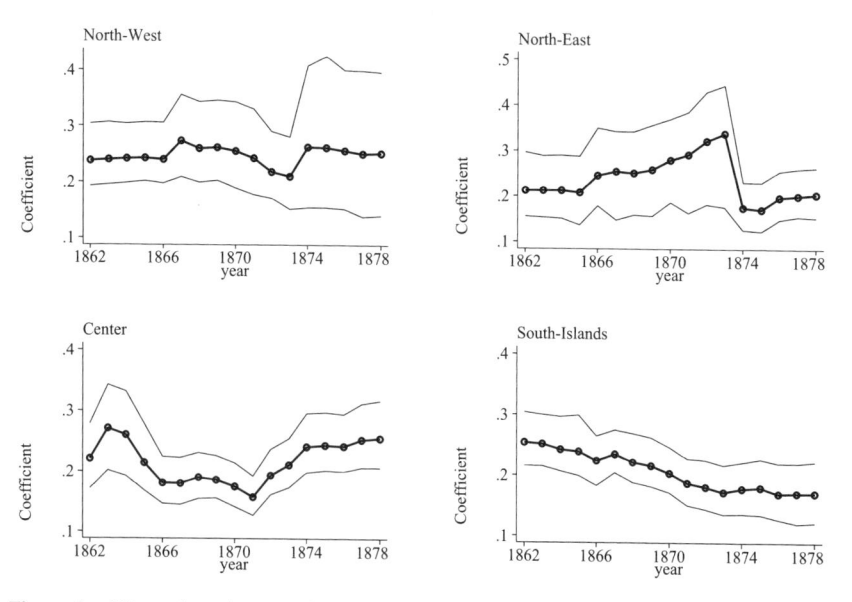

Figure 3. Dispersion of nominal wages, by macro-area—Master masons, 1862–1878

The evidence on the convergence of regional labour markets can be summarized as follows:

1. There is no evidence of convergence within the north-western and central regions, neither in the skilled nor in the unskilled labour markets.
2. In the north east, the dispersion of wages of unskilled workers slowly decreases. The same does not occur with skilled workers' wages, where the trend of the coefficient of variation is segmented.
3. The southern parts of the kingdom and its islands show the highest degree of convergence. For both occupations, the dispersion of wages declines monotonically over the whole period.
4. Overall, the trends observed in Figure 1 seem to be driven by the pronounced convergence observed in the southern and island areas.

Capital Market Unification

As in the case of the labour market, understanding capital market unification requires, in the first place, the selection of a Big Mac. We must, in other words, choose a financial asset frequently and substantially traded on as great a number of local markets as possible. The price of (interest rate on) bank loans has sometimes been used to assess the existence of a single market for capital. This does not seem to be the best choice. Data on *individual* unsecured loans are well kept secrets (bank archives contain only scanty price information), and, even if available, allowance for risk assessment would need to be made in order to compare like with like. Secured loans, such as mortgages, were still largely made *intuitu personae* and, at any rate, a secondary market for mortgage securities (*cartelle fondiarie*) developed only at the end of the century. A thick market existed, however, for such Government Securities as Consols (the so-called 'non-redeemable debt of the state', or *Rendita Italiana*—Italian Rent), the favourite outlay for middle-class savings. We therefore took the Rendita Italiana 5% to be our Big Mac for financial markets.

The Rendita Italiana 5% originated in August 1861 from the consolidation of the outstanding public debt of the previous states into a single sovereign debt of the Kingdom of Italy. The very accessible minimum size of the negotiable bond, the high yield, the perceived low default risk, the high liquidity provided by the thickness of the secondary market, and its being universally accepted by financial intermediaries as collateral for loans, all contributed to making the Rendita Italiana 5% by far the most popular security among Italian savers. It was widely distributed across social classes and geographic areas.[21]

In the 1860s and 1870s as many as seven (eight after 1870) main stock exchanges were active in Italy: Genoa, Turin, Milan, Florence, Naples, Palermo and Venice (after 1866), and Rome (after 1871). The most important one, both in terms of transaction volume and the number of listed securities, was the Genoa Bourse, followed by that of Milan. Out of a total number of listed securities varying from 30 to 50, only 7 were listed in more than 2 stock exchanges, and not all of them were simultaneously traded on any given day. The authors' analysis is based upon one weekly (Wednesday) observation of the closing (published) price for the Rendita Italiana (i) over the years 1869 to 1878 for all the existing stock exchanges but Palermo's, and (ii) over the period 1862 to 1878 for the stock exchanges of Florence, Genoa, Milan and Naples.[22]

To assess the extent to which arbitrage opportunities were exploited and a single market for financial assets was created, the authors closely followed the methodology outlined in the discussion of labour market convergence. Accordingly, the authors estimated the weekly CVs in the recorded prices for the Rendita Italiana 5% across all the available bourses. Fifty-two CVs (corresponding to as many weeks) were thus obtained for each of the years between 1862 and 1878, which were then summarized by the median value from each of the CV-series. The available evidence is plotted in Figure 4, showing the price-dispersion trend (as measured by the weekly median CVs) of the Rendita Italiana 5% across Italian exchange markets over the years 1862 to 1878.[23]

---

[21] Bonaldo Stringher reports that over the period 1860–1913 the Rendita Italiana 5% accounted for at least 80 per cent of the total value of transactions on the financial markets.

[22] The main sources for the years after 1869 are the weekly journal *L'Economista d'Italia* (of Florence-Rome), and the financial daily *Il Sole* (of Milan).

[23] The authors should mention that they are not reporting estimates of the standard errors associated with the median CVs. In this case, it is safe to assume that the available price data for the Rendita Italiana 5% are extremely close to exhausting their own universe. The authors therefore implicitly assumed negligible non-sampling errors (such as editing errors), thereby assimilating the CVs to the 'true' population parameters rather than to their estimates.

Lessons from Italy's Monetary Unification

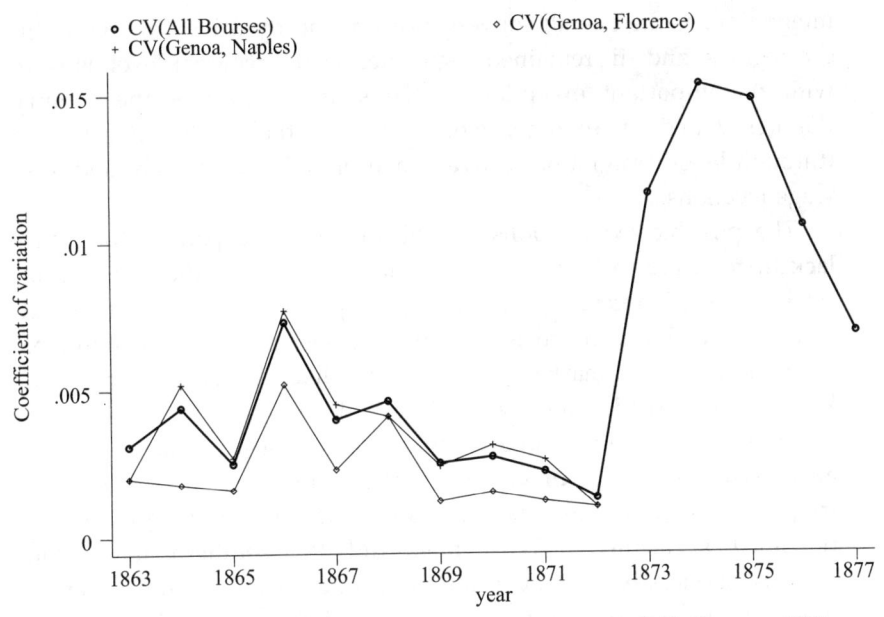

Figure 4. Dispersion of prices of the Rendita Italiana 5% — Available bourses, 1863–1877.

The time path of financial market unification appears in Figure 4 to be characterized by four phases:

1. Slow divergence in the three years following political unification (from 1863 to 1866).
2. A faster convergence pace from 1867 to 1872.
3. A shock of some kind that clearly hits the market in the second semester of 1873. It is followed by two years during which each individual market seems to be going its own way (rapid increase in divergence).
4. Fast resumption of the convergence process that takes place from 1876 onwards.

Was Convergence Slow? If So, for What Reasons?

Understanding the Pattern of Labour Market Unification

In the two decades following the political and monetary unification of the country, the market for masons' services (both skilled and unskilled) (i) showed a very low pace of convergence towards national

327

integration, as the overall convergence was mostly driven by the southern regions, and (ii) remained segmented at the regional level as well, with the important exception of the southern part of the country (Figures 2 and 3). In other words, only in the south did arbitrage (through labour migration) actively take place between high- and low-wage locations.

The possible explanations for this convergence pattern (or rather lack thereof) are to be found among factors affecting the cost of arbitrage (transaction costs). They are typically of two types: (i) transport, insurance, and related costs, and (ii) barriers created by institutions, customs, language, market power and the like. As far as labour markets are concerned, transport and related costs can be neglected in explaining Italy's labour market behaviour as they are likely to be (i) an inverse function of time, and (ii) higher in the south, where 'arbitrage' did actually take place, than in the north, where markets remained segmented.[24] Why, then, did the southern market for masons' services become ever more integrated, while a similar trend is only partially observed in the north east and not at all in the two other macro-areas of the country? A priori, two possible explanations stand out: (i) the long-lived political and, to some extent, monetary, unification of the south,[25] (ii) the diversity of land-tenure contracts.[26]

All other things being equal, long-established, uniform, well-understood institutions result in lower information and similar costs of migration within the area where such conditions apply, relative to the costs of moving outside the area itself. As institutional changes take a long time to be appreciated and accepted, it might be argued that it was more than one or two decades before migration across the borders of the former independent Italian states took place in numbers large enough to affect wage determination. Workers simply preferred to move within the boundaries of their former countries. Of the four macro-areas into which the authors have divided the peninsula, only the one labelled 'South-Islands' consisted almost entirely of a single pre-unity state. The other three macro-areas in Figures 2 and

---

[24] This is the case if, for instance, transport costs are approximated by the development of the rail network.
[25] One of the authors developed this intuition in the course of a conversation with Gabriel Tortella, to whom they are indebted. It should be recalled that, with the exception of scarcely-populated Sardinia, the whole of the South-Islands macro-area had belonged to the Bourbon Kingdom of the Two Sicilies.
[26] See Sereni, *Capitalismo e mercato*, and Sereni, *Capitalismo nelle campagne*.

3 were all divided up by the borders between the previous states. If migration across the former borders was perceived to be more costly than movements within previous borders, then an explanation could be found for wage convergence in the south, and lack of it elsewhere.

But this explanation is hardly convincing in the light of the subsequent labour market history. In the 1890s and 1900s, southern Italians emigrated in very great numbers to the Americas. Emigration was both permanent and seasonal, as in the case of Argentina. In emigrating, southern Italians moved across much wider institutional and cultural barriers than those involved in migration to central and northern Italy. Given large enough incentives, southern Italians were easily persuaded to move across the Atlantic. It is therefore difficult to argue that the feeling of 'going abroad' when moving outside the former Bourbon Kingdom plays a major part in explaining the observed dispersion pattern by macro-area (Figure 2). The phenomenon must be otherwise explained.

Both the persistence of a segmented labour market for unskilled construction workers in the north-western and central areas, and the market-unification drive in the south are most likely due to differences in land-tenure regimes. During the nineteenth and the first part of the twentieth centuries, construction typically provided a link between agriculture and manufacturing occupations, drawing—part-time at first—from the former, and eventually leading to the latter. Therefore under-employed agricultural labour was, with occasional exceptions, the main source of unskilled construction labour. The extent of time during which workers were allowed to leave the fields depended, however, on the organization of the farm, in other words on agrarian institutions. Only where workers could absent themselves from agriculture for relatively long periods of time (weeks or months) could they move from their home villages far enough to take advantage of higher wages in the construction industry, wherever they might happen to be offered them. And only by them doing so could arbitrage leading to labour market unification effectively take place. In the northern and central areas of the peninsula, land tenure institutions were such that workers moved only locally, usually within distances consistent with a daily return home. A substantial proportion of southern peasants, on the other hand, worked the land under conditions permitting longer periods of absence from home.

Italy's land tenure regimes were multifarious and complex and are the subject of innumerable studies.[27] While it is impossible here even to begin to review the literature on the subject, the key stylized facts for understanding labour market behaviour are easily spelled out. By the middle of the nineteenth century, the northern and central regions had developed (i) various forms of co-participation in expenses and revenues by tenants and landlords (particularly efficient were share-cropping contracts prevailing in Tuscany and Umbria), and (ii) long leases to capitalist tenants whose farms mostly employed permanent fixed-wage workers. In both cases there were indeed slack periods when one or more members of the peasant household, temporarily under-employed, wished to supplement their income by working outside the farm. But daily presence on the land was often required either by contract or by the need to care for a small family-owned plot. Before the diffusion of the bicycle, therefore, the typical agricultural worker offered his hodman's services only to those construction sites that were located within, say, 16 kilometres of his residence. The land tenure contracts in the northern and central areas, ultimately reflecting a fairly adequate population to land ratio, seem therefore to be directly responsible for the segmentation of the market for unskilled construction labour. This market segmentation accounts for the lack of convergence in the north-western and central areas in the mid-1860s, and again in the mid-1870s (Figure 2) in the Turin and Florence areas during the construction booms in both towns.[28]

In the southern parts of the former Papal States (Latium and Abruzzi) and in the whole of the former Kingdom of the Two Sicilies, land tenure regimes differed considerably from those in the northern and central parts of the Peninsula. The diffusion of large estates (*latifundia*) and of single-cropping (mostly grain) rather than multi-cropping was consistent with the employment of most of the work force as day labourers, often hired daily in the town square by the landlord's agents. Employment was highly seasonal, leaving the worker unemployed for long stretches of time. Hence the incentive for adult males to look for gainful occupation outside agriculture, and their willingness in doing so to travel long distances, inasmuch as the opportunity cost of an extended absence from home was minimal. An extreme instance

---

[27] For reviews of the issues involved, see Bevilacqua, *Storia*; Giorgetti, 'Contratti'; and Cafagna, *Dualismo*.
[28] See Insolera, 'Urbanistica'.

of this attitude was found in later years in the large number of people available for seasonal employment in the southern hemisphere during Europe's winter. Under these conditions, arbitrage between local markets for unskilled labour could develop. Judging from the levels of the coefficients of variation in the early 1860s, soon after unification markets were more segmented in the south than anywhere else in the country. While the north-western and central areas made little or no progress towards higher market integration, progress did however take place in the southern part of the country. The reasons for the fairly good market integration of the north east can be explained by the existence in parts of the region of land tenure and labour contracts similar to those in the south.[29]

If agrarian regimes go a long way towards explaining the behaviour of the markets for unskilled labour in the four macro-areas of the country, the same does not hold for skilled labour markets. The master mason's profession was highly regulated at the local (municipality) level. An entrance examination was required over which provincial authorities and the local masons' craft organization retained joint control, as they subsequently did over the master masons' contracts and wages. Preference in local employment was given to locals, or to 'foreigners' holding a local licence.[30] This is hardly surprising in view both of the trust component in the master mason's job and of the market power enjoyed by local professional organizations (the old arts and crafts guilds).

The strength of such a market power, however, was not the same across the country. In particular, the vitality of the local communities and of the crafts organizations is well known to have been much lower in the south than in the rest of the country. It is therefore likely that in the territory of the former Kingdom of the Two Sicilies, the regulatory power of the local bodies would yield to market pressures more easily than in the more compact and organized central and northern regions.[31]

---

[29] In parts of the north east such as the Po Delta and some areas east of Venice, large mono-cultural (sugar beet, tobacco) estates prevailed with labour regimes (seasonal day labourers) not dissimilar to those in the south. Further investigation into the extension of such contracts is needed before coming to a conclusion about the similarities of the two labour markets.

[30] We have found evidence of out-of-province candidates for the Milan examination in the 1870s, probably attracted by the relatively buoyant construction industry there. See De Vecchi and Treu, *Organizzazioni*.

Understanding the Integration of Financial Markets

Monetary unification *per se* is likely to have had a favourable impact on financial market convergence as it eliminated exchange rate risk and made prices at the various stock exchanges readily comparable. The process of consolidation of the debt of pre-unity states into the sovereign debt of the Kingdom of Italy, however, did not favour market unification. As the stock of outstanding debt by northern states, particularly Piedmont, largely outweighed those of the Pope's and Bourbons' states, the bulk of Rendita Italiana ended up by being concentrated in the northern and central areas of the country. This fact in itself was responsible for thicker secondary markets for the Rendita in those areas relative to the rest of the country. Moreover, the stock exchanges of Genoa and Turin were not only more efficiently organized than most of the others but traders there had closer business (and information) connections with the Paris Bourse, the actual price-setter for Italian government bonds. Thicker markets, a relatively efficient organization, and proximity to the main Continental Stock Exchange are the reasons behind the comparatively fast creation of a single market for financial assets in the north. The speed of convergence of the Florence prices of the Rendita with those of Genoa (the largest and best organized Italian bourse at the time) is faster than that of Naples with Genoa. Such core-periphery differentials in convergence speed also characterize today's European Union.

Figure 4 shows that little, if any, convergence in financial assets prices was obtained at the overall national level in the twenty-odd years after political unification. This result is likely due to the offsetting forces driving the markets in opposite directions. On the one hand, market unification was promoted by both decreasing transaction costs and government regulation. The transaction costs of arbitrage were reduced by rapidly decreasing communication costs resulting from the huge investment drive by the new kingdom in railways, roads and harbours. Of paramount importance was the rapid spread of telegraph lines and the enormous decrease in the cost of telegrams. At the time of political unification, Italy possessed 12,000 kilometres of telegraph lines; this grew to almost 50,000 a decade later. In 1878 it became mandatory for

---

[31] Note that our findings here are similar to those in Rosenbloom's 'Occupational Differences' on the US labour market, where organized, skilled construction workers, while exploiting within-region arbitrage opportunities, prevented greater inter-regional arbitrage.

every town with a municipal centre to possess a telegraph station.[32] Shortly before unification, sending a 20-word telegram cost the colossal sum of 20 lire (a sum equivalent to more than 20 days' wages for an unskilled male worker). In 1871 the cost of the same telegram was down to 1 lira.[33] Government regulation of such matters as price fixing and stockbroker qualifications and accountability promoted transparency within and across stock exchanges, thereby lowering the information and contract enforcement costs of arbitrage. Market regulation by the government also played a role in improving the conditions for market unification. In particular, regulators sought to standardize price formation and contracts among the various regional stock exchanges, and to lower asymmetries of information by setting standards for the brokerage profession.

If these trends promoted market unification, other forces were at work to throw as much sand as possible into the gears of the process. If the national economy benefits from technical and institutional changes promoting lower communication and non-tariff barriers to trade, a number of individuals stand to lose in the process. Protected local markets create rent positions, and it is only natural that those enjoying them should fight for their preservation. This was the case in mid-nineteenth century Italy, as it is the case in today's Europe. During the process, threatened local vested interests in the financial intermediation industry put up as stern a resistance to change as was possible. They resisted both the effects of lower communication costs (typically by refusing to install telegraph stations within the premises of the local bourses) and the government's efforts to increase transaction transparency. Ultimately, a clash developed between stockbrokers and regulators. In the early months of 1873, an Act of Parliament stipulated that only registered stockbrokers could legally perform financial market operations. The norm was meant to safeguard small savers, often from dishonest off-market self-styled brokers. As such it was expected to please official, registered stockbrokers and to loosen their silent opposition to more efficient and transparent markets. But the government, then in its last drive to achieve a balanced budget, muddled the matter by increasing both the transaction tax and the guarantee deposit required of the official stockbrokers. The latter reacted in a strong protest. Out of the 120 Genoa stockbrokers, 40 did not renew their regis-

---

[32] *L'Economista d'Italia*, 1878, p. 713.
[33] *L'Economista d'Italia*, 1871, p. 780.

tration and set out to perform off-market illegal operations. Their example was followed throughout the country. Price-fixing became difficult and often meaningless. The episode explains the upward blip in the CVs observed in Figure 4. Neither the government nor the stockbrokers being willing to compromise, the stock markets remained empty, as observers claimed at the time. The Act was revised only in 1876, after the fall of the Minghetti cabinet. A balanced budget had by then been achieved. The protest subsided and markets began to converge again.

'Lessons' for the European Union

About 140 years have passed since Italy's monetary and slow market unification. Does its history provide any useful economic insight into the on-going processes of European monetary unification and the creation of a 'single market'? Needless to say, a number of conditions in the EU today are different from those in mid-nineteenth-century Italy. Arguably, the existence of the European Central Bank and today's cheap and sophisticated communication technologies provide more favourable conditions for swift monetary and market unification than those existing in the 1860s. At the same time, back then Italy enjoyed the advantage over today's Europe of possessing a single central government. In spite of these and many other differences between the situations 'then' and 'now', Italy's historical case study underlines issues that can be usefully studied and analysed in the present European context.

Our study reminds us that—when discussing market unification—measurement issues should not be overlooked.[34] In particular, it is of paramount importance to make sure that we are measuring like with like. Even in the case of apparently well-defined Big Macs, we have seen that the job description of a 'mason' may vary from one locality to the other. More surprisingly, even a financial asset such as the Rendita Italiana 5% was not homogeneously defined across local stock exchanges. Needless to say, the problem becomes excruciatingly complex when dealing with a bundle of commodities (price indices and the like). Awareness of these measurement problems implicit in any discussion of market unification cautions scholars and policy-makers

---

[34] See Feinstein, 'Rise and Fall'.

alike against jumping to easy and often not fully warranted conclusions. We should also bear in mind that perfect price convergence will never be achieved: over time and space, every economy is always in a state of tension between such forces as local endowments, transaction costs, information asymmetries, vested interests that make for price divergence and arbitrageurs taking advantage of such differences and thereby producing price convergence.

On a more substantive ground, the first 'lesson' to be brought home from the study of nineteenth-century Italy is that actual (*de facto*) monetary unification is bound to be a much longer process than formal (*de jure*) unification. It took at least two decades and powerful exogenous shocks for the Italian lira to be unquestionably preferred by Italians over the traditional currencies, in spite of the obvious advantages of holding the former over the latter. The currency we use is such an intimate part of our daily life that parting from it entails a major change in deeply rooted habits, even in long-standing loyalties. Twenty years after changing over from 'old' to 'new' francs, the French were still routinely counting in terms of the former currency. As it is the case with the European Monetary Union after 1999, the Italian lira coexisted formally for a while (from 1861 to 1862) with the previous legal tenders at a fixed and irrevocable exchange rate. After 1862 the official currency of the kingdom became the only legal tender (as happened to the euro in 2002) but, as we have seen, ordinary citizens were very slow in changing over to the new currency. European monetary authorities seem to be well aware of the problem, when Mr Duisenberg candidly admits that 'we are still in the process of making the euro a currency in the minds of the people'.[35]

Probably the main set of 'lessons' to be drawn from the Italian case is that pre-existing economic conditions, habits and institutions are of crucial importance in shaping the pattern of market unification. More so as they are usually the playground for the vested interests that would probably be upset by larger and more efficient markets. The lack of internal labour migrations has often been cited as one major weakness of Europe as a single currency area. The time span examined in this paper precedes that of the great Italian domestic and international labour migrations. Land tenure contracts and, probably, cultural and linguistic barriers barred most agricultural labourers from moving around far enough to provide efficient arbitrage in the labour

---

[35] Barber, 'Bloodied', p. 12.

markets. It is likewise unlikely that in the near future the mason's wage will be equalized across Europe. In the case of master masons, these difficulties were compounded by the licence system, a form of protection for local insiders. Today's Europeans have gone quite far in the cross-recognition of diplomas and degrees, but powerful professional associations are still in the way of full mobility for highly qualified professionals. History shows that until such regulations are done away with, European consumers are unlikely to benefit fully from an unfettered single market for professional services.

It is by no means surprising that rent-seekers resort to any available means to oppose the advent of a larger single market. We have seen how Italian local stockbrokers sternly fought against open market measures; similar oppositions against the single market are emerging all over Europe. National stock exchanges and stockbrokers have, so far, retained their independence, merger projects having rapidly been shelved. Likewise, medical doctors, pharmacists, lawyers, notaries, accountants, tax consultants and several other professionals remain strongly entrenched in local customs and regulations as a way of excluding outsiders. Car-makers will not yield on the issue of exclusive dealership contracts. The list of sectors where traditions and local regulations are invoked and used as protective devices could fill many more pages. History shows that determined governments can do a lot to break those oligopolies that are in the way of the full completion of a single market. The Italian case also shows that government action is routinely met by strong protest that, as in the case of the stock exchanges in 1872, can actually disrupt the market mechanism. It is the fear of social unrest and of ultimately achieving perverse results that often makes authorities shy away from pushing their regulatory powers to their ultimate, and beneficial, consequences. Surely, the long disruption of business in the Italian bourses after 1872 was a costly outcome of government action. Yet, in historical perspective, its consequences can only be regarded as moderate, and worth suffering, relative to the long-run benefits of more open and better regulated markets. This is a political, rather than strictly economic, lesson from the past that today's European rulers might well regard as not entirely off the mark.

References

Archivio Storico della Banca d'Italia, Roma (Bonaldo Stringher, folder no. 53).

Boyer, George R., and Timothy J. Hatton. 'Regional Labour Market Integration in England and Wales, 1850–1913.' In *Labour Market Evolution*, edited by George Grantham and Mary MacKinnon, 84–106. London/New York: Routledge, 1994.

Barber, T. 'Bloodied, but Unbowed.' *Financial Times*, 26 November 1999: 12.

Barro, Robert J., and Xavier X. Sala-i-Martin. *Economic Growth*. New York: McGraw-Hill, 1995.

Bevilacqua, Piero. *Storia dell'Agricoltura*. Venezia: Marsilio, 1990.

Cafagna, Luciano. *Dualismo e sviluppo nella storia d'Italia*. Venezia: Marsilio, 1989.

De Cecco, Marcello. *L'Italia e il sistema finanziario internazionale 1861–1914*. Roma-Bari: Laterza, 1990.

De Mattia, Renato. *L'unificazione monetaria italiana*. Torino: ILTE, 1959.

De Vecchi, Giorgio, and Cristina Treu. *Le organizzazioni operaie edili in Lombardia 1860–1914*. Milano: Nuove Edizioni Operaie, 1979.

Di Rollo, Franca. 'Le retribuzioni dei lavoratori edili a Roma dal 1826 al 1880.' In *Archivio Economico dell'Unificazione Italiana*, Vol. 13, sec. 4, 1–31. Roma: IRI, 1965.

Ercolani, Paolo. 'Documentazione statistica di base.' In *Lo sviluppo economico in Italia*, edited by Giorgio Fuà, Vol. 3, 388–476. Milano: Franco Angeli, 1978.

Feinstein, Charles. 'The Rise and Fall of the Williamson Curve.' *Journal of Economic History* 48, no. 3 (1988): 699–729.

Giorgetti, Giorgio. 'I contratti agrari.' In *Storia d'Italia*, Vol. 5, Documenti, 699–758. Torino: Einaudi, 1973.

Insolera, Italo. 'L'urbanistica.' In *Storia d'Italia*, Vol. 5. Documenti, 725–86. Torino: Einaudi, 1973.

Levi, Giovanni. 'I salari edilizi a Torino dal 1815 al 1874.' In *Miscellanea Walter Maturi*, edited by la Istituto di Storia Moderna e del Risorgimento, 335–405. Torino: Giappichelli, 1966.

Martello, Tullio, and Armando Montanari. *Stato attuale del credito in Italia e notizie sulle istituzioni di credito straniere*. Padova: Salamin, 1874.

Ministero di Agricoltura, Industria e Commercio. Direzione Generale della Statistica. *Salari. Prezzi medi di un'ora di lavoro degli operai addetti alle opere di muratura ed ai trasporti di terra e mercedi medie giornaliere degli operai addetti alle miniere*. Roma.

O'Rourke, Kevin H., and Jeffrey G. Williamson. 'Late Nineteenth-Century Anglo-American Factor-Price Convergence: Were Heckscher and Ohlin Right?' *Journal of Economic History* 54, no. 4 (1994): 892–916.

Pakko, Michael R., and Patricia S. Pollard. 'For Here or To Go? Purchasing Power Parity and the Big Mac.' *Federal Reserve Bank of St Louis Review* 78, no. 1, (1996): 3–21.

Pittaluga, Giovanni B. 'La monetizzazione del Regno d'Italia.' In *Il progresso economico dell'Italia*, edited by Pierluigi Ciocca, 177–206. Bologna: Il Mulino, 1992.

Ripa di Meana, Carlo, and Mario Sarcinelli. 'Unione monetaria, competizione valutaria e controllo della moneta: è d'aiuto la storia italiana?' In *Monete in concorrenza*, edited by Marcello De Cecco. Bologna: Il Mulino, 1992.

Roccas, Massimo. 'L'Italia e il sistema monetario internazionale dagli anni sessanta agli anni novanta del secolo scorso.' In *Ricerche per la storia della Banca d'Italia—Contributi*, edited by Franco Cotula, Vol. 1, 3–67. Bari-Roma: Laterza, 1990.

Rosenbloom, Joshua L. 'Occupational Differences in Labour Market Integration: The United States in 1890.' *Journal of Economic History* 51, no. 2 (1991): 427–39.

Sannucci, Valeria. 'Molteplicità delle banche di emissione: ragioni economiche ed effetti sull'efficacia del controllo monetario (1860-90).' In *Ricerche per la storia della Banca d'Italia—Contributi*, edited by Franco Cotula, Vol. 1, 181–218. Bari-Roma: Laterza, 1990.

Sereni, Emilio. *Il capitalismo nelle campagne (1860-1900)*. Torino: Einaudi, 1947.

———. *Capitalismo e mercato nazionale in Italia*. Roma: Editori Riuniti 1966.

Spinelli, Franco, and Michele Fratianni. *Storia monetaria d'Italia*. Milano: Mondadori, 1991.

Supino, Camillo. *Storia della circolazione cartacea in Italia dal 1860 al 1928*. Milano: Editrice libraria, 1929.

Williamson, Jeffrey G. 'Globalization, Convergence, and History.' *Journal of Economic History* 56, no. 2 (1996): 277–306.

11.
Ideology and the Shadow of History:
A Perspective on the Great Depression
BARRY EICHENGREEN & PETER TEMIN

Introduction

History casts its shadow in a variety of different ways. Among them is the interpretation of past experience in shaping perceptions of the feasible and desirable. The makers of US foreign policy, seeking to respond to geopolitical problems in real time, use analogical reasoning as a guide, invoking historical analogies for guidance as to what should or should not be done. Struggling to come up with a response to the crisis in Kosovo, they invoked, rightly or wrongly, analogies with Munich and Vietnam. They codified the lessons of this history, as they perceived them, in the Wilson and Powell Doctrines, world views that worked to shape their perceptions of how to respond.[1]

What is true of foreign policy is also true of economics. Investors, operating in an environment where information is costly to assemble and process, use rules of thumb about how markets behave to make sense of events and anticipate price fluctuations, and derive those rules of thumb from their perceptions of historical experience. Thus, the fact that price-earnings ratios on the New York Stock Exchange are, at the time of writing, higher than they have been at any time since the 1920s is widely invoked by investment analysts who currently advise caution of their clients.

---
[1] May, *Lessons*. See also, for a more recent treatment of the same issues, Vertzberger, 'Foreign Policy'.

Yet another example is criticism of the International Monetary Fund for how it responded to the Asian crisis of 1997–8. The Fund was blinkered, it is said, by blind adherence to a model designed for a world of low capital mobility that had long since given way to a world of global financial markets. Instead of recognizing that countries were experiencing 'high-tech' financial crises rooted in the intrinsic volatility of international capital flows, the IMF continued to perceive that those suffering crises had brought their plight upon themselves by running recklessly expansionary monetary and fiscal policies. Swayed by analogies with the Latin American crises of the 1980s and drawing strong lessons from the earlier history of budget-deficit and current-account-deficit related crises under Bretton Woods, the IMF continued to prescribe monetary and fiscal austerity even where it was inappropriate. Wedded to the ideology of austerity, the mentality of Bretton Woods and the doctrine of 'financial programming', the IMF continued to press the traditional policy response long after it had been rendered anachronistic.

In this paper we explore the role of this ideological inheritance in the shaping of the actions of economic agents with reference to a particular historical experience, the Great Depression. The Depression is one of those seminal events in the development of the modern world economy on which policy-makers and market participants instinctually rely when formulating their conceptions of how market economies behave. In addition, and critically for our purposes, it is an unusually powerful illustration of the role of ideology and doctrine in the making of economic policy. Casting the experience of the Great Depression in this light has the further benefit of providing new insight into the nature of the great macroeconomic catastrophe of modern times.

We argue that the ideology of the gold standard led policy-makers to take actions that accentuated economic distress in the 1930s. This mentality and the actions and institutions it supported limited the ability of governments and central banks to respond to adversity. Indeed, they prescribed policies that made economic conditions worse instead of better. In response to balance-of-payments deficits and gold losses, governments could only deflate the economy, restricting credit with the goal of reducing domestic prices and costs until international balance was restored. Critical to this process was the effort to reduce wages, the largest element in costs. As F.C. Benham summarized the conventional understanding in 1931:

The loss of gold or the higher bank rate, then, can restore international equilibrium only by reducing internal prices. Of these, the most important is the price of labour. Wages and other incomes from labour may be reduced. This will have a double effect. On the one hand, wage-earners and others will have less to spend on everything, including imports. On the other hand costs will be reduced in all industries, including export industries. Imports will be checked and exports stimulated until the two flows once more balance.[2]

This mechanism had worked well before World War I, and it was seen as the path to economic stability in the chaotic post-war years. The hyperinflations of the early 1920s appeared to show what would happen if the gold standard was abandoned. It cannot be surprising that policy-makers in the 1920s were wedded to this defence against economic anarchy. It was, however, a world tragedy.

The Gold Standard Before the Great Depression

World War I was a shock to the world economy, as it was to Edwardian society. The by-gone world had been an international one. English and European consumers could buy goods from around the world and travel throughout it. Educated people—businessmen, bankers and their professional children—moved easily among capital and industrial cities from Moscow to Chicago, or at least from Berlin to New York. The authorities governing these cities promoted the economic stability that allowed persons and finance to move between them by adhering to the gold standard. The policy of buying and selling gold at a fixed price—adhering to the gold standard, in other words—appeared to guarantee both economic stability and civilized interchange.

The gold standard had this power for both real and symbolic reasons. It symbolized the mentality and patterns of conduct of intellectual and economic elites. It was integral to the emergence of what Keynes referred to as 'the investing class', whose members perceived saving and investing as a duty and a delight.[3] More concretely, saving and investing were encouraged by the stability of money values. Thrift was rewarded because there was no danger of the real value of a

---

[2] Sir William Beveridge, ed., *Tariffs: The Case Examined*; Benham, *Balance of Trade*.
[3] Keynes, *Economic Consequences*.

financial asset being inflated away.[4] The gold standard, which promised stable prices and restrained the financial freedom of governments, was the guarantor of this belief. Because the gold standard was an international system, it stabilized the value of money contracts worldwide. The exchange rate stability it provided encouraged unprecedented levels of foreign investment. That countries like Britain and France invested a quarter to a third of their savings abroad between 1880 and 1913, fuelling the expansion of the international economy, was a consequence of the gold standard and at the same time worked to enforce it.[5]

In order to maintain the policy of buying and selling gold at a fixed price, governments had to conduct their affairs within certain bounds. This disciplined behaviour in turn promoted economic stability in countries that adhered to the gold standard.[6] And the ability of governments to maintain this discipline marked the boundaries of the civilized world. The struggling countries of Latin America and Eastern Europe kept trying and failing to adopt the gold standard, making adherence to this policy a hallmark of a developed economy. Asian and African societies out of the orbit of European and American industry made no effort to join this club.

It seemed logical during and after World War I that reconstructing the gold standard (suspended during this war as in past wars) was essential to recover what was good in pre-war society. Even if internationalism would never be as absolute as before, the gold standard could still resume its dual functions. It could promote economic stability and delimit the range of modern society. Benjamin Strong, Governor of the New York Federal Reserve Bank, argued in a 1925 memo to Montagu Norman, Governor of the Bank of England, that British failure to restore gold payments 'would be followed by a long period of unsettled conditions too serious really to contemplate'.[7]

---

[4] As Keynes pointed out, 'so rooted...has been the conventional belief in the stability and safety of a money contract' that the law in many countries required those who oversaw trust funds to invest exclusively in gilt-edged bonds' (Keynes, *Tract on Monetary Reform*, p. 11).
[5] On foreign investment and the gold standard, see Feis, *Europe, The World's Banker*, White, *French International Accounts*, and Edelstein, *Overseas Investment*.
[6] Bordo and Rockoff, 'Gold Standard', pp. 389–428.
[7] Strong Memorandum, January 11, 1925, quoted in Temin, *Lessons*, p. 14.

Ideology and the Shadow of History

This is not to deny that there had been economic fluctuations under the gold standard. The Americans had roiled the financial markets during the election campaign of 1896, when William Jennings Bryan insisted, 'You shall not crucify mankind upon a cross of gold', and investors wondered if the United States would continue to honour its obligation to sell gold at its fixed price. The resulting panic sent interest rates soaring and disrupted international financial transactions. But this panic was short-lived; it was not in the forefront of many minds in the aftermath of the Great War. The United States had shown restraint in external relations; its domestic politics disturbed but did not derange the international economy.[8]

More vivid and revealing was another crisis of the pre-war gold standard: the Baring Crisis of 1890. Speculation in South American land had been encouraged amid a tremendous expansion of Argentinean government debt. Eventually the government of that country found itself unable to service the accumulated debt. The London firm of Barings was caught in the ensuing debacle. William Lidderdale, Governor of the Bank of England in 1890, understood his role in the world economy. The Argentineans could do what they wanted, but their excesses were not to threaten the gold standard. By involving a noted British firm in their dealings, they created conditions where their problems could generate panic in London.

To avoid a financial panic, Lidderdale accumulated reserves, discouraged thoughts that the Bank might run short, and encouraged creditors not to call in loans that might destabilize the markets. The first goal was accomplished by selling bonds to the government of Russia, borrowing through Rothschilds from the Bank of France, and securing guaranteed offers of loans from London joint-stock banks. The second was achieved by reaching an understanding with the banks not to liquidate loans they had made to bill brokers financing the American trade.[9] In this operation, Lidderdale was not so much exhibiting the power of the Bank of England to maintain the gold standard as revealing the need for both international and domestic cooperation in a joint effort.

The Great War was a larger shock than the Baring Crisis and appeared to policy-makers as beyond their range of historical experience. The Bank of England could raise funds to deal with the short-

---

[8] Calomiris, 'Greenback Resumption'.
[9] Powell, *Evolution of the Money Market*, p. 527.

lived increase in demand during the Baring Crisis, but it could not finance the war by such means. The government borrowed on its own, and the Bank of England used its powers of moral suasion to discourage London banks from undertaking transactions in precious metal. A key provision of the pre-war financial system, the right to import and export gold without restriction, was limited by the high wartime costs and hazards of ocean shipping. Central-bank stabilization of the dollar-pound exchange rate was substituted for gold flows.

Still, the war, like the Baring Crisis, was a temporary disruption. The lesson of history was clear: temporary modification of the gold standard was only to accommodate the needs of war and post-war reconstruction. Once reconstruction was underway, Britain should go back on the gold standard as she had done after defeating Napoleon a century earlier. But however clear the lesson, the dislocation of the Great War and its resultant inflation meant that resumption would not be straightforward.

The problem of post-war economic organization was recognized during the war in Britain. The Lords Commissioner of His Majesty's Treasury appointed the Cunliffe Committee to consider the question and report back to the government, which it did in 1918. Its report argued that the best defence against economic instability was the gold standard, and it invoked the stability of the past to predict that the same institution would generate stability in the future: 'In our opinion it is imperative that after the war the conditions necessary to the maintenance of an effective gold standard should be restored without delay.'[10] The restoration envisaged by the Committee was the free purchase and sale of gold at pre-war parities. Such expressions of the gold-standard ideology would pervade discussions in the 1920s.

But the end of American support for the pound in 1919 and its subsequent depreciation meant that adopting the Committee's recommendation would require deflation, as had similar policies after the Napoleonic Wars. Reluctant to impose the costs of reducing wages onto returning soldiers, the government postponed the resumption of pre-war parity for five years. This doubt about the usefulness of the gold standard at all times and in all conditions anticipated doubts that would deepen in the course of the 1920s to undermine the policies that grew from the dominant ideology.

[10] Great Britain, *First Interim Report*, p. 5.

The same modes of thought affected financial policies in France and Italy. But while the Italians tried to emulate Britain and deflate in order to restore the pre-war parity of the lira,[11] the French were unable to reform their internal fiscal system in order to reduce even government expenditures. French *rentiers* counted on German reparations to restore their traditional prosperity. Even when occupation of the Ruhr led to German passive resistance rather than increased reparations, the French parliament refused to relinquish its memories of pre-war prosperity.[12] In discussions about the value at which to fix the franc in 1926, one of the participants, Quesnay, hoped that they could 'maintain the gold value of French prices below world prices and thus facilitate the life of the country.'[13] The accomplishment of this goal, at least for a few years, generated a massive accumulation of gold in France and contributed to the crisis of the gold standard a few years later.

The Germans fell into a policy of financial excess, ending in hyperinflation. Their experience was considered one of the object lessons proving the value of the gold standard. When stability was restored in 1924 through the Dawes Plan, the mark resumed its pre-war parity. Adherence to the gold standard and its mentality was intense in Germany after the experience of hyperinflation.[14]

Opposition to deflation was endemic in Britain, although it was far more orderly than on the Continent. After the Labour Party was defeated in 1924, it adopted a programme of 'socialism now', which meant in practice a minimum wage and state-provided family allowances. These radical proposals were legitimated by the workers' contribution to the war effort; they were required because the reduction in costs required for the restoration of gold payments at the pre-war parity was threatening to reduce real wages.

Falling wages were noted most prominently in the coal industry, long a hotbed of labour activism. The demand for coal received a temporary boost in 1923 and 1924 during the French occupation of the Ruhr. The miners and management reached an agreement during that time whereby workers were guaranteed a minimum wage. But the resolution of the conflict on the Continent led to a renewed decline in the demand for British coal, and the agreement collapsed. The Prime

---

[11] Forsyth, *Crisis of Liberal Italy.*
[12] Schuker, *End of French Predominance.*
[13] Quoted in Mouré, 'Undervaluing the Franc Poincaré', p. 140.
[14] Feldman, *Great Disorder.*

Minister was brought into the renewed negotiations to repeat the mantra of the gold standard: ' . . . all the workers of this country have got to take reductions in wages to help put industry on its feet.'[15]

This is just one way of putting industry on its feet. But it is the only way open under the gold standard, since alternatives involving higher prices are not admissible. Calling for lower wages is the discourse of the gold standard because this call follows from the mechanics of the monetary system. Countries on the gold standard cannot devalue their currencies and allow the demand for exports to determine their exchange rate. They cannot expand the money supply to stimulate domestic demand, for doing so would push up prices, provoke gold exports, and weaken the exchange rate. For them, the only way to reduce prices is to reduce costs of production, and the largest of these costs is labour. It did however impose short-run costs to which the Prime Minister was alluding.

The unions were reluctant to bear these costs. They did not share the apocalyptic vision of the central bankers. They were not sufficiently secure to trade current sacrifices for purported future gains. They had participated in the war effort and now expected recompense. Their reluctance to agree to wage reductions rendered the restored gold standard of the inter-war years fragile and inflexible and transformed it from the guarantor of stability into the transmitter of the Great Depression.

Wages were less flexible after World War I in other countries as well. Borchardt argued that high German wages in the 1920s were the cause of Germany's economic collapse.[16] Post-war changes in labour-market institutions limited the flexibility of German wages in the second half of the 1920s.[17] The number of workers covered by collective contracts rose enormously between 1913 and the mid-twenties, although only a fraction of these contracts were national in scope.[18] This fragmented structure of collective bargaining was ill-suited for coordinating economy wide adjustments to macroeconomic shocks.[19] It

---

[15] Mowat, *Britain Between the Wars*, p. 292.
[16] Borchardt, *Perspectives*, Chap. 9.
[17] See Angell, *Economic Recovery*; James, *German Slump*.
[18] As of January 1928, 1.4 million workers were covered by Reich contracts, 3.4 million by district or regional agreements, and a still larger number by company- or plant-level contracts.
[19] Theory suggests that highly centralized and highly decentralized labour markets have the greatest capacity to accommodate shocks. Highly decentralized markets can raise or lower wages through competition. If wages are too high, unemployment will result, and the competition for jobs will bid them down. In centralized markets, the same outcome

was buttressed by compulsory arbitration, first introduced in wartime but reintroduced at the end of 1923 in response to the labour unrest incited by the hyperinflation. Ministry of Labour officials responsible for appointing these arbitrators were less than enthusiastic about wage reductions. Henrich Brauns and Rudolf Wissell were the labour ministers of the period; Brauns came from a Catholic tradition stressing the importance of just wages, while Wisell was a trade unionist himself. Thus, the spread of unionism, collective bargaining and compulsory arbitration supplanted decentralized labour markets without constructing a coherent alternative compatible with the imperatives of gold-standard adjustment.

The Gold Standard in Crisis

Like the Baring Crisis and the Great War before it, the Great Depression was a shock to this happy world. Like the war, it was not immediately apparent that it would be as severe and last as long as it did. Nor was it inevitable. It started out as an economic contraction like those before it. This recession was converted into the Great Depression by policies that accentuated the deflationary forces. Economic policies, in other words, did not act to alleviate the Depression in the early 1930s; they acted to intensify it.

Policies were perverse because they were designed to preserve the gold standard, not employment. Maintenance of the gold standard would in time restore employment, central bankers thought, while attempts to increase employment directly would fail. This was the lesson of history, both before the Great War and in its turbulent aftermath. The collapse of output and prices and the loss of savings as banks closed their doors were precisely what the gold standard promised to prevent. Reconciling outcomes with expectations consequently required interpreting these exceptional events in unexceptional

---

can be achieved through a single centralized decision to adjust wages. Problems arise when markets are neither highly centralized nor decentralized. Groups covered by collective bargaining are too large for the impact of their agreements on the labour market as a whole to be negligible but too small to have the incentive to take those impacts into account. When the time comes for wage concessions, no regional or industrial union will be willing to move first. See Calmfors and Driffill, 'Bargaining Structure'. This would seem to be an apt characterization of the German situation in the 1920s.

terms. Where the crisis was most severe, blame was laid on the authorities' failure to embrace the gold-standard mentality. The Federal Reserve and the Bank of England in particular had succumbed to the lure of managed money. Having refused to play by the rules of the gold-standard game, they had committed 'abuses of credit'. They had sterilized international gold flows, preventing them from exerting their normal stabilizing influence on credit conditions. This prevented prices and costs from adjusting.

Louis Germain-Martin, French Minister of Finance in 1932, 1934 and 1935, argued that the attempt to use monetary policy to manipulate prices, in violation of gold-standard strictures, had brought on the depression.[20] Cheap credit had fuelled an unsustainable boom, culminating in the inevitable crash, financial distress and depression. His adviser Charles Rist saw the slump as resulting directly from the artificiality of the preceding boom.

> [I]ncreased production would have provoked a general decline in the price level earlier if efforts had not been made from all sides to stimulate consumption artificially and to maintain it at a level superior to that corresponding to real income. It is there, in our view, that it is necessary to seek the specific origin of the present crisis.[21]

Similar views prevailed in Washington DC and in the regional reserve banks of the Federal Reserve System. Even as unemployment spiralled upward, Lynn P. Talley of the Federal Reserve Bank of Dallas wrote to George Harrison of the New York Fed saying that his directors were not 'inclined to countenance much interference with economic trends through artificial methods...'[22] Treasury Secretary Andrew Mellon notoriously advised President Hoover that the only way to restore the economy to a sustainable footing was to 'liquidate labour, liquidate stocks, liquidate the farmers, liquidate real estate... purge the rottenness out of the system...' As a result, Mellon continued, 'people will work harder, [and] live a more moral life'.[23] The puritanical strand of gold-standard dogma continued to carry the day. Hoover himself regarded the gold standard as 'little short of a sacred

---

[20] Germain-Martin, *Sommes-nous sur la bonne route?* pp. 20–1.
[21] Cited in Mouré, *Managing the Franc Poincaré*, p. 33.
[22] Talley to Harrison, letter, July 15, 1930, cited in Friedman and Schwartz, *Monetary History*, p. 372.
[23] Hoover, *Memoirs*, Vol. 3, p. 30.

formula'.[24] Any deviation he dismissed as 'collectivism', an all-embracing label for economic and social decay. And the failure of governments and central banks to embrace single-mindedly this liquidationist dogma only made things worse. As Clement Moret, the newly appointed Governor of the Bank of France, told his shareholders in January 1932,

> In order to bring the depression to its conclusion, it would have been necessary to stop the abuses of credit that have contributed so largely to the creation and spread of the crisis. In fact, there has been no movement towards a sufficient contraction of banking credits, so powerful were the efforts brought into play to maintain at any cost, by an artificial policy of cheap and easy money, the spirit of enterprise and the taste for speculation. This tendency has undoubtedly served to increase the disorders it was intended to mitigate.[25]

Karl Helffrerich, banker and one-time German finance minister, extended this thought in the sixth edition of his classic work, *Money*, arguing that abandoning the gold standard would make money a 'bone of contention between brutal interests'.

> [A] fight would result between the interests concerned, and this fight would, in the absence of an objective criterion, be decided in advance, not by reason and justice but by brute force only. On the one side we should have all those who owe money fighting for the greatest possible issue of money and for the largest possible diminution in the value of money, and on the other side we should have creditors and all those in receipt of fixed salaries, dividends, and wages who would be interested in the preservation and the increase in the value of money. The fight which would be waged round the value of money would, more than any other economic conflict between various interests, necessarily lead to the demoralization of economic and of social life.[26]

That the solution to the Depression might lie in rejecting gold was beyond the pale. The British Committee on Finance and Industry (the Macmillan Committee), reporting on financial problems in the summer of 1931, was prepared to entertain the heresy of a tariff before recommending that the gold standard be abandoned. British leaders were ready to turn their backs on nearly a century of free trade before jeopardizing sterling's hallowed status. Keynes, the committee's leading

---

[24] Warren, *Herbert Hoover*, p. 280.
[25] Cited in Mouré, *Managing the Franc Poincaré*, p. 37.
[26] Helffrerich, *Money*, p. 621.

Changes in Economic Regimes and Ideologies

intellectual light, 'was willing to try anything—a tariff, quotas, a national treaty on wages, profits and rents, foreign lending restrictions—anything except suspending the gold standard, which was too drastic to contemplate.'[27]

The gold standard consequently was not abandoned. Its rhetoric was deflation, and its directive was inaction. Central banks stood ready to withstand financial panics like the Baring Crisis but not to preserve production or employment. Federal Reserve officials inferred from low interest rates and excess bank reserves that no panic was in sight and counselled inaction. When there was a threat to the US commitment to gold in 1931, the Fed responded by raising interest rates sharply and driving the country deeper into depression.

Support for the gold standard, however, was not as strong as the Rock of Gibraltar. A Labour prime minister, no friend of the Bank of England, had occupied Downing Street since the summer of 1929. President Hoover announced in March 1930 that 'the worst effects of the crash on unemployment will have been passed during the next sixty days'.[28] When the recovery for which he hoped did not materialize, the odds on his re-election lengthened dramatically. Both the Bank of England and the Federal Reserve enjoyed independence of action, but their autonomy was not guaranteed.

The authorities may have been hesitant to abandon the gold standard, but the rise of unemployment rendered them equally reluctant to defend it. Balancing the budget was a conventional remedy, but governments were hesitant to raise taxes or cut support for veterans, pensioners and the unemployed given the present economic distress. Left-leaning governments like Britain's were least prepared to apply such cuts, but they were also particularly obliged to convince the markets of their fiscal rectitude if their defence of the gold standard was to succeed. If they failed to raise taxes, the markets would attack, and the government might fall for having failed to defend the financial foundations of the nation. If they did raise taxes, they might be blamed for failing to defend the interests of their core constituency and fall anyway. Currency traders saw that officials had no way out. As Philip Snowden, the Labour Chancellor, succinctly explained the sterling

[27] Boyce, *British Capitalism*, p. 293.
[28] *New York Times*, 8 March 1930; Warren, *Herbert Hoover*, p. 119.

crisis in his autobiography, 'The opposition of the Labour Party to the Budget proposals had given the impression abroad that the country was not united.'[29]

Nor were central banks prepared to raise interest rates as required to defend the system. When the sterling crisis struck London in July, the Bank of England, confronted by a 20 per cent unemployment rate, hesitated to raise its discount rate for fear of lengthening the dole queues. It waited nearly two weeks to raise the Bank rate. When the first increase failed to halt gold losses, the rate was raised again. But this was the final change until the suspension of convertibility on 19 September. According to Kunz, 'With business already very depressed, neither management nor labour nor their representatives in Parliament were willing to pay the price which such a high Bank rate would exact.'[30]

The authorities were cornered. If they hesitated to raise rates, the gold standard might succumb to market pressures. If they did raise rates, they might be forced from office by political pressures. Anticipating that the rate rise was politically unsustainable, the markets might attack anyway. Panic flights of hot money, unleashed by the realization that countries such as Britain had no escape from this dilemma, soon dwarfed the trade deficits and external debt service that dominated the balance of payments at other times. Central banks joined the fray, liquidating their own foreign securities to avoid capital losses in the event of a foreign devaluation. Even true believers like Herbert Hoover were forced to acknowledge that gold and financial flows had become 'a loose cannon on the deck of the world'.[31]

In this unstable environment the gold standard became an engine for deflation. Supplies of money and credit were linked to the gold and foreign exchange reserves of central banks. But as uncertainty mounted about the stability of key currencies, central banks liquidated their foreign exchange balances to build up their gold reserves. The share of foreign exchange in global monetary reserves fell to 11 per cent by the end of 1931, down from 37 per cent three years before.[32] The Bank of France sold its sterling- and dollar-denominated bonds and presented the proceeds at the Bank of England and the Fed for

---

[29] Snowden, *Autobiography*, 1934.
[30] Kunz, *Battle for Britain's Gold Standard in 1931*, p. 184.
[31] Hoover, *Memoirs*, vol. 3, p. 67.
[32] Nurkse, *International Currency Experience*, Appendix A.

conversion, forcing those central banks to defend their gold hoards. They restricted credit, destabilizing commercial banks and depressing prices, production and employment. Bank closures disrupted the provision of credit to households and firms, forcing the former to cut their consumption, the latter to curtail production.[33] Deflation magnified the burden of outstanding debt, forcing debtors to curtail their spending still further in the effort to maintain their credit worthiness.[34] As the gold-exchange standard collapsed back into the kind of pure gold-based system that Moret associated with financial stability, markets were destabilized as never before.

The gold-standard ideology extended to the advisers of the governments and central bankers. Lionel Robbins, the youngest member of the Macmillan Committee, argued in 1934, 'If it had not been for the prevalence of the view that wage rates must at all costs be maintained in order to maintain the purchasing power of the consumer, the violence of the present depression and the magnitude of the unemployment which has accompanied it would have been considerably less.'[35] As always in the rhetoric of the gold standard, lower wages would have allowed the deflation required by the monetary system.

In the end, what led to the system's downfall was not just agitation on the Left but the challenge to the hegemony of gold-standard ideology from the very fact of economic and financial distress. The more governments rededicated themselves to gold-standard policies, the more economic conditions worsened. As the patient's condition continued to deteriorate, even true believers began to consider unconventional remedies. So long as France, Switzerland and the Benelux countries resisted the worst effects of the Depression, they could ascribe the plight of their neighbours to their failure to cleave to gold-standard orthodoxy. Once their own economies were infected and repeated doses of deflation only aggravated the condition, not even the most sacrosanct of economic doctrines was secure.

---

[33] The most influential recent statement of this mechanism is Bernanke, 'Macroeconomics of the Great Depression'.
[34] This is the famous debt-deflation view of the Depression. Fisher, 'Debt-Deflation View of the Great Depression'.
[35] Robbins, *Great Depression*, p. 186.

Going Off Gold

As the Depression deepened, opposition to this ideology gathered strength. Yet the central bankers and political leaders who espoused the gold standard clung desperately to their faith in the face of economic reality and even the disintegration of the gold standard itself.

The British, caught on the horns of this dilemma, abandoned their commitment to exchange sterling for gold at a fixed rate in the fall of 1931. The decision was earth-shattering. For Jackson E. Reynolds, President of the First National Bank of New York, it was 'like the end of the world . . .'[36] The famous comment of Tom Johnston, former parliamentary secretary for Scotland and Lord Privy Seal—'Nobody told us we could do that!'—is celebrated precisely because it summarizes the prevailing sense of astonishment.[37]

This dilemma was hardly unique to Britain. As a result of the banking crisis that set the stage for the British devaluation, the German government restricted transactions in foreign exchange. Even though Weimar did not devalue, the free currency convertibility that was the hallmark of the gold standard was no longer allowed. Yet Brüning, like the Bank of England, could not free himself from the ideology of the gold standard. Nor could other German politicians. They continued to speak of Germany as being on the gold standard because the mark was maintained at parity, even though currency controls violated the fundamental activity of the gold standard—as noted in the Cunliffe Commission and elsewhere—and made the maintenance of parity a purely administrative matter.[38] Haunted by memories of hyperinflation and by Helfferich's words, Brüning continued to pursue policies designed to compress spending and preached the deflationary rhetoric of the gold standard. His decree reducing all prices was issued in December, 1931, six months after Germany effectively abandoned gold.[39]

---

[36] Cited in Kunz, *Battle for Britain's Gold Standard in 1931.* p. 113.
[37] Moggridge, *Return to Gold*, p. 9; Cairncross and Eichengreen, *Sterling in Decline*, p. 5.
[38] Borchardt, 'Could and Should Germany Have Followed Great Britain?'
[39] Brüning of course had mixed motives. The goal of restoring prosperity vied with the aim of ending reparations. Brüning could argue that the gold standard forced him to take deflationary actions whose results he then could use as evidence against Germany's ability to pay reparations. But these added complications do not diminish the importance of the gold-standard ideology. For Brüning could not have undertaken to prostrate the

Across the ocean, Mellon and Hoover remained staunch in their belief in the curative powers of the gold standard as the economy collapsed around them. The Fed raised interest rates sharply in October 1931. Friedman and Schwartz acknowledged the power of the gold standard in this action in the course of their account of the American contraction:

> The Federal Reserve System reacted vigorously and promptly to the external drain, as it had not to the previous internal drain. On October 9, the Reserve Bank of New York raised its rediscount rate to 2 per cent and on October 16, to 3 per cent — the sharpest rise within so brief a period in the whole history of the System, before or since. The maintenance of the gold standard was accepted as an objective in support of which men of a broad range of views were ready to rally.[40]

Even after losing the election of 1932, Hoover kept trying to enlist the president-elect in support of the gold standard. As late as February 1933, Hoover tried to chide Roosevelt into a commitment to support the gold price of the dollar, arguing that devaluation would lead to 'a world economic war, with the certainty that it leads to complete destruction, both at home and abroad.'[41]

None of these people appear to have escaped from their ideology under even the most extreme pressure. Brüning and Hoover maintained their deflationary policies for as long as they were in office, and they continued to champion them even after they lost power. Twenty years later, Hoover repeated his 1932 claim that maintaining the gold standard had been good for the United States: 'We have thereby maintained one Gibraltar of stability in the world and contributed to check the movement of chaos.'[42] Brüning said he had fallen 100 metres from the goal.[43] He meant the end of reparations, not the recovery of employment, but he revealed no doubt that the proper policy had been to stay within the rhetoric and framework of the gold standard even after abandoning convertibility itself.

German economy without support from the rhetoric of the gold standard. And one suspects his motives may have been no more mixed than those of Secretary Mellon who was so eager to liquidate everything in sight. See James, *German Slump*, pp. 32–5.

[40] Freidman and Schwartz, *A Monetary History*, pp. 317, 382.
[41] Hoover, 'Lincoln Day Address', pp. 1136–8.
[42] Hoover, *Memoirs*, p. 189.
[43] James, *The German Slump*, p. 35.

Ideology and the Shadow of History

Given the hold of the gold-standard mentality on central bankers and politicians, it took a change of leadership to change policy. The ideological constancy of Brüning and Hoover is only the most famous example of members of Keynes' 'investing class' who clung to their ideology during many lean years. It took pressure from the labouring classes to change public policies, by changing leaders if their rhetoric proved inviolate.

Unemployment in the early '30s rose to cataclysmic proportions. The effects were legion, from the physical hardship of feeding a family to the demoralizing effect of being out of work. The post-war world allowed two forms of protest. One was mass demonstrations. They were tried on some occasions, but the pervasive unemployment made strikes less attractive and powerful as an expression of labour's will.

The second form of protest was the vote. Limitation of the franchise before the Great War was one way in which the ideology of the gold standard could rule without challenge. But the gradual extension of the franchise had given workers in industrial societies an avenue to express their views. Not as often as they may have liked, perhaps, but enough to voice their opposition to the gold standard after two or three years of economic contraction.

German voters began to abandon the traditional political parties soon after the Depression began. The Socialists were as committed to the gold standard as Brüning, which they showed by rejecting calls within their party for more expansionary policies.[44] German voters transformed the Nazis from a fringe party to a presence in the Reichstag in the 1930 election by increasing their seats from 12 to 107. The voters then vented their spleen on the traditional parties in July, 1932, when the Nazis won 230 seats. Voting analysis has not found a strong correlation between unemployment and Nazi votes in these elections, but it is hard to argue that the spectacular rise in the Nazi vote was independent of the economic crisis. The link was there, filtered through the rhetoric of protest rather than taken straight as a function of unemployment.[45] No one could mistake the rhetoric of the Nazis for the rhetoric of the gold standard.

---

[44] Woytinsky, *Stormy Passage*, pp. 462–72.
[45] Voters did not vote the Nazis into a majority position. In fact, they decreased their support for the Nazis in the second election of 1932 when Brüning's successors made the first tentative steps toward abandoning the rhetoric and policies of the gold standard. Instead the voters conferred enough respectability on the Nazis to allow Hindenburg, the

American voters had to wait longer. So long as Hoover retained office, the investing classes shaped policy. Given a choice in 1932, the workers voted for someone who sounded not at all like the dour afficcionados of the gold standard, someone who heralded 'reflation', not deflation, as the cure for America's ills. Roosevelt fulfilled their mandate by abandoning the gold standard shortly after taking office in March 1933, and then refusing to contemplate a return at the World Economic Conference in July. Called to salvage what could be saved of the tattered gold standard, the conference had little promise in the horrendous conditions of 1933. Roosevelt blasted it before it even opened, signalling to the other members of the international investing class his sharp turn from the rhetoric of the gold standard. In Roosevelt's words: 'The world will not long be lulled by the specious fallacy of achieving a temporary and probably an artificial stability in foreign exchange on the part of a few large countries only... The sound internal economic situation of a nation is a greater factor in its well-being than the price of its currency.'[46]

In France, where the mentality of the gold standard was particularly strong, this change was still three years in coming. The Bank of France possessed large gold reserves, and its appetite for more gold had contributed to the disintegration of the gold standard at the beginning of the 1930s. Despite multitudinous changes in government, the French barred anyone who disagreed with gold-standard rhetoric from power even after most of the world abandoned gold and began an economic recovery as a result. They organized the remaining true believers into a gold bloc in the aftermath of the abortive World Economic Conference, and they repeated the tired rhetoric of the gold standard in the face of continued economic decline.

Weimar President, to invite the Nazis into the government. It was all the Nazis needed to take over German society and cause endless grief to their own and many other people. See Hamilton, *Who Voted for Hitler?* and Childers, *The Nazi Voter*.

[46] Nixon, *Franklin D. Roosevelt*, p. 269. The ordeal of the Depression had altered discourse so that now the gold standard was 'artificial'. Previously, deviations from gold-standard orthodoxy were said to yield 'artificial' results.

Conclusion

There now prevails a remarkable degree of consensus among specialists about the causes of the Depression. The literature focuses on the gold standard as the mechanism that turned an ordinary business downturn into the Great Depression.[47] The constraints of the gold-standard system hamstrung countries as they struggled to adapt during the 1920s to changes in the world economy. Central bankers held to gold-standard policies as the world economy continued to decline. They continued to kick the world economy while it was down until it lost consciousness.

Workers of course were a different matter. They were asked to bear the costs of achieving this stability, as Benham so clearly noted, and their lack of enthusiasm created new difficulties in the maintenance of the gold standard in the inter-war period. Wages lacked the flexibility they once possessed in the increasingly structured and politicized labour markets of the inter-war period. The fluidity of labour costs was limited by the spread of unionism, the growth of internal labour markets and personnel departments in the United States, and a general preoccupation with the relationship of one's wage to that of other workers. For this reason, the conventional gold-standard adjustment mechanism no longer operated as before.

In addition, even pre-war levels of flexibility might not have sufficed to resolve the turmoil of the 1930s. The deflationary shock in 1929 was superimposed on radical shifts in the pattern of international settlements, requiring extensive changes in prices and costs for external balance to be restored. But these problems did not penetrate the consciousness of those beholden to the gold-standard mentality, who refused to question the advisability of pursuing the deflationary route. The Victorian and Edwardian virtues of thrift, reliability, stability and cosmopolitanism were invoked ritually as attributes of the monetary system. Gold was moral, principled and civilized; managed money, the opposite. The former was preserved by deflation, and the rhetoric of deflation was to cut wages. Only 'speculators' disagreed. This rhetoric delegitimized the arguments of those who dared question the merits of gold convertibility.

---

[47] Eichengreen and Sachs, 'Exchange Rates'; Temin, *Lessons*; Eichengreen, *Golden Fetters*.

In other segments of society, and in the working classes in particular, opposition to gold-standard ideology and policies boiled over in the 1930s. Workers who suffered unemployment when central banks raised interest rates had few ways of making their objections felt before the Great War. The war transformed this situation by encouraging unionization, impelling extensions of the franchise, and improving the electoral prospects of the socialist and labour parties. Political leaders asked for the first time whether repeated doses of the standard deflationary corrective might undermine their political security. Once they hesitated, the market pounced, destabilizing the currency, the exchange rate and the economy. The need to defend the gold standard with deflationary initiatives became all the more pressing.

But the same working-class pressure that aggravated the Depression by breeding doubts about governments' willingness to stay the course and heightening the need for deflationary action also provided the means of escape. When officials wedded to the gold-standard ideology refused to see the light, voters turned them out of office in favour of others less wedded to the status quo. These new leaders abandoned the gold standard, even though the central bankers with whom they had to work remained reluctant to embrace the new policies of reflation.

The ideology of the gold standard had developed during the long boom of the late nineteenth and early twentieth centuries. It survived World War I and promised a safe haven for ships of state buffeted by stormy social, political and economic seas. But rather than keeping the economies afloat in the 1930s, it helped to sink them.

The world economy, most observers agree, is endowed with powerful self-correcting tendencies. When activity turns down, its inner workings provide a tendency for it to bounce back. Only sustained bad policies can drive the world economy so far off this path that it loses its capacity to recover.[48] And only a hegemonic ideology can convince leaders to persist in such counterproductive policies.

The gold standard provided just such a hegemonic ideology. Its rhetoric dominated discussion of public policy in the years before the Great Depression, and it sustained central bankers and political leaders as they imposed ever greater costs on ordinary people. The mentality of the gold standard proved resistant to change even under the most

---

[48] Perhaps the clearest recent statement of the conventional view among mainstream economists, as applied to the Great Depression, is Bernanke, 'Macroeconomics'.

pressing of economic circumstances. 'What is astonishing,' Basil Blackett observed in 1932, 'is the extraordinary hold which what is called the gold mentality has obtained, especially among the high authorities of the world's Central Banks. The gold standard has become a religion for some of the Boards of Central Banks in Continental Europe, believed in with an emotional fervour which makes them incapable of an unprejudiced and objective examination of possible alternatives.'[49]

Countries only began the struggle to restore prosperity under new leadership, that of individuals who had not been party to the rhetoric of the gold standard in previous lives. Thomas Kuhn argued years ago that scientific revolutions often take place when old scientists who steadfastly adhered to an old paradigm are replaced by fresh faces.[50] So it was with the gold standard. It proved easier in the 1930s to replace leaders inculcated with this ideology than to convert them.

Ultimately, this political class and the gold-standard ideology with which it was imbued contained the seeds of their own destruction. As one contemporary put it, 'The hard-boiled deflationists and bitter-end liquidationists of this era simply overplayed their hands. They recognized no limit of endurance on the part of the public, no end to the amount of punishment that the people could take . . . They had been run over by a steam roller they had not seen coming, namely, the human equation. They still think it wicked that this steam roller came along.'[51] The world paid a high price before the mentality of the gold standard was flattened by this human steam roller, removing the obstacles to economic recovery.

---

[49] Blackett, *Planned Money*, p. 71. Not only on the Continent. Even at the depths of the Depression, people like Lionel (later Lord) Robbins could call for further deflation. Robbins continued to believe that 'no really impartial observer of world events can do other than regard the abandonment of the gold standard by Great Britain as a catastrophe of the first order of magnitude'. Robbins, *Great Depression*, p. 117.
[50] Kuhn, *Structure*.
[51] Edie, *Dollars*, p. 227.

References

Angell, James. *The Economic Recovery of Germany.* New Haven: Yale University Press, 1990.

Benham, F.C. 'The Balance of Trade.' In *Tariffs: The Case Examined*, edited by William Beveridge, 244–60. London: Longman, 1932.

Bennett, Edward W. *Germany and the Diplomacy of the Financial Crisis, 1931.* Cambridge: Harvard University Press, 1932.

Bernanke, Ben. 'Nonmonetary Effects of the Financial Crisis in the Propagation of the Great Depression.' *American Economic Review* 73 (1983): 257–76.

──────. 'The Macroeconomics of the Great Depression: A Comparative Approach.' *Journal of Money, Credit and Banking* 27 (1995): 1–28.

Beveridge, Sir William, et al. *Tariffs: The Case Examined.* London: Longmans, Green (popular edition), 1932.

Blackett, Basil P. *Planned Money.* London: Constable and Co, 1932.

Borchardt, Knut. 'Could and Should Germany Have Followed Great Britain in Leaving the Gold Standard?' *Journal of European Economic History* 13 (1984), 471–97.

──────. *Perspectives on Modern German Economic History and Policy.* Cambridge: Cambridge University Press, 1991.

Bordo, Michael, and Hugh Rockoff. 'The Gold Standard as a "Good Housekeeping Seal of Approval".' *Journal of Economic History* 56 (1996): 389–428.

Boyce, Robert W.D. *British Capitalism at the Crossroads, 1919–1932.* Cambridge: Cambridge University Press, 1987.

Caillaux, Joseph. *The World Crisis: The Lessons Which it Teaches and the Adjustments of Economic Science Which It Necessitates.* London: Cobden-Sanderson, 1932.

Cairncross, Sir Alec, and Barry Eichengreen. *Sterling in Decline: the Devaluations of 1931, 1949, and 1967.* Oxford: Blackwell, 1983.

Calmfors, L. and Driffil, J. 'Bargaining Structure, Corporatism and Macroeconomic Performance.' *Economic Policy* 6 (1988): 13–62.

Calomiris, Charles W. 'Greenback Resumption and Silver Risk: the Economics and Politics of Monetary Regime Change in the United States, 1862–1900.' In *Monetary Regimes in Transition*, edited by Michael Bordo and Forrest Capie, 86–132. Cambridge: Cambridge University Press, 1993.

Childers, Thomas. *The Nazi Voter: The Social Foundations of Fascism in Germany, 1919–1933.* Chapel Hill: University of North Carolina Press, 1983.

Clarke, Stephen V.O. *Central Bank Cooperation, 1924-31.* New York: Federal Reserve Bank of New York, 1967.

Edelstein, Michael. *Overseas Investment in the Age of High Imperialism.* New York: Columbia University Press, 1982.

Edie, L.D. *Dollars.* New Haven: Yale University Press, 1934.

Eichengreen, Barry. *Golden Fetters: The Gold Standard and the Great Depression.* New York: Oxford University Press, 1992.

Eichengreen, Barry, and Jeffrey Sachs. 'Exchange Rates and Economic Recovery in the 1930s.' *Journal of Economic History* 45 (1985): 925–46.

Feldman, Gerald. *The Great Disorder.* New York: Oxford University Press, 1993.

Feis, Herbert. *Europe: The World's Banker.* New Haven: Yale University Press, 1930.

Fisher, Irving. 'The Debt-Deflation View of Great Depressions.' *Econometrica* 1 (1933): 337–57.

Forsyth, Douglas J. *The Crisis of Liberal Italy.* Cambridge: Cambridge University Press, 1933.

Friedman, Milton, and Anna J. Schwartz. *A Monetary History of the United States, 1867–1960.* Princeton: Princeton University Press, 1963.

Garraty, John A. *The Great Depression.* New York: Harcourt Brace Jovanovich, 1986.

Germain-Martin, Louis. *Sommes-nous sur la bonne route?* Paris: Payot, 1934.

Gilbert, Seymour Parker, *Report of the Agent-General for Reparations Payments.* Berlin: Office for Reparation Payments, 10 December 1927.

Great Britain. *First Interim Report of the Commission on Currency and Foreign Exchanges After the War.* British Parliamentary Papers, Cd. 9182, 1918.

Hamilton, Richard. *Who Voted for Hitler?* Princeton: Princeton University Press, 1982.

Hawtrey, Ralph. *A Century of Bank Rate.* London: Longmans, Green, 1938.

Helfferich, Karl. *Money.* New York: The Adelphi Company (trans. Louis Infield), 1927.

Hoover, Herbert H. 'Lincoln Day Address, February 13, 1933.' *Commercial and Financial Chronicle* 136 (1933): 1136–8.

———. *Memoirs.* New York: Macmillan, 1952.

Hume, J. 'The Gold Standard and Deflation.' In *The Gold Standard and Employment Policies Between the Wars*, edited by Sidney Pollard, pp. 122–45. London: Methuen, 1970.

James, Harold. *The German Slump: Politics and Economics, 1924–1936.* Oxford: Clarendon Press, 1986.

Keynes, John Maynard. *The Economic Consequences of the Peace.* London: Macmillan, 1919.

———. *A Tract on Monetary Reform.* London: Macmillan, 1923.

———. *The General Theory of Employment, Interest and Money.* London: Macmillan, 1936.

Kuhn, Thomas S. *The Structure of Scientific Revolutions*, second edition. Chicago: University of Chicago Press, 1970.

Kunz, Diane B. *The Battle for Britain's Gold Standard in 1931.* London: Croom Helm, 1987.

May, E.R. *Lessons of the Past.* New York: Oxford University Press, 1973.

Moggridge, D. E. *The Return to Gold 1925.* Cambridge: Cambridge University Press, 1969.

———. *British Monetary Policy, 1924–31.* Cambridge: Cambridge University Press, 1972.

Mouré, Kenneth. *Managing the Franc Poincaré.* Cambridge: Cambridge University Press, 1991.

———. 'Undervaluing the Franc Poincaré.' *Economic History Review* 49 (1996): 137–53.

Mowat, Charles L. *Britain Between the Wars.* Chicago: University of Chicago Press, 1955.

Nixon, Edgar B, ed. *Franklin D. Roosevelt and Foreign Affairs,* January 1933-February 1934, Vol. I, Cambridge, MA: Harvard University Press, 1969.

Nurkse, Ragnar. *International Currency Experience.* Geneva: League of Nations, 1944.

Powell, Ellis T. *The Evolution of the Money Market.* London: The Financial News, 1915.

Robbins, Lloyd. *The Great Depression.* London: Macmillan, 1934.

Schuker, Stephen A. *The End of French Predominance in Europe.* Chapel Hill: University of North Carolina Press, 1976.

Snowden, Philip. *An Autobiography.* London: Nicholson and Watson, 1934.

Temin, Peter. *Lessons from the Great Depression.* Cambridge: MIT Press, 1989.

Vertzberger, Yaacov Y.I. 'Foreign Policy Decisionmakers as Practical Intuitive Historians: Applied History and its Shortcomings.' *International Studies Review* 30 (1986): 223–47.

Warren, Harris Gaylord. *Herbert Hoover and the Great Depression.* New York: Oxford University Press, 1959.

Wheelock, David C. *The Strategy and Consistency of Federal Reserve Monetary Policy, 1924–33.* Cambridge: Cambridge University Press, 1991.

White, Harry D. *The French International Accounts, 1880–1913.* Cambridge, MA: Harvard University Press, 1933.

Williamson, Philip. *National Crisis and National Government: British Politics, the Economy and Empire, 1926–1932.* Cambridge: Cambridge University Press, 1991.

Woytinsky, W.S. *Stormy Passage.* New York: Vanguard, 1961.

PART THREE
Welfare, Well-being and Individual Economic Security

The essays in this Part deal with the nexus of issues arising from modern economic growth's diverse and changing significance for individuals' sense of personal well-being and security, as well as from its differential impacts upon the levels of economic welfare experienced by individuals within the affected populations. Although the focus is upon key aspects of economic and social welfare policy in the developed economies, the discussion recognizes the implications of these issues for the developing world. Indeed, approaching these problems from an historical perspective enables one to appreciate better the different ways in which they affect societies at different levels of economic and demographic development.

The central questions the authors address involve matters of measurement as well as policy. How should we measure economic welfare? Is the traditional metric of national income adequate to capture the improvement (or deterioration) in the quality of life over time? If not, what areas of social infrastructure are revealed to be most relevant to the construction of human happiness? Is it possible, or indeed appropriate, to formulate policies that concentrate on these components rather than on the traditional aspiration of maximizing economic growth or even, as with an older branch of welfare empiricism, minimizing the social costs of growth.

Avner Offer's paper raises fundamental questions for evaluating social developments in past and present, and thinking about future possibilities. Offer notes that there is no single metric that should dominate our consideration of welfare. The design of appropriate measures is contingent on value judgements about what is good and bad, how to measure the strength of positive and negative elements, and how to balance them. Offer rehearses a number of alternative measures, all of which have one idea in common — the need to be more inclusive in measuring social welfare — even if they diverge in the direction, extent and evaluation of added components. Bads as well as goods matter. Moreover, more focus needs to be placed on the experience of individuals relative to the norm, rather than to the movement of some fictive average. Of course, as Offer recognizes, the idea of the norm is itself contingent. Every approximation to the social welfare function is a cultural construct, in which notions of what matters, why and to what extent they matter, are shaped and reshaped by history.

A striking result produced by Offer's survey of an array of 'alternative' welfare indicators, assembled for a number of modern societies observed during the latter half of the twentieth century, is their strong curvilinear relationship with measures of economic welfare such as GDP per capita: both international cross-section and time-series observations of average levels of self-avowed satisfaction (or 'human happiness') do not go on rising with increases in absolute average real income. There is, on the other hand, a strong positive association between individuals' relative income status within their own social and economic milieu, and the level of personal satisfactions or 'happiness' they report. Among the interpretations that can be placed on these findings, the relationship between human welfare and economic welfare can be read as being historically contingent. In an initial phase of economic growth, the elimination of basic deprivations and the satisfaction of basic needs yield high payoffs in terms of human satisfactions. But, eventually more GDP per person provides only diminishing or negligible gains in satisfaction, possibly because it is accompanied by increasing congestion and competition for scarce 'positional' goods, and because affluence brings an abundance of psychic rewards that induce habituation.

Recently, economic historians have sought to move beyond the empirical and normative limitations of national income measures of growth and welfare in past societies by making use of data that were gathered about the heights and weights of members of particular subgroups in the population. Two essays debate the benefits of reading these anthropometric measurements as indicators of human welfare. Roderick Floud, one of the pioneers of historical height analysis, argues that anthropometry remains a powerful tool of welfare measurement. Height disparities across and within populations suggest that there is something to be explained and that the gaps reflect divergences in patterns of nutrition and morbidity. When age-specific height is allied with age-specific weight observations, these may be formed into a body mass index (BMI) that is potentially a more revealing indicator; modern medico-physiological research has associated changes in the BMI with certain alterations in nutritional and health status.

Consistent with Offer's finding that economic growth creates diminishing marginal gains in economic welfare, BMI statistics suggest that the relationship between economic growth and individual social welfare is far from linear. Obesity is no less telling a social phenomenon than is stunting. Indeed, Tim Leunig and Hans-Joachim Voth argue that it is more informative, especially with regard to the general health status of the population. Since individuals have greater control over weight than height, BMI measures have the added advantage of being rooted in social and cultural consciousness. They can therefore be integrated into a more complex story, in which historical contingencies may play a more readily perceptible role.

These essays raise some important points of disagreement regarding the scope for future applications of anthropometric indicators. The divergences between the appraisals of Floud, on the one hand, and Leunig–Voth, on the other, turn in considerable part on whether or not the population whose condition is to be gauged has already passed into the stage of development where the effects of real further increases in real income are negligibly weak. But the authors of the two essays join in emphasizing that any meaningful comparisons among movements in anthropometric measures constructed for societies at widely separated points in time, or at different stages of economic development, need to be made with great caution. Account must be taken of the complex, non-linear nature of the relationships among those physical dimensions of the human condition and the population's command over material resources as measured by average levels of real income, and also changes both in levels of exposure to disease and the state of knowledge about how best to cope with the assaults incurred by the human immune system.

The consumption of health care offers yet another perspective on the complex relationship between economic growth and material welfare as that is mediated through the condition of the human body. Past or present, most people have preferred health to illness and 'fitness' to disability. Given these preferences (as close to universal cultural constants as can be found), people who perceive themselves to be afflicted with ill health will as a rule invest their time and money in seeking the aid of healers and medicines that are regarded by others in their social setting to be the most effective—at least the best forms of 'cure' to be had within their means. Of course, nothing in this assures that those health care choices will be as well informed as they might be, let alone efficacious.

Recently, in the developed, high-income societies, where 'scientific medicine' is widely considered to be clearly superior to all the alternative forms of health care, 'alternative medicine' has been gaining in popularity—particularly among middle- and upper-income consumers. The essay by Anne Digby and Sheila Ryan Johansson explores the significance of this trend, which on its face might appear somewhat paradoxical. To what extent should this growing interest in alternative forms of health care be interpreted as a 'retrograde' development, a manifestation of growing scepticism and even hostility to the dominance of science in modern society? In what respects might its continuation pose issues for public policy in the field of health care?

One such policy issue arises from the view of alternative medicine as lacking the scientific foundations of licensed medical practices, and therefore as posing special risks to those consumers who may be diverted from seeking 'proper' care, that is to say (putatively) more accurate diagnoses and more effectual therapeutic treatments. A rather different regulatory issue is raised by those who see the trend towards legitimizing 'alternative' forms of treatment for general consumption as having the potential to add new sets of claims to the ones already straining public health care systems, and to raise the costs of private health insurance.

Digby and Johansson offer a new perspective on these matters. Looking back to the European scene in the Middle Ages, they point out that the diagnoses and treatments offered by medical practitioners who based their procedures upon 'science' at that time were providing what was generally viewed to be a dubious, 'alternative' form of health care. It is not only the changing perceptions about the strengths and deficiencies of the alternative medical regimes that must be considered, but also the possibility that assessments of the relative importance of the two may undergo significant revisions. Several centuries later, when the superiority of what is today known as 'scientific medicine' had been broadly conceded, the practitioners of 'regular' medicine were still unable to treat successfully many of their patients' diseases, or to meet the particular individual needs of their individual patients—no matter what the amounts that they came prepared to spend.

Consequently, in Digby and Johansson's view, other (alternative) approaches to medical care survived in Western societies as a 'backup system' to scientific medicine. Sometimes it functioned to provide treatment for those who were unable to afford 'the best'. But increasingly, alternative medicine offered form(s) of care that addressed comparatively minor health problems which, although not life-threatening, nonetheless caused discomfort and otherwise diminished the patient's sense of well-being. By and large, the latter are conditions to which lower priority has been assigned by the medical establishment and health service authorities in the West, and which are typically treated at lower expense. The relationship between the two forms of medical care that presently exists in the developed economies therefore is judged by Digby and Johansson to be dominantly that of useful complements, rather than antithetical substitutes—despite the persistence of some professional tension between the two groups of medical practitioners.

In the developing world, to which their essay then turns, the prevailing situation is shown to be considerably more complicated. As a consequence of scientific medicine having been introduced into those societies both as a superior and as a foreign form of health care, its evaluation vis-à-vis 'traditional', indigenous practices of 'healing' became entangled with other contentious issues. In the ensuing cultural rivalry, the alien medical practices—being in some instances promoted and in others more coercively reinforced by the policies of Western colonial regimes—threatened to displace traditional medicine entirely.

The present policy problems regarding the place of indigenous medicine in these societies are not only enmeshed in their political and cultural histories, but are made more difficult to resolve by the extremely limited resources that these countries are able to devote to delivering modern ('scientific') medical care to their citizens. Programmes of that kind not only have to proceed under stringent financial constraints in these regions, but Digby and Johansson insist also that care be taken to avoid destroying respect for the traditional healers—if only because, for some time to come, it is they who will continue to offer the most affordable and readily accessible forms of health care for the mass of the population.

Part of the reason for the spread of complementary medicine in richer societies has been increasing longevity. Older persons may benefit more from the pain-reducing benefits of herbal medicines; palliative and hospice care also tend to be concentrated among the elderly. Elderly health care is, however, a clear example of the errors of assuming a generic model for all rich societies. Institutional structures, cultural heritage, and political realism produce different solutions to what is becoming increasingly a common policy issue world-wide — how to care for the elderly. Thus, in Britain, the rationing of many services for those over 60 or 65 is viewed as essential to the continued financial coherence of a state-run health care system; whereas in the United States, although health maintenance organizations (HMOs) doubtless would like to move in the same direction, they are constrained by the political will and power of the Gray Panthers. Nonetheless, in both countries, the elderly are the most expensive to care for and thus the ageing of their population creates financial and policy issues.

Mark Thomas and Paul Johnson argue that the problems of ageing, while not necessarily different in form now from in the past, are certainly different in scale and clearly demand new societal solutions. Old people are living longer, with higher expectations of quality as well as quantity of life, and will for the next thirty years grow as a share of total population. As age at voluntary retirement declines, financial pressures of paying for old age will intensify. The challenge for policymakers is to design a system that will allow sufficient flexibility to meet these financial challenges over the next generation within a system that has evolved over a century or more of history. A historical perspective makes it clear that past solutions are unlikely to provide much appeal to present or future generations; it also emphasizes the role of state institutions in constraining the range of possible solutions. A brief reading of the development of pension policy in Britain and the US shows not only that the state in each country has developed its own approach to financing old age, but also that over time these approaches have become entrenched and perhaps ossified, as institutional sclerosis abetted by political pressures has set in. It may well be that the problem of how to pay for old age can be solved with only minor changes in policy. Any such modifications, however, have to be consonant with public perceptions of the institution's traditional commitments — if only out of due recognition of the power of interest groups, and the politicians who cater to them, to derail any very ambitious reforms that would appear to break faith with previous generations of contributors.

Social welfare programmes and policies in much of the West are also under challenge at the start of the new century from another direction. Both within Europe and the United States there is negotiation of a new form of federalism. Curiously, the systems appear to be moving in opposite directions. In the US, the political resurgence of states' rights and the decline in the political power of the central state has led to a devolution of federal responsibilities for management of key components of the welfare state, under the slogan 'welfare reform'. In newly federalized Europe, however, the challenge is to develop policy structures that minimize differences across national boundaries. The ideology of a single labour market within the European Union, dependent on free labour mobility, is inconsistent with the persistence of different national welfare systems that have different rules of entitlement and differ in the generosity of the support they offer, and also in the obstacles they interpose to the trans-border portability of pensions and other benefits.

Peter Solar and Richard Smith's essay calls attention to the existence of forces that are tending to press towards the emergence of one or another among the extreme solutions for this problem—federalization of social welfare programmes or individualization of social welfare systems. But they also observe that national interests may militate against universal voluntary acceptance of either of those alternatives or, indeed, of a collective decision to create a harmonized system of benefits. The authors recall that an analogous situation existed in early modern England at the time that a national Poor Law policy was first established. The locus of jurisdiction in the English system was the parish, which had the effect of internalizing the costs and benefits of support for the needy within the local community, and minimized disaffection arising from the transfer of income to 'strangers'. There was a recognized need for measures that would encourage parishes to accept inflows of migrants who were attracted thither by opportunities for employment; and correspondingly to reduce the incentives for workers in labour-surplus parishes to remain there in order to retain their claim to local poor relief under the Act of Settlement.

Solar and Smith suggest that a modern-day counterpart to the solution that was found under the Old Poor Law regime would be something along the lines of a European 'welfare passport' that would facilitate transfers of support from the home countries of intra-EU emigrants. Such a scheme, they argue, would address the dual problems of welfare free-riding and impediments to labour mobility. But, as with the Old Poor Law, an institutional innovation of that kind would take time to develop into a reliably working system.

Although history might teach policy-makers the need for patience, its lessons also justify the conclusion that there are perils in delaying action until most if not all of the doubts and uncertainties surrounding alternative proposed responses to a pressing problem can be resolved. Making an early start along one or another line that preserves the flexibility needed to undertake subsequent corrective changes in policy direction would prevent the formation of vested interests in policy stasis and thereby offer the best hope of meeting the still more difficult economic challenges that will be faced in the century ahead.

12.
Economic Welfare Measurements and Human Well-being
AVNER OFFER

Introduction

Richard Easterlin asked memorably, 'Does Economic Growth Improve the Human Lot?'[1] This chapter suggests that 'it all depends—on history'. In 1948, a standard System of National Accounts (SNA) was adopted by the United Nations.[2] Its broad and rapid acceptance facilitated international and inter-temporal comparisons, and generated a competitive preoccupation with economic growth, which continues among economists and economic historians to the present day. Extended into the past, it allowed the measurement of modern economic growth back to its beginnings.[3] The primary purpose of the SNA was not to monitor human welfare, but to provide an efficient measure of cyclical changes in total economic activity. In that role it is an enduring success. Its persistence has some of the attributes of technological 'lock-in' and path-dependence. The same applies to its more problematic role as a welfare measure: during the 1950s and the 1960s, the output measure of GDP per head, or its annual rate of change, also became a normative benchmark for economic and even social performance, the higher the better.

The 'golden age' of 1950 to 1970 had barely taken off when the welfare value of economic growth began to be queried.[4] Books like John K. Galbraith's *The Affluent Society*, Vance O. Packard's *The Waste*

---

[1] Easterlin, 'Economic Growth'.
[2] Studenski, *Income of Nations*.
[3] For example with great authority by Charles Feinstein for the UK.
[4] Kapp, *Social Costs*.

Makers, David Riesman's *Abundance for What?* and E.J. Mishan's *The Costs of Economic Growth* sold well in the late 1950s and early 1960s. They were followed by the anti-materialist 'counter-culture' of the 1960s, and the anti-growth environmentalism of the 1970s. The discipline of economic history was also affected. In Britain, the 'pessimists' in the 'standard of living' debate argued that material improvement was compatible with a decline in well-being. In the United States, the debate on the economics of slavery suggested that efficiency was compatible with human degradation.

The debate on economic growth is usually regarded as an expression of conflicting values. But it might also be the case that the sources of human welfare are historically contingent. As the two decades of the post-war age (c. 1950–1970) came to an end, attention began to shift towards the costs of affluence, ecological, social and psychic. In the poorest of countries, priority was claimed for a set of basic needs over the sacrifices necessary for maximizing GDP. Hence, from the late 1960s onwards, the quest for alternatives to GDP as measures of welfare.

'Alternative' measurements of welfare have followed three approaches. The first involves 'extending' the national accounts, to incorporate non-market goods and services, and to eliminate detrimental components. A second approach identifies social norms, and evaluates their satisfaction by means of 'social indicators'. A third approach has targeted mental states directly, with surveys of reported subjective well-being, and research on the dynamics of hedonic experience. Cumulatively, these three approaches suggest that the pursuit of welfare is not always satisfied by economic growth alone, and may require different measures at different times.

Extended Accounts

The micro-economic foundations of the SNA are insecure. The obstacles to the measurement of economic welfare at the micro level are formidable. Much of the difficulty arises from the problem of disaggregation from market prices and quantities to household and to individual consumption.[5] Aggregating welfare upwards from individuals and households to the level of society is even less tractable. As

---

[5] Slesnick, 'Empirical Approaches'.

Amartya Sen puts it, 'personal real income theory translates readily into the theory of real national income [only] if the nation is viewed as a person.'[6] This 'welfarist' position, he says, is 'not outrageously realistic'. Since the nation is not a single person, a higher level of GNP might fail to deliver more 'welfare', even in the narrow utilitarian sense.

In the face of such doubts, the pervasive use of GDP per head as a social welfare measure is a puzzle. The assumption that society is a unitary actor does help to side-step some intractable problems: the difficulty of making interpersonal and intertemporal comparisons of welfare, of taking account of inequality, of compensating losers for Pareto improvements, and of evading Arrow's impossibility theorem. One explanation might be an assumption that underneath we are all pretty much the same, and share a repertoire of innate needs.[7] When SNA is defended as a measure of welfare, it is on pragmatic grounds, by pointing to positive correlations, often implicit ones, with social indicators such as health, life expectation, and education.[8] The unitary actor assumption also has a compelling appeal for international comparisons. And sometimes there is an *a priori* preference from doctrine or self-interest for market-friendly policies that can be justified as maximizing GDP.

Unlike the SNA, systems of 'extended accounts' are mostly designed to measure welfare. They start out with the SNA core, and make adjustments on consumption and capital accounts: they typically eliminate some commodities and services which are seen not as final goods in themselves, but as 'regrettable necessities'. Finally, they impute a value to sources of welfare from outside the market. Early estimates were produced in the late 1960s, by Kendrick and Sametz.[9] Nordhaus and Tobin's 'Measure of Economic Welfare' (MEW) of 1972 was very influential.[10] This measure eliminated 'regrettables', such as commuting, police, sanitation, road maintenance, defence and the

---

[6] Sen, 'Welfare', p. 36.
[7] Stigler and Becker, 'De Gustibus', pp. 76–7; Diener and Suh, 'Measuring Quality', pp. 445–6.
[8] Abramovitz, 'Retreat;' Dasgupta, *Inquiry*; Olson and Landsberg, *No-Growth Society*; Lebergott, *Pursuing Happiness*; Beckerman, *Defence*.
[9] Kendrick, 'Studies;' Sametz, 'Measurement'.
[10] Nordhaus and Tobin, 'Is Growth Obsolete?'

disamenities of urban life from total output. On the positive side, Nordhaus and Tobin imputed values for household production, and for time available for leisure.

Extended accounting of this and similar kinds has continued into the 1980s and the 1990s, and has included estimates for the United States, Britain, Europe and Australia. [11] Some of these contained retrospective historical accounts, going back to 1950 for Britain, 1869 for the United States, and all the way to 1788 for Australia.[12] These indices indicate that extended welfare has been positively correlated with GNP over the long run, though the actual growth rates have differed.[13]

The most compelling implication is that more welfare is derived from non-market than from market activities. Typically the imputed value of leisure equals or exceeds the value of GDP, and household production adds another 25 to 45 per cent. About two-thirds of output arise outside the market. This salience of non-commodities casts doubt on the welfarist assumption that all well-being can be priced. Leisure and housework dominate the index, and are relatively slow to change. Hence, the summary indicators are not much use for monitoring cyclical fluctuations.

Extended accounting relies heavily on the allocation of time. There is also a strand of research which takes time-use as the measure of welfare. This lends itself both to micro and to macro applications.[14] Gershuny and colleagues have been attempting to devise an encompassing system of accounting based on time use, with a wide international coverage, and going back to the early 1960s.[15]

The concept of sustainable consumption goes back to Hicks, who defined it as the maximum value of consumption which would leave the individual afterwards as well-off as before.[16] In their study of 1972, Nordhaus and Tobin attempted to estimate 'sustainable' welfare, which they took as consumption plus net investment.[17] They acknowledged the need to take account of the depletion of non-renewable natural

---

[11] Kendrick, 'Studies'; Zolotas, *Economic Growth*; Eisner, *Total Incomes*; Nordhaus, 'Reflections'; Beckerman, 'Comparable Growth'; Crafts, 'Thatcher Experiment'; Snooks, *Portrait*.
[12] Crafts, 'Thatcher Experiment'; Eisner, *Total Incomes*; Sametz, 'Measurement'; Snooks, *Portrait*.
[13] Nordhaus, 'Reflections'.
[14] Juster and Stafford, *Time*; Gershuny and Halpin, 'Time Use'; Robinson and Godbey, *Time for Life*; Schor, *Overworked American*.
[15] Gershuny et al., 'The Time Economy'.
[16] Hicks, *Value*, p. 172.
[17] Nordhaus and Tobin, 'Is Growth Obsolete'?

resources. This had been anticipated by Kapp in 1950, and several estimates were produced during the 1970s.[18] Weitzman provided theoretical underpinning: national product net of asset depletion also described the discounted sustainable productive potential of the economy.[19] A more normative and radical approach was pioneered by Zolotas in 1981. He incorporated pollution and natural resource depletion into a set of extended accounts for the United States for the period 1950 to 1975, and also imputed shadow costs to some social detriments.[20] His index of the economic aspects of welfare (EAW) rose progressively more slowly than GNP, and he envisaged a time, a generation hence, when an increment of GNP would produce no welfare at all. He argued that this was a systemic feature: 'beyond a certain point, economic growth may cease to promote social welfare. In fact, it would appear that, when an industrial society reaches an advanced state of affluence, the rate of increase in social welfare drops below the rate of economic growth, and tends ultimately to become negative.'[21]

Concern over inequality has motivated a good deal of the effort to devise measures of welfare.[22] Atkinson's influential index provided a measure for evaluating the effect of income inequality on welfare, which could be adjusted to the amount of inequality tolerated (or desired).[23] This has been applied to extended accounts by Beckerman, Crafts, and Jackson et al.[24]

After a hiatus in the 1980s, Daly and Cobb continued to develop the Zolotas model: they incorporated inequality (based on Gini coefficients) into a new measure, the Index of Sustainable Economic Welfare (ISEW).[25] This had the effect of depressing the index: inequality has worsened since the 1970s, and it offset the benefits of economic growth.[26] The principle of 'sustainability' in the rubric referred primar-

---

[18] Kapp, *Social Costs*; Kneese, *Economics*; Drechsler, 'Problems'; Meyer, 'Greening'.
[19] Weitzman, 'Welfare Significance'.
[20] Advertising, commuting, and 'corrrective' spending on health and education. Crime and divorce were also considered as bads, but kept out of the accounts.
[21] Zolotas, *Economic Growth*, p. 1.
[22] Another has been the measurement of household consumption; see Slesnick, 'Empirical Approaches'.
[23] Atkinson, 'Measurement'.
[24] Beckerman, 'Comparable Growth'; Crafts, *Economic Decline*, pp. 58–60; Jackson, *Economic Welfare*.
[25] Daly and Cobb, *Common Good*.
[26] Crafts, *Economic Decline*, pp. 58–60.

ily to the depletion of non-renewable resources. Daly and Cobb also removed the imputation for leisure time, on the grounds that it dominated the index and was conceptually unsound. It was this item mainly that had tended to offset the increase in inequality in less radical accounting exercises.[27] While GNP continued to grow, the American ISEW declined overall by about 25 per cent between the 1975 and 1990, and the British one by almost 50 per cent during the same period.[28] Later versions (Figure 1) show smaller declines. The innovation has caught on, and ISEW measures are available for Australia, Austria, Chile, Germany, Italy, the Netherlands, Sweden, the UK and the USA.[29] All except Italy record ISEW growth until the 1970s, with stagnation or decline afterwards. ISEW is explicitly normative, where SNA is only so implicitly. An American variant, the 'Genuine Progress Indicator', is bolder still, and introduces imputations for divorce and crime.[30] For all their defects, these measures are effective ways of articulating a normative position on economic change.

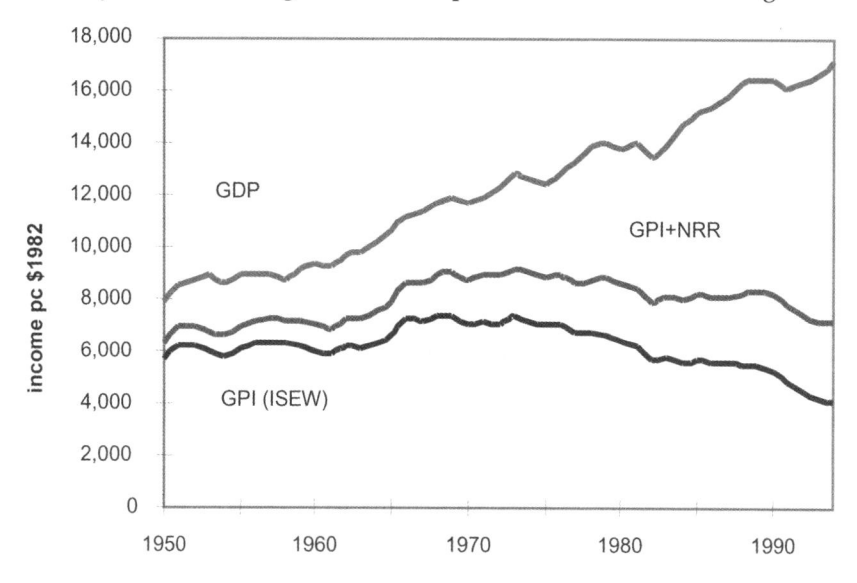

Figure 1. GNP and index of sustainable economic welfare (ISEW), USA 1950–c. 1995.

[27] Daly and Cobb, *Common Good*, pp. 412–13; Crafts, *Economic Decline*, compare Table 4, p. 20 and Table 17, p. 59.
[28] Cobb et al., *Progress Indicator*; Jackson and Marks, 'Economic Welfare'.
[29] Friends of the Earth, website.
[30] Cobb et al., *Genuine Progress*.

If we are to think of society as a unitary actor, then according to the ISEW, the growth in economic activity since the mid-1970s has been producing a *reduction* in aggregate welfare. Since the 1970s, from this perspective, the pursuit of further growth has been irrational. It is only myopia and habit which allow it to continue in the face of negative welfare returns. The problems of aggregation should be borne in mind, and the imputation of environmental depletion is open to criticism. For Britain, however, the inflection point remains even without this imputation.

Extended accounting is approaching official recognition. Following two decades of research and consultation, in its last revision of the SNA, the United Nations introduced guidelines for an optional set of 'satellite' environmental accounts, designed to integrate with the main core SNA.[31] 'Sustainability' has become a normative public policy objective in the UK.[32] This perspective of diminishing returns to economic growth is also captured in a different research programme, the measurement of normative social indicators.

Social Indicators

An abiding idea is that access to certain goods constitutes a precondition of welfare. Early examples in Britain were the Poor Law, compulsory primary education, and B.S. Rowntree's 'Poverty Line' of 1901. In the 1960s and early 1970s this approach re-emerged as the 'social indicators' movement. This was also inspired by the idea that real welfare was not captured by the SNA indicators.[33] Typically the goods in question consisted of nutrition, housing, education, health and life expectations, environmental quality, crime, and poverty levels. They might also include such objectives as the freedoms of movement, expression and political organization. Implicit in social indicators is some notion of adequacy: there is too little of some things, such as nutrition, housing or education; or too much of others, such as poverty, inequality or crime. Social indicators are rarely scaled in the metric of money, or set within an accounting framework.

---

[31] Meyer, 'Greening'.
[32] Great Britain, Department of Environment, *Sustainable Development*; and *Sustainability Counts*.
[33] Bauer, *Social Indicators*.

By the early 1970s, several leading countries and international bodies had published one-off or serial collections of social indicators.[34] This enterprise has not abated. Social indicators relied implicitly on a social-democratic consensus, with an egalitarian bias and a quest for social inclusion, as in the Scandinavian 'level of living' surveys.[35] But there was a lag between impulse and execution, and by the time social indicators were delivered, the impetus of social democracy was spent. Priorities for social expenditure had already been set in the 'golden age' period of expansion and the 1970s were a period of fiscal retrenchment. Social consensus swung away from equality and towards competition, from the left towards the right. The absence of a coherent accounting framework was another disadvantage.

In developing countries, deprivation was not relative but absolute. In the 1970s a 'basic needs' movement identified a bundle of goods that might claim priority over economic growth.[36] Morris argued that if encompassing was beyond reach, there was a virtue in parsimony. He introduced an unweighted 'Physical Quality of Life Index' (PQLI), made up of infant mortality, literacy and life expectation at age one, as a single measure of welfare.[37] Economic historians adopted the same principle by taking anthropometric measures, primarily heights, as a welfare index.[38]

What followed shows how social indicators not only depend on norms, but can also help to create them. The focus on basic needs came into conflict in the 1980s with the World Bank/IMF 'structural adjustment' policy, and with the increasing market orientation within development economics. The results of these programmes have been mixed, but the impression was that costs fell often disproportionately on the poor. In the late 1980s, dissatisfaction with the 'structural adjustment' programme inspired the creation of a new social indicator, the Human Development Index (HDI).[39] This is made up of income per head, life expectation at birth, and an education indicator, expressed in a single figure between 0 and 1. It has gained wide acceptance, and may have played some role in the partial retreat of the World Bank

---

[34] Terleckyj, *Quality of Life*.
[35] Nordic Council, *Living and Inequality*.
[36] Miles, *Human Development*, pp. 153–6.
[37] Morris, *Measuring the Condition*.
[38] Floud et al., *Nutritional Status*; Fogel, 'Economic Growth'. See also Floud, and Leunig and Voth, in this Volume.
[39] Desai, 'Human Development'.

and its acknowledgment of poverty as a policy objective.[40] Morris's updated index of 1996, which covered a longer time-span, also exposed the ambiguity of the links between growth and welfare.[41]

It is interesting to compare HDI and GNP with Sen's 'capabilities' approach, which has attracted a great deal of discussion. Sen moved from an axiomatic 'welfarist' position to the view that income alone does not satisfactorily capture welfare. In keeping with liberal values, he has not privileged any particular good. Even under indigence it was necessary to respect individual priorities.[42] Well-being constitutes having the 'capabilities' to achieve valuable 'functionings'. Both of these categories extend beyond the purely economic. Sen has not embodied his approach in any metrics, but it has influenced the Human Development Index. 'Alternative' approaches, especially Sen's capability/functioning approach, and the various 'sustainability' measures are congruent to some extent with non-utilitarian ethical frameworks — Eastern, Jewish, Greek, Christian, 'Enlightenment', Romantic — which teach that acquisitiveness may be self-defeating, and which highlight other welfare criteria: virtue, stoicism, altruism, approbation, self-realization.

The most compelling justification for the SNA as a measure of welfare is its correlation with social indicators which enjoy normative consensus as 'good things'. Hence, it is instructive to test the claims that this correlation exists. What such tests indicate is that the correlation is strong under conditions of indigence, but loses its power at surprisingly low levels of real income. In Figure 2, three such indicators are plotted against income per head. These are Morris's Physical Quality of Life Index (3 indicators), Estes' Index of Social Progress (36 indicators in 10 subgroups), and Slottje's Multidimensional Quality of Life Index.[43] All three suggest a strong diminution of welfare returns to income at around $2500–3000 US in 1981 prices. A logarithmic curve provides the best fit. The HDI already incorporates such a turning point in its premises, by including income per head in its arguments, with a diminishing return to incomes higher than the whole-sample average.

[40] World Bank, *Poverty Reduction*.
[41] Morris, 'Measuring the Quality'.
[42] Sen, 'Capability'.
[43] Morris, *Measurement*; Estes, *Social Progress*; Slottje, *Quality of Life*.

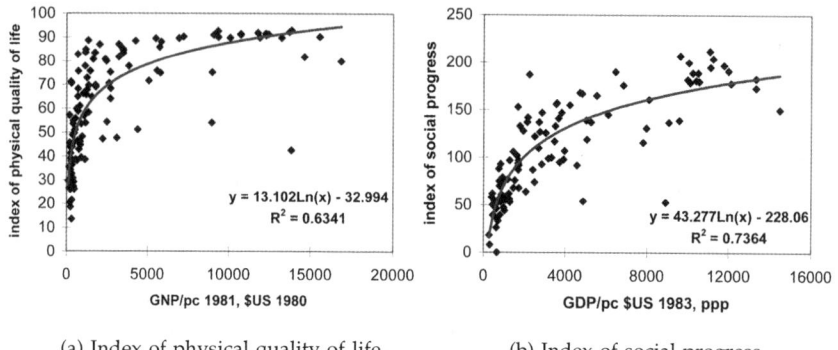

(a) Index of physical quality of life.

(b) Index of social progress.

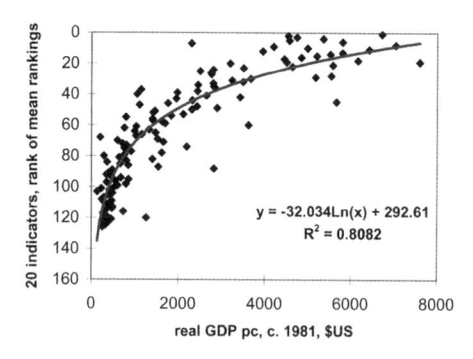

(c) Rankings of multidimensional quality of life index.

Figure 2. Social indicators and income per head, 1981, 1983. Selected countries.

Notes:
(a) Simple average of indices of infant mortality, literacy, and life expectation at age 1.
(b) Average of normalized indices of 10 domains, based on 36 indicators. The domains are: education, health, women's status, defence effort, economics, demography, geographic, participation, culture, and welfare effort.
(c) Index of 20 indicators for: political rights, civil liberty, household size, militarism, energy consumption, female and children labour participation rates, roads, telephones, life expectancy, infant mortality, medical services, nutrition, literacy, media access, GDP. Rank of mean rankings.

Sources:
(a) Morris, 'Measuring the Changing Quality'.
(b) Estes, *Trends in World Social Development*, Table A2, p. 186–8.
(c) Slottje et al., *Measuring the Quality of Life*, Table A. 2.2, pp. 96–9.

Table 1. Measures of the relation of welfare to income per head, c.1870–1973.

Welfare units per 1990 dollar of GDP per head, 1870–1973

	UK	USA	France	Germany
1870	1.2	1.8	2.2	2.0
1913	1.0	1.0	1.5	1.2
1950	0.9	0.7	1.1	1.5
1973	0.6	0.5	0.5	0.5

HDI* per 1990 dollar of GDP per head, 1870–1973

	UK	USA	France	Germany
1870	1.1	1.5	1.7	1.7
1913	1.0	0.9	1.3	1.2
1950	0.9	0.7	1.1	1.4
1973	0.6	0.5	0.6	0.6

Income Elasticity of Welfare Index

	UK	USA	France	Germany
1870–1913	0.5	0.3	0.4	0.3
1913–1950	0.7	0.3	0.2	0.9
1950–1973	0.3	0.1	0.1	0.1

Income Elasticity of HDI*

	UK	USA	France	Germany
1870–1913	0.7	0.4	0.6	0.5
1913–1950	0.8	0.6	0.6	2.2
1950–1973	0.3	0.3	0.3	0.2

Notes: Welfare index is made up of (% school enrolment+life expectation) 2. HDI* is the Human Development Index, with the income element untruncated. Index units multiplied by 100. The indices are bounded variables but are well short of the maxima even in 1973.
Source: Calculated from Crafts, 'Human Development Index'.

A visual examination of the figures indicates that some countries achieve very high levels of welfare indicators on very low incomes, and that others persist in low welfare indicators on high incomes. These three exercises in social indicators research echo the extended accounts findings of a curvilinear relation between income and welfare.

These data are cross-sections at one point in time. Similar patterns also appear to obtain over the long term. The contribution of economic growth to welfare may have been underestimated for the earlier periods of economic development, as has been noted by Crafts.[44] A corollary is that its contribution to welfare may be overestimated for the period of affluence. This is suggested by some very crude measures in Table 1. This table takes two measures of welfare, (a) an ad hoc welfare index made up of percentage school enrolment and life expectation,[45] and (b) the Human Development Index. For both measures, the corresponding purchasing power of a 1990 dollar and the income elasticity (in 1990 dollars) are calculated. In the four countries measured, there is a downwards trend in the welfare purchasing power of income over time, although the income elasticity of welfare tends to peak in the inter-war years. In brief, then, dollars deliver diminishing returns in simple welfare measures over time, as well as in the cross-section.

It could be argued that the simple development indices are misleading, in that the measures used are exhausted under affluence. Measures like HDI and PQLI are oriented strongly towards the priorities of indigence. The most extensive social indicators study so far puts this possibility to the test.[46] Easterly used a panel dataset of 81 indicators covering up to four time periods (1960, 1970, 1980 and 1990), in seven domains.[47] Each of these indicators was regressed on income per head, with fixed time effects. The criterion for robustness was an impact on the quality of life indicator that was significant, positive and more important than exogenous shifts. Exogenous shifts capture the effect of global socio-economic progress which may arise from the diffusion of knowledge or of norms. Three methods were used. In the first, all data were pooled, and only time effects were included in the regression. Thirty-two out of eighty-one indicators passed this test. When country fixed effects were added, the number of robust indicators fell to 10. With a first-differences IV estimator to establish causal effects, only 6 indicators survived out of 69. Three variables alone passed all three tests: calories per head, protein per head, and telephones per head. The first two, however, are known to be problematic

---

[44] Crafts, 'Human Development Index'.
[45] A more reliable measure than notional literacy, which peaks early in the process of development.
[46] Easterly, 'Life during Growth'.
[47] (1) rights and democracy (2) political stability and war (3) education (4) health (5) transport and communication (6) inequality, and (7) 'bads'.

once adequacy has been reached.[48] This comprehensive study confirms that the relationship of well-being and income per head is weak, both in cross-section and over time.

Association between health outcomes and economic status has long been observed within countries.[49] It is not entirely clear how much ill-being arises simply from material deprivation, and how much from the psychic costs of exclusion. There are good descriptive indicators of inequality, such as the Poverty Line, the Lorenz Curve, the Gini Coefficient, Atkinson's index and Pareto's alpha. What is lacking are standard, simple, social indicators of the *consequences* of inequality for affluent societies, an index of deprivation and detriment similar perhaps to the PQLI or HID. Such indices are currently under construction.[50] It is also possible, of course, that causation is not exclusively from low status/income to poor health, but also the other way round, from poor health to low status/income.

The HDI has the prestige of UN approval, is widely used and quoted, and has also been used retrospectively for historical evaluation.[51] The United Nations has now also laid down a standard for a 15-item 'minimum national social data set'.[52] But unlike HDI or PQLI, the components do not lend themselves to aggregation, indexation or a focal-point summary figure. These indicators are oriented towards development. They are essentially catch-up indices, calibrated to current best practice. They fail to address the original impulse of the social indicators movement, which was finding a way of measuring welfare in *affluent* societies; not only the welfare of the poor in those societies, but also of those who are working, healthy, and reasonably well-off. How does economic growth affect such people, and is it worth the cost?

---

[48] Offer, 'Body Weight'.
[49] Black et al., *Black Report*; Marmot, 'Social Differences;' Smith, 'Healthy Bodies;' Wilkinson, 'The Epidemiological Transition'.
[50] Index 99, 'Final Consultation'.
[51] Costa and Steckel, 'Trends in Health'; Crafts, *Economic Decline* and 'Development Index'.
[52] UN, 'Social Statistics'.

Psychological Indicators

Economic resources are not final goods, but intermediate ones. Pigou conceded that 'welfare consists of states of consciousness only and not material things', and Irving Fisher wrote, 'human beings are ever striving to control the stream of their psychic life by appropriating and utilizing the materials and forces of nature'.[53] From this viewpoint, to understand the economy, more needs to be known about the mind. Psychological approaches attempt to reach directly into the experience of welfare. They test the validity of the national accounting measure of welfare in two ways: 'static' measures estimate the correlation between SNA goods and psychological indicators of well-being. 'Dynamic' approaches probe deeper into the hedonics of satisfaction.[54]

Like 'human development', the static 'happiness' approach has also produced a measurement standard. This constitutes survey data on responses to a simple question about current subjective well-being on a bounded ordinal scale (1–3, 1–5, 1–7 or 1–10). One variant is the following survey question: 'Taking one thing with another, how would you describe your feeling today? Very satisfied, quite satisfied or not so satisfied?' The response to questions of this kind is known as 'Subjective Well-being' (SWB). The stock of surveys of this kind is very large. Some time series go back as far as the 1940s.[55] The indicator is crude, but this is not necessarily a defect. It has a defensible empirical validity.[56] A common theme in this literature is that levels of reported well-being are remarkably high in affluent societies. Those describing themselves as unhappy or very unhappy are typically fewer than 15 per cent.[57]

Richard Easterlin was originally impressed by an apparent lack of relation between country income levels and SWB.[58] This was challenged by Veenhoven, who identified a curvilinear relation, rather like the social indicators in Figure 2.[59] A recent comparison of countries was carried out by Diener et al. (Figure 3a).[60] They found that SWB

---

[53] Pigou, *Economics of Welfare*, p. 10; Fisher, *Interest*, p. 3.
[54] Kahneman et al., *Hedonic Psychology*.
[55] Veenhoven, *Database*.
[56] Veenhoven, 'Satisfaction Research'; Diener and Suh, 'Differences'.
[57] Veenhoven, 'Study', Table 2, p. 26.
[58] Easterlin, 'Does Economic Growth?'
[59] Veenhoven, 'Is Happiness Relative?'
[60] Diener et al., 'Factors Predicting'.

rose moderately but significantly with income, with a large variance, of which 37 per cent was explained. Subsequent analysis of the same data indicated an inflection point at the 75th percentile: above that level, income did not provide any increment to subjective well-being.[61] But cross-sections do not establish convergence over time. In fact, for the United States, France and Japan, SWB changed hardly at all since 1946, over a period in which real incomes per head have more than doubled (Figure 3b).[62]

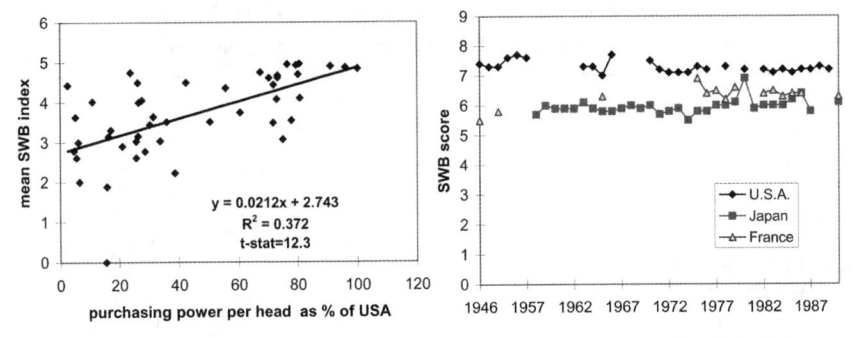

(a) SWB and income, cross-section, early 1990s. (b) SWB over time, USA, France, Japan. Scale 0 to 10.5 is neutral midpoint.

Figure 3. Subjective well-being, income and time. Selected countries.
Sources:
(a) Diener et al., 'Factors Predicting', Table 1, p. 856.
(b) Diener and Suh, 'Measuring Quality of Life', Table 1, p. 211.

This result has been confirmed by surveys of SWB at the individual level. SWB has been correlated with an array of socio-economic determinants and domains. This approach was first applied in cross-section on an American national sample in the early 1970s.[63] The predictive power of each individual determinant of global well-being was low, and even all of them together accounted for only about half of the variance. Income on its own counted little for happiness, and the relation is again curvilinear: the effect is stronger at lower incomes. The positive effect of income is stronger in cross-section than over time. A large longitudinal study in the United States found a very modest relation of income to well-being ($r=0.12$), with a curvilinear form, flattening out at

---

[61] Diener and Suh, 'Differences', Fig. 22.1.
[62] Diener et al., 'Income and Subjective Well-Being'; 'Predicting Subjective Well-Being'; 'Quality of Life'; Blanchflower and Oswald, 'Well-Being'.
[63] Campbell et al., Quality.

about $6000–8000 (1971 to 1975).[64] Interestingly, a rise of income over time for particular individuals produced no improvement at all in well-being. Among the determinants of SWB, the quality of relationships, of leisure and of work experience counted considerably more for aggregate well-being than income and consumption measures.[65] Materialism, a preoccupation with economic well-being, was negatively correlated with SWB, and especially so in those who believe that more money would make one happier.[66]

Table 2. Happiness in the United States (ordered probit), 1972–1994.
Dependent variable = Reported Happiness on a three-point scale. N=26,668.

Variable	Coeff.	Std.error
Unemployed	−0.379	0.041
Self-employed	0.074	0.023
Male	−0.125	0.016
Age	−0.021	0.003
Age squared	2.77E−04	3.00E−05
Education: High school	0.091	0.019
Associate/Junior college	0.123	0.04
Bachelor's	0.172	0.027
Graduate	0.188	0.035
Marital status: Married	0.38	0.026
Divorced	−0.085	0.032
Separated	−0.241	0.046
Widowed	−0.191	0.037
No. of children: 1	−0.112	0.025
2	−0.074	0.024
3 or more	−0.119	0.024
Income quartiles: Second	0.161	0.022
Third	0.279	0.023
Fourth (highest)	0.398	0.025
Retired	0.036	0.031
School	0.176	0.055
At home	0.005	0.023
Other	−0.227	0.067

Source: Di Tella et al., 'Macroeconomics of Happiness', Table 3, p. 20.

---

[64] Diener et al., 'Income and Subjective Well-Being'.
[65] Campbell et al., *Quality*, p. 80; Levy and Guttman, 'Multivariate Structure'; Argyle, 'Causes and Correlates', pp. 356–9; Headey and Wearing, *Understanding Happiness*, pp. 78–9.
[66] Ahuvia and Friedman, 'Macromarketing Model', pp. 154, 161.

The determinants of SWB have more recently been investigated on very large samples over time, in both the United States and in Europe.[67] The findings are consistent with previous ones. They show little variation of SWB over time. Absolute income counts for little but relative income (that is position in the ladder of earnings) has significant influence on well-being, from the second quartile upwards. Misery, that is strong negative divergences from the reference case (white, married, female, employed), is caused primarily by three conditions: non-white race, unemployment and non-marriage. There are also a number of consistent but weaker effects, such as age (U-shaped). Gender makes no difference. In the European sample there are also very strong country effects. The magnitude of the coefficients is remarkably similar from one large sample to another, which indicates that however crude SWB is as a measure of well-being, its components are surprisingly robust. Table 2 is typical.

The positive cross-sectional correlation of income and SWB *within* countries has long suggested a link from static to dynamic approaches, and to the 'relative income hypothesis', which states that what counts is not absolute income, but relativities.[68] From this point of view, even a large rise in income will leave no impact on well-being, if distribution is unchanged. For example, the large rise in American, French and Japanese incomes since the war has hardly changed their SWB scores (Figure 3b). The reason for this, it is argued, is that as incomes increase, so do consumption norms.[69] Consumers become habituated to new levels of consumption. Scitovsky reviewed psychological research on arousal and habituation to probe the dynamics of diminishing returns,[70] and questioned whether American acquisitiveness was in fact increasing welfare. The Dutch 'Leyden Approach' to welfare research has also found that the welfare increment declines substantially as income increases. Earning norms drift up with income, though not all the way. A more vivid metaphor, which applies to all three measurement approaches to welfare, is the 'hedonic treadmill': income has to rise in order to sustain satisfaction at a constant level.[71]

---

[67] Di Tella et al, 'Macroeconomics of Happiness;' Blanchflower and Oswald, 'Well-Being'.
[68] Duesenberry, *Consumer Behavior*; Hirsch, *Limits to Growth*.
[69] Easterlin, 'Raising the Incomes'.
[70] Scitovsky, *Joyless Economy*.
[71] Van Praag and Fritjers, 'Measurement of Welfare'; Coleman et al., *Social Standing*, ch. 17; but see Diener et al., 'Income and Subjective Well-Being', 'Predicting Subjective Well-Being'.

The World Values Survey permits a cross-sectional test of the importance of the effect on subjective well-being of relative and absolute income. Figure 3 indicates that in the cross-section absolute income is quite highly correlated with subjective well-being scores. But the same dataset also makes it possible to distinguish whether it is relative or absolute income that produces well-being.

The three waves of this survey (in the early 1980s, and early and mid-1990s, covering forty-six countries in all) record both relative and absolute income levels. The effect of income on subjective well-being was analysed in regressions with a very large sample of 87,806 observations, which included a maximum of 38 variables (some of them sub-categories). It was found that both absolute and relative income delivered strongly diminishing returns of well-being. Taking relative incomes first, for an individual to move from the fourth to the fifth income decile raised well-being by 0.11 units, but from the ninth to the tenth, only 0.02 units, although in absolute terms the latter was the much larger increase. Comparing absolute income internationally, a 10 per cent increase in per capita incomes at half the US level would increase average individual well-being by only 0.0003 of the same units, while net gains became zero before US levels were achieved.[72]

The low responsiveness of well-being to income under affluence may arise because people are simply born happy or unhappy, and most are happy already. Longitudinal studies indicate that personality is a strong predictor of SWB.[73] One review concludes that happiness is more a trait than a state.[74] A study of separated identical twins suggests that neither social and economic status, educational attainment, family income, marital status nor religious commitment could account for more than three per cent of the variance in 'happiness'. About half the variance was associated with genetic variation. Subsequent re-testing suggested that about 80 per cent of the stable element in well-being was heritable.[75]

Culture provides another element of stability. Affluent industrial societies with similar levels of income per head report very different levels of subjective well-being, with a gradient coming down from the Nordic countries, which have very high levels, the English-speaking

---

[72] Helliwell, How's Life?', pp. 15–16.
[73] Headey and Wearing, *Understanding Happiness*, pp. 84–5.
[74] Stones et al., 'Happiness.'
[75] Lykken and Tellegen, 'Happiness'; Stones et al., 'Happiness', p. 135.

countries at an intermediate level, the Catholic middle and south of Europe lower still, and Japan lowest of all.[76] Inglehart regards this gradient as representing an adaptation or adjustment to affluence. He classifies societies on two value orientation dimensions, the pursuit of economic security and deference to traditional authority. As societies become more affluent, they move gradually away from both. This implies that the experience of affluence reduces concerns about economic security, and that culture adapts, albeit slowly, to changes in economic endowment.[77]

In affluent societies, culture appears to affect SWB more strongly than income. Japan and Australia had comparable incomes per head in the early 1990s but Australia scored an SWB of 1.02 (mean of 60 countries at 0), with Japan at the other end of the affluent country distribution, at −.86. Once controlled for 'individualism', the correlation of income and SWB disappeared.[78] This suggests that the hedonic ideal of individual welfare, utility or happiness might be an ethnocentric cultural construct that is peculiarly Nordic, Anglo-Saxon or Protestant. European surveys of SWB over time have produced very large country coefficients.[79] The long-term persistence of SWB scores in particular countries even brings to mind the idea of 'national character'.

An early inspiration of the social indicators movement was the 1960s 'rediscovery of poverty', which redefined it as a relative rather than absolute form of deprivation. Easterlin has hypothesized that expectations are formed by comparisons with parents, and that demographic cycles mean that (in the United States, at least, since World War II) different cohorts have different expectations.[80] Satisfaction has moved pro-cyclically for young adults, with those of the 'golden age' exceeding their own modest expectations, while the successor 'baby boom' having its higher expectations disappointed. A related perspective is Inglehart's long-standing study of 'post-materialism'. The argument here is that the post-war cohorts have shifted their preferences from economic to non-economic rewards, as a result of their experience of economic security.[81]

---

[76] Inglehart et al., *Human Values*, Table V18.
[77] Inglehart, *Modernization*, ch. 3.
[78] Diener et al., 'Factors Predicting', pp. 860–2.
[79] Di Tella et al., 'The Macroeconomics of Happiness.'
[80] Easterlin, *Birth and Fortune*.
[81] Inglehart, *Modernization*.

A different psychological approach is to investigate the hedonic dynamics of satisfaction. In welfare economics, it is assumed axiomatically that the consumer is well-informed, self-aware, consistent and acquisitive. These assumptions are necessary if 'revealed preference' is to equal welfare.[82] Other approaches do not have such confidence in the cognitive abilities of the consumer. That individual choice might fail to maximize welfare is an old but neglected theme in welfare discourse. The Victorians distinguished between the deserving poor, who had suffered from adversity, and the feckless and undeserving, who had brought about their own misfortune. B.S. Rowntree made a distinction between 'primary poverty', which was caused by the shortfall of subsistence resources, and 'secondary poverty', caused by impulsive consumption and poor resource management.[83] This is brought out by the difference between a 'social indicator' poverty line, which focuses on normative consumption, and a money metric one, which merely measures access to resources. Economists committed to rational choice might regard 'secondary poverty' as reflecting legitimate lifestyle choices.[84]

Empirical research into the determinants of choice queries the empirical validity of the axioms of rationality. This is not very damaging to SNA welfare measures, since, as we have seen, their microfoundations are already insecure. These lines of research have not so far provided direct measures of the validity of welfare aggregation, but rather implicitly query the premises of consumer sovereignty. This effort has highlighted a sequence of systematic and recurrent deviations from normative optimizing choice behaviour.[85] The most robust ones appear to be asymmetric valuation of gains and losses, and the 'endowment effect' by which goods increase their value once they have entered into possession. If correct, these findings cast further doubt on the possibility of compensating losers, and on the notion of 'opportunity cost'. Research in the hedonics of satisfaction continues. It stresses that satisfaction depends on habituation, anchoring, contrast and temporal effects; that the experience of satisfaction varies with time, and changes between decision, experience and retrospection.[86]

---

[82] Sen, 'Income Comparisons'.
[83] Rowntree, *Poverty*, ch. 5.
[84] Hagenaars et al., 'Patterns of Poverty', p. 26.
[85] Rabin, 'Psychology'.
[86] Kahneman, 'Objective Happiness', pp. 14–21.

Under affluence, SWB appears buoyant and quite stable, and responds quite sluggishly to economic indicators, both stagnation and growth. It is poorly correlated with income in affluent societies, and highly correlated in poor countries, confirming the diminishing returns to income detected in social indicators research.[87] Both extended accounting and static psychological indicators suggest that well-being is derived to a great extent *outside* the market, from human relations in the workplace, the family, and from other forms of attachment. The psychic payoff of rising absolute income is small, but gains from relative income are considerable. There are high levels of satisfaction with stable attributes such as personality, gender and nationality. Stability and habituation appear to promote well-being.

This also suggests that novelty may undermine it. New rewards are compelling, while their costs are not yet known. Economic competition is driven by novelty and innovation, which stimulate myopic rather than informed choices. In the absence of prior experience, new forms of stimulation are highly compelling. Innovation devalues existing prudential conventions and norms, and is to that extent destructive of existing psychic and social capital. Diener found that SWB is inversely related to the pace of economic growth.[88] Cheap alcohol, drugs, tobacco and fast food are all innovations which it has taken society decades to adjust to and cope with.

Conclusion

'Alternative' measures of welfare provide a great variety of indicators, in cross-section and over time, international, intra-national and individual. A common pattern emerges: the relation of economic welfare and welfare overall is historically contingent. They all suggest a curvilinear relationship between economic welfare and human welfare. Using extended accounting and social indicators, international comparisons suggest an historical cycle of two periods. In the first, economic growth provides high welfare payoffs, as basic deprivations are remedied and basic needs are satisfied. In the second phase, GDP goods provide diminishing, steady or even negative returns, depending on the measure used. This pattern can be fitted to different curvilinear curves.

---

[87] Veenhoven, 'Satisfaction Research', p. 25.
[88] Diener et al, 'Income and Subjective Well-Being'; 'Predicting Subjective Well-Being'.

A logistic curve model was first proposed by Xenophon Zolotas in 1981. He described three phases in the relation of income and welfare—of privation, steady improvements and declining ones, respectively.[89] More graphic metaphors might be the economy of deprivation and the economy of satiation; or the economy of pain followed by the economy of pleasure. For social indicators the logarithmic curve relation of welfare to income provides a good fit. The three studies presented in Figure 2, as well as the HDI, all have in common the initial steep rise, followed by an increasingly flat trajectory.

Subjective individual welfare also follows a similar log-normal or power curve response to economic welfare.[90] The cross-sectional international comparative relation of subjective well-being with income is positive, linear and fairly weak; it disappears when controlled for relative income. The temporal relation for individual countries is almost completely flat. This is consistent with low psychic welfare returns to rising economic growth, the classic 'hedonic treadmill'.

If it is true that GDP goods and services have delivered and are delivering diminishing welfare returns, the question is: Why? It is premature to attempt to answer it here, but a few observations might be ventured. Both ecological and psychological approaches have one notion in common, namely that affluence produces congestion. In both cases, the affluent economy produces more than it can absorb. The ecology cannot absorb the extra energy, the extra traffic, the extra pollution, without incurring costs that equal or exceed the benefits. Likewise, the abundance of psychic reward under affluence leads to satiation and habituation. These are simple-minded metaphors that require much greater analysis and empirical study.

But policy cannot wait. Alternative accounting of welfare is pragmatically motivated, and even at this stage, it has some implications for policy:

(a) In the most advanced economies, the increased supply of GDP goods and services is not the highest priority.
(b) For policy to find a coherent focus, it requires a better understanding of hedonic dynamics.

---

[89] Zolotas, *Economic Growth*, Fig. 1, p. 16.
[90] Kahneman, 'Objective Happiness', p. 17; van Praag and Frijters, 'Measurement', pp. 419–20.

High levels of well-being are already pervasive, and it is manifestly difficult to improve them much further by raising incomes overall. What is needed is a more systematic targeting of *ill-being*, its determinants, and the economic costs of its amelioration, to make the reduction of ill-being the focus of international competition: of such things as life expectation, material deprivation, the prevalence of crime and the severity of punishment, ethnic, social and political exclusion and repression, family structure and breakdown, mental health, suicide, morbidity, education, quality of working life, job security, access to health care, urban congestion and sprawl, and perhaps also of the quality of personal and social interaction.[91] It might be more useful to shift the focus of measurement from happiness to unhappiness. There is a view that ill-being does not belong on the same dimension as well-being.[92] 'Prospect theory' argues that losses are more acutely experienced than gains. Unemployment and discrimination have a more powerful effect on well-being than material gains.[93] It may be easier to reach consensus about welfare bads than about welfare goods.

This does not mean that GNP goods have lost their relevance permanently. A society dependent on exponential growth for a stable experience of well-being might suffer badly if growth is withdrawn. Many societies have yet to arrive at that state of abundance, and can still anticipate large welfare returns to growth, and a shift away from GDP goods towards leisure or short-term gratification might eventually return us to the economy of pain. Longer life expectation, high dependency rates and shorter working lives suggest that material scarcity could be a problem in the future as much as in the past. In other words, we should recognize the possibility that the determinants of human well-being are themselves historically contingent. How contingent? This is one of the challenges for economics and history in the twenty-first century.

---

[91] Doyal and Gough, *Human Need*.
[92] Bradburn, *Psychological Well-Being*; Diener and Emmons, 'Positive Affect'.
[93] Campbell et al, *Quality*, Fig. 2–5, pp. 52–3; Blanchflower and Oswald, 'Well-Being', p. 20.

References

Abramovitz, Moses. 'The Retreat from Economic Advance: Changing Ideas about Economic Progress.' In *Progress and its Discontents*, edited by Gabriel Almond, Marvin Chodorow and Roy Harvey Pearce, 253–79. Berkeley: University of California Press, 1982.

Ahuvia, Aaron C. and Douglas C. Friedman. 'Income, Consumption, and Subjective Well-Being: Toward a Composite Macromarketing Model.' *Journal of Macromarketing* 18, no. 2 (1998): 153–68.

Ainslie, George. *Picoeconomics: The Interaction of Successive Motivational States within the Person*. Cambridge: Cambridge University Press, 1992.

Argyle, Michael. 'Causes and Correlates of Happiness.' In *Well-Being: The Foundations of Hedonic Psychology*, edited by Daniel Kahneman, Ed Diener and Norbert Schwartz, 353–73. New York: Russell Sage Foundation, 1999.

Atkinson, Anthony B. 'On the Measurement of Inequality.' *Journal of Economic Theory* 2, no. 3 (1970): 244–63.

Bauer, Raymond A., ed. *Social Indicators*. Cambridge, Mass.: MIT Press, 1966.

Beckerman, Wilfred. *In Defence of Economic Growth*. London: Jonathan Cape, 1974.

———. 'Comparable Growth Rates of "Measurable Economic Welfare": Some Experimental Calculations.' In *Economic Growth and Resources*, vol. 2, edited by R.C.O. Matthews, 36–59. London: Macmillan, 1980.

———. 'Is Economic Growth Still Desirable?' In *Explaining Economic Growth: Essays in Honour of Angus Maddison*, edited by Adam Szirmai, Bart van Ark, and Dirk Pilat, 77–100. Amsterdam: North-Holland, 1993.

Becker, Gary S. and Casey B. Mulligan. 'The Endogenous Determination of Time Preference.' *Quarterly Journal of Economics* 112, no. 3 (1997): 729–58.

Black, Sir Douglas, Margaret Whitehead, Peter Townsend, et al. *Inequalities of Health: The Black Report*. Harmondsworth: Penguin Books, 1988.

Blanchflower, David G. and Andrew J. Oswald. 'Well-Being Over Time in Britain and the USA.' NBER Working Paper no. 7487, 2000.

Bradburn, Norman M. *The Structure of Psychological Well Being*. Chicago: Aldine, 1969.

Campbell, Angus, Philip E. Converse and Willard L. Rodgers. *The Quality of American Life: Perceptions, Evaluations, and Satisfactions*. New York: Russell Sage Foundation, 1976.

Clark, Andrew E. and Andrew J. Oswald. 'Unhappiness and Unemployment.' *Economic Journal* 104 (1994): 648–59.

Cobb, Clifford, Ted Halstead and Jonathan Rowe. *The Genuine Progress Indicator: Summary of Data and Methodology*. San Francisco: Redefining Progress, 1995.

Coleman, Richard P., Lee Rainwater and Kent A. McClelland. *Social Standing in America: New Dimensions of Class*. London: Routledge & Kegan Paul, 1979.

Costa, Dora L. and Richard H. Steckel. 'Long-Term Trends in Health, Welfare, and Economic Growth in the United States.' In *Health and Welfare During Industrialization*, edited by Richard H. Steckel and Roderick Floud, 47–90. Chicago: University of Chicago Press, 1997.

Crafts, Nicholas, F.R. 'Was the Thatcher Experiment Worth It? British Economic Growth in a European Context.' In *Explaining Economic Growth: Essays in Honour of Angus Maddison*, edited by Adam Szirmai, Bart van Ark and Dirk Pilat, 301–26. Amsterdam: North-Holland, 1993.

———. *Britain's Relative Economic Decline 1870–1995: A Quantitative Perspective*. London: Social Market Foundation, 1997.

———. 'The Human Development Index and Changes in Standards of Living: Some Historical Comparisons.' *European Review of Economic History* 1, no. 3 (1997): 299–322.

Daly, H. and J. Cobb. *For the Common Good: Redirecting the Economy Towards Community, the Environment, and a Sustainable Future*. London: Green Print, 1989.

Dasgupta, Partha. *An Inquiry into Well-Being and Destitution*. Oxford: Clarendon Press, 1993.

Dasgupta, Bilplab. *Structural Adjustment, Global Trade and the New Political Economy of Development*. London: Zed Books, 1998.

Desai, Megnhad. 'Human Development: Concepts and Measurement.' *European Economic Review* 35 (1991): 350–7.

Diener, Ed, and Robert A. Emmons. 'The Independence of Positive and Negative Affect.' *Journal of Personality and Social Psychology* 47, no. 5 (1985): 1105–17.

Diener, Ed, Ed Sandvik, Larry Seidlitz, et al. 'The Relationship between Income and Subjective Well-Being: Relative or Absolute?' *Social Indicators Research* 28 (1993): 195–223.

Diener, Ed, Marissa Diener and Carol Diener. 'Factors Predicting the Subjective Well-Being of Nations.' *Journal of Personality and Social Psychology* 69, no. 5 (1995): 851–64.

Diener, Ed, and Eunkook Suh. 'Measuring Quality of Life: Economic, Social and Subjective Indicators.' *Social Indicators Research* 40, no. 1–2 (1997): 189–216.

———. 'National Differences in Subjective Well-Being.' In *Well-Being: The Foundations of Hedonic Psychology*, edited by Daniel Kahneman, Ed Diener and Norbert Schwartz, 434–50. New York: Russell Sage Foundation, 1999.

Di Tella, Rafael, Robert J. MacCulloch and Andrew J. Oswald. 'The Macroeconomics of Happiness.' LSE Centre for Economic Performance, The Labour Market Consequences of Technical and Structural Change, Discussion Paper no. 19, 1997.

Doyal, Len and Ian Gough. *A Theory of Human Need*. Basingstoke: Macmillan Education, 1991.

Drechsler, L. 'Problems of Recording Environmental Phenomena in National Accounting Aggregates.' *The Review of Income and Wealth* 22 (1976): 239–52.

Duesenberry, James S. *Income, Saving, and the Theory of Consumer Behavior.* Cambridge, Mass.: Harvard University Press, 1949.

Easterlin, Richard A. 'Does Economic Growth Improve the Human Lot? Some Empirical Evidence.' In *Nations and Households in Economic Growth: Essays in Honor of Moses Abramowitz*, edited by Paul David and Melvin W. Reder, 89–125. New York: Academic Press, 1974.

――――. *Birth and Fortune.* London: Grant McIntyre, 1980.

――――. 'Will Raising the Incomes of All Increase the Happiness of All?' *Journal of Economic Behavior and Organization* 27 (1995): 35–47.

Easterly, William. 'Life During Growth.' *Journal of Economic Growth* 4, no. 3 (1999): 239–76.

Eisner, Robert. *The Total Incomes System of Accounts.* Chicago: University of Chicago Press, 1989.

Elster, Jon. *Ulysses and the Sirens: Studies in Rationality and Irrationality.* Revised edn. Cambridge: Cambridge University Press, 1984.

Estes, Richard J. *Trends in World Social Development: The Social Progress of Nations, 1970–1987.* New York: Praeger, 1988.

Fisher, Irving. *The Theory of Interest as Determined by Impatience to Spend Income and the Opportunity to Invest It.* New York: Macmillan, 1930.

Floud, Roderick, Kenneth W. Wachter and Annabel Gregory. *Height, Health and History: Nutritional Status in the United Kingdom, 1750–1980.* Cambridge: Cambridge University Press, 1990.

Fogel, Robert W. 'Economic Growth, Population Theory, and Physiology: The Bearing of Long-Term Processes on the Making of Economic Policy.' *American Economic Review* 84, no. 3 (1993): 369–95.

Friends of the Earth website, http://www.foe.org.uk/progress/

Galbraith, John Kenneth. *The Affluent Society.* Boston: Houghton Mifflin, 1958.

Gershuny, Jonathan, Sally Jones and Patrick Baert. 'The Time Economy or The Economy of Time: An Essay on the Interdependence of Living and Working Conditions.' Unpublished typescript, Universities of Oxford and Bath, 1991.

Gershuny, J., and B. Halpin. 'Time Use, Quality of Life, and Process Benefits.' In *In Pursuit of the Quality of Life*, edited by A. Offer, 188–210. Oxford: Oxford University Press, 1996.

Great Britain, Department of the Environment. Government Statistical Service. *Indicators of Sustainable Development for the United Kingdom.* London: HMSO, 1996.

――――. *Sustainability Counts: Consultation Paper on a Set of 'Headline' Indicators of Sustainable Development.* 1998.

Hagenaars, Aldi, Klaas de Vos and Ashgar Zaidi. 'Patterns of Poverty in Europe.' In *The Distribution of Welfare and Household Production*, edited by Stephen P. Jenkins, Arie Kapetyn and Bernard M.S. van Praag, 25–49. Cambridge: Cambridge University Press, 1998.

Headey, Bruce and Alex Wearing. *Understanding Happiness: A Theory of Subjective Well-Being.* Melbourne: Longman Cheshire, 1992.

Helliwell, John F. 'How's Life? Combining Individual and National Variables to Explain Subjective Well-Being.' NBER Working Paper no. 9065, July 2002.

Hicks, John. *Value and Capital*. Oxford: Oxford University Press, 1946.

Hirsch, Fred. *Social Limits to Growth*. London: Routledge & Kegan Paul, 1977.

Index 99 team with Clive Payne and David Firth. 'Final Consultation: Report for Formal Consultation Stage 2: Methodology for an Index of Multiple Deprivation.' Unpublished paper, University of Oxford, 1999.

Inglehart, Ronald. *Modernization and Postmodernization: Cultural, Economic, and Political Change in 43 Societies*. Princeton: Princeton University Press, 1997.

Inglehart, Ronald, Miguel Basáñez and Alejandro Moreno. *Human Values and Beliefs: a Cross-Cultural Sourcebook: Political, Religious, Sexual, and Economic Norms in 43 Societies; Findings from the 1990–1993 World Value Survey*. Ann Arbor: University of Michigan Press, 1998.

Jackson, Tim and Nic Marks. *Measuring Sustainable Economic Welfare — A Pilot Index, 1950–1990*. Stockholm: Stockholm Environment Institute, 1994.

Jackson, T., N. Marks, J. Ralls, et al. *Sustainable Economic Welfare in the UK, 1950–1996*. London: New Economics Foundation, 1997.

Juster, F. Thomas and Frank P. Stafford, eds. *Time, Goods and Well-being*. Ann Arbor, Michigan: Survey Research Center, Institute for Social Research, University of Michigan, 1985.

Kahneman, Daniel, Ed Diener and Norbert Schwart, eds. *Well-Being: The Foundations of Hedonic Psychology*. New York: Russell Sage Foundation, 1999.

Kapp, K.W. *The Social Costs of Private Enterprise*. Cambridge, Mass: Harvard University Press, 1950.

Kendrick, J. 'Studies in the National Income Accounts.' National Bureau of Economic Research, *47th Annual Report*, 1967.

Kneese, A. V., R.Y. Ayres and R.C. d'Arge. *Economics and the Environment: A Material Balances Approach*. Washington, DC: Resources for the Future, 1970.

Lebergott, Stanley. *Pursuing Happiness: American Consumers in the Twentieth Century*. Princeton: Princeton University Press, 1993.

Levy, S., and L. Guttman. 'On the Multivariate Structure of Well-being.' *Social Indicators Research* 2 (1975): 361–88.

Loewenstein, George and Jon Elster, eds. *Choice over Time*. New York: Russell Sage Foundation, 1992.

Loewenstein, George. 'The Fall and Rise of Psychological Explanations in the Economics of Intertemporal Choice.' In *Choice Over Time*, edited by George Loewenstein and Jon Elster, 3–34. New York: Russell Sage Foundation, 1992.

Lykken, David, and Auke Tellegen. 'Happiness is a Stochastic Phenomenon.' *Psychological Science* 7, no. 3 (1996): 186–9.

Marmot, Michael. 'Social Differences in Health Within and Between Populations.' *Daedalus* 123, no. 4 (1994): 197–216.

Meyer, Carrie A. 'The Greening of National Accounts: The Role of Ideas in a Theory of Institutional Change.' Working Paper in Economics no. 97/03, George Mason University, 1997.

Miles, Ian. *Social Indicators for Human Development*. London: Frances Pinter, 1985.
Mishan, E.J. *The Costs of Economic Growth*. Harmondsworth: Penguin Books, 1967.
Morris, Morris David. *Measuring the Condition of the World's Poor: The Physical Quality of Life Index*. Oxford: Pergamon, 1979.
——. 'Measuring the Changing Quality of the World's Poor: The Physical Quality of Life Index.' Working Paper No. 23/24, Brown University Center for the Comparative Study of Development, Providence, RI, 1996.
Nordhaus, William D., and J. Tobin. 'Is Growth Obsolete?' In *Economic Growth. Fiftieth Anniversary Colloquium V*, 1–80. New York: NBER, 1972.
Nordhaus, William D. 'Reflections on the Concept of Sustainable Economic Growth.' In *Economic Growth and the Structure of Long-Term Development*, edited by Luigi Pasinetti and Robert M. Solow, 309–25. Basingstoke: Macmillan, 1994.
Nordic Council. *Level of Living and Inequality in the Nordic Countries: A Comparative Analysis of the Nordic Comprehensive Surveys*. Stockholm: Nordic Council and the Nordic Statistical Secretariat, 1984.
Offer, Avner. 'Body Weight and Self-Control in the United States and Britain since the 1950s.' *Social History of Medicine* 14, no. 1 (2001): 79–106.
Olson, Mancur, and Hans H. Landsberg, eds. *The No-Growth Society*. London: Woburn Press, 1975.
Pigou, Arthur Cecil. *The Economics of Welfare*. London: Macmillan, 1920.
Packard, Vance O. *The Waste Makers*. London: Longmans, 1960.
Rabin, Matthew. 'Psychology and Economics.' *Journal of Economic Literature* 36, no. 1 (1998): 11–46.
Riesman, David. *Abundance for What? and Other Essays*. London: Chatto, 1964.
Robinson, John P. and Geoffrey Godbey. *Time for Life: The Surprising Ways Americans Use their Time*. University Park, Pennsylvania: Pennsylvania State University Press, 1997.
Rowntree, B.S. *Poverty: A Study of Town Life*. 4th edn. London: Macmillan, 1902.
Sametz, A.W. 'The Measurement of Economic Growth.' In *Indicators of Social Change: Concepts and Measurements*, edited by Eleanor B. Sheldon and Wilbert E. Moore, 77–96. New York: Russell Sage Foundation, 1968.
Schor, Juliet B. *The Overworked American: The Unexpected Decline of Leisure*. New York: Basic Books, 1991.
Scitovsky, Tibor. *The Joyless Economy*. New York: Oxford University Press, 1976.
Sen, Amartya. 'The Welfare Basis of Real Income Comparisons: A Survey.' *Journal of Economic Literature* 17, no. 1 (1979): 1–45.
——.'Capability and Well-Being.' In *The Quality of Life*, edited by Martha Nussbaum and Amartya Sen, 30–53. Oxford: Oxford University Press, 1993.
Slesnick, Daniel T. "Empirical Approaches to the Measurement of Welfare." *Journal of Economic Literature* 36 (1998): 2108–65.
Slottje, Daniel. *Measuring the Quality of Life Across Countries: A Multidimensional Analysis*. Boulder, Col.: Westview, 1991.

Smith, James P. 'Healthy Bodies and Thick Wallets: The Dual Relation between Health and Economic Status.' *Journal of Economic Perspectives* 13, no. 2 (1999): 145–66.

Snooks, Graeme D. *Portrait of the Family Within the Total Economy: A Study in Longrun Dynamics, Australia 1788–1990.* Cambridge: Cambridge University Press, 1994.

Stigler, George J., and Gary S. Becker. 'De Gustibus Non Est Disputandum.' *American Economic Review* 67, no. 2 (1977): 76–90.

Stones, M.J., Thomas Hadjistavropoulos, Holly Tuuko, et al. 'Happiness has Traitlike and Statelike Properties: A Reply to Veenhoven.' *Social Indicators Research* 36 (1995): 129–44.

Studenski, Paul. *The Income of Nations; Theory, Measurement, and Analysis: Past and Present.* New York: New York University Press, 1958.

Terleckyj, Nestor E. *Improvements in the Quality of Life: Estimates of Possibilities in the United States, 1974–1983.* Washington, DC: National Planning Association, 1975.

United Nations Social and Economic Council. Working Group on International Statistics and Co-ordination. 'Social Statistics: The Follow-up to the World Summit for Social Development.' Unpublished paper, 24 January 1996.

United Nations Development Programme. *Human Development Report 1998.* New York: Human Development Report Office, United Nations Development Program, 1998.

Van Praag, Bernard M.S., and Paul Fritjers. 'The Measurement of Welfare and Well-Being: The Leyden Approach.' In *Well-Being: The Foundations of Hedonic Psychology*, edited by Daniel Kahneman, Ed Diener and Norbert Schwartz, 413–33. New York: Russell Sage Foundation, 1999.

Veenhoven, Ruut. *World Database of Happiness.* http://www.eur.nl/fsw/research/happiness/

———. 'Is Happiness Relative?' *Social Indicators Research* 24 (1991): 1–34.

———. 'Developments in Satisfaction Research.' *Social Indicators Research* 37 (1996): 1–46.

———. 'The Study of Life Satisfaction.' In *A Comparative Study of Satisfaction with Life in Europe*, edited by Willem E. Saris, Ruut Veenhoven, Annette C. Scherpenzeel, et al., 11–48. Budapest: Etvs University Press, 1996.

Weitzman, Martin. 'On the Welfare Significance of National Product in a Dynamic Economy.' *Quarterly Journal of Economics* 90, no. 1 (1976): 156–62.

Wilkinson, Richard. 'The Epidemiological Transition: From Material Scarcity to Social Disadvantage?' *Daedalus* 123, no. 4 (1994): 61–77.

World Bank, *Poverty Reduction and the World Bank.* Annual, Washington DC.

Zolotas, Xenophon. *Economic Growth and Declining Social Welfare.* Athens: Bank of Greece, 1981.

13.
The Human Body in Britain
Past and Future
RODERICK FLOUD

Introduction[1]

As Britain enters the twenty-first century, the bodies of its citizens continue to change, as they have done for at least the last two centuries. Men and women in early adulthood who, only a hundred years ago, could have expected to die while in their 60s can now confidently expect to live well into their 80s. They, and their children, are much taller and fatter; diseases which killed or maimed them as late as the 1950s, such as smallpox and polio, are now only memories; hernia repairs and hip and knee replacements have removed pain and increased years of active life. Smoke and lead pollution has greatly diminished, leading to healthier and longer lives; malnutrition in childhood, with its long-term effects on health and on intelligence, has greatly diminished.

It is easier to recognize the changes of the past than it is to accept that they are still continuing and are likely to do so for the foreseeable future. All of us have a natural tendency to believe that the world that is familiar to us is also close to the bounds of possibility. But there is no evidence that this is so, as major changes to our bodies continue to occur. Studies based on British people with life insurance show, for example, that a man aged 30 in 1980 could expect to live until the age of 80.2, a woman aged 30 until the age of 84.7. Only 19 years later, in 1999, such a man could expect to live until the age of 85.4 and such a

---

[1] I am grateful to Bernard Harris and to many participants at the Conference on Economic Challenges of the 21st Century in Historical Perspective for their helpful comments on earlier versions of this chapter.

woman until the age of 88.4. Even the life expectancy of 80- and 90-year-olds themselves is still increasing.[2] During the same period, the gap between the expectation of life of men and of women, which had been substantial, began to shrink; only time will tell whether this trend will continue.[3]

Average height and weight continue to grow, although young men in Britain are still about 6 centimetres shorter on average than young men in the Netherlands, leaving plenty of room for further growth.[4] More speculatively, performance in school examinations continues to improve, perhaps as a result of better nutrition and declining pollution as well as improved teaching and changes in the national curriculum. Death rates for a number of major illnesses are higher in Britain than in some other European countries, again suggesting that there is room for improvement.

These changes are sometimes presented as causes for concern. The 'burden of the aged' worries politicians across the world; projected pension costs for longer years in retirement and growing health care costs for an ageing population are seen as threats to national social security budgets. In a number of countries such fears have led to moves to raise pensionable ages. Increasing height seems, in the United States and other developed countries, to be accompanied by increasing girth and fears that childhood obesity will lead to increasing morbidity and mortality. These fears are expressed within a general climate of concern about the possible malign effects of economic growth on the environment and our quality of life. To other commentators, by contrast, the changes are seen as benign, the product of increased wealth and consumer choice which will themselves overcome any problems; higher incomes during working life will, for example, allow higher savings to finance longer retirements.

Future change in our bodies is thus a source of both fascination and controversy. It is clear, however, that we do not yet fully understand the interactions and causal chains between changes in the economy, nutrition, consumption habits, savings preferences, health-care methods and other factors, which have contributed to the changes in our bodies that we have experienced and expect to continue to occur.

---

[2] Institute of Actuaries.

[3] Ibid. In 1980, for example, the expectation of life at age 40 for a man was 4.6 years shorter than for a woman, while by 1999 this gap had shrunk to 4 years.

[4] Steckel and Floud, *Health and Welfare*.

Some of these interactions, indeed, operate over very long periods. There is increasing, although still controversial, evidence about the impact of maternal, foetal and childhood nutrition on future morbidity and mortality, suggesting that we are still experiencing the consequences of events that occurred 80 or more years ago and that events now will still be having repercussions late in the twenty-first century.[5]

Changing Bodies, Nutritional Status and the Standard of Living

This short chapter cannot do more than touch on such issues. What it sets out to do is to provide some new evidence on one of these complex phenomena, the changing height, weight and body mass of the population. In so doing, it contributes to a sub-discipline which has come to be known as 'historical anthropometry', based on the belief that change in our bodies is significant as an indicator of nutritional status. This term, invented by human biologists, itself encompasses much of what historians have described as the 'standard of living' of the population. As L.R. Villermé (1782–1863), who occupied in France much the same position as a pioneer of public health as Edwin Chadwick did in Britain, wrote in 1829:

> Human height becomes greater and growth takes place more rapidly, other things being equal, in proportion as the country is richer, comfort more general, houses, clothes and nourishment better and labour, fatigue and privation during infancy and youth less; in other words, the circumstances which accompany poverty delay the age at which complete stature is reached and stunt adult height.[6]

A modern restatement was that by Eveleth and Tanner:

> A child's growth rate reflects, better than any other single index, his state of health and nutrition, and often indeed his psychological situation also. Similarly, the average value of children's heights and weights reflects accurately the state of a nation's public health and the average nutritional status of its citizens, when appropriate allowance is made for differences, if any, in genetic potential. This is especially so in developing and disintegrating countries. Thus a well-designed growth study is a powerful

---

[5] See, for example, Waaler, 'Height, Weight', and Barker, *Fetal and Infant* and Barker, *Mothers, Babies*.
[6] Villermé, 'Mémoire sur la taille', p. 585, as quoted in Tanner, *A History*, p. 162.

tool with which to monitor the health of a population, or to pinpoint subgroups of a population whose share in economic or social benefits is less than it might be.[7]

This chapter explores evidence on the changing shape of the British human body, in particular its height and weight, in order to throw light on the past and possibly the future standard of living of the British population. Economists and historians were initially resistant to the view that nutritional status and changes to the shape of the human body could be used as measures of alterations in living standards. But by the end of the 1990s, concepts of the proper scope of studies of living standards have greatly widened. As Crafts puts it:

> Both development economists and economic historians have become increasingly concerned to develop measures of living standards that are more comprehensive than real wages or real GDP per head. Partly, this is because attention has increasingly turned to the lives that people lead rather than the incomes that they enjoy and partly because in most circumstances a substantial element of well-being is derived not on the basis of personal command over resources but depends on provision by the state.[8]

Crafts considers four approaches: 'heights, the Human Development Index (HDI), the Quality of Life Index and imputations to GDP growth.' He argues that:

> ...they do offer something useful by way of supplementing existing income measures and do tend to confirm that real wages and/or real GDP are not the whole story.[9]

Crafts remains sceptical about the use of height data as an index of welfare *per se*, but is prepared to accept them as diagnostic of situations in which economic growth and rising real wages may be '...misleading indicators of changes in living standards'.[10] Other economic historians, including Charles Feinstein, have gone even further in accepting the validity of height data as indicative of changes in living standards.[11]

---

[7] Eveleth and Tanner, *Worldwide Variations*, p. 1.
[8] Crafts, 'Quantitative Economic History', p. 11.
[9] Ibid., p. 12.
[10] Ibid., p. 14.
[11] Feinstein, 'Pessimism Perpetuated'.

Height, Weight and the Body Mass Index

The vast majority of studies of historical anthropometry in the first 20 years of the life of the subject were about changes and variations in heights. This was always unsatisfactory, both to those who wrote and those who read the studies. As human biologists know, height is an excellent indicator of the nutritional status of children, but it has deficiencies as a more general measure of the nutritional status of the whole population. The most serious flaw is that height does not change after the late teens, while nutritional status and the socio-economic environment certainly do. Carefully handled, measurements of the height of adults can be excellent indicators of the nutritional status of those adults at a time when they were infants and children, but they are less and less informative about the nutritional status of those adults as they grow older.

It was always apparent, therefore, that it would be desirable to add other measurements to those of height. This became even clearer with the publication in 1984 of Hans Waaler's 'Height, Weight and Mortality: the Norwegian Experience'. Most studies by human biologists had hitherto concentrated on the exploration of growth and nutritional status in childhood, but Waaler and several others, in particular Barker and Marmot in Britain, now turned their attention to the long-term consequences of nutritional status, in infancy, childhood and adolescence, for the morbidity and mortality of adult populations.[12] They were able to demonstrate that height, weight and body-mass were all, together and independently, influential on morbidity and mortality.

Historians have been rather slow in grasping the implication of these findings, not only for studies of demographic history but also as a stimulus to the collection of data on weight as well as height.[13] With the exception of the work of Robert Fogel and his colleagues in the United States, there have been few studies of changing weight and body mass index (BMI) and of their relationship to morbidity and mortality.[14] The primary difficulty seems to lie in the paucity of data. Fogel and his colleagues are able to exploit the unrivalled coverage and

---

[12] Waaler, 'Height, Weight'; Barker, *Fetal and Infant* and *Mothers, Babies* and, for example, Marmot and Elliott, *Coronary Heart Disease*.
[13] The Body Mass Index (BMI) is calculated as weight in kilograms divided by the square of height in metres, and therefore cannot be directly observed.
[14] The most notable exceptions are Fogel, 'Economic Growth', and Costa and Steckel, 'Long-term Trends'.

complexity of the Union Army pension records of individual soldiers, but few if any other countries possess such records.[15] Height was measured and recorded across Europe and other continents as a guide to the likely stamina of potential army recruits and as a means of identification, but weight was thought to be much less useful for either purpose and was rarely recorded.[16]

Table 1. The number of observations in published sources by birth cohort, gender and age of those measured. Each observation is of a group of individuals with the specified characteristics of date of birth, age and gender. Children are aged 18 and younger, adults 19 and older.

Birth Cohort	Male Adults	Male Children	Female Adults	Female Children
1810s	17			
1820s	4	4		4
1830s	4			
1840s	5	10		
1850s	24	9	3	
1860s	27	62	10	40
1870s	17	54	2	53
1880s	21	5		5
1890s	19	63	2	54
1900s	28	38	15	37
1910s	26	36	7	25
1920s	13	29	8	24
1930s	7	47	6	39
1940s	8	44	8	40
1950s	6	34	6	34
1960s	4	15	4	15
1970s		10		10

However, even if individual records of the measurement of weight in the nineteenth or earlier centuries are rare, there do exist in Britain (and possibly in other countries) a large number of disparate observations of the height and weight of different groups of the population at different periods. In total, British published sources provide about 1000 observations of the mean height and weight at particular ages of groups of males, the earliest relating to men or male children born

---

[15] A possible exception is the pension records of the British army in World War I, currently being investigated by Bernard Harris, Eilidh Garrett and colleagues.

[16] Even when weight was recorded, it usually included some clothing. A discussion of the necessary adjustments to measured weights can be found in Floud, 'Height, Weight', pp. 8–9.

between 1810 and 1819. There are also about 500 observations of the mean height and weight of groups of females, the earliest relating to women or female children born in the 1820s.

Table 1 shows the distribution of the number of observations across time periods and by the age-group of those measured. Unlike the individual height data which have been used in the majority of studies of anthropometric history, each of these observations is itself a mean of a number of individual measurements of individuals. These data thus have the significant disadvantage of lacking information on the variation around the means and of dampening the variation which might otherwise occur in the observations of BMI.[17]

It must be emphasized that hardly any of the data which can be gathered were drawn from random or systematic samples of the British population. Indeed, no such sample was compiled until the early 1980s. The data come from a variety of sources, socio-economic classes, regions and age-groups. As to the last, men, women and children were measured at different ages and different times. Following intense discussion in the early stages of the analysis of historical height data, it has become customary to organize the data into birth cohorts; as an example, men measured when aged 20 in 1880, and therefore born in 1860, are grouped with men aged 40 in 1900 (and thus also born in 1860), rather than with men aged 20 in 1900.[18] This practice implicitly reflects the fact that, in measuring height, we are dealing with the consequences of events in early life, so that the reference should be to the date of birth rather than to the date, possibly many years later, at which the measurements were made; this ensures that cohorts with different environmental experiences are kept distinct.[19] It could be argued that this logic would lead to a different treatment of data on weight and BMI, since these reflect partially events and environments long after birth, but the practice of using birth cohorts is so well established that it is followed here for the sake of consistency.

---

[17] This is because BMI is, in what follows, calculated from dividing means of means of weight by the square of means of means of height.

[18] See Floud, Wachter and Gregory, *Health, Height and History*, p. 132, for a discussion of the distinction between birth and recruitment cohorts.

[19] Gregson and Grubb, 'Anthropometric versus Conventional', criticize some scholars for forgetting, or failing to emphasize, the fact that height reflects childhood events. However, the use of birth cohorts implicitly recognizes this fact.

Table 2. Mean heights of adult males (in metres), from published sources, Britain 1820–1979.

Birth cohort	Age 19–25	Age 26–30	Age 31–35	Age 36–40	Age 41–50	Age 51–60	Age 61–70	Age >70	Mean of Means
1800–19		1.68					1.74		1.71
1820–39					1.73	1.73			1.73
1840–59	1.71	1.71	1.72	1.73					1.72
1860–79	1.71				1.75	1.74	1.67		1.72
1880–99	1.73	1.75	1.74	1.74	1.74				1.74
1900–19	1.73	1.70					1.71	1.68	1.71
1920–39	1.75				1.74	1.73	1.71		1.73
1940–59	1.76	1.75	1.75	1.75	1.74				1.75
1960–79	1.76	1.76							1.76

Note: *Height, Health and History*, table 4.1, can be used to calculate mean heights for the 24–29 age group by birth cohort as follows:

1800–19	1.71 metres
1820–39	1.70 metres
1840–59	1.69 metres
1860–79	1.70 metres

The new results which most closely parallel and complement the evidence from individual heights presented in *Health, Height and History* are those for the heights of groups of adult males (in metres), shown in Table 2.[20] The average heights of the birth cohorts, shown in the final column headed 'mean of means' in Table 2, show an increase from the birth cohort of 1800 to 1819 to that of 1820 to 1839, falling back slightly in the cohorts of 1840 to 1859 and 1860 to 1879, before rising into the twentieth century (although with an apparent fall in the cohort born in the first 20 years of that century). This pattern is similar to that found in the individual height data; in particular, it confirms the decline in the middle of the century which has become the subject of some controversy. The absolute levels found in the group data are, however, consistently higher by some 1–2 centimetres than those derived from the individual data and reported in Table 4.1 of *Health, Height and History*.[21] It seems likely that this stems from the fact that

---

[20] It should be noted that, from the 1830s to 1881, some of the group data—drawn from the published reports of the Army Medical Department—were in fact spliced with the individual data and reported as such in Table 4.1 of Floud, Wachter and Gregory, *Health, Height and History*. The data used in Table 2, however, were calculated by Rosenbaum (1988) using somewhat different methods from those used in *Health, Height and History*. Table 3, of course, also uses data drawn from other sources.

[21] Floud, Wachter and Gregory, *Health, Height and History*, pp. 140–9.

Table 2 includes data from non-military sources and thus, to some extent, includes men from higher social groups than the working classes who provided the bulk of army recruits.

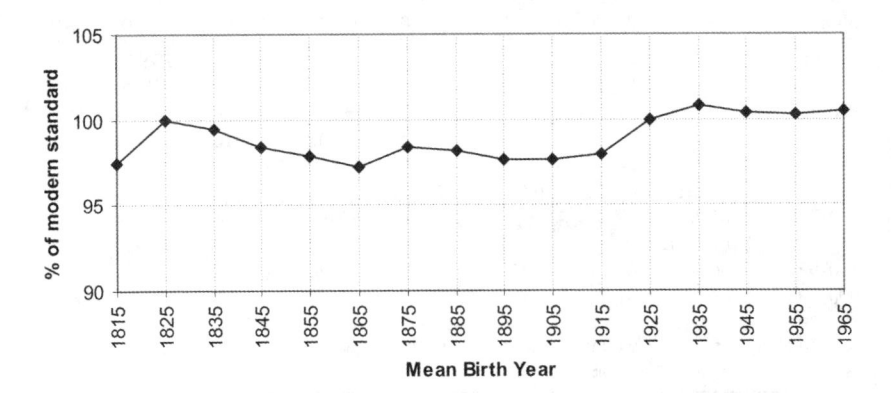

Figure 1. Adult male heights, Britain 1810–1969.

Figure 1 presents the data on adult male heights in a different way, by calculating each observation — now for 10-year birth cohorts — as a percentage of the modern British standard; this has been drawn from observations of the relevant age-groups in the past 20 years. The decline in adult male heights, for adults from birth cohorts of the 1820s to those of the 1860s, is clearly shown. While there are less than 10 observations for each of the adult birth cohorts of the 1820s, 1830s and 1840s, the mean heights for those periods are consistently greater — though perhaps too high in relation to the modern standard to be wholly believable as indicators of national levels — than those for the 1850s and 1860s. The cohorts of the 1870s and 1880s show increased height, but thereafter there is a return to the levels of the 1850s and 1860s, before significant growth occurs between the 1910s and 1920s. Male children also show a substantial decline in mean height between the 1840s and the 1870s, followed, as with male adults, by an improvement and then a renewed decline before improvement occurs again from the 1910s onwards. There are insufficient observations for adult females in the relevant birth cohorts to draw any conclusions, but there is a slight fall between the 1860s and 1870s among female children, paralleling that found for male children.[22]

---

[22] Comparable figures showing results for female adults and male and female children can be found in Floud, 'Height, Weight'.

Welfare, Well-being and Individual Economic Security

Table 3. Mean weight of adult males (in kilograms), from published sources, Britain 1800–1979. (All values corrected for weight of clothing, either by Roberts' method or, for figures in brackets, by Quetelt's method. See Floud, 'Height and Weight'.)

Birth cohort	Age 19–25	Age 26–30	Age 31–35	Age 36–40	Age 41–50	Age 51–60	Age 61–70	Age >70
1800–19		61.94 (58.50)					73.97 (74.15)	
1820–39					69.71 (70.13)	70.80 (71.16)		
1840–59	62.49 (63.31)	64.52 (65.22)	67.96 (68.47)	69.98 (70.38)				
1860-79	61.03 (61.93)				73.67	75.16	62.19	
1880–99	66.00	68.48	69.28	70.42	71.19			
1900–19	63.45	61.02					74.85	70.85
1920–39	66.08				77.53	77.50	76.28	
1940–59	71.40	73.80	76.70	78.65	78.84			
1960–79	71.40	77.35						

Table 4. Mean BMI of adult males, from published sources, Britain 1800–1979. (All values corrected for weight of clothing, either by Roberts' method or, for figures in brackets, by Quetelt's method. See Floud, 'Height and Weight'.)

Birth cohort	Age 19–25	Age 26–30	Age 31–35	Age 36–40	Age 41–50	Age 51–60	Age 61–70	Age >70
1800–19		21.91 (20.70)					24.58 (24.64)	
1820–39					23.38 (23.52)	23.76 (23.88)		
1840–59	21.31 (21.51)	21.94 (22.18)	22.84 (23.01)	23.38 (23.51)				
1860–79	21.03 (21.06)				24.02	24.42	22.38	
1880–99	22.03	22.32	22.71	23.12	23.46			
1900–19	21.07	21.03					25.60	25.05
1920–39	21.54				25.63	25.89	26.09	
1940–59	23.00	24.00	24.98	25.90	26.10			
1960–79	23.04	24.93						

These data collectively show, therefore, a decline in heights in the middle of the nineteenth century, as described in *Health, Height and History*. What is perhaps most surprising is that the recovery from these levels appears to have been more prolonged than was suggested in that book, with a further decline or at least stability at the end of the century. It has to be remembered that there were no army recruitment or other individual data for birth cohorts after 1881, and it is possible that we were misled, in *Height, Health and History*, into an incorrect interpolation between those earlier birth cohorts and the evidence of various surveys in the inter-war period. The implication is that growth in heights was faster, in the period around World War I, than has hitherto been believed.

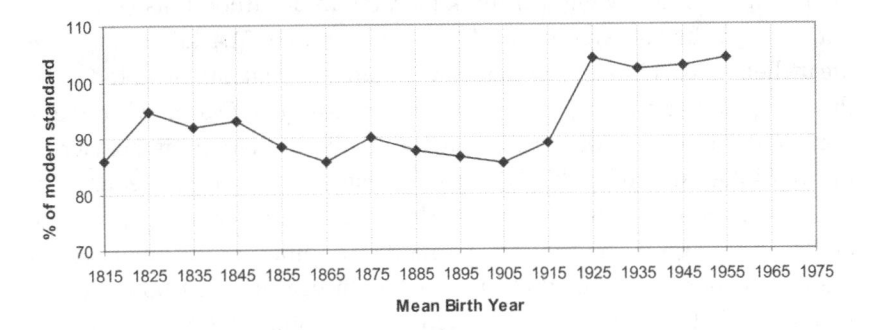

Figure 2. Adult male weights, Britain 1810–1969.

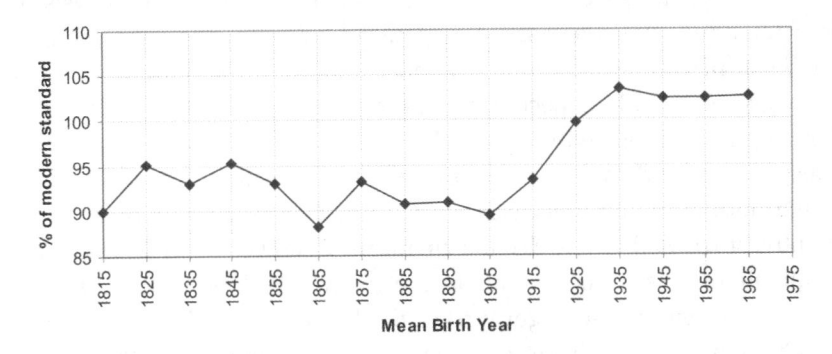

Figure 3. Male Adult Body Mass Index, Britain 1810–1969.

The new data also make it possible to consider not only height but also weight and body mass, with results for adult males shown in Tables 3 and 4. As explained above, there are no comparable data for individuals and these data must stand on their own. It must be re-emphasized that, for the nineteenth-century birth cohorts, adjustments for the weight of clothing are significant, as both tables show. The tables do show substantial increases in both weight and BMI, but these occurred somewhat after increases in height, most significantly in the period after World War I. It is important to stress that the absolute average levels of height and weight, and of BMI, were significantly less, in the mid- to late nineteenth century, than today. It may not seem very striking to say that men and women were, at that time, only 2–3 per cent shorter and 10–15 per cent lighter than today, but these are large differences by the standards of variations in average height and weight over time and between populations. In the male birth cohort of 1840 to 1859, for example, men attained a mean height of 171 centimetres and a mean weight of 68 kilograms in adulthood, as compared with current British values of 176 centimetres and 71.4 kilograms.[23] A mean height of 171 centimetres is the same as that attained today by the Bulgarian, Hungarian, Romanian and Russian (Moscow) populations, but all but one of these populations, the Romanian, is heavier by up to 4 kilograms than the British mid-nineteenth century mean.[24] The closest analogue in the modern world to the British male populations of 150 years ago is the modern Romanian population. In other words, the British population of the mid-nineteenth century was both stunted and wasted, but particularly wasted, when compared to the modern British population.[25]

So far as changes over time are concerned, the results of analysis of data for adult males are shown, again as percentages of the modern standard, in Figure 2 for weights and in Figure 3 for BMI.[26] The data are consistent with expectation and modern evidence in that both weight and BMI rise with age, as Tables 3 and 4 demonstrate for adult males. The new data show that, for males, the decline in mean heights in the middle of the nineteenth century was paralleled, perhaps even slightly surpassed, by a decline in mean weights; as an arithmetical result, there was a similar fall in mean BMI. Following this decline, male adult height rose slightly from the birth cohort of the 1860s, but weight remained much more stable or even declined until the end of the century, as it did with adult females. This finding, if confirmed by

---

[23] Knight and Eldridge, *Survey*, Tables 2.1 and 3.1.
[24] Eveleth and Tanner, *Worldwide Variations*.
[25] The terms 'stunted' and 'wasted' are used in their technical sense of 'significantly below mean height and weight'.
[26] Tables 1–3 show mean height, weight and BMI attaining values of over 100 per cent of the modern standard, in most cases from the birth cohorts of the 1920s onwards. The most likely explanation for this phenomenon is that the published data sets are drawn predominantly from relatively prosperous groups of the population, or perhaps geographical areas, and that working-class groups are under-represented. It is impossible, given the number of observations and the information available, adequately to control for this difficulty, but there is no reason to suppose that it varies significantly over time. Comparable figures for adult females and male and female children can be found in Floud, 'Height, Weight'.

other evidence, is both surprising and significant. It suggests that, whatever the causes (whether improvement in nutritional status, or the reduced exposure of the young population to disease after the 1860s) that were responsible for the increases in height, those factors were not sufficiently strong to induce similar increases in weight.[27]

After the beginning of the twentieth century, the increase in the weight of both adult males and adult females was much more dramatic than the increase in height, and this led to substantial changes to BMI; this was particularly apparent between the birth cohort of 1900 to 1909 and that of 1930 to 1939, by which latter date modern levels of BMI had largely been attained. There was then possibly a slight dip in BMI in the birth cohorts of the 1950s and 1960s, caused by a slightly greater increase in heights than in weights at that time, but recent indications are that weight and BMI are both increasing, leading to some widely popularized fears of the impact of obesity on health.

The position with children is less clear-cut and is particularly affected in the case of females by small sample sizes. Male child heights and weights appear to have fallen, as with male adults, in the middle of the nineteenth century before rising again in the latter years of the century, but the same pattern is not observable for females. For both male and female children, however, it appears that the rise in both heights and weights began during the last quarter of the nineteenth century but was particularly marked between the birth cohorts around the start of the twentieth century and those of the 1930s. Height and weight rose together over those years, giving rise to an upward trend in BMI which was less steep than for adults at the same period, but confused by a sawtooth pattern which may again reflect small sample sizes.

Increase in height and weight during childhood and adolescence is also faster today than it was in the nineteenth century, although growth in height ceases at an earlier age. The numbers of observations at particular ages are too few, among the published data sets, to calculate full growth profiles, but the heights and weights which were attained in early adulthood, around the age of 19, in the male birth cohort of 1840 to 1859 are today attained at the age of 15. Similarly, the average height and weight of men of that cohort in their early 30s is

---

[27] On non-nutritional factors affecting height distributions, see, for example, Voth and Leunig, 'Did Smallpox Reduce Height?' and discussion by Leunig and Voth in this Volume.

now attained, for height, at the age of 16 and for weight at the age of 21. Differences in physical appearance from today were thus particularly great in late adolescence and early adulthood.

It must always be remembered that average figures, such as those just quoted, are merely a representation of the underlying distributions of individuals' heights, weights and BMI. Unfortunately, the lack of individual observations makes it impossible to calculate the full underlying distributions, but it is possible to suggest their underlying shape by inference from modern distributions. This is particularly easy in the case of height, because of the normality of height distributions and the fact that they have a common standard deviation among males of about 6.4 centimetres. A mean height for the male birth cohort of 1840 to 1859 of 171 centimetres therefore implies that about 16 per cent of that cohort had a height of less than 164.6 centimetres and that 2.5 per cent of the cohort had a height of less than 158.3 centimetres. Inference from modern distributions of weight and BMI is more complex, because it cannot be assumed that historical distributions had the same shape as those of today. However, a modern distribution of BMI with a mean of 21.4, a level typical of the younger adult age-groups among mid-nineteenth-century cohorts, has 33 per cent of the distribution with a BMI of less than 20, taken to be the current definition of underweight. This confirms the inference that significant fractions of nineteenth-century populations were severely stunted and wasted by the standards of today.[28] The data do not, however, support the conclusion that Victorian male adults were significantly better nourished, and therefore less stunted or wasted, than women and children; nor do they show that Victorian male children were better nourished than their female siblings.

The Future

The implications of the data presented in this chapter are both considerable and complex. Change in our bodies in the past has been very significant, to the extent that we now look entirely different from our ancestors, we live much longer and we are healthier during our lives.

---

[28] If the published observations are biased towards the higher socio-economic groups, this would be an underestimate of the true extent of stunting and wasting in the whole population.

Such change has accompanied the massive changes in economy and society which we know as modern economic growth. We can infer from these co-occurrences that continued economic growth will bring further changes to our bodies and that, moreover, the changes in the bodies of those still living will affect them and their children well into the twenty-first century.

As an example, consider the implications of the growth in heights that took place in the early and middle years of the twentieth century. It is likely that improvements in nutritional and health status, which this growth suggests have occurred, have been a contributory factor in the recent increase in life expectancy in Britain; it is the men and women who were children in the first 30 years of the century who are now dying and contributing to the mortality statistics. Consider also the fact that young men and women in Britain are now substantially shorter than similar men and women in several other European countries, such as the Netherlands, Sweden and Norway, despite the fact that in the nineteenth century the British were taller than the citizens of these countries. If the cause of the current disparity is the greater income inequality within Britain, then the reduction of that inequality could quite easily lead to changes in access to resources that will be reflected by a substantial increase in the average height of the British. If, again, nutritional status in childhood is linked to mortality and morbidity in later life, then increasing height would betoken further increases in life expectancy during the coming century.

What we cannot yet do is to demonstrate the exact causal connections which link all these phenomena; nor can we therefore adequately model their likely consequences. While Robert Fogel has begun the task of developing such models in his description of the concept of 'technophysio evolution', there is much to be done in exploring the relationships between these complex variables and the proxies which are often all that we can use to measure them.[29] The scope and magnitude of the task are sufficiently great to occupy generations of scholars. All that we know is that, in the study of the changing human body as in so many areas of economic, social and technological development, 'We ain't seen nothing yet'!

[29] Fogel, 'When Will Humanity?' and 'Economic Growth'.

References

Barker, D.J.P. (ed.) *Fetal and Infant Origins of Adult Disease.* London: BMJ Publishing Group, 1992.

──────. *Mothers, Babies and Disease in Later Life.* London: BMJ Publishing Group, 1994.

Costa, Dora L., and Richard H. Steckel. 'Long-term Trends in Health, Welfare and Economic Growth in the United States.' In *Health and Welfare during Industrialization,* edited by Richard H. Steckel and Roderick Floud, 47–90. Chicago: Chicago University Press, 1997.

Crafts, N.F.R. 'Quantitative Economic History.' L.S.E. Working Papers in Economic History 48/99, 1999.

Eveleth, P.B., and J.M. Tanner. *Worldwide Variations in Human Growth.* Cambridge: Cambridge University Press, 1976.

Feinstein, C.H. 'Pessimism Perpetuated: Real Wages and the Standard of Living in Britain during and after the Industrial Revolution.' *Journal of Economic History* 58 (1998): 625–58.

Floud, Roderick. 'Height, Weight and Body Mass of the British Population since 1820.' National Bureau of Economic Research, Historical Paper 108, November 1998.

Floud, R.C., K. Wachter and A. Gregory. *Height, Health and History: Nutritional Status in the United Kingdom, 1750–1980.* Cambridge: Cambridge University Press, 1990.

Fogel, R.W. 'When Will Humanity Finally Escape from Chronic Malnutrition?' The 1997 Nestlé Lecture on the Developing World.

──────. 'Economic Growth, Population Theory and Physiology: the Bearing of Long-term Processes on the Making of Economic Policy.' In *Classics in Anthropometric History,* edited by J. Komlos and T. Cuff, 23–62. St Katharinen, Germany: Scripta Mercaturae Verlag, 1998.

Gregson, M.E., and F. Grubb. 'Anthropometric versus Conventional Economic Measures of the Standard of Living: A Search for Theoretical Consistency.' Unpublished paper presented to the meetings of the Economic History Association, September 1997.

Institute of Actuaries, Continuous Mortality Investigation Bureau, 1999.

Knight, I., and J. Eldridge (for the Office of Population Censuses and Surveys and the Department of Health and Social Security). *Survey of Adult Heights and Weights.* London: Stationery Office, 1984.

Marmot, Michael, and Paul Elliott (eds.). *Coronary Heart Disease Epidemiology: From Aetiology to Public Health.* Oxford: Oxford University Press, 1992.

Rosenbaum, S. '100 Years of Heights and Weights.' *Journal of the Royal Statistical Society* Series A, 151 (1988): 276–309.

Steckel, Richard H., and Roderick Floud (eds.). *Health and Welfare During Industrialization.* Chicago: Chicago University Press, 1997.

Tanner, J.M. *A History of the Study of Human Growth.* Cambridge: Cambridge University Press, 1981.

Villermé, L.R. 'Mémoire sur la taille de l'homme en France.' *Annales d'hygiène publique* 1 (1829): 551–99.

Waaler, Hans T. 'Height, Weight and Mortality: the Norwegian Experience.' *Acta Medica Scandinavica* 679 (Supplement) (1984): 1–56.

14.
Height and the High Life:
What Future for a Tall Story?
TIMOTHY LEUNIG & HANS-JOACHIM VOTH

Introduction: The Fading Usefulness of Stature

Height itself is not a 'good'. It provides precious few immediate benefits, and beyond a certain point height appears to be a 'bad'.[1] It is useful to economic historians not for what it is, but insofar as it serves as an indicator of health status and living standards in a wider sense. Three conditions need to be satisfied for historians to find height a useful measure. First, adult heights are only of interest at a more than anecdotal level if direct information on health status and living standards is unavailable or insufficient. Second, even then, height will only be useful if other indirect indicators do not show greater predictive power and/or greater data availability. Third, it must be the case that heights are a robust indicator of health and well-being, something that cannot be taken for granted in all periods.

The first two conditions have been broadly satisfied for a significant number of historically important periods. This has led to the production of a number of useful anthropometric studies for various countries, covering different periods.[2] The evidence that height is a well behaved indicator in these periods is not, however, wholly convincing, with evidence that gains in height and well-being may be uncorrelated, or even in conflict.[3] We argue that, for future historians, these

---

[1] Note, however, that the number of sexual partners is correlated with an individual's height—though many other factors may be involved. Furthermore, an individual's height does positively affect their adult income, even correcting for education levels. Meyer and Selmer, 'Income Inequality'; pp. 222–3.
[2] Steckel, 'Stature'.
[3] Crafts, 'Some Dimensions'.

conditions will be reversed. For the vast majority of countries better direct and indirect data will undermine the popularity of stature as a proxy for either health or living standards more generally. In contrast, however, for those countries in which data remain poor or unavailable, height can be used as a relatively reliable indicator of health and well-being. This is because the specific factors that can cause systematic divergence will decline in importance.

Future economic historians will have what are, by the standards of today's historians, quite remarkable data for all developed and many developing countries. We have high quality evidence on incomes, prices, working hours and conditions, consumption, mortality, morbidity, literacy, and so on and so forth. The single most important reason why we will become less concerned with adult heights in OECD countries is that we are able to observe directly just about everything that we might, as economic historians, be interested in.

It is worth remembering that historians today use height not because the medical evidence claims that it is the most reliable indicator of health status, but because it is frequently the only measure that was recorded by contemporaries. It is simply the case that the army and the prisons measured height, rather than weight or skinfold thickness. In recent years one of the largest gains in data quality and understanding has been in health. Around the world health information today is much better than at any other point in history. Health surveys and medical records generate data on an unprecedented scale. Mortality risk and various measures of morbidity are tracked closely over time and in cross-sections. Over the past 30 years, an average of 270,000 medical articles have been published each year, the vast majority of them based on original empirical research. Height itself is not used very often in modern-day medical studies as an indicator of mortality, and shows poor predictive power in many cases. There is some doubt, for example, as to the correlation between height and mortality. Work on Union Army recruits by Costa and Fogel and Wimmer implies that the two are positively correlated.[4] Their results are in line with research by Waaler, who found a U-shaped relationship between stature on the one hand, and mortality risk on the other.[5] In contrast, a World Health Organization (WHO) study found that American veterans from the twentieth century appear to live substantially longer if

---

[4] Costa, 'Height', Fogel and Wimmer, 'Early Indicators'.
[5] Waaler, 'Height'.

they are shorter.[6] The so-called Framingham Study, analysing data on 2,019 men and 2,585 women over a period of 36 years, failed to find any association between all-cause mortality and stature in general, and height and cardiovascular disease in particular.[7] A large random sample of the US population, containing 13,031 respondents, also showed that heart disease and height are not associated.[8] On the other hand, alternative measures of health status such as body mass index (BMI, defined as weight divided by the square of height), waist to hip ratio (WHR), and skinfold thickness (normally measured at the triceps) consistently show high predictive power for mortality.[9] It therefore comes as no surprise that there are many more medical studies using weight measures as a predictor of mortality than those using stature — the main medical literature database, MEDLINE, lists 1,806 articles over the period 1966 to 1999 linking mortality and height, while there are 21,296 papers examining weight as a risk factor. As the medical community dedicates substantially more effort to collecting and analysing weight data than height data, future historians, insofar as they are concerned with anthropometric measures, are likely to redirect their attention from height to girth.

Third, whilst it is true that many populations are markedly taller than their ancestors, it is also true that height gains have slowed dramatically, and may have stopped altogether in some cases. Mainland China, arguably one of the largest economic success stories of the past 20 years, saw no gains in average stature in its urban population between the 1980s and the 1990s.[10] In Sweden, height gain for the 1943 cohort was still significant compared to the 1933 cohort while later cohorts show sharply lower rates of growth.[11] Height gains of Californian children of Japanese origin born between the 1950s and the 1970s have almost come to a standstill.[12]

Nor is this slowdown a passing phenomenon. Figure 1 plots mean heights by income, as well as the height gain per additional $1,000. The evidence is from a cross-country regression of adult heights on

---

[6] Those 175.3 centimetres or shorter live 4.95 years longer than veterans who are taller than 175.3 centimetres. Samaras and Storms, 'Impact', pp. 259–67.
[7] Kannam et al., 'Short Stature', pp. 2241–7.
[8] Liao et al., 'Short Stature', pp. 678–82.
[9] Kalmijn et al., 'Association', pp. 395–402. Yuan et al., 'Body Weight', pp. 824–32.
[10] Xu at al., 'Comparison'.
[11] Cernerud and Lindgren, 'Secular Changes'.
[12] Greulich, 'Some Secular Changes'.

income, ancestry, inequality (measured by the Gini coefficient), and dummy variables for student populations and military samples.[13] While richer countries clearly have taller populations, it is evident that as incomes rise the gain in height becomes smaller and smaller for every additional unit of purchasing power. A population that sees incomes rise from $2,000 to $3,000 would normally expect to see the average height of the population rise by some 1.6 centimetres. To achieve the same gain in height, the US today would have to increase average incomes by more than $9,000.[14] The spectacular height gains of the past that left younger generations towering over their parents are therefore likely to come to an end, first in OECD countries, later in others. Further, to the extent to which country incomes converge, cross-country height differences will decline.[15] Even constant income gaps (in absolute terms) would reduce the international differentials, as the 'height penalty' for being a few thousand dollars poorer declines with rising incomes. The same will be true for the gap between rich and poor within countries.

Three possible reasons can be suggested for the apparent slowdown in height gains. First, it is possible that populations in today's affluent countries are approaching a genetically-determined maximum height. Evidence for such a 'speed limit' for the human body is paltry, but it cannot be ruled out. Second, additional income is spent to an ever-decreasing extent on increasing nutrient availability once the most blatant nutritional shortcomings have been remedied. While food expenditure may be a normal good, nutrients appear to be an inferior good even in today's Third World.[16] As Adam Smith observed:[17]

> The rich man consumes no more food than his poor neighbour. In quality it may be very different, and to select and prepare it may require more labour and art; but in quantity it is very nearly the same...

Some goods with high income-elasticities, such as healthcare and better housing, may also facilitate height gains. Others, such as most

---

[13] The data is from Steckel, 'Stature', Table 4, interpolated on the basis of his regressions in Table 3. Steckel, 'Stature', see also Steckel, 'Height'.
[14] Maddison gives per capita GDP of 18,317 US-$ in 1989: Maddison, 'Monitoring the World Economy'.
[15] The empirical evidence in favour of convergence is ambiguous. Pritchett, 'Divergence'.
[16] Wolfe and Behrman, 'Is Income?'; Behrman and Deolalikar, 'Is Variety?'. This lends further support to the revisionist literature associated with the work of Seckler, 'Malnutrition' and Srinivasan, 'Undernutrition'.
[17] Cited by Clark et al., 'British Food', p. 221.

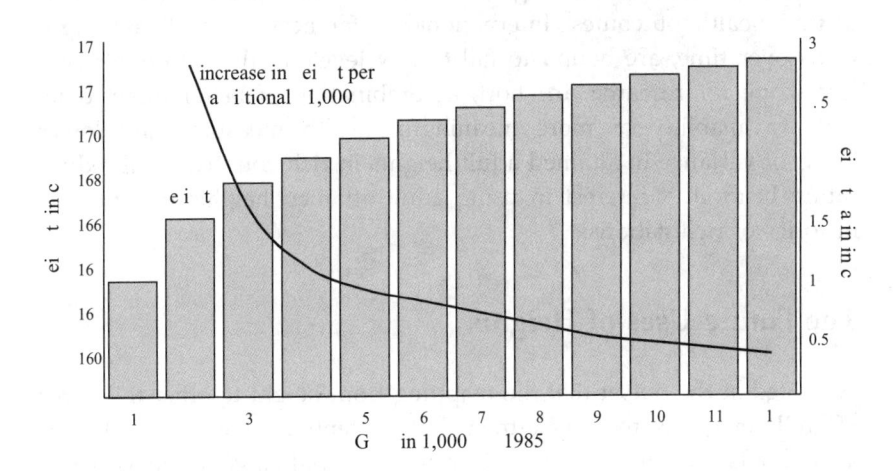

Figure 1. Height and GDP.

consumer durables, have no obvious health benefit. Indeed, affluence beyond a certain limit may lead to behavioural and dietary changes that reduce the human body's likelihood of attaining its genetic potential. High levels of net nutritional status, that is the body's energy balance after accounting for the needs of basic hygiene, work and keeping warm, may owe more to inactivity than to healthy diets. Lower levels of physical activity, typical in industrialized countries, may inhibit the production of growth hormones in adolescents. Finally, a taste for unhealthy dietary habits is often associated with high incomes. There is some evidence, for example, that vegetarians grow more slowly than their peers.[18] The argument that affluence reduces growth should not be taken too far: we know that people in developed countries today stop growing at an earlier age than in previous centuries, suggesting that final attained height is not ultimately constrained by insults, whether from lack of exercise or too much junk food.[19]

The attraction of adult heights alone as a research topic seems likely to fade in the future. Amongst historians of our own age, there will be 'catch-up' growth in research on other health measures such as weight, WHR and BMI. Not only are data on these being collected on a greater

---

[18] Vegetarian children (of different age groups) were 0.2 to 2.1 centimetres shorter than their peers. O'Connell et al., 'Growth'.
[19] Floud, Wachter and Gregory, Height, p. 22.

scale than in the case of height, but they are also more useful in predicting health outcomes. International differences, as well as height gains over time, are bound to fall to low levels in the future, offering less scope for research. In short, a combination of better direct data, better availability of more meaningful health measures and lower levels of variance in attained adult heights in rich countries will reduce future historians' interest in using adult attained heights to write the histories of rich nations.

The Future Uses of Heights

We noted at the outset that the mapping from height to other measures of well-being has recently attracted the attention of economic historians. Crafts has shown that stature in industrializing Britain was less correlated with other measures of the standard of living, such as life expectancy, infant mortality, literacy or real wages, than any one of these measures was with all others.[20] In the US, for example, there appears to be a puzzling decline in average stature during the middle of the nineteenth century, at a time when all other indicators of living standards are pointing upwards.[21] There are two main reasons why trends in height may systematically diverge, at certain points in time, from overall trends in the standard of living. First, exposure to disease may change in such a way as to reduce height, but improve well-being. The transition of many infectious diseases from deadly epidemics to benign childhood illnesses probably reduced heights, but clearly improved living standards.[22] Second, changes in the availability of consumer goods — through improved transport and goods innovation, for example — may lead to changes in consumer behaviour that impair height, even if the standard of living, broadly defined, has not suffered.[23]

The causes of such divergence are unlikely to operate in the postwar era. *L'unification microbienne*, the unification of the globe by disease, has been achieved long ago. Similarly it seems unlikely that there are any communities left where food consumption is running at extremely high levels simply because there are no other consumer

[20] Crafts, 'Some Dimensions'.
[21] Komlos, 'Anomalies'.
[22] Voth and Leunig, 'Did Smallpox?'
[23] Komlos, *Nutrition*.

goods available to purchase. There is therefore little reason to expect that future changes in heights will move in a 'perverse' fashion with changes in living standards.

We foresee two areas in which conventional data will either be unavailable or unreliable. In both cases there is at least a reasonable chance that the history of heights will prove to be a useful means by which economic historians are better able to explain the past. The first area is social history, and in particular family history, in the developed world. The second is the economic history of those countries or areas in which other data are scarce or too unreliable to be trusted.

Analysing Social Policy: the Heights of Children

We have already noted that gains in adult heights have slowed dramatically in most developed countries. Furthermore, given that many people reach their final heights substantially earlier than before, it appears that they have a long 'reserve' growth period that is no longer needed. The process of growing earlier, and more quickly, does not appear to be over—the rise in child heights by age in both England and Scotland continues.[24] It is noticeable that children's growth patterns are not perfectly smooth, but exhibit periods in which growth is checked and later catches up. So long as age-specific data—rather than just final height data—are collected, the variation in height gain offers future generations of social historians a potentially valuable source of information.

An extreme example demonstrates that the timing of growth may continue to be of interest even if final attained heights are not. During the Dutch Hunger Winter of 1944/5, the retreating German forces essentially starved the population of western Holland, a society already lacking food and fuel and under heavy psychological stress. As a result there was a cessation of growth among children. In the period after 1945, however, Dutch standards of living were sufficiently high that most children were able to make up entirely for their lost winter of growth.[25] It would be wrong to conclude that because the final attained heights of children of this generation recovered from their early insult, their standard of living was not affected by the events of 1944/5.

---

[24] Rona and Chinn, *National Study*, p. 32.
[25] Floud, Wachter and Gregory, *Height*, p. 19.

Rather, the pause in growth in 1944/5 is historically interesting and demonstrates severe problems in that society, problems that are not negated by the later height catch-up. The same is true for an individual's growth patterns. There is, for example, increasing evidence that reversible growth hormone deficiency (GHD) can have psychosocial causes. Children from disadvantaged family backgrounds are more likely to suffer reduced production of insulin-like growth factor 1 (IGF-1) without organic cause. Once placed in better care, they quickly return to normal levels of IGF-1 and growth hormone production, and experience catch-up growth with other children.[26] A similar case of severe stunting involving a 6.4-year-old boy who suffered from psychosocial GHD recently occurred in Britain.[27] In some cases, extreme stunting (sometimes termed 'psychosocial dwarfism') indicated extreme forms of psychosocial deprivation. Albanese et al. found that of 11 pre-pubertal children treated for growth failure without apparent organic cause, six had been sexually abused.[28] In all of these cases, later periods of above average height gain do not alter the fact that the earlier periods of height shortfalls indicate that something is wrong.

In contemporary life, welfare workers use growth shortfalls as an indicator of severe problems at an individual level. It is unlikely that economic and social historians of the future will do likewise. Rather, they are likely to use larger samples to detect smaller but more widespread height shortfalls that indicate more widespread social problems. Although smaller, these differences are not tiny: at the start of the 1960s, the Government's Chief Medical Officer for Education found that children in the poorer districts of Liverpool and Sheffield were between 1.5 and 6.6 centimetres shorter than children from more affluent parts of the same cities.[29] A substantial 'social gradient in height' among pre-school children continues to exist into the modern era.[30] A widespread programme of height measurement—or, better still, of weight or skinfold thickness—would allow social policy-makers today, and social historians tomorrow, to analyse policies that are otherwise hard to assess.

[26] Nieves-Rivera et al., 'Reversible Growth Failure', pp. 107–12.
[27] Stanhope et al., 'Physiological Growth Hormone Secretion', pp. 335–9.
[28] Albanese et al., 'Reversibility', pp. 687–92.
[29] Ministry of Education, *Health*, p. 11.
[30] Department of Health and Social Security, *Second Report on Nutritional Surveillance*, pp. 75–81, 95–7.

It is easy to think of family-oriented policies whose effects are hard to gauge. One example would be the current UK government's plan that, for low-wage families, child-related benefits should not be paid to the mother, as at present, but to the wage-earner, usually the father, via the wage packet. This is part of their programme to 'make work pay'. The move has, however, been strongly opposed by groups such as the Child Poverty Action Group, who argue that money is more likely to reach the child if paid to the mother. Direct evidence on this question is hard to come by. We cannot use aggregate income measures, or market-based data, because the whole question revolves around the allocation of resources within the family. Using age-specific height data before and after such changes may allow us to understand better the internal dynamics of family income distribution and, if done contemporaneously, might allow policy-makers to design public policy better in order to achieve the objectives set for it. An early attempt was made to analyse the withdrawal of free school milk using this methodology. Indeed, it was for this purpose that the *National Study of Health and Growth* was created. Unfortunately, it began data collection after the cessation of free milk, severely limiting its ability to create data to answer this question.[31] This approach has been used more successfully in South Africa. In the early 1990s pension coverage for blacks was increased dramatically.[32] One-third of black South African children live with an elderly person. Research showed that pensions received by women had a statistically significant effect on the height of female children in their households. This effect was large—sufficient to bridge more than half the gap between South African and US girls of the same age. The effect was smaller and insignificant for boys in such households, and the pension rise had no effect on the stature of children of either gender when it was received by men. Notice that it does not matter that any height shortfall will be made up later, nor that child height shortfalls have no long-term health consequences. All that is needed is the basic inference, accepted by all medical and public health authorities, that if a child is not getting taller, something is wrong.

---

[31] On the basis of smaller trials, no evidence was found that free school milk raised child heights. Rona and Chinn, *National Study*, chapter 13.
[32] Duflo, 'Child Health'.

Height can also be used to assess the efficacy of public policy in a wider sense. We know, for example, that in the eighteenth century, members of the upper class were on average some 9 centimetres taller than the poor. In the 1980s, the difference between men in class I/II and IV/V was 3 centimetres, substantially less than in the eighteenth century, but by no means a trivial height difference.[33] Since even the lower classes in England nowadays are well-fed by historical standards, the persistence of such differences is something of a puzzle.[34] This is especially true since the economy today is characterized neither by extensive heavy manual labour nor child labour. It therefore appears that neither nutrient intake nor (work-related) energy expenditure is directly responsible. There are a number of potential theories that may explain this finding. First, claims on energy intake, such as keeping warm, may have responded less flexibly to increased incomes than nutrient consumption itself—Britain still has a well-known problem of 'fuel poverty', the extreme manifestation of which is the early death of old-age pensioners as a result of inadequately heated homes. Second, there is a host of other environmental factors that are known to impact terminal heights. Medical research has shown that high concentrations of lead in drinking water lead to stunting in children—every increase by 10 micrograms/dL reduces the height of 7-year-old children by 1.57 centimetres.[35] High nitrate concentrations have also been hypothesized to produce similar effects, but the evidence is not always convincing.[36] To the extent to which the replacement of lead pipes has taken longer in poorer parts of Britain, for example, the continuing sensitivity of height with respect to class can be explained.

Age-specific height data can be used to assess the effects of long-run social changes. Two examples include the rising number of lone parent households and rising inequality in work patterns, with the growth of both no worker and dual worker households in many western countries. We know, for example, that at the whole nation level, the secular rise in child heights ceased temporarily in the period 1979 to 1986 in both England and Scotland.[37] During this period positive

---

[33] Floud, Wachter and Gregory, *Height*, p. 199.
[34] Note also that the group of men, aged 16 to 64 in 1980, would not yet have been affected by differences in access to health care—the rise in private health care as a result of NHS inadequacies occurred later.
[35] Ballew et al., 'Blood', pp. 623–30.
[36] Gatseva et al. 'Physical Development', pp. 108–14.
[37] Rona and Chinn, *National Study*, p. 31.

height gains continued to be recorded within social groups, but these within-group rises were negated by the redistribution of the population from taller to shorter groups. This was particularly important in England, where many of the newly unemployed had previously been skilled manual workers.[38]

Collecting data on the height of children should allow us to understand the link between inequality and height shortfalls more fully. At present there is a debate as to whether inequality per se causes height shortfalls, through some sort of psychosocial mechanism, or whether inequality is only correlated with such shortfalls because it indicates the presence of (absolute) poverty.[39] If it is the former, we would expect that, *ceteris paribus*, for any given income level, areas with lower inequality would have taller children. In Britain there are very good data on income inequality by area. The Inland Revenue publishes annual figures giving the mean and median income of taxpayers for each of the UK's 407 local councils.[40] These show much variation: some areas are poor but equal, others poor and unequal, a third group is rich and equal while the remainder are both rich and unequal.[41] There are even more locationally specific data for unemployment, with most local council employment services recording unemployment at ward level, where each ward contains between 6 and 12 thousand adults.[42] In addition, the Index of Local Conditions, a measure of deprivation, is available at the level of local council enumeration districts.[43] With an average of just 300 adults each, these enumeration districts are tiny, and mean that there exists remarkably good evidence for the location of both the most deprived areas, and the most unequal areas in Britain.[44] Furthermore, since almost all primary school children attend their closest school, it is possible to map these measures of

---

[38] Ibid., p. 33.
[39] See Harris, *Height of the Schoolchild*, for a fuller discussion.
[40] Borough, District or Unitary Authorities, Bailey, ed., *Inland Revenue Statistics*, p. 32 and table 3.14, pp. 48–52.
[41] For example, respectively, Sedgefield, County Durham (median income £10,900, mean to median income ratio 1.14), Craven, Yorkshire (£9,350/2.17), Spelthorne, Surrey (£16,400/1.15) and the City of London (£29,800/2.87), Bailey, ed., *Inland Revenue Statistics*, table 3.14, pp. 48–52.
[42] The data are compiled and released by most council employment services on a regular basis.
[43] The data are collected by the Department of the Environment, Transport and the Regions.
[44] Based on the London Borough of Hammersmith and Fulham.

deprivation into school-based data with remarkable precision. This should make it possible to assess whether, through psychosocial mechanisms, children's development is slowed by inequality at the local, regional or national level.

In the light of these suggested uses for child height data the authors regret both the ending of universal height measurement in the UK, and that nationwide data were not properly kept when the policy was in force. The authors correspondingly endorse the recommendation of the UK Joint Working Party of Child Health Surveillance that all children be measured at ages five, seven and nine, and argue that the data should be available to researchers at school level. Of the three ages, the most important is five, on entry to school. At this point height more closely reflects the realities of home life than at later ages, where height is also affected by the stresses of interacting, perhaps for the first time, with non-family members on a regular basis.

It would, of course, be possible to use biological indicators other than height to assess both the effects of changing social conditions and policies, and the links between poverty, inequality and children's development. The choice of height, weight, weight for height, skinfold thickness and so on is essentially a pragmatic one. Historians will use whichever has been collected previously; governments should collect the data in a cost-effective manner. In this decision height retains some advantages. Compared with weight-based measures it does not suffer from reversal, and the cessation of height gain is easier to interpret.[45] Weight loss, unlike height loss, can be a positive choice on the part of the child, and excessive weights for some can make average weights misleading. Height is also relatively quick and easy to measure, and needs less specialized equipment or training than, say, measures such as skinfold thickness. We note that the UK Joint Working Party of Child Health Surveillance recommended that children's heights, rather than other auxological measures, should be recorded, but historians will be able to make use of any such data to answer important questions about the conditions under which families exist and thrive.

---

[45] In contrast, weight can be lost through a conscious decision by parents or children, perhaps for fashion or health, or inadvertently, especially if warmer weather leads children to forsake the television in favour of more physical outdoor activities. Such weight losses are harder to interpret, both in health and social terms.

Analysing Political Change: Heights in Transition Economies

The second instance where height data will continue to interest future economic historians is where they are the only reliable data available. One unambiguous advantage of using heights is that even when bureaucrats choose not to record the data at the time, the data can be recorded with a reasonable degree of accuracy some years later. Once a person has attained their final height, they remain at that height until at least middle age; furthermore their peak height can be gauged reasonably accurately even when they are old.[46] Self-evidently this is not true for income data, but furthermore it is not true for other auxological measures, including those that involve weight data, such as the waist to hip ratio, and those that measure subcutaneous fat levels, such as skin-fold thickness. This ability to collect data that were not recorded contemporaneously is useful for historians of societies that do not record more traditional standard of living data accurately, either because of omission or deliberate error.

Subsistence-based economies are one example where both individual and national income data may rest on heroic assumptions. In addition, cash economies (and advanced economies with large black market sectors in which transactions go entirely unrecorded to escape taxation), and economies where the government's administrative apparatus is very weak, may suffer from very poor and incomplete data collection. Thus in many countries both individuals and — sometimes — the state have an incentive to lie about GDP. If individuals are self-certifying income that may later be used for tax assessment purposes they have a clear incentive to understate their income. More generally the relationship between the state and its citizens will affect the quality of statistical data. For example Atkinson and Micklewright report a fall in the response rates to the Polish Household Survey following the imposition of Martial Law.[47] If the state itself is a recipient or potential recipient of overseas assistance, they too may have an incentive to under-report the level of national income. In contrast we

---

[46] Evidence exists that the turning point for height is around the ages of 35–40, with people growing trivial amounts in the previous decade, and shrinking trivial amounts in the following decade. By the age of 70, people are on average one inch shorter than when they were 25. Floud, Wachter and Gregory, *Height*, p. 163.

[47] Atkinson and Micklewright, 'Economic Transformation', p. 16.

know that, for political reasons, the East European communist bloc substantially overstated the standard of living prior to the fall of the Berlin Wall, and many western experts are sceptical about the income and growth figures produced by the remaining communist countries, China, Cuba and North Korea.[48]

The ability to collect height data long after the historical events whose effects we wish to understand may be especially useful in understanding the economic history of economies that have undergone a transition from communism to capitalism, especially if new countries are born in the process. National income data will almost certainly be available for the communist period, but may be unusable for three reasons. First, under communism it may have been falsified for political purposes. Second, the prices used to construct the GDP estimates may be far from market prices. Third, data for the new nation itself may simply not be available for the period prior to independence, when it was part of a larger political unit. National income figures for the transition period, in contrast, may well suffer from under-reporting — the black economy is more likely to flourish — and from different methods of accounting for the production of large industrial companies whose survival is based on the continuance of soft credit. In these circumstances economic historians retain the ability, half a century or so after the beginning of transition, to collect the heights of the current adult population of different ages, and so construct a consistent measure of the standard of living in the communist, transition and post-transition economy. The income levels of these countries suggest that heights may prove responsive to changes in economic conditions. At the end of the communist period, the official figure for GDP per head in the USSR was $2,055.[49] Figure 1 makes it clear that typical countries with an income of around $2,000 still have 6–8 centimetres of growth to gain to reach 'western' levels, and that relatively slight falls in income at these levels can be expected to yield quite substantial falls in attained heights.

---

[48] Such scepticism proved well founded for the USSR. Official Soviet figures give growth, 1928 to 1984, at 9.7 per cent per annum, whereas US estimates — now accepted as much more reliable — give a figure of 4.8 per cent. The power of compound interest is such that Soviet estimates suggest national income grew by a factor of 178 over this period, while US estimates suggest a factor of just 14. Gregory and Stuart, *Soviet and post-Soviet Economic Structure*, p. 235.

[49] All figures are for 1988. *Economist Vital World Statistics*, p. 34.

The quality of conventional GDP data for the countries of Eastern Europe is sufficiently high to allow economic history to be written based on conventional measures. This is, however, less true for the former Soviet Union, where the problems of general under-reporting and non-market prices are much more pervasive. In addition, the Russian Federation is today made up of 89 constituent parts. It is at least plausible that, at some stage, some of these constituent parts will successfully establish themselves as independent nations. Whether that process is painless or bloody, it seems unlikely that historians will find it easy to assemble accurate series for living standards for such new nations prior to their independence. Even without historians measuring people in middle age, the widespread use of conscription may, as for so many countries historically, offer relatively good quality height data for such nations. Changes in genetic composition as a result of Russians leaving the far-flung provinces of the former Soviet Empire should be relatively easy to overcome—last names alone should provide a robust indicator of ethnic origin. In summary, the absence of reliable conventional data combined with the potential availability of height statistics, means that a height-based history of the former Soviet Union will surely prove as attractive as measuring the heights of individuals during the British Industrial Revolution.

The 'height history' of the transition from communism to capitalism may also interest social and economic historians for another reason—its link to the different values of communist countries. The claim of many such countries was not that their growth rates were the highest in the world, but that they had 'developed country' health indicators despite 'less-developed country' levels of income. Today the most vigorous defender of the second way is Cuba, which is able to boast infant mortality rates just 18 per cent worse than OECD levels, even though its level of GDP per head is 85 per cent below OECD levels. Similar comparisons can be made in Asia, where the East Asian market economies have infant mortality rates 65 per cent higher than their planned neighbours, despite having income levels that are four times as high.[50] We would correspondingly expect planned economies to have substantially better height profiles than their income levels would

---

[50] The market economies consist of Hong Kong, Indonesia, South Korea, Malaysia, Papua New Guinea, the Philippines, Singapore and Thailand, while the planned economies consist of Burma, Cambodia, China, North Korea, Laos and Vietnam. *Economist Vital World Statistics.*

suggest.[51] The causes of this performance seem to be two-fold. First, planned economies have broadly similar relative poverty profiles to those of richer OECD nations; that is, they are far more egalitarian than capitalist nations at similar levels of development.[52] Second, they have made the conscious choice to spend substantially more on health care than capitalist nations: a case of public affluence and private squalor. Thus we find that Eastern Europe had 60 per cent more doctors per head of population in 1988 than did OECD nations, while the planned Asian economies had more than three times as many doctors than their capitalist Asian neighbours. In each case, the capitalist half of the comparison is at least five times richer than the communist half.[53]

Both of these aspects of communist countries, relatively low inequality and relatively high spending on health care, are likely to decline at least in the transition stage. This means that writing the history of transition in terms of height will give a very different story from writing the story in terms of GDP per head. In particular, if under communism most people have a sufficiently healthy start to life that they are able to approach more closely their full height potential than would be expected from their income alone, then heights will be vulnerable to the introduction of a market economy. In the early stages of transition we might expect both income and heights to fall, as the demolition phase of transition occurs. But even in the medium term, as average GDP per head rises above the communist level, the rise in inequality might lead us to expect average height to remain at less than its communist level for a considerable period of time. This is an example of where we might expect the height and income stories systematically to diverge, but it is at least arguable that both will offer meaningful stories. A history in GDP will mirror capitalist values and

---

[51] We find, for example, that in 1965, 8-year-old Moscovite boys were the tallest of eight European nations for which we have comparable data. Boys from Naples were shortest. By 1980 Dutch boys were tallest, with Moscovites slipping to fifth place, albeit still ahead of boys from Brussels, Athens and Naples. Boys were taller in 1980 than in 1965 for all groups except Moscovites. In a study of 16-year-old boys, Czechs were as tall or taller than Danes in both 1965 and 1980, while boys from Warsaw were taller than those of Brussels. In all cases the communist countries had substantially lower levels of national income than the non-communist countries. Eveleth and Tanner, *Worldwide Variation*, pp. 30–2. A more detailed height history of Poland is given in Bielicki and Szklarska, 'Secular Trends'.

[52] Atkinson and Micklewright, 'Economic Transformation'.

[53] *Economist Vital World Statistics*, pp. 34, 216.

capitalist expectations, while a history in height will place much greater weight on those things which communist regimes emphasized, such as equality and public services.

A multi-country height history of the former communist states would have a further advantage. By looking at those nations for whom we have good data, we may be able better to calibrate the effect of known changes in income levels, growth rates, unemployment and inequality on heights. By better understanding what causes height changes, it will be easier to interpret changes in heights in conditions where we have only limited amounts of other data.

Conclusion

As the average height of an adult population ceases to rise, the history of adult heights must cease with it. We believe that we are fast reaching such a point for most OECD countries. In those countries the tall story will turn towards the shortest, and use the height of children to answer a different, but by no means less important, set of questions. Average adult heights will, in contrast, remain potentially interesting in countries whose income levels have not reached those of the West. Just as for the history of Britain in the Industrial Revolution, our interest in height inevitably increases as the availability of other data declines. Wherever possible, historians will follow the medical experts in deciding which anthropometric indicators are most worthwhile, and in all cases they will be forced to work with whatever form of data is left by one generation for the next. That much, at least, will never change.

Note. As Newton wrote, 'If I have seen further it is by standing on the shoulders of giants', and we thank Liam Brunt, Nick Crafts, Roderick Floud, Tam Fry, Bernard Harris, Clive Osmond, James Tanner, Linda Voss and participants at the 1999 Conference to honour the work of Charles Feinstein for their help in writing this paper. Needless to say, we alone are responsible for our opinions and our errors.

References

Albanese, A., G. Hamill, J. Jones et al. 'Reversibility of Physiological Hormone Secretion in Children with Psychosocial Dwarfism.' *Clinical Endocrinology* 40 (1994): 687–92.

Atkinson, A.B., and J. Micklewright. 'Economic Transformation in Eastern Europe and the Distribution of Income.' In *Economics for a New Europe*, edited by A.B. Atkinson and R. Brunetta, 147–74. New York: New York University Press, 1991.

Bailey, D. (ed.). *Inland Revenue Statistics*. London: The Stationery Office, 1998.

Ballew, C., L. Khan, R. Kaufmann et al. 'Blood Lead Concentration and Children's Anthropometric Dimensions in the Third National Health and Nutrition Examination Survey.' *Journal of Pediatrics* 134 (1999): 623–30.

Behrman, J., and A. Deolalikar. 'Is Variety the Spice of Life? Implications for Calorie Intake.' *Review of Economics and Statistics* 71, no. 4 (1989): 666–72.

Behrman, J., and B. Wolfe. 'More Evidence on Nutrition Demand: Income Seems Overrated.' *Journal of Development Economics* (1984): 105–28.

Bielicki, T., and A. Szklarska. 'Secular Trends in Stature in Poland: National and Social Class-specific.' *Annals of Human Biology* 26, no. 3 (1999): 251–8.

Cernerud, L., and G. Lindgren. 'Secular Changes in Height and Weight of Stockholm Schoolchildren Born in 1933, 1943, 1953, and 1963.' *Annals of Human Biology* 18 (1991): 497–505.

Clark, G., M. Huberman and P. Lindert. 'A British Food Puzzle, 1770–1850.' *Economic History Review* 48 no. 2 (1995): 215–37.

Costa, D. 'Height, Weight, Wartime Stress, and Older Age Mortality: Evidence from Union Army Records.' *Explorations in Economic History* 30 (1993): 424–49.

Crafts, N.F.R. 'Some Dimensions of the Quality of Life in Britain during the Industrial Revolution.' *Economic History Review* 50, no. 4 (1997): 617–39.

Duflo, E. 'Child Health and Household Resources in South Africa: Evidence from the Old Age Pension Program.' *American Economic Review* 90, no. 2 (2000): 393–8.

Eveleth, P.B., and J.M. Tanner. *Worldwide Variation in Human Growth*. Cambridge: Cambridge University Press, 1990.

Floud, R.C., K.W. Wachter and A. Gregory. *Height, Health and History: Nutritional Status in the United Kingdom, 1750–1980*. Cambridge: Cambridge University Press, 1990.

Fogel, R. and L. Wimmer. 'Early Indicators of Later Work Levels, Disease, and Death.' NBER Working Paper on Historical Factors in Long Run Growth 38. Cambridge, MA, 1992.

Gatseva, P., A. Aleksandrova, N. Ivanova et al. 'The Physical Development of Children Living in a Settlement with a High Nitrate Content in the Drinking Water.' *Problema Khig* 22 (1997): 108–14.

Gregory, P.R., and R.C. Stuart. *Soviet and post-Soviet Economic Structure and Performance* (5th edition). New York: HarperCollins, 1994.

Greulich, W. 'Some Secular Changes in the Growth of American-born and Native Japanese Children.' *American Journal of Physical Anthropology* 45 (1976): 553–68.

Harris, B. *Height of the Schoolchild.* Buckingham: Open University Press, 1991.

Kalmijn, S., J. Curb, B. Rodriguez et al. 'The Association of Body Weight and Anthropometry with Mortality in Elderly Men.' *International Journal of Obesity and Related Metabolic Disorders* 23 (1999): 395–402.

Kannam, J., D. Levy, M. Larson et al. 'Short Stature and Risk for Mortality and Cardiovascular Events. The Framington Heart Study.' *Circulation* 90 (1994): 2241–7.

Komlos, J. *Nutrition and Economic Development in the Eighteenth-Century Habsburg Monarchy: An Anthropometric History.* Princeton: Princeton University Press, 1989.

⸺. 'Anomalies in Economic History: Towards a Resolution of the "Antebellum Puzzle".' *Journal of Economic History* 56 (1996): 202–14.

Liao, Y., D. McGee, G. Cao et al. 'Short Stature and Risk of Mortality and Cardiovascular Disease: Negative Findings from the NHANES I Epidemiologic Follow-up Study.' *Journal of the American College of Cardiology* 27 (1996): 678–82.

Maddison, A. *Monitoring the World Economy.* Paris: OECD, 1995.

Meyer, H.E., and R. Selmer. 'Income, Eucational Level and Body Height.' *Annals of Human Biology* 26, no. 3 (1999): 219–27.

Nieves-Rivera, F., L. Gonzalez de Pijem and B. Mirabal. 'Reversible Growth Failure among Hispanic Children: Instances of Psychosocial Short Stature.' *Puerto Rican Health Science Journal* 17 (1998): 107–12.

O'Connell, J., M. Dibley, J. Sierra et al. 'Growth of Vegetarian Children: The Farm Study.' *Pediatrics* 84 (1989): 475–81.

Pritchett, L. 'Divergence, Big Time.' *Journal of Economic Perspectives* (1997): 3–17.

Rona, R.J., and S. Chinn. *The National Study of Health and Growth.* Oxford: Oxford University Press, 1999.

Samaras, T., and L. Storms. 'Impact of Height and Weight on Life Span.' *Bulletin of the World Health Organization* 70 (1992): 259–67.

Seckler, D. 'Malnutrition: An Intellectual Odyssey.' *Western Journal of Agricultural Economics* (1980).

Srinivasan, T. 'Undernutrition: Concepts, Measurements, and Policy Implications.' In *Nutrition and Poverty*, edited by S. Osmani, 97–120. Oxford: Clarendon Press, 1992.

Stanhope, R., P. Adlard, G. Hamill et al. 'Physiological Growth Hormone (GH) Secretion During Recovery from Psychosocial Dwarfism.' *Clinical Endocrinology* 28 (1988): 335–9.

Steckel, R. 'Stature and the Standard of Living.' *Journal of Economic Literature* 33, no. 4 (1995): 1903–40.

⸺. 'Height and Per Capita Income.' *Historical Methods* 16, no. 1 (1983): 1–7.

The Economist Book of Vital World Statistics: A Complete Guide to the World in Figures. London: Hutchinson, 1990.

United Kingdom, Department of Health and Social Security. 'Second Report by the Sub-Committee on Nutritional Surveillance (Committee on Medical Aspects of Food Policy).' *Reports on Health and Social Subjects*, no. 21.

United Kingdom, Ministry of Education. *Health of the Schoolchild 1960–1. Report of the Chief Medical Officer of the Ministry of Education for 1960–1.* London: HMSO, 1962.

Voth, H.-J., and T. Leunig. 'Did Smallpox Reduce Height?' *Economic History Review* 49, no. 3 (1996): 541–60.

Waaler, H. 'Height, Weight and Mortality: The Norwegian Experience.' *Acta Medica Scandinavica*, Supplement 679 (1984): 1–56.

Xu, Y., S. Liang and D. Liu. 'Comparison of Stature Growth Curves in Children and Adolescents.' *Chung Hua Yu Fang I Hsueh Tsa Chih* 31 (1997): 212–14.

Yuan, J., R. Ross, Y. Gao et al. 'Body Weight and Mortality: A Prospective Evaluation in a Cohort of Middle-aged Men in Shanghai, China.' *International Journal of Epidemiology* 27 (1998): 824–32.

15.
Producing Health in Past and Present:
The Changing Roles of Scientific and Alternative Medicine
ANNE DIGBY & SHEILA RYAN JOHANSSON

Introduction

Twentieth-century medical care has been increasingly based on theories and practices associated with western scientific medicine, and an implicit assumption has been that this efficacious form of medicine, provided by scientifically trained practitioners, would steadily displace any of its competitors. In many developing countries, however, 'alternative' medicine in the form of traditional healing remains resilient. This paper is unusual in applying the term 'alternative medicine' to traditional healing and to folk medicine, but justifies this usage in relation to its application to a long-run analysis of pluralistic forms of medical care in both developing and developed countries.

In developed countries alternative forms of medicine are thriving. During the 1980s, for every 20 people in Great Britain who consulted a general practitioner through the National Health Service, one person sought help from an alternative practitioner. Since then utilization rates have grown by ten per cent a year or more; at this rate patients will soon be as likely to use one system of healing as the other. This resurgence of alternative medicine is perceived as a policy problem for the twenty-first century.[1] To the extent that it is thought of as unscientific, the increasing popularity of alternative medicine may imply more quackery or consumer fraud. And, if alternative medicine is crowding out scientific medicine, then the formidable levels of disease control

[1] Sharma, 'Using Alternative Therapies', pp. 127–39.

that underpin high levels of life expectancy may also be threatened. But this popularity of alternative forms of medicine can also be seen as a beneficial development because it involves complementarity rather than substitution.[2] As economists might suspect, unorthodox forms of medicine exist because they satisfy a demand for forms of healing that scientific medicine cannot—or will not—deliver. This paper argues that in both developed and developing countries maximizing the production of health-related welfare may require the continued existence of these two different—but complementary—medical systems. Rival practitioners may regard alternative systems of care as potential substitutes for one another (in which case the better system should eliminate the other), but in reality the loss of either system would reduce the production of health-related human welfare.

Pursuing Health

Scientific medicine defines 'health' largely in negative terms as the absence of disease; in contrast alternative medicine defines 'health' as a positive state of feeling well. Somewhat surprisingly, influential institutions such as the United Nation's World Health Organization (WHO) have officially declared that 'health' should be conceptualized in positive terms as the individual attainment of complete physical, mental and social well-being, and not simply the global equalization of disease control.[3] In Britain, for example, there is popular awareness both of positive and negative meanings of health.[4]

The central goal of most forms of alternative medicine is to increase the individual patient's sense of well-being. Alternative practitioners think of themselves as experts in 'whole-person' medicine,[5] because

---

[2] Economists give the concepts 'substitutes' and 'complements' precise mathematical meaning in the context of demand theory and production theory. In this paper the concepts are used in a more general sense that, nonetheless, shares the same intuitive meaning. When A and B are substitutes, having more of A reduces the need for B. When A and B are complements, the opposite is true. Even economists sometimes employ the terms in this looser fashion. (See David and Hall, 'Heart of Darkness'; Wibble, *The Economics of Science*, pp. 322–7.)

[3] 'Health' is a vague concept with (at least) half a dozen alternative definitions. In contemporary health research specialists tend to define 'health' in a way that privileges their professional concerns and the standard methods of measurement used in their own fields. (See Johansson, 'The Politics of Discourse Synthesis', pp. 43–53.)

[4] Charlton and Murphy (eds.), *The Health of Adult Britain*, p. 3.

[5] Dillard and Ziporyn, *Alternative Medicine*, p. 15.

they look beyond the obvious symptoms of disease to find out why a patient does not feel well. Explaining why will usually involve understanding the individual's lifestyle, attitudes and unique constitution, which means that no two patients are perceived as being alike. For the sufferer alternative medicine thus offers a wide range of individualized approaches to feeling better. In contrast, scientific medicine today is based on preventing and treating specific diseases through standardized methods of care involving medical technology and powerful pharmaceuticals. Interestingly, this relatively impersonal treatment contrasts with the more holistic care that could be found, for example, in an earlier variant of scientific medicine — that of British primary healthcare. At best, this was characterized by general practitioners' attentive and humane treatment of their patients — itself facilitated by long-term continuity of care based on doctor's knowledge of individual patients and their family circumstances.[6] Treated with less instrumentality or haste, the doctors' sympathetic attention left patients feeling cared for, and their problems understood. This has been succeeded by contemporary scientific medicine which, despite its superior efficacy, may leave the patient feeling less the subject of treatment than its object. Individuals in developed countries who have been kept disease-free (or have been restored to that state) because of preventive or curative scientific medicine may therefore go in search of positive health by turning to alternative forms of medicine. These are generally perceived as a complement to, and not as a substitute for, scientific medicine.

In many developing countries also, different forms of medicine are used as complements within a system of medical pluralism. Typically, western scientific medicine in health clinics will be a resort for acute conditions, for 'white man's diseases', and when surgery is needed. (However, western medicine may be delivered in a culturally insensitive way so that its effectiveness is curtailed.)[7] Traditional healing will be used for 'local diseases', or for chronic and puzzling ailments. The latter may also be employed after western treatments have 'cured' the patient, in order to address the significance of the sickness and its causes.[8] Scientific medicine does not attempt to answer the 'why me?' cry of the afflicted, so that traditional healing may act as a valuable complement

---

[6] Digby, *The Evolution*.
[7] Johansson, 'Cultural Software', pp. 47–50.
[8] Matse, 'A History of Disease'.

in attempting to assign meaning to disease, in either an individual or a social context. In these varied ways traditional medicine continues to play a central role in the production of health-related forms of welfare.

Within any historical context alternative systems of health care give consumers more freedom to use their own resources to pursue health as they see fit. But when consumers do not know how to evaluate the efficacy of different forms of medical care, their lack of expertise renders them vulnerable to deception and fraud by unscrupulous professionals. The medical market is ill-equipped to produce, test and deliver abstract knowledge about effective disease control in response to price signals from individual consumers in need of immediate care. Such knowledge is a public good best produced by institutions capable of allocating the necessary material and social resources to basic research. From its inception scientific medicine was based on 'research' but this does not necessarily produce a continuing stream of useful innovations. Without continuing competition from alternative forms of care, medical science might well have ossified, and adhered blindly to established theories of disease instead of evolving dynamically.

Understanding how alternative systems of care contribute to the production of health-related well-being can most fruitfully be done in specific contexts. The importance of context gives history its relevance to understanding the present, including the policy issues related to the public provision of scientific care and/or the formal regulation of 'unscientific' medicine. Because the relationship between information and innovation, markets and mentalities, health and healing is not timeless and universal, it is best understood in context. For example, what we recognize as scientific evolved within a Western European cultural framework; it was not imposed on ordinary people as a side-effect of colonialism or imperialism. Thus, western medical science could increase health-related human welfare in Europe by controlling disease without necessarily diminishing perceived well-being. But when western medicine was introduced as a foreign system of healing, it was frequently embedded in a wave of cultural disruption inimical to security and self-esteem.[9] In some non-western historical contexts 'health' may increase in the biological sense (as various diseases come under increased medical control), while decreasing in another sense (because psycho-cultural disorientation is felt as a loss of 'well-being').[10]

---

[9] Watts, *Epidemics in History*. See also Arnold, *Colonizing the Body*.
[10] Ibid., pp. 1–5. See also, Turshen, *The Political Economy*.

Different circumstances require different policies. To the extent that health policy must be context-sensitive, the history of scientific medicine and the alternatives to it become as relevant to the present as the latest models based on the most recent statistics. This paper looks first at the development of scientific and alternative medicine focusing on a European context, and within this in more detail on an English case study, before widening its geographical and cultural locus to Asia and Africa. It ends with a discussion of South Africa.

Medicine as Science in the European Past

It is often argued that medicine, even western medicine, only became 'scientific' in the last hundred years. Since the adjective 'scientific' came into general use in the last half of the nineteenth century, this view has the virtue of literal truth.[11] But the noun 'science' is far older, and so is medicine's official status as a science. In Ancient Rome *scientia* generally referred to all those systems of belief whose characteristics were rigour and certainty. This made them worthy of trust in some sense, and legitimized the sale of professional expertise to non-experts.[12] Medicine became this kind of science in Western Europe about 900 years ago, when it was first taught at various universities alongside law and theology, which were also classified as sciences.

Previously, medical care in Europe was based on traditional folk medicine (in all its local diversity) to which the Greeks and Romans had added information about new drugs and surgical procedures. This stock of knowledge was subsequently devalued by Christianity, which tended to favour the idea that the best healing was spiritual healing.[13] The upshot was that by AD 1000 medieval healers, including some who were priests, combined religion, magic and medicine in a way that had similarities with traditional healers in modern developing countries. European folk medicine had some positive effects, not least in giving meaning to the occurrence of sickness, in encouraging coping strategies, and in capitalizing on the *placebo* effect.[14] Moreover, some folk

---

[11] Lindberg, *The Beginnings*, p. 4.
[12] Nutton, 'Roman Medicine', pp. 39–70.
[13] Rawcliffe, *Medicine and Society*.
[14] Root-Bernstein, *Mud, Maggots*; Dillard and Ziporyn, *Alternative Medicine*, p. 37. Any treatment that works less than 68 per cent of the time is thought to be working by chance and/or wishful thinking.

443

medicines were based on plant extracts that, when later scientifically tested, were found to be efficacious in a modern clinical sense.

In early medieval Europe richer Europeans could more easily obtain the services of healers with the best reputation but, since reputation was inseparable from a talent for self-promotion, consumers did not know precisely what they were buying. Historical mortality data indicate that those adults who belonged to wealthy elites did not seem to have lived any longer, on average, than ordinary peasants, despite having multiple material advantages.[15] Like other Europeans, elite groups had a life expectancy at birth in the neighbourhood of 30 years.[16] The descriptive literature on the health of medieval and early modern elites suggests that from infancy onwards their comparatively short lives were beset by recurrent disease.

In pursuit of better health care for themselves Europe's ruling supported the creation of a new system of medicine.[17] Between AD 1100 and 1500 dozens of universities were founded in Europe, and about 50 of them eventually taught medicine as a science, where graduates could earn degrees as bachelors of medicine and doctors of medicine.[18] Medicine was based on the study of authoritative texts which were inherited from the ancients, so that research consisted of recovering, translating and interpreting these canonical texts, and elaborating on the general equilibrium theory of disease they contained. Health was perceived to be the product of the balance between the body's four humours: blood, bile, phlegm and choler. Humoural disequilibrium was the cause of all disease and the key to its prevention. The humours could be kept in balance through 'regimen' or lifestyle — including appropriate diet, exercise, sleep, sexuality and state of mind. When lost, equilibrium could be restored by generic healing techniques

---

[15] Ordinary people in England had a life expectancy at age 25 of circa 30 years from AD 1300 to 1500 (Smith, 'Plagues and Peoples'). At the same time males belonging to England's ducal families had a life expectancy at age 20 years of circa 24 years; females, who were less subject to violent death, had a value of circa 30 years, closer to the average. (See Hollingsworth, 1957, 'A Demographic Study'.) Elite mortality data for the early modern period is summarized by Woods and Williams, 'Must the Gap Widen?'

[16] Groups with a life expectancy at birth of circa 30 years survive half of the ever born to the threshold of adulthood, and half of all those suriving adults lived to the age of 40 to 45 years. Only 10 per cent of the ever born live as long as 70 years.

[17] Lindberg, *Western Science*. The precise circumstances which led to the creation of medical programmes in various medieval universites remain poorly understood.

[18] For the dates and location of medieval European universities teaching medicine see Nutton, 'Medicine', p. 154.

including bleeding and purging. Since individual patients had different constitutions and medical histories, what successfully restored equilibrium to one patient might not work for another. Hence the need for frequent medical supervision from a physician who knew his patient as an individual. Physicians also gave advice to their patients on every aspect of life, based on the training in astrology they received, which gave their health advice a mathematical foundation.[19] Medicine as a medieval science therefore seems to have had more in common with 'whole-person' healing than with disease-specific medicine.

As long as the university medicine remained expensive, ordinary people continued to treat themselves, or receive treatment in the home. There women (and sometimes men) used knowledge passed down from generation to generation. When domestic expertise failed, local healers (some of whom were also women) were called in to treat symptoms that would not disappear.[20] In addition, midwives were called upon for help in managing pregnancy and childbirth. Although women were an integral part of medieval health care, they were excluded from the formal study of physic in universities. Fortunately, babies could be delivered, broken bones set, wounds treated, boils lanced, hernias repaired, teeth pulled, fevers nursed, all without the benefit of a general equilibrium theory of disease or attendance by a learned physician.

Physicians competed in the urban medical market with leading empirics who boasted of their ability to cure specific diseases using secret remedies. The curative expertise of empirics involved a willingness to experiment with new drugs and, in their sale of medical care, empirics 'tested' most of the new drugs coming into Europe after 1500 as part of the expansion of trade with the Far East, Africa and the 'New World'. Because exotic drugs were profitable, empirical medicine stayed commercially successful. From the 1400s onwards the consumer's demand for empirical medicine forced institutionalized medicine to offer students more courses on the treatment of specific diseases. Nevertheless, the practitioners of learned medicine continued to denounce empirical medicine as an inferior substitute for health care based on theory.

---

[19] Rawcliffe, *Medicine and Society*, p. 218.
[20] Ibid, chapters 8 and 9.

Halfway through the millennium Western Europe was convulsed with the intellectual ferment of the Renaissance, Reformation and Counter Reformation—in the course of which medicine as a science was revolutionized. Reformers such as Paracelsus proclaimed that medical truths could only be discovered by studying nature, not ancient texts. And, to the extent that observation and experiment were increasingly accepted as the foundation of genuine knowledge about natural processes including disease, text-based and theory-oriented medicine no longer seemed to be a real science. During the scientific revolution of the seventeenth century[21] the remodelling of medicine as a new science (that is, commonly spoken of as a new kind of natural philosophy) was most far-reaching in England, not least because English university medicine had remained more purely scholastic (text-based and theory-oriented) and resistant to change for much longer than in continental Europe.[22]

Leading philosophers such as John Locke legitimized the idea that in theory, medicine could do without theory and still be a science. Locke's friend, the physician Thomas Sydenham, had inspired Locke's philosophizing by working along empirical lines in his own private practice and in London's hospitals. Sydenham radically transformed traditional bedside methods for treating specific diseases; he became known as the English Hippocrates and the father of clinical medicine. To Sydenham the physician's challenge was to list and classify individual diseases, and discover the specific drugs that cured them; for example, chinchona bark containing quinine cured the ague (malaria) and iron cured the green sickness (anaemia).

As an empirically-oriented science English medicine began to outstrip continental medicine, partly because the most innovative physicians were willing to dispense with theory as the basis of their claim for superiority over alternative practitioners.[23] Most of those eighteenth-century physicians who hoped to make a successful medical living had no choice but to keep one foot in hospital-based medicine and one foot in England's thriving medical market.[24] Significantly, however, elite members of society used the new form of medicine as their preferred form of health care but when it let them down, they were quite

---

[21] Hall, *Revolution in Science*; Shapin, *Scientific Revolution*.
[22] Cook, 'New Philosophy', and Cook, 'Living', pp. 111–136.
[23] Lindberg and Westman, 'Introduction', pp. 1–15.
[24] Digby, *Making a Medical Living*.

willing to use various forms of alternative medicine as well. However, the majority of the population still relied on unorthodox or alternative practitioners, unless they could obtain the charitable services of an orthodox practitioner.

Was this early modern medicine more scientific than the earlier scholastic medicine? In abstract terms that depends on how 'science' is defined. A Newtonian would see the new medicine as still being unscientific because it was not based on general laws expressed in mathematical terms. If experimental methods are valued more highly than equations, then this medicine was genuinely scientific because it was based on observation and experiment.[25] The new medicine contributed novel ways of preventing, treating and curing diseases.[26] By 1600 lives threatened by bloody flux (severe diarrhoea) could be treated with new and more effective drugs such as iapec (imported from Brazil); by 1700 syphilis could be prevented with condoms, and treated with guiacum (a New World anti-bacterial bark) as well as with mercury, whilst scurvy could be prevented and cured with citrus fruits; and after 1720 smallpox could be prevented through inoculation (a new procedure imported from Turkey). Even the medicine of regimen was adapted along more disease-specific lines to prevent and treat such chronic diseases of middle age as gout. England's leading surgeons also became more sophisticated in developing new instruments and techniques to make operations faster and safer. During the eighteenth century technological progress in surgery was extended from abnormal to normal childbirth. As male-dominated medical science invaded and conquered reproductive medicine, maternal mortality dropped by more than half from the late seventeenth century through the eighteenth century. But, at the same time, this devalued the alternative practitioner—the female midwife.[27]

From the late seventeenth century death rates for those adults belonging to elites began to decline, and their life expectancy levels to rise. Between 1675 and 1800 the English aristocracy, along with non-titled elites, added between 10 and 15 years to their average life spans.

---

[25] Continuing debates between historians of science are discussed by Shapin in *The Scientific Revolution*. The historians' failure to agree over what 'science' means continues to have a negative influence on the history of medicine. In particular it has impeded the development of illuminating comparisons between European and non-European medical systems. See Staal, *Concepts of Science in Europe and Asia*.
[26] See Johansson, 'Death and the Doctors'.
[27] Digby, *Medical Living*, pp. 261–3, 269.

Instead of a life expectancy at birth of 30 to 35 years, they reached a level of 45 to 50 years by 1800. This rise of life expectancy involved declining death rates from infancy to later middle age, and even old age. Ordinary people lagged behind elite groups, adding about four years to earlier levels of life expectancy.[28] While it was only the elite groups who could afford the new medicine, the relationship between medicine, mortality and the rise of elite life expectancy remains problematic. However, it is possible to state with confidence that, as medicine-the-new-science concentrated on the prevention and treatment of specific diseases, its whole-person elements became less important. Old truths such as 'every patient is unique' were orphaned and subsequently adopted by alternative forms of medicine.

Orthodox and Unorthodox Medicine

The division between different kinds of medicine is signalled by language which is culturally and socially created. This poses a conceptual dilemma because dichotomous terms such as mainstream/alternative; insider/outsider; orthodox/unorthodox; or scientific/alternative medicine themselves construct and perpetuate a binary opposition. Equally, such terms obscure changes in the historical contours of, or permeability in the boundaries between, medical 'systems'. And the official recognition which may be accorded by modern state or social insurance schemes to one, rather than the other, has also tended to obscure their problematical character or historically contingent construction.[29]

Britain's Medical Act of 1858 gave official recognition to doctors who had trained, and gained a qualification, in western techniques of surgery or medicine. Recognition gave definite advantages, notably that only those on the new medical register could now have access to public appointments in medicine—such as those of poor law medical officers, or medical officers of health. The legislation of 1858 did not fulfil the hopes of the medical profession at the time, since they had wished to proscribe alternative forms of medicine. Parliament took the view that consumer preferences should be prioritized over the sectional interests of an occupational group, with the result that the medical

---

[28] Johansson, 'Death and the Doctors'.
[29] See 'Alternative Medicine in Europe'.

market remained highly competitive; registered doctors had to compete against alternative practitioners whether these were herbalists, bonesetters, chemists, midwives or sellers of patent medicines.[30] However, the provision in 1858 that only the registered doctor should hold a public appointment under central or local government brought more substantial advantages in the twentieth century, since practice under the National Health Insurance Scheme of 1911 and the National Health Service of 1948 were also reserved for them.

Orthodox scientific medicine thus assumed a very powerful position in publicly-funded British healthcare. Variants and alternatives could be made available to patients, but the scope for these was small, as when, for example, registered practitioners who where themselves homeopaths could practise homeopathy on their own NHS patients. In addition, under the development of an internal market in the NHS during the 1990s, registered practitioners (who were fund holders), could recommend alternative practitioners to their patients, with this care funded on a discretionary basis by the local health authority. A more liberal attitude to alternative health care exists in Europe: in France a medical doctor may recommend non-standard remedies and the social security system picks up the bill for them;[31] and in Germany or Austria alternative remedies can be paid for through agreed mechanisms in social insurance schemes. It appears that where social security or social insurance payments are concerned, alternative medicine has a rather stronger position in continental Europe than in Britain.

Free biomedical care to everyone in Britain was brought by the establishment of the National Health Service in 1948. But this reform did not eliminate the medical market or the sale of alternative forms of care. Medical students may study the sociology or psychology of patient-practitioner interaction; but the majority of their training is directed at how to deliver effective, standardized methods of clinical care for specific diseases. In biomedicine the extent to which each patient can be seen as a unique individual requiring time-intensive forms of care is limited, both because of the clinical imperatives of the practitioner and, in public forms of medical care, by the costs involved. Alternative medical practitioners frequently focus on ambiguous symptoms, and minor — if chronic — medical problems in their patients, not

---

[30] Digby, *British General Practice*, pp. 32–7.
[31] Ramsey, 'Alternative Medicine in France'.

least because sufferers are themselves prepared to pay for such holistic care and attention. Alternative medicine therefore flourishes as a true complement to scientific medicine, because access to the latter is not limited by costs.

Since 'socialized medicine' must deliver high quality curative care to the entire population on a relatively tight budget, the scarcity of medical resources creates covert forms of rationing, which in the British case is leading to discrimination against older patients. Mammograms to detect breast cancer are routinely given to women between the ages of 50 and 64 years, but older women must request this service, even though the risk of breast cancer rises with age. Those aged over 60 are refused heart transplants, yet two-thirds of those treated for heart attack in NHS hospitals are more than 65 years old.[32] In a recent Gallup poll amongst those aged 50 or more, 5 per cent had been refused a treatment on the grounds of age, and 10 per cent thought that they had been treated differently because of their age.[33] This is a serious policy problem, both because Britain has an ageing society, and because this involuntary and discriminatory differential in take-up subverts the universal access laid down in one of the NHS's founding principles.

Voluntary patterns of utilization of NHS provision may also reflect cultural differences in the British population. For example, women immigrants from the Caribbean have maintained a limited preference for using what they call 'bush' remedies, instead of prescription drugs, because the production and delivery of those remedies remains completely under their control.[34] In this contemporary sub-cultural context, folk medicine promotes a sense of well-being (including a healthy regard for Caribbean traditions) without preventing the delivery of scientific care for acute medical problems through the NHS. In this case a reliance on home remedies does not involve a sub-optimal substitution of a folk medicine for newer, perhaps more effective remedies. In that sense there is no health problem which needs addressing through policy.

---

[32] *Turning Your Back on Us.* A recent policy decision has raised the age limit for mammograms to 70.
[33] *Independent*, 9 November 1999.
[34] Thorogood, 'Caribbean Home Remedies'.

In the contemporary world the division between officially recognized mainstream medicine and traditional medicine takes the different form of monopolistic, tolerant, parallel or integrated models. In the first type, western biomedicine may be given a monopoly (as in Madagascar); in the tolerant variant, traditional medicine may not be officially recognized but healers are free to practise it; in the third parallel type, there are two equal but separate recognized systems (as in India); and in the integrated form traditional healing and biomedicine are merged in both medical education and in later practice (as in China and Vietnam).[35] A country may supersede one model with another, as is happening in South Africa.

Medicine and Health Care in Non-Western Contexts

Since context matters so much in determining the extent to which different systems of healing are substitutes or complements, the impact of western scientific medicine on the health of people must be evaluated on a case-by-case basis. When western medicine was introduced to India, China, Japan and most Islamic countries, they already possessed systems of medical care based on the study of written texts which were taught in well-organized schools. For example, in India the European doctors who arrived during the seventeenth and eighteenth centuries displayed a qualified respect for the achievements of formal Ayurvedic (Hindu) medicine and Unani (Muslim) medicine. Initially, there was even a certain amount of hybridization between indigenous and western systems of health care, despite the cultural assumption of superiority on the part of western-trained physicians.[36] But by the 1850s a *de facto* commitment to complementarity between medical systems had been weakened by racism and formal imperial rule, and later by the self-confidence of doctors who perceived their training as being in 'genuinely' scientific medicine. By this time western medicine had made real progress with respect to the treatment of specific diseases such as dysentery, malaria and smallpox, as well as the clinical management of fever cases. From the early 1800s some ambitious Indian medical students recognized and responded to these developments by

---

[35] Bodeker, 'Medicinal Plants'.
[36] Harrison, 1994. *Public Health in British India*, pp. 40–1.

actively seeking training in western medicine,[37] in much the same spirit as earlier English medical students had gone to study in the excellent faculties of Renaissance Italy. Nevertheless, Hindu elites continued to use Ayurvedic practitioners as curers of first resort. Only when they failed to give satisfaction did they turn occasionally to western medicine as an alternative form of care, but without losing overall confidence in the value of their own medical heritage.[38] Traditional Indian medicine survived and, ironically, is now being consumed by Western Europeans as one kind of alternative medicine. In other words, what is perceived as orthodox or unorthodox varies not only according to its historical contexts, as we have already suggested, but also according to its cultural context.

In Sub-Saharan Africa traditional medical beliefs and practices were part of an oral tradition with many local variants. To western-trained doctors arriving in the nineteenth century, African approaches to healing seemed to be based on divination and magical practices, rather than on classic texts, so that in their eyes this did not constitute 'real' medicine. Only a few European physicians were willing to explore the medical potential of the local plants used by the local population to heal themselves, and thereby pay their respects to the empirical side of indigenous medicine. Within a colonial context most western doctors and missionaries could only perceive African healers as 'witch doctors', so that to them a logical policy was to encourage the substitution of western medicine, without regard to the culturally destructive side-effects of this substitution.[39] But in East Africa traditional healers were viewed as a residual category by colonial administrations and, rather than being banned, were restricted to practise within their own communities.[40]

The history of medicine in South Africa illustrates what can happen when scientific medicine is introduced into a society based on extreme racial inequality. The world's first heart transplant operation was performed in 1967 by Dr Christiaan Barnard in Groote Schuur Hospital, Cape Town. This spectacular demonstration of clinical excellence in 'high tech' medicine occurred in a country which denied the majority of its people basic human rights, including adequate access to modern

---

[37] Watts, *Epidemics in History*, pp. 200–12.
[38] Arnold, *Colonizing the Body*, pp. 3–6.
[39] South Africa, Cape Parliamentary papers, *Native Affairs* (series).
[40] Iliffe, *East African Doctors*.

health care. Severe sickness was heavily concentrated in the black and coloured (mixed race) communities where child malnutrition, infant stunting, rheumatic heart disease and tuberculoses were prominent in the 1980s.[41] Differences in life expectancy were extreme under apartheid. Although white South Africans had already achieved a life expectancy at birth of 67 years (65 for men and 70 for women) during the 1950s, for South Africans of Asian descent the same figure was 55 years, and for coloured South Africans it was 44 years.[42] For Africans no estimates were provided, because the majority of the population were not even part of the data-gathering system of the apartheid state. Data from other African countries suggest that life expectancy at birth for the black population of South Africa was perhaps between 30 and 40 years.[43] These contrasting levels of life expectancy in one country at one time were a demographic manifestation of the overtly racist ideology of apartheid, which had magnified existing social and economic differences between ethnic groups, including those in medical care.

Ironically the National Health Services 'Gluckman' Commission of 1944 had outlined a unitary system of health care for the entire nation, irrespective of race.[44] This mid-century recognition of the pressing need to provide better health care for black Africans, not least because they made up the vast majority of the labour force, had already forced through a long-contested admission of black medical students to the University of the Witwatersrand, where the first black doctors graduated in 1946. Alongside the Gluckman Report this inaugurated hope that a more efficient, as well as a more equitable, health care system might be created. But for the government that won power in 1948 such an egalitarian system of medicine had no place within an apartheid regime. Subsequently, the government invested tax revenues in forms of western health care that were heavily skewed towards curative care in urban areas. Particularly in more remote rural areas, where clinics and hospitals were few and far between, traditional medicine was not a complement to scientific medicine, not least because it was still virtually the only kind of health care available. But even when western medicine was available, indigenous healers retained a powerful

---

[41] Savage, 'The Political Economy;' Department of National Health, *Health Trends*.
[42] Chimera, *Demographic Patterns*; *Household Survey*, Pretoria.
[43] *UN Demographic Yearbook*, p. 706. Data provided for Tanganyika/Tanzania and Zambia in the same table indicates a life expectancy at birth between 35 and 45 for Black Africans.
[44] South Africa UG 30.44 *Report on the Provision of an Organized National Health Service*.

presence, so that today it is estimated that four-fifths of the black South African population continue to consult traditional healers. In southern Africa healers give meaning to illness within a shared cultural context that increases the ability of the sick, and those who care for them, to get through difficult times. Healers were (and are) seen to have an especially strong competitive advantage over western medicine in chronic illness, mental illness and also in forms of sickness that have vague and ambiguous symptoms.[45] Indeed, the continuing respect and custom given to indigenous healers by the majority of the population pose the question of whether such indigenous medicine should be seen as alternative or mainstream medicine.

It is possible to argue that the tremendous range of life expectancy differentials found in apartheid South Africa was simply a reflection of underlying economic and social inequality, not of differential access to medical care. However, countries such as China, Costa Rica, Sri Lanka and the state of Kerala in India have demonstrated that it *is* possible to deliver good health at small cost to low-income populations by carefully and equitably investing resources in health care.[46] In each case a life expectancy at birth at or near 70 years has been delivered to ordinary people, who live on *per capita* incomes one-tenth or less of those typical of developed countries. But delivering high levels of life expectancy to relatively poor, predominantly rural people requires government policies that put low-tech, preventive forms of scientific medicine (especially those geared to controlling infectious diseases) above 'high-tech' curative care such as heart operations. It also requires policies that are culturally sensitive to the views of local people about what they themselves see as the most important forms of health care.[47]

Letting the medical market allocate care according to the purchasing power of consumers in developing countries may perpetuate health-related medical inequalities. In the past formally-trained biomedical doctors have concentrated in urban areas where they focus on curing paying patients, while the practice of rural medicine is not seen as equally challenging or rewarding. Indigenous medicine as an alternative form of health care was seen as having only a limited efficacy or else, quite literally, was not seen at all. Interestingly, this situation is changing as western pharmaceutical companies recognize the

---

[45] Matse, 'Swaziland'; Honwana, 'Spiritual Agency'.
[46] Halstead, Walsh and Warren, *Good Health*.
[47] Rohde et al, *Reaching Health*. See also Caldwell, 'Introductory Thoughts'.

healing properties of South African plants customarily used by African healers, and attempt to gain access to this knowledge as an expeditious alternative to lengthy laboratory trials involving thousands of plant species.[48] This hybridization of indigenous and western medicine has also operated with transmission of knowledge going in the opposite direction. For example, in neighbouring Botswana traditional healers have mixed herbs with patent medicines in treating what were perceived to be 'European diseases' acquired by migrant labourers in the gold mines of South Africa.[49]

Post-apartheid South Africa is responding to these kinds of complexities by adopting new health care policies which embody traditional medicine as a valuable complement to western medicine, and not as an inferior and outmoded substitute. In giving traditional practitioners formal professional recognition, a new government is recognizing the potent intersection of medicine and culture. It is also attempting to meet the economic challenges of the twenty-first century — not least by redressing the inequities and past neglect of its political economy of health. In 1994 the first democratically elected government committed itself formally to redress the grossly-skewed delivery of medical services. Health care centres are being set up that offer free care to all children under seven years of age, and on graduation medical students are being required to give a year's service to the treatment of rural populations. A national system of primary health clinics and community health centres is being built.[50] But the ANC government of the 'New South Africa' also appreciates the continuing respect that ordinary Africans have for their indigenous healers. The Ministry of Health is negotiating with traditional healers over the conditions for their formal recognition as health care professionals. Effectively, a policy decision has been made that western and indigenous medicine should be complements, not substitutes, in the production of health-related forms of human welfare in the twenty-first century. A unitary health system with a more efficient distribution of resources is recognized as being an imperative in optimizing human development within what is the wealthiest and most technologically developed country in Africa.

---

[48] *Mail and Guardian*, 25–31 August 1995; *The Times Saturday Supplement*, 3 October 1998.
[49] Mushingeh, 'A History of Disease'.
[50] Policy statement, Pretoria.

Conclusions

At the beginning of the new millennium, scientific medicine might appear to have a hegemonic potential. Its past achievements attest to its power in that smallpox has been eradicated, whilst other scourges of the past—including diphtheria, measles or polio—have substantially lost their terror, as modern vaccines control their mortal impact. However, the advent of evidence-based medicine has led to a review of the efficacy of other well-used procedures and medications, sometimes with highly critical evaluations. More strikingly, the emergence of frightening new diseases, such as AIDS, has highlighted the limitations of scientific medicine. In Africa, the worst affected continent, two-thirds of the world's HIV infections are concentrated in only 10 per cent of its population; AIDS deaths are estimated to have reached two million per year.[51] Indeed, in South Africa international organizations have recently reduced their life expectancy estimate by 10 years because of the large—and increasing—numbers of HIV and AIDS sufferers.

Disparity in national disease controls within a shrinking globe has also resulted in an alarming importation of so-called 'tropical' diseases into temperate countries through international air traffic. In both developed and developing countries newly drug-resistant strains of diseases pose significant threats, especially within hospitals (through infection from surgery), and within the community (through the spread of tuberculosis). Equally, there has come a recognition of the fallacies of earlier over-optimism by colonial medical services and international health organizations about disease eradication in a continent such as Africa. Now a greater weight is given to the political and socio-economic contexts in which health campaigns are waged, together with more realistic objectives in the control of bilharzia, sleeping sickness or malaria. Yet today one out of the three million people who die of malaria live in Africa despite decades of effort there by those in scientific medicine. For many in developing countries the ravages of disease remain, both because of limited access to medical treatments, and because of low income levels which restrict nutritional intake, thus making malnourished bodies more vulnerable to some diseases. The limitations of the 'vertical' vector-based campaigns of disease elimin-

---

[51] *Independent*, 19 November 1999.

ation are therefore giving way to broader-based 'horizontal' campaigns to raise the health status of the population. In policy discussions measures of preventive public health—such as the provision of clean water supplies—are increasingly recognized as having a strategic and more cost-effective role than much curative medicine.

In developed countries the authority of formally-trained physicians has diminished in a post-professional era; while the power of the patient as medical consumer has been enhanced by an information revolution. This has forced the perception amongst those with a public responsibility for health that 'top-down' methods of health education need to be modified by 'bottom-up' approaches, in that changes of lifestyle are less likely to be doctor-led than to come from the individual. An emphasis on positive health or well-being, rather than on the negative condition of an absence of disease, has tended to enlarge cultural horizons and increase the range of therapeutic options. In most advanced economies during the late twentieth century the reviving fortunes of alternative therapies suggest patients' recognition of the limitations of scientific medicine's exclusive focus on the physical body, and their selective preference for more holistic alternative therapies. Paradoxically, one result of scientific medicine's success in curing acute or infectious conditions has been its contribution to an ageing population with incurable chronic conditions best palliated by alternative therapies, at least so far.

Alternative systems of medical care specialize in the production of positive 'health'. In contrast, during the last 500 years scientific medicine has specialized in reducing the prevalence of deadly diseases, and has increasingly neglected the production of 'health' as a positive feeling of well-being. Since feeling good involves treating minor ailments and troubling conditions that affect many lives, alternative medicine has been able to occupy a significant market niche. In one sense folk/traditional/alternative medicine, as the most ancient form of medicine, has survived by making people feel better even when their diseases could not be cured. Alternative medicine is not necessarily highly efficacious in treating many of the specific diseases that keep life expectancy at birth levels between 20 and 40 years, instead of a potential 60 to 80 years. To argue that alternative medicine is just as good as (or better than) western scientific medicine in every respect is a recipe for keeping premature mortality unnecessarily high. But abolishing or undermining confidence in folk medicine would also undermine health-related welfare. As long as it does no harm, alternative medicine, however 'unscientific', is not a policy problem, except in clear cases of fraud. To survive in the face of competition from scientific medicine, alternative medicine has itself adapted by responding to a demand for forms of care that scientific medicine was unable or unwilling to deliver.

Deeply rooted in the historical record has been a dialectic between alternative/traditional and biomedical/scientific systems. In this discussion of the nature and relationship of different forms of health care the complexity of the terminology has indicated the fluidity of orthodox and unorthodox forms. Alternative systems of health care can be seen either as a complement or as a substitute for a medical system whose practitioners have their qualifications recognized or privileged by the state and associated with science. Formally recognized physicians almost always perceive their rivals as promoting an inferior system of healing to mainstream medicine, which could be eliminated without a loss of health-related welfare. In this situation, as we have seen, orthodox practitioners may put pressure on governments to regulate or even suppress the delivery of unorthodox forms of care. But consumers who can afford it persist in treating alternative systems of healing as complements and for good reason.

This historical survey of scientific/orthodox medicine and alternative/unorthodox medicine has suggested the limitations of a binary model since it has shown that rival medical 'systems' can act as partners in the production of health, even to the point of producing a hybrid form of medicine. Policy-makers need to appreciate this complex interdependence as they consider health care options for the twenty-first century.

Note. We thank our conference discussant, Dr Charles Webster, for his very helpful comments, and are grateful to the Editors and conference participants for their constructive suggestions and support. Anne Digby also acknowledges the financial support of the Wellcome Trust for her researches into medical pluralism in South Africa, 1840–1960.

References

'Alternative Medicine in Europe Since 1800.' Special issue of *Medical History* 43, no. 3 (1999).
Arnold, David. *Colonizing the Body. State Medicine and Disease in Nineteenth-Century India*. Berkeley: University of California Press, 1993.
Bodeker, Gerry. 'Medicinal Plants, Traditional Knowledge and Health Service Development in Africa: Issues at the Interface.' Unpublished paper given at the Recovery of the History of Indigenous Medicine in Africa Conference, held at Oxford Brookes University, June 1999.
Caldwell, J. 'Introductory Thoughts on Health Transition.' In *What We Know About Health Transition: The Cultural, Social and Behavioural Determinants of Health*. Canberra: Health Transition Centre, Australian National University, 1990.
Charlton, J., and M. Murphy, eds. *The Health of Adult Britain 1841–1994*. Vol. 1 (Chapter 1–14) Office For National Statistics. Decennial Supplement No. 12. London: The Stationery Office, 1996.
Chimera, D. *Demographic Patterns in South Africa*. Johannesburg, 1995.
Cook, Harold. 'The New Philosophy and Medicine in Seventeenth-Century England.' In *Reappraisals of the Scientific Revolution*, edited by D. Lindberg and R. Westman, 397–436. Cambridge: Cambridge University Press, 1990.
_____. 'Living in Revolutionary Times: Medical Change under William and Mary.' In *Patronage and Institutions: Science, Technology and Medicine at the European Court, 1500 to 1750*, edited by B. Moran, 111–36. Rochester, New York: The Boydell Press, 1991.
David, Paul A., and B.H. Hall. 'Heart of Darkness: Public-Private Interactions Inside the R&D Black Box.' Stanford Institute for Economic Policy Research. Discussion Paper, March 1999.
Department of National Health and Population Development. *Health Trends* (1994).
Digby, Anne. *The Evolution of British General Practice, 1850–1948*. Oxford: Oxford University Press, 1999.
_____. *Making a Medical Living. Doctors and Patients in the English Market for Medicine, 1720–1911*. Cambridge: Cambridge University Press, 1994.
Dillard, J., and T. Ziporyn. *Alternative Medicine for Dummies*. Foster City, CA: IDG Books Worldwide, 1998.
Hall, R. *The Revolution in Science 1500–1750*. London: Longman, 1983.
Halstead, S., J. Walsh and K. Warren. *Good Health at Low Cost*. New York: The Rockefeller Foundation, 1985.
Harrison, Mark. *Public Health in British India. Anglo-Indian Preventive Medicine*. Cambridge: Cambridge University Press, 1994.
Hollingsworth, T.H. 'A Demographic Study of British Ducal Families.' *Population Studies* XI (1957): 4–26.
Household Survey, 1994. Pretoria, 1994.
Iliffe, John. *East African Doctors*. Cambridge: Cambridge University Press, 1998.

Johansson, Sheila Ryan. 'Cultural Software, Institutional Hardware and Health Information Processing in Social Systems.' In *What We Know About Health Transition. The Cultural, Social and Behavioural Determinants of Health*. Canberra: Health Transition Centre, Australian National University, 1990.

———. 'The Politics of Discourse Synthesis in the Literature of Health Research.' *Social Epistemology*, 10 (1996): 43–53.

———. 'Death and the Doctors. Medicine and Mortality 1600–1800.' Cambridge Group for the History of Population and Social Structure, Working Paper Series, No. 7, 2000.

Lindberg, D. *The Beginnings of Western Science. The European Scientific Tradition in Philosophical, Religious and Institutional Context, 600 BC to AD 1450*. Chicago: University of Chicago Press, 1992.

Lindberg, D., and R. Westman. 'Introduction.' In *Reappraisals of the Scientific Revolution*, edited by D. Lindberg and R. Westman, 1–15. Cambridge: Cambridge University Press, 1990.

Mail and Guardian, 25–31 August 1995.

Matse, P.M. 'A History of Disease and Medicine in Swaziland.' PhD diss., University of Cambridge, 1996.

Mushingeh, A.C.S.M. 'A History of Disease and Medicine in Botswana, 1820–1945.' PhD diss., University of Cambridge, 1984.

Nutton, Vivian. 'Roman Medicine, 250 BC to AD 200.' In *The Western Medical Tradition 800 BC to AD 1800*, edited by L. Conrad, M.. Neve, V. Nutton, et al., 39–70. Cambridge: Cambridge University Press, 1995.

Policy Statement. Pretoria, ANC Department of Information and Publicity, 26 March 1998.

Ramsey, Matthew. 'Alternative Medicine in France.' *Medical History* 43, no. 3 (1999): 286–322.

Rawcliffe, Carol. *Medicine and Society in Later Medieval England*. Stroud: Sutton Publishing Limited, 1997.

Rohde, J. et al. *Reaching Health for All*. Delhi: Oxford University Press, 1993.

Root-Bernstein, R., and M. Honey. *Mud, Maggots, and Other Medical Marvels: The Science Behind Folk Remedies and Old Wives' Tales*. New York: Macmillan, 1997.

Savage, M. 'The Political Economy of Health in South Africa.' In *Economics of Health in South Africa*, edited by S. Westcott and F.A.H. Wilson. Johannesburg, 2 volumes, 1978/80.

Shapin, S. *The Scientific Revolution*. Chicago: Chicago University Press, 1996.

Sharma, Ursula M. 'Using Alternative Therapies: Marginal Medicine and Central Concerns.' In *New Directions in the Sociology of Health*, edited by P. Abbott and G. Payne, 127–39. London, Falmer Press, 1990.

Smith, Richard. 'Plagues and Peoples: The Long Demographic Cycle, 1250–1670.' In *The Peopling of Britain: The Shaping of a Human Landscape*, edited by P. Slack and R. Ward, 177–210. Oxford: Oxford University Press, 2002.

South Africa, Cape Parliamentary papers, *Native Affairs* (series).

South Africa, UG 30.44. *Report on the Provision of an Organized National Health Service for All Sections of the Union of South Africa* (Gluckman Commission).

Staal, F. *Concepts of Science in Europe and Asia.* Leiden: International Institute for Asian Studies, 1993.

The Independent, 9 November 1999.

The Independent, 19 November 1999.

Thorogood, N. 'Caribbean Home Remedies and their Importance for Black Women's Health Care in Britain.' In *New Directions in the Sociology of Health*, edited by P. Abbott and G. Payne, 140–52. London: Falmer Press, 1990.

The Times Saturday Supplement, 3 October 1998.

Turning Your Back on Us: Older People in the NHS. London: Age Concern, 1999.

Turshen, M. *The Political Economy of Disease in Tanzania.* New Brunswick, New Jersey: Rutgers University Press, 1984.

Watts, S. *Epidemics in History.* New Haven: Yale University Press, 1997.

Wibble, R. *The Economics of Science: Methodology and Epistemology as if Economics Really Mattered.* London: Routledge, 1999.

Woods, R., and N. Williams. 'Must the Gap Widen Before it can be Narrowed? Long-term Trends in Social Class Mortality Differentials.' *Continuity and Change* 10 (1995): 105–37.

UN Demographic Yearbook. New York, 1967.

16.
An Old Poor Law for the New Europe?
Reconciling Local Solidarity with Labour Mobility in Early Modern England

PETER M. SOLAR & RICHARD M. SMITH

Introduction

In the European Union today there exists a tension between national solidarity and the development of the single market. Despite efforts to create a single market for labour, the migration of EU citizens within Europe remains relatively limited, compared to that in the United States, and may even be declining.[1] Differences in language and culture and the persistent strength of local and family ties certainly play a role in keeping down labour mobility. The high levels of unemployment in receiving regions in the last quarter of a century may be another factor. So, too, must be the complications and costs of moving among countries with different systems of social welfare.

If there is a 'European model' of capitalism, then one important element is certainly the shared commitment of European nations to high levels of social welfare benefits and to the high levels of taxes and employer and employee contributions necessary to pay for them.[2] But this shared commitment is national in its scope and execution. National pension systems tend to favour those with a complete record of contributions. Persons moving from one country to another often

---
[1] For a recent survey of the evidence on labour mobility within Europe, see Brauerhjelm et al, *Integration*, ch. 4.
[2] For an overview of the European welfare state, see Buti et al, *Welfare State*, ch. 1. On the 'European model', see Freeman, 'The Large Welfare State'.

find that in the country that they are leaving they can cash out their own, but not their employer's or the state's, contributions. In the country to which they are moving they find it prohibitively expensive or even impossible to buy into the system. Eligibility for unemployment compensation in most countries depends on demonstrating a history of contributions. Although EU legislation dictating equal treatment of community citizens for social welfare does exist, it contains many loopholes.[3]

The development of the single market in Europe, pushed along by the introduction of the euro, is already leading firms to rationalize production across the EU, though not yet to the extent seen in the United States.[4] What this often means in practice is that when plants in one part of the union are closed or downsized, the firm loses the skills and experience of workers and managers. If it expands elsewhere, it must bear the costs of training new workers and managers. The workers and managers affected by closure or downsizing often face difficulties in finding comparable employment.

Two very different long-term solutions might be envisaged to reduce the barriers to migration posed by differing social welfare systems. One would be the harmonization of social welfare regimes across the Union and the eventual creation of a European welfare system. Income convergence among existing members might make it possible to move towards similar levels of contributions and benefits, though the entrance of the low-income countries of Central and Eastern Europe would delay such a process. As things stand, some member countries already fear an influx of labour from the poorer, eastern candidates. The harmonization of social security regimes would also follow the same logic, and face much of the same opposition, as the social chapter of the Maastricht Treaty.

The other long-term solution would be the effective individualization of social welfare. In principle, the current movements in many countries towards increasing the contributory and funded components of pension schemes should make pensions more easily portable across national boundaries. Treating other aspects of social welfare, such as health care and disability and unemployment compensation, as pure insurance schemes would have the same effect.

---

[3] Veil, *Report*.
[4] Brauerhjelm et al, *Integration*, ch. 2.

Both of these long-term solutions would be likely to run up against different national views on the appropriate scope and level of social welfare benefits and on the degree to which different societies deem it desirable to use such schemes to redistribute income. Even among countries at similar levels of income, both spending on social welfare and the degree of redistribution implicit in contributions, tax finance and spending differ greatly within Europe.

The redistributive component in current social welfare also raises the problem of who is to benefit from redistribution. Reactions to the recent wave of immigration have shown that solidarity with foreigners has its limits. So, too, has the pressure within a socially divided country like Belgium to regionalize some or all of its social welfare system. Until true Europeans start to be born, solidarity is likely to remain national or regional. Any scheme to promote labour mobility will have to take this into account.

The tension between the free movement of labour and the solidarities implicit in social welfare schemes is not a new phenomenon. The different national systems in Europe today arose out of two parallel developments in the late nineteenth and early twentieth centuries. Innovations in industry and in transport and communications led to the rationalization and localization of economic activity across Europe. These forces were increasingly contained and channelled by the rise of nation states, which used the schools, the media, the army and new national systems of social welfare to overcome regional and ethnic loyalties and so create loyal citizens.[5] Forging national solidarity was a long and difficult process in many European countries, and there is no reason to think that a strong and widespread sense of European solidarity will be any easier to achieve.

But for an example of the tensions between labour mobility and social solidarity that is more relevant to current European concerns one must look further back, to England in the sixteenth, seventeenth and eighteenth centuries. The English economy before the Industrial Revolution was precocious in many respects. One was its high degree of labour mobility, both over short and long distances. Another was its development of a nationally organized, but locally administered and financed, system of social welfare. Although the system of relief under the Old Poor Law has long had a bad press, from Smith, Malthus and the classical economists onwards, recent research on how it actually

---

[5] Stearns, *European Society*, pp. 231–41.

operated suggests a number of features that might be transposed to the Europe of the twenty-first century.[6] This research has itself benefited from seeing the Old Poor Law in the broader context of European experience with poor relief during these centuries.

The Old Poor Law as a Local Welfare System

Solidarity under the Old Poor Law was very local indeed. Each parish, which might contain a few hundred to a few thousand people, was responsible for its own poor. Throughout Europe in the pre-industrial period local churches played a crucial role in social welfare alongside family ties and institutions such as monasteries and guilds and fraternities.[7] The community that made up the religious parish was an important source of alms, and its priest or pastor was usually active in administering charity. Most charity went to residents of the parish. Strangers were sometimes succoured, but often driven from the parish to seek assistance elsewhere.

During the sixteenth century parish poor relief in England came to differ from that on the Continent in two crucial, though intimately related, respects.[8] First, the parish became a unit of civil administration. The distinction arose between civil and ecclesiastical parishes, which was important in an era of increasing religious pluralism. The 1536 statute on poor relief was notable in recognizing the parish as the appropriate unit of administration. In several spheres the parish as an administrative entity came to have authority not only over the members of the new and usually dominant Church of England, but also over members of the Catholic Church and the emergent Protestant sects.

The rise of the parish as a unit of civil administration was related to its increasing capacity for levying taxes, which is the second way in which England came to differ from the Continent. Poor relief in England came to depend not on the charity of parishioners. It was funded by local property taxes, as were roads and other activities of the civil parish. The over-riding importance both of the parish as a fund-raising and spending unit, and of 'outdoor relief' (help in cash or

---

[6] Solar, 'Poor Relief'; Smith, 'Charity'.
[7] Jütte, *Poverty*.
[8] The following paragraphs draw on Smith, 'Historic Roots'.

in kind to individuals in their homes) as 'indoor relief' (assistance given in centralized residential institutions, usually located in towns), set England apart from her European neighbours throughout the early modern period.

The willingness of parishes to resort to taxation in order to finance poor relief and their capacity for raising local taxes effectively may have their roots much earlier, in the fourteenth century. In 1334 the central government stopped relying on detailed tax lists to assess and levy taxes throughout the country. Instead it made local communities responsible for assessing and collecting a specified sum. Over the next two centuries parishes increasingly moved to using land as the basis for taxation, which had the effect of broadening the tax base. They developed methods for administering this land tax in which churchwardens came to occupy a key role. The methods used for collecting the king's taxes were gradually extended to raising revenue for local needs, mainly for the maintenance of the church fabric but sometimes for charitable and other purposes. During the early sixteenth century, religious strife and royal confiscations of monastic property and other church property, and even of some local charitable resources, undermined many of the existing charitable institutions. The availability of an equitable and well-established system of local taxation certainly facilitated the move, first through local initiative and then through national legislation, to tax-financed poor relief.

The existence of an effective local tax system in England probably also bolstered resistance to Crown initiatives for more centralized provision of relief. For example, a provision in the original 1536 bill for vagabonds to be employed on public works funded by an income tax did not survive. The subsequent parliamentary history of relief legislation suggests no over-dependence on centralized machinery for its implementation.

Along with the right to raise funds by taxation, poor relief legislation of the sixteenth century gave parishes the responsibility for dealing with their own poor. Who these poor were, that is the criteria for eligibility for relief from the parish, was gradually defined by legislation and jurisprudence over the sixteenth and seventeenth centuries. But the clientele was essentially local so that, given the small size of most parishes, the moral hazard problems of welfare administration were kept to a minimum.

Tax-financed poor relief on such a small scale also encouraged local elites to take a much broader approach to the welfare of the poor.[9] The concentration of landownership in England meant that the economic burden of the land tax fell mostly on a relatively small group of people, which also made decisions about employment, housing and investment that could influence the poor relief liabilities of the parish. Where the local elite was cohesive, these decisions internalized both benefits and costs to the relief system. English landlords had a greater incentive than their continental counterparts to keep local population and resources in balance, either by taking measures to restrain population growth or by promoting agricultural or industrial activities that would increase employment opportunities.

For its time English poor relief was quite elaborate and generous. Parish relief authorities dealt predominantly with cases of poverty arising from illness, old age and widowhood. They also dealt on occasion with the consequences for the 'able-bodied' of poor harvests, trade depressions and seasonal unemployment. At its peak in the late eighteenth and early nineteenth centuries, spending on relief may have reached a few per cent of national income. This is far, far below today's welfare state but was well above spending elsewhere in Europe at the time. Moreover, it accounted for a share of national income not again reached in England until the late nineteenth or early twentieth century.[10]

Local responsibility and funding meant that there was considerable variation across parishes in the organization, scope and generosity of relief.[11] It took many decades in the seventeenth century before some parishes even raised a poor rate. Difference in parish resources and the attitudes of local elites meant that there were always parishes which gave relief grudgingly, while others, sometimes just down the road, were models of generosity.

Mark Blaug once called the Old Poor Law a 'welfare state in miniature'.[12] In fact, it could be more accurately described as many, many miniature welfare states, each with its own administration, funding

---

[9] Solar, 'Poor Relief'.
[10] Lindert, 'Poor Relief'.
[11] King, 'Poor Relief'.
[12] Blaug, 'Poor Law Report', p. 229.

and clientele. Seen in this way, the situation in early modern England was an extreme version of the patchwork of social welfare systems in Europe today.

The National Coordination of Local Welfare Systems under the Old Poor Law

Local responsibility for relief raised a number of problems in a world where parish boundaries were easily and often crossed. Parishes that had few resources and many that were poor, or that were badly organized, or that were simply mean could end up exporting their poor to better-organized and better-funded parishes. Whilst the migrant poor had no formal claim on these parishes, various considerations led authorities in host parishes, in some cases, to provide some relief. In other cases they simply drove the foreign poor away, pushing the problem further down the road.

Such problems were not unique to England. Poor relief on the Continent was much better organized in the towns than in the countryside, with the result that urban poor relief authorities faced inflows of the rural poor.[13] The ill, the disabled and the old drifted to the towns in search of charity. Their numbers were augmented in times of harvest failure by the landless and the hungry. Such flows had the unfortunate side-effect of spreading epidemic disease.

In England, though not on the Continent, the problem of parishes that shirked their duties was largely solved during the sixteenth and seventeenth centuries by the development of mechanisms for enforcing local responsibility. In the sixteenth century national legislation gradually defined these responsibilities and gave parishes the means to meet them. Although the first major national legislation was enacted in the 1530s, it was very general and its implementation involved widespread experimentation at the parish level. The problems that arose in defining eligibility, raising funds and dealing with the migrant poor led to further legislation, culminating in the great codifying acts of 1598 and 1601. These acts laid the basis for a national system of locally administered and funded relief.

[13] Solar, 'Poor Relief'.

Yet the developments in the seventeenth century were arguably more important. England was not the only country in Europe to enact national legislation for poor relief in the sixteenth century. The social disruption caused by religious strife, population growth and economic change prompted a wave of experimentation and reform. This pan-European movement stressed the rational use of Christian charity and opened the way for a growing role for public authorities in the management of welfare provision.[14] But a crucial difference between England and the Continent was that much of continental (and Scottish and Irish) legislation on poor relief remained dead letter for want of effective implementation and enforcement.[15] In England, by contrast, the number of parishes raising a poor rate, a key indicator of local organization, increased steadily during the seventeenth century so that coverage was almost universal by the end of the century.[16]

The successful implementation of poor relief legislation in England was due to a number of factors. The English aristocracy and gentry were largely resident on their estates, at least for part of the year, which helped assure their involvement in local affairs. The English landowning class was also unusual in its aversion to smallholdings and subdivision. Land was increasingly let in large blocks and preference given to tenant farmers with capital and talent. These substantial farmers and the people who served both them and the landowners—the vicars, lawyers, doctors and shopkeepers—provided the manpower to administer local relief, and the importance of the voluntary labour that went into such activities should not be underestimated. In other countries, notably in Ireland, parish organization of relief and other activities proved to be impossible for want of dense and reliable local elites.[17] The Irish case also highlights the importance of the Church of England's relative hegemony.

These factors meant that most English parishes would have the manpower and resources to implement the Old Poor Law and that most would raise a rate and take care of their poor. It did not mean that *all* parishes would be willing to do so. From the seventeenth century onwards recalcitrant parishes were brought into line by the courts. On the basis of complaints both from the poor themselves and from

---

[14] Lis and Soly, *Poverty and Capitalism*, pp. 82–96.
[15] Leonard, *Early History*, pp. 293–300.
[16] Slack, *English Poor Law*, p. 26.
[17] Dickson, 'In Search'.

parishes bearing the costs of free-riding behaviour, magistrates at district and county level put both legal and social pressure on local elites to take effective care of their poor. The role of the magistrates was reinforced by their responsibility for carrying out Tudor and Stuart legislation to deal with harvest shortages. In times of dearth, they were charged with monitoring grain supplies and the working of grain markets. These intrusive polices gave way during the seventeenth century to reliance on parish doles to ensure that the poor had the cash to buy food when prices were high.[18]

Labour Mobility under the Old Poor Law

Most English parishes were much too small to be self-contained labour markets. Differences in demographic characteristics and in economic opportunities meant that some people would have to cross parish boundaries to find work. The high death rates in early modern cities required a constant inflow of migrants to sustain their populations. The development of rural industrial activity, in mining, ironworking or textiles, usually drew in workers from outside the parish. Even in agriculture, farmers often needed to recruit labourers from elsewhere, either to work year round or to help out at seasonal peaks.

Since the days of the classical economists, the Old Poor Law has been criticized for impeding the movement of labour in the English economy.[19] The focus of criticism has been on the settlement laws, which set out the criteria of eligibility for relief in a given parish and provided ways of dealing with those who were not eligible. In principle, every English man and woman had a parish of settlement, in which he or she was entitled to relief. They were not entitled to relief elsewhere and if they asked for it, they could be removed to their parish of settlement. The threat of removal, it was thus argued, discouraged people from leaving their parish of settlement.

Mobility was also allegedly restrained because parishes discouraged immigration for fear that migrants might acquire settlements and become chargeable to the parish. This was the case because settlement became not just a matter of birth. The settlement laws of the late seven-

---

[18] Smith, 'Historic Roots'.
[19] The following paragraphs draw on Redford, *Labour Migration*, ch. 5 and Slack, *English Poor Law*, pp. 35–9.

teenth century actually expanded the number of ways in which a migrant could acquire eligibility for relief (and restricted the ability of parishes to remove individuals). Under the 1662 act a settlement could be acquired by renting a house worth £10 a year or more, a condition unlikely to be met by more than a tiny fraction of potential migrants. Those without a settlement could be removed even if they were only likely to need relief. By 1692 settlements could also be obtained by paying local rates or, more pertinently for most migrants, by being bound as an apprentice or by being hired as a servant and working for a year in the parish. Although some parishes later in the eighteenth century used contracts of less than a year to limit the number of new settlements, the settlement laws of the late seventeenth century actually gave greater security to the migrant and probably made migration easier.

An important innovation of the late seventeenth century was the use of certificates from the parish of settlement acknowledging its responsibility for relief of a given migrant.[20] The 1690s legislation made it illegal to remove migrants with certificates until they actually applied for relief. The use of certificates became widespread in many parts of England and brought with it arrangements whereby parishes sometimes paid relief to their settled poor residing in other parishes. It made good sense for a parish to pay such non-resident relief where un- or underemployment was likely to be temporary, as in the case of trade depressions. Even where the parish of settlement could not be made to pay, it also made sense for industrial parishes that depended on skilled workers to tide them over temporary crises.

Those who suffered most from the settlement laws were not those seeking jobs but those who had little chance of earning a living. Beggars and young widows with small children were much more likely to find themselves being removed. The settlement laws were generally used by parishes to control migration rather than to prevent it. This control was all the more effective since the small size of most parishes minimized both the moral hazard problems of giving relief and the externality problem that could arise if some ratepayers' use of labourers from outside the parish displaced local residents onto the relief rolls.

---

[20] Taylor, 'Impact', and Taylor, 'Different Kind'.

The Old Poor Law did not solve all problems. Foreigners were completely outside the system. In practice this meant the Irish and, to a lesser degree, the Scots. In the late eighteenth and early nineteenth centuries some areas, notably London, Bristol, Liverpool, Manchester and other industrial cities, had to deal with relatively large inflows of Irish migrants.[21] These migrants had no entitlement to relief, though on occasion they were relieved. Sometimes they were removed to Ireland, but without anyone in Ireland taking responsibility for them, this proved a costly and not very effective solution.

By providing the English with an entitlement to relief and by developing mechanisms to deal effectively with migration, the Old Poor Law may be argued to have facilitated labour mobility in pre-industrial England.[22] On the Continent (and in Ireland) the poor had no legal entitlement to relief, even in their home parish. If, however, they did have at least a moral claim on their local community, then they would have been reluctant to stray far from home. This did not prevent movements of labour but it helps to explain why seasonal, rather than permanent, migration was so common in many poor regions of Europe. It also helps to explain why the desire to acquire and hold on to even small pieces of land was so strong on the Continent and in Ireland.

The End of the Old Poor Law

Although the Old Poor Law served the English economy well during the seventeenth and eighteenth centuries, it was ultimately abandoned when the much more restrictive New Poor Law was adopted in 1834. The reasons for its demise stemmed from the increasing integration of the English economy.

The Industrial Revolution led to greater spatial concentration of industry. The textile industries, among the biggest industrial employers, tended to become localized in a few areas: cotton in Lancashire, woollens and worsteds in West Yorkshire, hosiery in Nottinghamshire. Producers in outlying regions tended to suffer terminal decline. Moreover, industry became increasingly concentrated in

---

[21] Redford, *Labour Migration*, ch. 5.
[22] Solar, 'Poor Relief'.

the towns. In the countryside textile manufacture declined, though it was replaced in some areas by labour-intensive but very poorly paid activities such as straw plaiting.

These large and relatively rapid changes in industrial location made it clear that the parish was no longer the appropriate risk pool for poor relief. Parishes where rural industries had dried up were particularly hard hit. Even in the new industrial towns downturns in economic activity produced distress while at the same time reducing local resources. Increased residential differentiation within towns led to concentrations of the poor in parishes with weak tax bases, though this problem was not entirely new. In the eighteenth century legislation had been enacted to facilitate some redistribution of resources among London parishes.

The differential effects of industrialization on the burden of poor relief were exacerbated by selective migration. Country parishes, especially in the south of England, lost the young and able-bodied to the towns, whilst retaining responsibility for the old and infirm who remained.[23]

The increased burden of poor relief expenditure on agricultural parishes led to pressures from the landed elite for reform. The New Poor Law and its subsequent implementation were intended to restrict eligibility for relief, to provide for more redistribution among parishes, and to make it easier for migrants to obtain settlements, thus shifting more of the burden onto the towns.

Lessons from the English Experience of Poor Relief

What does the case of early modern England have to say about the future of Europe's fragmented social welfare system? The differences between these two cases are enormous. Welfare spending in the eighteenth century may have reached 1–2 per cent of GDP. Today it accounts for ten times that much. Relief in pre-industrial England was organized at parish level, with all the advantages that small scale brought for monitoring the behaviour of both ratepayers and potential recipients. Today large bureaucracies administer cumbersome national systems of benefits. But, despite these differences, some aspects of English experience with the Old Poor Law may have a certain resonance for Europe today and tomorrow.

[23] Williamson, *Coping with City Growth*, pp. 15, 22, 34–6.

First, English poor relief, despite its local funding and administration, was still a national system with recognized and enforced minimum standards. This was necessary to prevent lax parishes from effectively exporting their poor to more generous neighbouring parishes. While there is relatively little danger of social benefit-induced migration within the current EU-15, the accession of Eastern European countries with less developed welfare systems may present problems. The coming decades may even produce a rather different problem if rich countries with aging workforces and large pension liabilities start providing inducements for younger workers to immigrate from poorer countries that are also facing aging populations.

Second, the settlement laws helped facilitate and control migration in a world where the locus of solidarity was the parish. They provided relatively clear rules for distinguishing movements of labour that were economically desirable and that warranted a change in the parish of settlement. They also provided mechanisms, certificates and non-resident relief, that vouched for migrants by reaffirming the parish's responsibility for their welfare and that could help migrants over temporary difficulties. The thrust of current EU policy is to make it easy for migrants to obtain full and immediate access to the social welfare system in the host country. Not surprisingly, there is resistance from some member countries, especially those likely to be most affected by enlargement. An alternative arrangement, inspired by the English experience, might be a social passport committing the country of origin to fund some or all of the migrant's welfare needs over a clearly specified period of transition to social citizenship in the host country. Such a system would, of course, involve complicated questions concerning intra-country financial transfers and raise the possibility of 'removals' from one EU country to another. But it might go some way towards calming the passions surrounding immigrant workers, one of the clearest signs that solidarity in Europe remains predominantly national in scope.

Third, the fate of the national social security systems in Europe will be linked to the way in which the single market and single currency projects affect the pattern of industrial specialization. As firms consolidate and rationalize production within the EU, a major uncertainty is whether there will be big winners and big losers among Europe's regions or there will be winners all around as regions develop their own distinct specialities. If the process leads to polarization, then the further question arises as to whether or not people in declining regions will move to the jobs in the more dynamic regions. The English experience during the Industrial Revolution was that polarization occurred and that people went to the jobs. But this still made local poor relief untenable. If Europe in the early twenty-first century does become economically polarized and people do not move to the more dynamic regions, then social security systems in the countries left behind will come under enormous pressure. If people do move to the jobs, there will also be pressure on the less dynamic countries, but the migrants will become an important constituency for a system of social security that is more European in scope.

References

Braunerhjelm, Pontus, Riccardo Faini, Victor Norman, et al. *Integration and the Regions of Europe: How the Right Policies Can Prevent Polarization*. London: Centre for Economic Policy Research, 2000.

Blaug, Mark. 'The Poor Law Report Reexamined.' *Journal of Economic History* 24, no. 2 (June 1964): 229–43.

Buti, Marco, Daniele Franco and Lucio R. Pench. *The Welfare State in Europe: Challenges and Reforms*. Cheltenham: Edward Elgar, 1999.

Dickson, David. 'In Search of the Old Irish Poor Law.' In *Economy and Society in Scotland and Ireland, 1500–1939*, edited by Rosalind Mitchison and Peter Roebuck, 149–59. Edinburgh: John Donald, 1988.

Freeman, Richard. 'The Large Welfare State as a System.' *American Economic Review* 85, no. 2 (May 1995): 16–21.

Jütte, Robert. *Poverty and Deviance in Early Modern Europe*. Cambridge: Cambridge University Press, 1994.

King, Steve. 'Poor Relief and English Economic Development Reappraised.' *Economic History Review* 50, no. 2 (May 1997): 360–8.

Leonard, E.M. *The Early History of English Poor Relief*. Cambridge: Cambridge University Press, 1900.

Lindert, Peter. 'Poor Relief before the Welfare State: Britain versus the Continent, 1780–1880.' *European Review of Economic History* 2, no. 2 (Aug. 1998): 101–40.

Lis, Catharina, and Hugo Soly. *Poverty and Capitalism in Pre-Industrial Europe*. Hassocks, Sussex: Harvester Press, 1979.

Redford, Arthur. *Labour Migration in England 1800–1850*, third ed. Manchester: Manchester University Press, 1976.

Slack, Paul. *The English Poor Law 1531–1782*. London: Macmillan, 1990.

Smith, Richard M. 'Charity, Self-interest and Welfare: Reflections from Demographic and Family History.' In *Charity, Self-Interest and Welfare in Britain*, edited by Martin Daunton, pp. 23–50. London: UCL Press, 1996.

Smith, Richard M. 'The Historic Roots of English Parish-Funded Welfare,' manuscript, 1999.

Solar, Peter. 'Poor Relief and English Economic Development before the Industrial Revolution.' *Economic History Review* 48, no. 1 (Feb. 1995): 1–22.

Stearns, Peter, and Herrick Chapman. *European Society in Upheaval*, third ed. New York, Macmillan, 1992.

Taylor, James S. 'The Impact of Pauper Settlement, 1691–1834.' *Past & Present* 73 (November 1976): 42–74.

Taylor, James S. 'A Different Kind of Speenhamland: Nonresident Relief in the Industrial Revolution.' *Journal of British Studies* 30, no. 2 (April 1991): 183–208.

Veil, Simone, et al. *Report of the High Level Panel on the Free Movement of Persons.* Report to the European Commission, 18 March 1997.

Williamson, Jeffrey. *Coping with City Growth during the British Industrial Revolution.* Cambridge: Cambridge University Press, 1990.

17.
Paying for Old Age:
Past, Present, Future
MARK THOMAS & PAUL JOHNSON

Introduction

In this paper, we focus attention on one fundamental aspect of the economics of an ageing population—how to pay for old age, individually and collectively. Paying for old age is not a new problem. It does, however, raise more powerful and complex questions today than at the start of the twentieth century, and it will create further challenges in the decades ahead. Moreover, it is becoming an increasingly global issue, which, while still relating most forcefully to mature societies, is of growing concern to developing nations.[1] A historical perspective on the evolution of mechanisms to finance old age in the transatlantic world not only helps us understand how we got to the present situation, but may also help us understand how to approach these future challenges.

The basic issue is presented by Figure 1. The share of the elderly (using the standard definition of 65 as the threshold to old age) has risen consistently (and at very similar rates) over the twentieth century in both Britain and America. Less than 5 per cent of the population lived to 65 at the start of the century; with advances in nutrition, falling fertility and, especially, improvements in the disease environment, that share has tripled over the last hundred years. The American population, with its high rate of natural increase and high level of immigration, has always had a younger age structure than the British. But it is forecast that, by 2030, 20 per cent of US residents will be over 65.

---

[1] The share of the elderly in the global population was 6.8 per cent in 2000; this proportion is forecast to rise to over 12 per cent by 2050.

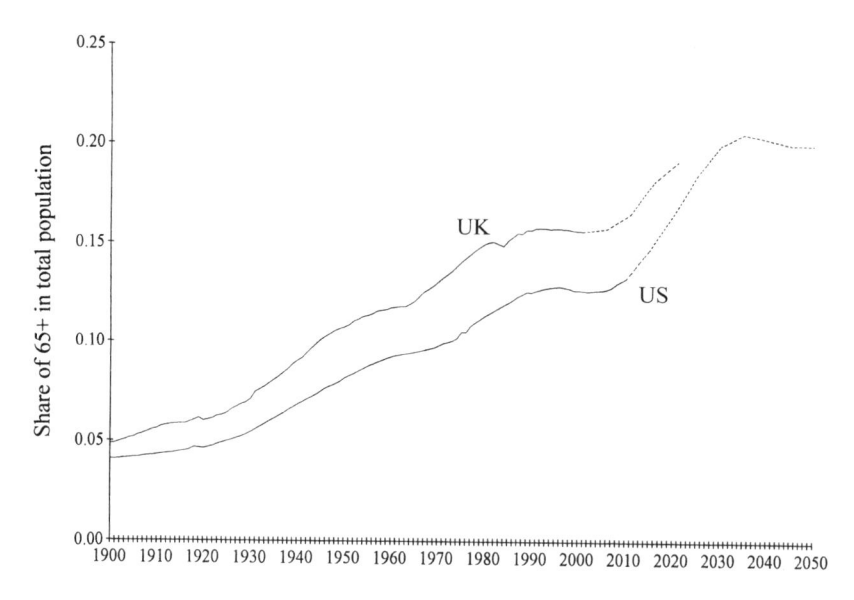

Welfare, Well-being and Individual Economic Security

Figure 1. The ageing of the population: the share of the elderly in the US and UK, 1900–2050.

Note: The elderly are defined as persons over 65 years of age.

Moreover, *within* the elderly the population is ageing. The very old (those over 85) accounted for 3 to 4 per cent of the elderly in 1900; that proportion currently stands at about 10 per cent. By 2050, as the US 'baby-boom' generation continues to age, their share in the population will have more than doubled.[2] These proportions are likely to be even higher in the UK.

The demographic challenge for a maturing society is not limited to increased longevity. Falling fertility rates tend to alter the population pyramid from the bottom up, creating a situation in which there are fewer younger workers to produce resources to support the burgeoning elderly. Figure 2 demonstrates the change. The age structure of the population in both the US and UK is becoming increasingly rectangular, rather than pyramidal as in 1900. The timing of this change is

---

[2] Recent figures from the US Census Bureau project that the very old will constitute 23 per cent of the elderly population by 2050 (middle projection); the high life expectancy series projects a share of 28 per cent. US Bureau of the Census, *Population Projections*, 1996.

Paying for Old Age

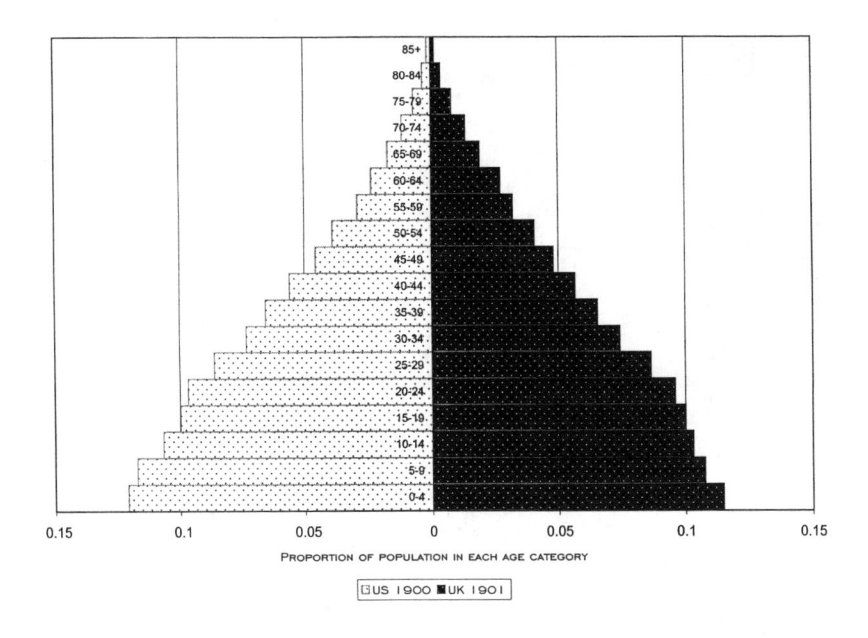

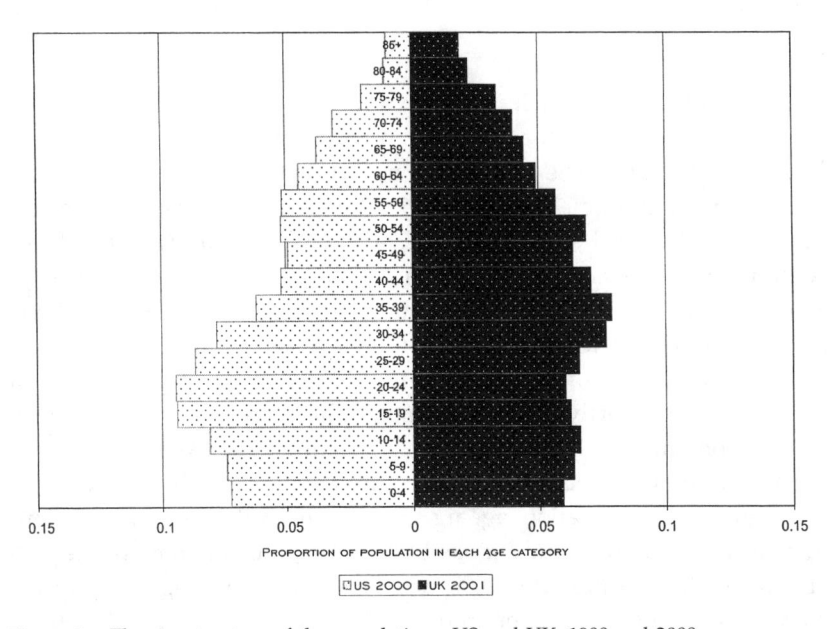

Figure 2. The age structure of the populations: US and UK, 1900 and 2000.

Figure 3. The Elderly Dependency Ratio: US and UK, 1900–2000.

Note: The dependency ratio is calculated as the ratio of persons over 65 to employed civilian workers.

mapped in Figure 3, which reproduces the elderly dependency ratio — the ratio of elderly to the civilian employed workforce — for the two societies since 1900. The two series moved in tandem for much of the century, rising from c.12 per cent in 1900 to 25 per cent by mid-century. They have diverged since 1960, with the level of elderly dependence continuing to rise steeply in Britain, while stabilizing in the United States. The entrance of the baby-boom generation into the labour force, along with the increased participation of women in the paid workforce, has kept the effects of ageing in check. That this has happened much less in Britain partly reflects demographic differences, and partly macro-economic fundamentals. The strength of the American labour market, at least as measured by its ability to produce jobs, has lowered the burden of population ageing, relative to British experience. But even in America, the future looks bleak. The probable track of the elderly dependency ratio after 2000 will take it to new heights — to over 40 per cent in 2030, and over 45 per cent by 2050.

Dependency ratios tend to understate the extent of the challenge of ageing to societies, since they take no account of rising resource consumption by the elderly over time. The age-profile of consumption of net resources follows a U-shape, with health care, education and the opportunity costs of parenting dominating at the youngest ages, and health care and the opportunity costs of adult supervision sharply increasing after the age of 75. So, shifting the age distribution towards the very old generates a per capita increase in resource consumption by the elderly. This trend is kept somewhat in check by the declining proportion of the young and the very young, who are also hungry consumers of resources. But note that the real costs of health care have risen in real terms over time, and most markedly so for the oldest generations. Thus, the continued increase in longevity, especially among the very old, is likely to intensify the challenge of paying for old age in the future.

What can history tell us about how such challenges have been met in the past? Can it prepare us for the onslaught of future problems by providing a road map for policy-makers, or at least a cautionary perspective from which to evaluate the depth and intransigence of future challenges? We begin to answer these questions by focusing on the provision for old age a century ago, before the introduction of social security and old-age pensions.

Past: How Was Old Age Financed Before Social Security?

In the era before social security, the main way in which both British and American households financed old age was by continued work. Labour force participation rates for elderly males were roughly 65 per cent in the US and 61 per cent in the UK in 1900.[3] These rates seem high compared to current levels (17.4 and 7.3 per cent in 1997, respectively), but actually understate the degree of labour force attachment a

---

[3] We use the conventional dating of the onset of old age at 65 years. Note that comparisons across countries and across time reflect compositional differences in the age structure of the population over 65. However, the lower participation rates for British workers are only marginally affected by cohort effects or mortality differences. Thus, the participation rates for 65- to 69-year-olds in 1900 were 68.9 per cent in the UK and 78.5 per cent in the US. Similarly, ageing has not been a significant factor in the decline in labour force participation of the elderly over the twentieth century. Note, however, that the industrial distribution of the labour force had a greater impact on the relative rates of participation, in particular, the dominance of agriculture in the US, with its comparatively elderly labour force. Johnson, 'Employment', has emphasized the importance of agricultural decline in shaping the twentieth-century profile of elderly participation in the UK; compositional effects played an even stronger role in the US after 1900.

century ago. There is a conceptual difference between being unattached from the labour market on the day of a census and permanent withdrawal (retirement).[4] Modern data indicate that it is not uncommon for elderly 'retirees' to re-enter the labour force, perhaps more than once in their lifetime. Such behaviour is not new; 35 per cent of male retirees in 1900 had re-entered the labour force by 1910. The rate of permanent retirement for American males over 65 years in 1900 was probably below 5 per cent.[5]

Continued work no doubt partly reflected precautionary concerns in an era with limited communal resources — the possibility that ill health of self or spouse could wipe out accumulated assets, for example.[6] But the primary motive was the continued need to earn income to escape poverty. Retirement at a level of even minimal comfort had to be self-financed; few workers accumulated enough to buy such leisure.

That is certainly the thrust of the evidence for working households at the end of the nineteenth century. The evidence is more detailed for American families, the subjects of numerous state and federal social surveys by governments eager to learn more about the impact of tariffs, immigration and other policies on the economic and social welfare of the average worker. In almost all such surveys, the median household was revealed to undertake no savings; only the upper echelon of workers (the top 10 to 20 per cent) achieved savings rates commensurate with the economy-wide average of 15 per cent. High deficits, financed by borrowing on credit, selling off assets, or spending down past savings, were a common feature in all these surveys.

Were we to take the logic of such surveys literally, we would conclude that the average American working household accumulated no savings for retirement (after all, the sum of zero savings over a lifetime is zero). However, this rests on the implausible assumption of complete

---

[4] Ransom and Sutch, 'Labor', have used this difference to suggest that retirement was a more common experience before 1930 than most historians have previously recognized; by treating older workers reporting six months or more of unemployment as effectively retired, they estimate that over 20 per cent of American males had retired by 1900. Robert Margo's statistical comparison of the retired and the long-term unemployed ('Labor Force') indicates that this is an invalid conclusion.

[5] See Costa, *Evolution*, p. 91, on re-entry, and Lee, 'Expected Length', on permanent retirement.

[6] In a survey of the aged poor in Massachusetts in 1908/9, one-quarter sustained losses in assets because of 'extra expenses for sickness and emergencies' (Commonwealth of Massachusetts, *Report*, p. 74).

persistence of savings levels over time. It is more likely that households saved in some years and not in others; moreover, the intensity and irregularity of unemployment among American workers suggest that households did not inhabit fixed points in the income hierarchy. Simulations of household accumulation using the abundant survey data and a more appropriate treatment of the persistence of income and savings suggest that the median household in 1900 accumulated about $2,750 by the time the household head reached the age of 65.[7] Such an accumulation could buy a 15-year annuity for two people for something less than $250.[8]

Such an amount was clearly not enough to finance retirement. The Massachusetts Old Age Commission of 1910 considered a 'pension . . . adequate for American standards of living' to be not 'less than $200' per person per year.[9] Other surveys of the period used $300 per person as the dividing line between security and 'danger'.[10] An accumulation of $2,750 was far below that necessary to maintain a reasonable standard of living beyond 65. The shortfall of assets was a problem not only for the bottom half of the wage distribution. The simulations for 1900 indicate that over 85 per cent of working households saved too little to meet the income level of $500 recommended by the most conservative commentators for this period.[11]

---

[7] See James, Palumbo and Thomas, 'Have American Workers?'.
[8] $247.34 to be exact. The 15-year basis is based on an expected lifetime of 11.5 years for males and 12.2 years for females at age 65 in 1900/2, plus the average difference in age between husband and wife of about 2.2 years.
[9] Massachusetts, Report, p. 231. The following paragraphs are based on Thomas, James and Palumbo, 'Have American Workers?'.
[10] Orloff, Politics, p. 147.
[11] Note that such calculations are only meant to be suggestive: the primary vehicle for asset accumulation, real estate, cannot readily be annuitized (although it earns 'income' by reducing the necessary outgoings on rent), while uncertain lifetimes may make such conversions unpalatable for risk-averse households. Indeed, annuities were an infrequent method of savings for both American and British families before the introduction of social security. Commercial insurance companies introduced annuity policies in the US before World War I, but they never caught on. Among 102 families of California streetcar workers in the 1930s, only one spent enough to secure commercial insurance to the amount necessary to buy an annuity paying $35 per month for man and wife after age 65 (Huntington and Luck, Living, p. 79). The Post Office offered annuities after 1910 on reasonably generous terms, but the public showed singularly little interest in their possibilities. A similar Post Office scheme in the UK also failed owing to apathy, despite policy changes designed to make the programme more attractive to working families. Friedman and Warshawsky, 'Annuity Prices', indicate that annuities remain unpopular as a means of financing old age in the US.

Much the same was true in the 1920s. In 1924, the Massachusetts Commission on Old-Age Pensions found that about a quarter of Boston elderly workers had neither income nor property.[12] Similarly, the National Civic Federation found that almost 30 per cent of 15,000 elderly surveyed from the north-eastern states 'had no property whatever'; if those in private and public institutions are included, the proportion rises to 35 per cent.[13] Note that these figures underestimate the situation faced by elderly workers, since both surveys incorporate information on upper middle-class households. If the top quartile of the distribution is excluded, the median wealth in 1925 was less than $1,000 and the average $2,450 ($1,180 in 1900 prices).[14] Retirement was simply not possible with wealth holdings like these.

The evidence for British households likewise indicates limited potential for self-financing of old age. A sample census of 24,000 elderly individuals in 1899 revealed that no more than 35 per cent (and probably less than 20 per cent) received income from property or savings.[15] Such incomes were themselves likely to be very small. Before 1914, manual workers had access to only three types of 'small saver' institutions—savings banks, building and co-operative societies.[16] The average value of accumulated deposits in these institutions in 1911 was £22.50. Moreover, not all these funds came from working-class savers; Paul Johnson estimates that working households accounted for 30 per

---

[12] Monthly Labor Review, 'Report'.

[13] Ibid.

[14] Note, however, that these figures relate to all elderly households and are not commensurate with the estimates of asset accumulation at age 65 cited above, given the probability of some asset decumulation after the onset of old age.

[15] *Departmental Committee on the Aged Deserving Poor*, Appendix II. Although the survey questionnaire explicitly asked about the level of income from savings and property for all households, the results were only reported for individuals with non-relief incomes below 10 shillings a week. 10.9 per cent of persons (12.8 per cent of males; 9.9 per cent of females) recorded some income from property. The figures quoted in the text were generated by assuming either that all persons with an income above 10 shillings a week held property (upper level), or that two-thirds of those earning above 20 shillings per week and one-third of those with between 10 shillings and 20 shillings per week had 'means'. Both are likely to be over-estimates. The report downplayed the role of savings in financing old age: 'many persons will probably have drawn upon their savings before they have reached the age of 65 . . . necessitated by a premature breakdown of health' (p. xxi). The report further suggested that less than 0.5 per cent of all elderly Irish persons received income from 'money invested in savings banks or elsewhere' (p. 71).

[16] The most common form of property in the test census was probably land and a cottage; this is suggested by the concentration of property holders in rural locations. Fewer than 5 per cent of males in large urban communities reported income from 'means'.

cent of savings banks deposits, 10 per cent of building society assets, and 75 per cent of co-operative holdings.[17] Working-class institutional accumulation c. 1900 amounted to something less than £4 per adult. This figure is averaged over all adults; in the absence of data on age-specific holdings, we cannot be certain that the elderly were not better provided for.[18] But other evidence suggests that they were not. Thus, the average value of the estates of the poorest 90 per cent of the population who died between 1899 and 1904 (at an average age of 57) was less than £16.[19] Similarly, 60 per cent of those over 70 passed the means test for receipt of old-age pensions once they were introduced in 1908, demonstrating an income somewhat less than half the average earnings of male manual workers. Hunt's comment, that 'as late as 1890 half of [all workers] were still either too poor, too reckless, or too uncertain of reaching old age to make adequate provision against eventual loss of earnings' seems to have lost none of its relevance by 1910 — or indeed by 1930.[20] A 2 per cent sample of manual workers in London in 1929/31 finds that only 14 out of 1,528 elderly-headed households reported receipt of an income from savings or from private means.[21] There is little systematic evidence of the use of life-cycle savings to finance retirement for British workers before 1939, despite the ungenerosity of the British social security system.

[17] Johnson, *Saving*, pp. 204-6.
[18] The authors did attempt to replicate the procedure used to generate accumulated assets by American working families by simple summation of the surplus of income over expenditure at each age from 25 to 65 for a survey of 1,024 British workers in textiles, metals, mining and glass-making in 1889/90. Ignoring interest and secular changes in wages, median savings would have yielded assets of £255, sufficient to purchase an annuity of 10 shillings per week for one member of the household at age 65. Such an annuity conforms to a replacement rate of 66 per cent on average manual earnings for all males c. 1890, 35 per cent on earnings of sampled male workers, and 23 per cent of family income of those surveyed. These results imply more aggressive saving behaviour than does other evidence for Victorian Britain; but note that these results are generated from a single cross-section of workers drawn from the top end of the earnings distribution, using a measure of savings highly sensitive to mis-reporting (as the difference between two reported variables, each possibly in error), on the assumption that all savings were life-cycle in character, with no correction for income-smoothing strategies. Even with these potential upward biases, the results indicate an insufficiency of savings to maintain a living standard appropriate to a couple drawn from the labour aristocracy.
[19] Chiozza Money, *Riches*, p. 51.
[20] Hunt, *British Labour*, p. 122.
[21] Baines and Johnson, 'Did They Jump?'

In the absence of guaranteed income from private savings or state-mandated social security, how did elderly households survive? Partly through continued work (albeit with declining incomes generated by falling productivity, rising sickness, disabilities and unemployment) and partly by outside sources of income.[22] The most important source of supplemental income for American households was earnings from family members. The living arrangements for the majority of elderly households at the end of the nineteenth century maintained the rural structure developed in the first flush of land abundance. In urban and rural communities alike, the extended family was the norm for elderly households. In 1900, over 60 per cent of the non-institutionalized population over 65 years lived with married or unmarried children; a further 10 per cent lived with other kin. Adult children who remained in the home subsidized their aged parents; the rooms of the children who left were rented out. Among cotton textile workers surveyed by the US Commissioner of Labor in 1889/90, the most common source of income for those households with an elderly head was the earnings of resident children (almost half of family income); income from boarders or lodgers contributed a further 17 per cent to the family coffers. Less than 6 per cent came from all other sources, including pensions and accumulated savings.

Child rearing thus constituted a form of asset accumulation in response to life cycle and precautionary (income insecurity) concerns. Moreover, given the economies of scale of household management and the relative risks inherent in raising a family and maintaining a monetary 'nest-egg' in an era of substantial economic instability, it may have been a more efficient method of providing for old age and its uncertainties than financial accumulation. Indeed, households headed by older workers (55 years and above) had the highest average per capita

---

[22] Most of the evidence for this relates to American households: census records reveal that elderly (male) workers spent at least 3.5 months out of work in 1900. The rise in 'days lost' was due both to increased sickness and disability as well as higher unemployment. Incomes reflect the combination of falling employment opportunities and declining productivity: a sample of workers in the US cotton industry in 1889/90 shows that males aged 65 and older earned an average annual income 56.7 per cent of 55- to 64-year-olds. Female headed households were even more vulnerable in an era of low labour force participation for married women. Widowhood was a key marker for poverty in both Britain and the US.

income of any decadal age group in the 1889/90 survey. This was partly due to the smaller family size of older households; but it also reflects the changing composition of family incomes.

Living arrangements were not so structured in the UK, whose agriculture was dominated by landless labour rather than the family farm, and whose urban land prices precluded the purchase and maintenance of large family homes. Only 20 per cent of households contained relatives other than children (a proxy for multi-generational or extended households) in 1851; this proportion fell to 15 per cent by 1951 and below 8 per cent by 1971.[23] A corollary of this was that most elderly men were head of their own household—84 per cent in both 1891 and 1951—similar to the 88 per cent estimated by Laslett for pre-industrial England.[24]

David Thomson has argued that historically it has been 'unEnglish behaviour to expect children to support parents'.[25] From the introduction of the Poor Law in 1601, destitute elderly people had a right to subsistence support, but it was the local community rather than the family on whom the obligation lay. Although the community had a legal right to recover expenses from the children of dependent elderly paupers, in practice this sanction was seldom applied.[26] This is not to say that family support was completely unknown among older Britons. The test census of 1899 reported that 55 per cent of those living on a non-relief income below 10 shillings a week (about 40 per cent of the total number surveyed) 'received assistance from children or others'; a further 17 per cent of the sample had no income but were 'maintained by friends or relatives'. Such figures suggest that at least 40 per cent of the 'aged poor' received some measure of financial support from children, other relatives and friends. But fragmentary evidence suggests that the financial transfers involved were small, certainly smaller than in the US. Thus, for the small number of British textile workers over 65 included in the 1889/90 worker survey, children's earnings accounted for about 30 per cent of family incomes. At the other end of the income scale, Colonel Milward's survey of non-workhouse elderly poor in South Warwickshire in 1898 found that a third depended in some measure on family support. The amounts involved were clearly insuffi-

---

[23] Wall, 'Regional'.
[24] Falkingham and Gordon, 'Fifty Years On.'
[25] Thomson, 'Welfare', p. 198.
[26] Thomson, 'I Am Not'.

cient in most cases — 60 per cent of those so helped also turned to supplemental sources of income (parish relief, etc.). In inter-war London, only 3.3 per cent of elderly-headed households reported being in receipt of allowances from relatives.

Inter-generational transfers were not available to everyone, even within the US. Not all workers married and procreated; not all parents could rely upon sufficient income support from their children. The importance of family support to financial viability for many Americans is made clear by the results of a survey of poverty in Massachusetts in 1908/9, which reveals a high correlation between destitution and the absence of family support. A third of those elderly who managed to escape dependency but who remained on the fringes of poverty received some form of family support; in contrast, over three-quarters of the dependent poor (those in receipt of public or private income transfers) had no adult children or near relatives 'able to aid at present'. For the institutionalized poor, the proportion was over 90 per cent: 60 per cent had no adult child living at the time of entrance into almshouse or benevolent society.[27]

How successful were these mechanisms for financing old age in the era before social security? If we measure success by ability to avoid dependence on private charity or the public purse, the answer is: not very, especially in the British case. Old age, as Charles Booth found, was a primary marker for poverty among British households at the end of the nineteenth century. Fully a third of elderly households were in receipt of poor law relief in 1891, a figure that changed little before 1908, when old-age pensions were introduced. The test census of the aged deserving poor indicated that 64 per cent of older Britons received an income below 10 shillings per week in 1899 (a little less than half of Rowntree's poverty line for a family of five).

Older Americans in general seem to have escaped these extremes of poverty, suggesting the comparative success of family strategies to avoid destitution. Only 3 per cent of Massachusetts' elderly were paupers in 1908; if those supported by private charity are included, the proportion rises to 6.5 per cent. According to the Massachusetts survey, about 11 per cent lived on less than $5 per person a week (about twice the poverty line in the UK). Other sources produce a higher proportion in poverty: in the 1920s, the National Civic Federation observed that 17 per cent of the non-dependent aged in north-eastern states had neither

---

[27] Massachusetts, *Report*, p. 61.

property nor income; in Massachusetts, 23 per cent had incomes below $100 ($48.50 in 1900 prices). Other surveys in the 1920s pointed to similar results.[28] These were enclaves of poverty, less widespread than in the UK, but testimony nonetheless to the fundamental insecurity faced by the elderly in the absence of state-guaranteed income.

(Historic) Present: How Has Old Age Been Financed Since the Introduction of Social Security?

The twentieth century has seen a revolution in the mechanism by which old age is financed, as state-run social insurance has increasingly replaced the patchwork quilt of financing systems that had evolved by 1900. The introduction of old-age pensions in the UK in 1908 began the trend towards consistent funding of old age without recourse to the perils of the Poor Law. Nonetheless, the evidence is that pensions were not much of an improvement over poor relief. The level of benefits was low, reflecting moral hazard concerns by some policy-makers; for an aged couple (over 70 before 1928, over 65 thereafter), the replacement rate was about 28 per cent of the median urban household's total income. Clearly, the financial position of elderly households was not altered radically by a programme that while reducing income insecurity did relatively little to assist in the expenses of everyday living.[29] The basic structures of the pension system have remained true to the original intent of modest financial support over the past ninety years.

The social security system that evolved in the United States also began hesitantly. There were originally two complementary programmes in place—Old Age Assistance, a joint programme between the federal government and the states, and Old Age (later, Old Age and Survivors—OASI) Insurance. Access to the latter was restrictive in the first instance; over time, however, the programme has grown by accretion both in terms of coverage and generosity. In 1940, only 2.2 per cent of men over 65 were beneficiaries under OASI; within ten years, 25 per cent were in receipt of monthly cheques; the proportion

---

[28] Orloff, *Politics*, pp. 146–8.
[29] Baines and Johnson, 'Did They Jump?', show that the old age pension provided no more than 75 per cent of a poverty line income in 1929/31; those workers who did retire appear to have suffered a substantial decline in disposable income.

491

reached 60 per cent by 1960, and had passed 90 per cent by 1970. The liberalization of social security has not been limited to expansive entitlements; benefits have also been increased in absolute and relative terms over time. The level of benefits was c.17.5 per cent of the median income of a 2-person family in 1948; by 1960 it had risen to 30 per cent, by 1969 to 44 per cent, and by 1980 to 66 per cent. Significantly, state financing has expanded to include medical expenses for the elderly (Medicare), introduced as part of the *mélange* of Great Society programmes in the 1960s, when advocates of social engineering seemed to have unbounded confidence in its curative powers.

Public provision has thus evolved very differently in the two countries. The irony of outcomes belying rhetoric is self-evident. Britain, in the vanguard of social progressivism and a pioneer of the Welfare State, has created a system of minimalist support for the elderly poor;[30] the US, with the intensity of the convert to welfare idealism (and with a political system that rewards and promotes special interests), has crafted a system that has largely eradicated poverty for the aged.

Private systems of retirement dovetail in expected ways with the pattern of public provision. Tax policies encouraged the growth of private pension plans in Britain and the US, with pivotal legislation in 1921 and 1942 respectively. But such plans grew more rapidly in the UK, in terms of numbers of plans, extent of coverage, and place of importance in paying for old age. Leslie Hannah records their early history.[31] By 1936, 12.5 per cent of the employed workforce was covered by occupational pension plans, a proportion that rose to 33 per cent in 1956, and which has hovered around 50 per cent for the past thirty years.[32] The diffusion of occupational pensions has been significantly lower in the US—the equivalent shares of the employed labour force being 6.1 per cent (1935), 26.5 (1956), and 35–40 (since 1965).

Occupational pension plans, therefore, remain much less important in the US than in Britain, especially in relation to social security. Currently in the UK, about half of pensioners' incomes originate from sources other than social security sources; the share for American

---

[30] The proportion of British old age pensioners in receipt of supplemental income to bring them above the poverty line has remained stable (at about 25 per cent) since the 1950s.
[31] Hannah, *Inventing*, pp. 31–40, 149.
[32] See Hannah, *Inventing*, p. 67, and Blundell and Johnson, 'Pensions', p. 168.

elderly households was 16 per cent in 1986.[33] The low rate of self-financing in the US suggests that the realities of state support have finessed popular rhetorical commitments to individualism. In Britain, by contrast, the high rate of self-financing indicates that the realities of individual need have trumped rhetorical political commitments to state provision.

With the development of such wide-ranging programmes of public (non-contributory) and private (contributory) insurance, it is perhaps unsurprising that almost none among the structures of old age support in place at the end of the nineteenth century have survived to today. Retirement is now the norm rather than the exception (Figure 4); most elderly live alone (or with their spouse) rather than with children or

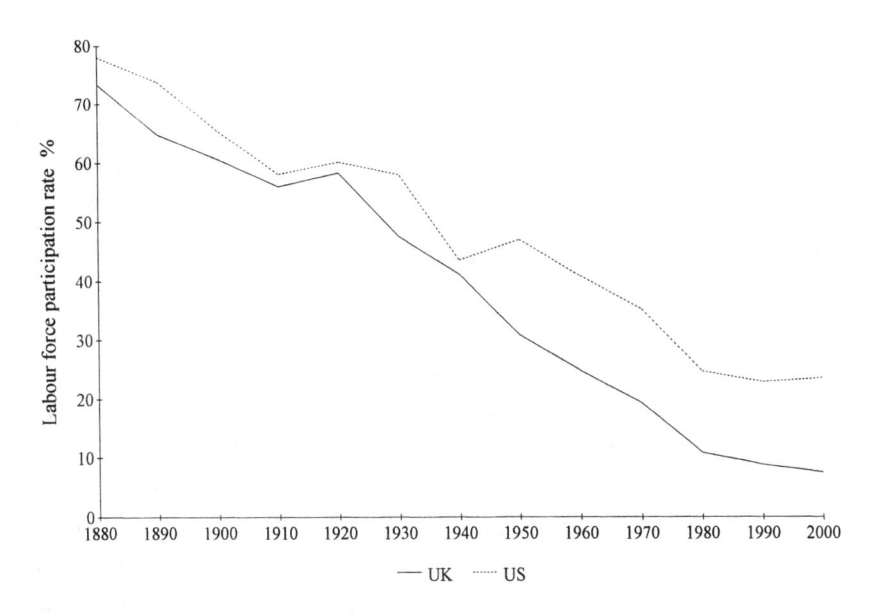

Figure 4. Labour force participation ratio of elderly males: US and UK, 1880–2000.

Source: Johnson, 'Employment and retirement', p. 116, supplemented by data from the *Annual Abstract of Statistics*; US: Costa, *Evolution of Retirement*, pp. 29–30, supplemented by data drawn from the Current Population Survey.
Note: Labour force participation is defined as being employed (or seeking employment) for some period during the year.

---

[33] See Blundell and Johnson, 'Pensions', p. 168, for the UK, and Hurd, 'Economic', p. 67, for the US.

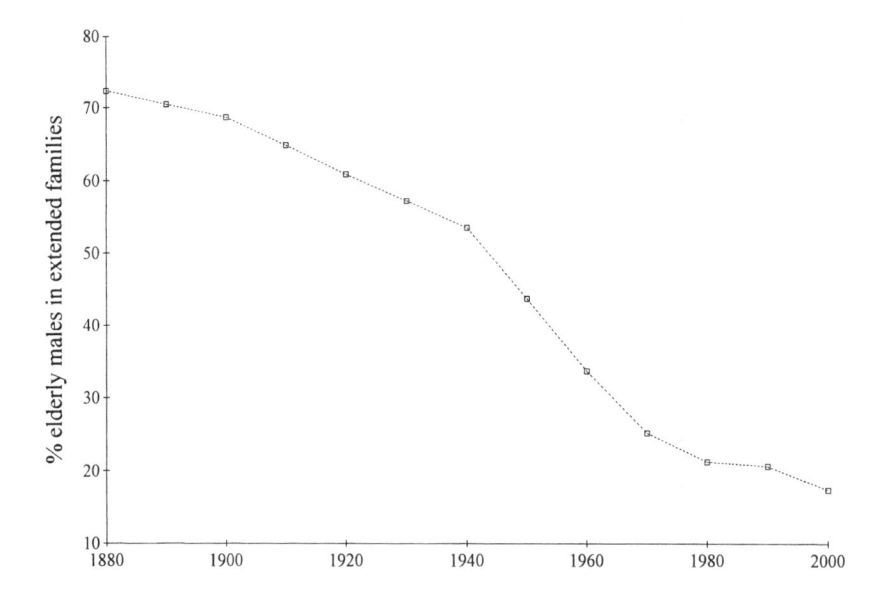

Welfare, Well-being and Individual Economic Security

Figure 5. Co-resident status of elderly males: US household, 1880–2000.

Source: Costa, *Evolution of Retirement*, p. 130, supplemented by data drawn from the Current Population Survey.
Note: Co-residence is defined as living in a non-institutional household with at least one family member besides the spouse.

other relatives (Figure 5); poor relief is dead and almshouses and benevolent homes are largely a thing of the past. Elderly poverty still exists, but to a much lesser extent than a century ago. Many of these trends predated the introduction of social security, but there is little doubt that social policy has accelerated the dismantling of the former system of old age support.[34]

[34] Thus, as Figure 4 indicates, the trend by which 'old people have shifted from living as relatives in family households to living alone or apart from related individuals' (Smith, 'Accounting', p. 87) began before the introduction of social security, although it accelerated after 1940. Hareven notes of two generations of workers in Manchester, New Hampshire: 'while the ... cohort (born before 1910) expected their children to assist them in old age, the ... cohorts (born between 1910 and 1929) did not expect to have to rely on their children for *economic* support. They prepared for old age through pension plans, savings, and home ownership and expected to rely on social security' ('Life-course Transitions', p. 120).

Thus, in both Britain and the US, labour force participation began its steady decline in the 1880s (Figure 4). Moreover, the rate was similar in the two countries between 1880 and 1940, despite very different national histories of public pension provision. The aggregate participation rate, however, hides some disparities. In the UK case, as Johnson points out, compositional effects in the structure of employment distorted the retirement path, especially with the contraction of agriculture which left behind a bastion of superannuated workers.[35] Curiously, adjusting the aggregate labour force participation to remove the effects of all sectoral shifts across industries reveals that the average within-sector rate only began to decline in the 1930s. This suggests that it was the Depression, rather than old-age pensions, that began the process of labour market separation for the elderly (note that the speed of falling labour force participation accelerated in the US in the 1930s). Farming has employed an older workforce in the US as well, and its relative decline since 1880 has undoubtedly accelerated the fall in overall participation.[36] But participation rates have declined at a similar rate for both on-farm and off-farm households from 1880 to 1990, indicating that the evolution of retirement predates the introduction of social security.

How should we explain these anomalies? At the highest level of generality, by understanding that retirement was a product of both labour demand and labour supply forces. On the labour supply side, the relative ungenerosity of the British old-age pension before 1945 suppressed the rate of voluntary withdrawal from the labour market, while the development of new vehicles for financing retirement in the US before 1936 (such as Civil War pensions) stimulated retirement. On the labour demand side, the increased difficulty that the elderly had in finding jobs, in the 1930s in particular, no doubt pushed many into involuntary retirement.

Figures 6 and 7 reproduce the trends in labour force participation for males in relation to the real value of old-age benefits. The figures appear to trace a common linkage between retirement and social security. Yet once again, there are instructive differences between the two countries. Social security payments as a fraction of previous earnings (the replacement rate) for aged couples in the US increased sharply in

---

[35] Johnson, 'Employment'.
[36] Note, however, that the migration of retired farmers to urban areas exaggerates the importance of declining agriculture in the US (Costa, *Evolution*, p. 23).

495

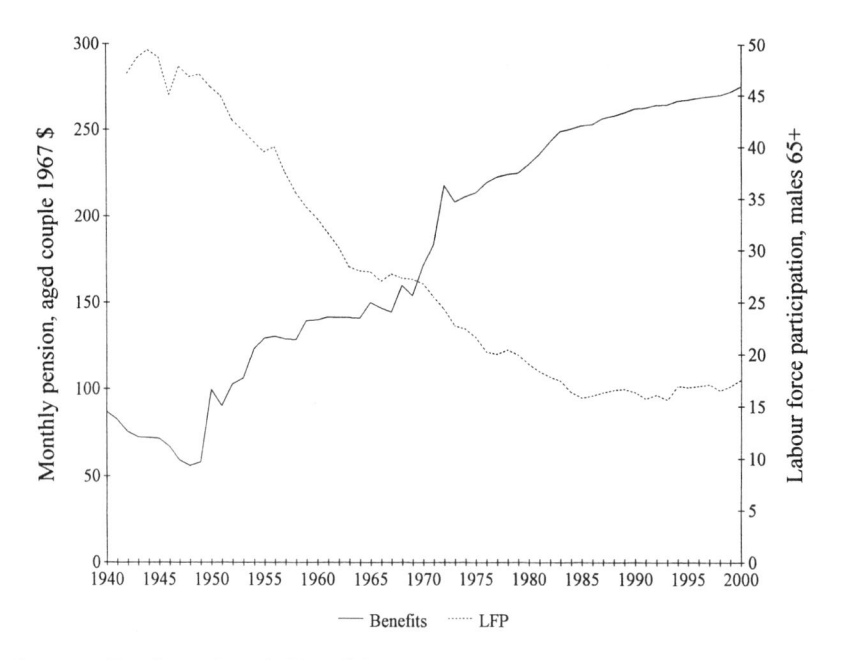

Welfare, Well-being and Individual Economic Security

Figure 6. Benefits and work: United States, 1940–2000.

Note: Labour force participation is measured by the CPS criterion of 'economic activity', defined as employed or seeking employment in the week preceding the annual Current Population Survey. The participation rate is consistently lower than the 'gainful worker' measurement of Figure 4.

the early 1970s (from 44 per cent in 1969 to 58 per cent in 1975) and have continued to rise slowly since. Not coincidentally, the period from 1969 to 1974 saw the steepest decline in the rate of poverty among elderly Americans; by the mid-1990s, the poverty rate was below 15 per cent, the replacement rate above 70 per cent. The replacement rate of benefits against median earnings has remained stable in the UK, at about 45 per cent for married couples. Yet the pace of retirement has progressed similarly in the two countries; moreover, the state with the less generous system of support has the lower rate of participation.

When evaluating retirement, it is well to recognize that it is a normal good, the demand for which rises as its (opportunity cost) price declines, as the relative prices of other goods (substitutes and complements) change, as tastes evolve, and as income increases. The replacement rate is, therefore, only one ingredient in explaining changes in labour market attachment by the elderly. Retirement has its benefits. The relative prices of many complementary activities (travel, entertain-

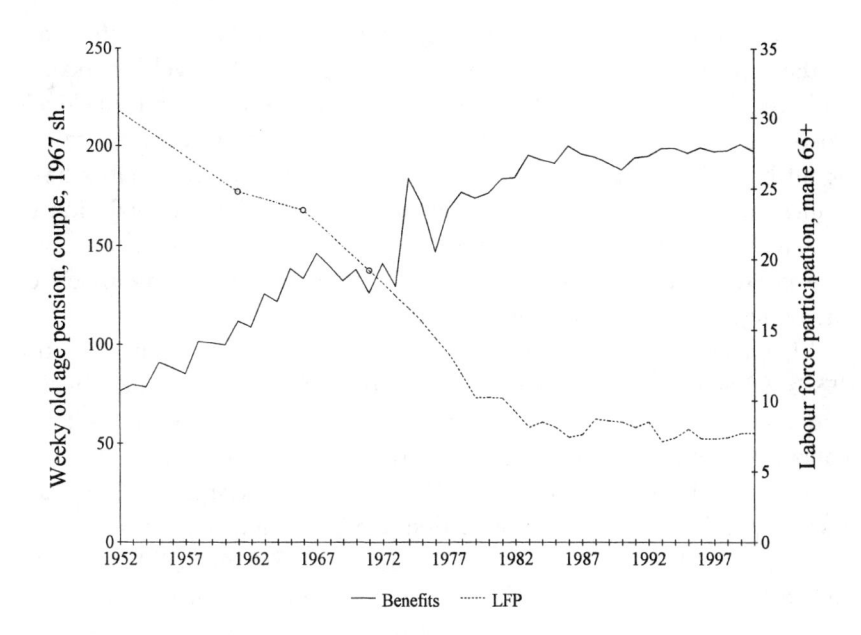

Figure 7. Benefits and work: United Kingdom, 1952–2000.

ment, cultural activities) have fallen over time; household income has increased; and any stigma that might once have attached to retirement has largely disappeared. The tax regime has only reinforced the downward trend in participation, especially in the UK, where the marginal tax on postponing retirement is close to 100 per cent in many cases.

Future: How Will the Next Generation (or Two) Cope?

We began this paper by noting the peculiar challenges to be faced over the next half-century as the population ages. The likely impact of this demographic shift has been described variously as a 'complex and formidable set of interrelated challenges', a 'looming old age crisis', and an 'agequake'.[37] For the US, UK and other developed countries, the immediate question is not, as one economist has asked, 'Can we afford to grow older?', because the long-run rate of economic growth significantly exceeds that of the population.[38] Unless ageing *per se* fundamen-

[37] OECD, *Maintaining*; World Bank, *Averting*; Wallace, *Agequake*.
[38] Disney, *Can We Afford?*

tally reduces the rate of economic growth,[39] it can be anticipated that in the future our societies will have higher per capita levels of income and wealth than today. If there is an 'old age crisis' looming in developed societies, it is not about the size of the economic cake, but rather about how this cake is cut. Demographic and institutional factors have coincided to create this pressing public policy dilemma. Its solution in turn will be shaped not only by future politics, but also by past history. The power of path dependence is clearly seen from a comparison of the policy options faced in the two societies.

Let us be more specific about the nature of the challenge. In the 1990s a historically high proportion of the population of both the US and the UK was of working age. The baby-boomers formed a large cohort of prime-age workers, while low fertility rates since the 1970s meant that there were relatively few child dependants. In 1990, the total dependency rate (the population aged 0–14 and 65 and over as a percentage of the working age population) was 51.7 in the US and 52.9 in the UK. The retirement of the baby-boomers after 2010 is projected to increase this rate to around 68.0 in both countries by 2030.[40]

Thus, in a period of forty years, the demographic regime will move from being unusually favourable, in the sense of having almost as many potential workers as non-workers, to being unusually demanding. Part of the burden of ageing on the working population will be lessened by the reduction in the demands of the young. But, given that the consumption of resources rises with age among the older population, the smaller share of the very young will not be sufficient to offset the costs associated with a large and increasing number of older people. Moreover, the consumption of resources by the elderly will certainly rise over time, as they themselves age. This is most obvious in the case of the cost of medical services. According to US figures for 1987, per capita health-care expenditures for those over 85 are 2.5 times greater than for 65- to 69-year-olds, and 6 times greater than for 19- to 64-year-olds.[41] UK figures show similar ratios: compared to the

---

[39] In theory, ageing could have a negative impact on growth through both labour market and capital market effects. Older populations may in aggregate possess fewer relevant skills than younger populations, and they may save less and consume more. Although there is evidence that age structure may be related to savings rates or growth rates for some countries and time periods, the underlying causal mechanism is unclear, and the empirical relationship is unstable. See, for instance, Dowrick, 'Demographic Change'.
[40] OECD, *Ageing*.
[41] Hobbs and Damon, *65+*, pp. 3–25.

average per capita hospital expenditure on people aged 16–64, those aged 65–74 and 75 plus consume 3.4 and 9.8 times this amount respectively. Compositional changes in the age structure may be expected to push up total medical expenses. On the basis of the 1987 figures, US per capita medical expenses will rise by about 20 per cent between 1997 and 2050; the figure for the UK is likely to be even greater.[42] Such figures surely understate the true added costs, since they assume that treatment technologies and costs remain static. Recent US experience vitiates this assumption. Between 1977 and 1987, the real cost of medical care for the elderly rose twice as rapidly as for 19- to 64-year-olds (54 per cent versus 26 per cent). Over the longer term, the contrast is even sharper. Between 1963 and 1987, average medical costs for 14- to 64-year-olds rose at an annual rate of 4.23 per cent per annum; for 65- to 74-year-olds, at 7.6 per cent; for 75- to 84-year-olds, at 8 per cent; and for the over 85 group, at 10.6 per cent per annum.[43] The combination of population growth, population ageing, and continuing costly resort to new biomedical technologies may cause the value of resources devoted to health care to more than quadruple by 2050. Moreover, medical expenses are only one part of the total added expense incurred by an ageing society.

Demographic imperatives are far from being the only factor that will affect the resource allocation decisions of future generations. Institutions matter too, and the institution that causes most concern is the pay-as-you-go public pension system in which each year's contributions from workers finance each year's payments to pensioners. For this type of pension to be sustained in the long run, successive birth cohorts must accept that they will pass through a phase of net contribution during working life, before entering a phase of net benefit during retirement. There exists, in effect, an implicit contract between birth cohorts or generations to honour transfer obligations. Population ageing impacts on this transfer system by increasing the size of the pensioner population relative to the contributing population; this means contribution rates have to rise to sustain a given level of pension. But this demographic effect is only half the problem faced by public pension systems today; they also have to come to terms with the problem of system maturity. From the 1950s to the 1970s politicians increased the generosity of public pensions, particularly in the US. This was

---

[42] Johnson, 'Retirement', p. 166.
[43] Cutler and Meara, 'Medical Costs', p. 240.

done at relatively low cost, because pensioner cohorts were small, and the number of contributors was increasing, with the maturation of the baby-boomers accompanied by a sharp rise in female labour force participation. The real value of pensions increased without a corresponding increase in the tax burden on contributors. But pension systems are now beginning to mature. There is no new group of contributors to enrol in the system in order to generate windfall gains. We now have to face up to the unpleasant fact that the extravagant promises about long-run pension benefits made in the 1970s can only be honoured if future generations accept historically unprecedented levels of social security taxation.

It is clear that many politicians and voters believe these past promises to be unsustainable. Poll after poll in the US has revealed the extent to which American workers discount the future of social security. In the UK, younger people declare strong support for the public pension system, but little confidence that they will receive an adequate state pension in their old age. Yet this pervasive scepticism about the future ability of social security to deliver an adequate retirement income has not been matched by a shift towards more individualistic methods of paying for old age. Although surveys indicate that workers with reduced faith in the survival of social security into their old age tend to have higher savings rates than the more sanguine, the aggregate personal savings rate in the US has been in sharp secular decline since the early 1970s (becoming negative in the national income accounts in mid-1999). Partly this is due to a misleading measurement convention: flow of funds data understate the level of savings by ignoring unrealized capital gains (especially an issue in the great bull market in the US of the last two decades), which are in turn driving buoyant expectations about the future. But partly it resides in the faith of Americans that government will solve the social security crisis and ensure continuity of the system of rewards that has supported their parents and grandparents through old age. This faith seems misplaced. There is no way in which a growing retired population can be supported at a given level of income without increasing that population's resource base. This is true regardless of whether the resources are provided through collective social security and tax systems, or through private transfers and saving. Put simply, this is the inevitable price of extended lifetimes.

In the UK the situation is different, but no less problematic. There is no social security financial crisis, because the pension replacement rate has always been low and, since 1980, has been gradually declining as a result of a switch from earnings to price indexation.[44] Public pension expenditure is projected to fall quite sharply in the second quarter of the twenty-first century, but so will the relative value of the public pension. The replacement rate of the basic pension, already down to around 15 per cent of average male earnings, is likely to fall to just 7 per cent by 2050.[45] Despite these projections, there has been no compensating surge of private pension saving; according to a recent survey, only 20 per cent of current workers are saving sufficient to attain a financially content retirement.[46]

Demographic and institutional developments mean that current systems for financing old age in the US and the UK are not in long-run equilibrium. Strategies for providing retirement incomes, which have changed enormously over the course of the twentieth century, must change again. A return to earlier, more individualistic, financial arrangements may at first sight seem attractive, but it is never easy, and sometimes impossible, to turn the clock back. Policies designed to return to an era of longer work-lives and inter-generational support systems appear doomed to failure.

One policy that has been advocated in order to increase the economic resources of older people and at the same time reduce public pension expenditure is to raise the retirement age. It is already predicted that the labour force participation of the elderly will stabilize and may even rise after the turn of the century, even without policy changes. Nonetheless, both US and UK governments are committed to raise the age of retirement. Legislation in the UK to take effect after 2010 will raise the retirement age for women from 60 to 65; in the US, social security reforms will raise the starting age for receipt of full pensions from 65 to 66 by 2005; between 2017 and 2022, a second gradual escalator will bring it to 67. But although governments can attempt to change labour supply conditions by raising the minimum pension age, it is not clear that they will be successful. Surveys of US workers indicate a substantial downward trend in the desired (and planned for) retirement age. Recent history offers little support for this as a solution.

---

[44] Johnson and Falkingham, *Ageing*, p. 142.
[45] Government Actuary, *National Insurance*.
[46] Natwest, *Pensions*.

In the US, the 1986 amendment to the Age Discrimination in Employment Act effectively prohibited mandatory retirement at any age, but despite the legislation, the average age of permanent withdrawal from the labour force has continued to decline, and involuntary unemployment rates among older workers remain above average. It is commonly asserted that employers are prejudiced against older workers; on the other hand the combination of social security and private pension incomes may encourage older people to set a reservation wage that prices them out of the labour market. A reduction in the value of social security pension entitlements would change this only if private pension savings do not rise to fill this potential income gap. The historical record shows that labour force participation rates for older men began their downward trajectory in both the US and the UK before the introduction of public pensions and of 'official' retirement ages, and it would be unwise to assume that government action will readily be able to reverse this long-run trend. The economics of retirement are unlikely to shift dramatically enough to change expectations quickly enough to alter the final outcome. Moreover, in a pay-as-you-go system, as long as the government maintains its commitment to benefit provision, there is little incentive for the current elderly to sacrifice leisure to postpone the system's default.

Another option would be to reduce public transfer expenditures by reinforcing the motivation for inter-familial exchange. The income and asset tests that restrict access to publicly financed long-term care in both the US and the UK could be revised to permit larger bequests to family members who provide a substantial level of care. On the other hand, the post-war rise in female labour force participation has increased the opportunity cost of caring for many women, and today, as in the past, many dependent elderly people have no relatives to provide care. Public provision in the UK arose in large part because of the inadequacy of family support strategies. The American system of intergenerational living arrangements has dwindled away in the past century. In neither society is there sustained evidence that families today are prepared to provide intensive social care or financial support for older relatives.

The most frequently discussed way of turning the clock back is to encourage or compel everyone to save for his or her own old age by making contributions to a private pension. We would argue that this is something of a misreading of history in the pre-social security era. Nonetheless, over the last thirty years occupational pension plans have had a good record in providing adequate retirement income for many workers, and so they appear to offer a model for the financing of old age in the future. However, twentieth-century traditions of 'welfare capitalism' are being transformed as labour markets become more flexible, and employment relationships become shorter. In the UK, today's pensioners have had an average of 3.5 different jobs during their working lives, but today's workers have experienced at least this number of jobs by the age of 30.[47] When labour contracts are short, it makes little sense to delegate pension saving to the employer, or to fix pension payments to the final salary offered in any particular employment. Little wonder, then, that defined-benefit pension programmes run by employers are in decline. In the US the number of participants in private-sector defined-benefit plans fell from 30 to 27 million between 1983 and 1989, while participation in defined-contribution plans rose from 25 to 36 million, largely because of the creation and expansion of employer-sponsored personal retirement (401 k) plans.[48] Yet while tax-advantaged individual retirement accounts may fit well with current labour market behaviour, they offer little by way of the inter-personal or inter-generational risk-sharing that exists in most defined-benefit plans, as well as in social security systems.

Defined-benefit pensions also restrict individual choice over when to retire, because they commonly provide massive financial incentives for individuals to retire at a particular age.[49] These rules have deep historical roots. Defined-benefit pensions were designed to reduce labour turnover, reward loyalty and provide an honourable exit route for redundant workers—a combination of golden handcuff and golden handshake.[50] A policy-led shift towards defined-contribution pensions (for instance by further extending the tax allowances on individual retirement accounts) could give older workers greater opportunity to make unconstrained choices between work and leisure. It might also raise savings rates. The freedom to choose a contribution rate, and to vary it over time, in theory should encourage the development of optimal life-time savings trajectories. Yet we should remember that today, as a century ago, savings are highly skewed. Most US workers make little or no use of tax-advantaged savings instruments, and in the UK

---

[47] Ibid.
[48] Scheiber and Shoven, 'Economics', p. 6.
[49] Lumsdaine, Stock and Wise, 'Pension Plan'.
[50] Hannah, *Inventing*; Sass, *Promise*.

most contributors to personal pensions make only the statutory minimum contribution of 4.8 per cent of income. Extending choice over retirement saving options will not necessarily increase the propensity to save, or the propensity to work.

Much depends upon whether governments can persuade people that their personal financial future really does depend on their current and future propensity to save. Put simply, the issue is whether governments can make credible threats that non-savers will be allowed to sink into poverty in old age. The historical record does not look persuasive; old age poverty has been a potent issue in the electoral politics of social security. The problem of credibility is particularly acute in the US where the earnings-related nature of social security pensions has created a massive political constituency of direct beneficiaries, and where single-issue politics gives real power to old age pressure groups such as the AARP. The 'social security crisis' in the US is therefore a political rather than an economic phenomenon: the social security fund is not in long-run financial equilibrium, but present and prospective pensioners actively resist cuts in pension levels, voters withdraw support from politicians who advocate higher taxes or contributions, and current workers fail to increase their personal savings, because they do not believe that future governments will tolerate mass old age poverty.[51] And if no political group is prepared to stomach default today, it is safe to say that the political will is likely to be even less tomorrow, when the proportion of elderly voters is even higher.

In the UK, the flat-rate nature of the public pension, its low replacement rate, and the high levels of enrolment in occupational pensions since the 1950s, together have produced a public pension system that is politically less entrenched than in the US. Nevertheless, there is little incentive in the UK for households with below-average income to save for old age, since they are unlikely to be able to accumulate sufficient assets to generate a pension income substantially greater than the social security minimum income.

---

[51] A recent survey of Americans indicates strong opposition to any major change in social security provision, including reducing automatic increases in benefits, raising the retirement age to 70, increasing the current payroll tax, or reducing prospective benefit rates at some date in the future. The only change that generated any positive response was reducing entitlements to benefits for retirees over $50,000 per annum. Younger workers were as supportive of the current system as current pensioners. Rother and Wright, 'Americans' Views', pp. 392–3.

Here may be the greatest historical continuity in the economics of old age financing. We suggested above that workers in both the US and the UK did not save enough to pay for their retirement in the era before social security. Self-financing remains inadequate for a disturbingly high proportion of the population. This is reflected in the highly-skewed distribution of private pension entitlements across the population in both countries. In 1987 the bottom income quintile of UK pensioners received only 3.5 per cent of total income from occupational pensions, and the median pensioner household drew only 13 per cent of income from this source.[52] In the US, three-quarters of retirees had no income from private pensions or annuities in 1986; among 65- to 69-year-olds in 1991, the net worth portfolio of the median household derived 6 per cent of its value from employer-provided pensions, compared to 38 per cent from social security entitlements (and 19 per cent from home equity);[53] close to 40 per cent of 51- to 61-year-olds in 1992 had no pension.[54] It is hard to resist the observation that in Britain a significant proportion of the elderly have never been able to save enough to finance old age, while in the US, a significant proportion assumed they would never have to save for retirement. Institutional arrangements, designed to solve one pressing social problem, are now at the root of another.

Social security entitlements, and their associated apparatus of retirement rules, tax incentives and asset tests, are proving to be much harder to revise than devise. Around each of these institutions there have developed significant vested interests which limit the scope for policy reversal. Governments are locked in to a set of institutional arrangements which were devised to respond to immediate social and economic problems, but which have acquired a rationale and a dynamic of their own. The longer reforms are delayed, the more abrupt will be the necessary adjustments. Closer analysis indicates that modest reforms introduced now can certainly accommodate the projected economic consequences of population ageing. Although a comparison of current pension or health care costs with those projected for 2030 or 2050 can look alarming, we should recognize that they imply rates of expenditure growth no faster than those experienced since World War II. Our societies have shown themselves to be highly adapt-

---

[52] Johnson and Falkingham, *Ageing*, p. 63.
[53] Poterba, Venti and Wise, 'Targeted Savings'.
[54] McGarry and Davenport, 'Pensions', p. 482.

able to large-scale economic, technological, demographic and geopolitical change over the last half-century. The challenge of an ageing population will be met, one way or another; institutional sclerosis, allied to electoral realpolitik, will limit the range of responses to those that can be accommodated within the political status quo. That is one of the inevitable lessons of history. The reform of social security will be no different from the reform of poor relief a century ago. The other lesson of this brief historical excursion is that it is neither possible nor desirable to embrace the structures of old age financing that existed before state support. Modest reforms are sufficient, necessary and possible. Delay, for whatever reason, will make reforms more difficult, less palatable, and more disruptive to the economic welfare of the baby-boomers and their offspring.

References

Baines, Dudley, and Paul Johnson. 'Did They Jump or Were They Pushed? The Exit of Older Men from the London Labor Market, 1929-31.' *Journal of Economic History* 59 (December 1999): 949-71.

Blundell, Richard and Paul Johnson. 'Pensions and Labor-market Participation in the United Kingdom.' *American Economic Review* 88 (May 1998): 168-72.

Chiozza Money, L.G. *Riches and Poverty*. London: Methuen, 1906.

Costa, Dora M. *The Evolution of Retirement: An American Economic History, 1880-1990*. Chicago: University of Chicago Press, 1998.

Cutler, David M., and Ellen Meara. 'Medical Costs of the Young and Old: A 40 Year Perspective.' In *Frontiers in the Economics of Aging*, edited by David A. Wise, 215-42. Chicago: University of Chicago Press, 1998.

Departmental Committee on Aged Deserving Poor, Cd. 67, 1900.

Disney, R. *Can We Afford to Grow Older*? Cambridge, Mass.: MIT Press, 1996.

Dowrick, S. 'Demographic Change, Investment and Growth in the Asia-Pacific Region.' *Asia Pacific Economic Review* 1 (1995): 20-31.

Ellis, Bryan. *Pensions in Britain, 1955-1975*. London: HMSO, 1978.

Falkingham, J. and C. Gordon. 'Fifty Years on: The Income and Household Composition of the Elderly in London and Britain.' In *Welfare and the Ageing Experience*, edited by B. Bytheway and J. Johnson, 148-71. London: Avebury, 1990.

Friedman, Benjamin M., and Mark Warshawsky. 'Annuity Prices and Saving Behavior in the United States.' In *Pensions in the US Economy*, edited by Zvi Bodie, John B. Shoven and David A. Wise, 53-77. Chicago: University of Chicago Press, 1984.

Government Actuary. *National Insurance Fund Long-term Financial Estimates*. London: HMSO, 1990.

Hannah, Leslie. *Inventing Retirement: The Development of Occupational Pensions in Britain*. Cambridge: Cambridge University Press, 1986.
Hareven, Tamara. 'Life-course Transitions and Kin Assistance in Old Age: A Cohort Analysis.' In *Old Age in a Bureaucratic Society*, edited by David Van Tassel and Peter N. Stearns. New York: Greenwood Press, 1986.
Hobbs, Frank B., and Bonnie L. Damon. *65+ in the United States*. US Bureau of the Census, Current Population Reports, Special Studies, P23–190. Washington, DC: Government Printing Office.
Hunt, E.H. *British Labour History, 1815–1914*. Atlantic Highlands, NJ: Humanities Press, 1981.
Huntington, Emily H., and Mary Gorringe Luck. *Living on a Moderate Income*. Berkeley, California: University of California Press, 1937.
Hurd, Michael D. 'The Economic Status of the Elderly in the United States.' In *Aging in the United States and Japan: Economic Trends*, edited by Yukio Noguchi and David A. Wise, 63–83. Chicago: University of Chicago Press, 1994.
James, John A., Michael P. Palumbo and Mark Thomas. 'Have American Workers Always Been Low Savers? Savings and Accumulation Before the Advent of Social Insurance: The United States, 1885–1910.' University of Virginia typescript, 2002.
Johnson, Paul. *Saving and Spending: The Working-class Economy in Britain, 1870–1939*. Oxford: Oxford University Press, 1985.
_____. 'The Employment and Retirement of Older Men in England and Wales, 1881–1981.' *Economic History Review* 47 (February 1994): 106–28.
_____. 'Retirement; Evolution and Macro-economic Implications.' *Reviews in Clinical Gerontology* 4 (1994): 161–7.
Johnson, Paul, and Jane Falkingham. *Ageing and Economic Welfare*. London: Sage, 1992.
Lee, Chulhee. 'The Expected Length of Male Retirement in the United States, 1850–1990.' *Journal of Population Economics* 14, no. 4 (2001): 641–50.
Lumsdaine, Robin L., James H. Stock and David A. Wise. 'Pension Plan Provisions and Retirement: Men and Women, Medicare, and Models.' In *Studies in the Economics of Aging*, edited by David A. Wise, 183–212. Chicago: University of Chicago Press, 1994.
McGarry, Kathleen, and Andrew Davenport. 'Pensions and the Distribution of Wealth.' In *Frontiers in the Economics of Aging*, edited by David A. Wise, 463–85. Chicago: University of Chicago Press, 1998.
Margo, Robert A. 'The Labor Force Participation of Older Americans in 1900: Further Results.' *Explorations in Economic History* 30 (1993): 409–23.
Massachusetts, Commonwealth of. *Report of the Commission on Old Age Pensions, Annuities and Insurance*. Boston: Wright and Potter, 1910.
Monthly Labor Review. 'Report of the Massachusetts Commission on Old-Age Pensions.' *Monthly Labor Review* 22 (1926): 679–81.
_____. 'Extent of Old-Age Dependency.' *Monthly Labor Review* 26 (1928): 960–2.

Natwest. *Pensions Index, vol. II*. Bristol: National Westminster Life Assurance, 1998.

OECD. *Ageing in OECD Countries*. Paris: OECD, 1996.

———. *Maintaining Prosperity in an Ageing Society*. Paris: OECD, 1998.

Orloff, Ann Shola. *The Politics of Pensions*. Madison, WI: University of Wisconsin Press, 1993.

Poterba, James M., Stephen F. Venti and David A. Wise. 'Targeted Savings and the Net Worth of Elderly Americans.' *American Economic Review* 84 (May 1994): 180–5.

Ransom, Roger, and Richard Sutch. 'The Labor of Older Americans: Retirement of Men On and Off the Job, 1870–1937.' *Journal of Economic History* 46 (1986): 1–30.

Rother, John, and William E. Wright. 'Americans' View of Social Security and Social Security Reforms.' In *Prospects for Social Security Reforms*, edited by Olivia S. Mitchell, Robert. J. Myers and Howard Young, 380–93. Philadelphia: University of Pennsylvania Press, 1999.

Sass, S. *The Promise of Private Pensions: The First Hundred Years*. Cambridge: Harvard University Press, 1997.

Schieber, Sylvester J., and John B. Shoven. 'The Economics of US Retirement Policy: Current Status and Future Directions'. In idem, *Public Policy Towards Pensions*, 1–39. Cambridge: MIT Press, 1997.

Smith, Daniel Scott. 'Accounting for Change in the Families of the Elderly in the United States, 1900-Present.' In *Old Age in a Bureaucratic Society*, edited by David Van Tassel and Peter N. Stearns. New York: Greenwood Press, 1986.

Thomas, Mark, John A. James and Michael P. Palumbo. 'Retirement Savings Before Social Security.' *National Tax Journal*, September 1999: 361–70.

Thomson, D. '"I Am Not My Father's Keeper": Families and the Elderly in Nineteenth-century England.' *Law and History Review* 2 (1991): 265–86.

———. 'The Welfare of the Elderly in the Past: A Family or Community Responsibility?' In *Life, Death and the Elderly: Historical Perspectives*, edited by M. Pelling and R. Smith, 194–221. London: Routledge, 1991.

US Bureau of the Census. *Population Projections of the United States by Age, Sex, Race, and Hispanic Origin: 1995–2050*. Current Population Reports, Series P25–1130. Washington DC: Government Printing Office.

US Department of Health and Human Services. *US Decennial Life Tables for 1979–1981*, vol. 1, no. 1. DHSS Publication no. 85–1150–1, August 1985.

Wall, R. 'Regional and Temporal Variations in the Structure of the British Household Since 1851.' In *Population and Society in Britain*, edited by T. Barker and M. Drake, 62–99. London: Batsford, 1982.

Wallace, P. *Agequake*. London: Nicholas Brealey, 1999.

World Bank. *Averting the Old Age Crisis*. New York: Oxford University Press, 1994.

Name Index

Abegglen, James, 119
Abramovitz, Moses, 108, 156n, 210, 373n.
Adlard, P., 426n.
Aghion, P., 147n.
Ahuvia, Aaron, 386n.
Albanese, A., 426
Aldcroft, Derek, 103n.
Aleksandrova, A., 428n.
Alexeev, Valery, 271
Allen, R.G.D., 248n.
Amann, R., 186n.
Amendola, M., 176
Amsden, Alice, 214, 215
Anderson, E., 169n., 170n.
Anderson, Michael, 117n., 118–19n.
Anfimov, A., 277n.
Angell, James, 346n.
d'Arge, R.C., 375n.
Argyle, Michael, 386n.
Arnold, David, 442n., 452n.
Arnold, E., 180n.
Arrow, Kenneth, 177–8, 186, 282
Arthur, W.B., 288n.
Ashby, A.W., 97
Ashton, T.S., 14
Aslund, A., 254n., 256n.
Atkinson, A., 375, 431, 434n.
Ayres, R.Y., 375n.
Azariadis, C., 82n.

Baert, Patrick, 374
Bailey, D., 429n.
Baines, Dudley, 487n., 491n.
Balcerowicz, L., 239
Ballew, C., 428n.
Barber, T., 335n.
Barker, D.J.P., 403n., 405
Barnard, Christiaan, 452–3
Barnett, Corelli, 103n., 120n., 247n., 250n.
Barro, Robert J., 104n., 323n.
Basanez, Miguel, 389n.
Bates, R., 283n.
Bauer, Raymond, 377n.
Bayoumi, Tamim, 221n.
Beason, Richard, 222n.
Becker, Gary, 46, 66n., 81n., 373n.
Beckerman, Wilfred, 373n., 374n., 375

Behrman, Jose, 422n.
Bekar, C., 144, 177n.
Ben-Amos, J.K., 86n., 93n., 94n., 95n.
Benham, F.C., 340–41, 357
Bernanke, Ben, 352n., 358n.
Beveridge, W.H., 242n., 340–41
Bevilacqua, Piero, 330n.
Bielicki, T., 434n.
Bienefeld, M.A., 51n.
Black, Sir Douglas, 383n.
Blackett, Basil, 359
Blanchard, Olivier, 235n., 236–8, 238n.
Blanchflower, David, 385n., 387n., 393n.
Blasi, J.R., 255n.
Blaug, Mark, 468
Bloch, Marc, 1
Blondal, Sveinbjorm, 222n.
Blonde, Bruno, 55n.
Bloom, David, 217n.
Blundell, Richard, 492n., 493n.
Bodeker, Gerry, 451n.
Boiko, B., 270
Bolino, August C., 112n.
Booth, Charles, 490
Borchardt, Knut, 346, 353n.
Bordo, Michael, 342n.
Borensztein, Eduardo, 215n.
Borland, J., 48n.
Bosworth, Barry, 216, 217n.
Boulton, Matthew, 89
Bowden, S., 250n.
Boyce, Robert, 350
Boyer, George, 321n.
Boyko, Maksim, 271n.
Brada, J., 240n.
Bradburn, Norman M., 393n.
Braudel, Fernand, 61
Braunerhjelm, Pontus, 463n., 464n.
Brauns, Henrich, 347
Braverman, Harry, 127
Brennan, G., 251n.
Brennan, Thomas, 60n.
Bresnahan, T., 144, 177
Brewer, John, 53n.
Brezhnev, Leonid, 279
Broadberry, Stephen, 2, 34–6, 103n., 104n., 105n., 106, 107, 108, 113n., 114n., 115n., 119n., 120n., 125n., 154n., 155n., 244n.
Brooks, K., 279n., 290n.

509

Name Index

Bryan, William Jennings, 343
Bruland, K., 191
Brüning, Heinrich, 353–5
Bundy, Colin, 305n.
Burnside, Craig, 220n.
Bush, Vannevar, 179
Buti, Marco, 463n.

Cafagna, Luciano, 330n.
Cairncross, Alec, 247n., 249n., 250n., 251n., 353
Caldwell, J.C., 454n.
Calmfors, L., 347n.
Calomiris, Charles W., 343
Calvert, M.A., 182n.
Campbell, Angus, 385n., 386n., 393n.
Campbell, Robert, 83n.
Cao, G., 421n.
Cargill, Thomas, 221n.
Carlaw, K., 144, 177n.
Carlin, Wendy, 224n.
Carlson, Leonard, 267n.
Carr, E.H., 239
Carr-Saunders, A.M., 115n.
Carter, Paul, 98
Cassis, Y., 181n.
Cernerud, L., 421n.
Chadwick, Edwin, 403
Chandler, A.D., 180–81, 184, 191
Chang, Chun, 87n.
Chapman, Herrick, 465n.
Charemza, W., 233n.
Charlton, J., 440n.
Childers, Thomas, 356n.
Chimera, D., 453n.
Chinn, S., 425n., 427, 428n.
Chiozza Money, L.G., 487
Chung, William, 223–4
Churchill, Winston, 243
Ciccone, Antonio, 213n.
Clark, Greg, 52, 52n., 63n., 422n.
Clark, Peter, 60n., 78n., 89n.
Cobb, Clifford, 375–6
Cobb, J., 375–6
Cohen, W.M., 168n., 191n.
Cole, W.A., 44n.
Coleman, Donald, 179n.
Coleman, Richard, 387n.
Collins, E.J.T., 61n.
Collins, Susan, 216, 217n.
Collyer, J., 83n.
Commander, S., 258n., 273n.
Conrad, Alfred, 11
Conte, Leandro, 4, 205–7
Converse, Philip E., 385n., 386n., 393n.

Cook, Harold, 446n.
Cooper, J., 186n.
Copeman, G.H., 119
Costa, Dora, 383n., 405n., 420, 484n., 493, 494, 495n.
Crafts, Nicholas, 3, 50n., 63, 73n., 198–200, 211n., 217n., 218, 221n., 374n., 375, 376n., 381–2, 383n., 404, 419n., 424n.
Cripps, Stafford, 249
Crush, Jonathan, 304n.
Csontos, L., 270n.
Curb, J., 421n.
Cutler, David M., 499n.

Dahlman, Carl, 219n.
Daly, H., 375–6
Damon, Bonnie, 498n.
Danilov, V.P., 275n., 280n.
Danilova, L.V., 277n.
Dasgupta, Partha, 178n., 373n.
Davenport, Andrew, 505n.
David, Paul, 2, 36–41, 108, 127, 135n., 137n., 138n., 139–40, 147n., 149, 153n., 154–5n., 156, 157n., 158n., 161n., 177, 178n., 191n., 283n., 286n., 288n., 440n.
Davies, Margaret Gay, 74n., 76n., 77n., 84–5, 93n., 95n., 99n.
Davis, C., 3, 200–201, 233n., 234, 253n., 254n., 258n.
De Cecco, Marcello, 320n.
De Mattia, Renato, 318n., 319
De Vecchi, Giorgio, 331n.
de Vos, Klaas, 390n.
De Vries, Jan, 2, 29–30, 31, 44n., 45n., 47n., 50n., 51n., 54n., 58, 59, 62n.
Deakin, Simon, 75
Deane, Phyllis, 44n., 59
Dearle, N.B., 241n.
Defoe, Daniel, 51–2
Denison, Edward, 110, 223–4
Deolalikar, A., 422n.
Desai, Meghnad, 378
Descartes, Rene, 12
Devine, W., 140n.
Dewald, Jonathan, 62n.
Di Rollo, Franca, 322
Di Tella, Rafael, 386, 387n., 389n.
Dibbits, Hester, 56n.
Dibley, M., 423n.
Dickson, David, 470n.
Diener, Carol, 384–5, 385, 387n., 389n., 391n.
Diener, Ed, 373n., 384–5, 384n., 385n., 386n., 387n., 389n., 391n., 393n.
Diener, Marissa, 384–5, 385, 387n., 389n., 391n.

Name Index

Digby, Anne, 5, 311n., 366–7, 441n., 446n., 447n., 449n.
Dillard, J., 440n., 444n.
Disney, Richard, 497n.
Dobb, M., 239
Doklad, 271n.
Douglas, Paul H., 142n.
Dowie, J.R., 244n.
Dowrick, S., 498n.
Doyal, Len, 393n.
Drechsler, L., 375n.
Driffil, J., 347n.
DuBoff, R., 140n., 141
Dubrovskiiz, S.M., 275n., 278n.
Duesenberry, James, 387n.
Duflo, E., 427n.
Dunlop, Jocelyn, 74n., 76, 77n., 78n., 79, 81, 93n., 97–8

Eads, G., 178n.
Eakins, Stanley, 212n.
Earle, Peter, 75n., 79n., 83n., 84n., 85n., 89n., 90–91
Easterlin, Richard, 371, 384, 387n, 389
Easterly, William, 382
Edelstein, Michael, 342n.
Eden, Sir Frederic Morton, 62
Edgerton, David, 181n.
Edgerton, David, 120
Edie, L.D, 359
Edwards, James, 119
Edwards, J.R., 117n., 118–19n.
Eichenbaum, Martin, 220n.
Eichengreen, Barry, 4, 207–8, 250n., 353, 357n.
Eisner, Robert, 374n.
Elbaum, Bernard, 87n.
Eldridge, J., 412n.
Eliott, V.B., 79n., 80
Elliott, Paul, 405
Ellman, M., 240n., 257n.
Emmison, F.G., 92n.
Emmons, Robert, 393n.
Ercolani, Paolo, 322n.
Ergas, H., 179n.
Ericson, R., 258–9
Erith, F.H., 97n.
Estes, Richard, 379, 380n.
Eveleth, P.B., 403–4, 412, 434n.
Everitt, Alan, 80, 94n.

Fabricant, Solomon, 136–7
Faini, Riccardo, 463n., 464n.
Fairchild, Cissie, 56

Falkingham, Jane, 489n., 501n., 505n.
Fayle, C.E., 242n.
Federico, P.J., 172n., 174n.
Feinstein, Charles, 50n., 107n., 148, 149–50n., 153n., 167, 232n., 244, 334n., 371n., 404
Feis, Herbert, 342n.
Feldman, Gerald, 345n.
Fernandez, R., 282, 284, 285
Finlay, Roger, 79n., 80
Finniston, M., 182
Fisher, Irving, 352n., 384
Fishlow, Albert, 44n.
Flamm, K., 179n.
Floud, Roderick, 5, 114–15, 311n., 364–5, 378n., 402n., 406n., 407n., 408–12, 423n., 425n., 428n., 431n.
Fogel, Robert, 53, 378n., 405–6, 415, 420
Fohlin, Caroline, 211n.
Foray, D., 191n.
Foreman-Peck, James, 3, 200–201, 245n., 249n., 250n.
Forsyth, Douglas J., 345n.
Franco, Daniele, 463n.
Fratianni, Michele, 318n.
Freeland, C., 255n., 257n.
Freeman, C., 170n.
Freeman, Richard, 463n.
Freudenberger, Herman, 50n.
Fridman, M., 277n., 278n.
Friedman, Benjamin, 485n.
Friedman, Douglas, 386n.
Friedman, Milton, 348n., 354
Fritjers, Paul, 387n., 392n.
Frost, Robert, 24
Fukuda, Shin-ichi, 217n.

Gaddy, C., 258n.
Gaffard, J.-L., 176
Gaidar, Yegev, 254–6
Galambos, Louis, 181
Galbraith, J.K., 371–2
Gao, Y., 421n.
Garrett, Eilidh, 406n.
Gatrell, Peter, 278n.
Gatseva, P., 428n.
Germain-Martin, Louis, 348
Gerschenkron, Alexander, 150, 198–200, 209–10, 211, 213, 214
Gershuny, Jonathan, 374, 374n.
Gilb, Corinne, 117n.
Giorgetti, Giorgio, 330n.
Glaziev, S., 186n.
Godbey, Geoffrey, 374n.
Goldin, Claudia, 109, 114n., 127, 154–5
Goldman, M., 257n.

511

Name Index

Goldstein, Morris, 225n.
Gonzalez de Pijem, L., 426n.
Goodman, Jordan, 59
Gorbachev, Mikhail, 253–4
Gordon, Colin, 119n., 489n.
Gough, Ian, 393n.
Gow, Ian, 119n.
Gowing, M.M., 247n.
Graham, Malcolm, 79, 80, 94n.
Grantham, George, 52
Granville, Brian, 256n.
Graves, Robert, 238
Greasley, David, 109n.
Greenwald, Bruce C., 87n.
Gref, Germain, 259
Gregory, Annabel, 378n., 406n., 407n., 408–12, 423n., 425n., 428n., 431n.
Gregory, P.R., 232n., 234, 252n., 432n.
Gregson, M.E., 407n.
Greulich, W., 421n.
Gros, D., 235n.
Grossman, Richard, 220n.
Grubb, Farley, 75n., 89n., 407n.
Grupp, Hariolf, 169
Guttman, L., 386n.
Guy, K., 180n.

Habakkuk, H.J., 125n.
Hadjistavropoulos, Thomas, 388n.
Hagenaars, Aldi, 390n.
Hall, B.H., 440n.
Hall, H.D., 247n.
Hall, R., 446n.
Halpin, 374n.
Halstead, S., 454n.
Halstead, Ted, 375–6
Hamill, G., 426
Hamilton, Richard, 356n.
Hancock, W.K., 247n.
Handy, Charles, 119n.
Hannah, Leslie, 149n., 492, 503n.
Harberger, Arnold, 138
Hardin, R., 283n.
Hareven, Tamara, 494n.
Harley, C. Knick, 50n., 211
Harris, Bernard, 406n., 429n.
Harrison, George, 348
Harrison, Mark, 451n.
Hart, Oliver, 82, 212n.
Hartley, L.P., 12
Hartmann, Heinz, 119
Hatton, Timothy, 321n.
Hayek, F.A. von, 185, 191, 239
Headey, Bruce, 386n., 388n.
Heim, C.E., 179n.
Heisenberg, Werner, 14

Helfferich, Karl, 349, 353
Helliwell, John, 388n.
Helpman, E., 144n., 146, 147n., 177
Herrigel, Gary, 113n.
Hicks, J.R., 176, 176n., 374n.
Hill, Bridget, 51n.
Hindenburg, Paul von, 355–6n.
Hirsch, Fred, 387n.
Hirschman, Albert, 44n.
Hobbs, Frank, 498n.
Hobsbawm, E.J., 44n.
Hoffman, Philip, 52n.
Hoffmann, Walther G., 107n., 171–2
Hollingsworth, T.H., 444n.
Honey, M., 444n.
Honwana, 454n.
Hoover, Herbert, 348–9, 350, 351, 354
Hornby, W., 247n.
Horrell, Sara, 45n., 52
Horrocks, Sally, 120
Hounshell, David, 145
Howitt, P., 147n.
Howson, S., 244n.
Huberman, M., 63n., 422n.
Hughes, T.P., 149n.
Hughes, R.A.W., 247n.
Humphries, Jane, 2, 33–4, 45n., 52
Hunt, E.H., 487
Huntington, Emily, 485n.
Hurstfield, Joel, 247n.
Hutchison, Michael, 221n.
Hutton, Graham, 124n.

Ickes, B., 258n.
Ide, Masasuke, 221n.
Iliffe, John, 452n.
Inglehart, Ronald, 389n.
Insolera, Italo, 330n.
Ioffe, G., 279n.
Ito, Takatoshi, 221n.
Ivanova, N., 428n.

Jackson, Tim, 375
James, Harold, 346n., 354n.
James, John, 485
James, William, 24
Jansen, J.C.G.M., 59
Jeeves, Alan, 304n.
Jennison, Florence T., 142n.
Jerome, Harry, 140
Jobse-van Putten, Jozien, 60n.
Johansson, Sheila Ryan, 5, 311n., 366–7, 440n., 441n., 447n., 448n.
Johnson, Paul, 492n., 493n.

Name Index

Johnson, Paul A., 5–6, 368–9, 483n., 486–7, 487n., 491n., 493, 495, 499n., 501n., 505n.
Johnston, Tom, 353
Jones, Colin, 62n.
Jones, J., 426
Jones, Sally, 374
Jorgenson, Dale, 157
Juster, F. Thomas, 374n.
Jutte, Robert, 466n.

Kahan, Arcadius, 277n., 278n.
Kahl, W.F., 78n.
Kahneman, Daniel, 384n., 390n., 392n.
Kalmijn, S., 421n.
Kamermans, Johan, 54–5, 62n.
Kannam, J., 421n.
Kantor, Shaw, 267n.
Kaplan, Steven, 61n.
Kapp, K.W., 371n., 375
Katz, Lawrence, 114n., 127, 154–5
Kaufmann, R., 428n.
Keck, O., 184n.
Kelatwang, Teresa, 299n.
Kellett, J.R., 78n.
Kendrick, John R., 107n., 136–7, 139, 143n., 373, 374n.
Kennedy, Paul, 243n.
Keynes, John Maynard, 246, 341, 342n., 349–50, 355
Khan, L., 428n.
Kim, S.R., 188n.
King, Gregory, 60–61
King, Steve, 468n.
Kline, S.J., 169n.
Kneese, A.V., 375n.
Knight, I., 412n.
Komlos, J., 64n., 424n.
Kornai, J., 185n., 232n., 233n., 238n., 258, 270n.
Kroumova, M., 255n.
Kremer, M., 238n.
Krugman, Paul, 209, 223
Kruschev, Nikolai, 279
Kruse, D., 255n.
Kuhn, Thomas, 359
Kunz, Diane, 351, 353
Kuznets, Simon, 11, 44n.
Kuznetsov, V.V., 273n.

La Porta, Rafael, 224n.
Lall, Ashish, 225n.
Lancaster, Kelvin, 46
Landes, David, 43n., 44–5n., 103n.

Landsberg, Hans, 373n.
Lane, Joan, 75n., 78n., 79n., 80, 83n., 89, 93n., 95n., 98n., 99n.
Lang, R.D., 89
Lardy, Nicholas, 226n.
Larson, M., 421n.
Laslett, Peter, 489
Lavoisier, A.-L., 59
Layard, Richard, 256n.
Lebergott, Stanley, 373n.
Lee, Chulhee, 484n.
Lee, Chung, 214
Lee, Jong-Wha, 215n.
Leonard, Carol, 3, 201–3, 267n., 268n., 270n., 271n., 272n., 273n., 275n., 279n., 285n., 288n.
Leonard, E.M., 470n.
Lerman, Z., 290n.
Leunig, Timothy, 5, 311n., 365, 378n., 413n., 424n.
Levi, Giovanni, 322n.
Levine, A.L., 103n.
Levine, Ross, 212n.
Levinthal, D., 168n., 191n.
Levy, D., 421n.
Levy, S., 386n.
Leybourne, Steven, 211n.
Liang, S., 421n.
Liao, Y., 421n.
Lidderdale, William, 343
Liefert, W.M., 272n., 273n.
Liepmann, Kate, 114n.
Lindberg, D., 443n., 444n., 446n.
Linder, Staffan B., 46n.
Lindert, Peter, 63n., 422n., 468n.
Lindgren, G., 421n.
Lipsey, R.G., 144, 177n.
Lis, Catharina, 470n.
Liu, D., 421n.
Lloyd, E.H.M., 242n.
Lloyd George, David, 244
Locke, John, 446
Lopez-de-Silandes, Florencio, 224n.
Luck, Mary Gorringe, 485n.
Lumsdaine, Robin, 503n.
Lykken, David, 388n.

McClelland, Charles, 117n.
McClelland, Kent, 387n.
McCloskey, D.N., 51n., 108
McCormick, Barry, 87–8, 90
MacCulloch, Robert, 386, 387n., 389n.
MacDonald, Ramsay, 243, 350
Macey, D.A.J., 270n.
McGarry, Kathleen, 505n.
McGee, D., 421n.

513

Name Index

McKendrick, Neil, 53n.
McKinlay, A., 250n.
MacLeod, Christine, 179n.
Maddison, A., 43n., 104n., 109–10, 174n., 216, 217, 422n.
Malcolmson, James, 87–8, 90
Malthus, Thomas, 45, 465
Mandela, Nelson, 301
Margo, Robert, 484n.
Marks, Nic, 375
Marmot, Michael, 383n., 405
Marshall, Dorothy, 78n.
Martello, Tullio, 320n.
Massie, Joseph, 79
Mathias, Peter, 73n.
Matse, P.M, 441n., 454n.
Matsuyama, Kiminori, 213n.
Matthews, Derek, 117n., 118–19n.
Matthews, R.C.O., 107n., 148, 149–50, 153n.
Mau, V., 240n., 254n.
Maw, James, 87–8, 90
May, E.R., 339n.
May, Julian, 299n., 300n.
Mayer, Colin, 224n.
Meara, Ellen, 499n.
Mellon, Andrew, 348
Meyer, Carrie, 375n., 377n.
Meyer, H.E., 419n.
Meyer, John, 11
Micklewright, J., 431, 434n.
Miles, Ian, 378n.
Mills, Terence, 211n.
Milward, Alan S., 251n.
Milward, Colonel, 489
Minami, R., 151–2
Minchinton, Walter, 85n.
Mintz, Sidney, 65n.
Mirabal, B., 426n.
Mishan, E.J., 372
Mishkin, Frederic, 212n., 220n.
Mitch, David, 64n.
Mitchell, Brian R., 59, 154n., 244
Moggridge, D.E., 353
Mokyr, Joel, 43n., 45n., 169n.
Montanari, Armando, 320n.
Moodie, T. Dunbar, 304n.
More, Charles, 112
Moreno, Alejandro, 389n.
Moret, Clement, 349
Moriya, Fumio, 151n.
Morris, Morris David, 378, 379, 380n.
Moure, Kenneth, 345n., 348, 349
Mowat, C. L., 243n., 345–6
Mowery, D.C., 179n., 180n., 181n., 183n.
Mui, Hoh-Cheung, 61–2
Mui, Lorna H., 61–2
Mumssen, C., 258n., 273n.
Murphy, Kevin, 213n.

Murphy, M., 440n.
Murray, Colin, 305
Murrell, P., 239n., 240n.
Mushingeh, A.C.S.M., 455n.
Muzumdar, Sucheta, 65

Naughton, Barry, 226n.
Ndatshe, Vivienne, 304n.
Nefedova, T., 279n.
Nelson, Richard, 120n., 177–8, 178n., 183n.
Nickell, Stephen, 214n., 224n.
Nieves-Rivera, F., 426n.
Nixon, Edgar B., 356
Noguchi, Yukio, 221n.
Nolan, P., 257n.
Noordegraaf, Leo, 50n.
Nordhaus, William, 161n., 373–5
Norman, Donald, 163n.
Norman, Victor, 463n., 464n.
North, Douglass, 43n., 214
Nove, Alec, 185n.
Nurkse, Ragnar, 351n.
Nutton, Vivian, 443n., 444n.

O'Brien, Patrick, 60
O'Connell, J., 423n.
Odling-Smee, John, 107n., 148, 149–50n., 153n., 371n.
Offer, Avner, 5, 363–4, 383n.
Okhawa, Kazushi, 126–7, 152n.
Olson, Mancur, 283n., 373n.
O'Mahony, Mary, 121n., 123–4
Orloff, Ann, 485n., 491n.
O'Rourke, Kevin H., 316
Oswald, Andrew, 385n., 386, 387n., 389n., 393n.
Overton, Mark, 56
Oxley, Les, 109n.

Packard, Vance O., 371–2
Pakko, Michael R., 321–2
Pallot, J., 268n.
Palumbo, Michael, 485
Paracelcus, 446
Pareton, Vilfredo, 25, 383
Park, Yung-Chui, 220n.
Parker, J., 256n.
Patten, John, 95n.
Pavitt, Keith, 180
Pench, Lucio, 463n.
Perkin, Harold, 117n.
Perotta, L., 274n.

Name Index

Petersen, Christian, 61n.
Pigou, A.C., 237n., 244, 246, 249, 384
Pilat, Dirk, 222n.
Piore, Michael, 113n.
Pittaluga, Giovanni B., 318n.
Plumb, J.H., 53n.
Pogrebinsky, A.P., 277n.
Pollard, Patricia S., 321–2
Pollard, Sidney, 53, 103n.
Popkin, S., 283n.
Popper, Karl, 239
Posel, Dorrit, 299n., 304
Poterba, James, 505n.
Powell, Ellis T., 343n.
Prais, S.J., 111n., 115n.
Pressnell, L.S., 251n.
Pritchett, L., 422n.
Putin, Vladimir, 259–60

Rabin, Matthew, 390n.
Rainwater, Lee, 387n.
Ramphele, M., 298n., 299n., 304n.
Ramsey, Matthew, 449n.
Randlesome, Colin, 119n.
Ransom, Roger, 484n.
Rapcyzynski, A., 238n.
Rashin, A.G., 276n.
Rawcliffe, Carol, 445n.
Reader, William, 115n.
Rebelo, Sergio, 220n.
Redford, Arthur, 471n., 473n.
Reynolds, Jackson E., 353
Ricardo, David, 45
Richardson, Peter, 223
Riesman, David, 372
Ripa di Meana, Carlo, 320n.
Rist, Charles, 348
Robbins, Lionel, 352, 359n.
Robinson, E.A.G., 247n., 248n.
Robinson, Joan, 14–15
Robinson, John, 374n.
Roccas, Massimo, 320n.
Rockoff, Hugh, 342n.
Rodgers, Willard L., 385n., 386n., 393n.
Rodriguez, B., 421n.
Rodrik, Dani, 213, 214, 225, 282, 284, 285
Rohde, J. et al, 454n.
Roland, G., 235n.
Rona, R.J., 425n., 427, 428n.
Roosevelt, Franklin D., 354, 356
Root-Bernstein, R., 444n.
Rose, Michael B., 74n., 98n., 99n.
Rosenbaum, S., 408n.
Rosenberg, N., 145, 179n., 180n., 183n., 184
Rosenbloom, Joshua L., 332n.
Rosovsky, Henry, 126–7, 152n.

Ross, R., 421n.
Rostow, W.W., 176
Rother, John, 504n.
Routh, Guy, 116n., 123n.
Rowe, Jonathan, 375–6
Rowntree, B.Seebohm, 390, 490
Rushton, Peter, 78n., 81, 85n., 86–7, 91–2, 95n., 96n.

Sabel, Charles, 113n.
Sachs, Jeffrey, 235n., 249n., 357n.
Sala-i-Martin, Xavier, 104n., 323n.
Samaras, T., 421n.
Sametz, A.W., 373, 374n.
Sanderson, Michael, 155n.
Sanderson, W.S., 286n.
Sandvik, Ed, 385n., 386n., 387n., 391n.
Sannucci, Valeria, 320n.
Sapir, J., 240n., 257n.
Sarcinelli, Mario, 320n.
Sass, S., 503n.
Savage, M., 453n.
Scharrenborg, R., 257n.
Scheiber, Sylvester, 503n.
Schmookler, Jacob, 169–70
Schneider, C.M., 186n.
Schneider, Juergen, 59
Schor, Juliet, 374n.
Schuker, Stephen A., 345n.
Schultz, T.P., 46n.
Schumpeter, Joseph A., 11
Schurr, S.H., 141n.
Schwart, Norbert, 384n.
Schwartz, Anna, 348n., 354
Scitovsky, Tibor, 387
Scott, James C., 283
Scott, J.D., 247n.
Scranton, Philip, 113n.
Seckler, T., 422n.
Seidlitz, Larry, 385n., 386n., 387n., 391n.
Selmer, R., 419n.
Sen, Amartya, 373, 379, 390n.
Senker, J., 169n.
Sereni, Emilio, 328n.
Serova, E., 267n., 271n., 272n., 273n.
Sewell, J.E., 181n.
Shammas, Carole, 56, 59, 60n., 63n., 64–5
Shapin, S., 446n., 447
Sharma, Ursula, 439n.
Shleifer, Andrei, 213n., 224n.
Shoven, John, 503n.
Shvanebakh, P.K., 277n.
Sierra, J., 423n.
Slack, Paul, 470n., 471n.
Slesnick, Daniel, 372n., 375n.
Slottje, Daniel, 379, 380n.

515

Name Index

Smith, Adam, 30, 45, 48, 49, 422, 465
Smith, Daniel Scott, 494n.
Smith, James, 383n.
Smith, K., 191n.
Smith, Richard, 5, 69–70, 444n., 466n., 471n.
Smith, S.R., 79n., 88n.
Snell, K.D.M., 75n., 87n., 91, 92n., 97n., 98
Snooks, Graeme, 374n.
Snowden, Philip, 350–51
Soete, L., 170n.
Solar, Peter, 5, 73–4, 369–70, 466n., 468n., 469n., 473n.
Soly, Hugo, 470n.
Song, Byung Khun, 98n.
Soskice, David, 81n., 88n.
Spechler, M.C., 278n.
Spinelli, Franco, 318n.
Srinivasan, T., 422n.
Staal, F., 447n.
Stafford, Frank, 374n.
Stanhope, R., 426n.
Stearns, Peter, 465n.
Steckel, Richard, 64n., 383n., 402n, 405n., 422n.
Steinherr, A., 235n.
Steinmuller, W.E., 158n., 159n.
Steuart, Sir James, 66
Stigler, George, 373n.
Stiglitz, Joseph, 232n., 239n., 240–41, 255n.
Stiroh, Kevin, 157
Stock, James, 503n.
Stolypin, Piotr, 202, 275, 27, 288
Stone, Lawrence, 79
Stones, M.J., 388n.
Storms, L., 421n.
Stringher, Bonaldo, 326n.
Strong, Benjamin, 342
Stuart, R.C., 232n., 234, 252n., 432n.
Studenski, Paul, 371n.
Suh, Eunkook, 373n., 384n., 385
Supino, Camillo, 320n.
Sutch, Richard, 484n.
Sydenham, Thomas, 446
Sylla, Richard, 211n.
Symons, L., 278n.
Szklarska, A., 434n.

Talley, Lynn P., 348
Tanner, J.M., 403–4, 412n., 434n.
Tawney, R.H., 235n., 241n., 245, 249
Taylor, James, 91n., 472n.
Tellegen, Auke, 388n.
Temin, Peter, 4, 149, 207–8, 342n., 357n.
Temple, Sir William, 66
Terleckyj, Nestor, 378n.

Thirsk, Joan, 51
Thomas, Mark, 5–6, 368–9, 485
Thompson, E.P., 53
Thomson, David, 489, 489n.
Thorogood, N., 450n.
Tobin, James, 373–5
Toniolo, Gianni, 4, 149, 205–7, 211n.
Toutain, Jean-Claude, 59
Townsend, Peter, 383n.
Trajtenberg, M., 144, 177
Treu, Cristina, 331n.
Turrell, Rob, 302
Turshen, M., 442n.
Tuuko, Holly, 388n.
Tylecote, A., 191n.

Van Atta, D., 270n.
van der Woude, Ad, 58, 59, 62n.
Van Praag, Bernard, 387n., 392n.
Vandenbroeke, C., 59
Veblen, Thorstein, 150
Vecchi, Giovanni, 4, 205–7
Veenhoven, Ruut, 384, 384n., 391n.
Veil, Simone, 464n.
Venti, Stephen, 505n.
Vershinin, V.F., 271
Vertzberger, Yaacov Y.I., 339n.
Villerme, L.R., 403
Vishny, Robert, 213n., 224n.
von Tunzelmann, Nicholas, 2, 35, 36, 39–40, 169n., 170n., 182n., 183n., 185n., 188n., 191n.
Voskuil, J.J., 59, 61n.
Voth, Hans-Joachim, 5, 51, 64n., 311n., 365, 378n., 413n., 424n.

Waaler, Hans, 403n., 405, 420
Wachter, Kenneth, 378n., 406n., 407n., 408–12, 423n., 425n., 428n., 431n.
Wade, Robert, 214–15
Wagner, Karin, 114n., 119n., 120n., 124n., 155n.
Walker, W., 182n.
Wall, Richard, 489n.
Wallace, P., 497n.
Walsh, J., 454n.
Wang, Yijiana, 87n.
Warner, W. Lloyd, 119
Warren, Harris Gaylord, 348–9, 350
Warren, K., 454n.
Warshawsky, Mark, 485n.
Watts, S., 442n., 452n.
Wearing, Alex, 386n., 388n.

516

Name Index

Wedel, J., 239n., 255n.
Weinstein, David, 222n.
Weir, David, 64n.
Weitzman, Martin, 375
Wells, Roger, 61n.
Westman, R., 446n.
White, Colin, 278n.
White, Harry D., 342n.
White, Lawrence, 212n., 220n.
Whiteford, Andrew, 299n.
Whitehead, Margaret, 383n.
Wibble, R., 440n.
Wiener, Martin, 103n., 120n.
Wilkinson, Richard, 383n.
Williams, Gertrude, 114n.
Williams, N., 444n.
Williamson, Jeffrey, 217n., 316, 474n.
Williamson, Oliver, 82n., 211
Wilson, Francis, 3, 203–5, 298n., 299n., 304n., 306n., 309n.
Wilson, P.A., 115n.
Wimmer, L., 420
Wise, David, 503n., 505n.
Wise, G., 181n.
Wissell, Rudolf, 347
Wolfe, B., 422n.
Wolff, Edward, 183
Woods, R., 444n.

Worger, William H., 302n.
Woytinsky, W.S., 355n.
Wright, Gavin, 2, 36–41, 120n., 127, 135n., 137n., 138n., 139–40, 147n., 149, 154–5n., 177
Wright, William, 504n.
Wrigley, C.C., 247n.
Wrigley, E.A., 43n., 62, 80

Xu, Y., 421n.

Yang, X., 48n.
Yarbrough, Anne, 88n.
Yeltsin, Boris, 204, 231, 254, 259, 270
Young, Allyn, 48–9
Young, Alwyn, 216, 217n.
Yuan, J., 421n.
Yudelman, David, 304n.

Zaidi, Ashgar, 390n.
Zeitlin, Jonathan, 113n.
Ziporyn, T., 440n., 444n.
Zolotas, Xenophon, 374n., 375, 392

Subject Index

AARP—see American Association of Retired Persons
Abruzzi, 330
Academy of Sciences (USSR), 186
Africa, 216, 217, 342, 445, 452
Africa, East, 452
Age Discrimination in Employment Act (US), 502
Ageing, 402, 409
   US-UK comparison, 479–82
Agriculture
   and apprenticeship in Britain, 1600–1750, 93–6, 98–9
   and British Industrial Revolution, 73, 99
   and Russian economy, 201–3, 367f.
   and South Africa, 309–10
   comparative labour productivity in, 1870–1990, 105–9
America, Colonial North, 49, 54, 63
American Association of Retired Persons (US), 504
Amgen, 183
Annales school, 22
Anthropometry (see also, Heights, Body-mass index), 5, 364–5, 401f., 419f.
Apartheid, 3, 204–5, 298f.
Apple Computing, 160
Apprentices
   number of, 17th and 18th centuries, 78–81
   number of, 19th and 20th centuries, 111–13
Apprentices, pauper, 96–9
Apprenticeship, 2, 11, 104, 128
   and British Industrial Revolution, 33–4, 73f.
   and rural-urban migration, England, 1600–1750, 93–6
   and poverty, 96
   transformation after 1870, 34–5
Ardleigh, 97
Argentina, 329
Asia, 184, 187, 248, 342, 443
Asia, East
   banking in, 219–20
   'developmental states' in, 214–22, 224
   economic growth, 21st century, 222–7
   'economic miracle', 3, 198–9, 209, 216–17
   financial crisis, 1990s, 3, 198, 208, 222, 340
   infant mortality rates in, 433
   labour supply in, 32, 227
   productivity growth in, 216–19
   technology in, 183, 186
Asia, South, 216
'Asian Tigers', 3, 199, 219, 234
Assymmetric information
   and apprenticeship, 87–9
   and East Asian financial crisis, 219–20
Australia
   welfare measurement in, 374, 376, 389
Austria, 218, 376, 449
Ayurvedic Medicine, 451–2

Bank of England, 342, 343–4, 348, 350, 353
Bank of France, 343, 349, 351–2, 356
Banks
   during Great Depression, 220
   East Asia, 219–20, 224–6
   Russian, 257
   US, 1930s, 221
Bantu, 311
Baring Crisis, 1890, 343–4, 347
Basutoland, 305
Belarus, 281
Belgium, 54, 59, 218
Benelux Countries, 352
Berlin, 341
Berlin Wall, 298
Bio-technology, 183
Body-mass index (BMI; see also, Anthropometry, Heights), 365, 405, 421, 423
   in Britain, 1800–1980, 406f.
Bolsheviks, 235, 239, 271
Botswana, 455
Brazil, 299
Bretton Woods, 340
Bristol, 93, 95, 473
Britain — see Great Britain
Bulgaria, 412

Canal Control Commission (UK), 242
Cape Town, 452

519

Subject Index

Capital
  as source of economic growth, 20th century, 124–7
Caribbean, 183, 450
Catch-up (see also, Economic backwardness), 35, 153, 199, 200–201
  technological, 150
Central banking (see also Bank of England, Bank of France), 343–4, 351–5, 358–9
Central Electricity Supply Board (UK), 149
Chartres, 54
Chicago, 341
Child Poverty Action Group (UK), 427
Chile, 376
China, 216, 222, 223, 225–6, 227, 421, 432, 451, 454
Church of England, 466, 470
Cisco Systems, 183
City of London, 40, 85
Cold War, 249, 252
Collective action, theory of, 282–3
Collectivism, 267–9, 272–3
Command Economy, 234, 235–6, 242, 252
  characteristics, 232–3
Communism, 180, 185, 235
Compaq, 183
Comparative systems, 2–3, 39–41, 198–200, 232–3
Computers
  as General Purpose Technology, 156f.
Consols, 325
Consumer Revolution, 18th century, 49, 53f.
Consumption
  and economic growth, 30–1, 44–6, 49, 53–62
  luxury goods, 65–6
  second-hand goods, 56
  strategic goods, 44–5
  transition to durables, 1600–1700, 55–7
  Z-goods, 46–7, 53–4, 61, 65
Consumption goods
  alcohol, 391
  beer, 60
  bread, 60–61
  coffee, 58–9
  durables, 31, 55–7
  sugar, 31, 57–9, 62, 64–5
  tea, 57–9, 62, 65
  textiles, 56, 57–8, 65
  tropical, 57–9
Consumption technology, 46
Contracts, theory of
  and apprenticeship, 11, 33, 82f.
  and transaction costs, 328–9
Construction Industry, Italy, 1862–80, 322–5, 329
Convergence
  price, 321f.
  wage, 327f.
Co-ordination failures, 26, 40, 213
Co-ordination problem, 48
Copenhagen, 315
Corn Laws, 205
Costa Rica, 454
Cottage industry, 30
Coventry, 80, 93, 94
Cuba, 432, 433
Cunliffe Committee, 1918 (UK), 243, 344, 353

Dawes Plan, 1924, 345
de Beers, 307
Deflation, 245
  and Great Depression, 344f.
Delft, 54
Demand (see also, Consumption)
  foreign demand and industrialization, 44
Denmark, 218
Department of Scientific and Industrial Research, 1916 (UK), 179
'Developmental state', 212, 214f.
Disease
  and anthropometric measurement, 402, 412–13, 424
  and theories of medicine, 439, 446–8
  AIDS, 205, 456
  cancer, 450
  'European', 455
  gout, 447
  smallpox, 447, 451
  syphilis, 447
Division of labour, 48–9
Dorset, 95
Du Pont, 181
'Dutch Hunger Winter' (1944–5), 425–6

Economic Controls in post-1945 UK, 249–52
Economic backwardness (see also, Catch-up, Gerschenkron), 150, 198–9, 209–14, 222, 226
Economic growth
  and happiness, 371, 384, 386
  and social welfare, 371f.
  and well-being, 377f.
  steady-state, 23
Economies of scale
  and technology, 180–81
Education
  and British economic decline, 1870–1914, 103

520

Subject Index

and economic growth, 32–3, 154–5
and labour productivity growth, 109–11, 120–8
and social welfare, 377
and 'human development index', 378
Elderly dependency ratio (see also, Ageing), 482–3, 498
  defined, 482
Electrification
  and US economic growth, 2, 37–8, 135, 140–41, 147, 157
Emancipation
  of Russian serfs, 1861, 275, 276
Employment, seasonal, 330–31
England (see also, Great Britain, United Kingdom), 60–61, 443
  human capital formation in, 2, 33–4
  labour migration, early modern, 465–6
  labour productivity in, 52
  medicine and disease, early modern, 446–7
  heights, modern, 425, 428
  poor relief, early modern, 465f.
  wages in, 50
Ergodicity, ergodic systems, 18, 19
Europe, 248, 249, 344, 366
  Eastern, 185, 258, 342, 433, 464, 475
  federalism in, 368, 476
  'Golden Age' (1950–73), 217–19
  health care in, 442, 449
  height measurements in, 406
  'industrious revolution', 29–32, 43f.
  labour migration in, 463, 474–6
  medicine in, 444–6
  poor relief administration in, 469, 470, 473
  rationalization of industry, interwar period, 149
  social welfare in, 474–6
  welfare measurements in, 387
European Bank for Reconstruction & Development (EBRD), 255
European Union, 4, 5, 271, 368, 463–4, 474–5
  single market, 4, 205, 315, 320–21, 334
  monetary union, 205–6, 315–16, 334–6

Federal Reserve Bank of Dallas, 348
Federal Reserve Bank of New York, 342, 348
Federal Reserve System, 348, 350, 354
Fernandez-Rodrik Model, 282–4
  and Russian resistance to land reform, 285f
Feudalism, 235

Finland, 218, 222
Finneston Report, 1980 (UK), 182
First National Bank of New York, 353
Flexible production, 159
  and training of labour, 114–15
Florence, 326, 332
Fordism, 128
Framingham Study, 421
France, 52, 54, 60, 61, 217, 248, 387, 449
  growth accounting in, 216, 218
  interwar financial policy, 345, 352, 356
  new goods in, 58–9
  overseas investment, 342
Frankfurt-am-Main, 315
Frelimo, 302

Galois Theory, 168
Gasprom, 258, 273
General Electric, 181
'General Gas Law', 20
'General Purpose Technology', 2, 36, 135–6, 144–7, 154–5, 158–9, 163–4
  and US economic growth, 36–8, 135f.
Genoa, 326, 332
Germany, 35, 54, 151, 185, 211, 217, 248, 252, 449
  apprenticeships in, 1870–1990, 110–15
  education, formal, in, 109–11
  growth accounting in, 216, 218
  human capital formation in, 2, 35, 103f., 184
  labour productivity in, 1870–1990, 105–8
  patents and patenting in, 1870–1990, 172, 173
  wages, interwar, 346–7
Georgia, 281
Gibraltar, 350, 354
Gini coefficient (see also, Income inequality), 299, 375, 383, 422
Glaxo, 181
Gold Standard, 4, 207–8, 243, 244, 316, 340f.
  and economic policy-making, 1930s, 243, 340f.
Gluckman Commission, 1944 (South Africa), 453
Gray Panthers (see also, AARP), 368
Great Britain (see also, United Kingdom)
  apprenticeships in, 1870–1990, 111–15, 155
  banking and industry in, 20th century, 189
  consumption patterns, 1600–1750, 58–9
  education, formal, in, 109–11, 155
  health care in, 439, 440, 448–50

521

Subject Index

heights in,
 during Industrial Revolution, 198, 419–20, 433, 435
 19th century, 406f.
 21st century, 402, 405
human capital formation in, 2, 34–5, 103f.
labour force participation in, 483–4, 493, 495–6
labour productivity in, 1870–1990, 111–15
life expectancy in, late 20th century, 401–2, 415
old age provision in, 368
overseas investment, 342
population structure, 479–82
post-war economic transition
 1918–25, 147, 231, 233, 238–9, 243–6, 249, 260–62
 1945–51, 231, 233, 239, 246, 248–52, 260–62
productivity growth, 1920s, 148
wartime economy (1914–18; 1939–45), 3, 200, 233, 235, 241–3, 247–8
welfare measurement in, 374, 376
Great Depression, 220, 340–41, 347f.
 and policy-making, 4, 207–8, 340f.
Great Yarmouth, 95
Growth accounting, 36, 106–8, 209, 216, 218, 222–4
Guatemala, 299
Guilds, 83–4

Hanwell, 98
'Hartley's Rule', 12
Health (see also, Disease, Medicine)
 defined, 440
 'European diseases', 455
Health and Morals of Apprentices Act, 1802, 78
Health Care
 and economic growth, 365–7, 383
 in South Africa, 453–6
 rising cost of, late 20th century, 498–9
Health Maintenance Organizations (HMOs), 368
Heights, weights (see also, Body-mass index, Waist-hip ratio), 5, 364–5, 401f., 419f.
 as index of social welfare, 404
 as proxy for health, 419–20
 growth hormone deficiency (GHD), 428
 height and mortality, 420–21
 heights in transition economies, 431–5
 poverty and, 428

social class differences, 428
Heisenberg Uncertainty Principle, 14
Hewlett-Packard, 184
Highland Park Plant, Ford Motor Company, 145
Historical economics, 6–7, 10f.
'History matters' (see also, Path dependency), 15–16, 22
Holland, 12, 59, 60, 61, 218, 376
 heights in, late 20th century, 402, 415, 425–6
 labour supply in, 51, 52
 probate inventories in, 54–6
 shops and retail distribution in, 62
Homeorrhesis, 22, 23
Hong Kong, 209, 217, 218, 219, 223
Household economy
 and the 'industrious revolution', 48f.
Household production (see also, Z-goods), 52
Housing
 and social welfare measurement, 377
Human capital
 accumulation, 103f., 183
 and productivity, 103f.
 and skill development, 322–4
 investment in, South Africa, 205, 307–8, 310–11
Hungary, 412
Hyperinflation, 341, 345, 353

Income inequality
 and anthropometric measurement, 429–30
 in transition economies, 434–5
 and health care provision, 453–5
 and social welfare measurement, 377
 in South Africa, 299–300
 indexes of (see also, Gini coefficient), 383
India, 299, 310, 451–2
 Gujarat State, 310
 Kerala State, 454
Indonesia, 216, 218, 223
Indentures, apprenticeship, 77–8, 85–6
 length of, 17th-century England, 90–92
Industrial Revolution, British, 2, 11, 31, 45, 49, 53, 73, 170, 172, 473–4, 476
 apprenticeship and, 33
 heights and standard of living in, 419–20, 433, 435
Industrialization, Russian, 238, 275
'Industrious Revolution', 29–32
 defined, 47
 and household production, 29–30

522

Subject Index

Industry
    and British Industrial Revolution, 73, 98, 473–4
    automobiles, 182
    comparative labour productivity in, 20th century, 105–9
    chemical, 35, 145
    coal, 241, 246, 250, 251
    cotton textiles, 44 n.6, 246
    elecrical engineering, 37, 182
    electrical supply, 37, 139–40
    petroleum, 169–70
    telecommunications, 170, 310, 332–3
    textiles, 51, 150–51
Information and Communications Technology (ICT), 136, 156, 158, 175
ICT revolution (see also, Third Industrial Revolution) 38, 136, 162–4
Inland Revenue (UK), 429
Institutional change
    and industrialization, 43
    and transition economies, 200, 214, 238, 240–41
International Business Machines (IBM), 160, 160 n. 39, 184
International Monetary Fund (IMF), 4, 208, 255, 257, 340
Ireland, 218, 470, 473
Italy, 218, 243, 248, 345, 376,
    capital market, late 19th century, 206, 325–7, 332–4
    currency reform, 4, 205–7, 315f.
    financial markets, late 19th century, 318–20, 326, 334–6
    labour market, late 19th century, 206, 320–25, 327–31
    monetary union, 205–6, 317f.

Japan, 183, 184, 192, 226, 252, 310, 387, 451
    electrification in, 136, 150–52
    financial system in, 220–21, 225
    growth accounting in, 216, 218, 222
    productivity growth, manufacturing, 1920s, 152–3
    welfare measurements in, 389

Kimberland, 302, 307
Königsberg, 54
Korea, South, 184–5, 209, 214–16, 218, 221
Korea, North, 432
Kosovo, 339

Labour migration
    and apprenticeship, 17th-century England, 93–6
    and British Industrial Revolution, 474
    and Russian agriculture, 287–9
    in European Union, 463, 475
    in South Africa, 204, 303–7
Labour mobility
    and poor relief in early modern England, 465–6, 471–3
Labour productivity
    in England, 1600–1750, 50
    relative UK-US, 20th century, 104–8
    relative UK-German, 20th century, 104–8
Labour supply
    and 'industrious revolution', 32, 49–53, 65
    and East Asian 'economic miracle', 32
    and US economic growth, 32
    elderly, US and UK, since 1880, 493, 495–6
    hours, US and UK, 1918–30, 154
    in South Africa, 302–7
Lancashire, 473
Land Act, 1913 (South Africa), 302
Land Code, 1996 (Russia), 270–71
Land Reform
    Russian, 267f.
    resistance to, in Russia, 280–82
Land Tenure
    Italy, 328, 330–31, 335–6
    Russia, 275–6, 280–81
    South Africa, 301–2, 309–10
Latin America, 189, 216, 217, 219, 340, 342
Latium, 330
'Law of One Price' (see also, Market integration)
    defined, 321
Learning-by-doing, 26, 44
Leisure
    and subjective wellbeing, 386
Lenin Prize, 178
Lesotho, 303–4, 305, 306, 307
Life expectancy
    and social welfare measurement, 373, 377, 378, 424
    and health care, 447–8, 453–4
    in Britain, late 20th century, 401–2, 415
    in South Africa, since 1950, 453
Liverpool, 425, 473
Lombardy, 317
London, 50, 61, 79–80, 89, 94, 95, 446, 473

Maastricht Treaty, 205, 464
Macmillan Committee, 1931 (UK), 349–50, 352

Subject Index

Madagascar, 451
Mafia, 189
Malawi, 303
Malaysia, 216, 223, 225
Management
  and technological change, 119–20
Manchester, England, 94, 473
Manchester, New Hampshire, 494 n. 34
Manhattan Project, 179
Market Economy, 213
  characteristics, 232–3
Market Failure
  concept of, 25, 219
  and education, 34, 35
  and human capital investment, 81–3, 89–91, 103
  and network externalities, 26
  and technological change, 177–85, 189–90
Market integration, 4, 315, 320f.
Market unification
  capital, Italy, late 19th century, 206, 325–7, 332–4
  labour, Italy, late 19th century, 206, 320–25, 327–31
  monetary, Italy, late 19th century, 318–20, 334–6
Markov Chain, 18–19
Marshall Plan, 249
Mass production
  and labour training, 35–6, 113–15, 154–5
  and British industry, post-1945, 124
  and US economy, 35, 124, 141, 182–3
  v. 'flexible production', 113–4
Massachusetts, 484 n.6, 485–6, 490–91
Massachusetts Old Age Commission, 1910, 485
Massachusetts Commission on Old-Age Pensions, 486
Max Planck Institutes (Germany), 184
Medical Act, 1858 (UK), 448
Medicare, 492
Medicine
  alternative and scientific, 5, 366–7, 439f.
  complementarity of, 367–8
  Ayurvedic (Hindu) and Unani (Muslim), 451–2
  folk, 443–4
  holistic, 440–42
  indigenous, 454–5
  and professions, 116
  in ancient societies, 443
  in medieval Europe, 444–5
  in Renaissance Europe, 446–7
  in early modern England, 447–8
  in modern South Africa, 451f.
Merck, 181

Mexico, 183
Microsoft, 184
Middle East, 216
Milan, 315, 426
Mining, Gold (South Africa), 302–7, 312
Ministry of Shipping (UK), 242
Ministry of Food (UK), 242
Ministry of Munitions (UK), 241–2
Monetary Union
  Austro-German, 316
  European (EMU), 315–16, 335
  Italian, 1862, 205–6, 317f.
  Latin American, 316
  Scandinavian, 316
Moscow, 278, 341, 412
Mozambique, 303–4
Munich, 315, 339

Naples, 326, 332
Narrative and economic explanation, 7, 20–23
National Land Committee (Russia), 273
National Health Insurance Scheme, 1948 (UK), 449
National Health Service (UK), 181, 250, 439, 448–50
National Health Services Commission, 1944 (South Africa), 453
National Civic Federation (US), 486, 490
Netherlands (see Holland)
Network Failure
  and technological change, 40, 187–90
New Economic Program, NEP (Russia), 281
'New Economy'
  in relation to 'industrious revolution', 31
'New Growth Theory', 176, 177
'New Household Economics', 46
'New Institutional Economics', 43 n.3, 214
New Poor Law, 1834 (UK), 473, 474
New York, 341
New Zealand, 181
  technological development in, 20th century, 188–90
Newcastle-upon-Tyne, 81
North American Free Trade Organization (NAFTA), 183
Northampton, 80, 94
Norway, 191, 218, 405, 415
Norwich, 94, 95
Nottingham, 94
Nottinghamshire, 473
Nutrition
  and heights, weights, 402, 412–13, 423
  and social welfare measurement, 377

524

Subject Index

Occupational distribution, 107–8
  in South Africa, 308
Organization for Economic Development and Co-operation (OECD), 174, 175, 210. 219, 222, 225, 422, 433, 434, 435
Office of Research and Development (US), 179
Old Age
  and economic policy-making, 5–6
  and health care, 368
  and poverty, 490–91
  financing of, 368–9, 479f.
Old Age Assistance (US), 491
Old Age & Survivors Insurance (US), 491–2
Old Poor Law
  and apprenticeship, 91–3, 97–9
  and labour migration, 34, 73–4, 369–70, 465–6, 462–3
  as welfare system, 5, 97–9, 369, 465f.
Oxford, 79–80, 93–4

Palermo, 326, 332
Pareto Optimality, 25
Paris, 59, 60, 332
Patents and patenting, 39–40, 168, 169–74
Path dependence
  concept of, 15–19, 20, 24
  and agrarian reform, 287–9, 291
  and economic transitions, 203
  and market failure, 24–6
  and measurement of economic growth, 371
  and policy-making, 197–8, 207–8
  and welfare systems, 505–6
Path independence (see also, Ergodicity), 17
Peasants' Land Bank, 1883 (Russia), 275, 277
Pensions, Old Age
  and retirement, 495–7
  and labour migration, 463–4
  defined benefit v. defined contribution, 503–4
  occupational, UK and US, 492–3, 503
  private, 492–4, 502–3
  state, 491–3, 499–500
Philippines, 216, 218, 223
Phillips Curve, 15
Piedmont, 317
Pilkington Glass, 181
Poland, 239–40, 254, 431
Poor Law (see also, Old Poor Law, New Poor Law), 377, 466, 467, 491
Poor Law Act, 1601, 76, 97, 99, 469

Poor Relief, 466f.
  indoor v. outdoor, defined, 467
  local administration of, 466–9
Population growth
  and industrialization, 43
Portugal, 218
'Poverty Line' (see also, Rowntree), 377
Poverty
  and old age, 490–91, 496
  and social welfare measurement, 379, 389
  child, 426–7
  'primary' v. 'secondary', defined, 390
Powell Doctrine, 339
Principal-agent problem, 188
Privatization, 239–41, 267, 285–9
Probate inventory
  and consumption, 54–7
Professional Associations, 117–19, 128
  accountancy, 116–19
  engineering, 116
  industrial management, 119–20
  law, 116
  science, 116
Professions
  and human capital investment, 115–20
Property rights, 200, 231, 234, 240, 268, 273–4
Proto-industrialization, 2, 30, 48
Public choice models, 178
Public goods (see also, Market failure), 177–8
Public science and technology, 179–81, 185f.

Quantity Theory of Money, 20

Relative income hypothesis, 387–8
Rendita Italiana, 325–7, 332–4
Rent-seeking, 210, 213
Research and development (R&D, see also, Technology), 174–7, 179, 180–82, 185–6, 190–2
  statistics of, 1920–90, 119–20
  and General Purpose Technologies, 144, 146
Retirement, 483–4, 493, 498
  age at, US and UK, 501–2
  and child-rearing, US, UK, 488–9
Risk aversion, 283
Rochford, Essex, 91
Romania, 412
Rome, 317, 326
Ruhr Valley, 345

525

Subject Index

Russia (see also, Soviet Union, Russian Federation), 211, 243
  agricultural reform in, 3, 201–3, 269
  command economy, 233, 252–4
  Constitution of, 1993, 271, 274
  economic reforms in, 3, 200–201, 231, 239–41, 254–62, 269
  industrialization in, 275
  land reforms in, 267f.
Russian Federation (see also, Russia), 299
Russian Revolution, 1917, 233, 243, 275

Sardinia, Kingdom of, 206, 317–8, 319
Savings
  by UK households, c. 1900, 486–7
  by UK households, c. 2000, 501, 505
  by US households, c. 1900, 484–6
  by US households, c. 2000, 500, 505
Science
  'Big Science', 179–80
Scotland, 54, 470
  heights in, late 20th century, 425, 428
Second Industrial Revolution, 172
Services
  comparative labour productivity in, 1870–1990, 105–9
Settlement Laws, 77, 472
  and apprenticeship, 91–3
  and labour migration, 471–3
Sheffield, 425
Shops and retail distribution, 61–2, 64
Sicily, 206, 317
Sierra Leone, 299
Singapore, 216, 217, 218, 219, 223
Skills
  and economic growth, 20th century, 122–7
  Italy, 1860–80, 323–4
Slavery, 302, 372
'Social capabilities' (see also, Abramovitz), 36, 104, 126–7, 210–11, 224
  defined, 210
Social indicators — see Wellbeing
Social welfare systems
  in early modern Europe, 466f.
  in modern Europe, 464–5
Socialism, 235
Soho (London), 89
South Africa, 3, 203–5, 443, 497f.
  labour supply in, 302–7
  medicine in, 452–6
  poverty in, 427
  Free State Province, 307
South America, 343
Soviet Union (see also Russia, Russian Federation), 178, 185, 247
  agricultural system, 279, 280–81, 285
  collapse of, 238, 239, 254
  economic system, 234, 235, 238–9, 253–4
  heights in, 432–3
  industrialization in, 238
  technological system in, 185–7, 190–91
  war economy, 1939–45, 248
Spain, 218
Sri Lanka, 454
St Petersburg, 278
Stamp Act, 1709, 77
Stamp Duty, 79
Standard of Living Debate, 49–50, 372
  and anthropometric evidence, 403–4
Statute of Artificers and Apprentices, 1563, 75–6, 84, 93, 95–6
  repeal of, 1814, 78, 78 n.14
Stock Exchange
  in Italy, 326, 333–4, 336
  New York, 339
Stolypin Reforms, 1906–11 (Russia), 202, 275
Structural change
  and apprenticeship, 93–6
  and British Industrial Revolution, 73
  and comparative labour productivity, 1870–1990, 105–6
Sweden, 218, 376, 415, 421
Swedish Match Trust, 1921, 151
Switzerland, 352
System of National Accounts (SNA), 371–3
  and extended social accounts, 373–7
  and psychological indicators, 390
  and quality of service provision, 161
  and social indicators, 379

Taiwan, 223
  technological development in, 188–90
Technical education
  in Britain, Germany, US, 103, 114–15
Technology
  and industrialization, 43
  and economic growth, 167f.
  and R&D, 39
  capital-saving, 140–41
  'Computer and Dynamo', 139, 156
  computer technology, 156f.
  co-ordination failures, 40
  'Dynamo Revolution', 37, 38, 135–6, 139, 145, 164
  General Purpose Technology (GPT), 135–6, 144–7, 154, 155, 177, 187
  defined, 144, 177
  computers, 158–9, 163–4
  electrification as an example, 149
  governmental failure, 185–7, 189–90

Subject Index

information and communications technology (ICT), 136, 156, 158, 175
ICT revolution, 38, 136, 162–4
laser, 169
market failure, 177–85, 189–90
network failure, 40, 187–90
public science and technology policy, 179–81, 185f.
role of state, 178f.
'Systems of Innovation', 39–41, 167f.
Telecommunications, 310, 332–3
Thailand, 214–5, 216, 218, 223, 224–5
Third Industrial Revolution (see also, ICT Revolution), 175
Transkei, 305
Transition
  economic, defined, 232–3, 235–8, 239–41
  economic, in Russia, 231, 234, 238–41, 252–62, 267, 269, 279
  economic, in South Africa, 297f.
  gradual v. abrupt ('big bang'), 3, 235, 238–41, 248–9, 252–5, 261
  political, in South Africa, 298f.
Treaty of Rome, 1960, 315
Trieste, 58
Truth and Reconciliation Commission (South Africa), 308–9
Turin, 326, 332
Tuscany, Grand Duchy of, 317, 319
Two Sicilies, Kingdom of, 317, 319, 330, 331
Tysoe, 97

Ukraine, 281
Unani Medicine, 451
Unemployment, 237, 463
  and social welfare measurement, 387
  in interwar period, 244, 245–6, 355, 358
  in post-1945 Britain, 251, 252
  in post-1989 Russia, 256
  in South Africa, late 20th century, 301, 310
United Kingdom (UK; see also, Great Britain, England)
  child care benefits, 427, 430
  electrification in, 1880–1940, 148–50
  growth accounting in, 216, 218, 222, 148
  Labour government and economic policies
    1924, 345
    1929–31, 350–51
    1945–51, 249–52
  old age financing in, 6, 479f.
  patents and patenting in, 1700–1960, 170–72, 173
  technological development in, 178–9
  technology policy in, 190–92
  productivity growth, 1920s, 148
United Nations, 371
USA, 35, 185, 218, 221, 222, 243, 339, 342, 464
  apprenticeship in, 1870–1990, 111–15
  economic growth, 20th century, 135
  education, formal in, 109–11
  electrification in, 2, 36–8, 135, 140–41, 147
  federalism in, 368
  financial crisis, 1930s, 222, 224
  growth accounting in, 216, 135–8, 152–3
  heights in, 421–2, 424
  'High Wage Economy', 1920s, 142–3, 146
  human capital formation in, 2, 35–6, 103f., 183
  labour force participation in, 483–4, 493, 495–6
  labour migration in, 463
  labour supply in, 32
  labour productivity in, 1870–1990, 105–8
  old age financing in, 6, 368
  patents and patenting in, 1860–1970, 172, 173
  population structure, 479–82
  productivity growth, 1920s, 36–8, 135, 136–8, 152–3
  'productivity paradox', 1960–90, 156–8
  technological development in, 179–80, 187–9
  technology policy in, 190–92
  war economy, 1941–5, 248
  welfare measurement in, 374, 376, 385–7, 388, 405–6
USSR — see Soviet Union

Venice, 317, 326, 332
Venice–Milan Railway, 1857, 317
Vienna, 58, 317
Vietnam, 339, 451
Vocational training (see also, Apprenticeship, Professionals), 2, 33, 103
  and labour productivity growth, 111f.
  market for, 81f.
  weakness, in UK, 182
Volga (river), 278

Wages
  Italy, 1860–80, 322–5
  US, 1920s, 142–3
  UK, 1920s, 153–4

Subject Index

Waist-hip ratio (WHR; see also, Body-mass index), 421, 423
Welfare, economic (see also, Well-being), 4, 364
  and economic growth, 5
  and inequality, 4
  measurement of, 373–7
  new goods and, 161
  relative to national income (GDP), 375–6
  relative to social welfare measurement, 364
Welfare, social (see also, Well-being)
  aggregation issues, 372–3
  anthropometric measures, 403–4
  measurement of, 363–4, 372f.
  psychological indicators, 384–91
  relative to economic welfare, 364, 372f.
  relative to economic growth, 371f.
  social indicators, 377–83
Welfare State, 468, 492
Well-being
  anthropometric measures, 403–4
  economic measures
    'Economic Aspects of Welfare' (EAW), 375
    'Genuine Progress Indicator' (GPI), 376
    'Index of Sustainable Economic Welfare' (ISEW), 375–6
    'Measure of Economic Welfare' (MEW), 373–4
  psychological indicators
    'Subjective Well-being' (SWB), 384–9, 390–91
  social indicators
    'Genuine Progress Indicator' (GPI), 376
    'Human Development Index' (HDI), 378–83, 392, 404
    'Index of Social Progress' (ISP), 379–81
    'Multidimensional Quality of Life Index', 379–81
    'Physical Quality of Life Index' (PQLI), 378–83, 404
    relative to GDP levels, 380–82
    relative to GDP growth, 382–3
Wilson Doctrine, 339
Witwatersrand, 302, 312, 453
World Bank, 202, 217, 219, 240–41, 255, 378–9
World Economic Conference, 1933, 356
World Health Organization, 420, 440
World Values Survey, 388
World War One, 178, 207, 231, 343–4, 347
World War Two, 179, 200, 231
World Wide Web, 163, 311

York, 93, 94, 95
Yorkshire, 473